Warped

Historical Materialism Book Series

The Historical Materialism Book Series is a major publishing initiative of the radical left. The capitalist crisis of the twenty-first century has been met by a resurgence of interest in critical Marxist theory. At the same time, the publishing institutions committed to Marxism have contracted markedly since the high point of the 1970s. The Historical Materialism Book Series is dedicated to addressing this situation by making available important works of Marxist theory. The aim of the series is to publish important theoretical contributions as the basis for vigorous intellectual debate and exchange on the left.

The peer-reviewed series publishes original monographs, translated texts, and reprints of classics across the bounds of academic disciplinary agendas and across the divisions of the left. The series is particularly concerned to encourage the internationalization of Marxist debate and aims to translate significant studies from beyond the English-speaking world.

*For a full list of titles in the Historical Materialism Book Series
available in paperback from Haymarket Books, visit:*
www.haymarketbooks.org/category/hm-series

Warped

Gay Normality and Queer Anti-Capitalism

By
Peter Drucker

Haymarket Books
Chicago, IL

First published in 2014 by Brill Academic Publishers, The Netherlands
© 2014 Koninklijke Brill NV, Leiden, The Netherlands

Published in paperback in 2015 by
Haymarket Books
P.O. Box 180165
Chicago, IL 60618
773-583-7884
www.haymarketbooks.org

ISBN: 978-1-60846-636-8

Trade distribution:
In the US, Consortium Book Sales, www.cbsd.com
In Canada, Publishers Group Canada, www.pgcbooks.ca
In the UK, Turnaround Publisher Services, www.turnaround-uk.com
In all other countries, Publishers Group Worldwide, www.pgw.com

Cover design by Ragina Johnson.

This book was published with the generous support of
Lannan Foundation and the Wallace Global Fund.

Printed in Canada by union labor.

10 9 8 7 6 5 4 3 2 1

Library of Congress Cataloging-in-Publication data is available.

I hear it was charged against me that I sought to destroy institutions...
(What indeed have I in common with them? Or what with the destruction of them?)
Only I will establish ...
Without edifices or rules or trustees or any argument,
The institution of the dear love of comrades.

WALT WHITMAN, *Leaves of Grass*

• • •

I pondered all these things, and how men [sic] fight and lose the battle, and the thing that they fought for comes about in spite of their defeat, and when it comes turns out not to be what they meant, and other men have to fight for what they meant under another name.

WILLIAM MORRIS, *A Dream of John Ball*

• • •

...for the embattled
there is no place
that cannot be home
nor is.

AUDRE LORDE, 'School Note'

• •
•

Contents

Preface

This book is meant to be both a political intervention and an empirically and theoretically rigorous work of scholarship. Since lesbian/gay liberation and lesbian/gay studies got started over forty years ago, the scholarly discipline has grown enormously in scale, status and sophistication, but this kind of hybrid of politics and scholarship has become more unusual. While many people in queer studies today try to engage with political issues in their less academic writings and speaking, and some persist in trying to integrate politics into their scholarship, the warring imperatives of an academic field and of political movements have made the combination an increasingly difficult one to pull off. I believe the attempt remains worthwhile and important. Political engagement can give scholarship a sense of proportion, focusing it on larger societal and human stakes, rather than the sometimes arcane preoccupations of rival academic schools. And sexual politics needs to be informed by theory and history. Otherwise mainstream sexual politics can become the prisoner of a narrow, complacent, conformist agenda, while radical sexual politics can despair of change and become embittered and insular.

In this spirit, this book makes an ambitious attempt to make sense of a wide range of other people's discoveries (I have not undertaken original fieldwork or research in previously untapped primary sources), and to draw conclusions from them for activism. Others will have to judge to what extent it has succeeded. I have done my best to be empirically accurate and theoretically consistent, but make no claim to academic serenity above the political fray. I also make no claim to have the last word on any specific issue. Rather, my hope is to stimulate dialogue and research on issues I think have been neglected in the last few decades: especially the connections between capitalism and the heterosexual norm, and between class and sexual politics. At certain points, my argument takes some daring leaps over social and cultural mediations that are vital to the links I am trying to make. I hope that others will be inspired to try to fill these gaps, even if this means modifying my hypotheses.

Although the book has not been a collective project and its flaws are solely my responsibility, it could never have been written or published without many people's help, so I have many people to thank. Thanks to the other organisers of and participants in the International LGBT Strategy Seminars in 1998, 2000, 2002 and 2009 at the International Institute for Research and Education (IIRE) in Amsterdam for stimulating discussions and helpful criticisms – especially to Terry Conway, a comrade, co-thinker and friend for many years – to my fellow IIRE lecturers and staff members for many forms of intellectual and practical support, and to the students (all of them activists) at the IIRE for their enthusiasm, dedication and stimulating comments and questions. Several people associated with the IIRE – comrades who have also become friends, notably Gilbert Achcar, Penelope Duggan and Pierre Rousset – gave me valued encouragement in pursuing the politics of sexuality as part of my work as Co-Director and later Fellow. Pierre in particular has been a model of engaged scholarship outside the academy.

Thanks to the editors of the journal *Historical Materialism* for persevering through the eight-year marathon that led to publication of the 2011 article ('The Fracturing of LGBT Identities under Neoliberal Capitalism'),[1] which was, in its turn, the starting point for this book, and which still (in revised form) makes up much of chapter 3 in particular. Paul Reynolds set the whole process in motion; Sebastian Budgen, Peter Thomas and the other editors of the Historical Materialism book series gave encouragement and help at the later stages. Two anonymous reviewers for the series made encouraging comments and helpful suggestions. Series editor Danny Hayward has patiently, persistently shepherded the book over many hurdles on the way to publication. Simon Mussell has been a thorough and sensitive copy-editor.

This book represents among other things an attempt to fuse that 2011 article on queer identities with earlier work – notably a 1996 article for *New Left Review* and my work as editor of the anthology *Different Rainbows* – on LGBT identities and politics in the dependent world. Any attempt to resist the prevailing Eurocentrism of queer studies involves a fight against steep odds – against US hegemony in the field (a phenomenon that I try to analyse), queer studies' continuing neglect (despite its rapidly expanding scope) of some corners of the globe, and my own inability to keep up with everything that is published. Crucial to this effort were the comments and criticisms of LGBT people in or from dependent countries, who kept me alert to the Eurocentrism so often implicit even in would-be radical queer approaches (including my own). Special thanks are owed to David Fernbach for shepherding both the *New Left Review* article and *Different Rainbows* from conception to completion, to the contributors to *Different Rainbows*, to the Asian, African and Latin American participants in IIRE sessions, and to the members of Lambda Istanbul who took part in a discussion with me there in 2011.

Various articles of mine on LGBT history and politics over the past two decades in various publications provided other material for this book. I have drawn on almost all of them, but most have been so thoroughly reworked as

---

[1] Drucker, Peter 2011, 'The Fracturing of LGBT Identities under Neoliberal Capitalism', *Historical Materialism*, 19(4): 3–32.

to be unrecognisable, so I have simply cited and footnoted them as appropriate. In any case, acknowledgement is due to the editors of the US socialist journal *Against the Current* for publishing many of them and for providing what has remained my political and intellectual home base since 1984. While submitting my work elsewhere has always involved the risk of running up against unforeseen political and ideological obstacles, I could always count on a sympathetic and intelligent reception from ATC, even after I found myself thousands of miles away in the substantially different social climate of the Netherlands (where the magazine *Grenzeloos* has become my home base in the even smaller world of Dutch critical Marxism). Bits of articles from *Against the Current*, particularly of 'Arab Sexualities' from 2008, have found their way into this book.

I owe ATC's editors a debt of gratitude, particularly David Finkel and Dianne Feeley for continuing to ask me for articles, and Alan Wald, who has made ongoing and intelligent efforts to link Marxism and queer studies in his own work as well as encouraging mine. The socialist feminist scholarship and activism of former ATC editor Johanna Brenner has been a continuing inspiration. And while his own work on the agrarian origins of US capitalism is remote from mine, Charlie Post, a frequent contributor to ATC, has provided insightful comments on what I am trying to do.

Of other articles of mine I have drawn on, 'Changing Families and Communities: An LGBT Contribution to an Alternative Development Path'[2] has been cannibalised here and there for some passages, mainly in chapter 6. I give thanks to the editors of *Development in Practice* for permission to reprint them here. Thanks as well to the editors of *New Politics* for permission to use some reworked passages, again mainly in chapter 6, from my article 'Reinventing a Queer Left',[3] originally published as part of a symposium that appeared in issues 45[4] and 46.[5]

Besides an attempt to engage with the dependent world, this book is also an attempt to engage with concerns of a younger generation than mine, one whose sexual identities and politics have taken shape since the 1990s. Born in the US in 1958, I am largely a product of the years of growing prosperity and Cold War ideology. I came out as a gay man during the years after the 1969

---

2 Drucker, Peter 2009, 'Changing Families and Communities: An LGBT Contribution to an Alternative Development Path', *Development in Practice*, 19(7): 825–36.

3 Drucker, Peter 2009, 'Reinventing a Queer Left', *New Politics*, 46, http://newpol.org/ reinventingqueerleft.

4 http://newpol.org/content/symposium-gays-and-left-part-i.

5 http://newpol.org/content/symposium-gays-and-left-part-ii.

Stonewall rebellion (although I was too young when it happened to experience it or even be conscious of it). As a gay activist in the 1980s, I tried to help maintain and deepen links that had been made in the 1970s between lesbian/ gay liberation, sexual radicalism more broadly, feminism and socialism, and took part in ACT UP in San Francisco and New York. By the time Queer Nation and transgender activism emerged in the early 1990s, however, my identity was pretty much formed, and I could only be a sympathetic but critical outside observer. In 1993, I moved to the Netherlands, which despite (or more likely because of) its fabled tolerance for gays is not a hotbed of queer radicalism, and my efforts to link up with what queer radicalism exists here have not always gone smoothly. I am all the more indebted to young queer comrades in other countries who have worked with me on these issues, notably Nina Trige Andersen in Denmark, Gabriel Girard in France and Quebec, Sérgio Vitorino in Portugal, and especially (before his untimely death from AIDS in 2005) Torvald Patterson in Canada.

An independent scholar like me necessarily incurs even more debts of gratitude. Despite benefiting from the advantages of a comfortable middle-class upbringing, an elite education and even a PhD, I was perverse enough to spend 25 years largely in movement jobs instead of trying to climb the academic career ladder. The choice brought me many rewards, and I do not regret it. But a project such as this book definitely suffers from my lack of access to an extensive university library in an English-speaking country. Special thanks are therefore due to the Dutch National Library in The Hague, a precious public resource that needs support and defence in its country's current climate of cutbacks and anti-intellectualism. I found other sources in the libraries of the IIRE and of the Atria Institute on Gender Equality and Women's History, which was often the only library in the Netherlands to possess a crucial book; my thanks to their staff. I am also grateful to Gilbert Achcar, Heather Berg (especially), Eileen Boris, Johanna Brenner, Arthur Bruls, Sebastian Budgen, Gisela Dütting, Penelope Duggan, Gabriel Girard, Dagmar Herzog, Steve Leinbach, Ghassan Makarem, David McReynolds, Paul Mepschen, Charlie Post, Catherine Sameh, David Thorstad and Alan Wald for their help in finding sources that Dutch libraries could not provide. Thanks as well to Hanno, Nancy and Peter Beck, Valerie Diamond, Winston Leyland and Joan Roe for gifts of useful books. Despite all this help, I have sometimes been forced to rely on second-hand sources; in each case the original author is mentioned in either the text or the footnote, while the footnote cites the source I actually consulted.

Johanna Brenner, Terry Conway, Dagmar Herzog, Ghassan Makarem, Paul Reynolds, Catherine Sameh and Alan Sears generously found time in their busy schedules to read all or part of a draft of this book and gave me valuable criticisms, comments and suggestions. I am sincerely grateful to them all for their input, even when I was perverse enough to ignore it. They are truly not to blame for the result. Although (perhaps foolishly) I did not ask Carolyn Magid, Nancy Wechsler or Anne Finger for feedback, I nonetheless owe them thanks for their formative influence on the socialist feminist politics that inspires the book.

I would like to express my special appreciation to the established scholars who, in a blurb for *Different Rainbows*, in an email, chatting in a corridor at a conference, or over lunch or dinner, have said something positive about my work or made it clear that they took the work seriously. This meant at least as much to me – perhaps even more – when (as was usually the case) it did not necessarily imply agreement with my approach or endorsement of any specific conclusion. These generous souls include Dennis Altman, Mark Blasius, Eileen Boris, Johanna Brenner, George Chauncey, John D'Emilio, Martin Duberman, David Halperin, Rosemary Hennessy, Dagmar Herzog, Theo van der Meer and Gloria Wekker. Their kind words have probably been more important in keeping me going than they can imagine. I would also like to acknowledge my debt to Gloria Wekker for the lines from Audre Lorde that became one of the book's epigraphs; they speak powerfully to feelings that I share with so many rebellious expatriates and migrants.

I am also grateful to friends who patiently listened to me babble on about what I was trying to do. Thanks, for example, to Enzo Traverso for his advice on shortening the title.

Finally, thanks and love to Christopher Beck, who encouraged my solitary work on this book even at the cost of our precious weekends. He is responsible for the fact that it at least has a main title that is possible to remember. As always, he did his best to make my prose readable and comprehensible, and keep me halfway sane throughout it all. After 33 years of this sort of thing, it is high time for me to dedicate something to him, so this book is for Christopher.

Rotterdam, March 2014

Introduction: What's at Stake?

Over the past forty years, lesbian/gay/bisexual/transgender (LGBT)[1] movements over much of the world have gone from strength to strength, victory to victory, to an extent that would have seemed almost unimaginable at the time of the 1969 Stonewall rebellion. The fact that same-sex sexual acts are now legal in all but a minority of countries may not seem out of line with global trends since the Second World War. But given the furious opposition that the first anti-discrimination laws provoked only a few short decades ago, the fact that the UN Human Rights Council in 2011 by majority vote endorsed protection of sexual minorities is a milestone. The fact that legal recognition of same-sex partnerships has been won or is being seriously considered not only in Denmark, post-apartheid South Africa and Argentina, but even in Britain, Iowa and Nepal, and that federal benefits have been won by same-sex married couples in the US,[2] surely exceeds almost anyone's expectations. By comparison with the 1960s and 1970s, when gay liberation 'touched very few',

---

1   In the rest of the book I will be making some fine distinctions that are not part of most people's everyday usage. Although the logic behind these distinctions will only become clear in the course of the argument, some terminological notes at the start may help. 'Same-sex' is the term used in this book to refer most broadly to desire and erotic relations between two people defined as male or two people defined as female. The term 'lesbian/gay' is used to refer to one, historically specific form of same-sex identity, dating largely to the period after World War II, which is discussed at length in chapter 2. 'Homosexual' or sometimes 'lesbian' refers to a somewhat different form of same-sex identity and behaviour, most prevalent in the period from the late nineteenth century to the 1950s, which is discussed at length in chapter 1. 'Transgendered' ('trans' for short) is used as a broad umbrella term for people who assume or are assigned a gender identity different from their perceived biological sex, whether they are defined as of the other gender, a third or fourth gender, or no gender, or as 'gender queers'. 'LGBT' is used as a broad term for all people with same-sex sexual identities, as well as for trans people even if they define themselves as straight, though not for people who experience same-sex desire or engage in same-sex behaviour without adopting a distinctive identity. Although the word 'queer' is sometimes used by others to refer generally to LGBT people, I try to reserve the word in this book to those who have self-identified as queer, mostly since the 1990s, who are often rebelling not only against the heterosexual norm but also against present-day 'gay normality'; queer identity is discussed at length in chapter 3. These distinctions may seem confusing at first, especially since other authors I cite do not always make them. Nevertheless, I hope that readers will be convinced of their usefulness in the course of the book.

2   As late as 2005, as seasoned an observer as Stephanie Coontz wrote that the US was unlikely to join the Netherlands, Belgium and Canada in instituting same-sex marriage (2005, p. 274).

as John D'Emilio has observed, beginning in the 1990s 'the world turned' for millions of LGBT people.[3]

While many factors have contributed to these victories, the power of LGBT mobilisation is definitely one of them. Almost no one is born into a LGBT community; this makes it all the more remarkable that strong movements, in which self-organisation and distinctive LGBT identities play a central role, have emerged from these communities. Since the turnouts for LGBT marches can seem improbable even to sympathetic people who are unfamiliar with LGBT activism, it is worth citing some figures that suggest how strong these movements have become. In the US, for example, between half a million and a million people turned out each time for national LGBT demonstrations in 1987, 1993, 1994 and 2000. In Paris in 2008, and Berlin in 2012, there were over half a million participants; over a million people took part in the final parade of Europride in Madrid in 2007. Over half a million took part in Rio de Janeiro's Pride in 2012; organisers in Saõ Paulo claimed 4 million event-goers in 2011.

Nor can these be seen merely as apolitical parades, although every big political demonstration takes on this character to some extent. Their organisers have consistently featured themes and demands meant to harness the numbers to specific goals. At many recent pride marches, the imminent prospect of winning same-sex marriage has clearly swelled the turnout. And this organising has always been done independently, without any substantial debt to other social movements or political organisations.

Yet many LGBT activists, and ordinary LGBT people, are not entirely happy with the movements they have built and the world that has been won. Admittedly, the development of same-sex politics has never been a smooth process. The history of movements for sexual freedom is not a narrative of steady process, but rather one of 'recurrent backlashes'.[4] LGBT movements in particular have certainly faced many backlashes; almost every victory has provoked one, sometimes a massive one. But that is not the main problem faced by the movement now. In fact, the backlashes, however intense, usually seem remarkably short-lived; a single electoral cycle is often enough to make the anti-gay right resign themselves to LGBT advances and give up on rolling back reforms when they return to office. The problem is not so much holding on to victories, as the form the victories take and the context within which they are embedded.

Perhaps some activists in 1968 or 1969 could have imagined that openly gay men would one day be allowed to serve in the US military; but living as they

---

3   D'Emilio 2002, p. ix.

4   Herzog 2011, p. 1.

were at the height of the movement against the Vietnam War, they would probably not have been thrilled at the prospect – or at the use of arguments for
sexual freedom to justify wars in western Asia. Even if they could have foreseen
legal recognition of same-sex partnerships and welcomed it as a step towards
full equality, they would probably not have given high priority to the estate and
tax planning for affluent same-sex couples that it has made possible – and still
less favoured cutting poor and low-income LGBT people's social benefits on
the grounds of their relationship with someone slightly less poor. And given
the inspiration those activists drew from black and immigrant struggles, they
would presumably have been distressed, if not appalled, to see how LGBT
people and immigrants are being pitted against each other today in much of
Europe, or how LGBT people are being pitted against Africans and Arabs on a
global scale.

The paradoxes surrounding LGBT victories are due in part to the defeats that
other movements have suffered in the same years, notably labour and poor
people's movements, anti-war movements and the political left. A victory like
partnership recognition would take a different shape if it were won in more
egalitarian and peaceful societies. Since in reality LGBT victories have been
and are being won in an increasingly unequal, polarised and violent world, the
victories have taken on a disturbing colouration. LGBT communities and lives
are the worse for this.

LGBT people may in a sense be freer today in much of the world than they
once were. But whatever freedom they enjoy is increasingly dependent on
and constrained by a commercial scene and marketplace that are much more
hospitable to people with money, whatever their sexuality, than to those without. What activists in the US civil rights movement once referred to as their
'beloved community' existed, though small, conflict-ridden and fragile, in early
post-Stonewall LGBT communities as well, complete with non-commercial
gathering places, music, literature, and an ethos of their own. Today, much less
of that is available, and it often comes with a price tag. And because especially
in the sexual realm the personal is political, LGBT relationships and lives have
also been affected. To the extent that they can rely less for emotional and practical support on their families of origin, LGBT people are particularly dependent on friends, and are therefore particularly harmed by what Alan Sears has
described and documented as the 'falling rate of friendship' in contemporary
capitalism.[5]

Connections between societal change and individual lives are rarely direct
or simple. But when community and friendship can be counted on less, sexual

---

5   Sears 2006/7, pp. 36–7.

passion and partnerships tend to be counted on more – and this is not good
for them. As Dagmar Herzog has cautioned, 'the relationships between sex and
love – their connections and disconnections – are not obvious, and never have
been'.[6] Certainly under capitalism, almost no human connection fits the norm
of loving relationships free of any conflict.

Ninety years ago, Bolshevik commissar of social affairs Alexandra Kollontai
warned, as the first flush of an earlier period of radicalisation began to sub-
side, of the growing hold of what she considered the bourgeois, possessive
ideal of 'all-embracing love', which extended 'the concept of property rights
to include the right to the other person's whole spiritual and emotional world'.
'People "in love" are unbelievably insensitive', she warned. People cling 'in a
predatory and unhealthy way to illusions about finding a "soul mate"...as
the only way of charming away, if only for a time, the gloom of inescapable
loneliness' – the loneliness they feel 'even in towns full of shouting, noise and
people, even in a crowd of close friends and work-mates'.[7] Across a long century of hopes crushed and hopes realised, Kollontai's words speak eloquently
today to the condition of LGBT people (and, of course, others too) in today's
ever-more-capitalist world.

This book is meant as a contribution to an alternative vision of LGBT life
and struggle: of loving same-sex relationships, of ways of fighting for LGBT
demands like partnership equality, and of queer politics. It is aimed at helping to rebuild a radical LGBT movement freed of the growing commercialism,
middle-class assimilationism, prejudice and complicity in imperial projects
that have increasingly characterised LGBT scenes and organisations in recent
decades. Such a renewed LGBT radicalism should combine the best of the early
lesbian/gay liberation of the 1960s and 1970s with the most valuable impulses
of the queer rebellions that have grown up since the 1990s.

As a theoretical foundation for a renewed LGBT radicalism, *Warped* draws
on the insights of left feminism, radical Freudianism, queer theory, transgender liberation, anti-racist critiques by radical queers of colour, and the transnational turn in queer studies. At the same time, I draw especially and centrally
on the Marxist tradition. In doing so, I buck the trend of the turn away from
Marxism that predominated in LGBT studies from the late 1980s to the early
twenty-first century. Joining in a tentative reassessment of Marxism in queer
studies that has been taking place in the last few years, I hope to show that
Marxist analyses are indispensable to radical queer responses to (specifically)

6   Herzog forthcoming.
7   Kollontai 1978, pp. 288, 242, 243, 240.

neoliberalism, capitalism, racism, imperialism, gender oppression and the heteronormative order itself.

My argument for a coherent revolutionary vision – centrally grounded in historical materialism but integrating key contributions from other paradigms as well – cannot be confined to politics narrowly defined. It demands a fresh look at LGBT life as a whole. *Warped* is therefore not merely a political manifesto or programme. It is also an argument for a particular approach to queer studies and for a reinterpretation of same-sex histories. My hope is to foster dialogue on all these issues. I do not expect to be vindicated across the board, but I trust that the LGBT movement will benefit from the debate.

Structure of the Book

This introduction outlines the political stakes involved in the questions that the book will take up and sets out key elements of the politics that inform the book as a whole. It suggests that LGBT people's victories over the past forty years are both real and important, on the one hand, and hopelessly tangled up in real and significant defeats, on the other. The increasing commercialisation of the gay scene, the drift to the right in LGBT movements and the weakness of a left alternative prompt a re-examination of the question of how sexual freedom should be defined. To clarify this, I consider Michel Foucault's contribution to understanding power at the micro level, Gayle Rubin's contribution to the fight against sex-negativity, and above all Herbert Marcuse's vision of a society freed from surplus repression and permeated by the erotic charge of polymorphous perversity.

I link these sexual conceptions of freedom to a broader social conception, in which a battle against the new commercial, nationalist and racialised gay normality has to be integrated into a fight against the neoliberal world order. Ultimately gay normality and neoliberalism can only be defeated by attacking their roots: that is, by a queer anti-capitalism. Although queer anti-capitalism will inevitably be a convergence of different left currents, I suggest that Marxists can make a specific and crucial contribution, not only through a working-class perspective, but also by drawing on Karl Kautsky's and V.I. Lenin's commitment to fighting non-class oppression, on a global conception of the fight for economic and sexual transformation, and on socialist feminists' view of independent women's and LGBT movements as integral parts of an anti-capitalist force. All these different insights should flow together into a transformative, intersectional rainbow politics.

Part 1 of the book tries to clarify the origins of neoliberal gay normality, developing a historical and social analysis of how we got to where we are today. It is preceded by a section on 'understanding same-sex histories', which reflects on what historical materialism can contribute to this analysis. Exposing the flaws in a biological determinist account of sexual orientation, I suggest that several key concepts of historical materialism are far more useful in understanding gay normality: *social totality*, for example, which can explain how particular sexual patterns are enmeshed in a larger economic, imperial, racial and gender order, and *reification*, which illuminates both the commercialisation of sex and the gay/straight binary. I combine these concepts in defining a 'same-sex formation': a distinctive combination of several different same-sex patterns (such as transgender, intergenerational and lesbian/gay) in which one pattern is culturally dominant, and which occupies a specific place in an overall mode of production (like feudalism) or capitalist regime of accumulation (like neoliberalism). No same-sex formation is uniform, however; each takes different forms in different regions, as part of a combined and uneven social construction of sexuality in our increasingly unequal world.

The basic argument of the prologue and chapters 1 and 2 is that the gay/straight binary as it is lived in much of the world today is not intrinsic to human sexual life, nor is it even always characteristic of sexuality under capitalism. The prologue shows how central transgender identities have been through almost all of human sexual history, rooted in the close connection between sex and kinship, and how central intergenerational relationships were to the civilisations of the ancient Greek and Roman and medieval Islamic worlds, China and Japan. I present evidence that in the first centuries of capitalism, beginning in England, the Netherlands and France in the seventeenth and eighteenth centuries, a distinctive, commodified form of transgender relationships prevailed; I define the same-sex regime of these early bourgeois societies as 'molly-dominant'. The prologue also describes the impact of European colonialism on the construction of sexuality in the rest of the world, and the rise in Europe of separate men's and women's spheres and same-sex romantic friendship.

In chapter 1, I argue that the distinction between heterosexuality and homosexuality took clear shape only in a later, specific regime of capitalist accumulation, classical imperialism, towards the end of the nineteenth century. This was part of a series of processes that included imperial expansion, the rise of pseudo-scientific racism, the invention of a working-class family wage, the celebration of heterosexual romance, the first wave of feminism and the medicalisation of sexuality. Even then, homosexuality was conceived in a way that was often as much transgender-related as gay, and linked to 'sexual inversion'. I define the same-sex regime of this period as 'invert-dominant'. This invert-dominant regime also took hold in regions of Latin America and Asia which were incorporated into global capitalism but not directly colonised, while South African mining areas and the colonised Arab region developed distinctive same-sex patterns less subject to the emerging hetero/homo binary. Growing European repression of homosexuality provided the impetus for the first homosexual rights movements, allied in Germany with the socialist movement and reflected in the pioneering sexual reforms of the Russian Revolution. The rise of Nazism and Stalinism led to sexual reaction, however, which was mirrored even in imperialist democracies through the 1950s.

In chapter 2, I argue that only in the course of the twentieth century did the gay/straight binary, founded on the idea that same-sex desire is 'innate to a certain subset of individuals',[8] take the form seen in North America and Western Europe by the 1970s, following the maturation of the Fordist regime of accumulation. I call the same-sex regime in which this binary prevailed, and transgender and other patterns were marginalised, 'gay-dominant'. It depended on rising wages, a welfare state, a transition from old conceptions of manhood and womanhood to a more 'performative' definition of gender, the second wave of feminism and pervasive sexualisation linked to a commercial scene. Fordism also provided a basis for racial liberalism and decolonisation. In many neo-colonial countries, and in the Soviet bloc, China and Cuba, however, the basic conditions for lesbian/gay communities were absent; there the binary was imposed instead through the promotion of heterosexuality and the repression of homosexuality. By the 1960s, in Western Europe and the Americas a new wave of resistance appeared – lesbian/gay liberation – linked to socialist, feminist, anti-imperialist and anti-racist movements, and to the Nicaraguan, Mexican, Brazilian and South African left, which briefly challenged the gay/ straight divide.

Part 2 of the book (chapters 3 and 4) gives an overview of gay normality in the contemporary, neoliberal period. My conclusion in chapter 3 is that lesbian/gay identities have continued to spread and that LGBT people have continued to carve out social space for themselves under neoliberalism since the 1970s, but that in doing so they have increasingly been 'warping', that is, adapting to fit into an increasingly fragmented working class, a gender order ('public patriarchy') where direct male domination of women is camouflaged in superficially gender-neutral institutions, an intensifying global hierarchy and an unequal world. Especially in some regions where LGBT rights have become most solidly established and particularly among the middle class, gay identity

---

8   Herzog 2011, p. 186.

has morphed into a new gay normality, characterised by growing ghettoisa-tion, gender conformity, the exclusion of trans people and sexually margin-alised queers, a racist and Islamophobic integration in dominant nations and the formation of normative families founded on marriage. I call this current same-sex regime 'homonormative-dominant'. The superficial multiculturalism characteristic of neoliberalism barely masks growing racial inequality, fuel-ling waves of homophobic reaction in the Islamic world and Africa, as well as among racialised others. Meanwhile low-income and rebellious LGBT people have formed an oppositional subculture of gender and other queers.

The analysis presented in chapters 1, 2 and 3 makes it possible to trace same-sex formations in a multi-dimensional sequence across the recent history of capitalism, as set out in the following schema:

Accumulation regimes	Classical imperialism	Fordism	Neoliberalism
Global order	Colonialism/ semi-colonialism	Neo-colonialism	Neoliberal globalisation
Racism	Pseudo-scientific racism	Racial liberalism	Neoliberal multiculturalism
Gender	Manhood/ womanhood	Performative gender	'Public patriarchy'
Same-sex formation	Invert-dominant regime	Gay-dominant regime	Homonormative-dominant regime

But the different levels of each accumulation regime are emphatically not automatically coordinated or synchronised with one another. In particular, racial, gender and sexual changes proceed unevenly and contingently, often lagging far behind changes in the productive order.

Chapter 4 explores the political dimension of gay normality, tracing the rightward trends that gathered momentum around the world from the 1970s, increasingly took hold of LGBT movements in many countries by the dawn of the twenty-first century, and accelerated with the post-2001 'war on terror'. The chapter analyses the origin and dynamics of the homophobic, often funda-mentalist right, of a new gay right that has enthusiastically embraced neoliber-alism, of a gay, social-liberal centre and centre-left that have largely made their peace with neoliberalism, and of a radical left that has so far failed to present an adequate alternative to gay normality or to link up with queer resistance.

The chapter also looks at some features of the queer radicalism that has grown up since the 1990s that have helped perpetuate its marginality and inhibited the development of an effective queer anti-capitalism.

Part 3 especially is meant as a contribution to the development of an effective queer anti-capitalism and a global rainbow politics. Chapter 5 takes the five features of gay normality given in chapter 3 and turns them upside down to chart the axes of a radical queer sexual politics:

Neoliberal gay normality	Radical queer sexual politics
Stable lesbian/gay minority / neoliberal ghetto	Blurring the boundaries / polymorphous perversity
Gender conformity	Subverting gender / third-wave socialist feminism
Exclusion of gender & other queers	Queer inclusion / trans and youth liberation
Homonationalism	Global and anti-racist solidarity
Homonormative families	Queering intimacy & domesticity / polyamory / love-comradeship

This agenda for a radical sexual politics is closely connected to a socialist feminist programme for reproductive freedom. It focuses particularly on cutting-edge struggles like those of trans people and queer youth, and solidarity campaigns against Islamophobia, cuts in aid to poor countries and the 'pinkwashing' of Israel as a supposedly pro-gay state. It also starts from visions of queer kinship and queer 'families of choice' to define a radical yet unitary approach to the issue of same-sex partnership, opposing the privatisation of care and the transmission of class privilege, while exploring new ways of supporting parents and other caregivers and creating flexible forms for intimate relationships.

Chapter 6 starts by recognising that a queer sexual politics cannot be a merely personal or cultural project, but requires a social transformation that LGBT people cannot bring about on their own. Queers need allies. To be effective allies, broader, class-based and other social movements need to be 'queered' so that they address basic LGBT needs like housing for queer relationships, and safety and independence for queer youth. Movements around healthcare from ACT UP to the South African Treatment Action

Campaign are discussed as exemplary cases of queered social movements. Chapter 6 also explores LGBT labour activism, linking the queering of unions to challenges to bureaucracy and class collaboration, and discusses the queering of the global justice movement and of the anti-capitalist left. It concludes with a vision of queering democracy so that it may become inclusive of all those whom neoliberal democracy today excludes, and embraces all the realms of life that neoliberalism declares out of bounds to democracy.

Repression and Freedom

Yet a queer anti-capitalist alternative has still barely begun to take shape. Even today, when neoliberal capitalism as it took shape in recent decades is clearly in crisis, LGBT organisations are still rarely forging strong links with the labour movement or the political left. That could hardly be expected while the left and labour globally are still in such deep disarray, and even new activist currents like insurgent young Arabs, the Spanish *indignad@s* and Occupy are so embattled.

Perhaps an alternative discourse is beginning to emerge in the movements for sexual rights, 're-linking these movements with universal struggles for social justice'.[9] Yet there are still constraints, not only to many still-rightward-moving mainstream LGBT organisations, but even to much of the radical queer activism of the past two decades. As Cathy Cohen concluded regretfully in the mid-1990s, there were still few signs of a 'truly radical or transformative politics'.[10] Like Cohen, I advocate a more multi-dimensional radical sexual politics with roots on the left, one that foregrounds 'one's relation to power, and not some homogenized identity' and emphasises exploitation and 'the systemic nature of power'.[11] I also emphatically agree with Jasbir Puar's insistence that 'queerness . . . must consistently, not sporadically, account for nationalism and race within its purview'.[12] Recognising that queer politics can go beyond the sexual and cultural implicitly challenges it to realise a more far-reaching potential. As Dennis Altman has written, gay liberation 'cannot exist in a vacuum and only ask "Is it good for the gays?" ' It needs to make politics central and 'get global'.[13]

---

9   Makarem 2011, p. 98.
10   Cohen 2005, p. 22.
11   Cohen 2005, pp. 22, 28.
12   Puar 2007, p. 221.
13   Morton 1996, p. 29.

Haneen Maikey of the Palestinian LGBT group Al Qaws has carried this multidimensional approach a step further, rejecting the division between LGBTQ and 'friends'. She has said that Al Qaws' goal 'isn't building bridges between the LGBTQ community and society but to swim in the same river to change its course together'. At the same time, Maikey insisted on the need to fight the constraints imposed by 'patriarchy's institutions and ... pure heterosexuality', which 'limits our choices'.[14] I wholeheartedly agree. Similarly, Maria Gabriela Blanco of the Venezuelan Revolutionary Alliance for Sex-Gender Diversity has said that its members 'are not defined solely by our sexual orientation and gender identities ... because we are also women [and men], afro-descendants, indigenous, poor, and Chavista', seeing their struggle as part of a fight against a unified system.[15]

No single word – neither 'queer' nor any other – can fully encompass the broad discourse that is needed by the LGBT left.[16] Nevertheless, the reality is that the word 'gay' has increasingly, perhaps irremediably, been claimed by the mainstream. Perhaps it is now more promising – without disparaging people who prefer to identify as lesbian or gay, and without taking the parameters of existing queer-identified radicalism as our sole starting point – to try to give a new connotation to 'queer'. After all, queer still implies, as it has done since its emergence as a current in the early 1990s, rebellion and gender bending. It still evokes subversion of the gay conformism that is steadily being consolidated in more and more parts of the globe. But to be saved for a politics of social transformation, the concept of queer needs to be redefined in a way that makes it broader, more global and more welcoming to large numbers of LGBT people, especially LGBT working people. In Johanna Brenner's words, 'we have to recapture the radical potential of sexual politics *and* integrate these issues into other struggles'.[17] It should be possible to do this at least in part under a queer banner, since, in Judith Butler's words, 'queer' is 'never fully owned, but always and only redeployed, twisted, queered from a prior usage and in the direction of urgent and expanding political purposes'.[18]

Among other things, the directions of LGBT activism will depend to a great extent on how activists consciously or unconsciously define sexual freedom. Most theorists of sexual liberation have counterposed the idea of freedom to that of repression, whether psychic, social or political. In psychological terms,

---

14   Maikey 2012.
15   Blanco, Spronk and Webber 2012.
16   Schulan 2012, p. 153.
17   Brenner 2000, p. 273.
18   Butler 1993a, p. 228.

Herbert Marcuse was the most promising of the left Freudians who tried to synthesise Sigmund Freud's theory of sexual repression with a Marxist understanding of oppression and liberation. In recent decades, Michel Foucault has been more influential with his rejection of what he called 'the repressive hypothesis' in favour of an approach focused on power at the micro level, in the interstices of all human relationships. Gayle Rubin, rightly seen as a foremother of contemporary queer theory, has made original contributions to understanding and combating the pervasiveness of sex-negativity. Looking in turn at the contributions of these three thinkers can enable us to appreciate both the importance of freedom for radical sexual politics and the dynamics that a simple conception of repression or freedom cannot fully grasp.

Marcuse set out to do justice to the radical implications of Freud's theory, which in Rubin's words had been 'radically repressed' for half a century.[19] He went further than anyone had before in linking the psychological repression that Freud had theorised to the social and political repression that Karl Marx had focused on. The two are in fact linked: the Freudian unconscious is 'reproduced and maintained by the relations of the society'.[20] In Freud, as in Marx, repression is the result of forces beyond any one person's control or comprehension, so that both make nonsense of the bourgeois ideology of the free individual.[21] But Marcuse was unique in the way that he started from the terms of Freud's own theoretical system and proceeded to turn it inside-out.

In tension with the popular view of Freud as an advocate of less sexual repression, Marcuse noted that for Freud 'a repressive organization of the instincts underlies *all* historical forms of the reality principle in civilization'. Marcuse agreed with Freud that no functioning society was compatible with the immediate gratification of all human impulses. But he argued that Freud confused socially necessary self-restraint, above all in a technologically developed economy, with what he called 'surplus-repression': the 'restrictions necessitated by social domination' above and beyond what was needed to sustain society as such. While people need to be induced to sublimate their desires in the interests of a coherent social response to the 'brute *fact* of scarcity', he wrote, far more sublimation is required now by the 'specific *organization* of scarcity' demanded by alienated labour under capitalism.[22]

---

19   Rubin 2011, p. 47.
20   Padgug 1989, p. 63 (citing Zillah Eisenstein).
21   Althusser 1971, pp. 218–19.
22   Marcuse 1966, pp. 34–6.

For Marcuse, the paradoxical proof that most sexual repression today is needless in a society of relative abundance[23] was what he called 'repressive desublimation'. Capitalism had reached the point at which it had to stimulate desire, at least to some extent, in specific forms conducive to profitable production, rather than simply stifle desire. But this desublimation was repressive, and the satisfaction peculiarly unsatisfying, because it was forced into narrow channels of acquisition and performance. It went together with the 'de-eroticisation' of the environment, because free-floating erotic energy in the wider social environment would in systemic terms be wasted, inasmuch as it would not lead people to purchase or perform. The result under capitalism was a 'localization and contraction of libido' and the reduction of erotic pleasure to the mere pursuit of orgasms.[24]

In a non-capitalist society where human needs could be satisfied without the cycle of alienated labour, payment, purchase and performance, however, far less erotic energy would need to be either repressed or channelled towards profitable activity. Most repression and repressive desublimation could give way to what Marcuse called 'self-sublimation', in which eroticism, in pursuing pleasure, 'transcends it to others, searching for fuller gratification'. The liberated erotic energy of non-genitally-obsessed 'polymorphous perversity' could infuse a panoply of human relations, including 'new and durable work relations'.[25]

There are weaknesses in Marcuse's work: his conception of eroticism as 'a universal energy that exists prior to or outside of social life', and his failure to address the historically varied ways in which sexuality is shaped by changing economic and gender relations.[26] Simply assuming an instinctual sexuality that could be liberated from the constraints of class domination, he left unresolved the question of just what should be liberated. Marcuse's sexual vision foresaw 'the release of a hidden or blocked essence', neglecting the need for conscious intervention in claiming and shaping sexual expression.[27]

---

23   In recent decades, the concept of abundance has been subjected to a radical ecological critique. Marcuse understood abundance, however, not as an endless accumulation of things, but as an adequate relationship between the availability of products and services and the socially constructed array of human needs in a given society. In this sense, abundance in a rationally, justly, sustainably organised society would be compatible with a vastly lower production of cars, washing machines, plane flights, and so on.

24   Marcuse 1964, pp. 75, 73.

25   Marcuse 1966, pp. 211, 155.

26   Hennessy 2000, p. 44.

27   Weeks 1981, pp. 3, 10.

Yet Marcuse did explicitly recognise (if not emphasise) that the reality principle has taken different historical forms, even if he himself failed to investigate the specific forms it had taken. In fact, his account shed a great deal of light on one of those forms, namely, the sexual formation of capitalism in the age of Cold War prosperity. And if the potential for liberation he identified seems less evident today, that is not due to any increase in absolute scarcity in the world (at least not yet – who knows what the consequences may be of the ecological devastation capitalism is producing?) Rather it is a consequence of an increase in alienation, inequality and domination under neoliberalism, a social order that he never witnessed in its fully-fledged form. If Marcuse's objective of transforming genital heterosexuality into liberated polymorphous eroticism seems more remote today, it can at least inspire resistance to the relentlessly advancing alienation of erotic life, and promote a defence of those sexual formations that are most 'perverse' according to the logic of neoliberal capitalism.

What Marcuse clearly recognised is that the 'political moment...can be of key importance in nuancing the regulation of sexuality'.[28] That recognition is less clear in the work of Michel Foucault, whose influence on recent queer thought has been far greater. On the other hand, Foucault's approach has the advantage of emphasising facets of sexual repression and freedom that Marcuse's tended to obscure. Precisely because of his suspicion of accounts that derived all the contours of sexual life from political and economic structures, Foucault emphasised the importance of the micro level, the subtle exchanges and gradations of power in sexuality, and of the pluriformity of sexual desires and practices. Without particularly identifying with feminism as a political project, he provided feminists with useful tools for revealing the many ways in which the personal is political.

Foucault also developed a conception of sexual freedom that was distinctive in its understanding that social and political repression is only one of a number of mechanisms that shape and constrain sexual formations in the interests of maintaining power relations. He saw that sexuality is socially constructed through continual processes of 'the stimulation of bodies, the intensification of pleasures, the incitement to discourse, the formation of special knowledges, the strengthening of controls and resistances'. He thus put in question what he called the 'repressive hypothesis'. He made clear that dominant forces have shaped sexual life through 'polymorphous techniques of power': as much by

---

28   Weeks 1981, p. 15.

inciting, intensifying, redefining, categorising and regulating sexual forms as by rejecting, blocking and invalidating them.[29]

Foucault's neglect of class and state power followed from his conception of power in general, which he believed was inherent in any form of economy, knowledge or sex. 'Power comes from below', he wrote; that is, 'there is no binary and all-encompassing opposition between rulers and ruled at the root of power relations'. While he accepted that the power relations in workplaces, families and other groups crystallise 'wide-ranging effects of cleavage', he asserted, '[m]ajor dominations are [only] the hegemonic effects that are sustained by all these confrontations'.[30] For Foucault, therefore, any major shifts in power structures were ultimately the result not of their own internal dynamics or of collisions between them, but simply of an accumulation of small-scale convergences and shifts.

Foucault's conception of power seems almost designed to rule out the conception of sexual constraint and erotic liberation that Marcuse put forward. In Marcuse's view of repressive desublimation, a man who buys a pornographic magazine, for example, is sexually unfree insofar as his libido has been channelled by the power structures of his society into a form that is conducive to capital accumulation by the publishing company and that perpetuates the distorted relations that the magazine reproduces. In a liberated society as Marcuse conceived of it, the man could instead infuse a broad array of social relations with that erotic energy, not focusing them narrowly on the models' sexual attributes or on the sexual acts he fantasises performing with them. For Foucault, by contrast, since he argued that power came from below, the man, the models and the photographers themselves are the ultimate source of the gender and sexual norms crystallised in the magazine, which could only be changed by an accretion of micro-level changes. The conception of freedom and the possible scope for freedom in this paradigm seem far more limited than in Marcuse's.

Foucault's approach thus underestimated the importance of the power of capital and the state, of men over women, and of white over non-white people.[31] Ultimately, it was incompatible with any idea of a global relationship of forces between oppressor and oppressed that could be changed in major ways (for better or worse). A queer left needs to embrace Foucault's insights into the micro level without neglecting the macro.

---

29 Foucault 1978, pp. 105–6, 111.
30 Foucault 1978, p. 94.
31 Poulantzas 1980, p. 44.

Gayle Rubin has paid ample attention to the macro level of repression, in the form of the sex-negativity she sees as pervasive. She was justified in citing Foucault's statement that he aimed less at dismissing the repressive hypothesis as 'mistaken' than at 'putting it back within a general economy of discourses on sex'.[32] Rubin herself has returned again and again to the analytic matrix of 'an extremely punitive social framework' that she has portrayed as structuring sexuality in 'Western' societies.[33] This highlights the ongoing reality of sexual repression. Rubin has done a great service to historians of sexuality with her catalogues of atrocities against sexual deviants. This book too draws on her examples, which are frequently appalling. Any sexual radicalism worthy of the name has to acknowledge and combat such horrors.

But Rubin has gone too far towards restoring repression to the central place from which Foucault sought to dislodge it. Recent historians have shown that many of the most notoriously sex-negative societies of the last few centuries were not really as sex-negative as their reputations: the Massachusetts Puritans, the English Victorians, or even the Nazis.[34] The powers that be always have many other, more subtle means at their disposal for disparaging, discouraging or regulating sexual dissent and deviance. Foucault was right: as a core explanation, repression does not stand up very well.

Rubin's own approach since the early 1980s has been to define sexuality as a 'vector of oppression' with 'its own intrinsic dynamics', not comprehensible in terms of class, race, ethnicity, or gender.[35] In fact, recognising the reality of repression does not in itself bring us any closer to identifying the direction of a vector of sexual oppression at a specific historical moment, or the logic structuring at a specific historical moment a hierarchy of sexualities – because the direction of the vector and the logic of the hierarchy are usually external to the sexual realm. They reflect the interests and ideologies of dominant economic, social and political forces. And combating the power of those forces demands far more than the 'campaign against prohibitions' that sexual politics has largely been reduced to since the 1970s.[36]

For this reason, Foucault mocked the idea that merely speaking about sex was somehow transgressive and subversive, hastening the advent of a better future. He urged a 'counterattack against the deployment of sexuality' that, rather than focusing on the free expression of sexual desire, would 'counter the

---

32   Foucault 1978, p. 11.
33   Rubin 2011, p. 147.
34   See D'Emilio and Freedman 1997, pp. 3, 5, 22–5, 27; Gay 1999; Herzog 2011, pp. 67–72.
35   Rubin 2011, p. 164.
36   D'Emilio 2002, p. 62.

grips of power with the claims of bodies, pleasures, and knowledges, in their multiplicity and their possibility of resistance'.[37] Here Foucault seemed to converge with Marcuse in defending those sexual formations that are most 'perverse' in the eyes of the dominant forces.

Foucault's sceptical spirit can help us look back to the lesbian/gay radicalism of the 1970s not only with nostalgia, but also with a critically honed historical sense. Certainly there is much to celebrate in the experimentation and transgressive spirit of the 1970s, before AIDS and a growing conservatism reined it in.[38] The impulse to rebel against the mimicking of heterosexual romance and family formation is even more timely today than it was thirty or forty years ago. Having multiple sexual partners and a wide range of sexual practices are hard-won rights that should be defended. With the benefit of hindsight, however, we can see that these rights can be compatible with marital domesticity, a mainstream career and a lifestyle founded on overconsumption.

It is not clear that 'the claims of bodies, pleasures, and knowledges' that Foucault defended equip us to freely lead our sexual lives much better than a simple assertion of the rights of repressed desire. One can, like Kollontai, celebrate sexual pleasure founded on something other than 'all-embracing love' – friendship, caring or comradeship, for instance – while still seeing its most radical potential as dependent on weaving it into a wider social fabric.

Daniel Bensaïd has complained that queer theorists who have inherited Foucault's mantle often seem to sing the praises of 'a shifting shimmer of singularities' rather than promoting a 'dialectic of difference, which is essential to establishing a relationship of forces in the battle against oppression'.[39] A dialectic of difference and a relationship of forces require the context of a wider social fabric. Unfortunately, in this time of crisis and entrenched repressive desublimation, queer activists are engaged in a wearing war of position against conservative impulses that are pervasive in the gay commercial scene and solidly rooted in institutions like marriage. This makes it hard for queers to imagine a major, qualitative improvement in the balance of forces. And it makes the dialectic of difference that should make this blessed event possible seem rather abstract.

Fighting against the many mechanisms of sexual normalisation and defending sexual freedom remain crucial in this situation. In resisting the forces of normalisation, self-organisation by their victims is crucial. This insight into the organisational side of sexual liberation can be traced back to Karl Marx,

---

37   Foucault 1978, pp. 6–7, 157.
38   Shah 2011/2012 (citing Amber Hollibaugh); Altman 1982, esp. pp. 172–207.
39   Bensaïd 2001, p. 42, my translation.

diversity ≠ freedom

inasmuch as he was the first to see self-organisation and self-emancipation as the central elements of a strategy for human liberation. Tragically, in the course of the twentieth century, the tradition Marx founded became identified with movements that had little or nothing to do with self-emancipation. Reinventing the concepts and tools for self-organisation and the exercise of power from below are indispensable to sexual liberation in the twenty-first century.

Alongside the importance of winning sexual freedom through self-organisation by the sexually oppressed, sexual liberation requires a radical definition of the substance of freedom. In this respect, we can learn key lessons from Marcuse, Foucault and Rubin. Drawing selectively on the best of their work, we can define sexual freedom in a way that welcomes the diversity of bodies and pleasures, without viewing diversity alone as the be-all-and-end-all of freedom; that intransigently combats the repression of sexualities that do not deny others' freedom, and at the same time resists the many more subtle techniques through which power incites, manipulates and distorts sexualities; and that is sensitive to the ways power is deployed even in personal relations, while understanding the ultimately determinant role of global power structures in setting the parameters of freedom. In chapter 5, I will return to the task of sketching a radically queer sexual politics that gives substance to this conception of sexual freedom. At this point, however, it is the impact on sexual life of those global power structures that we need to analyse.

Neoliberalism and Gay Normality

The LGBT mainstream has proved insufficiently resistant to the seductions of 'freedom' as defined by the dominant culture, and radical queers have not yet managed to offer a compelling alternative. However, there is one thing that queer radicals increasingly grasp in the twenty-first century: that LGBT struggles today have to be situated in the context of neoliberalism, the specific period of capitalism the world has been in for about thirty years now. We need to give overturning neoliberalism and its gender and sexual dimensions pride of place in our conception of sexual liberation. Neoliberalism's current crisis can be used and is being used to restore a utopian dimension to LGBT politics, in keeping with the insight that linked to sexual desire, another kind of 'desire – desire for something different – is also central to any project of emancipation'.[40]

---

40   Lybeck 2009, p. 29.

For decades under neoliberalism, legal equality has been, in Lisa Duggan's words, 'an empty shell that hides expanded substantive inequalities'.[41] This reality has been concealed behind a 'truce' between the gay mainstream and capital, which welcomes gay 'consumers and professionals in return for acquiescence and accommodation'.[42] By the 1990s, this truce had clearly left its mark on queer politics and queer studies. As Kevin Floyd wrote, 'what was once a healthy queer skepticism about the Marxist tradition...congeal[ed] into something more automatic, dismissive, phobic'.[43]

Some queers have (approvingly or critically) affirmed the existence of a link between gay identity and capitalist consumerism, as when Michael Warner declared, 'Post-Stonewall urban gay men reek of the commodity. We give off the smell of capitalism in rut'.[44] In fact, the decades of neoliberal privatisation and deregulation have also to some extent been decades of what Sears has called 'moral deregulation', in which some of the sexual restrictions that acted as barriers to capital accumulation have been cleared out of the way. This has facilitated a proliferation of LGBT clubs, bars, saunas (for gay and bisexual men), publications, chat sites and more. Undeniably, this sexual liberalisation has expanded sexual possibilities. New gay and lesbian niche markets have become the dynamic centre of spaces in which men and women can explore, act out and celebrate their same-sex desires. Working-class LGBT people in the wealthiest countries have particularly benefited from opportunities for sexual exploration and enjoyment that were once the preserve of the rich.

But whatever queer market enthusiasts imagine, neoliberal moral deregulation has not only expanded sexual possibilities but also fostered new kinds of conformism. The spread of commercial venues and the shrinkage of leisure time and public resources have crowded out some community-based, non-profit LGBT spaces that lack slickness. The days when gay men went to dance at the New York Gay Activists Alliance Firehouse now seem remote. While more grassroots community groups are vital for relatively small geographical and other communities, large community institutions have often edged closer to the businesses that they depend on for funding and 'professional' staff. In the Netherlands, for example, the annual Pink Saturday pride events have been eclipsed by Amsterdam Pride, which from its inception has been run by the Gay Business Association.

---

41 Vaid, Duggan, Metz and Hollibaugh 2013.
42 Hennessy 2006, p. 389.
43 Floyd 1998, p. 171.
44 Floyd 1998, p. 187.

The gay commercial world itself may be big, but it is no model of diversity. While there are profits to be made from LGBT niche markets, there are far more in uniform spaces targeting consumers with the most effective demand, where people with the wrong bodies, the wrong clothes, the wrong sexual practices, the wrong gender or the wrong colour skin are viewed as bad for branding and marketing, and are regularly excluded. The growth of the commercial scene has thus entailed a rise in stigmitisation and marginalisation for many LGBT people.

In an economy of greater inequality, moreover, participation in a commercialised scene requires the ability to pay, and only those who can pay fit in. Finally, and paradoxically, even when commercial spaces serve as outlets for behaviour and imagery perceived as daring, extravagant or transgressive, the contrast between these spaces devoted to consumption and the outside world helps confine sexual daring to the realm of 'private life' and 'free time'. Carryings-on that may be admired in a club on Saturday night could mean big trouble at work or on many neighbourhood or city-centre streets on Monday morning (except to a very limited extent in workplaces or neighbourhoods that are themselves sexualised). Even people who are 'out' at work and in public usually nonetheless self-ghettoise all sorts of actions and images that are central to their sense of LGBT identity, which they manifest only in truncated form in the wider world. This is repressive desublimation on a scale never witnessed by Marcuse. All this means that in more and more parts of the world, neoliberalism has laid the foundation for a new gay normality.

Duggan has defined the politics of this reconciliation with everyday life under neoliberalism as the '*new homonormativity*'. If heteronormativity is the institutionalisation of heterosexuality through the implicit assumption that people are straight unless otherwise labelled, homonormativity is a mind-set that does not 'contest dominant heteronormative assumptions and institutions but upholds and sustains them'.[45] At the same time, homonormativity delivers 'a demobilized gay constituency and a privatized, depoliticized gay culture anchored in domesticity and consumption'.[46] These identity-based politics 'not only eschew class politics, but . . . naturalize capitalism'.[47]

---

45   Duggan 2002, p. 179.

46   Duggan 2003, p. 50. She added the disclaimer that heteronormativity and homonormativity are not equivalent: 'there is no structure for gay life, no matter how conservative or normalizing, that might compare with the institutions promoting and sustaining heterosexual coupling' (Duggan 2003, p. 95, n. 14).

47   Duggan 2003, p. 79. Duggan was on less solid ground when she stated that 'neoliberalism is not a unitary "system", but a complex, contradictory cultural and political project' (2003,

The dynamics that link the reality of LGBT lives under neoliberalism to the growing political differentiation among LGBT people are extremely complex. In chapter 3, I go into more detail about the steady rise over the past half-century of the gay commercial scene and the increasing integration of LGBT people into a neoliberal world order. This is the social constellation that this book is attempting to analyse. Its political consequence is the 'warping' of LGBT movements to which the book is meant to help formulate an alternative.

In the last analysis, I argue, the victories of LGBT movements since the 1960s have made possible the emergence of lesbian/gay petty-bourgeois layers leading relatively comfortable lives in neoliberal societies, which in turn has made possible the development of homonormative ideologies and politics in a tolerated corner of a heteronormative world. At the same time, the growth of layers of younger LGBT working-class and marginalised people, with lower incomes and less economic security, has been crucial for a queer rebellion against the new gay normality. This helps explain the paradoxes of victory and defeat of the past forty years. In hindsight, the lesbian/gay upsurges of the late 1960s and 1970s bore the seeds of both ongoing queer resistance and the new homonormativity. Their victories were in part genuine victories for all LGBT people, and in part victories specifically for an emergent lesbian/gay elite that reaped disproportionate benefits from them. Now the agendas of gay normality and queer resistance are parting company, at different rhythms in different parts of the world, with many LGBT individuals still combining elements of both in their consciousness.

The picture is further complicated by a number of other factors. The possibility of an openly gay petty bourgeoisie depends on the space that exists for openly lesbian and gay lives, which varies enormously from continent to continent, country to country, and region to region. Where even middle-class LGBT people cannot safely be open about their sexuality, they may succumb in all sorts of ways to conservatising pressures, but their adaptation cannot be described as genuinely homonormative. On the other hand, many working-class and poor LGBT people, even in regions where LGBT rights are relatively well established, have sexual lives and relationships that are not particularly

---

p. 70). Like any regime of accumulation whose sway has extended across continents for several decades, neoliberalism is indeed complex and contradictory, and requires specific institutional mediations. As the economists I cite in chapter 3 have shown, however, it is the manifestation of a deep-rooted, persistent drive by capital to respond to the crisis of profitability afflicting capitalism since the 1970s. Grasping this reality is crucial in enabling us to understand the stubborn hegemony of the neoliberal consensus among virtually every major political force in the world.

transgressive by the standards of their time and place. A whole range of other factors – race, nationality, ethnicity, religion, gender, disability, family history, sexual inclination, intellectual conviction, individual psychology – can influence people's choice to (not) identify with left-wing and/or queer perspectives.

All these complexities make clear the pitfalls of a queer voluntarism, prevalent in some radical queer circles, which views the divide as pivoting on a personal ethical choice. This voluntarism often sets an unreasonably high standard for activism, demands of all LGBT people an immediate and full rejection of racism, sexism and 'classism', dismisses hard-won working-class gains as evidence of co-optation, and often fosters too little patience for dialogue or organising with those outside the charmed circle of the enlightened. Most LGBT people are too busy with the business of day-to-day survival to be ideologically pure, at least as long as their own lives do not confront them with inescapable choices. There is a slow process of sorting-out that is underway, which cannot be forced, though it can be encouraged and supported. True radicalism consists of mobilising people when they can be mobilised, on the specific issues on which they can be mobilised, so as to set a dynamic in motion that can lead to more far-reaching changes.

Fortunately for the resistance to neoliberalism and specifically to homonormativity, there are still many LGBT people that the lesbian/gay right and centre are not about to integrate, people that radical queers should be able to reach if they go about it intelligently. Class and race are obviously crucial factors that divide even most 'normal gay' people from the new gay right. Most LGBT people are working class – in the broad sense of having to work for an employer in order to survive – and the limitations of politics that the lesbian/gay mainstream have to offer them have become 'more and more obvious'. Existing lesbian/gay leaderships 'advocate for their own class agenda in an endlessly infuriating way'.[48] One result is that open queers are more often active in, and bring queer perspectives to, other movements.

Imperialism is another key factor in politicising LGBT people. Even the sometimes intense repression experienced by LGBT people in countries like Lebanon and Palestine fail to convince most of them to side with the US, Israeli and European 'liberal' forces that are assaulting their nations. This leads some LGBT people to reject 'the "us versus them" of the war on terror'[49] – sometimes even replacing this false 'us versus them' with the real 'us versus them' of class and of progressive opposition to empire.

---

48   Hollibaugh and Singh 1999, pp. 85–6.
49   Puar 2007, p. 215.

The challenge of developing a genuinely radical queer politics, presented in this way in the full extent of its different dimensions, is a daunting one. It is not enough simply to assert the necessity of tackling many different tasks. For political activists, the temptations are great to dismiss one task or another as peripheral. LGBT trade unionists, for example, can be tempted to dismiss small queer activist groups as marginal, irrelevant and unhelpful. Radical queer activists can be quick to dismiss trade unions, traditional social movements and political parties as hopelessly old-fashioned and in thrall to hetero- and/ or homonormativity. This book tries to make the case that a comprehensive understanding of the class, racial, gender and sexual dynamics of today's neoliberalism, including their structural anchoring in capitalism and their complex imbrication with forms thrown up by centuries of historical development, leaves us no alternative but to accept the full complexity and diversity of queer struggles.

We can see now that 'heterosexual hegemony' is both stubbornly persistent and strikingly diverse in the forms it takes. As Antonio Gramsci saw, hegemony has always relied not only on 'consent, legitimation, and "common sense"', but also on 'denial, silencing, and coercion'.[50] Today we see, as with bourgeois hegemony in capitalist societies generally, how variable the mix of consent and coercion in heterosexual hegemony can be. In Zimbabwe, coercion is still very much foregrounded. In Denmark, 'common sense' is more effective today in identifying same-sex desire as something 'perfectly normal' and yet not the norm, that is, as the domain of a protected but permanent minority.

A broad queer resistance to neoliberalism and gay normality will have to take widely different forms as it grows up in different places and circumstances in the course of different fights. No one identity, ideology or political current can or should dominate it. It should have room for people who self-identify as lesbian, gay, bisexual, trans, intersex[51] or queer, for anarchists, greens, militant social democrats, left-wing feminists and anti-racists, and more. Leslie Feinberg has observed that like rivers, 'movements are driven by many political currents.

---

50   Kinsman 1987, p. 33.

51   Intersex people are those whose genitals and/or other reproductive organs are perceived at their birth or later as complicating an unambiguous classification as male or female, whether or not an attempt is made to 'correct' this ambiguity through surgery and/or treatment, and whatever gender identity the person is assigned or assumes in later life. Many theorists and activists today recognise intersex people by using the acronym LGBTI. Since I have found it difficult enough to fully include trans people when referring to LGBT people, and impossible to do full justice to intersex people as well in all these contexts, I have stuck, with apologies, to 'LGBT'.

Which currents determine the course of the river for a time is also affected by external factors, like prevailing winds, storms, the inexorable pull of the moon and the resulting tides'.[52]

Increasingly, however, queer radicalism is defining itself as not only anti-neoliberal, but also anti-capitalist. This does not imply subscribing to any blueprint of a socialist alternative, much less following the lead of any organisation. Rather, it entails accepting the growing weight of evidence that neoliberal policies are not simply mistaken or the result of a temporary advantage enjoyed by right-wing forces; rather, in this prolonged time of crisis, they are the result of the inherent, systemic logic of global capitalism. Moreover, queer anti-capitalism implies a commitment by queers to join with others to resist the tremendous power that the system confers on capital.

One can be anti-capitalist in this way without being Marxist. One can even make use of the helpful analytical tools that historical materialism offers without identifying politically as a Marxist. Within the emerging array of queer anti-capitalist currents, however, I believe that queer Marxists – as long as they devote themselves to working within and building broader frameworks, without trying to impose any sectarian agenda or separate group interests – have a special and key contribution to make.

The Return of Marxism?

The movement for lesbian/gay liberation, born out of the New Left of the 1960s, inevitably tried in its first decade or two to engage with Marxism. Names like 'Gay Liberation Front', pervasive for a few years from 1969 into the early 1970s, indicate the strength of the connection. They also suggest the kind of Marxism that was mostly engaged with – one more linked to anti-imperialist guerrilla struggles and radical nationalism than to the traditions of working-class socialism. Still, the engagement was a serious one, leading lesbian/gay activists to wrestle with issues of Marxist strategy and theory well into the 1980s. Even after Marxism became much less fashionable, the radical left retained some Marxist references, as well as significant influence on LGBT activism into the last decade of the twentieth century. At the same time, however, LGBT movements have 'warped', twisting away from the left-wing worldviews that characterised many early twentieth-century 'sex reformers' and post-1968 lesbian/gay liberationists.

---

52   Feinberg 1998, p. 61.

The rightward trend that took hold of LGBT organisations in many countries by the 1990s still does not seem to have exhausted itself – even after 2008, as the outbreak of a global economic crisis has shaken the myth of a capitalist 'best of all possible worlds' and shown the urgency of long-neglected class issues. But at least debates that a few years ago seemed almost definitively closed are now being re-opened. LGBT activists who raise class issues or ask Marxist-sounding questions can no longer be so easily dismissed.

Given the immense challenges for social organising and political practice, there may initially be more openings for academic and theoretical discussions of class and capitalism. There have been scholarly efforts all along to link Marxism and queer studies. These have included Rosemary Hennessy's landmark book *Profit and Pleasure* (2000) – unfortunately published when academics were, in her words, 'galloping away from Marxism in one direction or another, disparaging its fundamental concepts . . . as the last vestiges of modernity's "grand narratives"'.[53] As a result, *Profit and Pleasure* received far less attention than it deserved. It is symptomatic now in the deepening crisis, as Floyd suggested in 2010, that people in queer studies are paying more attention to Marxism's 'explanatory power'.[54] Floyd was vindicated barely a year later when the leading queer studies journal GLQ published a special issue on the crises of capitalism, complete with a silhouette of Karl Marx on the cover, in which most of the articles referred in one way or another to Marxist concepts.

This book means to seize this occasion in several ways. It aims at joining the discussion in queer studies by going more deeply into contributions that historical materialism can make to the study of same-sex sexualities and LGBT identities. It tries to convince Marxists that following these discussions is important and urgent. And I hope it will give radical, LGBT activists tools to shift the movement's debates and practice back to the left.

I start from the understanding that there no longer exists (if there ever did) a single, unified Marxist politics. In almost every one of the fiercest debates that have divided LGBT movements since the 1970s, people have claimed the authority of Marxism for opposite positions. This reflects in part the deep divisions between different Marxisms over the past century: between advocates of reform and advocates of revolution, between partisans of grassroots democracy and of top-down guidance by a supposedly scientifically informed vanguard, between those who have embraced movements like feminism and those who have tended to suspect movements other than labour of petty-bourgeois deviations.

---

53   Hennessy 2000, p. 28.
54   Floyd 2010, p. 2.

The dominant trend within the Marxist left – not only during the heyday of Stalinist homophobia from the 1930s to the 1950s, but well beyond it – has been heteronormative.[55] Even in many Marxist organisations today whose positions on LGBT liberation are good on paper, and whose leaders' personal opposition to heterosexism is clear and sincere, the heterosexuality of their members tends to be assumed and the heteronormativity of their internal culture persists.[56]

In the rest of this introduction, therefore, I try to set out the theoretical foundations of the specific kind of Marxism that I believe LGBT movements need. This Marxism can never be a monolith; it will remain what Bensaïd has called it, an 'archipelago of controversies, conjectures, refutations and experiences'.[57] But at a minimum, it can and must be non-reductionist, non-Eurocentrist and anti-economistic, and founded on the basic imperative of self-organisation of all the oppressed. I believe that this Marxism is particularly indispensable to an understanding of sexual and gender oppression and dissent,[58] and that a sexual dimension also has to be integrated into other progressive movements if they are to be effective. As Hennessy put it, we need 'to imagine and form collective class agency that does not reify "the proletariat", foreclose sexuality, or relegate it to a secondary status'.[59]

I especially want to contribute to renewing the socialist feminist debates of the 1970s and 1980s, in support of socialist feminists who have continued to insist that capitalism is in its essence a *gendered* mode of social production and reproduction that needs to be combated as such. I also support the integration into Marxist politics of key insights from other paradigms that have been important for queer politics, such as the radical Freudianism pioneered by Marcuse among others, the radical libertarianism of Foucault, and the queer activism (especially anti-racist queer activism) linked to some extent to recent queer theory.[60]

Merely to outline this very full agenda is to push against the limits of queer studies' still tentative return to engagement with Marxism. For some of us, the renewed openness to discussions of Marxism among some queer currents is the fulfilment of a dream that we cherished for many lonely years. Yet our

---

55   Kinsman 1987, p. 14.
56   For an attempt by one international Marxist current (mine) to understand and combat these dynamics, see Fourth International 2003, *Part IV: Public Profile and Internal Life*.
57   Bensaïd 2013, p. 301.
58   The term 'sexual and gender dissent' is borrowed from Healey 2001.
59   Hennessy 2000, p. 231.
60   Camfield 2014 makes a similar plea.

enthusiasm has to be tempered by an awareness of the limits of the openings there have been so far. The tide may be rising, but even if it is, so far it is hardly halfway up the beach.

Too often even today, 'the relationship between sexual identities and capitalism remains for the most part ... unexplored – even unspeakable'. Perhaps the taboo on Marxism has been weakened. And the critical tone of queer discussions of Marxism is fully justified; the tradition's weaknesses on sexual politics are undeniable. Those Marxists who *have* tried to link capitalism to sexual identities have too often failed to acknowledge just how 'complex, indirect, and historically variable' the relationship is.[61] Many critics have justifiably 'interrogated the historical lapses of political economy and Marxism in thinking gender, race, and sexuality'.[62] As one Marxist has sourly commented, some Marxists treat '*Capital* as if it were a lemon, as if by squeezing it hard enough all the categories of social life would come dripping out'.[63] Even some LGBT Marxists have been 'seduced into an essentially heterosexist project where gay issues are sidelined'.[64]

Marxism's unique strength is its understanding of the dynamics of capitalism, and of the key role the working class can play (and sometimes does play) in resisting the power of capital. But its special claim to LGBT activists' and theorists' attention hinges on its effectiveness in creating a multidimensional, radical sexual analysis and politics that address nationalism, race and gender, as well as class and capital. And critical Marxists have been working for decades to hone its effectiveness, not only in the heady years of the 1970s and early 1980s, but in the more difficult decades since. Particularly since the 1980s, the increasingly clear inefficacy of earlier forms of working-class organisation has spurred them to pay attention to other potential agencies of social transformation, such as indigenous peoples, women and LGBT people. This book is aimed at showing that the reinvention of a class-based politics of anti-capitalist transformation can only take place in interaction with non-class-based currents like radical queers.

Historical experience – not only in Russia in 1917 and France in 1968, but more recently labour's role in toppling dictatorships from Brazil to Poland to South Korea to Tunisia and other countries – has demonstrated the working class's tremendous potential power. But we see today that neoliberalism has increasingly fragmented and weakened labour movements. Consequently,

---

61   Hennessy 2000, p. 4.
62   Rosenberg and Villarejo 2012, p. 2.
63   Rubin 2011, p. 303.
64   Edge 1995, pp. 3–4.

many of the strongest forms of resistance to neoliberalism have had non-class bases. Anti-neoliberal movements organised around non-class identities have not always taken progressive forms. The parallel crises of capitalism and of non-capitalist alternatives have favoured the development of 'non-rational (sometimes irrational) reactions' in the shape of religious, national and other identity-based movements.[65]

In the English-speaking world, left-wing activists describe such movements, more or less pejoratively, as 'identity politics'. Some Marxists are totally dismissive of it, describing identity-based movements as 'cries for help rather than carriers of programmes', calls for 'some "community" to belong to in a world of social isolates; some refuge in the jungle'.[66] Even LGBT Marxists sometimes apply this dismissal to LGBT identity politics. It can in fact be a 'barrier to solving class-based injustices' by fostering 'group loyalty across class lines' and mostly benefiting middle-class leaderships.[67] And ultimately, attempts to 'live sexually liberated lives under the current material circumstances will always come up against the real limitations of people's daily existence'.[68]

But the 'current material circumstances' are not reducible to capitalism or class oppression alone. Non-class identities need to be analysed concretely, case by case, particularly distinguishing imposed identities from freely chosen ones, fixed identities from fluid ones, monolithic identities from crosscutting ones. Identities' potential as sources of strength and sites of resistance needs to be acknowledged.[69] The possibility needs to be held open of deploying identities in ways that do not petrify them, but rather seize upon whatever in them is most dynamic and open-ended. And non-class identities cannot be fully grasped if seen only as divisions sown by the ruling class in the interests of perpetuating its rule. While employers and right-wing politicians can and do take advantage of every kind of prejudice, this is not an adequate explanation of the power of the heterosexual norm, or of the persistence of anti-LGBT prejudice even in the absence of direct or visible ruling-class influence.

As Hennessy has argued, unmet affective and sexual needs are only part of a much larger domain of 'outlawed needs', which are 'the monstrous outside to capitalism that haunts it'. A major challenge in building a movement against capitalism is thus to intervene at the points where 'labor and desire meet'.[70]

---

65   Löwy 1998, p. 63.
66   Hobsbawm 1994, p. 342.
67   D'Emilio 2002, p. 143.
68   Wolf 2010, p. 276.
69   Crenshaw 1993, pp. 1242, 1297.
70   Hennessy 2006, pp. 389, 391.

This means recognising that 'a politics without sexuality is doomed to failure or deformation'.[71]

Culture, class, community and desire have in fact always been key to working-class organising itself. Class politics is also fundamentally about culture and community, about working people as 'full members and sharers in collective life'.[72] Every serious study of working-class movements and politics has demonstrated that class is 'lived through race and gender'.[73] Identity politics has often enriched rather than displaced people's understanding of class. So class organising is impossible without taking account of the way class is actually lived, through race, gender, and sexuality in particular – including issues like family life that queer politics addresses.[74] This is no easy task. The whole second part of this book is devoted to figuring out how to meet this challenge in a number of ways. But no left that fails to confront it can succeed today.

Failure to recognise the interdependence of class and other identities exacerbates the trend of 'identity-based political formations drifting rightward into neoliberalism's embrace, while being denigrated and dismissed' on the left: 'a self-propelling, self-defeating, utterly antiproductive spiral of political schism'.[75] The neglect of class in identity politics is paralleled by the tendency of economism – a single-minded focus on class and other economic factors – to neglect everything else. The ferocity of the clash between economism and identity politics often conceals the fact that each of them is peddling a rival brand of reformism, each resisting in its own way the radical potential that a synthesis of class-based and other movements could yield.

Non-Marxist queers too should ask themselves some hard questions. For example, after decades of a retreat from class in the academy in the midst of intensified class conflict, is it possible now in LGBT circles to talk seriously about the labour movement and left-wing parties? To tackle head-on and consistently the barriers to participation in queer activism by working-class people and by the poorer four-fifths of the earth's population? To suggest that Lenin, whatever he did wrong, nonetheless made significant contributions to anti-racism, national liberation and fights against non-class forms of

---

71   Padgug 1989, p. 55.
72   Duggan 2003, p. 83.
73   Krupat 1999, p. 24 (citing Robin D.G. Kelley).
74   Duggan 2003, pp. 85, 83.
75   Duggan 2003, p. 71.

oppression in general?[76] To discuss socialist feminism and a possible world beyond gendered capitalism? The publication of this book is meant to help pry open debate on these questions. Time will tell, of course, how much and what sort of discussion will be forthcoming.

There is resistance to such discussions even among radical queers. While queer studies has increasingly foregrounded a critique of neoliberalism, even taking an anti-capitalist position and using Marxian analytic categories, it still often shuns the historical tradition of the left 'as a model [even a critically reshaped model] for new political engagement'.[77]

Even if Marxists can offer a critically reshaped model of engagement, they have no legitimate claim to a monopoly of queer radicalism. Just as resistance to neoliberalism is and must be far broader than the ranks of those committed to overthrowing capitalism, so Marxists should hope only to be accepted as one tendency among several trying to build a global, mass, class-conscious, anti-racist, feminist queer politics. They can show that they have useful insights to contribute without winning everyone over to their full perspective. However, Marxists can try to play the role of the backbone of a new queer politics, in two ways. On the one hand, starting from an appreciation of the vital importance of broad outreach to LGBT working people, Marxists can help guard against queer radicals' tendency to sub-cultural self-isolation. On the other hand, starting from an appreciation of the harm done by centre-left versions of neo-liberalism with a human face, Marxists can help guard against leftists' strong temptation (whatever their sexualities or ideologies) to join in a kinder, gentler form of accommodation.

Closer attention to capitalism might 'return "queer" to … some of the political promise from which it has in recent years become unmoored'.[78] And who knows, despite the seriousness of the challenge we face, perhaps restoring broader horizons to 'the politics of pleasure will serve to deepen the pleasures, as well as to widen the possibilities, of politics'.[79]

---

76   The GLQ special issue on the crises of capitalism, for example, contained only one, pass-
      ing, negative reference to Lenin (Crosby et al. 2012, p. 142 – unless one counts two cita-
      tions of Althusser's Lenin and Philosophy).

77   Lecklider 2012, p. 184.

78   Crosby et al. 2012, p. 136 (citing David Eng).

79   Halperin 2002, p. 103.

Against Racism and Empire

Within the Marxist tradition, its encounter with the second wave of feminism probably did more than anything else to spur explicit exploration of the connections between class and non-class oppressions and struggles. Yet in a previous phase of Marxist renewal, in response to a crisis in the early twentieth century with the rise of imperialism and the collapse in 1914 of the Second International, labour's relationship to national and anti-racist movements provoked equally deep divisions and profound rethinking. In queer studies' engagement today with radical activism too, the most central political concerns relate to struggles against racism and imperialism.

The link with anti-racism is particularly compelling. Racism 'of any kind has necessarily always been also about sex'[80] – though the other way around, sexuality's connection with ' "race" is still something that can be overlooked'.[81] Foucault's key insight that twentieth- and twenty-first-century racism has shifted its emphasis from determining who will die to granting or denying the means to live[82] helps make clear how racism is deployed today in such sexualised domains as fertility and health.[83] Born as it was in the first months of the post-Cold War world, queer activism also from the beginning intermittently took part in anti-imperialist actions, in the US, for example, playing a visible role in demonstrations against the 1991 Gulf War.[84]

Yet specifically Marxist approaches to anti-racism and anti-imperialism have been strikingly absent so far from the discussion in queer circles. In fact, the predominant picture of Marxism among queer radicals (inasmuch as there is one) is that Marxism may have useful insights to contribute on class and economics, but virtually none on race, ethnicity or gender. Rubin, for example, despite calling the neglect of Marx 'a tragedy' in 1994 and hoping for a revival of interest in his work, has continued to uphold the position she staked out in 1982: 'Marxism is most successful in the areas of social life for which it was originally developed – class relations under capitalism'[85] – and by implication, should approach other areas of social life with modesty and restraint. This picture does not do justice to the achievements of the sophisticated Marxism that has developed since the 1970s, largely under the impact

---

80   Herzog 2011, p. 70.
81   Wekker 2006, p. 5.
82   Foucault 1978, pp. 135–45.
83   Puar 2007, p. 200 (citing Rey Chow).
84   Stryker 2008, p. 135.
85   Rubin 2011, pp. 303, 179.

of radical feminism and anti-racism – or even to the classical Marxism of the Second and Third Internationals.

The works of Karl Kautsky, the leading theorist of Second International Marxism in Europe before the First World War, contain a number of striking statements about the importance for socialist politics of non-class identities like nation and sex. In 1900, Kautsky wrote that the working class could not free itself without 'making an end to all oppression and exploitation', and thus had to be 'the advocate of all ... oppressed classes, oppressed nations, and an oppressed sex'. 'The need for freedom, for self-determination, is as natural as the need for food', he wrote later; socialists had to be 'the most tireless champions of the freedom of all who were oppressed, not merely the wage-earner, but also of women, persecuted religions and races, the Jews, Negroes and Chinese'.[86]

Lenin, before the First World War an orthodox Marxist follower and admirer of Kautsky,[87] was echoing this authority when he wrote his well-known lines in 1902 insisting that a Marxist must be not a 'trade union secretary, but the *tribune of the people*, who is able to react to every manifestation of tyranny and oppression, no matter where it appears, no matter what stratum or class of the people it affects'.[88] Lenin's statements on the key importance of non-class struggles became even more forceful after the outbreak of the First World War in 1914. He identified a narrow economism as one symptom of the desertion of revolutionary politics that had discredited and hobbled the Second International in the face of war.

In 1916, for example, in response to the Irish Easter Rising, Lenin wrote:

> To imagine that social revolution is *conceivable* without revolts by small nations in the colonies and in Europe, without revolutionary outbursts by a section of the petty bourgeoisie *with all its prejudices*, without a movement of the politically non-conscious proletarian and semi-proletarian masses against oppression by the landowners, the church, and the monarchy, against national oppression, etc. – to imagine all this is to *repudiate social revolution*.[89]

As a Marxist, Lenin saw the strategic role of the working class in a socialist transformation as central. But drawing on and deepening Kautsky's insights,

86   Kautsky 1900; Kautsky 1918.
87   See Lih 2006.
88   Lenin 1961.
89   Lenin 1970.

he was also convinced that semi-proletarian and non-proletarian movements were indispensable.

Lenin's conviction was important, after the foundation of the Third (Communist) International in 1919, in making Communists worldwide take anti-racism, anti-imperialism and the right to self-determination seriously. The consequences were visible for decades in anti-racist movements, in the US and South Africa, for example, and in dozens of struggles for national liberation. Pressure from the Communist International made it possible for US Communists to converge in the early 1920s with New York's African Blood Brotherhood.[90] Its legacy made it possible decades later for South African Communists to work closely with the African National Congress, and the US Socialist Workers Party in the mid-1960s with Malcolm X.[91] Recognising this fact by no means requires dodging the question of Lenin's contribution to the preconditions for Stalinist tyranny,[92] nor does it entail accepting any of the variants of 'Leninist' ideology that were largely manufactured after Lenin's death. A Marxist approach can nonetheless be useful in joining queer politics to anti-racism and anti-imperialism – and help is badly needed, given the limitations of queer activism to date in speaking compellingly to the racially oppressed or the peoples of the dominated countries.

Queer anti-racism would benefit from greater engagement with Lenin's theory of imperialism, which helps explain the global hierarchy that traps the great majority of the world's peoples in economic dependence and domination. It could also be informed by Marx's concept of the 'industrial reserve army', which later Marxists have used to help explain the racialisation of economic divides. For Marx, the existence of a large section of the working class that was structurally paid lower wages and subjected to more frequent unemployment ensured that the class as a whole produced through technological change 'the means by which it is itself made relatively superfluous' and put 'a curb on [workers'] pretensions'.[93] More recent Marxists have stressed that some workers are made even more superfluous and allowed even fewer pretensions than others.

Racism helps justify the existence of a disproportionately non-white reserve army and to stigmatise those who constitute it. Today, as a result of neoliberal globalisation, immigrant workers from the dominated countries have joined

---

90   Draper 1986, pp. 324–31.
91   On the SWP and Malcolm X, see Breitman 1967.
92   See Farber 1990.
93   Marx 1976, pp. 781–802, esp. 783, 792.

the reserve armies of the US and Europe.[94] Thus, in most imperialist countries today, the reserve army is racially defined. When 'class-based responses to the insecurities of life under capitalism appear impractical, white workers will seek to defend themselves as whites against the racialized threat of the reserve army of labor'[95] – a potent source of racism.

A better understanding of the dynamics of racism and empire can clarify the potential and limits of queer radicalism. This book suggests that queer politics today in the countries I will call 'imperialist'[96] can best be understood as a reaction against the gay normality that increasingly prevails there. However, this dynamic is very different in different regions. There are countries like the Netherlands and Denmark where gay normality is clearly hegemonic, despite the obvious continuing strength of heteronormativity in the wider societies; in these countries, a queer critique of homonormativity is a precondition to any serious radical LGBT politics. In some other locations – South Africa,

---

94   Magdoffs 2004.

95   Post 2007b. Post has also noted that the reserve army consists disproportionately of women and immigrants, so that in the absence of class responses workers can defend themselves in equally reactionary ways as 'males, native-born or straight' (2007a).

96   A word is needed here in defence of the terminology I will use: 'imperialist' or '(economically) dominant' countries on the one hand, and '(economically) dominated' or 'dependent' on the other. Calling the world's richest countries 'developed' or 'advanced' and the poorest ones 'less developed', as even Marxists sometimes do, would seem to imply that poverty somehow results from a failure of capitalism to develop fully, whereas history shows that as capitalism develops, inequality tends to intensify. The term 'underdeveloped', which Walter Rodney (1972) used as a verb to describe what Europe did to Africa, seems in practice to have the same unfortunate and false connotation as 'less developed' for many people who are unfamiliar with it. Hennessy's term 'overdeveloped' has the advantage of highlighting waste and overconsumption in rich countries, but the disadvantage of seeming to overlook the poverty that exists even in rich countries and the exploitation of its own working classes that is central to capital's accumulation there. To the term 'dependent' the objection might be made that imperialist capital is as dependent on the resources and cheap labour of poor countries as these countries are on the imperialist centres, but in fact it is not. Multinational capital continues to extract the great bulk of its profits from Europe, North America and Japan, while dominated countries depend on the global market for a huge proportion of their income. Capital's reliance on the BRICS (Brazil, Russia, India, China and South Africa) and other 'emerging economies', while increasing, is still limited. In fact, the gap between the average incomes of imperialist countries and the average incomes of dependent countries has deepened since the 1980s (especially if one leaves aside China and India – two countries where domestic inequality has been increasing sharply) (Thoresen 2012, p. 25). And capital is virtually indifferent to vast areas of the planet and the billions of people who live there.

Argentina, Mexico, Spain and the US, for example – enclaves of emerging gay normality, signalled by the passage of same-sex marriage, exist alongside large areas where LGBT people are often very much on the defensive. In these countries, explicit radical queer organising may be called for at some times and places, while at others any LGBT organising at all may be implicitly radical.

Finally, in many dominated countries, where homonormativity is much weaker or absent, a radical sexual politics may be able to develop in greater continuity with the initial radicalism of lesbian/gay liberation. This suggests that while an explicitly queer outlook is essential in some countries as a militant response to homonormativity, and is important in at least some parts of other countries, in much of the dependent world a radical LGBT politics cannot be defined mainly as anti-homonormative in LGBT people's specific national or regional contexts. This helps explain why the word 'queer' has not yet caught on as broadly in these countries.[97] Yet it has been picked up there too, particularly by trans people, as when the Indian group Stree Sangam in 2002 changed its name to LABIA and its self-definition from a 'lesbian and bisexual women's group' to a 'queer and feminist collective of lesbian, transgender and bisexual women', defining its politics as 'contesting the heteronormative constructs of both gender and sexuality'.[98]

At the same time, gay normality continues to spread, even to unexpected places. Turkey's Republican People's Party, for example, the heir to the party that dominated the country in the first half of the twentieth century, proposed in 2012 adding LGBT rights protection to the country's constitution. Coming from an embattled opposition party, the proposal was certain to be rejected. Even if it had been adopted, its top-down nature would not have transformed Turkish society at a stroke or brought the country's (generally radical) LGBT movement to power. Yet the mere fact that it was made shows the depth of a dynamic towards gay normality at work below the surface.

I also believe that LGBT people's struggles, even in parts of the dependent world where there is not much of a 'normal' gay ghetto, are in part directed against a *global* homonormativity: an attitude among the emerging global lesbian/gay elite that defines other sexualities as derivative or even inferior. Many LGBT people in dominated countries sense this condescension; the most radical activists among them rebel against it. A truly global sexual radicalism can be defined as 'queer' in this sense. It can also draw on Gloria Anzaldúa's

---

97   At least among activists or a broad LGBT public. Jackson has noted, however, the rising influence of queer studies in Asia: at the first International Conference of Asian Queer Studies in Bangkok in 2005, over 160 papers were presented (2009, p. 388, n. 3).

98   Shah, Raj, Mahajan and Nevatia 2012, pp. 189–90.

linkage of the queer to 'borderlands' inhabited by 'the squint-eyed, the perverse, the queer, the troublesome, the mongrel, the mulatto, the half breed, the
half dead; in short those who cross over, pass over or go through the confines
of the "normal"'.[99]

A truly global sexual radicalism remains to be created, however. The movement for lesbian/gay liberation began its breakthrough in the late 1960s at a
moment of crisis for the capitalist world order, often identifying its goals with
those of movements for liberation from imperialism. However, the later, rapid
expansion of LGBT identities and rights on a global scale has coincided with
a period of several decades in which capital responded offensively to its economic and geopolitical crisis, with a series of structural transformations and
policy shifts that constitute neoliberal globalisation. The international LGBT
movement structures that have grown up in these decades are generally dependent on funding and other resources from Western Europe and other rich
countries. As a result, however sincere the impulses of solidarity that motivate
their leaders, as organisations they have often been more influenced by contemporary ideologies of globalisation than by earlier ideas of anti-imperialism.

In such conditions, 'colonial structures of knowing and seeing remain in
place within a discourse of an "international" lesbian and gay movement'.[100]
LGBT activists from the dominated countries have often found themselves
contending, against the organisational odds, that 'the Western gay is not seated
at the top of the evolutionary tree',[101] that there is no 'triumphant progress and
transfer of sexual forms and identities from the West to the Rest',[102] or that they
need not 'recreate them[selves] in a Western mold'. When they say to 'Western
gay people, "We are like you"', they 'must remember to add, "only different"'.[103]

Sex and Feminism

An analysis of gender relations, at least as much as of racism and national
oppression, must be at the heart of a radical sexual politics. In their different ways, Marxists and feminists have long understood that the bourgeois
individual 'depends on the labor of those who enable his or her existence',
whether in factories, offices or homes, and that sexual relations are 'part and

99   Shah 2005, p. 721.
100   Gopinath 1998, p. 117.
101   Jackson 1989, p. 358.
102   Wekker 2006, p. 226.
103   Altman 1996, p. 81 (citing Shivanda Khan), 90 (citing Eduardo Nierras).

parcel of the social relations' that make labour possible in all these locations.[104] Politically, this means that sexuality has been a central battleground in fights for and against gender equality.[105] Theoretically, this struggle requires 'a feminist historical materialism ... flexible in its openness to ... sexuality, historical in its emphasis on ... the construction of gender and race, and dialectical in its emphasis on contradiction'.[106]

A feminist historical materialism presupposes an understanding of the basic concept of gender. Marx and Engels saw divisions between men and women as biological and therefore prior to social categories like capital and labour. But socialist feminists since the 1960s have, like most feminists, distinguished social gender – a term largely popularised in the 1950s with a somewhat different agenda by sexologist John Money[107] – from biological sex. At the beginnings of gay liberation, Altman borrowed this crucial insight from Kate Millett; David Fernbach backed it up with anthropological evidence and explored its meaning for gay oppression.[108] Rubin expressed the insight in a classic essay by paraphrasing a passage from Marx's *Capital*: 'A woman is a woman. She only becomes a domestic, a wife, a chattel, a playboy bunny, a prostitute, or a human Dictaphone in certain relations'.[109] Many Marxist feminists' conception of gender reflects the complex ways in which 'capitalism integrates and employs pre-capitalist power relations to create hierarchies of exploited and oppressed, digging trenches and raising barriers'.[110]

By the 1970s, for the most radical wing of the lesbian/gay movement, a fundamental critique of gender became key to their self-understanding as advocates of liberation and not merely of equal rights within the existing system. Their goals became dismantling the heterosexual family institution that was a source of oppression for both women and gays, and entirely transcending the categories of 'masculinity' and 'femininity'. In a seminal article, Iris Young stressed that with women playing a crucial role both on the bottom rungs of the waged workforce and in the reproduction of labour outside it, their oppression is central to production relations as a whole. Returning to the conception of the division of labour in Marx and Engels as an even more fundamental category

104   Jakobsen 2012, pp. 25, 27.
105   D'Emilio and Freedman 1997, p. xviii.
106   Sangster and Luxton 2012, p. 304.
107   Jordan-Young 2010, pp. 12–13.
108   Altman 1971, pp. 83, 93, 205–8, 213–17; Fernbach 1981, pp. 15–60, 69–91, 111–12.
109   Rubin 2011, p. 34.
110   Arruzza 2013, p. 126.

than class, Young posited the gendered division of labour as a key category.[111]
A feminist historical materialism thus takes as a starting point 'the socially
necessary and socially organized labor through which humans reproduce
themselves – not only the production of things but the work involved in using
those things to renew life'.[112]

In the socialist feminist synthesis, women under capitalism play key roles
as unpaid reproducers of labour power, as cheaper paid labour power, as a
disproportionate part of the industrial reserve army and as organisers of consumption. Socialist feminists have frontally attacked the male bias implicit
in many earlier forms of Marxism. They have noted that although women do
most of the world's socially necessary labour, 'much of it is rendered invisible'.[113]
Housework in particular is 'a key element in the process of the reproduction
of the laborer', and a crucial way of integrating women into 'the surplus-value
nexus which is the sine qua non of capitalism'. Each class society has its own
way of moulding the 'biological raw material' of sex, procreation and care-
giving into a mode of social reproduction.[114] Nancy Chodorow has focused on
emotional nurturing as another central form of female reproductive labour,
one that shapes and distorts male and female personality structures.[115]

At the same time, feminists today are increasingly 'attuned to the intersections of race, class and sexuality within gender'.[116] Black feminists focused
on the struggle against racist discrimination and violence in particular, like
Kimberlé Crenshaw and Patricia Hill Collins, have pioneered the 'intersectional
analysis' that insists on the inextricable enmeshment of power structures and
oppressions founded on class, 'race', gender and sexuality. Socialist feminists
had already warned against assuming that all women have 'a common and unified situation', specifically urging analysis of racial tensions among women and
workers, and in the society at large.[117] In the ensuing years, non-white feminists
'exposed the assumptions of universality in feminist theory',[118] so that intersectional analysis could continue where early feminists left off. They explored

---

111 Young 1981, pp. 49–51.
112 Brenner 2000, pp. 76–7.
113 Hennessy 2000, p. 6.
114 Rubin 2011, pp. 37, 39. Rubin preferred 'sex/gender system' to 'mode of reproduction' on
     the grounds that replacing machinery is also a form of economic reproduction (2011,
     pp. 39–40). In the context of this book, I think it is clear enough that 'social relations of
     production and reproduction' are relations of class and gender.
115 Barker 2012, p. 141.
116 Stryker 2008, pp. 3–4.
117 Young 1989, pp. 55, 52.
118 Brenner 2000, p. 255.

their own situation in 'a location that resists telling', showing how the tools of feminism and anti-racism were inadequate in isolation from one another, even in addressing the oppressions that were central for them.[119]

There are 'multiple and intersecting systems of power that largely dictate our life chances' and 'regulate and police the lives of most people'. This insight has important implications for sexual politics. Sexual deviance has been used in a host of ways, for example, to demonise women, including 'promiscuous' straight non-white women[120] – a demonisation that also works as a ' "controlling image" for white working-class women'.[121] Recognising such dynamics can provide the basis for a sophisticated analysis of 'who and what the enemy is and where our potential allies can be found', and a new political identity that is 'truly liberating, transformative, and inclusive'. The 'multiplicity and interconnectedness of our identities', Cohen has written, 'provide the most promising avenue for the *destabilization and radical politicization*' of all identity categories.[122]

A truly intersectional approach goes beyond acknowledging that important links among gender, racism, class and sexualities exist; it insists on the need for a fully-fledged transversal politics revolving around new, liberating 'ties that bind'.[123] Gloria Wekker, for example, has preferred not to use the word 'lesbian' at all as an all-embracing category for women loving women because of its 'Euro-American situatedness', 'unwanted baggage' and neglect of the many ways in which 'black female sexuality has historically been maligned and vilified'.[124] This is only one example of the new light that intersectional politics can shed on seemingly old issues. In Duggan's words, LGBT people have to go beyond single-issue politics: 'We don't lead single-issue lives'.[125]

Unsurprisingly in view of its origin among black feminists, intersectional analysis has so far focused mainly on the intersection of 'race' and gender in

---

119   Crenshaw 1993, pp. 1242, 1252.

120   Cohen 2005, pp. 25, 42.

121   Brenner 2000, p. 303; see also Kinsman 1987, pp. 44–5.

122   Cohen 2005, pp. 42, 25, 45.

123   Collins 1998, pp. 936, 930 (citing Nira Yuval-Davis). Himani Bannerji is, of course, right that non-white, working-class women's 'social experience is not, as lived, a matter of intersectionality', but 'felt or perceived as being all together or all at once', and cannot be conceived theoretically as 'outside of capital' (2011, pp. 41–3). But intersectional analysis does not necessarily imply that it can be. Danièle Kergoat's proposed alternative of 'consubstantiality' or 'coextensivity' risks neglecting the relative autonomy of different dimensions of identity (Kergoat 2009).

124   Wekker 2006, pp. 69–70.

125   Vaid, Duggan, Metz and Hollibaugh 2013.

imperialist countries. Integrating Marxist insights could help expand its reach further. Marxists can help (and are helping) to turn class and economics from the neglected stepchild of intersectional analysis to a fully equal dimension, adding in crucial links like the racialised reserve army of labour. While intersectional analysis has been making headway in what is today called 'postcolonial studies', a Marxist understanding of imperialism and commitment to fighting it can help spread intersectional politics more broadly in mass movements in the dependent world. The result should be an internationalist class politics that is also a global rainbow politics.

Understanding Same-Sex Histories

The Marxist tradition has always included a political dimension as well as a method of historical and social analysis. The introduction to this book focused on the political dimension, arguing for the relevance of anti-capitalism and of Marxism to a radical sexual politics today. This section stakes a claim for the usefulness, in fact indispensability, of the historical materialist method in making sense of sexual histories.

In this book, I invent and use a new central category to understand same-sex histories: 'same-sex formation'. A same-sex formation is a specific hierarchy of different same-sex patterns (like the transgender, intergenerational and lesbian/gay patterns) in which one pattern is culturally dominant (if not necessarily most prevalent). Each same-sex formation (or regime) occupies a specific place in a particular mode of production (like feudalism) or capitalist regime of accumulation (like classical imperialism). Using this category we can see that lesbian/gay identity, far from being eternal, only acquired hegemony over other same-sex patterns (in what I call the 'gay-dominant formation') when it took its place in the global Fordist regime of capitalist accumulation, from roughly the 1940s to the 1970s. The same-sex regime that preceded the gay-dominant formation was different in many ways; the regime we are living with today (which I call 'homonormative-dominant'), under neoliberalism, has been undermining the centrality of lesbian/gay identity. After the historical development of these successive same-sex formations is sketched out in Part 1 of the book, the concept of the homonormative-dominant same-sex formation underpins a critical dissection of today's gay normality in Part 2 and the elaboration of a queer anti-capitalist alternative in Part 3.

In putting together the concept of a same-sex formation, I have drawn on other historical materialist concepts that people have applied to sexual life before me. By contrast with the weak (if popular) arguments of biological determinists, this section shows how historical materialism offers several concepts that are valuable in understanding sexual histories. The concept of 'reification', for example, helps us understand the commodification of sex and the homo/hetero binary, both of which have been increasingly central to each successive same-sex formation under capitalism. The concept of 'social totality' can be used to explain how a same-sex formation fits into coherent though contradiction-ridden modes of production, and imperial, racial and gender orders. Correctly understood, a materialist conception of social totality also makes clear that no same-sex formation is uniform. Each formation takes different forms in different regions, as part of what I call the 'combined and uneven social construction' of sexuality. These four ideas – same-sex formation, reification, social totality, and combined and uneven social construction – are the gist of what this section explains and explores.

A Paradigm, Not a General Theory

Sexual life, once a largely unexplored continent for historical materialism, has long since ceased to be so. In the 1970s and early 1980s, lesbian/gay historians, using Marxist and feminist analytical tools among others, began to chart the emergence of lesbian/gay identities.[1] In Gayle Rubin's recollection, in fact, from the late 1960s through the mid-1970s Marxism in various forms was the 'dominant paradigm' among progressive intellectuals.[2] Historical materialist categories have been supplemented and then to a large extent supplanted in queer studies by Foucauldian approaches since the 1980s and queer theory since the 1990s. But elements of the contributions of the first, Marxist-influenced generation of historians and theorists still survive to some extent within a broad range of social constructionist perspectives.[3] Most historians and theorists – if not necessarily most LGBT laypeople – still agree that the lesbian/gay identities that emerged by the 1970s were unique, clearly distinguishable from any of the same-sex sexual patterns that existed before the last century or so, and from many that still exist in various parts of the world.

Since the 1980s, however, parallel with the retreat from Marxism in politics, scholarly approaches to sexual history have increasingly been divorced from

---

1 For example, Fernbach 1981; D'Emilio 1983a and 1983b.

2 Rubin 2011, p. 276.

3 To cite one example, David Halperin recalled his bemusement in 1990 in finding his work described as Foucauldian, while to his mind Foucault had at the time less influence on him than New Historicists, French structuralists, radical sociologists, cultural anthropologists, feminist theorists – and Marxists (2002, pp. 7–8). I use the term 'social constructionism' simply as the opposite of 'essentialism': a view of sexual identities as biologically determined or otherwise transhistorical. Social constructionism, by contrast, starts from the premise that 'sexual identities are not "given" by nature but are culturally constituted or produced' (Halperin 1990, p. 10). Thus, I do not think of social constructionism as a specific school of thought contrary to Marxism or any other. Although 'social constructionism' as a term has fallen out of fashion over the past twenty years, the essentialist-constructionist debate remains relevant (Halperin 2002, p. 12). Like John D'Emilio, I have the impression that, ironically, in the same years that social constructionism has virtually 'swept essentialism from the [academic] playing field', essentialism has strengthened its hold as the routine assumption of most LGBT people, except for a queer-identified minority (2002, p. 222).

sexual politics in the wider world, and both have largely given up on earlier attempts to engage with Marxism, in connection with the 'erasure' of labour from academic queer theory.[4] In 1993, for example, queer theorist Michael Warner asserted that 'class is conspicuously useless' for understanding sexuality.[5] Even Rubin, who in 1975 called for a Marxian 'political economy of sex' that would analyse kinship and sexual relations as 'always parts of total social systems', concluded in 1982 that the problems most specifically concerned with gender and sexuality were not 'amenable' to Marxist analysis after all.[6] Now attitudes may be changing. More space may be opening up for a 'social constructionism that is...deeply aware of political economy',[7] an approach that insists on theorising, historicising and situating desire in 'larger histories of gender, family and production'.[8] In short, more people may at last be ready for a 'political economy of sexuality'.[9]

For historical materialism, theorising and historicising desire cannot mean constructing a general theory of sexuality. 'Sexuality' is itself a relatively recent historical construct, combining in one field such distinct elements as the anatomy, biology and sociology of human reproduction, the sexual characteristics associated with social gender, the kinship relations of which marriages and other (partly) sexual partnerships form a part, licit and illicit eroticism and romance. Within this wide array, the boundaries between 'sexual' and 'nonsexual' relations are culturally determined, and the dividing lines between them are set by conflicts.[10] The linkage between all these different elements – not to mention their importance in defining our individual sexuality as 'the essence of our individual being'[11] and a 'repository of personhood, agency, and personal identity'[12] – is neither self-evident nor constant across history, societies or cultures.

Historical materialism has no key at its disposal to unlock all these mysteries at once. It can only provide a method by which the basic matrix of gender and kinship can be understood in the context of specific modes of production and reproduction. Within this approach, sexual relations and ideologies can be

---

4   Hennessy 1994, p. 104.

5   Hennessy 2000, p. 54.

6   Rubin 2011, pp. 63, 179.

7   Wekker 2006, p. 3

8   Adam 1985, p. 658.

9   Altman 1996, p. 91.

10   Chauncey 1989, p. 317.

11   Weeks 1981, p. 12.

12   Wekker 2006, p. 103.

understood as by-products of the shifting social and cultural formations that result from the combination of different modes.

In capitalist societies, uniquely in human history, the increasing separation of the family, the site of biological and social reproduction, from the production process forms the basic matrix of gender and kinship. Yet this basic matrix is not equally predominant in all capitalist societies, and can take very different forms. Sexual relations and ideologies under capitalism have become a driving force of economic growth through the power of sexualised advertising, and a focus of politics through spreading debates over marriage, abortion and homosexuality.[13] Yet sexuality is even more diverse than gender and kinship. It responds to the imperatives of different regimes of capitalist accumulation and different combinations of capitalist with non-capitalist elements, which are inherited from the past and preserved or transformed by the dynamics of capitalism in a particular region and time. As a result, not only can historical materialism not provide any general theory of sexuality, it cannot even lay a foundation for a 'universalistic history of homosexuality'[14] or a static, general theory of sexuality under capitalism.[15] Instead, as always in historical materialist research, the study of sexuality needs to focus on the concrete analysis of concrete social formations.

Change, Diversity and Structure

The first key point to establish is that there is no such thing as a transhistorical 'homosexuality' to be explained by any theory – least of all a biological one. Despite the biological determinism that pervades much of the media worldwide, there is strong support among scholars for a social and historical approach to understanding same-sex desire and behaviour. Putting most science journalists to shame, Sherry Wolf has picked apart the fallacies underlying studies that conclude there must be a 'gay gene'. She has looked insightfully and in depth at studies of childhood sexual development, finding that the 'prevalence of a sexual binary in most gay gene studies flies in the face of both long-standing empirical research and at least some LGBT people's lived

---

13   Herzog 2011, p. 3.

14   Weeks 1981, p. 97.

15   My confidence in this statement is backed up by Nicos Poulantzas' conclusion that there cannot be any general Marxist theory of the state (1980, pp. 16–19) either, and that even the Marxist theory of the capitalist state cannot be isolated from the specific forms of state (liberal, interventionist, fascist, Bonapartist, etc.) (1980, pp. 24–5).

experience: much of sexual identity is fluid and not fixed'.[16] The variety of LGBT people's life stories even in a specific society today goes far beyond what binary definitions can explain. In any event, biological studies that purport to explain sexual orientation have not been replicated, and even twin studies 'are open to serious critique and contrary interpretations'.[17] All these studies reflect the enduring legacy of nineteenth-century sexology.[18] Simon LeVay's attempts to demonstrate the existence of a 'gay brain', in particular, reveal 'a kind of psychic dimorphism that would have made even Freud blush'.[19]

People who have gone more deeply into the biological and neurological evidence have often reached similar conclusions. Rebecca Jordan-Young's long and detailed examination of hormones' supposed role in hardwiring gender and sexual orientation in the human brain – with masculinity and femininity as neurological 'package deals' and LGBT people as recipients of a package delivered to a different address – has concluded that 'the evidence simply does not support the theory'. In fact, 'the data aren't just weak, they are broadly contradictory'. Unlike genitals (in most cases), brains cannot be reliably sorted into male and female by observers who do not know which is which. LeVay's famous study used brains from a small sample of men, overwhelmingly men who had died of AIDS, and provided no evidence that brain development had preceded identity formation.[20]

Often in these studies, definitions of masculine and feminine sexuality vary and shift. Sexologist John Money and colleagues consistently characterised genital arousal as masculine in studies in the 1960s, only to turn around in a 1982 study and call it (in certain circumstances) 'stereotypically feminine sexual behavior'. Studies of sexual orientation in animals other than humans use different and even contradictory definitions of 'gay' from one study to the next (e.g. sometimes only counting males that mount other males; at other times only counting males who are mounted). In humans, studies sometimes define 'gay' by arousal, sometimes by behaviour and sometimes by romantic involvement, with different results. Many researchers exclude a high proportion of subjects whose sexual orientation is 'inconsistent'; others interpret any sign of same-sex attraction or response as evidence of homosexuality.[21]

---

16   Wolf 2009, pp. 217–18.
17   D'Emilio 2002, pp. 161–2.
18   Beccalossi 2012, pp. 227–30.
19   Herdt 1994, pp. 16–17.
20   Jordan-Young 2010, pp. xi–xiii, 39–40, 197, 49, 105.
21   Jordan-Young 2010, pp. 135, 53, 148, 153, 156–7, 171, 173.

Materialists do accept that human sexuality, like that of other animals, has deep connections to physical reproduction. Biological sexuality is 'the necessary precondition for human sexuality'. But it is 'only a precondition, a set of potentialities, which...becomes transformed in qualitatively new ways in human society'. A key characteristic of human sexuality is 'the unique role played in its construction by language, consciousness, symbolism, and labor'.[22] The scientific evidence supports a similar conclusion: 'the brain and the neuroendocrine system...develop and change in a constant dialectic with social and material "inputs"'.[23]

The diversity of human sexual behaviour almost defies conception. Although same-sex erotic behaviour is virtually universal in human societies,[24] just what same-sex forms exist and are considered acceptable or even conceivable varies enormously from one society to the next. These different forms are 'neither innate nor *simply* acquired', but shaped by 'forms of fantasy both private and public, conscious and unconscious, which are culturally available and historically specific'.[25] To cite one striking example: until the twentieth century, the extensive repertory of Thai sexual practices did not include fellatio or even kissing. Until recent decades, 'Thai sexual partners did not kiss but placed cheek (*kaem*) against cheek and sniffed'.[26]

The overwhelming majority of same-sex sexual formations in past cultures were in some demonstrable way different from what is now seen globally as lesbian/gay identity.[27] 'The New Guinea bachelor and the sodomite nobleman are only tangentially related to a modern gay man'.[28]

In many cultures, people have had same-sex sexual relationships with one another without being seen as a particular kind of person. Afro-Surinamese women who call themselves each other's *mati* had and have long-term, intense, often open sexual relationships with each other in between or alongside their sexual relationships with men, but a *mati* is not a distinctive kind of woman equivalent to 'lesbian'.[29] In many societies, including ancient Mediterranean ones now viewed as the origins of the modern 'West', same-sex relationships

---

22   Padgug 1989, pp. 56–7.

23   Jordan-Young 2010, p. 237.

24   Ford and Beach 1951.

25   Meyerowitz 2002, p. 35 (citing Teresa de Lauretis).

26   Jackson 1989, pp. 394–5 n. 76.

27   Greenberg has provided the most comprehensive survey available of the range of same-sex patterns (Greenberg 1988).

28   Rubin 2011, p. 157.

29   Wekker 1999, p. 120.

that were intergenerational or status-defined (where, for example, youths or male servants could be penetrated sexually but masters could not) did not confer a distinct sexual identity on either of the partners. Chinese culture for centuries did not posit 'an innate sexual essence, but concentrated rather on actions, tendencies, and preferences'. Instead of saying what a man ' "is", Chinese authors would usually say whom he "resembles" or what he "does" or "enjoys" '.[30]

However, the extreme reading of social constructionism – asserting that before the nineteenth century there were only same-sex acts, but no same-sex identities[31] – cannot survive even a superficial examination of pre-colonial Asian or African cultures. Still less tenable is the claim that the contemporary Islamic world[32] knows same-sex acts but no same-sex identities, which is belied by LGBT organising today from Turkey to Palestine and Lebanon to Indonesia. Many non-European languages have centuries-old words for people who habitually engage in same-sex sex, not just for particular sex acts. Yet most people in history with same-sex identities – in the great majority of cases transgender identities – could not be defined as 'lesbian' or 'gay'. The terms 'lesbian' and 'gay' exclude not only many people who have same-sex sex – pretty much everywhere in the world, many heterosexually married men who have sex with men do not identify as gay – but also many of the trans people who have same-sex identities. Only an awkward, portmanteau expression like lesbian/gay/bisexual/transgendered (LGBT) is at least somewhat inclusive.

On the other hand, identities and communities that clearly are lesbian and gay have emerged in one country after another. Analyses that see capitalism as crucial to the rise of a lesbian/gay identity are bolstered by the fact that capitalist development has often eventually been accompanied by the emergence of lesbian/gay communities. Yet the variety of LGBT identities around the world is greater than any historical materialist account so far has been able to explain.

This book is not aimed at attempting the impossible: providing an unattainable general theory, theorising the incredible diversity of human sexual

---

30 Hinsch 1990, p. 7.

31 Halperin has pointed out several times that Michel Foucault never made this assertion, although it has been attributed to him (2002, pp. 8–9).

32 In this book, I use 'Islamic world' to mean not a world wholly defined by Islam as a religion, but rather the 'Islamicate world' as defined by Marshall Hodgson (Amer 2005, pp. 215–16, n. 1): a wide expanse of Muslim-majority countries in which Christians, Jews and unbelievers, as well as Muslims, share many elements of a common culture, including many non-religious features and some that even predate Islam.

regimes throughout history, or even giving a complete overview of sexual regimes in all capitalist societies. Its main aim is to shed light on the historical and social basis of, and the political challenges posed by, the forms taken by same-sex sexualities since the late 1970s under one specific regime of accumulation, namely, neoliberalism. This is in itself a vast enough task. It requires coming to grips with a series of methodological problems.

First, a focus on 'same-sex' is by no means self-evident. Even in contemporary capitalist India, for example, *hijras*, who according to centuries-old traditions have no gender at all, and gay men, who often see themselves as much the same as gay men in London or New York, are rarely spontaneously inclined to amalgamate their sexual lives under a rubric like 'same-sex'. Homosexuality and transgender identity are recent US and European constructs 'imposed on the infinite varieties of human sexual and gender diversity',[33] within which the hetero/homo binary is a 'stunningly recent creation'.[34] The otherwise arbitrary choice to amalgamate and focus on same-sex sexual relationships can only be justified by the growing tendency of capitalist societies over the past century and a half to classify human sexual relations and even individual human beings along these lines. This book argues that understanding why and how this has been happening enables us to deepen our understanding of contemporary gendered capitalism in general.

Second, the forms taken by same-sex sexualities under neoliberalism are both linked to, and fundamentally different from, the forms they took when 'homosexuality' was first identified and defined in Western Europe in the nineteenth century. They are also closely linked to, and yet surprisingly different from, the forms they took in the lesbian/gay communities that took shape in the 1950s, 1960s and 1970s. Making these assertions seem plausible, let alone explaining how they can be true, is a big challenge.

The concepts of gay and straight, historically recent as they are, have now become so embedded in billions of people's sense of their own identities and in a whole pseudo-scientific discourse that even many radicals need convincing that human beings have not always been divided this way. Not only do we have a hard time understanding the logic of other organisations of sex, 'we have an even harder time understanding our own inability to understand'.[35] The process of lesbians' and gay men's coming out, gradually expanding their self-definition to include vaster LGBT communities, and demanding and winning rights seems so ineluctable that by now its subjects can hardly be perceived,

---

33   Healey 2001, pp. 63–4.
34   Chauncey 1994, p. 13.
35   Halperin 2002, p. 3.

by themselves or by hundreds of millions of others around the world, outside the framework of this powerful narrative of progress. The hundreds of millions of others who seem to resist it, notably in the name of Christianity or Islam, by insisting on the wrongness of 'homosexuality' (a concept unknown to Jesus or Mohammed) play their part in the drama as the benighted rear-guard so convincingly that they tend in many ways to confirm the discourse that they mean to reject.

Even theorists can find it hard to be 'as rigorously historicist ... as our historiographical principles might require'. Yet care in avoiding overuse of categories like 'gay' and 'homosexuality' is crucial to understanding sexual history. The fact of same-sex sexual attraction across different histories and societies no more establishes 'the transhistorical reality of "homosexuality"' than the fact that feudal peasants, like proletarians, worked with their hands establishes the transhistorical reality of 'proletarianism'.[36]

Nevertheless, even sophisticated historians who consciously and explicitly reject essentialism may sometimes read back the contours of today's gay normality into earlier periods. Some have suggested, for example, that the late-nineteenth-century invention of 'homosexuality', or the early eighteenth-century emergence of urban 'sodomite' subcultures in London, Paris and the Netherlands, or even same-sex subcultures in Italian cities during the Renaissance[37] constituted the origin of gay people as we now know them. These accounts tend, though to a lesser extent than biological determinism, to exaggerate the duration and solidity of today's gay normality.

Without denying the seeds of the present that were sprouting in the past, I tend rather to stress the permanence of change and key differences between same-sex regimes in different epochs, in the interest of alerting us to the tensions at work and changes underway today. 'Constant metamorphoses' in sexual patterns[38] and historical events can 'powerfully shape the construction of what otherwise appear to be "traditional"' sexual patterns.[39]

Recent queer theorists have tended to look less at historical and social preconditions than at a range of discourses, which persist, overlap and are often available to individuals as alternative and/or complementary ways of defining

---

36 Halperin 2002, p. 59 (citing Henry Abelove).
37 '[T]he Renaissance planted the first seeds of a new identity and social status for homosexuality' (Saslow 1989, p. 105).
38 Faderman 1991, pp. 8–9, 306–7.
39 Roscoe 1994, p. 371.

their sexual identities.[40] I think there is a great deal of truth in this approach as well. Even a single, consistent sexual regime can offer scope for different kinds of sexual relationships and identities to co-exist. Moreover, even in today's overwhelmingly capitalist world, there are still chunks of non-capital-ist modes of production that have been incorporated into the capitalist order (from traditional indigenous forms of communal production in the Andes to typically Stalinist forms of factory management in Russia). On a global scale, same-sex sexualities should be seen 'not as a monolithic domain but as a mul-tiplicity of beliefs and practices, elements of which can move independently of each other'.[41] Changes in capitalist accumulation regimes also proceed very unevenly, so that Fordist and pre-Fordist elements are still very much present in today's neoliberal economy. Changes at the level of imperial, racial, gender or sexual formations are not in perfect synch with economic changes.

Even phenomena (like the ancient Athenian polis or medieval chivalry) that have been historically superseded can still leave cultural and ideological lega-cies. All this explains how, even in this neoliberal world, an incredible range of sexual discourses can be present and vital and can provide usable imagery for individuals.

Yet recognising the great range of imagery available to individuals and of discourses present in the world does not require us to see them all as equally powerful or equally meaningful everywhere. A woman-loving woman in present-day Mexico City might see herself as the heir to a pre-Colombian sha-man, say, but that does not enable her to live the life that a pre-Columbian shaman lived, or to assume an identity consistent with that life. In the world in which we live, some structures are dominant and powerful, while others are subaltern and relatively powerless. We need to analyse the dominant struc-tures to understand what identities are possible when and where, and how much they signify when and where they are permitted to exist. While 'human experience exceeds social theories', social change still happens and needs to be explained.[42] While sexual formations and ideologies are not as stable as capitalism, neither are they as fleeting and relative as images and discourses.

Whether they cite Marx, Foucault or both, historians' analysis of lesbian/ gay identity has linked its emergence to the development of modern, indus-trialised, urbanised societies. This link is broadly accepted by leading scholars

lower status

---

40   See, for example, Halperin 2002, pp. 108–36. Chiara Beccalossi has recently stressed the
     continuity and coexistence of different models in nineteenth- and twentieth-century sex-
     ology (2009, pp. 8–9).

41   Boellstorff 1999, p. 496.

42   Van der Meer 1994, p. 176.

working in a social constructionist framework.[43] Some historians have linked its emergence specifically to the development of capitalism.[44] Recently, there have been signs of greater openness in queer thought to a 'direct engagement with Marxism that emphasizes its explanatory power'.[45]

Yet there is no one-to-one correspondence between economic and social developments and shifts in sexual, cultural and political identities. In LGBT communities, as in the world at large, there is a whole set of institutions that produce (among other things) sexual ideology and identity, mediate the underlying class and social dynamics, and represent (to use French Marxist Louis Althusser's definition of ideology) 'the imaginary relationship of individuals to their real conditions of existence'.[46] To analyse how all these ideological structures – from newspapers and magazines to porn videos to publishing houses to websites and chat rooms to queer studies departments to small business associations to sports clubs and beyond – function ideologically under one set of productive relations, and tend to function differently under another, would go beyond the scope of this book. Yet a key point in Althusser's definition is that the word 'real' is as important in it as the word 'imaginary': it implies that social 'relations do exist ... independent of our will ... independent of mind, independent of thought',[47] and independent of the ideological structures that constantly construe them.

Totality and Reification

Nevertheless, no aspect of capitalist culture, including sexual culture, exists in complete isolation from the mode of production as a whole. Fundamental shifts in capitalism are detectable, however indirectly, at the level of gender and sexual regimes as at other levels. Sexuality and work are 'equally involved in the production and reproduction of *all* aspects of social reality, and cannot easily be separated out from one another'.[48] This basic understanding can give us the audacity, even in the absence of fully worked-out mediations, to point out some trends that correspond to changing class dynamics in LGBT communities.

---

43   Halperin 1990, p. 8.
44   D'Emilio 1983a; Rosenberg and Villarejo 2012, p. 3.
45   Floyd 2009, p. 2.
46   Althusser 1971, p. 162.
47   Hall 1985, p. 105.
48   Padgug 1989, p. 61.

Here the Marxist concept of totality, central to György Lukács' conception in *History and Class Consciousness*, is invaluable. For historical materialism, gender and sexual structures can and should also be seen as integral parts of a gendered capitalist totality. They are not merely local aspects of a social formation – though too many Marxists have treated them as such – but instead are central to the process of capitalist accumulation, just as economics, politics and ideology cannot be understood as separate domains, but only as parts of a structured whole. 'The *economy* cannot be transparently abstracted from the *state* or the *family*'.[49] Production, reproduction and consumption are all gendered and sexualised from their inception.

As Althusser stressed, however, 'totality' does not mean that developments at one level of capitalism are expressed simultaneously at other levels. Capitalist social formations do not in fact develop in this synchronous way, either at different levels (economic and cultural, for instance) or in different regions (North America and Africa). Marxist feminists in particular reject this logic of 'expressive causality' in which every aspect of a society is supposed to 'emanate from one central cause'.[50] The unevenness of capitalist development and the relative autonomy of different levels need to be taken into account in the role of sexuality in the totality as well: for example, the slower pace and lesser extent to which the category of homosexuality initially influenced working-class as opposed to middle-class men.[51]

One useful term of Althusser's to conceptualise the inextricable linkage of production, reproduction, gender and sexuality is 'overdetermination': the way in which different causes operating at different levels of a society converge to produce a historically and geographically unique result that class dynamics alone could never account for. This concept allowed Althusser to insist on determination by social relations of production 'in the last instance', while acknowledging that 'the lonely hour of the "last instance" never comes', because the impact of class (and gender) are always mediated and complicated by politics, ideology, culture and history.[52] The idea of overdetermination hardly resolves everything. Yet it is useful in clarifying how capitalism's central contradictions are 'enacted and inflected' in history.[53]

A social totality, while ridden by contradictions and complicated by the relative autonomy of different instances, is nonetheless driven onwards by the

---

49   Duggan 2003, p. xiv.
50   Hennessy 2000, p. 26.
51   Foucault 1978, p. 121; Chauncey 1994, p. 27.
52   Althusser 1979, p. 113.
53   Hennessy 2000, pp. 86–7.

central determining role of social production and reproduction, of class and gender dynamics.[54] A non-reductionist historical materialism faces multiple challenges. It has to recognise the relative autonomy of different levels of a social formation. It has to recognise that class and gender are inextricably at its core – which includes understanding class as 'always mediated by other social differences'[55] and heteronormativity as enmeshed with gender, race, class, and nation.[56] Yet it has to avoid succumbing to a methodological pluralism that simply sees the contingent interplay of a variety of factors.[57]

Rubin is right that neither Marxism nor feminism can singlehandedly be 'the ultimate and complete account of all social inequality'.[58] The point, however, is to synthesise them, and incorporate the strengths of other paradigms into the synthesis, so as to produce a totalising historical materialist account

---

54   Queer theorists have rejected this global, structured totality in favour of what they call a 'scavenger' totality – essentially a random accumulation (Crosby et al. 2012, pp. 146, 138–9). In fact, queer theorists' attempts to engage with the concept of totality sometimes seem like a long series of attempts to evade it. Duggan, for example, has written about 'provisional, shifting, totalities … [m]oving beyond the Marxist notions of the relative autonomy of culture'. Even Floyd has asked, 'Must we choose between characterizing global capitalism as either heterogeneous or unified?' I would respond: if we want to radically change the world, then yes, we do. What Judith Halberstam has called a 'scavenger methodology, combing information culled from people with information culled from texts' (Wekker 2006, p. 81) – a frequent and fruitful approach taken by radical and queer anthropologists – by no means necessarily implies a conception of a 'scavenger totality'.

55   Hennessy 2000, p. 58. At one point Hennessy seemed to suggest that it does not matter to capital *which* social differences mediate its class relations; capitalism requires an unequal division of labour, she wrote, but not heteronormative families or even a gendered division of labour (2000, p. 105). I would argue that capitalism needs to be understood not as an abstract blueprint of an economic order, but as a historically shaped whole. While it can change in many ways from one regime of accumulation, period and part of the world to another, it cannot, even in the face of overwhelming social pressure, simply shuck off and replace the whole set of oppressive relations that formed the historical conditions for its emergence.

56   Jakobsen 2012, p. 24.

57   I would thus take some distance from Duggan's conclusion that because capitalist institutions, practices and social relations 'changed over time and varied across space', 'capitalism has never been a single coherent "system"' (2003, p. x). We need to distinguish, on the one hand, between gendered capitalism's varying imbrications with different modes of production and the resultant social, political and cultural phenomena, which are historically contingent, and major social transformations that result from capitalism's inherent laws of motion. While no capitalist society is pure, the increasing global dominance of capital has increased the weight of capitalism's intrinsic dynamic.

58   Rubin 2011, p. 180.

powerful enough to grasp reality. We need an understanding of gendered capitalism as a unified system of which oppression in all its forms is 'a *core* attribute', in which the analysis of each form of oppression is 'an integral part of a revised marxism, rather than merely married to marxism'.[59]

A post-modern critic of Marxism might charge that this is simply an alibi for old-fashioned economic reductionism. In fact, the opposite is true. An analysis that fails to grasp how vital sexism, sexual oppression, racism and imperialism are for the global functioning of capitalism can never ground any of these forms of oppression as something of more than merely local importance. In this sense, by renouncing the causal link between culture and economy, 'cultural materialism' ends up being the 'other side of the coin of economism'.[60] Conversely, a thorough analysis demands that each of the key types of oppression be understood as integral to the whole.[61] In short, a complex understanding of totality is the necessary foundation of an intersectional politics.

Another key concept from Lukács is *reification*, the reduction of human beings and human social relations to things. Reification in the broadest sense did not begin with capitalism; slavery is an obvious example of treating a human being as a thing, in the Romans' term as a 'speaking tool'. But capitalism is unique in the range of 'things' it defines, brings to market, puts a price on, and turns into embodiments of vast, complex social realities, from a 'derivative' that puts a price on someone's ability to keep up payments on a home six years from now, to an hour of sex with a Brazilian transwoman for a Parisian business executive. Capitalist ideologues portray this reification as the bearer of a historically unprecedented freedom of choice. What this obscures is the essential freedoms that reification denies, such as the freedom to continue living in one's home even if a multinational closes the factory where one works, or the Brazilian transwoman's freedom to have sex how and with whom she likes, unconstrained by economic necessity.

Marx had shown in *Capital* that commodities are fetishised in capitalist societies; people attribute an almost magical power to them, which tends to conceal the social relations that make them commodities and give them their social function. Jamie Gough and Mike MacNair have shown how this Marxist conception of commodity fetishism can be linked to a conception of sexual fetishism: attraction to specific attributes of people or things, to 'abstracted aspects of people', ranging from the leather or rubber they wear to particular body parts. With the growth of sexual 'markets', they argued, a sexual partner's

---

59   Young 1981, pp. 44, 62.
60   Hennessy 2000, pp. 80, 94.
61   Young 1989, p. 56.

gender became 'the most important fetish'. Lesbians and gay men thus emerged as '*carriers* of particular fetishised sexualities'.[62]

Lukács deepened Marx's insight about commodity fetishism by further developing the concept of reification: an overarching term for the ways in which relations between human beings are disguised in capitalist societies as relations with, or even between, things. Lukács specifically cited marriage as an example of how every 'natural form' and all human 'physical and psychic qualities' are subjected to this process of reification.[63] We even tend to reify sex in general as 'a thing-in-itself'.[64] Kevin Floyd has cited the binary that divides human beings into 'homosexuals' and 'heterosexuals', two categories that only emerged under capitalism, as an example of reification. Only under capitalism have people come consistently and centrally to classify their own desire according to the sex of the people at whom it is directed, abstracting maleness and femaleness from the network of kinship and social ties in which other societies embed them. Male and female bodies are thus reduced to things that can and must be obtained, notably by acquiring all sorts of other things (from one's own gym body to the right brand of deodorant). This application of the concept of reification to gender and sex helps explain people's fierce attachment to their gender and sexual identities.

Reification can be understood as a form of ideology, which 'naturalizes differences (between men and women, whites and blacks, straight and gay, able and disabled, rich and poor, etc.)'. Ideology cannot be reduced to propaganda, or to a state of mind produced by propaganda; it is an inevitable by-product of living in a class and gendered society. Even desire and pleasure are completely enmeshed under capitalism with ideology. Sensations 'never speak for themselves'; when 'they are recruited by ideology, sensations and pleasures can be powerful ways to naturalize the historical social relations identities rely on'.[65] Or in David Halperin's phrase, there is 'no orgasm without ideology'.[66]

This is not to say that changing the social relations will automatically or quickly change people's sensations or pleasures. The process takes place over the course of a lifetime, so that in each individual's experience, sexuality has 'something intractable'.[67] Still, individuals' accounts of their own desires inevitably define them in terms of the specific kinds of ties between human

---

62   Gough and MacNair 1985, pp. 26, 42, 50, 26, 50.

63   Lukács 1972, pp. 93, 100.

64   Ross and Rapp 1983, p. 67.

65   Hennessy 2000, pp. 19, 72.

66   Halperin 2002, pp. 102–3.

67   Rubin 2011, pp. 281–2.

beings that can be conceived within their particular society. Desire is 'a way of linking personal reality to cultural ontology', in a space 'halfway between the private and the public' – especially in a capitalist society with its ideology of individualism.[68]

The main challenge for the historical materialist study of sexuality under capitalism is to trace the mutations of sexual reification and of rebellion against it in interaction with changes in capitalist production, its global political economy and its gendered reproduction. This means charting the ways in which these basic historical and material determinants of sexuality are mediated through politics, the broader culture, the media and community institutions. Ultimately, it means mapping the impact of all this on the enormous variety of individual psychologies and individual lives. These are the challenges that this book aims to help tackle.

In chapter 1 of this book, I argue that the division of human beings into 'heterosexuals' and 'homosexuals' is not permanent or universal even under capitalism. It only arose in the last quarter of the nineteenth century with the formation of a global imperialist system, in particular locations of that system (imperialist countries where the second industrial revolution was taking place), as a specifically heterosexual family structure and a conception of heterosexual romance became central to social reproduction and consumption. And even after the distinction emerged, the fact that a sexual relationship was same-sex was not necessarily central to how people perceived it. The specific roles people took on in sex and their departures from gender norms may have been more important, so that the 'simple polarities of "homosexual" and "heterosexual" obscure rather than lay bare the complexity of a sexual system'.[69] The reification of desire as 'homosexual' was initially, in the late nineteenth century, ascribed to individuals who sexologists called 'inverts' – they might today, in many cases, be called transgender – only later to largely middle-class people who self-identified as homosexual but not as inverts, and only from the mid-twentieth century to masses of people who self-identified as lesbian or gay.

Moreover, at other locations of the imperialist system in the same period, some same-sex patterns survived – like South African 'mine marriages', Afro-Surinamese 'mati' relationships, and relations between men and youths in much of the Arab region – that supposed a vision of sex as a realm of activity rather than identity, one in which sexual fulfilment counted for more than the

---

68   Herdt 1994, p. 77.
69   Chauncey 1989, pp. 315–16.

gender of one's partner.[70] While not all of these patterns have endured, those that do survive have elements with the potential to contribute to an alternative vision of sexual life, one not organised around a gay/straight binary. This eroticised, non-reified world anticipated by Marcuse might even dispense with the very conception of sexuality as a separate domain, separated out from the broad spectrum of human ties and feelings.

Of course, individual desire and psychology are very resilient. They are shaped over the course of lifetimes, not totally transmuted by the social developments of a decade or two. In some cases, the winds of erotic fashion undoubtedly have shallower causes than profound socioeconomic change, and it would be a mistake to read too much into them. Individual psychology is a product not just or even mainly of an individual family constellation, but of a specific interplay of history, class, gender, ethnicity and other factors. Any particular matrix of sexual relations has a range of individual desires built into it.[71] And the enormous number of determinants that shape any one individual's sensations and pleasures make it ultimately impossible to 'tame the wild profusion of existing things'.[72] In the last analysis, we are 'woefully ignorant' of the reasons behind an individual's desires, especially desires that implicitly dissent from the dominant sexuality.[73]

A materialist approach can examine historically *different* sexual patterns under capitalism, without privileging any particular one. At the same time, although Marxists like Clara Zetkin and Alexandra Kollontai wrote insightfully about sexual life within a purely Marxist framework, more recent historical materialist treatments of the subject have almost always engaged critically with other approaches, such as psychoanalysis, feminism, Foucauldianism, post-colonialism and queer theory. A rigorous historical materialist approach to sexual life is not only compatible with an engagement with other social constructionist approaches, but in fact requires it.

Same-Sex Formations

In this book, I use the concept of 'same-sex formation' or 'same-sex regime' – much as Althusser used the concept of 'social formation', a historically specific combination of several different modes of production in a particular

70   Wekker 2006, pp. 13, 214.
71   Davis and Kennedy 1989, p. 436.
72   Rubin 2011, p. 248; Foucault 1973, p. xv.
73   Herdt 1994, p. 72.

society[74] – to describe the way in which one same-sex pattern is taken as the dominant and preferred one among several coexisting sexual patterns. In ancient Athenian slave society, for example, a particular kind of intergenerational relationship between active, adult male citizens and receptive citizen youths was the dominant same-sex formation, although male prostitution, intense emotional bonds between male friends, sexual use of male slaves, and sexual penetration of transgendered *kinaidi* all existed alongside it. In neoliberal Europe and North America today, similarly – and due to their global dominance, worldwide – a particular form of homonormative relationship culminating in same-sex marriage is increasingly the social norm, although many sorts of transgender, gay, queer and other same-sex patterns exist alongside it.

The question remains as to what logic governs the transition from one same-sex formation to another. One of this book's central arguments is that sexuality under capitalism has been shaped to a great extent by different regimes of capitalist accumulation over the last century, which in their turn were products of successive waves of contraction and expansion of the global economy. Alongside the business cycle of boom and bust lasting several years, which Marx theorised in *Capital*, later economists have identified a longer cycle lasting several decades, during whose expansive phases recessions are relatively short and mild and expansions longer and more vigorous, and during whose recessive phases recessions are relatively deep and prolonged and expansions relatively short and weak.[75] The long crises that characterise the recessive phases of long waves tend to be periods of far-reaching economic and social reorganisation, in which new regimes of accumulation restore previously depressed average rates of profit. The major examples I will examine are the classical imperialist regime of accumulation shaped in the long recessive phase from the early 1870s to the mid-1890s, the Fordist regime of accumulation shaped in the period of and between the First and Second World Wars, and the neoliberal regime of accumulation shaped in the long recessive phase beginning in the early 1970s.[76]

---

74   For example, Althusser 1971, p. 159.

75   See Mandel 1995.

76   The concept of Fordism has been largely associated with the French 'régulation' school. Many of the basic elements of what regulationists call the Fordist regime of accumulation are also to be found in Mandelian long-wave theory or the 'social structure of accumulation' approach. These different schools differ from one another particularly in relation to the causes of the rise and decline of different modes of accumulation. While important, these debates are not directly relevant to this book.

These different regimes of accumulation have not been comprised only of narrowly defined economic structures. Each one has entailed a specific global division of labour, a specific way of structuring relations between central (generally richer) and peripheral (generally poorer) regions of the global system, and thus a specific planetary division of regions, states and nations between those that are economically dominant (imperialist) and others that are economically dominated or dependent. At the same time, because capitalism has always been not only a class-based mode of production but also a gendered mode of reproduction, each shift to a new regime of accumulation has also entailed major shifts in gender relations and family structures.

I will argue that each shift to a new regime of accumulation has also triggered – though not necessarily all at once, at the same pace or evenly across the globe – new racial configurations and new sexual regimes. The different forms of racism that have accompanied capitalism throughout its four centuries of existence have responded to and perpetuated deep-rooted aspects of its productive structures, from its profound enmeshment with chattel slavery from the seventeenth to nineteenth centuries, to its subjugation and subordination of Africans, Asians and Latin Americans, to the historically unprecedented degree of inequality resulting today from neoliberal globalisation.

Moreover, because different sexual regimes have been so closely linked to gender roles and relations, the major shifts in gender relations entailed in the emergence of a new regime of accumulation were bound to have an impact as well on cross-sex and same-sex formations. The rapid and disorienting changes in sexual regime that ensue help to explain the recurrent historical periods when sexuality has been 'more sharply contested and more intensely policed'.[77] It is in these periods 'when an older system is in disarray and a new one is forming' that political movements for sexual change are most likely to catch on.[78]

The three same-sex regimes this book focuses on are an 'invert-dominant regime' arising in the late nineteenth century under classical imperialism, a 'gay-dominant regime' arising in the mid-twentieth century under Fordism, and a 'homonormative-dominant' regime today under neoliberalism. None of these same-sex regimes has corresponded exactly, temporally or geographically, to the regimes of accumulation to which they are linked. This is partly because economic production and gendered reproduction are not necessarily synchronised, and sexual patterns do not immediately change as the social foundations of gender do so. Moreover, while classical imperialism, Fordism and neoliberalism began to take shape as soon as the modes of accumulation that

---

77 Hennessy 2000, p. 199.
78 D'Emilio and Freedman 1997, p. xviii.

preceded them went into crisis, they took recognisable form only gradually and unevenly. I mentioned earlier Althusser's critique of an 'expressive' use of the category of totality, in which formations at every level correspond neatly to one another. Reality does not work like that. In general, a particular regime of accumulation, above all at the levels of economic production and gendered social reproduction, creates the conditions for the corresponding racial and sexual formations, but this does not mean that the corresponding formations immediately or necessarily come into existence.

So, for example, homosexuality became widely visible as such in Western Europe only in the 1890s with Oscar Wilde's trial in England and the founding of the Scientific-Humanitarian Committee in Germany, although it had roots in the depression that began in the 1870s and European imperial expansion from the 1880s. Lesbian/gay communities became widely visible in North and Latin America and Western Europe only in the late 1960s, although they had roots in a systemic crisis that began in the 1910s and social transformations that came with and after the Second World War. And although the clearest marker of today's gay normality, same-sex marriage, is a twenty-first-century phenomenon, its roots are in the recessive long wave that began in the 1970s and the spread of neoliberalism from the early 1980s.

Nor does the emergence of a new regime of accumulation in one part of the world necessarily imply that it will become dominant in other regions quickly, or ever. Even when an accumulation regime is dominant almost everywhere, as neoliberalism is now, it can still incorporate other capitalist accumulation regimes or even non-capitalist elements into its functioning, with a myriad of possible consequences at different levels of different social formations.

With all these caveats, the correspondence between regimes of accumulation and same-sex formations provides evidence for a basic historical materialist assertion: the material relations of production and reproduction constitute the fundamental matrix underlying all of social reality. It also has political implications. In the political introduction, I argued that especially in a period like this one, anti-capitalists cannot afford to neglect sexual and racial identity politics, because particularly when progressive class-based movements are weak, what are called the 'culture wars' in the US are often the wellspring of politics. This is vital in day-to-day and year-to-year struggles. But if economic long waves are ultimately determinant for the shift from one same-sex formation to another, then on a scale of decades and centuries sexual radicals cannot afford to neglect the dynamics of capitalist economies. In other words, consistent queer opponents of homonormativity have to be at least anti-neoliberal if not anti-capitalist.

The analysis of same-sex formations has other political implications as well. Negatively, it means that the mutations from invert-dominant to gay-dominant to homonormative-dominant regimes have marked a steadily if unevenly increasing ghettoisation of same-sex desire. Despite growing tolerance of LGBT people in many countries, even despite some straight-identified people's willingness to acknowledge their own same-sex desires, the development of family structures and sexual ideologies has, if anything, solidified the boundaries between straight and LGBT people. Positively, each same-sex regime has generated forms of rebellion and resistance. In the era of classical imperialism, there are examples from Suriname to Morocco and beyond of people who persisted in same-sex relationships that failed to fit the category of 'homosexuality', while allied sex reform and Communist movements offered political prospects to pathologised inverts. In the Fordist era, the radicalisation in the late 1960s and early 1970s included lesbian/gay liberationists' rebellion, consciously linked to broader revolutionary currents, against the hardening binary. And today, in the age of gay normality, LGBT people whose lives adapt them poorly to neoliberalism have increasingly been defining *their* identities in non-homonormative ways: queer ways.

Combined and Uneven Social Construction

In addition to the difficulty of providing an analysis of same-sex sexualities under capitalism that does justice to temporal and social continuities and discontinuities, I face the difficulty of providing an analysis that at least approximates being global. While a genuinely global analysis is more than I can manage, I do attempt to include evidence from enough regions to avoid the pitfalls of focusing exclusively on either the world's richest regions or those whose cultures are largely derived from Europe (the two factors that are usually combined to form the ideological construct of 'the West'). I have tried to make the realities of the dependent world in particular an integral part of the account.[79]

---

79   The unevenness of LGBT studies reflects more than global disparities of wealth and power. This book refers to South Africa and Thailand more than contemporary Italy, for example – not because Italy is poor or dependent, or for that matter because it has no LGBT life, but because of cultural and historical factors that have held back the growth of LGBT studies there. It also inevitably reflects the hegemony of the US in queer studies worldwide, even in the study of LGBT people elsewhere – itself a historical phenomenon

There is a strong tendency to tell the history of homosexuality as 'a progressive, even teleological, evolution from pre-modern repression, silence, and invisibility to modern visibility and sexual freedom'.[80] Besides being a simplistic and in many ways false narrative of progress, the dominant account of LGBT people in the world today is Eurocentric. Insofar as it does not define LGBT identities as eternal and unchanging, the dominant account portrays them as 'Western' discoveries, of which the rest of the world is now reaping the benefits. It either establishes a distinction between the 'modern' and the 'pre-modern' that functions as a strategy of exclusion, or perpetuates the 'hoary colonialist notion that non-European cultures represent the cultural childhood of modern Europe', or implies a 'Eurocentric progress narrative' that at the very least fails to take enough account of messy transnational realities.[81]

However it does so, the dominant account generally credits 'the West' with pioneering the emancipation of LGBT people who have always been everywhere, living in fear and silence. Even queer theory has often been 'as relentlessly Atlantic-centric in its view of the world as the mainstream culture it critiques'.[82] Whatever their variants, the Eurocentric narratives of queer studies make it almost possible to grasp and appreciate, for example, the 'variety, distribution, and longevity of same-sex patterns in Islamic societies'.[83] It is all too easy to reduce sexual lives in the poorer four-fifths of the world to a 'false "other"' and thereby 'erase the complexities and inconsistencies of an overarching model'.[84]

Many historians realise that this picture is a distortion. But this does not eliminate the mind-set that perpetuates it, whether explicitly or, more often and effectively, implicitly. The way to avoid these pitfalls is not to deny difference, or to recognise difference in a way that denies different sexual regimes' parallels, interactions and development from one to another. It is true that earlier sexual forms persist, and that no single pattern is ever wholly dominant. But this does not mean that all historical models are operative 'at every historical moment', that specific models are never hegemonic, or that one model's

---

that reflects more than the exceptional size and wealth of US universities, as I discuss in chapters 2 and 3.

80   Roscoe and Murray 1997, pp. 4–6.
81   Halperin 2002, pp. 18–20, 13–14.
82   Altman 2000, p. 138.
83   Roscoe and Murray 1997, pp. 4–6.
84   Green 1999a, p. 8.

dominance cannot have a decisive impact on how the others function. To deny this would be to impose 'a new and more insidious universalism'.[85]

The truth is that LGBT communities and identities *are* part of a global reality, but in a far more complex and contradictory way than the radiation from centre to periphery of a newfound way of life, or of the pioneering emancipation of an age-old way of life. The Marxist concept of 'combined and uneven development', which describes the ways in which high-tech and older technologies and systems of production can co-exist in economically dominated countries, suggests a way forward.

In the past, I have used the term 'combined and uneven social construction' to describe processes, linked today to neoliberal globalisation, that are constantly generating worldwide sexual difference. This term has a significant advantage in that it avoids any implication of a uniform process moving more or less quickly in a single direction, which the idea of 'globalisation' seems to suggest. The idea of combined and uneven social construction, by contrast, can help us understand how different indigenous starting points, different relationships to the world economy, and different cultural and political contexts can combine to produce very different results – while still producing identifiable common elements of LGBT identities in one country after another. It can help us understand how some indigenous sexual patterns can be preserved within a global economy and culture, changing to a certain extent their forms or functions; how new forms can emerge; and how indigenous and new forms can be combined.[86]

The initial definition of 'homosexuality' in capitalist societies, which was the identification and treatment of a pathology, was embedded in the global expansion of a gendered and sexualised capitalism, which identified many non-capitalist societies as hotbeds of homosexuality. In fact, pre-colonial and pre-capitalist sexual cultures had extraordinarily rich and varied forms of same-sex eroticism, in some cases expressed in open, socially accepted forms of same-sex behaviour or identity in historical periods when 'sodomites' were still being burned alive in Europe. With the arrival of colonialism and capitalism, this discovery was used to legitimate conquest and to map out a programme for transforming the conquered societies in ways that fit the imperatives of capital.[87]

---

85   Halperin 2002, pp. 12, 21.
86   For an initial attempt to apply the idea of combined and uneven development to same-sex sexual formations, see Drucker 1996.
87   Bleys 1995.

Later, in imperialist countries after the Second World War, geographical displacement, rising wages, the development of a welfare state and legal victories redefined the heterosexual norm from a strict taboo on 'the love that dare not speak its name' to a situation where LGBT people are considered 'abnormal' more in a statistical than in a pathological sense – and in the sense that they are still more or less marginal to the family institutions through which society reproduces itself. However, this process of redefining the heterosexual norm was not uniformly replicated in economically dominated countries. Varied indigenous sexual cultures combined with different modes of insertion into the world market to produce widely divergent heterosexual norms and widely variant LGBT formations.

Thailand, a country that was fully incorporated into the world capitalist market without ever being formally colonised, is a particularly striking case of the impact of capitalism on sexual developments in a distinctive social formation, independently of European or North American cultural influence. Peter Jackson has argued cogently in his work on Thailand that LGBT formations in dependent countries have not always emerged from a single, foreign capitalism, but through 'hybridizations' derived equally from 'local capitalisms that have revolutionized local premodern cultures', as capitalism 'produces novel cultural forms again and again in each society in which it takes root'.[88] What same-sex patterns emerge in a particular society is 'not a foregone conclusion'; it involves 'unexpected outcomes'.[89]

As I have argued elsewhere, these outcomes can be sorted into several broad patterns, including the suppression of indigenous same-sex eroticism by colonialism, its adaptation to better fit the requirements of dependent capitalist development, its repression by neo-colonial regimes, and the relative greater prominence of transgender patterns in conditions of dependent development.[90] This means that no LGBT identity today can be *purely* indigenous. In a global capitalist system with far-reaching social and cultural consequences, the idea of absolutely pure, authentic same-sex identities is as untenable as a false universalism.[91]

Of the different factors at work in combined and uneven social construction – indigenous sexual regimes, economic and social development, cultural

---

88   Jackson 1989, pp. 387, 364.

89   Rofel 1999, p. 470.

90   I have developed this analysis at greater length elsewhere (Drucker 2000a, pp. 15–16, 20–5).

91   Neil Garcia has argued convincingly against the idea that 'cultures are by nature circumscribed by impermeable boundaries' (1996, pp. xvii–xviii).

globalisation and political change – I have argued that cultural globalisation and the rise of the 'global gay'[92] may be the least essential. Cultural borrowings are frequent, of course – cultural industries are part of the broader political economy[93] – but they are no proof of influence, let alone causation. Deep-going social processes like urbanisation are far more central to identity formation than access to European magazines and Hollywood movies.[94] A materialist analysis would even suggest that the poor countries' economic dependence, by helping to hold back and distort economic growth, has delayed the emergence of a specifically lesbian/gay identity.

Thanks to mass migration, moreover, the peoples of these different parts of the world increasingly live side by side, mostly in the imperialist countries: another crucial factor in shaping sexual regimes. The role of capital and of capitalist states in structuring migratory flows needs to be integrated into a transnational understanding of sexuality.[95] This applies to both international migration and the movement from countryside to cities characteristic of sexual dissidents worldwide, in the course of which 'the purportedly premodern and the seemingly postmodern...intersect'.[96] For international migrants, migration involves, alongside the economic, social and cultural impact of their destination country on the countries left behind, a process in which the diaspora 'creates the homeland' – a fact equally relevant to queer diasporas.[97]

So far, LGBT studies has not managed to define its field of study in a way that does justice to all these different global parameters. At first, it almost exclusively studied North America and Europe. In more recent decades, as part of what is called 'the transnational turn', the study of same-sex formations in Latin America, Africa and Asia has flourished, but in ways that usually either borrow basic categories from earlier, Eurocentric works, or that look at their regions in relative isolation. In this book, I attempt to begin from an insight that, as far as I am aware, has not yet been treated as central to the study of LGBT regimes: that their development has always been a global process, but one in which, at every stage, *both* the rich, dominant, imperialist countries *and* the poor, dominated, economically dependent countries were central to these regimes' transformations.

---

92   Altman 1996, pp. 77–8.

93   Duggan 2003, p. 78.

94   Adam, Duyvendak and Krouwel have pointed out that even 'similar cultural practices have quite different meanings' in different cultures (1999, p. 348).

95   Arguelles and Rich 1989, pp. 442, 450.

96   Herzog 2011, p. 205.

97   Puar 2007, pp. 170–2 (citing Brian Keith Axel and David Eng).

So while this book focuses on same-sex sexualities under neoliberal capital-ism, in trying to give an adequate account I have been forced to give it a broad scope in both time and space. Making sense of LGBT sexualities today requires me to explain how they are both the same as and different from same-sex for-mations in non-capitalist societies, in capitalist societies in which same-sex formations were not 'gay', and in the capitalist societies of the 1960s and 1970s in which these sexualities were 'gay' in a somewhat different sense. Making sense of LGBT formations in any one part of the world today requires me to explain how virtually every part of today's world is linked to the rest, economi-cally, socially and sexually, in a hierarchy that is characterised by often brutal domination and inequality, whose globalisation is as productive of difference as it is of homogenisation.

An emphasis on combined and uneven social construction is in tension with an account of a same-sex formation as a global totality. The same-sex regime that is globally dominant – today, I argue, neoliberal homonormativity – is by no means locally dominant in every corner of the planet. Even within a single country – South Africa, for instance – the same-sex regime in a predominantly white, middle-class gay disco in Cape Town is very different from the regime two women in a relationship face in Soweto or in rural KwaZulu. I believe that both the global and the local are relevant to sexual politics in each situation, in ways I will try to show, but what is politically decisive varies in different times and places.

These methodological parameters have implications for the organisation of Part 1 of this book. At first glance, the sequence of chapters and sections is chronological: first pre-capitalist societies (prologue), then pre-gay same-sex formations in capitalist societies (prologue and chapter 1), then lesbian/gay sexualities under Fordist capitalism (chapter 2), then LGBT sexualities under neoliberalism today (chapter 3). In fact, since capitalism and its different regimes of accumulation prevailed in different parts of the world at different times, examples from chronologically earlier periods sometimes appear later than examples from chronologically later periods. Moreover, since capitalist regimes of accumulation have sometimes allowed or even compelled the pres-ervation of non-capitalist or differently-capitalist elements within an over-arching global order, even the chapter on sexualities under neoliberalism has to discuss phenomena that at first sight 'fit' into earlier periods. I do my best to make clear as I go along why and how the different pieces of the jigsaw belong where they are placed.

As Theo van der Meer has pointed out, there is no such single entity as homosexuality, and the homosexuality of a hundred years ago is not the homosexuality of today.[98] Moreover, there is *still* no single same-sex sexual pattern today. The same-sex sexuality of a Dutch gay professional man is far removed from that of an Indonesian tomboy – whether she lives in Jakarta or in Amsterdam. And neither of them is more modern than the other; neither represents the end of the story. The story is still unfolding.

---

98   Van der Meer 2007, p. 19.

PART 1

Origins of Gay Normality

••

Prologue: Before Homosexuality

Understanding the neoliberal homonormativity that queers are up against today, and how we can fight it, requires understanding where it came from. Part 1 of this book uses the concept of same-sex formations developed in the previous section to trace the origins of today's gay normality, both before and under capitalism. In the prologue, after sketching out a range of pre-capitalist same-sex formations in which transgender and intergenerational patterns were usually hegemonic, I argue that the 'molly-dominant' regime of European early bourgeois societies, from the late seventeenth to early nineteenth centuries, was itself characterised by the dominance of a very distinctive transgender pattern. In this formation, 'mollies' and 'sapphists' mimicked emerging bourgeois conceptions of love and free choice, rooted in an emerging society defined by 'freedom' of contract.

Something similar applies to the 'invert-dominant' regime described in chapter 1, which flourished in the period of classical imperialism from roughly the late nineteenth to mid-twentieth centuries. The 'homosexual' who was first invented in this period was in fact usually a gender-nonconformist 'invert', whose relationships formed a pendant to the emerging culture of heterosexual romance that greased the wheels of working- and middle-class family formation. These histories make clear the uniqueness of the 'gay-dominant' regime that arose after the Second World War, described in chapter 2, in which – for the first time in history – masculine but same-sex-identified gay men and feminine lesbians became the norm. This period saw the consolidation of the sexual binary and gender conformism that queers are battling against today.

A vast array of same-sex formations existed in human societies before the rise of imperialism in the late nineteenth century. For the purposes of this book, there are only a few points that can and need be made about them in this prologue. One point is that all of them – all the hugely varied indigenous sexual formations of Eurasia, the Mediterranean world, Africa and the Americas – had a key feature in common: they were not based on a hetero/homo binary.[1] A second point, discussed at some length below, is that they had pervasive connections with kinship and with men's dominance over women as a consistent constituent element of both cross-sex and same-sex patterns. A third is that patterns that today under neoliberalism are seen as 'queer' – as foreign to lesbian/gay normality as it is increasingly understood and accepted – were central to most same-sex relations in human history. Notably,

---

1 Massad 2007, p. 40.

transgender or intergenerational relationships were at the heart of many if not most same-sex formations. Transgender identities have been central through almost all of human sexual history, rooted in the close connection between sex and kinship. Intergenerational relationships were central to the civilisations of the ancient Greek and Roman and medieval Islamic worlds, China and Japan.

This prologue also describes the rise in the first centuries of capitalism of transitional same-sex forms, which broke with previous sexual history in unprecedented ways and yet still did not involve a hetero/homo binary. Beginning in the early bourgeois societies of England, the Netherlands and France in the late seventeenth, eighteenth and early nineteenth centuries,[2] a distinctive, commodified form of transgender relationships prevailed in a 'molly-dominant' same-sex regime. While this regime began to take root in some parts of the world that European states colonised, other same-sex formations were brutally suppressed. The transitional same-sex regime of early modern Europe also entailed the rise of separate men's and women's spheres and same-sex romantic friendship. The different transitional forms would all persist, have an ongoing impact and be radically reconfigured in the late nineteenth century.

Besides these political points, this prologue also serves to show with a few examples the usefulness of a historical materialist approach in making sexual history comprehensible. The concept of same-sex formations is meant to be applied mainly to the sexual regimes of different periods of capitalism, but in this prologue I suggest that it can be more broadly useful. For example, it can help us understand the place of transgendered *kinaidi / cinaedi* in ancient Greek and Roman sexual regimes in which intergenerational patterns were dominant, or understand the place of commercial ties between Japanese male merchants and actors in a sexual formation where relationships between samurai and their young squires were the model. I also suggest that the concept of combined and uneven social construction can illuminate the development of sexual formations in regions of the Americas and Asia that were ruled from feudal or early capitalist Europe.

The uniqueness of modern same-sex formations based on a distinction between 'homosexuals' and 'heterosexuals' is the first necessary point to grasp before any of the others. This is a commonplace in queer studies today. Yet I suspect that it may still be difficult for many readers to understand, given

---

2   My conception of 'early bourgeois societies' draws on Hal Draper's definition of 'bourgeois' as referring to 'the broader and more varied social relationships that cluster around the capitalist class' (Draper 1978, p. 169) – although Charlie Post has made me aware of the problematic character of 'bourgeois' in reference to France in periods when it had no capitalist class.

how deeply the division between 'gay people' and 'straight people' has by now shaped so many people's common-sense understanding of sexual life. Analysing a few of the innumerable other ways of conceiving and living sexual desire and behaviour should help dispel this common sense.

Kinship and Patriarchy

If and when same-sex sexual relations have been tolerated in a society, they have had to adapt to, and be ideologically justified in terms of, the society's gender and kinship systems. Kinship plays an important role in all class societies, as a key link between the gender relations that always structure social reproduction and the property relations that regulate production. In this sense, as Gayle Rubin has convincingly argued, kinship and the traffic in women are a key locus of women's oppression, and a central factor structuring the psychology of individual women and men in sexist societies.[3] In Michel Foucault's terms, the family involves an interchange of sexuality and alliance, with alliance involving marriage and the 'transmission of names and possessions'.[4] At the same time, they are always part of 'total social systems', in which sexuality, economics, and politics interact.[5]

Kinship was particularly important and constricting in pre-class societies where the family was a key production unit, and the first division of labour, the one based on gender, was the main or only one.[6] Many pre-class societies had extraordinarily elaborate marriage rules and clan structures, sometimes extending far beyond the nuclear unit of man, woman and children.[7] In such societies, kinship was often 'the idiom of social interaction', economic, political and ceremonial as well as sexual.[8] A wide range of same-sex social and emotional ties and sexual patterns has fitted into such kinship patterns. Often same-sex eroticism has been shaped into some quasi-kinship category, particularly by assigning to people social genders different from their perceived

---

3 Rubin 2011, pp. 43–7.

4 Foucault 1980, p. 106.

5 Rubin 2011, pp. 63, 65. I agree with Hennessy that kinship is inadequate as 'the sole lens for examining the oppression of women' (2000, p. 181). But if kinship is a key link between production and reproduction, then a focus on it does not necessarily obscure 'changes in the division of labor globally' (Ibid); nor should kinship relations be seen as mere 'cultural relations' (Hennessy 2000, p. 59).

6 Young 1981, p. 53.

7 Wekker 2006, p. 76.

8 Rubin 2011, p. 41.

biological sex. Transgender, intergenerational and other non-gay same-sex systems 'articulate homosexuality *within* kin logic'.[9]

Given the historically pervasive subordination of women, kinship structures have sometimes drastically restricted women's sexual possibilities. In many cultures and regions, open sexual relationships between women were beyond their reach. As Adrienne Rich has written, many of the ways in which men have oppressed women have also served specifically to repress lesbianism: 'men's ability to deny women sexuality or force it upon them; to command or exploit their labor to control their produce; to control or rob them of their children; to confine them physically and prevent their movement'; even genital mutilation.[10] In those parts of the world where women were most dependent on men, sexual relationships between women grew up only in unnoticed corners of households and villages, where women who were segregated from men bonded with each other, perhaps even including unnamed, unspoken sexual bonding.

Yet, as a number of feminists have pointed out, an extreme system of compulsory heterosexuality for women by no means characterised all pre-capitalist societies.[11] In many cultures, paradoxically, women have benefited from resistance to the idea that 'sex' can happen between women at all, particularly where male penetration or ejaculation is the criterion for it. As a result, in cultures like the Southern African Basotho, deep kissing or even cunnilingus between women might not be seen as sex.[12]

In most societies throughout history, kinship structures have been all-important for men as well as women, notably in negotiating relationships to class and other power structures. Families are significant in forming and changing modes of production, above all because they are central in 'the production of people and their capacities for work, compliance and resistance'.[13] In China, all members of a family share in its *mianzi* ('face'), which is 'indispensable to social status'; people who cause their family to lose status thereby undermine their own.[14] In other societies too, people's status, wealth and power often depend on those of their family. Even in neoliberal societies today, the state and capital rely on families sharing resources with members who

---

9   Adam 1985, p. 668.
10   Rich 1983, pp. 183–5.
11   For example, Blackwood 1986.
12   Epprecht 2009, pp. 1266–7 (citing Jane Kendall).
13   Seccombe 1992, p. 9.
14   Rofel 1999, p. 464.

would otherwise need social support. This makes families shock absorbers for the damage that the market can wreak.

Alongside kinship, religion has played a crucial role in structuring most societies. It has not just been a way of meeting people's spiritual needs and making sense of good and evil, life and death. It has also been the foundation of identity, family life and customs. Among the indigenous peoples of the Americas, for example, sexual life, cross-sex and same-sex, was embedded in a spiritual framework.[15] But religion has never been socially or politically neutral. It has always been political, from the Conquistadors to the Iranian Revolution to the Pope's visit to Cuba. Notably, religions have often reflected and reinforced women's social and sexual subordination.

But although LGBT people in the Americas and Europe who have wrestled with Christian homophobia might not credit it, the effect of religion on same-sex possibilities has not always been negative. By contrast with the patriarchal deities of Judaism, Christianity and Islam, both Hinduism and indigenous African religions have androgynous deities that can be invoked to explain or justify human androgyny or gender ambiguity. Gloria Wekker has contended that there is 'an essentially egalitarian, non-rigid gender ideology embedded within the folds' of indigenous African and African-derived religions. This helps explain the wealth and authority that is possible for some women within the tradition of female same-sex marriages in Dahomey, Nigeria, Sudan and Kenya.[16]

Transgender

Some of these religions provide ways of expressing transgender identity, through the idea of possession by deities of the other sex. Transgender roles in indigenous Hausa religion in Nigeria have Dahomeyan and Yoruba counterparts elsewhere in West Africa.[17] Religious transgender patterns also existed among southern African peoples, including peoples that had *sangomas* or 'rain queens',[18] and the Shona of present-day Zimbabwe whose traditional animist

---

15   D'Emilio and Freedman 1997, p. 7. Katz has compiled many accounts of same-sex relations among indigenous North Americans (1976, pp. 281–327).

16   Wekker 2006, pp. 85, 185, 216–18. Wekker has noted that both she and Audre Lorde have been taken to task for suggesting that these marriages sometimes had a sexual component (2006, p. 272, n. 17).

17   Murray 1997, pp. 222–4.

18   Drucker 1996, p. 79.

belief in ancestor spirits allowed for men's possession by the spirits of their 'aunties'.[19] Information about sexual relations between women among the Ashanti of Ghana and Zimbabweans suggest a shared, religiously founded conception of some women as having 'a "heavy soul" – a "masculine soul that likes to lie down with women"'.[20] Transgendered shamans were apparently associated with androgynous deities before Islam spread through Indonesia in the fifteenth century, in the Philippines before the Spanish,[21] and in indigenous Siberian society in the pre-1917 Russian Empire.[22]

Throughout human history, many transgender same-sex relationships have involved assigning a distinct gender and sexual identity to at least one partner different from his or her perceived biological sex. Sometimes in these relationships, for example, a man who is penetrated sexually may no longer be considered masculine and becomes a person of the 'other gender' or a 'third gender' – a 'transgendered' person. (A man who penetrates other men sexually is often still considered a typical man, however, and may often be expected to marry a woman and have children). However, this is only one variant of a very wide range of identities that are placed under the umbrella 'transgender'. Transgender is primarily a gender category, not a sexual one, so that many transgendered people 'don't fit into other people's sexual orientation categories'. They may be 'of any sexual orientation', 'specifically attracted to transgender people', asexual or 'autosexual' (taking pleasure in their own bodies).[23] There are many words in use around the world that put gender identity in question in various ways. All these words for trans people, which often refer to only one partner in a same-sex relationship or encounter, are used instead of or alongside 'bisexual' (which might sometimes be used for a non-transgendered partner), 'gay' and 'lesbian' (which do not necessarily put men's masculinity or women's femininity in question).

Transgender relationships have always been the most common same-sex pattern.[24] In many pre-capitalist cultures, transgendered people played special military and/or social roles. Often transformations of gender and sexual practices have gone together. The variety of transgender formations has been extraordinary. In some cultures, trans people have simply been reassigned from

---

19   Hoad 1999, p. 567.
20   Wekker 2006, pp. 77–8, 122.
21   Drucker 1996, p. 79.
22   Healey 2001, p. 8.
23   Stryker 2008, p. 16.
24   Clellan Ford and Frank Beach found transgender more than any other same-sex pattern among the 76 societies they studied, with examples on every continent (1951, p. 130).

masculine to feminine or vice versa; in other cultures, trans people have been defined as a third or even fourth gender; in still others, they have been defined as non-gendered. Male-to-female trans people in different societies could be seen as the wives of cisgendered (non-transgendered) men, or as more or less honoured prostitutes, or as asexual. The cardinal rule was that gender was the primary determinant: 'individuals' gender rather than their genitalia determined their sexual object choice'.[25]

Although the sexual division of labour was often crucial to pre-class societies, in some there was little or no hierarchical difference between men and women. Thus, male-to-female trans people did not necessarily lose status through their transformation.[26] On the contrary, they sometimes enjoyed prestige as healers, conciliators or bearers of knowledge. This was the case with Native American transgendered berdaches, who in a number of indigenous North American societies had both '*productive specialization*' and '*supernatural sanction*'. They were 'accepted and integrated members of their communities', with equal status, often enjoying special honours and viewed as possessing 'exceptional productivity, talent and originality'.[27]

But male domination in many societies, even pre-class societies, has had implications for sexual regimes. Lower status for women has turned male-to-female transgender identity into a degradation, and female-to-male transgender identity into a form of upward mobility,[28] where it has been permitted, or an unacceptable escape from female inferiority, where it has not. In some societies, in some circumstances allowing a few women to rise to male status has been viewed as advantageous to the family, as in Balkan cultures where, as late as the mid-twentieth century, families without sons allowed or even encouraged daughters to dress and live as men so as to fill the role of warrior head of the household that would otherwise have been vacant. In these Balkan cases, however, these transgender roles were seen as emphatically not sexual: the trans women who assumed them were called 'sworn virgins', allowed to express attraction to women but not act on it, and if they got pregnant they were to be punished by death or at least loss of status and forced marriage.[29]

At the same time, by segregating women from men in order to keep them from power, from activities restricted to men, and from men other than their fathers, husbands or masters, some male-dominated societies have tended to

25   Loos 2009, p. 1320.

26   Trevisan 1986, p. 62; Greenberg 1988, pp. 42–5, 65.

27   Roscoe 1994, pp. 332, 370, 335.

28   Herdt 1994, p. 60.

29   Grémaux 1994, pp. 247, 257, 261, 244, 253, 268–70.

promote female bonding. This female bonding, including sexual activity, has
the potential in male-dominated societies to be felt or seen as a form of wom-
en's resistance, 'both the breaking of a taboo and the rejection of a compulsory
way of life'.[30]

Transgender remained an especially strong tradition in South and Southeast
Asia, perhaps because Hinduism preserved elements of earlier, kinship-based
cultures even after the rise of centralised states. Indian cultural traditions were
tolerant towards androgyny, as is evident from the androgynous character
of major Hindu deities such as Siva, Vishnu and Krishna,[31] and spread with
Hinduism as far as Bali.[32] The transition to class society in South Asia probably
helped to bring about the severe constriction of women's public life now characteristic of Hinduism, and also probably lowered the status of male-to-female
trans people.

In any event, the rise of class society required fitting trans people into a
more elaborate division of labour and a more developed hierarchy. In some
cases, the existence of people located outside rigid kinship structures could
have advantages from the viewpoint of a wider class society. This seems to have
been the case with the South Asian transgendered *hijras*. *Hijras* were traditionally drawn from the ranks of those who were seen as unqualified for male
or female status, family formation and thus full personhood: intersex people,
eunuchs (either from birth or emasculated by other *hijras*; those living as *hijras*
but resisting emasculation faced disapproval and pressure), sexually impotent
males, or women unable to menstruate. Living together in groups under the
direction of a *hijra* guru and with no caste and kinship status to uphold, *hijras*
were 'freed from the constraints of respectable behavior and nearly invulner-
able to social control by those outside their community'.[33]

In religious terms, *hijras*' consciously accepted outsider status made them
'ascetics' or 'renouncers', able to 'transform an incomplete personhood into a
transcendent one' and 'the dross of lost virility into the gold of divine power'.[34]
They were supposed to be under the protection of the goddess Bahuchara
Mata and to be endowed with her powers, including the power to bless or
curse.[35] Economically, they functioned as paid performers at weddings and

30   Rich 1983, pp. 183–97.
31   Nanda 1994, pp. 375–6.
32   Agustine et al. 2012, p. 306.
33   Nanda 1994, pp. 380–5, 392.
34   Nanda 1994, pp. 394–5.
35   Nanda 1994, pp. 373, 386–7; Kumar 1993, pp. 86–90.

births (traditionally of boys) – thus ensuring the persistence of a male lineage from which they were excluded – and to some extent as prostitutes.[36]

Strikingly, a somewhat similar transgender social role existed for Byzantine eunuchs, despite their embedding in the different ideological framework of Christianity. Over a period of almost a thousand years, eunuchs were defined broadly as not only men who had been castrated but all men who could not procreate and were thus marginalised from kinship structures. This made them ineligible for supreme power but all the more suited for a wide range of social roles, as brokers, secretaries, envoys, singers, doctors, political advisers and administrators. Church spokesmen defended and even exalted the institution of eunuchs, responding to the argument that castration was unnatural by asserting that 'ascetics choose a life beyond nature'.[37]

A related tradition existed in Thailand. The Thai word *kathoey*, which primarily means intersex, has also been used to describe transvestites and other men who take on feminine roles. Despite the existence of Buddhist texts viewing transvestism and male prostitution as sinful,[38] Thai Buddhist ethical literature contained only one prohibition relative to *kathoeys*, interestingly enough: the prohibition of magic transforming a *kathoey* into a man or vice versa. Thai traditions, which allowed married men to keep concubines and visit prostitutes, permitted *kathoeys* to fill these roles as well.[39]

Societies in the Americas with large concentrations of African slaves often made possible the persistence of African transgender patterns among the enslaved. Perhaps gender relations among slaves – in which enslaved women as well as men did heavy labour, men had little or no power as heads of households, and a 'dual marriage structure' gave white owners as well as black male slaves sexual access to female slaves – allowed both genders 'expressive and "mothering"' behaviour and gave women scope to be sexual.[40]

Class Trumps Kinship

In many Eurasian slave-based economies, however, in which slaves were torn from their kinship and community ties, age-defined or class-defined sexual relationships between males were common and often dominant in their

---

36 Drucker 1996, p. 80.
37 Ringrose 1994, pp. 85–6, 90, 96–7, 106.
38 Hinsch 1990, pp. 96–7.
39 Jackson 1989, pp. 20, 26, 37.
40 Wekker 2006, pp. 161, 106–7.

same-sex formations. In these cultures, males who were sexually penetrated were supposed to be socially inferior to, or at least younger than, the men who penetrated them. This was the hegemonic same-sex pattern in the countries of Greek or Latin culture along the Mediterranean, the Persian-Arab-Islamic world and the Chinese empire.[41]

The ancient Greeks, for example, defined sex as penetration, and penetration as domination. The 'proper targets' of desire for an adult male citizen, who in principle was also the head of a patriarchal household, were women, youths, foreigners and slaves. Male citizens in ancient Athens were distinguished from slaves and foreigners by freedom 'from servility, exemption from torture, and corporeal inviolability' – including, at least as adults, freedom from sexual penetration. They were also distinguished by their equal right to penetrate, to the point that Solon reputedly established public brothels open to all citizens as one of the founding acts of Athenian democracy.[42]

In this respect as in others, the Arab caliphate was the heir to the Mediterranean social order of the ancient Greeks and Romans, as well as the Persian Empire it had conquered. Despite explicit condemnations of *liwat* (sodomy) in the Koran, men's desire for male youths pervaded much of medieval Arabic love poetry and classical literature. The Koran, later Islamic religious texts and medieval Arabic love poetry confirm that Arabs in the first centuries of Islam simply did not classify human beings as homosexual or heterosexual.[43] Arabic did not even have a word for 'the sort of bisexuality that was considered as the unmarked, most common form of sexual practice'.[44] Instead, references to male-male sexual relations in medieval Arabic sources fell into an age-defined pattern: when the beloved was not a youth between 15 and 20 years old, he was almost always a slave, an artisan, a labourer or transgendered.[45]

Intergenerational patterns were equally hegemonic in the same-sex formation of medieval Iran, where lust for male youths was seen as such an intrinsic part of adult male desire that an eleventh-century advice manual urged

---

41   Greenberg 1988, pp. 91, 164.

42   Halperin 1990, pp. 30, 96, 100. The ancient Greeks' ephebophilia (male desire for pubescent youths) was distinctive in the emphasis they placed (at least in Athens and a number of other city-states, and only among citizens) on the educational function of an older lover's passion for his young beloved. Foucault stressed the 'admiration, gratitude, or affection' that youths were supposed to feel for their ancient Greek lovers (1990, p. 223), though he questioned whether the Greeks' privileging of ephebophilia was due solely to 'pedagogical concerns' (p. 195).

43   Massad 2007.

44   Amer 2005, p. 224.

45   Peirce 2009, p. 1333.

marriage mainly as a way of safeguarding a man's religion against homoerotic impulses. As in ancient Greece, the age when facial hair was just beginning to sprout was seen in Iran as particularly desirable, while the growth of a full beard marked the transition from being the object to the subject of desire.[46] This kind of intergenerational homoeroticism apparently spread with Arab-Persian-Islamic culture, for example, into Turkey, Albania, Central Asia, Afghanistan and the Indian subcontinent, where classical Urdu poets celebrated it.[47] Evidence from Central Asian regions under imperial Chinese rule suggests that the tradition of Sogdian dancing boys dates to pre-Islamic times.[48] Same-sex traditions also persisted among the Muslim Swahili peoples of the East African coast.[49]

In East Africa alone, interestingly, the higher status of women led to the adaptation of the Islamic male-male pattern to women.[50] In medieval Arab regions, by contrast, sex between women – generally conceived as 'rubbing' rather than penetration – was sometimes the subject of erotic tales, but often was not taken terribly seriously. 'Rubbing', which medical authorities said could be an 'innate and lifelong' predisposition for some women, was sometimes even viewed as a sort of insurance against adultery with men, which was seen as a far graver sin. Erotic practices between women like kissing and caressing were treated lightly, and not viewed as 'sodomy' (liwat). Medieval Arabic romances sometimes portrayed love between women as deep and passionate, but they almost invariably showed the women marrying men in the end – the women's own preferences being of no practical significance.[51]

The same-sex sexual regime of Ottoman society too was predominantly intergenerational, with a rich same-sex sexual life embedded in patriarchal mores. Intergenerational relationships cut across communal divides, with the formal supremacy of Islam allowing for much social and sexual interaction, including same-sex interaction, between Muslims, Christians and Jews.[52] Ottoman Jews followed the same patterns as Muslims. Same-sex relations between women, while more difficult and less attested, were feared particularly among widows.[53]

---

46   Najmabadi 2005, pp. 159, 15.

47   Drucker 1996, pp. 81–2.

48   Hinsch 1990, pp. 61–2.

49   Mburu 2000, p. 181.

50   Greenberg 1988, pp. 179–82.

51   Amer 2005, pp. 216–17, 22–3, 228.

52   Drucker 2012, pp. 143–5.

53   Peirce 2009, pp. 1332–3 (citing Yaron Ben-Naeh).

Imperial China too for millennia had a same-sex formation in which intergenerational relationships founded on status differences predominated.[54]

A key feature of these intergenerational regimes was the lack of any permanent identity linked to same-sex object choice, particularly of the adult male who penetrated youths or younger or lower-status males. Privileged adult males saw themselves as entitled to satisfaction of their sexual desires as an integral part of their privilege, and the gender of their sexual objects as being of no great significance. Ancient Greek and Roman, classical Arab and Persian,[55] and imperial Chinese sources even identified individual adult men who were exclusive or strong partisans of either women or male youths as exceptional and even odd, since most adult men were assumed to be capable of being sexually aroused by both. Any preference they did have was generally ascribed to a liking 'for particular human body parts, independent of the sex of the person who possesse[d] them'. The texts contained little or no suggestion that adult men would be desirable to any other adult men of comparable status;[56] among free, non-transgendered males, only youths were seen as objects of desire.[57]

This regime had consequences both for the youths who were the objects of desire and for the possibilities of friendship and love between men. For the youths, sexual submission to privileged adult males did not involve assuming a specific identity and was not necessarily perceived as dishonourable, on two conditions: (1) that it never be motivated by a desire for penetration (as opposed to respect or affection); and (2) that it never happen once full adulthood was reached (unless it involved submission to someone as exalted as a Chinese emperor). For privileged adult men, their feelings for youths might include intense passion, but could not be identified with friendship (any more than desire for a woman could be), because friendship was only possible between equals. Sex was about penetration, and therefore superiority and inferiority: it was 'not the sort of thing you would do to someone you really love'.[58]

Ottoman sexual culture too saw men's sexual drive as not only natural but in need of immediate satisfaction – within the parameters of patriarchal power relations.[59] Since marriage entailed the segregation of wives and was not founded on romantic love, privileged Ottoman men did not generally experience their extramarital liaisons as sources of conflict or pain. In ancient

---

54   Hinsch 1990, pp. 20–2.
55   Najmabadi 2005, p. 20.
56   Halperin 2002, pp. 90, 97–8, 95.
57   Halperin 1989, p. 44.
58   Halperin 2002, pp. 145, 121.
59   Thanks to Özlem Barin for this point.

imperial China too, since marriage was seen as 'the bonding of two lineage groups' rather than a romantic union, Chinese wives were expected to accept a husband's female concubine and, by the same token, his 'dalliances with a male slave'.[60]

Nonetheless, powerful men's sexual preferences for youths could be seen, especially in times of societal crisis, as threatening to marriage or procreation, and accordingly could be regulated, restricted or banned. The Chinese ban on 'sodomy with consent' decreed in 1740 under the Qing dynasty was part of a general crackdown on the perceived licentiousness of the preceding Ming dynasty. After a period of initial severity, however, this provision was enforced only intermittently or not at all.[61]

One striking, recurrent pattern is the persistence and even prevalence of transgender relationships even in societies where some other same-sex pattern was hegemonic. We will see that this was the case in late nineteenth- and early twentieth-century Europe and North America, where the new, broad category of 'homosexuality' in fact largely overlapped with what was then called 'sexual inversion' and would now often be viewed as transgender relationships. A similar pattern seems to be re-emerging in the twenty-first century, where 'queer' often means 'gender queer'. Something similar took place in many ancient societies where intergenerational or status-defined same-sex formations were hegemonic, but coexisted with, subordinated and reshaped transgender patterns. This underscores that while class and other status differences constitute central structuring elements, gender always underlies them and remains crucial. Moreover, alongside other forms of resistance to unequal social relations, resistance to the gender roles and identities assigned to individuals seems to be a constant.

This was the case, for example, in the ancient Greek and Roman worlds. In ancient Athens and other Greek city-states, while the idealised form of male same-sex relations was ephebophilia – desire, courtship and sex between an adult citizen and a pubescent citizen boy – adult male citizens could also sexually penetrate transgendered men called *kinaidi* (or in Rome, where the pattern was similar, *cinaedi*), whose desire to be penetrated revealed their gender deviance. The same applied to the female category of *tribades*, women whose desire to penetrate other women was only one aspect of their identification as 'phallic... hypermasculine or butch'.[62]

---

60   Hinsch 1990, pp. 19, 49.

61   Hinsch 1990, pp. 139–45, 162; Ng 1989, pp. 88–9.

62   Halperin 2002, pp. 33, 122 (citing Craig Williams), 37, 51.

Forms of transgender identity also existed in many Arab countries, where there have traditionally been terms for adult male-to-female trans people: *hassas* in Morocco, *köçek* in Turkey, *khanith* in Oman, *khusra* in Pakistan, and so on.[63] As among the ancient Greeks, receptive sexual behaviour that was not terribly stigmatised among male youths (as long as it was discreet) became a marker of transgendered identity, and shameful, in an adult male.[64] Pre-colonial Indonesia also provides examples of complex combinations of intergenerational and transgender formations: along with transgendered *waria*, intergenerational relationships were common in western Sumatra and, as early as the eighteenth century, in Muslim boarding schools in central and eastern Java.[65]

In imperial China, the intergenerational relationships between the scholar/ gentry and boy actors could also have a transgender dimension, as the boy actors often played female roles on stage. Eunuchs, sometimes (though not always) stereotyped as effeminate, also took passive roles in sex with powerful adult men. One seventeenth-century tale described a younger male 'wife' devoted to her husband to the point of castrating herself to preserve her feminine features. Another seventeenth-century story generalised that 'a man can become a woman and a woman can become a man'.[66]

Ancient Greece and Rome, Islamic empires and China all had highly developed commodity production and exchange, and accordingly prostitution, including male prostitution. Just as female prostitutes were viewed as inferior to married women because of their more precarious embedding in class hierarchies, however, male prostitutes clearly did not have the status of court favourites. In imperial China, acting and male prostitution were clearly linked to their mutual disadvantage; some Chinese male actors even had bound feet.[67]

Feudalism

Feudalism fits into the broad category of societies in whose sexual regimes class and status trumped gender and kinship. Yet the feudal mode of production had distinctive features that help account for capitalism's emergence from

---

63   Roscoe and Murray 1997.
64   Peirce 2009, p. 1331 (citing Everett Rowson).
65   Oetomo and Emond 1992, pp. 7, 3–4.
66   Hinsch 1990, pp. 148, 43–4, 12; Ng 1989, pp. 82, 84.
67   Hinsch 1990, pp. 72, 152–6.

feudalism in Europe and capitalism's failure to emerge in Asian empires that not only were far wealthier but also had far more extensive commodity production and exchange.[68] The fragmented nature of political power in feudal societies allowed quasi-bourgeois economic and social relations to flourish and achieve local dominance, even in urban enclaves that were physically and economically dwarfed by the surrounding feudal rural order, in a way that would have been impossible in more centralised states. This characteristic fragmentation had consequences for feudal sexual regimes as well. Beginning as early as fourteenth-century Italy, it made possible the emergence of urban same-sex regimes.

Feudal Japan, whose mode of production paralleled feudal Europe's in many ways, is an interesting case in point. It had a distinctive sexual regime in which intergenerational relationships between adult samurai and adolescents constituted the social ideal of male love.[69] Male-male sexual relations were intricately regulated in seventeenth- to mid-nineteenth-century Tokugawa Japan to maintain the hierarchy between samurai and their adolescent servants and acolytes.[70] Idealised devotion between samurai could make 'youth' a purely conventional term, however: although a youth traditionally became a man at about the age of 19 in a ceremony in which his forelocks were shaved, one story described two samurai who began their relationship as a 19-year-old man and a 16-year-old youth, but still preserved their roles as 'man' and 'youth' at the ages of 66 and 63.[71]

Sexual relationships between adult Buddhist monks and their adolescent novices shared many of the features of idealised samurai intergenerational relationships. Feudal Japan from the tenth to the nineteenth centuries had a tradition of tales of love between Buddhist monks and boy acolytes, with many love poems by monks included in imperial poetic anthologies.[72]

In the course of these centuries, a commodified same-sex subculture also grew up in Japanese towns, involving relationships between adult male merchants and transgendered boy kabuki actors who prostituted themselves. 'Townsmen took over the practice of male love from the samurai and Buddhist elite', and developed relationships between merchants and boy kabuki actors playing female roles.[73] However, there was a clear sense that these crass

---

68 Anderson 1979b, pp. 410–30.
69 Schalow 1996, pp. 14–16.
70 Loos 2001, p. 1321 (citing Gregory Pflugfelder).
71 Schalow 1989, pp. 120, 125–6.
72 Schalow 1996, p. 14.
73 Miller 1996, p. 99; Schalow 1996, p. 15.

relationships fell short of the ideal of samurai male love, which the participants in urban male relationships nonetheless sometimes tried to mimic; many stories focused on a youth's 'transcendence of the financial transaction and his entry into the emotional realm of *ikiji*, "shared masculine pride" '. Patronising kabuki boy actor prostitutes was seen as shameful for samurai.[74]

This Japanese feudal same-sex formation had some parallels in early forms of European feudalism. Although Christian moral strictures prevented the open celebration of male love between European knights and pages, European monarchs with male sexual favourites included Edward II in England and Henri III in France, as well as popes like Julius III.[75] The relations of domination and subordination between lords and serfs may have made possible forms of same-sex sexual relations that need not involve explicit naming. Evidence from tsarist Russia, where feudal relations persisted longer than in Western Europe, is in any event suggestive. Russian bathhouses were used as early as the seventeenth century for sexual relations that reflected the power imbalance between older and/or wealthier males, and younger and/or subordinate ones.[76]

The existence of intergenerational sexual relationships between Russian Orthodox monks and their young novices was an open secret. Sexual relations between older and younger monks were notoriously common in tsarist Russia even in the early twentieth century, and provided occasions for well-publicised trials of Orthodox clerics in post-1917 Soviet Russia, such as the 1919 trial of Bishop Palladii. Russian Orthodox penances for 'sodomy' were comparable to those for male-female adultery: lenient by comparison with Western European Catholic practices of recent centuries, but not that different from Western European penances up to the early thirteenth century. Russian Orthodox monastic rules, like Western European ones, took for granted that young novices would be sexually tempting to older monks.[77] Accounts of these Russian relationships are reminiscent of descriptions of love affairs between older and younger Catholic monks in Western Europe in the early medieval period.[78] Those in charge of women's monastic communities were also aware of same-sex sexual temptations – justifiably, to judge by one twelfth-century

---

74   Schalow 1989, pp. 122, 121.
75   Saslow 1989, p. 92.
76   Healey 2001, pp. 22–3, 26.
77   Healey 2001, pp. 21–2, 25–6.
78   Boswell 1980, pp. 187–93, 218–26, 244–50.

erotic poem sent from one nun to another – although harsh penalties were reserved for women who penetrated each other with a 'material instrument'.[79]

At a certain point, however, Western European sexual developments diverged from Japanese or Russian ones in some key ways. This was due in part to an economic and ecological crisis of Western European feudalism involving overpopulation, the exhaustion of agricultural land and intensifying class conflict. In this crisis, people who fell outside the norms of feudal society – Jews, Muslims, heretics, unmarried women ('witches'), as well as 'sodomites' – became scapegoats. From the thirteenth century a range of new and crueller penalties for 'sodomy' were enacted. Late medieval same-sex subcultures were driven deep underground by persecutions that were part of the general fourteenth- to seventeenth-century witch-hunts.[80]

The generalisation of commodity production and exchange in Europe nonetheless undermined sexual regimes based on feudal kinship hierarchies. Prostitution spread – mainly female, but also sometimes male – and covert communities of men sexually available to other men arose, in northern Italy as early as the fourteenth century, and in France in the fifteenth century.[81]

In some urban areas of late medieval Europe, pockets of intergenerational same-sex formations emerged. This applied notably to northern Italy, which by medieval European standards was exceptionally urbanised (rivalled in this respect only by Flanders). Households were separated from production in these cities to an extent that was untypical of feudal societies, making possible a profusion of same-sex sexual possibilities that prefigured later bourgeois societies. In fifteenth-century Florence, for example, 17,000 individuals (mostly males, out of a total population of 40,000) were charged with sodomy over a period of 70 years. The intergenerational pattern was clear from the indictments: about 90 percent of the receptive partners were 18 or younger, 93 percent of the penetrating partners 19 or older.[82] In the Dutch province of Holland too, many of the sodomy trials before 1675 were for sex with adolescents.[83]

Medieval northern Italy had a certain historical and cultural continuity with ancient Rome. The Florentine regime (and presumably regimes further north in Western Europe) was nonetheless distinct from the ancient Roman one, inasmuch as even the active partner was seen in Florence as having a

---

79   Brown 1989, pp. 69, 496, n. 12, 72–4.

80   Boswell 1980, pp. 269–302; see also Van der Meer 1994, p. 140.

81   Ross and Rapp 1983, p. 65; Greenberg 1988, pp. 330–1.

82   Halperin 2002, p. 115.

83   Van der Meer 1994, p. 148.

distinctive, exclusive and shameful sexual orientation.[84] This suggests that a new sexual regime was emerging, if only in an urban enclave, distinct from either the dominant feudal sexual regime or the ancient status-based one.

Early Bourgeois Regimes

With the emergence of bourgeois society following the Dutch and English revolutions, the rise of the bourgeoisie in late French absolutism, and eventually the French Revolution,[85] families, emotional ties and same-sex formations were transformed. The Protestant Reformation reflected an incipient change in the character of the family, as it became increasingly divorced from production.[86] Production was separated from kinship relations on a far broader scale than in medieval northern Italy, creating two distinct 'spheres of social life'. This would be one of the defining characteristics of capitalism.[87]

The no-longer-productive family acquired a new task as the 'guardian of... capital': a wife had to 'not only be a good housewife but also the helper and friend of her husband' so that his savings would 'be handled with care and skill' and rapid accumulation ensured. Women's tasks thus shifted from domestic production to housekeeping and emotional nurturing. Relationships between husbands and wives, parents and children in middle-class families were increasingly seen as based not only on religion and natural male authority but also on affection. Protestants preached 'the new moral ideal of a love that embraced both the flesh and the soul', linking love and marriage (which the feudal sexual regime had separated).[88] Marriage constituted for the Protestants an ideal of freedom, involving 'not wide-open libertinism but disciplined activity',[89] and defined marriage and the family as in a new sense private.[90]

---

84   Halperin 2002, pp. 38–41.
85   My account implicitly supposes that the Dutch, English and French revolutions were all 'bourgeois revolutions' by Charlie Post's 'minimal' definition: that their resolution of class conflicts had the development of capitalist property relations as an 'unintended consequence' (2012, p. 249). I remain unconvinced by his argument that the French Revolution did not fit even this minimal definition.
86   Seccombe 1992, pp. 233–4.
87   Young 1981, p. 48.
88   Kollontai 1978, pp. 282–4.
89   Jakobsen 2012, p. 23.
90   Duggan 2003, p. 6.

Notions of love, desire and free choice became fundamental to bourgeois and even aristocratic marriage in north-western Europe beginning in the seventeenth and eighteenth centuries. A more or less free choice of partners gained acceptance, and increasingly 'the words *love* and *marriage* were used in the same sentence'[91] (though, of course, people still tended to marry within their class).[92] By the nineteenth century, the link between sexual love and marriage became integral to 'bourgeois familial ideology',[93] whose ideas of romance and marriage have been making capitalism '(sometimes) survivable' for at least some sections of the population for several centuries.[94]

These conceptions of love and freedom should not be confused with a conception of equality, however. Protestant churches (except for their radical fringes) were as clear as Catholics in their view that men were the heads of the household and the holders of authority in public life. What happened in this period was not the overthrow or weakening of 'spousal hierarchy', but its 'reconstruction . . . on new material foundations'[95] – a redefinition of the family as 'a discrete unit . . . a "little commonwealth" ruled by its own patriarch'.[96]

In the wake of these developments, a new same-sex regime arose. It was a transitional regime: very different from feudal same-sex formations, yet still far removed in many ways from conceptions of homosexuality that would emerge in late nineteenth-century imperialist Europe. The main protagonists in this new regime were 'mollies' or 'sapphists'. As in many other same-sex regimes past and present around the world – and by contrast with the predominantly intergenerational regimes common in slave and feudal societies – its dominant pattern was transgender. In crucial ways, however, the relationships of mollies and sapphists were different from most other forms of transgender relationships in history. Their same-sex relations were commodified, something to be bought and sold. Those who engaged in these relations lived mostly in cities – rural sodomy cases in the eighteenth-century Netherlands, for example, were more likely than urban ones to involve sex with boys – while trans people in other cultures often lived in the villages where most human beings in history have lived.

Whereas trans people in many cultures have been part of elaborate kinship networks and often had stable marriages to people of the same sex, these

---

91   Coontz 2005, pp. 134, 124.
92   Trumbach 1989, p. 134.
93   Weeks 1981, p. 26.
94   Crosby et al. 2012, p. 132.
95   Seccombe 1992, p. 243.
96   D'Emilio and Freedman 1997, p. 4.

European trans people were largely detached from rather than integrated into traditional kinship networks. European same-sex subcultures were more or less associated with prostitution for money rather than any kind of socially sanctioned marriage; in the Netherlands, for example, there was considerable overlap between male same-sex and female prostitutes' milieus.[97] Crucially, these subcultures were at odds with, rather than being sanctioned by, the dominant Christian religion.

Although intergenerational and other same-sex patterns coexisted with this commodified transgender one, we can say that as a whole the same-sex formation of early north-western European bourgeois society was 'molly-dominant'. By the early eighteenth century, subcultures of 'mollies' emerged in London, Paris and Amsterdam: a minority of 'markedly effeminate men' who were seen as 'a species of outcast woman'. It became less common in this regime for a youth to take on an active role on reaching adulthood.[98] There were similar networks in major Dutch cities, with special meeting places and a 'true sexual market', whose members gave each other girls' names.[99] Somewhat later in the eighteenth century, a subculture of female 'sapphists' or 'tommies' emerged in London, where at the end of the eighteenth century some began to cross-dress as a way of attracting women.[100]

Changes in marriage, the family and gender roles had a significant, if indirect and complex, influence on the same-sex formation, to judge by the fragmentary evidence that has reached us. The evidence from the persecutions of sodomites in Renaissance Florence suggest that the men who had sex with male youths were sensitive to the youths' beauty and subject to sexual passion, but not that this led to longer-term romantic relationships. By contrast, records of persecution in the 1690s and early eighteenth century in London include accounts of imitation marriages, complete with romantic trappings.[101] In the Netherlands too, there is evidence of lasting romances and at least one improvised marriage contract.[102] There are similar accounts from Paris by the early eighteenth century.[103]

While there is evidence of earlier European settings where men could go in search of sex with male youths or with male-to-female trans people, the emer-

97   Van der Meer 1994, pp. 172, 152–3.
98   Trumbach 1989, pp. 130, 137, 139.
99   Huusen 1989, pp. 144, 147, 145.
100   Trumbach 1994, pp. 111–14, 121–2.
101   Norton 1992, pp. 100–2.
102   Van der Meer 1994, pp. 164–6.
103   Merrick and Ragan 2001, p. x.

gence of social and romantic subcultures in the seventeenth and eighteenth centuries was a novelty. So was the mollies' capacity, still rare at the time, for collective action: a pitched battle with the police in London during a raid in 1725 prefigured resistance by drag queens and hustlers in the US (notably in the Stonewall rebellion) over two centuries later.[104]

Comparable same-sex scenes emerged in the cities of late feudal Russia by the 1860s, first in St Petersburg in the elite consumerist settings of Nevskii Prospekt and the adjoining Passazh gallery of shops, and a little later along the Moscow boulevards. As in Western Europe, prostitution was a prominent feature of these scenes, while male-male sexual encounters in the bathhouses in this period also became more commercialised, and many of the prostitutes were transgendered. Moreover, as 'the ties of the patriarchal village were loosening and breaking', 'the oxygen of sophisticated city life' gave some Russian women the courage to adopt masculine dress and behaviour and pay court to other women.[105]

The new regime characterised by commodified transgender patterns differed in yet another way from most kinship-based transgender regimes, although the difference is slippery. Whereas being penetrated was key to the identity of ancient Greek *kinaidi* and male-to-female trans people in a range of other cultures, in the modern Western European commodified transgender pattern, effeminacy was often ascribed to any men who engaged in 'habitual sodomy', whatever sexual role they played. Sodomites were seen as 'punished with an effeminate appearance', since they had failed in masculine restraint and become like women, 'insatiable, that is, unmanly'.[106]

---

104   Feinberg 1998, p. 102.

105   Healey 2001, pp. 11, 30–1, 39–41, 26–9, 33–5, 39–41.

106   Van der Meer 1994, pp. 192–3, 185. The blurred distinction between active and receptive partners has led some scholars, including Rictor Norton, Randolph Trumbach and Theo van der Meer, to describe this regime as 'egalitarian'. This characterisation seems questionable on several grounds. First, Trumbach has explained the regime's emergence by asserting that relations between men and women generally were becoming more egalitarian in this period – an assertion refuted by Wally Seccombe's research, to take one example (see note 95 above). Second, trial records show that several defendants did express a preference for the receptive role, which one explained by saying that he 'had a female constitution'. Presumably men who penetrated such men were more likely to come from outside the circle of 'habitual sodomites', either because they were being paid or were wealthier men slumming, and thus less likely to be perceived or to perceive themselves as transgendered. Trial records also show that adherence to a specific sexual role was widely expected and alternation viewed as particularly heinous; one Amsterdam prosecutor even wrote (falsely) that only sodomites who played both penetrating and

While trans people in many cultures have had well-defined roles in tra-ditional religions, for example, as shamans, in early bourgeois Europe trans people were condemned and persecuted by Christian churches, as well as by the civil authorities. These persecutions were intermittent but persistent. French records, for example, show a series of burnings of 'sodomites' from 1519 to 1783. As one Paris police official observed cynically after the French Revolution, however, punishment under the old regime 'fell not on the most criminal but on the least protected'. It could hardly be otherwise when those notorious for keeping 'minions' included the sixteenth-century king Henri III, and when Louis XIV's mistress reported him a century later to have replied when urged to persecute 'those detestable vices' more vigorously, ' "So I must begin with my brother?" ' By the eighteenth century, the death penalty was exceptional and release in response to a patron's plea was common.[107] In England, there were waves of persecution at the end of the seventeenth century, in the 1720s, and the first third of the nineteenth century.[108] In the Netherlands, where a wave of persecution in 1730–1 began a series of at least eight hundred sodomy trials up until 1811, most upper-class suspects 'either got away or were not prosecuted at all'.[109] Still, the threat of draconian penalties was enough to keep the subcul-ture covert and hidden.

In Western Europe by the eighteenth century, the religious impetus behind the intermittent medieval persecution of 'sodomy' began to be overlapped, and to some extent rivalled, by attempts at social and sexual control by the growing state apparatus, justified in part by secular, would-be scientific ideology. The category of 'abnormality' first supplemented and then gradually supplanted the category of 'sin'. Medicine and the state increasingly worked hand in hand, with Italian forensic doctors, for example, doing rectal examinations as early as the seventeenth century to detect signs of penetration.[110] Scientists gradu-ally edged out the role of Christian confession with warnings of the dangers of female 'hysteria', masturbation and contraception.[111] The state's growing role in the eighteenth century in policing sexual life was reflected not only in waves of

---

receptive roles were put to death (Van der Meer 1994, pp. 160, 162). This suggests that Jeffrey Weeks was right to conclude that 'a wide variety of men from all sorts of social classes participated in the subculture, but very few organised their lives around them', and those who did were largely 'the relatively few "professionals" ', who were more often and more clearly transgendered (1981, p. 110).

107   Merrick and Ragan 2001, pp. 20, 23, 93, 98–9, 124–6, 31.
108   Weeks 1981, p. 100.
109   Van der Meer 1994, pp. 139, 145; Huusen 1989, pp. 143–9.
110   Beccalossi 2012, p. 51.
111   Halperin 1990, p. 26 (citing Foucault).

persecution of sexual undergrounds, but also in its usurpation of the church's traditional role in regulating marriage, as in the English Marriage Act of 1753.[112]

Bourgeois ideas of privacy and free consent helped change Enlightenment thinkers' perspectives on sexual life, though only gradually and partially. Although the 1765 article on sodomy in the *philosophes' Encyclopédie* was a reiteration of traditional, harsh penalties, a general desire for more humane laws led other philosophers eventually to propose decriminalisation. In the 1780s, Nicolas de Condorcet argued that this 'vile, disgusting vice' nonetheless did 'not violate the right of any other man' and that its 'true punishment is scorn'.[113]

While the papers of the French revolutionary National Assembly's Committee on Criminal Legislation have not survived, arguments like these may have led to the decriminalisation of same-sex acts (though not with minors or in public) in 1791. Some contemporaries were unsure, however. Then as later, decriminalisation without a wider array of LGBT rights changed the rationale and forms of repression, but did not eliminate it. A Parisian court in 1794 sentenced two men to a year in prison for 'the crime against nature', and the higher court that heard their appeal asked the Convention's Committee on Legislation for guidance, since this was 'a crime of which the horror it inspires has prevented mention in all the laws'.[114] This was the limited kind of decriminalisation that French revolutionary and Napoleonic conquests brought to much of Western Europe, including the Low Countries and some parts of Italy and Germany. By 1848, decriminalisation had also reached Spain and a number of other German states.[115]

The French revolutionary model did virtually nothing to increase women's sexual freedom, in any event, since it reaffirmed their subordination and dependence. The Napoleonic Code of 1804 defined women, like children and the insane, as incompetent.[116] In both France and the countries it influenced, moreover, same-sex relations were prosecuted vigorously as 'public indecency' after decriminalisation, for example, in the Netherlands in the decades after 1811.[117] Much of Latin America adopted this same model of formal

---

112   Weeks 1981, p. 24; Adam 1985, p. 664.
113   Merrick and Ragan 2001, pp. 155–7, 160–1.
114   Merrick and Ragan 2001, pp. 171, 221–3, 227–8.
115   Beachy 2010, p. 807.
116   Latimer 2005, p. 7.
117   Van der Meer 1994, pp. 141–2.

decriminalisation and intermittent persecution, for example, Brazil in 1830 not long after its independence from Portugal.[118]

The tides of revolution and reaction made a tremendous difference to the subsidence or resurgence of persecution in the eighteenth and early nineteenth centuries, as they have later. The same period in which same-sex relations were decriminalised in much of continental Western Europe witnessed a crescendo in repression of same-sex relations among males in Britain, the headquarters of resistance to revolutionary change in Europe. From 1805, the number of public hangings for 'sodomy' increased, with several almost every year in the following decades. Members of the British elite threatened with the harsh sodomy laws or intolerant social climate often took refuge in more tolerant countries like France or Italy.[119] Even English radicals who tended to sympathise with the French Revolution joined in anti-same-sex polemics, for their own purposes: the radical MP John Wilkes accused his aristocratic enemies of sodomy, radical printer William Benbow focused on sodomy among clergymen, and the periodical *Black Dwarf* wrote that 'it would be most uncharitable to call [aristocratic dandies] men'.[120]

Colonialism and Same-Sex

The European sexual regime in which the commodified transgender pattern and its persecution played a prominent role spread unevenly to the Western Hemisphere. In regions of settler colonialism, for centuries there were no large cities comparable to London or Paris, and apparently nothing comparable to the molly-dominant regime. In colonial New England, for example, there was apparently only episodic repression of incidental same-sex acts, without any significant same-sex subculture.[121]

In regions of the Americas, where a European minority ruled over a majority of subjugated indigenous people and enslaved Africans, however, the imposition of European rule was accompanied by the imposition of European sexual mores. The prohibition of many indigenous sexual practices was part of a far-reaching process of making colonised societies serve their conquerors' needs, while the disruption of kinship structures facilitated the establishment of exploitative forced or waged labour. The sexual customs of the conquered

---

118   Green 1999a, p. 21.
119   Crompton 1985.
120   Clark 1995, pp. 143, 154–5.
121   D'Emilio 1983b, p. 10.

peoples were often repressed on the grounds that they were brutal, primitive, un-Christian or mired in 'a corruption of morals past all expression'.[122]

Since societies without states, including those in much of North America, were particularly vulnerable to European conquest and domination, their same-sex regimes – often transgender-dominant – were most likely to disappear through subjugation, conversion and assimilation. The existence of same-sex eroticism among the indigenous peoples of the Americas was even used as a pretext by the Spanish for exterminating them or, at the very least, for conquering, dispossessing and converting them. The Spanish conquerors of Mexico 'treated "sodomy" as a special Indian sin and hunted it down and punished it as such on a grand scale'.[123] A chronicle of the Spanish invasion of Central America shows them setting their dogs on berdaches, for example.[124] In Cuba, Spanish colonists castrated indigenous Caribs they accused of sodomy.[125]

In Brazil, the Inquisition in 1591–3 accused a slave of having brought the practice of sodomy from the area of modern Angola or the Congo.[126] Between 1587 and 1794, in Brazil 4,419 people were denounced for sodomy before the Inquisition, of whom 30 were burned at the stake and many others sentenced to hard labour, exile, seizure of property or public whipping.[127] The Portuguese also burned 'sodomites' in sixteenth-century Goa.[128] Nor were Protestant churches more accepting. Missionaries on Tahiti, for example, condemned its king's 'vile affections' with male youths.[129]

Enslaved Africans transplanted to the Americas were condemned as 'lewd, lascivious and wanton', in need of white supervision, supposedly unworthy of sexual contact with whites yet subjected to it just the same by white slave-owners.[130] Yet indigenous sexual regimes were not always completely wiped out by colonisation, even in the Americas where Christianity became the dominant religion almost everywhere. Despite the suppression of slaves' political and social structures and their very languages, they retained elements of transgender regimes reflected in West Africa's Dahomeyan and Yoruba religions.

122   D'Emilio and Freedman 1997, p. 7.

123   Mejía 2000, p. 46.

124   Saslow 1989, p. 103.

125   Lumsden 1996, p. 46.

126   Trevisan 1986, p. 55.

127   Green 1999a, p. 21.

128   Greenberg 1988, p. 311.

129   Besnier 1994, pp. 290–1.

130   D'Emilio and Freedman 1997, pp. 35–7.

Same-sex patterns survived in Haiti, for example, reflecting the belief in possession by deities of a different gender in the *voudun* religion.[131] Similar beliefs in cross-gender possession by androgynous deities found their way into the *candomblé* religion that originated around 1830 in Bahia, Brazil, many of whose inhabitants were, like Haiti's, slaves brought from the ancient Dahomeyan kingdom of West Africa.[132] In Cuba, *santería*, derived mainly from the Yoruba religion, became 'a favoured form of gender transcendence',[133] while many Cuban Catholics made vows to Catholic saints modelled on Yoruba deities.[134]

The expansion of tsarist Russia brought large parts of Islamic Central Asia under its sway by the mid-nineteenth century, regions where intergenerational traditions predominated. In Uzbekistan and Turkmenistan, young male prostitutes called *bachi* were traditionally recruited for brothels or dancing troupes. In the early twentieth century, tsarist officials stepped up prosecutions for 'sodomy' particularly in Central Asia, adopting a repressive attitude towards the 'savage morals of the native population'.[135] Like earlier European colonists, the Russians cited the prevalence of same-sex sexual formations in Central Asia as evidence of its inhabitants' depravity and lack of civilisation, and as justification for their conquest. Early nineteenth-century English and French travellers to Iran expressed the same disgust at young males dressed as female entertainers.[136]

Romantic Friendships

One last same-sex pattern within early bourgeois regimes deserves special mention, because it would be important for the later development of homosexuality. This was the pattern of same-sex romantic friendship, whose sexual component was often deniable but whose passionate intensity was clear.

While the persistence of medieval and early modern repression of 'sodomy' was uneven in newly bourgeois Western European societies, the spreading conceptions of privacy, intimacy and romance had a more consistent impact on the less explicitly sexual aspects of the same-sex formation. As production was gradually separated from the domestic realm, earlier conceptions of

---

131   Murray 1990, p. 516.
132   Trevisan 1986, pp. 171–4.
133   Arguelles and Rich 1989, p. 445.
134   Lumsden 1996, p. 43.
135   Healey 2001, pp. 159, 8, 96–8.
136   Najmabadi 2005, p. 35.

a hierarchy in which men were superior and women inferior tended to give way to conceptions of separate, complementary men's and women's spheres, which fostered same-sex emotional ties without defining them as sexual. This regime's 'separation of masculine work from the feminine home became a marker of middle-class status'. By the late 1790s, among the English middle class it entailed 'self-control for men and chastity for women', setting them off from the 'dissolute aristocracy', 'debauched plebeians' and supposed sexual licence of the French Revolution.[137]

Within this regime, women were supposed to be loyal to 'heart values' rather than masculine 'muscle values' and 'rational values'. For women who lived in a separate women's world, intense, romantic friendships between women became possible. Historians have described intense friendships between eighteenth- and nineteenth-century women – in some cases unmarried women who shared homes and even beds – that were accepted and even idealised by their societies.[138] The idealisation of the relationship between Eleanor Butler and Sarah Ponsonby, who eloped together in 1778 and lived together for years in Wales, is a well-known example.[139]

From a middle-class point of view, both true domesticity and romantic friendship were impossible for the working class, since working men's labour barred them from middle-class men's public pursuits, and working women's labour prevented them from creating idealised homes. But working-class people often saw things differently. Nineteenth-century working-class men increasingly staked a claim to full citizenship. And plebeian women established networks of their own, like the English 'friendly societies', which set their own standards of respectability within which female bonding was possible. A few of these women earning independent wages opted to live together rather than marry men, like Irish female street-sellers in England or the two London milliners sharing a business and lodgings in 1789 who had been 'intimately acquainted' for fifty years.[140]

Same-sex romantic friendship, whether or not it had a genital component, fit neatly into early capitalist conceptions of manhood and womanhood alongside a narrow understanding of sex as procreative, so that even intensely emotional and physical same-sex bonds could sometimes be seen as asexual. In other cases, mid-nineteenth-century homoeroticism had barely maintained a tantalising ambiguity around its sexual manifestations, as Walt Whitman

---

137   Clark 1995, pp. 2, 7, 43–4.
138   Faderman 1991, pp. 18, 1.
139   Trumbach 1994, pp. 133–5.
140   Clark 1995, pp. 35–9.

did in his Calamus poems. While Whitman's vision of male love was typical
of his time, his implicit challenge to 'the very order of male power' made him
exceptional.[141] Whitman's boldness was made possible by a period of relative
tolerance in the rapidly growing metropolises, a permissive mid-century interval between early nineteenth-century and late nineteenth-century repression. Between 1796 and 1873, for example, only 24 indictments for sodomy
were handed down in New York City, usually involving use of force or dispar-
ity in ages.[142] Evidence from Brazil suggests that something similar may have
occurred there, where the gardens of the central Largo do Rossio in Rio de
Janeiro in the 1870s were largely 'abandoned ... to the perversity of boys'.[143]

Perhaps there was an interval of unusual tolerance in the US due to the post-
revolutionary weakening of traditional elites and the separation of church
from state, the underdevelopment of the pre-Civil War state, and the feeble-
ness of social control (for white men) along the frontier. In any event, some
homoerotically-inclined mid-nineteenth-century US male writers saw Western
frontier areas as a site for 'homoerotic cowboy romance', a counterpart to the
Byronic image of Greece: 'a place where personal liberty, political liberty, and
erotic attraction were joined'. A taboo on genital sexuality made possible an
otherwise extraordinarily great latitude for the expression of male friendship,[144]
with both long-term sexual ties and casual sex common notably among cow-
boys and men in the army.[145] The eroticisation of Native American men in this
period also contrasted with the more unrelievedly genocidal racism of the
later-nineteenth-century US.

The invention of the homo/hetero binary later in the nineteenth century
would transform all these same-sex elements inherited from the past. Yet they
have all survived, albeit in often unrecognisable forms and in radically new
configurations. The transgender and intergenerational patterns, predominant through millennia of history, are still part of queer landscapes today.
Eighteenth-century mollies and sapphists were the precursors of nineteenth-
century 'inverts', the first form of 'the homosexual', while same-sex romantic
friendship in some ways prefigured early middle-class homosexuality, as well
as later lesbian/gay and homonormative patterns. But the advent of imperialism would recombine all these elements within a radically new framework.

---

141   Martin 1989, p. 182; see also D'Emilio and Freedman 1997, pp. 123, 127–9.
142   D'Emilio and Freedman 1997, p. 123 (citing Michael Lynch). Katz has documented many
      same-sex romantic relationships during this period (1976, pp. 445–510).
143   Green 1999a, p. 19.
144   Martin 1989, pp. 174, 173, 180.
145   D'Emilio and Freedman 1997, p. 124.

Imperialism and Inversion

As we have seen, human beings organised their sexual lives for millennia, and as recently as the mid-nineteenth century, without distinguishing between 'heterosexuals' and 'homosexuals'. This hetero/homo binary took clear shape only in a specific regime of capitalist accumulation, classical imperialism, towards the end of the nineteenth century. This was an indirect result of major changes in capitalism, which over time led to a shift to a very different same-sex formation, following and in interaction with a long recessive wave in capitalist development. Systemic responses to the long depression included imperial expansion, the rise of pseudo-scientific racism, the invention of a working-class family wage, the celebration of heterosexual romance, the first wave of feminism, and the medicalisation of sexuality. Even once homosexuals emerged as a distinct category of people, they were often perceived in a way that defined them as gender and sexual 'inverts', as much like present-day transgendered people as like present-day lesbians and gays. The same-sex regime of this period can thus be characterised as 'invert-dominant'.

The invert-dominant regime also took hold in regions of Latin America and Asia that were incorporated into global capitalism but not directly colonised. Intensifying European colonialism involved the suppression of many indigenous same-sex forms in Africa and Asia, while European sex tourism helped spread the new European forms of homosexuality. But the combined and uneven social construction of sexuality produced different same-sex patterns in different areas of the global sexual order. South African mining areas and the colonised Arab region developed distinctive patterns ('outliers') less subject to the emerging hetero/homo binary. Growing European repression of homosexuality provided the impetus for the first homosexual rights movements, allied in Germany with the socialist movement and reflected in the pioneering sexual reforms of the Russian Revolution. The rise of Nazism and Stalinism led to sexual reaction, however, which was mirrored even in imperialist democracies through the 1950s. Some elements of the invert-dominant regime, particularly its enmeshment with rising inequality, racism and empire, prefigured today's gay normality; other elements were vastly different.

As the new regime took shape in Europe and North America in the later decades of the nineteenth century, the scope for romantic friendships between men and between women that had existed in the mid-nineteenth century narrowed. A phenomenon like the earlier eroticisation of Native American men by white men in the US West became almost inconceivable. Growing repression and stigmitisation became central to the sexual order of classical imperialism.

Crisis and Restructuring

The two decades following 1873, like the years after 2008, were a time of prolonged economic slump around the capitalist world. This did not mean then, any more than it does now, that there was no economic expansion anywhere. Rather, as economist Alfred Marshall put it in 1888, there was a prolonged 'depression of prices, a depression of interest, and a depression of profits'.[1] A depression of profits posed a threat to the entire mechanism of capital accumulation, which is vital to the functioning of the system as a whole. Overcoming this challenge required a drastic restructuring of the world economy. When profitability and more rapid accumulation were restored in the 1890s, it was on the basis of a different economic regime. To this economic regime corresponded, eventually, a new sexual regime, one whose organising concepts were for the first time (though in a somewhat different sense from today) 'heterosexuality' and 'homosexuality'.

The restructuring of capitalism involved, among other things, a concentration and centralisation of capital that restricted the scope of competition: a process widely confirmed by economists otherwise critical of Marx.[2] Large corporations 'owned by shareholders, employing hired managers and executives, began to replace real persons and their families owning and managing their own enterprises'. These corporations combined further into trusts and cartels, often put together by financiers based in banks and brokerages, meant to bridle competition and maintain profit margins. At the workplace level, Taylorism or 'scientific management' was increasingly used to extract higher production from fewer workers in less time, increasing the direct control of capital and decreasing the autonomy of labour.[3] Capital relied less on families to discipline its workforce, and more on an emerging managerial layer and the repressive and organising power of the expanding state.

At the global level, pressure from capital was instrumental in this period in spurring Western European states and the US to colonial expansion. Notably from the 1870s to 1915, almost all of Africa, the entire Pacific region and the remaining Spanish possessions were gobbled up or re-divided among the

---

1   Hobsbawm 1987, p. 36.
2   Hobsbawm 1994, p. 103.
3   Hobsbawm 1987, pp. 10, 43–5.

British, French, German, Belgian, Italian, Dutch and US colonial empires. One result was a 'more European century' than there had ever been in human history. While 'bourgeois civilization had always gloried in the triple triumphs of science, technology and manufactures', in 'the era of empires it also gloried in its colonies'.[4] As the colonised and semi-colonial world was forced into a 'cage of international specialization', furnishing raw materials for imperial industry and consumption, another consequence was an unprecedented degree of inequality. While per capita gross national product between 1750 and 1800 in what are now the imperialist countries was roughly comparable to that in what are now the dominated countries, it was about twice as high by 1880, over three times as high by 1913, and five times as high by 1950.[5]

This was the international constellation that led Marxists at that time to write of 'imperialism', in a specific sense going beyond the empire-building that had characterised many states over the preceding millennia. Lenin viewed this international dimension as so central to the new structure of capitalism that it justified using 'imperialism' to describe the new regime of accumulation as a whole: the 'division of nations into oppressed and oppressor nations ... forms the *essence* of imperialism', he wrote.[6] And while some features of this regime have disappeared in the subsequent Fordist and neoliberal periods, others have persisted: the corporate form of economic organisation, the key role of finance capital, the ongoing process of concentration and centralisation, and the growth of economic inequality, which has reached even greater extremes under neoliberalism.

There is continuity as well as discontinuity between the racism of the age of classical imperialism and racism today. Then as now, growing inequality and a global hierarchy of regions and peoples generated ideologies and prejudices that 'explained' and naturalised the new state of affairs. But the racism that grew up from the 1870s was exceptionally blatant and ideologically intricate; as biology was invoked to explain inequality, the idea of 'race' 'penetrated the ideology of the period almost as deeply as "progress"'.[7] Despite the abolition of the African slave trade and slavery, the African racial inferiority that had been asserted under slavery was reaffirmed with the colonisation of Africa and the disenfranchisement and reduction to virtual serfdom of former African-American slaves in the US South. The model of racial inferiority was

---

4   Hobsbawm 1987, pp. 45, 18, 70.
5   Hobsbawm 1987, pp. 64, 15.
6   Lenin 1964, p. 409.
7   Hobsbawm 1987, p. 32.

extended much further, moreover, to Asians whose empires in earlier centuries had still been widely admired by Europeans.

The racism that characterised this period was pseudo-scientific, open and often rigidly formalised. In the US, for example, there were grotesque legal rulings that established the 'one-drop-of-blood' principle (classifying as 'coloured' anyone with one African or African-American great-great-grandparent), defined Chinese immigrants in California as (Native American) 'Indians' (so that they could not testify in court against 'whites'), and determined that Sikhs' remote 'Aryan' origin did not make them 'white'.[8] This racist codification lived on in Nazi Germany's proceedings adjudicating who was a full or half-Jew, and even after the Second World War in apartheid South Africa's four-race scheme. It went hand in hand with capital's new emphasis on 'scientific' management and bureaucratic control of society.

The gender dimension of capitalism was also reconfigured in this period. The initial phases of industrialisation had piggybacked on existing family and community forms, as women and children who were massively pulled into the waged workforce often worked alongside or near their husbands and fathers in a system of 'patriarchal cooperation'. Over the course of the nineteenth century, however, more women and children went to work in large factories, undercutting men's wages.[9] Given the long working day and the separation of social reproduction from production (which, as noted in the prologue, is a core characteristic of capitalism), this increasingly overstretched the family that was necessary to reproduce the labour force.

In the later stages of industrialisation, which roughly coincided with the advent of imperialism, this problem was partially solved through increasing differentiation within the working class, with at least an upper crust of working men earning a 'family wage' that enabled their wives to be full-time housewives and mothers. In this stratum, the fact that a wife could stay home was 'the visible proof, before society, that the family was not pauperized'.[10] Higher male wages in Britain from the 1850s increased the burden of housework, as there were more clothes and dishes to wash and rooms to clean. This isolated women from a working-class culture which by the 1870s had become increasingly masculine. Even radical English working-class women came to reject the radical demand for free love and female public equality, instead organising themselves as wives, demanding that husbands bring home their wages rather

8   Puar 2007, pp. 175–7.
9   Clark 1995, pp. 20–3, 206, 23–4.
10   Hobsbawm 1987, p. 198.

than spending them on drink, and defining themselves as 'militant mothers defending their families'.[11]

An intensified ideology of innate male-female differences accompanied this change. 'Masculinity was reconstituted to reflect the machine, the motions of which the worker was required to adapt', and capital 'sought to discipline and regularize workers as steady, reliable, emotionless, hard, and instrumental'.[12] For their part, working-class men increasingly tended to 'conflate ... achievement in the world of paid work with proving their manhood'.[13] In combination with the rise of the family wage, this helped the ideology of separate men's and women's spheres spread from the middle classes to a somewhat broader layer of the working class. A new emphasis on the rituals of courtship and domestic life led to the 'invention of heterosexuality' (a previously unknown concept), and of homosexuality as its pendant – though initially, in a culture of intense gender differences, 'homosexuals' were usually viewed in large part as gender-dissident. In this way, 'heteronormative sexual identity and its perverse others' gradually took shape at the height of nineteenth-century imperialism.[14]

The new industrial discipline and the new 'scientific' racism accompanied an emphasis on the importance of a disciplined, 'normal' sexuality focused on physical and social reproduction of the labour force. New professional groups took charge of imposing order on the disorder of industrial society. The 'increasingly professionalized middle class, together with reform-minded capitalists, mobilized on virtually every front to ameliorate class animosities, regulate borders, police working class and African-American communities, monitor vice and morality, and strengthen the state's capacities to legislate in all of these areas'.[15] Imposing sexual discipline was an integral part of this agenda: as the middle class 'idealized the internalization of sexual controls for themselves', they 'sought to re-establish external controls over workers and the poor'.[16] Antonio Gramsci, who in Italy only witnessed this later stage of industrialisation, observed: 'The new industrialism wants monogamy: it wants the man as worker not to squander his nervous energies in the disorderly and stimulating pursuit of occasional sexual satisfaction'.[17]

11   Clark 1995, pp. 257, 269–70, 185–7, 220–3, 227–9, 249–50, 184.
12   Adam 1985, p. 663.
13   Willis 1999, p. 2.
14   Hennessy 2000, p. 97.
15   Valocchi 1999, p. 209.
16   D'Emilio and Freedman 1997, p. 142.
17   Adam 1985, p. 666.

At the same time, the conviction took hold, in the words of one British prime minister, that 'an empire such as ours requires as its first condition an imperial race'. The idea of 'white manhood' served to racialise masculinity.[18] Therefore, as one reverend proclaimed, 'the purity of the family must be the surest strength of a nation', so that 'sins of the flesh undermined both the self and the nation'.[19] Crusades for 'female purity' and against prostitution in this period were also strongly racialised, and were linked to efforts to regulate the mass migration between countries. It was no accident that the evil being combated was called the 'white slave traffic' (slavery presumably being worse when it was imposed on white women), or that the traffickers were identified in the US as 'a foaming pack of foreign hellhounds ... the moral and civic degenerates of the French, Italian, Syrian, Russian, Jewish or Chinese races'.[20]

The impact of industrialisation on women was differentiated, as some women were shanghaied into the workforce in some periods, while others were excluded from it at other times. Particularly where a family wage system of higher wages for the male 'breadwinner' was established for at least a layer of the working class, the culture conceived of the worker as male, 'ethnic-majority' and 'a family man'.[21] The central, blue-collar bastions of the trade-union movement were most likely to be overwhelmingly male and, at least before the migrations to industrial centres of ex-slaves and colonised people, white.[22]

This meant lower wages for those women, mostly the poorest and often immigrant or black or indigenous, who still had to work for wages,[23] and for the growing ranks of (in principle young, unmarried ones, since many employers refused to hire married women) women with factory, office and retail jobs.[24] There were millions of them: 34 percent of women over the age of 10 in Britain in the 1880s and 1890s, for example. In Germany, there were 174,000 female shop-assistants by 1907, five times as many as 25 years earlier. In Britain from 1881 to 1911, the number of female office workers rose from 6,000 to 146,000,[25] while the number of women trade union members rose from 37,000 in 1886 to 357,956 in 1914. In Catalonia, in the first half of the twentieth century women

---

18   D'Emilio and Freedman 1997, p. v.
19   Weeks 1981, pp. 125, 87, 106.
20   Rubin 2011, pp. 70–3, esp. 73.
21   Fraser 2009, p. 101.
22   Krupat 2009, p. 12.
23   Reddy 1998, p. 360; Sangster and Luxton 2012, pp. 290–1.
24   D'Emilio and Freedman 1989, p. 189.
25   Hobsbawm 1987, pp. 199–201.

were the large majority of textile workers.[26] Meanwhile black and immigrant women became a growing proportion of the reserve of cheap labour. Capitalism is the first economic system to require that not all productive people be employed, and gender and 'race' are easily adaptable criteria for defining a reserve army of labour. The role of women, blacks and immigrants as a secondary labour force became '*an essential and fundamental characteristic*' of capitalism.[27]

Eros in Women's Sphere

At the same time, the family wage system relegated other working-class women to the home and the existing, separate women's sphere already occupied by many middle-class women. The new wave of industrialisation required mothers to bear and rear 'the next generation of soldiers and workers, the Imperial race'.[28] Imperial ideology often influenced middle-class women's movements, as in Germany in 1908, when a new leadership of the League of German Women's Organisations adopted a racist, nationalist programme focused on raising the German birth rate.[29] Nationalist impulses continued under the Weimar republic to characterise some German feminist groups, which identified women's emancipation with ethical responsibility and 'a uniquely masculine ability to control one's desires' in the interests of a transcendent national cause.[30]

Practical pressures pushed some working-class families towards adopting a middle-class model of female domesticity. Given the length of the nineteenth-century working day, a division of labour in which one partner worked at home and the other for wages was preferable to one in which two adults worked long factory hours.[31] In this layer of the working class, housewives moved from being their husbands' partners in production to being dependent on their husbands for 'support', while providing the privatised household labour needed to reproduce factory labour. The ideology of femininity, which 'defined women as nonworking', served to justify their economic marginalisation.[32] A man's ability to support a wife was evidence of his manhood, self-sufficiency and

---

26   Arruzza 2013, pp. 30, 44.
27   Young 1989, p. 58.
28   Kinsman 1987, p. 49 (citing Anna Davin).
29   Steakley 1989, p. 255.
30   Lybeck 2009, pp. 38–9.
31   Brenner 2000, p. 29.
32   Young 1989, pp. 59 (citing Ann Foreman), 68, n. 46.

virility; women showed their womanliness not only through good housekeeping, but also by accepting family tasks as their 'emotional and sexual destiny', and being emotionally responsive and sexually submissive.[33] And for all women, once waged work became in principle an option, lower wages and job insecurity pushed them to get married or stay married.[34]

At the same time, there was a linkage between 'housewifization and colonization', rooted in an older international division of labour that has historically 'bound the woman of leisure to the peasant and slave woman'. In this period, it took the form of a linkage between middle-class and more prosperous working-class housewives, the poorer, often racially oppressed or ethnically distinct women who were their servants, and colonised women who produced 'colonial wares' for these families' consumption.[35]

For working-class women, the ideology of domesticity also held out the hope of protection from sexual dangers. Industrialisation had resulted in what Anna Clark has called a sexual crisis, with rising rates of illegitimacy, desertion and bigamy in once rigidly policed Calvinist Scotland as well as libertine London.[36] Greater geographical and occupational mobility made it easier for men to abandon women they had seduced. Especially for men in barracks, on ships or in shanty towns on the edges of cities, 'short-term cohabitation or prostitution were common, legal marriage the exception'. In these conditions, many working-class women's desire for respectability had practical motives, often remote from middle-class ideology,[37] even when they could afford no servants and few colonial wares. The 'moralization of the poorer classes'[38] also affected these women's husbands; sexual respectability became for them 'a hallmark of the labour aristocrat, anxious to distance himself from the "bestiality" of the casual working poor'.[39]

Domesticity gave some women opportunities to develop their own personal lives and even a distinct sense of their sexual needs. In the later nineteenth century, however, other middle-class women in increasing numbers sought individual self-development through professional careers. As more educational opportunities and professions opened up to women, many of them were initially practised in women's separate sphere. Some of these professional

---

33 Weeks 1981, pp. 39, 68, 42.
34 Hennessy 1994, pp. 100–1.
35 Hennessy 2000, p. 200 (citing Maria Mies).
36 Clark 1995, pp. 6, 42–3, 45–50.
37 Weeks 1981, pp. 64, 66, 72.
38 Foucault 1978, p. 122.
39 Kinsman 1987, p. 47.

women were feminist 'moral chauvinists', who believed that 'male values created the tragedies connected with industrialization, war and mindless urban-
ization', and that women, with their 'superior sensibilities', had to 'straighten
the world out again'.[40] Crusading middle-class women were both responding
to the rise of an industrial, imperial order and shaping a society to fit it. They
were working to restore some of the sexual controls lost as a more 'mobile and
heterogeneous society' weakened the authority of church and community. In
so doing, they tried on behalf of their class to create 'a semblance of order'
between the irresponsible new rich and the unruly industrial workers.[41]

Feminists joined in championing 'female self-defence against venereal disease, against overbearing male sexual demands, and excessive pregnancies'.[42]
A female socialist like Alexandra Kollontai was scathing about male hypocrisy and the double standard, which she saw as springing from 'the principles
of private property and the unwillingness of men to pay for the children of
others'. She believed that the 'distortion of the sex drive' by capitalism led
to a man's approaching 'any woman, though he feels no sexual need for her
in particular, with the aim of gaining his sexual satisfaction and pleasure
through her'.[43]

The most radical feminists, and a socialist like Kollontai, rejected marriage
as a longer-term variant of prostitution. The analogy between marriage and
prostitution had much in common with anarchist Emma Goldman's argument that for the bourgeois moralist, 'prostitution does not consist so much
in the fact that the woman sells her body but rather that she sells it out of
wedlock'.[44] For some upper- and middle-class women, 'Boston marriages' with
each other even became a possible alternative to legal, heterosexual marriage,
although these partnerships were rarely seen as sexual. While these relationships fit into the culturally sanctioned mould of female romantic friendship,
since these women could support themselves they were no longer economically compelled to marry men. Between 1880 and 1900 in the US, about 50
percent of college-educated women remained unmarried (to men), compared
with 10 percent of women in general;[45] three-quarters of women who received
PhDs between 1877 and 1924 stayed single.[46] In Europe, the pattern was much

40   Faderman 1991, p. 24.
41   D'Emilio and Freedman 1997, pp. 144, xvii, 57, 150–1.
42   Weeks 1981, pp. 163–4.
43   Kollontai 1978, pp. 228–9, 263–4, 286.
44   Rubin 2011, p. 83.
45   Faderman 1991, pp. 12, 14.
46   D'Emilio and Freedman 1997, p. 190.

the same:[47] a large number of female university students in late nineteenth-century Germany, for example, became outspoken feminists who lived in life-long female partnerships.[48] Many of these women consciously aimed to stay autonomous and single.

Such female couples flourished, for example, in US settlement houses offering services to the poor, run by middle-class women who, 'eschewing men, felt they had married each other for life'.[49] At their best, these female partnerships offered not only 'a communion of kindred spirits', but also 'relationships of equals in terms of finances, responsibilities, decision-making – all areas in which the husband claimed precedence and advantage in heterosexual marriage'.[50] Yet these relationships were usually discreet. 'The female separatism that they inherited from Victorian society and that a vigorous feminist movement affirmed safeguarded their relationships from the taint of deviance'.[51]

Single-sex female schools and colleges were growing rapidly in this period – in France girls' *lycées*, which were non-existent in 1880, had by 1913 a third as many pupils as boys' *lycées*; there were a quarter of a million girls in secondary school in Germany by 1910, and in Russia by 1900.[52] These institutions were often breeding grounds of such female partnerships. In a period when women were pioneering new public roles and professions, girls' schools encouraged 'an idealized love for an older, publicly successful woman'. The new, large girls' schools and colleges of the late nineteenth and early twentieth centuries were 'attuned to the needs of an expanding industrial and imperialist economy', preparing their graduates for careers in teaching, medicine and social work. Female friendships were seen as fostering the discipline and autonomy that women professionals would need, while teacher-pupil relationships were expected to combine 'practical information, moral advice, and personal affection'.[53]

As long as the partners in these relationships were white and middle-class, and no actual penetration was known to have taken place, even verbal outpourings and physical expressions of intense affection were not perceived

47   Hobsbawm 1987, pp. 215–16.
48   Lybeck 2009, p. 32.
49   Smith-Rosenberg 1989, p. 266.
50   Faderman 1991, p. 18; see also D'Emilio and Freedman, pp. 192–3.
51   D'Emilio 1983b, p. 95.
52   Hobsbawm 1987, pp. 203–4.
53   Vicinus 1989, pp. 213–14, 217, 221.

as sexual,[54] including holding hands, kissing and caressing.[55] In both Italy and Britain in the late nineteenth and early twentieth centuries, physicians expressed concern about the prevalence of erotic relationships (called 'flames' in Italy) in girls' schools.[56] This pattern of schoolgirl crushes existed far beyond the bounds of the white middle class in imperialist countries, in relationships between 'mummies' and 'babies' in female boarding schools as far away as Lesotho.[57]

By contrast, there were often a few working-class women who, resisting their exclusion from the workforce and public world, managed to pass as men, sometimes forming sexual relationships and even marriages with other women[58] – or in the case of the nineteenth-century female-born San Franciscan Jack Garland, erotic relationships with young men.[59] Given the meagre wages and intense social constriction of working women in the nineteenth century, the option of moving somewhere else, cutting their hair and passing as men offered substantial advantages. It lightened the 'triple load' of a working-class woman once capitalism had 'made her a wage-worker without having reduced her cares as housekeeper or mother'.[60] As one such woman said on her exposure in Milwaukee in 1914, 'The woman who must work is a slave'.[61]

Although as in earlier centuries these women's main motives were seldom sexual, they sometimes became other women's lovers or husbands. Intense romantic and sometimes sexual ties are also attested in the nineteenth and early twentieth centuries between female prostitutes and between women prisoners. Otherwise, open intense ties between working-class women only became possible for a few of them very late in the nineteenth century.[62]

The Hetero/Homo Binary

Gradually in the late nineteenth and early twentieth centuries, however, as the early industrial accumulation regime gave way to the world of the family wage

54 Newton 1989, p. 284.
55 D'Emilio and Freedman 1997, p. 126.
56 Beccalossi 2012, pp. 73–6, 108–11.
57 Wekker 2006, p. 185; Epprecht 2009, p. 1265.
58 Adam 1985, pp. 661–2.
59 Stryker 2008, p. 119. See Katz for accounts of passing women in the nineteenth-century US (1976, pp. 209–79).
60 Kollontai 1978, p. 252.
61 D'Emilio 1983b, p. 97.
62 Faderman 1991, pp. 42–3, 45, 37–9; see also D'Emilio and Freedman 1997, pp. 124–5.

and the female reserve army, the culture of separate male and female spheres eroded. In their place, the central discourses and practices of modern heterosexuality developed on a mass scale: 'romance, marriage, weddings, family values and traditions, eugenics, and social purity campaigns'.[63] As Jonathan Katz has shown, the end of the nineteenth and the beginning of the twentieth century was the period in which heterosexuality was invented as a social and sexological category.[64]

At least by comparison with the previous sexual regime, in which women who were made respectable by their class status and domesticity were expected to be sexually passive and ignorant, the new heterosexuality offered a certain expansion of sexual possibilities. There was a new openness to women's pleasure and participation in sex, at least in receptive and responsive ways seen as appropriate to their gender. At the same time, institutionalised heterosexuality reinforced the redefined sexual division of labour at home and in the labour market, and helped 'consolidate forms of desire that would be crucial in the marketing and consumption of commodities'.[65] As women acquired more education and new employment options, the new heterosexuality also kept their independence in check. There were male sex reformers and sexologists who set out to make 'the daughter's quest for heterosexual pleasures, not the mother's demand for political power, personify female freedom'.[66]

Ideologically, the development of Darwinian social thought prodded sexology towards gender and sexual essentialism.[67] Social Darwinism joined an eternal heterosexual norm to a permanent social hierarchy. In the US, the dominant perception was that both non-Europeans and the lower classes were immoral.[68] But the middle classes were determined to share the enlightenment they had achieved. As a result, the Victorians were 'the first people in history to try to make marriage the pivotal experience in people's lives and married love the principal focus of their emotions, obligations and satisfactions'.[69]

All these shifting identities were complicated by the long recessive period in the capitalist economies of the last quarter of the nineteenth century. Economic troubles and social conflict fuelled anxiety about threats to the nation and fostered nationalism and anti-Semitism. The 'natural order' and family were

63   Hennessy 2000, p. 22.
64   Katz 1995.
65   Hennessy 2000, pp. 25, 104.
66   Smith-Rosenberg 1989, p. 272.
67   Herdt 1994, p. 28.
68   Kinsman 1987, p. 45.
69   Coontz 2005, p. 177.

also seen as being under siege. This made the classification of 'abnormal' sexuality seem more important in the 1870s, 1880s and 1890s, in conjunction with burgeoning campaigns against masturbation and for 'social purity'.

The First World War accelerated changes in gender roles and sexuality. Especially in Europe, the demand for female industrial labour brought more women into the public sphere, increased gender equality, and divided cross-sex couples for long periods, 'if not forever'.[70] The male population was decimated, allowing or forcing many women to fend for themselves.[71] Similar changes occurred during and after the Second World War, especially in countries like the US where men were mobilised for years, almost a third of a million women served in the US military, and women's participation in wage labour soared.[72] In these circumstances, for a few brief years, officers of the US Women's Army Corps were ordered to avoid speculating about sex between female personnel and, when it was discovered, to pursue discharges only of women who were 'not amenable to successful guidance'.[73] Because the military and war industry badly needed women to fill traditionally masculine occupations, independent women and love between them were 'undisturbed and even protected'.[74]

Gender and sexual liberalisation followed each war, in the 1920s and again in the 1940s. Psychologists like Sigmund Freud and anthropologists like Margaret Mead with her study of Samoans' sexual freedom to experiment, Bronislaw Malinowski and Ruth Benedict helped provide this sexual liberalism with an ideology (though Malinowski did not share the others' tolerance of homosexuality).[75] Yet within several years after each war, the loosening of family forms and sexual mores was reined in, resulting in the sexual conservatism of the 1930s and 1950s. In the economic hard times of the 1930s, for example, women were discouraged from competing with men for jobs, with ideologues insisting that work 'defeminised' a woman.[76] Even the social programmes of the US New Deal, for example, were premised on and aimed to reinforce a male-breadwinner family.[77]

Same-sex patterns were reshaped from the 1870s to the 1940s as part of the reification of sexual object choice and the establishment of the hetero/homo

70   Herzog 2011, p. 45.
71   Latimer 2005, pp. 8, 20–2.
72   See Bérubé 1983 and D'Emilio and Freedman 1997, p. 289.
73   D'Emilio 1983b, p. 28.
74   Faderman, pp. 120, 123.
75   Meyerowitz 2010, pp. 1064–9.
76   Faderman, pp. 119, 94, 97.
77   Self 2012.

binary. For the first time, homosexuality became the domain of a specifically and systematically identified set of people, initially and mainly people whose desired gender was intensely reified, but eventually extending to most people engaging in same-sex activity, who were also increasingly defined by their gendered desire. Material preconditions for this change were large-scale, rapid urbanisation – which multiplied the size of urban communities and loosened their members' family ties – and available jobs at wages seen as decent. In a seminal article, John D'Emilio has explained how capitalist development in this way created the conditions for the rise of a distinct category of 'homosexuals'.[78] The rise of wage labour and the resulting individual economic independence made new institutions and relationships possible outside prescribed family and religious patterns.

Popularisation of ideas of heterosexual romantic love made marriage more painful for those whose strongest sexual and emotional bonds were with people of the same sex. They were pressured in a new way before entering into a cross-sex marriage to 'pretend' to be 'intimate, passionate, seductive, playful, sexual, physical and even jealous'.[79] Some men, who might have earlier gone to male-to-female trans people for sex, began looking for sex, romance and even longer-term relationships with other men, while lesbian romance and relationships began to be possible alternatives to heterosexual marriage for some women.

While social and romantic ties had existed in London's commodified transgender underground as early as the end of the seventeenth century, by the late nineteenth century particular bars in European and North and South American big cities became associated more broadly with lesbians and homosexual men. Men organised underground drag balls, and lesbian couples (generally discreet) became more common. By the 1890s, several cafés in Paris near the Place Pigalle became gathering places for lesbians.[80] In Berlin, a large network of bars, clubs, bathhouses and guest houses allowed homosexuals to at last 'remove their masks', to the point where some 'homosexuals from the provinces set foot in such bars for the first time and burst into violently emotional tears'.[81] In the US, an observer described male homosexuals by 1915 as 'a community distinctly organized'.[82]

---

78   D'Emilio 1983a.
79   Chou 2000, p. 194.
80   Rubin 2011, p. 157.
81   Rubin 2011, p. 353 (citing Magnus Hirschfeld).
82   D'Emilio 1983b, p. 12.

The trend intensified in the 1920s in Central and Western Europe and the us, with Paris, Berlin, Budapest and New York as notable centres for homosexual subcultures.[83] British lesbians met soul mates through wartime jobs like ambulance driving.[84] A white working-class lesbian subculture also emerged in the 1920s in big us cities like Chicago, and persisted in more difficult times in the 1930s. Bars were in general a central institution for sexual and gender dissent in this period, although in the us they only fully re-emerged with the repeal of Prohibition in 1933, and even then they faced constant sexual repression under state liquor-licence regulations.[85]

There was a specifically African-American lesbian culture in New York's Harlem, where there was a degree of tolerance that even allowed butch/femme couples to 'marry' in large private ceremonies. There was also considerable evidence of bisexuality among Harlem's female entertainers and female members of its upper crust.[86] In Washington DC, African-American men met one another 'under the shadow of the White House'.[87] Together with a certain latitude for black homosexuality in the 1920s, there was a degree of sexual fluidity[88] in locations where the hetero/homo binary had not fully crystallised. White homosexuals and bisexuals came to Harlem in the 1920s and 1930s in search of the exotic, the forbidden and perhaps even sex with black men – though many 1920s Harlem clubs that catered to white homosexuals excluded blacks.[89] In early twentieth-century California, Asian men were viewed more unambiguously as sources of evil and corruption, importing 'unnatural' sexual practices and contaminating young white males. The police court judge who declared in 1914 that most of the 'Hindus' in Sacramento's poor neighbourhoods were 'Sodomites' was simultaneously drawing the boundaries of the white race, normal masculinity and proper heterosexuality.[90]

By the late 1940s, in us cities like Los Angeles and New York parties at private clubs attracted hundreds of men, often ex-servicemen, in search of same-sex sex.[91] Wherever communities were formed, gathering places were of course crucial, with specific bars – however dangerous in periods of repression –

83   Herzog 2011, pp. 56–7.
84   Faderman 1991, pp. 63–4 (citing Radclyffe Hall).
85   Rubin 2011, p. 345; Chauncey 1994, pp. 173, 334–49.
86   Faderman 1991, pp. 80–1, 184.
87   D'Emilio and Freedman 1997, p. 227.
88   hooks 1990, p. 196.
89   Garber 1989, p. 329.
90   Shah 2005, pp. 703–4, 715, 705.
91   D'Emilio 1983b, p. 32.

playing a role worldwide as places to socialise, dress and behave in keeping with one's gender identity, and to find sexual partners.[92] Communities also came together around cultural forms that acknowledged their existence. Beauty contests among drag queens became a common feature of transgendered life in North and Latin America, South Africa and Southeast Asia. Sport became a binding element among lesbians and female gender dissenters in both dependent and imperialist countries. Football in particular (and softball in the US)[93] was a favourite pastime among butch lesbians and those who would later be called 'transmen', from Lima to Soweto. In India too, sport provided a space where they could feel at ease with their 'abnormal' bodies or behaviours and even begin low-risk sexual exploration.[94]

Inversion and Homosexuality

The homosexuality emerging from the 1870s to the 1940s should be distinguished from the lesbian/gay identity that only took shape in imperialist countries after the Second World War, and in other countries even later. Later developments should not be read back into earlier conceptions of homosexuality, which took fragmented and contradictory forms. Rather than creating 'a homogeneous gay community with a singular collective identity', capitalist development 'gave rise to a proliferation of same-sex communities of desire ... distinguished by class, color, sexual practices, and gender style'.[95]

The homosexuality of the era of classical imperialism has to be understood as a shifting combination of three different components, with blurred boundaries and gradations between them. First, the early bourgeois culture of same-sex romantic friendships was influenced in its last decades by new phenomena like women's education and professional careers. Second, the commodified transgender pattern that for centuries, beginning in late seventeenth-century urban north-western Europe, had dominated the early bourgeois same-sex formation, was inflected under imperialism by new mechanisms of bureaucratic control and by pseudo-scientific ideology. And third, a slowly emerging but still atypical proto-gay sexual pattern, still enmeshed with gender dissent, romantic friendship and intergenerational patterns, and still largely limited even in the middle decades of the twentieth century to middle-class layers in

---

92   Faderman 1991, pp. 161–3.
93   Faderman 1991, pp. 161–2.
94   Shah, Raj, Mahajan and Nevatia 2012, p. 213.
95   Valocchi 1999, pp. 210–11.

imperialist metropolises, partly prefigured the more performative, less polarised gender order of Fordism.

Of these three, the transgender component predominated in most milieus for most of the period, as the gender order of early capitalism persisted among the bulk of the population. Homosexuality was most often seen as 'a kind of inborn gender inversion', and was called 'a "hermaphrodisy of the mind"'.[96] This was how many homosexuals – some of whom in a later period might just as well be called trans men and women – saw themselves. Sexologists and lay people sometimes tried to distinguish different types within the new category of homosexuals. But the overriding focus in this period on people who were called 'inverts' justifies defining the same-sex regime as a whole, straddling the different patterns that existed within it, by analogy with the molly-dominant regime of the eighteenth and early nineteenth centuries, as 'invert-dominant'.

The continuity between the new homosexuality and the already existing commodified transgender pattern is clear. Working-class and poor people even in imperialist countries tended well into the twentieth century to focus on conceptions of manhood and womanhood rather than binary conceptions of sexuality,[97] invariably associating 'male homosexual behaviour with effeminacy and probably transvestism as well'.[98] Before the early twentieth century, the idea that gender identity and sexual orientation are 'two related but separate systems'[99] while not entirely unknown – the Italian sexologist Arigo Tamassia suggested a distinction between them as early as 1878[100] – was relatively rare.

George Chauncey has shown that even in the first half of the twentieth century most working-class men who had sex with other men still did not identify as homosexuals or see themselves as part of a distinct community; a distinct community and identity were still largely the preserve of the transgendered 'queens', 'fairies', 'pogues' or 'cocksuckers' (as they were called in the US) whom masculine working-class men penetrated. The masculine men – 'husbands', 'trade', 'wolves' – were often married to women,[101] or engaged in sex with other men for money or social benefit without taking on any distinctive identity. By 1890, some women 'had joined the sexual underworld of big cities such as New York ... wearing tuxedos and waltzing with other more feminine-looking

---

96   Hekma 1994, p. 214.
97   Foucault 1978, p. 121.
98   Weeks 1981, p. 101.
99   Newton 1989, p. 292.
100   Beccalossi 2012, p. 53.
101   Chauncey 1989, pp. 296, 298–9, 303; Chauncey 1994, pp. 87, 96.

women'.[102] One self-described 'androgyne', 'hermaphrodite' and 'fairy' in New York reported the formation as early as 1895 of a Cercle Hermaphroditos 'to unite for defense against the world's bitter persecution'.[103] Chicago police in 1911 described men who 'mostly affect the carriage, mannerisms, and speech of women'.[104]

In short, before the 1920s, in the US scene the transgender pattern was pervasive, colouring the identity of many of those defined as homosexuals and defining many of their clients or partners as non-homosexual. Working-class women in sexual relationships with one another – and the world of butch/femme lesbian bars in the US as late as the 1950s was very much working class – were defined as lesbians by late nineteenth- and early twentieth-century sexologists who conflated the term with 'men trapped in women's bodies', or at least with some degree of masculinity.[105] Lesbian femmes, though very much a part of the lesbian world, were not always seen as 'real' lesbians. The class correlations in the US between gender dissenter and working class, and between homosexual and middle class, were also racial correlations: one veteran of the Harlem scene of the 1930s and 1940s recalled that 'we were still Bull Daggers and Faggots and only whites were lesbians and homosexuals'.[106]

In Paris too, many women emerged from the First World War used to wearing their hair short, wearing men's clothes and projecting a masculine image. For some women in the 1920s, these became markers of lesbianism, which released them from 'predetermined schemas of femininity'. Singer Suzy Solidor, a 'confirmed bachelor' with a 'changeling body', was an icon of this lesbian milieu.[107] In the late 1930s, a British lesbian said that though 'officially a woman', she was really 'in a half way position'.[108] In the same period in Germany, Magnus Hirschfeld's studies of same-sex relations among largely working-class men led him, while recognising the great diversity of same-sex desire and behaviour, to focus particularly on a transgender 'third sex' model.[109]

In South American cities, same-sex scenes grew up in Argentina and Brazil before the First World War, as industrialisation and urbanisation gathered speed, fostering the growth of transgender undergrounds similar to those

102   Faderman 1991, pp. 57–9.
103   Stryker 2008, p. 41.
104   D'Emilio and Freedman 1997, pp. 227–8.
105   Davis and Kennedy 1989, p. 427.
106   Garber 1989, p. 331.
107   Latimer 2005, pp. 23–9, 8, 123, 129.
108   Weeks 1981, p. 221.
109   Drucker 1997, p. 37.

of Europe and North America. Such transgender communities appeared in Argentina not long after they did in the US – before the First World War in Buenos Aires – complete with the dress codes, slang and festivities that characterised them elsewhere.[110] In Brazil, for decades the 'macho fuck[ed] the bicha without being reduced to the bicha's status, much less being emotionally involved'.[111] In Cuba, where Havana as the Caribbean's largest city by far was by the late nineteenth century a centre for male prostitution, drag queens or effeminate homosexuals – maricones or locas – encountered 'repugnance and ridicule' from most Cubans but became objects of desire for some ' "real" men'.[112]

Due to the later incorporation of women into the waged workforce, Latin American lesbian milieus apparently emerged later than male invert ones. Lesbian scenes into the late twentieth century were often reminiscent of the butch/femme patterns of North America in the 1950s. In Mexico, lesbian 'machas' and 'colonels' continued to have formal weddings with 'femmes' – who often took care of children from previous cross-sex marriages, since early marriage was common.[113] Even later in Peru, a group of soccer-playing, working-class lesbian machas who encountered middle-class lesbian feminists suspected their middle-class sisters of wanting to turn them into femmes.[114]

A similar underground lesbian culture existed in the black South African township of Soweto.[115] Men who were called 'moffies' in the 'coloured' community of South Africa's Cape region also had transgender features. Transgendered skesanas had an analogous position in townships in the Johannesburg region, largely among men of Zulu origin.[116]

Unlike in earlier centuries, trans people were increasingly defined not only by themselves, religious strictures or popular culture, but by medicine, which classified them as 'inverts' – though most British doctors resisted the new category longer than those in continental Europe or the Americas, for fear of undermining morality or the law.[117] Sexology created a new caste of specialists with a socially legitimated claim to intervene in people's sexual lives. Kevin Floyd has suggested that the sexology of inversion in particular was a response to 'increasing and unmistakable contradictions' in Victorian sexual ideology.

110   Bao 1993, pp. 192, 208.
111   Trevisan 1986, p. 36.
112   Lumsden 1996, pp. 33–5.
113   Drucker 1996, p. 89.
114   Drucker 1996, p. 90.
115   Drucker 1996, p. 89.
116   Gevisser 1994, pp. 18, 28.
117   Beccalossi 2012, pp. 26, 55.

Paralleling the rise of the 'scientific' management of production and 'scientific' racism, it was a form of ' "scientific management" of anxieties about changing gender norms'.[118]

Sexologists played a major role in constructing a model of 'inversion' that was central to the new same-sex regime. Experts explained that in a minority of people, their 'tertiary' sexual characteristics (erotic drives), and often their 'fourth-order' characteristics (mannerisms, occupations and clothes), diverged from their 'primary' ones (genitals) and sometimes their 'secondary' ones (like breasts or facial hair). Some scientists replaced the earlier conceptions of a sexual hierarchy or separate sexual spheres with the idea of a sexual continuum with 'infinite gradations', both anatomical and behavioural, in which most people fell more towards one side or the other, but some, 'sexual intermediates', fell in the middle.[119] In the 1870s and 1880s, the Germans Karl Westphal and Richard von Krafft-Ebing and the Italian Tamassia linked signs of male effeminacy to 'congenital' deviance and 'degeneration'.[120] This kind of sexology was practised beyond Europe, for example, with the Brazilian doctor Francisco Ferraz de Macedo publishing a study in 1872 on the identification of 'passive sodomites'.[121] It also extended to an activist like the German Karl Heinrich Ulrichs, who described himself as a 'Uranian' with 'a woman's soul confined by a male body'.[122]

In short, these were not concepts of homosexuality distinct from gender dissent. In this way, sexology reinstalled a 'heterogender paradigm' within the new ideology of desire. For supposed experts well into the twentieth century, 'sexual inversion' and 'congenital homosexuality' were virtually synonymous. For lesbians, this meant that for much of the twentieth century, sexologists and many lay people 'could only conceive of the "real" lesbian who desires another woman by engendering her as "mannish" or butch'.[123] The Italian criminal anthropologist Cesare Lombroso, for example, stated that one member of each lesbian couple, whose clothes, appearance and even to some degree genitals were masculine, usually played the 'male part'.[124] Leslie Feinberg later recalled that the gay bars in the early 1960s in northern New York State and southern

118   Floyd 1998, pp. 174, 179.
119   Meyerowitz 2002, pp. 3, 21–8.
120   Hekma 1994, pp. 224–6; Healey 2001, pp. 81–2, 86–7; on Westphal and Tamassia, see Halperin 2002, pp. 127–8.
121   Green 1999a, pp. 39–44.
122   Halperin 2002, p. 128.
123   Hennessy 2000, pp. 101–2.
124   Beccalossi 2012, pp. 134, 139, 119.

Ontario 'were also transgender bars'.[125] In practice, distinctions between 'transgender' and 'homosexual' were far more fluid in the late nineteenth and early
twentieth centuries than they later became.[126]

The impact of the discourse of inversion on people's lives could be devastating. One woman in upstate New York, who in 1855 had safely published an
account of her life as a 'female hunter', was by 1883 confined in an insane asylum for her 'paroxysmal attacks of erotomania'. Walt Whitman, in his last years
in the 1880s, felt compelled for the first time to deny the sexual dimension
of the male intimacy he had celebrated for decades in his poems.[127] Italian
doctors resorted to excision or cauterisation of the clitoris as a supposed cure
for female sexual inversion.[128] Medical and psychiatric 'treatment of homosexuality' took place in the dependent world as it did in Europe and North
America; a wide array of medical and psychiatric treatments, ranging from
insulin injections to electroshock, were used in a country like Brazil from the
1920s to 1940s.[129] This was on the model of 'treatments' conducted, for example,
in the US under the California Sex Deviates Research Act of 1950, under which
male sex offenders in California prisons were castrated and experimented on
with sex hormones.[130]

Yet sometimes the sexologists' interventions converged with the wishes of
the people now referred to in the press as nature's 'rare blunders'. Some homosexuals, accepting the idea that their erotic drives and their genitals were out
of synch, expressed the desire to change their sex. Following rapidly on from
the development of endocrinology in the early twentieth century,[131] some
doctors became willing to give hormones to people they called inverts. As
early as 1902, a self-proclaimed invert in New York prevailed on a doctor to
castrate him, while another in Oregon in 1917 succeeded in getting a hysterec-
tomy. By the 1920s, a few more doctors, many of them in Germany, were willing to attempt more extensive sex-reassignment surgery. Hirschfeld, at once
a sexologist, a champion of homosexual rights and a discreet member of the

125 Feinberg 1998, p. 23.
126 Stryker 2008, p. 34.
127 D'Emilio and Freedman 1997, p. 129. For other US medical accounts of inversion, see Katz
     1976, pp. 258–79, 371–4.
128 Beccalossi 2012, pp. 7, 134–5.
129 Green 1999a, pp. 107–8, 138–42.
130 Stryker 2008, p. 42. See Katz for a compilation of accounts of such 'treatment' in the US
     (1976, pp. 129–207). Theo van der Meer's forthcoming account of medical castration of
     homosexuals in the Netherlands shows that this practice was more common in the 1950s
     than under the German occupation.
131 Jordan-Young 2010, pp. 22–3.

community himself, had several such operations performed at his Institute for Sexual Science. Others were performed elsewhere in Europe later in the 1930s. In the US, however, doctors still overwhelmingly refused surgery unless patients were clearly intersex (born with ambiguous genitals).[132]

In what Foucault has called a ' "reverse" discourse', more homosexuals and trans people in this period began to see and describe themselves as inverts.[133] Sexologists had a strong influence on the 'inverts' themselves.[134] 'Inverts' and 'perverts' sent a sexologist like Krafft-Ebing 'their life histories, their anguished self-examinations, and their angry social critiques', to the point that sexology was 'an intensely collaborative enterprise between the doctors and the perverts'.[135] For many of them, Krafft-Ebing's work was 'a kind of gospel'.[136] Sexologist Havelock Ellis was particularly popular with lesbians in the 1920s, like novelist Radclyffe Hall and Ellis's French translator Claude Cahun, who picked up his conception of cross-dressing as inversion.[137] Ellis also worked closely with the homosexual writer John Addington Symonds. Pioneering Italian sexologist Pasquale Penta supported Hirschfeld.[138] Sexologists even helped make lesbian communities possible by separating off 'the lesbian from the rest of womankind'. Some women 'perceived real benefits in presenting themselves as congenital inverts' – above all, if they were 'born into the "intermediate sex", no family pressure or social pressure could change them'.[139] In adopting the label of 'intermediate sex', middle-class New Women of the 1920s even 'sought to use male myths to repudiate male power'.[140]

Yet while some sexologists were more conservative and some more progressive, most, while perhaps not simple villains, were no heroes of sexual liberation.[141] All of them reinforced the pseudo-scientific ideology and social impact of their field. As an emerging social structure, sexology strengthened the power of the state and medical establishment to impose and enforce sexual categories.

Although by the Second World War, US army psychiatrists (middle class by definition) viewed same-sex 'active and passive partners...as equally

132   Meyerowitz 2002, pp. 33, 35–7, 17–18, 5, 15, 18–20, 30, 33–5, 39.
133   Foucault 1978, p. 101.
134   Chauncey 1989, pp. 313–14.
135   Rubin 2011, pp. 293, 352.
136   Beachy 2010, p. 817.
137   Latimer 2005, pp. 15–17, 88–9, 61.
138   Beccalossi 2012, pp. 174–84, 163–4, 14–15.
139   Faderman 1991, pp. 41, 35.
140   Smith-Rosenburg 1989, p. 265.
141   Beccalossi 2012, pp. 174–84, 163–4, 14–15.

homosexual',[142] the model of inversion was still strongly entrenched among lesbians in the military as well as working-class lesbians in the 1950s. Lesbians were either butches ('inverts') or femmes ('real women') – and many males with same-sex desires 'saw themselves as "nelly queens" in pursuit of "real men"'. 'Being neither butch nor femme was not an option if one wanted to be part of the young or working-class lesbian subculture'; 'kiki' or 'bluff' lesbians who hesitated or alternated between the roles faced rejection or even threats of violence.[143] Among a group of 'fairies' in early twentieth-century Rhode Island, an attempt to penetrate another fairy was viewed as inappropriate and had to be surreptitious.[144]

Individuals' reasons for choosing one role or another varied. Sometimes what 'felt sexually most natural' was decisive. At other times, the crucial factor was butches' rejection of perceived female 'weakness, passivity and powerlessness'. Other young lesbians, for whom the rules had little 'intrinsic meaning', accepted them as the price of community membership.[145] Among men too, effeminacy could be as much adopted as 'natural'.[146]

This does not mean that lesbian butch/femme relationships simply mimicked cross-sex ones. Madeline Davis and Elizabeth Kennedy have pointed out the striking paradox of 1950s butches in the US: masculine in their self-presentation and behaviour, in sex they emphatically saw their role as giving pleasure to their female partners, sometimes as 'stone butches' supposedly not experiencing any pleasure at all themselves. This was hardly the dominant pattern of working-class male heterosexuality in their time or society.[147]

Only several decades after sexologists first began applying the concept of 'female sexual invert' to working-class women did they extend it to middle-class and upper-class women. As the feminist movement grew, soon feminism began to be equated with inversion,[148] as part of a 'heterosexual counter-revolution' against feminism.[149] As early as 1867, an article in a British medical journal warned that the US women's rights movement was making women masculine and fostering 'those dark crimes not to be named of Christian men'.[150]

142 Valocchi 1999, p. 214.
143 Faderman 1991, pp. 167–8.
144 Chauncey 1989, p. 300.
145 Faderman 1991, p. 171–2.
146 Weeks 1989, pp. 205–6.
147 Davis and Kennedy, pp. 432–3.
148 Faderman 1991, p. 39.
149 Kinsman 1987, p. 54.
150 Beccalossi 2012, pp. 88–9.

'The driving force in many agitators and militant women who are always after their rights', wrote one later opponent of feminism, 'is often an unsatisfied sex impulse, with a homosexual aim'.[151] Feminists often reacted defensively, as when a Cuban feminist leader in 1928 called lesbianism a crime against nature.[152]

Once middle-class women too could be seen as lesbians their relationships became suspect, even those that had not previously been seen as sexual. In the US in the 1920s, one woman wrote that businesswomen hesitated to share apartments, adding that 'the ethics of homosexual relationships is the most serious problem the business or professional woman has to face today'.[153]

Although Ellis saw school 'flames' as temporary and harmless, not as signs of 'real congenital perversion',[154] he warned that feminine women with a weakness for female inverts needed to be shielded from unwholesome influences so that they could develop as normal women.[155] One 1928 novel drew a contrast between a US women's college in 1913, when crushes between students were seen as 'the great human experience', and the situation seven years later: 'Intimacy between two girls was watched with keen distrustful eyes'. This marked a 'general closing off of most affectional possibilities between women', Lillian Faderman has noted – soon romantic friendship would 'breathe its last' – and the opening up of new sexual possibilities for lesbians.[156] Some early-twentieth-century lesbians embraced the discourse of inversion specifically because they 'desperately wanted to break out of the asexual model of romantic friendship'.[157]

Although the same-sex regime of the classical imperialist era had a definite heterosexual norm and an identifiably homosexual minority, sexual inversion predominated not only among the working class and poor, but also in upper bourgeois strata. Among upper-class lesbians in Paris between the world wars, while class status and economic privilege gave them scope for sexual dissent, their personal relationships 'followed the conventions of nineteenth-century Victorian domesticity'.[158] Yet while the identification of lesbians with

---

151 D'Emilio and Freedman 1997, p. 193. Even the left-wing British *New Statesman* in 1928 blamed lesbianism on suffragist 'man-hating' as well as the First World War (Weeks 1981, p. 230, n. 91).
152 Farber 2011, p. 189.
153 D'Emilio and Freedman 1997, p. 194.
154 Vicinus 1989, p. 227.
155 Smith-Rosenberg 1989, pp. 270–1. See also Beccalossi, pp. 199–200.
156 Faderman 1991, pp. 45, 49, 35, 4, 305.
157 Newton 1989, p. 283.
158 Benstock 1989, pp. 339–40. Benstock has pointed out that many upper-class lesbians saw their privilege and their gender-dissident domesticity as in line with right-wing and

economically independent women did not make lesbianism a feasible option for many working-class women, Paris lesbians in the 1920s included women with both aristocratic and plebeian backgrounds and impulses. Their class diversity overlapped with a diversity of sexual patterns. Lesbian bohemians whose economic status was less secure and whose lives were less would-be-conventional, like surrealists Claude Cahun and Marcel Moore, were sometimes less clearly inverted or more inclined to play with gender ('shuffle the cards') in proto-queer ways.[159]

Middle-Class Homosexuality

While sexual inversion can be seen as in continuity with the commodified transgender pattern, it also needs to be seen as a challenge to, and even a head-on assault on, the mid-nineteenth-century culture of same-sex romantic friendship. The newly emerging conception of sexuality included not just reproductive sex, but all aspects of erotic desire and self-identification that could shape gendered interaction and consumption. As the reach of sexuality broadened, so did the category of homosexuality.

As long as the focus was on production and class hierarchy, the capitalist societies of the nineteenth century were less concerned with gender roles and heterosexuality than with 'manhood'. Like masculinity, manhood was a social construction; but it was 'fundamentally patriarchal and procreative',[160] emphasising the kind of rigid personality structure that was required for male participation in the production process and for reproduction of the working class. Socioeconomic trends from the 1890s to the 1920s propelled a shift away from this version of manhood among the middle classes, however. As self-employment declined and labour was increasingly de-skilled, 'an impersonal work and political order ignored men's individual values, skills, and reputation'. Traditional manliness was less in demand than 'tact, teamwork [and] the ability to accept direction', and thus new 'definitions of masculinity had to be

---

patriarchal ideology. There was no necessary link between gender dissent and right-wing politics, however. As we have seen, someone like Brand who preached love between equals could be right wing, whereas someone like Hirschfeld who championed 'third sex' theories was outspokenly left wing. Latimer has rightly emphasised class privilege rather than any sexual pattern as decisive in the right-wing sympathies of Paris lesbians like Brooks and Nathalie Barney (2005, pp. 138–9, 144).

159   Latimer 2005, pp. 4–6, 13, 101.

160   Floyd 1998, p. 173.

constructed.[161] Exclusive heterosexuality was one aspect of middle-class men's 'attempt to rescue their masculinity' from its crisis.[162]

The changing structure of capital and the growth of an increasingly managerial and professional middle class helped foster a shift in the construction of gender under capitalism, from conceptions of 'manhood' and 'womanhood' focused on the innate character required for production and reproduction, to conceptions of masculinity and femininity that were (in Judith Butler's term) more 'performative',[163] defined to a greater extent by patterns of consumption, dress and everyday behaviour.[164] Floyd has shown that the 'performative' masculinity and femininity that Butler has analysed are not eternal, but arose under specific historical conditions. A masculinity and femininity focused on everyday behaviour and clothing proved better suited to the capitalism that developed from the late nineteenth century and its new corporate organisation. It was overdetermined by a set of changes in capitalism including the 'mechanization and consequent de-skilling of work' and 'the production boom brought on by technological efficiency'. In this same period, declining birth rates and advancements in birth control made procreation less crucial as a focus of at least middle-class sexuality, and sexual desire and object choice more crucial.[165]

By the early twentieth century in the imperialist countries, the centralisation of capital in many sectors also entailed a shift from price competition to other forms of competition, notably advertising that sought to seduce competitors' customers. Middle-class consumption was particularly crucial to capital accumulation in the expansive long wave that lasted from the mid-1890s to the mid-1910s, though even the working class in imperialist countries began to acquire gas-cookers and get to know 'the bicycle, the cinema and the modest banana'.[166] The shift to a consumer economy promoted a focus on 'pleasure, self-gratification, and personal satisfaction that easily translated to the province of sex'.[167] The transition to performative gender among middle-class people was thus linked to 'engineered production and engineered desire-inducement': a more consumption-oriented capitalism needed gendered

---

161   Coontz 1988, p. 339

162   Valocchi 1999, p. 212.

163   Butler 1999.

164   Floyd 2009, pp. 57–66.

165   Hennessy 2000, p. 99.

166   Hobsbawm 1987, p. 53.

167   Hennessy 2000, p. 103.

desires to stimulate demand for fashion, novels, films and commercialised sport.[168]

Longer education for the middle classes also expanded and highlighted the social category of youth, strongly associated with modernity, novelty[169] and sex. Popular culture became 'saturated with sex' to an even greater extent in the imperialist countries in the interwar period.[170] 'Advertising came into its own as an industry in the 1920s, as executives consciously strove to incite desire'. This was the beginning of 'media...saturated with sexual images that...channel individuals toward particular visions of sexual happiness, often closely linked to the purchase of consumer products'.[171]

The growing incitement of desire and more performative character of gender fostered new definitions of sexuality based on gendered object choice, mainly at first among the middle classes, reinforced by the rapid spread among them of psychoanalytical visions of sexuality.[172] Over time the authority of theorists of inversion like Westphal and Krafft-Ebing gradually yielded to that of psychologists like Ellis and Sigmund Freud, who distinguished between gender identity and sexual orientation.[173] Freud was especially influential in seeing heterosexuality as being culturally necessary but not 'pregiven', as 'psychological not biological'[174] – though curiously, he sometimes saw an inherited component in lesbianism if not in male homosexuality.[175] In any event, Freud saw human beings as naturally having a 'certain degree of anatomical hermaphroditism' and 'an original disposition to bisexuality', strongly opposing 'the attempt to separate homosexuals from other persons as a group of a special nature'.[176] A certain ambivalence is visible in his writings: although he described homosexuality as an 'arrest of development' and thus not 'mature', he rejected the idea that there could be a 'single kind of sexual life for everyone' as a 'source of serious injustice'. His view of homosexuality was 'normalising' but not 'pathologising'.[177]

---

168 Floyd 1998, pp. 173–5.
169 Hobsbawm 1987, p. 169.
170 Coontz 2005, p. 198.
171 D'Emilio and Freedman 1997, pp. 278, xvii.
172 Floyd 2009, pp. 43–5, following Foucault 1978, pp. 118–23.
173 Herzog 2011, pp. 31–2.
174 Weeks 1981, pp. 152–4; Downing 1989, p. 34. Downing has maintained that Freud's writings on same-sex desire were deeply informed by his own feelings for Wilhelm Fliess and Carl Jung (1989, pp. 13–29).
175 Beccalossi 2012, pp. 223–4.
176 Freud 1938, pp. 558, 560, n. 1.
177 Robinson 2001, p. 92.

Freud acquired great influence particularly in the US, following lectures there in 1909, and the notion that sex drives were omnipresent and all-powerful spread. While earlier sexologists had promoted a view of inversion as genetic, Freud's influence was by the 1920s lending credence to views of homosexuality as acquired[178] – and to attempts at 'cures' that Freud himself, seeing homosexuality as 'nothing to be ashamed of, no vice, no degradation', refused to attempt.[179] The new psychology rose together with new middle-class attitudes, and provided them with an ideology. Foucault has characterised clinical psychology and psychiatry as a bourgeois science, which depended on the middle classes for its initial circle of clients.[180]

Yet so pioneering was Freud's conception of homosexuality that even many Freudians accepted it only partially and reluctantly – even though Freud disliked feminism, saw it as a chief manifestation of his lesbian subjects' sexual 'abnormality',[181] and aimed to defend clearly distinct gender roles. Ellis for his part, while hesitant to 'dogmatise rigidly concerning the respective spheres of men and women' and supportive of some feminist demands,[182] wrote that woman naturally 'breeds and tends; man provides', and that the 'female responds to the stimulation of the male...just as the tree responds to the stimulation of the warmest days in spring'.[183] Freud too 'tied a woman's sexual desires inevitably to the activating presence of a man'.[184] As with Freud, however, Ellis was embraced, especially in English-speaking countries, for his equation of sex with 'all that is most simple and natural', as well as for his insistence that 'sex penetrates the whole person'.[185]

The influence of Freud and Ellis helped spread the concept of homosexuality among the middle class. The new category of homosexuality was increasingly applied not only to more or less transgendered people and gender dissenters, but also to many others in same-sex relationships (however shocked these people sometimes were and however indignantly they sometimes protested). 'The old veneration of same-sex friendships...was tossed aside', so that by the 1920s men too faced 'the stigma of being labelled "homosexual" if they

---

178 D'Emilio and Freedman 1997, pp. 223–4, 226.
179 Downing 1989, p. 43.
180 Healey 2001, p. 89.
181 Faderman 1991, p. 130.
182 Beccalossi 2012, pp. 193, 196–9.
183 Weeks 1981, p. 147.
184 D'Emilio 1983b, p. 93.
185 D'Emilio and Freedman 1997, pp. 224–6.

expressed affection for someone of the same sex'.[186] Homosexuals were seen to include not only the already-transgendered and those who had previously seen themselves as same-sex romantic friends, but also a small but growing group of people who began to self-identify as homosexuals. This kind of same-sex identity emerged in developed capitalist countries in the late nineteenth and early twentieth centuries mainly among middle-class layers.

In the US in the 1920s, one sociological study of 2,200 (mainly middle-class) women showed that 50.4 percent of them had intense emotional relationships with other women, of which half were either 'accompanied by sex or recognized as bisexual' – a theme explored by male novelists like Sherwood Anderson and Ernest Hemingway. As the ideal of heterosexual companionate marriage took hold, its failures were sometimes blamed not only on men's lack of consideration or sexual skills, but also on women's threatening lesbianism.[187]

The growing visibility of homosexuality reflected the increasing ability of middle-class men and women (particularly women with education and professions) to live independently of their families and to defy convention. As early as 1898, a US observer noted that many 'men of perverted tendencies...held together by mutual attraction' tended to be 'men of education and refinement,...men of professional life and men of business and affairs'.[188]

In Germany from the 1890s, a homosexuality defined as masculine was notably championed by the middle-class Community of the Special founded in 1896 by Adolf Brand, which portrayed male homosexuals as 'masculine ideals for young men instead of pathological, pitiable cripples'.[189] In an age that was obsessed with the imperialist projection of 'such masculine traits as strength, courage, hardness, and military aggressiveness', the Community laboured to dissociate homosexuality from effeminacy and associate it with an aristocratic (if not wholly asexual) concept of 'ideal friendship'.[190] In the 1930s, the Japanese naturalist Minakata Kumagusu privately and discreetly propagated a 'Pure Way of Men', drawing on Japanese tradition to construct an emphatically masculine and nationalist homosexuality comparable to that of the German Community of the Special. At the same time, he expressed contempt for 'faggots' who haunted parks in search of men who would penetrate them.[191]

---

186   Coontz 2005, pp. 197, 206.
187   Faderman 1991, pp. 63, 65, 90–1.
188   Adam 1985, p. 667.
189   Hekma 1994, pp. 227–8.
190   Steakley 1989, pp. 242, 251–2.
191   Miller 1996, pp. 135–71.

Some of the best-known middle-class European homosexual men of the late nineteenth and early twentieth century, like Oscar Wilde, Paul Verlaine and the Dutch writer Louis Couperus, though not portraying themselves as hyper-masculine, were 'only partially inverted': they were all married to women, and though dandyish rarely or never cross-dressed.[192] Yet while they were not inverts, nor were they gay men in the later sense, and not only because they were married to women: among these middle-class men too, sexual relation-ships with other self-identified homosexuals were still the exception rather than the rule. Wilde's and Verlaine's most intense same-sex relationships were with significantly younger men with ambiguous sexual identities.

As part of this emerging middle-class homosexuality, there was a homo-sexuality that crossed class lines: middle-class men like Oscar Wilde were fascinated by 'rough trade' and 'feasting with panthers': stable-lads, news-paper sellers, bookmaker's clerks. This was an important bond in Wilde's noto-rious romance with Lord Alfred Douglas.[193] The same was true of André Gide, whose friendships with other self-identified homosexuals consisted largely of a common pursuit of working-class or Arab youths or of desirable, often non-homosexually-identified middle-class young men.[194] Yet a penchant for unequal relationships across class, ethnic or age divides was not necessarily linked to right-wing elitism. Unlike Brand and Kumagusu, Wilde, Verlaine and Gide all identified with the left.

Middle-class homosexuals in this period went in search of working-class men who supplemented their income by being paid for sex, like English Post Office messenger boys (involved in a major scandal in 1889–90) or Guardsmen.[195] In England, upper- and middle-class men identified their working-class sex part-ners as masculine to the point that they distinguished between 'homosexuals' and 'men'; in relations between the two 'the cash nexus inevitably dominated'.[196] As late as the mid-1960s, in the US the exchange of money separated 'queers' (who paid) from 'peers' (whose heterosexual masculinity was protected by being paid): 'the boy sells a service for profit ... the queer is to accept it with-out show of emotion' and violence could be used to enforce respect for these demarcations.[197] Yet these cross-class encounters could involve a form of 'sexual colonialism' or 'an often sentimental rejection of one's own class values

---

192   Hekma 1994, p. 233.

193   Ellmann 1988, pp. 389–91.

194   Sheridan 1998.

195   Weeks 1981, pp. 109, 112–13.

196   Weeks 1989, pp. 202–4.

197   Rubin 2011, pp. 326–7 (citing Albert Reiss).

and a belief in reconciliation through sexual contact'[198] – or all of these mixed together.

In their early forms, these middle-class homosexual milieus could sometimes be seen as attempts to preserve middle-class masculinity and the earlier cultures of same-sex friendship or mentorship from the taint of inversion. The male invert's 'effeminacy represented in extreme form the loss of manhood middle-class men most feared in themselves'.[199] Many middle-class homosexuals in particular found working-class inverts threatening.[200] Gide even wrote that inverts alone 'were guilty of some of the accusations levelled at all homosexuals'.[201] Yet middle-class homosexuals' recognition of and even insistence on their own 'specialness' set them apart from earlier same-sex friends. It meant that they were pioneering a new definition of the relationship between gender and sexuality, a homosexual self-definition that formed a pendant to the emerging culture of heterosexuality. The presentation of 'heterogendered differences as fixed and natural opposites' led to the conceptualisation of homosexual identity as 'supplementary "other"'.[202] This made the middle-class homosexual circles of the early twentieth century precursors in some ways of later lesbian/gay communities, and in some ways precursors of neoliberal homonormativity.

An entire generation and several decades were needed, however, before the new category of homosexuality took hold, even among middle-class people. For women, this meant that people were often slow to perceive lesbian possibilities, with a generation's lag between the development of male homosexual and lesbian subcultures.[203] In Germany in 1909, for example, a proposal to criminalise lesbianism was rejected on the grounds that it was too difficult to distinguish lesbian acts from physical affection between 'normal' women. Only in the 1910s and 1920s did all-female institutions like girls' schools become places where 'lesbianism was suspected of being rampant'.[204] As late as 1921 in Britain a proposal to criminalise lesbianism was defeated by arguments that it would be wrong to draw women's attention to its existence.[205]

---

198   Weeks 1989, p. 203.
199   Chauncey 1994, p. 115.
200   Valocchi 1999, p. 211.
201   Sheridan 1998, p. 377.
202   Hennessy 2000, p. 25.
203   Weeks 1981, p. 115.
204   Herzog 2011, pp. 41, 34–5.
205   Weeks 1981, p. 105.

By the 1920s, however, a distinct pattern of sexual romances between women emerged among middle-class married women like Virginia Woolf and Vita Sackville-West. Given their marriages to men and more explicit sexual connections, these women's romances were a break from the earlier pattern of Boston marriages. Yet they were only possible thanks to the understanding attitudes of the women's husbands (Sackville-West's had his own homosexual life) in a bohemian milieu. Among lesbians in Paris too, though they were less likely to be married to men, tolerance was greater in their bohemian milieu than in the population at large. This bohemianism had antecedents in the earlier, anti-bourgeois (though not anti-capitalist) dandyism of Charles Baudelaire, mirrored by lesbian artist Romaine Brooks and homosexual impresario Sergei Diaghilev. Like social work to an earlier generation of women bonding with women, literature and the arts offered bohemian lesbians an alternative to marriage. For many lesbians in this milieu, expatriation added to their sense of freedom and the 'utopian potential of alienation'.[206]

Sex and Empire

As capitalism expanded, it changed the reality, meaning and relationship to the state of territory and history. In the new global capitalism, not only 'firms but nations competed' – 'nation' in the sense of 'a more or less homogeneous territorial state, internationally sovereign, large enough to provide the basis of national economic development, enjoying a single set of political and legal institutions'. 'States therefore created "nations"'.[207] The emerging capitalist state unified and homogenised its land, as Nicos Poulantzas has shown, by organising it into the working space of its army, police, prisons, bureaucracy and schools. It transformed historical memory by turning history into 'the forward course of the nation' and wiping out signs of other peoples' pasts. Violence was often part of the process. Genocide is a modern 'form of extermination specific to the...cleaning up of the national territory by means of homogenizing enclosure', expelling ' "foreign bodies"...beyond space and time'.[208]

Much still needs to be done to map the links between new sexual identities and empire.[209] The sexual character of colonial conquest and rule remained in

206   Latimer 2005, pp. 80, 44–5, 60, 33, 41–2.
207   Hobsbawm 1987, pp. 42, 22, 150.
208   Poulantzas 1980, pp. 113, 107, 114.
209   Hennessy 2000, p. 148.

any event as evident in the classic period of nineteenth- and twentieth-century imperialism as it had been in the centuries of pre-capitalist European expansion. Travel to European colonies in the Middle East, Asia and Africa provided opportunities for men 'seeking same-sex encounters away from the watchful eyes of their communities of origin – encounters whose excitement was often heightened by the sense of exoticism surrounding the partners'.[210] Colonial Tangiers was a favourite site for European same-sex tourism.[211] Even Southern Europe was viewed as a region of homosexual promise for Northern European men: Byron celebrated the charms of Mediterranean men,[212] Thomas Mann explored his own homoeroticism in Italy, and many British men were 'particularly taken' with Italians of their own sex.[213] In fact, southern Italian men had a reputation for openness to same-sex encounters, not only in their native region but also in certain neighbourhoods of New York.[214]

Polarised gender roles, the norm of monogamous heterosexual marriage and the hetero/homo binary were 'weapons in the imperial arsenal' in the nineteenth and early twentieth centuries.[215] Imperialism entailed the spread not only of the new category of homosexuality, but also of its official persecution. Many laws against sex between males on the books in much of Africa and Asia today are copies of an old British law repealed in Britain in 1967. The British were responsible for criminalising 'sodomy' in India in 1833.[216] Persecution of indigenous same-sex relations was widespread in Britain's African colonies.[217] Europeans and North Americans suppressed the Polynesian transgendered *māhū* in New Zealand and Hawaii, though *māhūs* survived in parts of Polynesia where colonisation was less intensive.[218] Even in Canada, the 1859 statute that punished 'buggery' with the death penalty followed an English model, and later Canadian criminal provisions for at least a century after 1869 were often 'borrowed almost word for word' from England.[219]

---

210 Herzog 2011, p. 33.
211 Mitchell 2011, p. 679, n. 2 (citing Gordon Waitt and Kevin Markwell).
212 Drucker 2012.
213 Beccalossi 2012, pp. 18–20; see also Mitchell 2011, p. 679, n. 2 (citing Stephen Clift, Michael Luongo and Carry Callister).
214 Chauncey 1994, pp. 74–5.
215 Loos 2009, p. 1315.
216 Joseph and Dhall 2000, p. 160.
217 Mburu 2000, pp. 182–4.
218 Besnier 1994, pp. 295–6.
219 Kinsman 1987, p. 92.

There was a long colonial tradition of seeing Asia as the site of 'carefully suppressed animalistic, perverse, homo- and hypersexual instincts'.[220] In Russia, a conservative critic described homosexuality in 1909 as once confined to the 'less-civilised' Arabs and Caucasian mountain tribes.[221] In Cuba too, one anthropologist in 1906 blamed the 'abominable vice' of homosexuality on Asian immigrants.[222]

The repression of same-sex regimes occurred even where European imperialism took semi-colonial forms rather than the form of direct conquest and rule. At least for privileged men, pre-nineteenth-century Greece under Ottoman rule, like the Ottoman lands as a whole, was sexually 'freer than liberated Greece was to be'.[223] The Greek national state, established in the 1820s and consolidated over the course of the nineteenth century, would be religiously intolerant and sexually repressive, with the power of the Orthodox clergy acting as a brake on the development of an open homoerotic life. The current European ideological prism, which in general does no justice to the historical 'variety, distribution, and longevity of same-sex patterns in Islamic societies',[224] makes no sense at all of the sexual repression that nationalism and Europeanisation brought to the former Ottoman Balkans.

If the process of homosexual identity formation was rocky and irregular in Europe and North America, it was many times more so in the dominated regions reshaped rapidly by imperialism in the late nineteenth and early twentieth centuries. On balance, the evidence tends to confirm Jarrod Hayes's conclusion: 'Whereas colonial discourses represent precolonial cultures as being more patriarchal than the colonizing one', colonisation in practice meant the 'imposition of a specifically European form of patriarchy, the nuclear family headed by men'.[225] However, the binary of heterosexuality and homosexuality took different forms in the countries of dependent capitalism.

While middle-class men in the most urbanised areas of Latin America began moving towards more reciprocal homosexuality before the Second World War, as in North America and Western Europe, the invert-dominant model still prevailed in the early 1970s in Brazil's north and northeast, in rural areas and

220   Puar 2007, pp. 87.
221   Karlinksky 1989, p. 355.
222   Farber 2011, p. 189.
223   Crompton 1985, p. 336.
224   Roscoe and Murray 1997, pp. 4–6.
225   Hayes 2000, p. 276.

among the urban poor. The Afro-Brazilian religion *candomblé* reinforced this pattern, with many of the *candomblé* priests being transgendered.[226]

Southeast Asian cases are particularly complex, as European influence over Southeast Asia began early but proceeded slowly, with the conquest of Indonesia and the Philippines being completed only in the nineteenth and twentieth centuries and Thailand never being formally colonised at all. Yet Thailand's incorporation into the world market began as early as the seventeenth century, although the transition from feudalism to capitalism proceeded slowly until the late nineteenth-century abolition of serfdom and beyond.[227] From the 1850s, however, while semi-colonial Siam was subordinated to European imperialism, it retained political independence as it 'entered the imperial world economy ... as the "rice bowl" of Southeast Asia', exporting rice to European colonies like British Malaya and Dutch Java, in a process that actually reinforced the authority of Thai elites.[228]

The impact of social change on Thai sexual culture was gradual. The Thai tradition of transgendered *kathoeys* predated any contact with Europe.[229] The abolition of slavery in the late nineteenth century, however, helped create the conditions for the domestic sex trade as 'a major local industry over a half century before the era of international sex tourism'. By the 1930s, there was a same-sex sex trade in which teenage boys catered to Thai adult men, and prostitution by *kathoeys* catering to non-transgendered adult male *seua bai* ('bi-tigers'). By the early 1960s, nationally distributed newspapers were fostering 'the rapid dissemination of gay and *kathoey* identity' in Thailand.[230] The spread of transvestite beauty contests, common in much of contemporary Latin America but presumably not a tradition of ancient Southeast Asia, was one indication of how the Thai *kathoey* pattern took on more commodified forms without losing its indigenous character.[231] In much of South and Southeast Asia, pre-colonial transgender relationships were incorporated into a domestic and global sexual market.[232]

---

226   Green 1999a, pp. 6–7 (citing Peter Frey and Ruth Landes).
227   Jackson 1989, p. 45.
228   Jackson 2009, pp. 367, 370.
229   Jackson 1989, pp. 48–51.
230   Jackson 2009, pp. 377, 364, 378–84, 371–2, 363, 365, 377. This took place before US troops were stationed there – a factor often wrongly seen as central to the emergence of Thai LGBT identities.
231   Jackson 1989, p. 195.
232   Altman 2000, pp. 141–2, 149–50.

This history has led Peter Jackson to the conclusion that Asia's LGBT formations developed along paths that diverged 'from *both* Western queer cultures *and* the premodern gender and sex cultures of their own societies'. Notably, it was in Japan and Thailand, which 'escaped direct colonization and self-modernized, that Asia's first modern homosexual economies emerged' – *before* European colonies like India and Indonesia, where direct European colonisation 'retarded' the development of homosexual subcultures.[233] Even in India, British influence was uneven, with the emasculation of *hijras* being banned in some Indian states that were only under indirect British rule but not in others. Independent India extended the legal ban on emasculation to the whole country but enforced it only sporadically, while the economics of dependent capitalist development greatly increased the scope for *hijra* begging and prostitution.[234]

In Japan, rapid capitalist development following the Meiji Revolution of 1868 led by the early twentieth century to a new paradigm that 'condemned as uncivilized all sexual acts...outside state-sanctioned monogamous marriage'.[235] Despite a centuries-old tradition of same-sex love, in the new paradigm homosexuality was defined as abnormal. It was only discussed in 'a sparse and wholly imported medical literature that consigned same-sex relations to the realms of psychopathology'. The resulting 'long and adamant silence' about same-sex relationships continued for much of the twentieth century.[236] In China, the concept of homosexuality was adopted only in the early twentieth century as European scientific terminology spread.[237]

The imperialist same-sex formation in the dependent world was distinctively shaped by international sex tourism, though this was predominantly cross-sex. Same-sex sex tourism dates back to rich Europeans visiting Bali in the 1920s,[238] following on same-sex tourism to North Africa in the 1890s.

---

233 Jackson 1989, pp. 359–60, 366. I am delighted by Jackson's demonstration that the 'thought experiment' I once described as 'improbable' (Drucker 2000a, p. 16) – evidence of the rise of lesbian/gay identity even in the absence of 'outside cultural influence' – is not only feasible but decisive (1989, p. 369).
234 Nanda 1994, pp. 414–16.
235 Loos 2009, p. 1317.
236 Schalow 1996, p. 12; Miller 1996, pp. 135–6.
237 Hinsch 1990, p. 165.
238 Altman 2000, p. 146.

Outliers

The establishment of a hetero/homo binary in the imperialist heartlands towards the end of the nineteenth century thus had parallels in many parts of the world that imperialism dominated, though with specific features. However, other regions of the dependent world had sexual patterns that seemed to diverge far more than did urban Latin America, China or Southeast Asia from the newly defined heterosexuality and homosexuality of Western Europe and North America. By contrast with the consolidation of heterosexual families and romance in these regions and the invert-dominant same-sex regime that formed its pendant, other parts of the world preserved conceptions of people as 'multiple, malleable, dynamic, and possessing male and female elements'.[239] In South African mining areas, the Dutch South American colony Suriname and the Arab region, for example, in keeping with their specific places in the global capitalist political economy, a variety of same-sex patterns developed that were outliers in the global invert-dominant regime.

These outlying patterns were by no means limited to 'rural, "folk" and precapitalist pockets' with 'radically different articulations of homosexual desire'.[240] Moreover, on closer examination even regions of the dependent world where sexual relations were seen as traditional were often far from immune from the changes brought by imperialism. Embedded in the imperial economy, these sexual patterns still expressed a commitment to distinctive forms of sensual desire, creativity and playfulness.[241] They can thus be seen as 'outliers', not in the sense of lying outside the bounds of imperialism, but in the sense of lying outside the sway of the hetero/homo binary within a global system in which the binary increasingly prevailed.

Suriname, for example, as Gloria Wekker has pointed out, was not 'on the margin of the world system but, historically, squarely in the system's foundation'.[242] This was even more obviously true of the South African mines. While traditional transgender patterns were often stamped out, especially in Christianised regions, aspects of them sometimes resurfaced, distorted and spatially displaced, in the unisex labour forces of plantations, mines and later factories in which metropolitan capital exploited workers drawn from the hinterland. By contrast with traditional transgender patterns, this sometimes

---

239   Wekker 2006, p. 192.
240   Adam 1985, p. 659.
241   Epprecht 2009, p. 1267 (citing Zackie Achmat).
242   Wekker 2006, p. 56.

resulted in regimes where some people were doubly, ambiguously or flexibly gendered.

In analysing the different sexual dynamics in colonial hinterlands and in plantations, mines and factories directly dominated by metropolitan capital, it helps to see that the imperial order already constituted a global whole (a totality), though one that was unevenly structured and far from monolithic. On a global scale, capital and capitalist production were already predominant and capitalist relations increasingly pervasive almost everywhere. The market was being imposed from the outside even on remote areas, as African villagers were forced to pay colonial taxes and Indian villagers were obliged to buy British textiles. And some villagers were workers recruited for mines and factories, but were sent home when not needed at a given moment, thus relying on traditional means of subsistence that were convenient for colonial governments.

At first glance – and in reality too – the sexual patterns of rural Africa and Asia remained by far the most common ones in the era of classical imperialism, and were rooted in indigenous sexual regimes that predated capitalist penetration. Even African and Asian plantation, mine and factory workers were often only one generation removed from the village, often returned to it, and situated their primary family and sexual lives there, while sexual relations they engaged in and around their workplaces were influenced and defined by traditions 'back home'. Yet even in remote villages, supposedly unchanged family and sexual traditions did not necessarily have the same content or meaning in the framework of a global imperial order. Sexual relations in the centres of colonial capitalist production need to be understood even more in the context of the economic and imperial systems in which they were embedded.

T. Dunbar Moodie's account of South African 'mine marriages' from the earliest years of the twentieth century through the 1970s provides a fascinating case study of these dynamics. Older miners' relationships with their younger, male 'mine wives' – who were not only exclusive same-sex sexual partners (usually penetrated between the thighs), but also domestic helpers – were based on traditional forms of adolescent cross-sex sexual play (*metsha* in Xhosa, *hlobongo* in Zulu), but caught on and persisted due to their convenient fit with the colonial linkage of capitalist mine with rural reserve. The younger men became 'wives' at the mines – for financial reasons, to earn bride price – in order to become 'husbands and therefore full "men" more rapidly at home'. By expressing an attachment to indigenous village sexual patterns, these relationships expressed a certain resistance to taking on a purely proletarian way of life. Yet the emotional component of same-sex relationships – which, as we have seen, emerged in late seventeenth-century north-western Europe only with the rise of bourgeois society – was present in these mine marriages too.

Although gold miners could and did have female girlfriends in nearby towns as well, they returned to 'our boys' at night: 'We loved them better'. Attempts by white management to suppress mine marriages led to very proletarian forms of revolt: wildcat strikes and demonstrations in 1916, and again in 1941. Only higher wages and weakening ties to rural areas after 1973 gradually put an end to them.[243] At the same time, women left behind in rural Lesotho were sexually involved with one another too.[244]

The unique form of same-sex sexuality in twentieth-century Suriname – 'mati' relationships – was a comparable outcome of colonial capitalism. Originating before 1900 and first attested in 1912, the *mati* pattern was the result of the development of mining (first gold, and later bauxite, crucial for the US in the Second World War) and rubber industries that drew Afro-Surinamese men for months at a time to the Surinamese interior while women stayed in urban coastal areas. Combined with the gender and sexual legacy of slavery, this led working-class women to have sexual relationships with women as well as men, 'either simultaneously or consecutively', while typically having children. Given that the men were often absent, the women could develop tight partnerships, caring for one another and their children, while needing relations with men (having 'bedroom obligations') to conceive the children – important economically for the mother's future security as well as their status – and, given women's subordinate place in the colonial economy and the public sphere, for money. Sometimes women who were each other's *mati* were a man's co-wives. The upshot was that about half the women on one Afro-Surinamese working-class street had had same-sex relationships in the 1940s or later. Jamaican working-class female 'Man Royals' also had relationships and children with men while being sexually active with women. There have been similar accounts about other Afro-Caribbean communities.[245]

Although both women in such relationships generally had jobs and children, there was clearly a transgender dimension to them, with many *mati* agreeing that in every relationship one partner would play the male role. Often this transgender dimension went together with substantial age differences, in which older women eroticised their differences with 'young doves' or 'young chickens' and took pleasure in moulding and training them. But a distinctive feature of these relationships, in line with the tradition of simultaneous or consecutive cross-sex and same-sex relationships, was that neither

---

243   Moodie 1989, pp. 413, 420–4; see also Hoad 1999, pp. 568–9, Epprecht 2009, pp. 1265–6.
244   Epprecht 2009, p. 1265 (citing Judith Gay).
245   Wekker 2006, pp. 1–2, 31, 38, 172, 33, 148–50, 114–15, 57, 35, 41–2, 220–1 (citing Makeda Silvera).

138

CHAPTER 1

partner had either a wholly transgendered or a homosexual identity. Rather, *matis* were flexibly gendered, so that one woman or both took on a particularly strong, masculine persona at one time or another. The same colonial constellation produced similar *mati* patterns among Afro-Surinamese men, linked to the relatively great numbers of male sex workers and the frequency with which even prominent married men were spotted at male *mati* parties.[246]

The case of the Navajo transgendered *nádleehé* Hastíín Klah (1869–1939) shows how imperialism could influence sexual regimes on reservations even when it did not rely on their labour force for capitalist production. Although the US Christian authorities were hostile to Navajo traditions generally and transgender identity in particular, Klah's skills as a shaman were highly valued as the Navajos 'returned to traditional religion in response to the stresses of reservation life'. With confinement to the reservation, Navajo men lost the prestigious traditional activity of raiding, while the economic scope for trans artisans widened. Before Klah's time, Navajo weaving had been secular and done by women; Klah created 'an entirely new artifact – large weavings depicting ceremonial designs' – which were bought by wealthy art collectors and museums.[247] Historical factors – and notably the impact of imperialism – were thus crucial to the shaping of his twentieth-century berdache role.

Despite direct European colonisation, the Islamic world too proved resistant at first to the newly developed heteronormativity of the imperialist period, developing a distinctive same-sex regime that combined traditional intergenerational patterns with colonial ones. This led to a widespread belief in Europe that, as one French naval doctor put it in 1893, 'The Arab is an inveterate pederast',[248] and to attempts at suppression. During the French colonial mandate, for example, an article derived from Vichy legislation against 'unnatural sexual intercourse' was added to the Lebanese penal code.[249] The European vision of an endemic Arab homosexuality reflected the imposition of an emerging European heteronormative view of human sexuality on a part of the world that had never known it, where despite the condemnation of specific

---

246 Wekker 2006, pp. 193–4, 185–6, 193, 252, 271, n. 12. Wekker has suggested that the prevalence of gender-polarised relationships may be a kind of optical illusion, simply because relationships 'structured according to this principle are more visible than others' (2006, p. 197). My response would be, in keeping with my overall focus on what is socially dominant in a same-sex regime, that what is publicly visible matters more in defining a gender and sexual order than private arrangements between individuals, which often diverge from the predominant public norms.

247 Roscoe 1994, pp. 357–9.

248 Aldrich 2003, p. 16

249 Makarem 2011, p. 99.

acts Islam co-existed with rich same-sex cultural traditions. The homosexual identities that French and other European colonial officials and visitors projected onto Arabs were for many Europeans evidence of Arab inferiority.

The Islamic world itself changed with the partial adoption of heteronormative sexualities as part of late nineteenth- and twentieth-century attempts at autonomous development. Joseph Massad has described a host of modern Arab attempts to deny, downplay or condemn traditional Arab openness to same-sex desire. For example, erotic poetry focusing on youths or men, widespread in Arabic literature for centuries, 'disappeared completely as a poetic genre' around the late nineteenth century, while in the twentieth century many Arab critics denounced ninth-century poet Abu Nuwas's famous praise of youthful male beauty.[250] Among Jews too, as European colonisers attributed homosexuality to a decadent Arab culture, both traditionalist rabbis in Muslim countries and the modernisers of the Alliance Israélite Universelle increasingly tended to attribute same-sex relations among Jews to Muslim influence.[251]

In late nineteenth- and early twentieth-century Iran as well, as Afsaneh Najmabadi has shown, 'heteronormalization of eros and sex became a condition of "achieving modernity"'. In the last decades of the Qajar dynasty's rule (until 1925), the male object of desire disappeared from painting, and homoerotic verse was increasingly censured. This was part of a process in which romantic as opposed to merely procreative heterosexuality was exalted so that educated women could act as the mothers and wives of a regenerated nation; veiling and women's segregation were seen both as obstacles to modernisation and as causes for men's lust after male youths. Late Ottoman reformers similarly tried to institutionalise monogamous heterosexuality.[252] Hindu nationalists in India too rejected transgender and same-sex attachments – as Muslim.[253]

Yet more or less beneath the radar of colonial officials and Muslim or nationalist modernisers, the pattern of same-sex encounters between male adults and youths persisted. It acted as a magnet for Europeans who saw North Africa and the Middle East as sites of escape from their home countries' constraints. French writers – from Gustave Flaubert to Gide to Jean Genet – described sexual encounters with Arab males.[254] The Jews of the Islamic world, who had not traditionally had a binary view of human sexuality any more than Muslims had, were no more immune than Muslims to the temptations of sex between

---

250   Massad, pp. 35, 102; Makarem 2011, p. 99.

251   Peirce 2009, p. 1336.

252   Najmabadi 2005, pp. 3, 26, 163, 7, 156, 183, 193, 56, 150, 160 (citing Deniz Kandiyoti).

253   Loos 2009, p. 1316.

254   Aldrich 2003; Sheridan 1998.

males. One Frenchman commented in 1909, 'The Arabic and Jewish youth of Tunis readily prostitute themselves to foreigners'.[255]

Unlike the young Guardsmen and stable-lads of England, however, the youths of Tunis and other towns of the Islamic world had a tradition of their own, which persisted even in interaction with the imperial sexual order. By many accounts, this tradition allowed youths (up to a certain age) to play non-masculine roles without being seen as inverts, to be frank about their same-sex desires, to be proud of their beauty, and even to be actively seductive.

A New Sexual Politics

While in some locations of the imperialist system men and women persisted in same-sex relations without adopting homosexual identities, in others politics became an increasingly significant factor in consolidating homosexual or gender-dissident identities. This was the case in Germany, the Netherlands and England from the end of the nineteenth century, where sexual and gender dissent was linked to 'sex reform' movements with feminist and socialist overtones.

The emergence of same-sex identities and communities was never a steady progress towards a clearly conceived objective. Often it was a response to 'moral panics' and waves of persecution that arose in the wake of the periodic crises punctuating capitalist development. The long depression of the last quarter of the nineteenth century saw persecutions including the trial of Wilde, which in Ellis's words 'aroused inverts to take up a definite stand'.[256] Ellis's own book *Sexual Inversion* was banned as obscene after a trial in 1898.[257] Wilde's trial was a direct impetus for the founding of the German Scientific-Humanitarian Committee in 1897. More generally, it was Prussia's and the German Empire's anti-same-sex legislation that gave the impetus to the rise of sexology and the formation of a homosexual movement and identity there, as opposed to countries like France where decriminalisation had occurred a century earlier.[258] In Italy too, unification led to the extension of criminalisation to parts of the peninsula where the Napoleonic Code had eliminated it. Together with the major role of secular science in combating the anti-national (and supposedly 'unmanly') Catholic Church, this helps explain the flourishing state of

255   Aldrich 2003, p. 62.
256   Weeks 1981, p. 103.
257   Beccalossi 2012, pp. 185–91.
258   Beachy 2010, p. 836.

Italian sexology – though decriminalisation in 1889 eliminated any impetus for a homosexual movement.[259]

German same-sex organising was fuelled by the extension of Prussia's repressive law after German unification in 1871 to parts of Germany where homosexuality had been decriminalised. Initially applied only to anal sex, the German ban was extended by an 1876 ruling to cover oral sex.[260] US states also extended existing sodomy laws to cover oral sex.[261] New repressive laws were also adopted in Britain and Austria in the crisis years. In England, for example, the 1885 Labouchère amendment criminalised same-sex acts like mutual masturbation that had not previously fallen under the criminal law.[262] Lagging behind, Denmark passed new legislation against male prostitution in 1905,[263] and the Netherlands in 1911 raised the age of consent for same-sex relations from sixteen to twenty-one.[264]

The decades in which a gradual, partial, uneven transition was occurring from the molly-dominant pattern to inversion to proto-gay homosexuality were decades of political struggle over sexuality. Much of it took place under the banner of 'sex reform'. Feminists were split between those like the British suffragist Christabel Pankhurst, who demanded 'votes for women and chastity for men', and those who took up emerging conceptions of heterosexuality, campaigned for contraception to free women from the fear of pregnancy, and advocated marriage founded on love and mutual sexual satisfaction rather than procreation or economic security. The more daring pro-sex feminists and other sex reformers defended premarital sex for women as well as men, at least as a preparation for a pleasurable marriage.[265]

Divisions among politicised homosexuals paralleled divisions over sexuality in the first wave of feminism. More conservative men could see penetrating an invert, like penetrating a female prostitute, as a natural outlet for a powerful male sexual drive. Neither sexual act necessarily involved mutual pleasure or affection, since the class privilege of and payment by dominant men could make them indifferent to or even contemptuous of the person being penetrated. These relationships straddled class divides in a hierarchical and transactional way. Middle-class or bourgeois homosexuals might also hark

259   Beccalossi 2012, pp. 36–7, 50, 27.
260   Beachy 210, pp. 807–9.
261   Shah 2005, p. 717.
262   Weeks 1981, p. 87.
263   Herzog 2011, p. 77.
264   Van der Meer 2007, p. 141.
265   Herzog 2011, pp. 11, 17–18.

back to earlier ideals of male friendship, even tracing them back to classical antiquity, while despising inverts. Others, more progressive, joined sex reform movements alongside pro-sex feminists and others who opposed persecution of sexual minorities in general. The vision of male 'comradeship' in Walt Whitman's poetry, influenced by the democratic ideology of the Civil War-era United States, was important in shaping progressive homosexual men's self-image. Through Whitman's influence on Edward Carpenter, this vision, cross-pollinating with the ideas of the labour movement, influenced conceptions of same-sex love in Britain.[266]

Many of these progressives, like those drawn to Hirschfeld's Scientific-Humanitarian Committee, based their position on 'third sex' theories that defined homosexuality as congenital inversion, whether or not they shared his social democratic political leanings. While it was meant to be a broad group of advocates of legal reform, the Scientific-Humanitarian Committee's founding can be considered as the emergence of a homosexual community onto the public stage. With its establishment, an attempt began to use the pseudo-scientific categories of inversion to undermine the sexual norm, in the interests of sexual and gender emancipation – an attempt that influenced the parties of the Second and Third Internationals before Stalinism cut off the interaction, and which in some ways prefigures today's radical gender queers.

The petition the Scientific-Humanitarian Committee launched for the repeal of the anti-same-sex Paragraph 175 of the German penal code, promoted through a wide range of campaigns and publications, was finally presented to the Reichstag in 1922. In all these campaigns, third sex theories were given particular importance. The Committee's informational brochure on homosexuality, published in 1903, was even entitled *What Should the People Know about the Third Sex?*[267] This focus on inversion was picked up in regions where bourgeois society was underdeveloped. In tsarist Russia, for example, such pioneering Western European writers as Ellis, Hirschfeld and Carpenter were all translated and published before 1917.[268]

Progressive sex reform efforts formed a contrast with those of the German Community of the Special, who celebrated an often self-consciously aristocratic ideal of male-male friendship. The political differences reflected class differences. Working- and lower-class people tended to be involved in transgender relationships at a historically later period, while middle- and upper-class people tended to move earlier towards patterns that were, ambiguously

---

266   Rowbotham 1977a.
267   Lauritsen and Thorstad 1995, pp. 8–15.
268   Healey 2001, p. 104.

and partly, more reciprocal. Political alignments in Wilhelmine and Weimar Germany were particularly associated with class affiliation.[269]

Working-class homosexual activists could link up with a persistent strain of feminism and sexual libertarianism among early nineteenth-century socialists, notably the Owenites and Fourierists. Charles Fourier, in particular, urged tolerance of lesbianism. Friedrich Engels observed that 'the traditional bonds of sexual relations, like all other fetters, are shaken off' in 'times of great agitation', and Fourier's ideas in particular had a certain influence on Marx and Engels.[270]

Nonetheless, there was a homophobic strain in early Marxism. Engels's *Origins of the Family* (1884), in particular, reflected the period in which the cult of heterosexual romance enjoyed its greatest triumph. Engels subscribed to the cult by declaring that 'sexual love is by its nature exclusive', and that under socialism, with the abolition of the double standard, monogamy 'at last becomes a reality – also for men'.[271] Marx and Engels were unable to 'move beyond the "natural" appearance of the existing and developing heterosexual social forms of sexual life to reveal how these, too, were historical and social creations'.[272] Engels even condemned the ancient Greeks for 'the abominable practice of sodomy'.[273] There were also homophobic remarks in Marx and Engels's letters, including Engels's jokingly expressed relief that even if anal sex were decriminalised in Germany 'we, personally, are too old to have to fear that... we shall have to pay physical tribute to the victors'.[274] As Sherry Wolf has commented, there is 'no sense in trying to polish a turd here'.[275]

The rise of mass labour and socialist parties made socialists' attitudes of greater importance for sexual politics. From 1880 to 1906, politically organised labour movements became the norm in imperialist countries: while in 1880, Germany was exceptional in having one, by 1906 the US was seen as exceptional in lacking one.[276] The rise of these movements largely overlapped with the invention of heterosexuality and the triumph of heteronormativity. Like the rest of their societies, the European parties of the late nineteenth- and early twentieth-century Second International, even at their most radical,

---

269   Herzer 1995.
270   Weeks 1981, pp. 167–8.
271   Engels 2000.
272   Kinsman 1987, p. 25.
273   Engels 2000.
274   Engels 1988, p. 295.
275   Wolf 2009, pp. 77–8.
276   Hobsbawm 1987, pp. 116–17.

accepted and institutionalised the heterosexual norm. Moreover, their brand of Marxism was largely 'trapped . . . within a narrow economism' and 'mainly dismissed sexuality as merely superstructural'.[277]

Yet within this context, the early record of the Second International's flagship, the German Social Democratic Party (SPD), was relatively positive. The SPD was at the forefront of the fight to repeal Germany's anti-same-sex Paragraph 175 in the years before the First World War. SPD leader August Bebel, whom Hirchfeld had befriended, introduced a repeal bill in the Reichstag in 1898, making possible a full debate,[278] and gained widespread attention with his speeches on the issue that year and again in 1907. Speeches against Paragraph 175 by SPD Reichstag member Adolph Thiele took up thirty-four pages of the Scientific-Humanitarian Committee's 1905 Yearbook. Eduard Bernstein defended Wilde (himself an iconoclastic socialist) in the pages of the SPD's theoretical journal Die Neue Zeit in 1895. Bernstein rejected the idea that homosexuality was unnatural, writing that 'same-sex intercourse is so old and so widespread that there is no stage of human culture we could say with certainty [was] free from this phenomenon'. Hirschfeld reciprocated the left's support, calling at the outbreak of the German Revolution in November 1918 for a 'true people's state with a genuinely democratic structure' and a 'social republic'.[279]

In other countries too there were links between the socialist left and the defence of homosexual rights. In England, Wilde, though he only briefly and elliptically defended homosexuality at his trial (when his conviction was a foregone conclusion), contributed to the linkage of sexual and political radicalism with his Soul of Man under Socialism.[280] Carpenter was a leading figure in a series of small socialist groups from the 1880s even as he spoke publicly as a homosexual. Although Carpenter's book Homogenic Love was only printed privately in 1894 and never sold openly,[281] his Towards Democracy, inspired by Whitman's vision of 'comradeship', was a 'modern bible' for early English socialists, despite vicious attacks made on him because of his sex life and writings.[282] Carpenter was also the first president of the British Society for Sex Psychology, founded in 1914. In the US, Emma Goldman, who made a point of

---

277   Padgug 1989, p. 55.

278   Beachy 2010, p. 824.

279   Lauritsen and Thorstad 1995, pp. 11–12, 65–8, 27–8.

280   Weeks 1981, pp. 172–3, 181–2, 114, 92; see Wilde 1990.

281   Beachy 2010, p. 826.

282   Rowbotham 1977a, pp. 69–70, 88–92.

meeting Carpenter when she arrived in Britain in the 1920s, was noted for her defence of homosexuality.[283]

There is another side to the story, unfortunately. The German Social Democrats succumbed to the temptation to appeal to prejudice when there were same-sex scandals among the German Empire's aristocratic elite, notably in 1907. (That same year the Austrian *Kriminal-Zeitung* boosted its circulation by pursuing its own homosexual scandals, calling like the German Social Democrats for repeal of the anti-same-sex law (in Austria Paragraph 129 (b)) while darkly warning of the power of high-placed homosexuals).[284] More profoundly, socialists were credulous about 'scientific' biology and medicine, which contradicted the left's distinctive emphasis on historical and social factors. They also praised working-class 'manliness', often ignoring the female half of the working class. And in the early twentieth century, the SPD was only beginning to develop an analysis of imperialism generally, and was uncertain about its relationship to the German imperial state in particular. This limited its ability to grasp the gendered capitalism of its time in all its facets, as well as having fatal consequences when war broke out in 1914.

Russian Revolution

This is the background to the record of the Bolsheviks in power from 1917 to the early 1930s on questions of same-sex desire and practices, in conjunction with the sexual geography of the territories they governed. Pre-1917 tsarist Russia comprised an 'entire atlas of Europe's "geography of perversion"', from transgendered indigenous shamans in Siberia, to transgendered youthful dancers and prostitutes in Muslim Central Asia, to the young sexual minions of Orthodox priests in the country's monasteries, to men who cruised one another in St Petersburg's fashionable shopping arcade off the Nevskii Prospekt. Taken as a whole, these co-existing sexual forms provided a showcase of 'combined underdevelopment'.[285]

The Bolsheviks did not set out to replace this sexual life existing under tsarism with a wholly new, rational, free sexual world. There were bound to be both links and discontinuities between the Bolsheviks' revolutionary ambitions and their modernising practices. For example, some sources in the Soviet regime noted that male same-sex circles and relations often included partners

---

283   Weeks 1981, p. 161; Lauritsen and Thorstad 1995, pp. 34–6, 93–6, 40–1.
284   Spector 2007, pp. 21–4.
285   Healey 2001, pp. 252 (paraphrasing Bleys 1995), 8, 31, 10 (citing Laura Engelstein).

who were transgendered and others who were emphatically masculine, but they rarely suggested that this could or should be changed.[286]

In this respect as in others, the Bolsheviks were influenced by German Social Democracy, and thus strongly by Hirschfeld's theories and campaigns. The Bolsheviks decriminalised same-sex sexual acts when they took power, which the tsarist government had decided to continue criminalising when it revised its penal code in 1903. Though not the victory of a movement of sexual or gender dissenters (since none existed), decriminalisation in the 1922 Soviet Russian penal code was no accident. It was the outcome of a long and serious discussion. The new code completely avoided terms like 'sodomy' or 'unnatural', and made no distinction between same-sex and cross-sex acts. It even abandoned any fixed age of consent, accepting consent to any sexual act from the age of ' "sexual maturity" . . . to be determined by medical opinion in each case'.[287]

Throughout the 1920s, Bolshevik government leaders also supported the World League for Sexual Reform, whose affiliates (almost all in Europe) had 190,000 members. The League campaigned for decriminalisation worldwide (as well as for birth control, female equality and the right to divorce); the Soviet Union sent delegates to its congresses in 1921, 1928, 1929 and 1930. The Bolshevik government made possible 'an impressive volume of research and discussion' on what one Soviet biologist called the 'infinite quantity of intermediate sexes'. These basic facts are worth reiterating, if only because some recent scholarship has managed to overlook them.[288]

Dan Healey's indispensable work has made clear that early Bolsheviks in key positions had a range of views on sexual issues, and that opposing views were widely expressed and debated throughout the 1920s, with no single or official position.[289] The Bolsheviks' post-revolutionary debates were rooted in divergent pre-revolutionary approaches, some of which were benighted by the contemporary standards of international social democracy.

---

286 Healey 2001, pp. 9, 40–2.
287 Healey 2001, pp. 108, 115–25.
288 Lauritsen and Thorstad 1995, p. 74; Herzog 2011, p. 54; Healey 2001, pp. 128, 166. The tsarist penal code had anticipated the Soviet legal concept of 'sexual maturity', but only applied it to 14- to 16-year-olds (Herzog 2011, p. 38). Simon Karlinsky has done his best to obscure these basic facts, arguing that homosexuals were freer under tsarism than in the 1920s (see, for example, Karlinsky 1989). Lauritsen and Thorstad's brief account was, on the whole, far more balanced and accurate.
289 Healey 2001, p. 127.

Lenin, while attacking sexual prejudices due to religion, patriarchy and out-dated laws, apparently preferred to link sex to 'the serious in love' (by which he seems to have meant mainly parenthood), and believed that diverting energy from class struggle to sexual liberation was 'corrupt and degenerate'.[290] He also reportedly opposed Kollontai's proposal in 1919 to add a note on the withering away of the family to the party programme, and made disparaging remarks about Clara Zetkin and Kollontai's efforts to promote sexual free-dom.[291] Bolsheviks also 'actively rebuffed feminist aspirations'. For example, People's Commissar for Health Nikolai Semashko, in many ways a champion of sexual emancipation, deplored the way that some women would 'crop their hair, drink, smoke and swear', ignoring their 'constitution, designed for the functions of childbirth'. Soviet doctors often described transgendered people as pathological, but their same-sex partners as 'normal'.[292]

Yet the Bolsheviks' principled commitment to women's equality not only allowed women to rise under Soviet rule to positions they could never have occupied in Western Europe at the time, but also created considerable space for women perceived as masculine in workplaces and the Red Army, some in positions of command or authority. At least some of these women formed sexual relationships with other women and were accepted as 'happy, well-adjusted Lesbians'. In Bolshevik Moscow in the 1920s it was also possible, at least for a time, for the private arts circle Antinoi to stage 'readings of con-sciously homosexual poetry, recitals of music by "our own" composers, and even an all-male ballet'.[293] Openly homoerotic work that was produced and published in Russia in the 1920s included the poetry of Nikolai Kliuev, Mikhail Kuzmin and Sophia Parnok.[294]

In several cases in the 1920s, Soviet courts even accepted same-sex mar-riages (in which one partner was transgendered) as 'legal, because concluded by mutual consent' – a practice to which no one in the Health Commissariat's Expert Medical Council objected. While the Soviet abolition of regulated pros-titution created some new difficulties for sex workers with a same-sex clientele, and male prostitutes ended up plying their trade mainly in public toilets, it was motivated by revulsion at the brutal exploitation common in tsarist brothels;

---

290 Healey 2001, pp. 112–14. Healey has warned that these supposed remarks of Lenin's 'come to us heavily mediated, published five years after they were said to have been uttered'.

291 Kollontai 1978, pp. 202–3.

292 Healey 2001, pp. 6, 144–8.

293 Healey 2001, pp. 61–2, 143–4, 47.

294 Karlinsky 1989, pp. 359–60.

it would hardly have been possible to make an exception for male prostitutes and for prostitutes who identified as lesbians.[295]

In sum, 'Fragmentary evidence suggests that emancipatory and medical views were preferred (when no public disturbance, or politically disloyal act took place) over likely police preferences for a tougher line'.[296] Kollontai expressed the most advanced views, both during her tenure as Commissar for Social Welfare and for several years afterwards. While she never directly addressed same-sex issues, her focus on abolishing the 'enslavement of women' led her to challenge current gender norms head-on. She advocated making not only domestic work but also 'care of the younger generation . . . a social-state concern', 'so the obligations of parents to their children wither away gradually until finally society assumes the full responsibility'. And she interpreted this demand in a radical way: 'Maternity does not in the least mean that one must oneself change the nappies, wash the baby or even be by the cradle'.[297]

Nor did Kollontai's attention to issues of housework and childcare distract her from sexual issues. On the contrary, this was the field in which she became most famous (or infamous) in Bolshevik debates. In fact, it was her unwavering commitment to women's economic independence that gave her a basis to consistently defend women's sexual freedom, rather than succumbing to reliance on sexual purity and monogamy as had Christabel Pankhurst and Engels. Kollontai argued that humanity was living through 'an acute sexual crisis', that 'sexual problems are undoubtedly some of the most crucial' and becoming 'an urgent and burning issue'. Her hostility to marriage was revealed by her arguments against criminalisation in the fight against prostitution: if prostitutes were arrested, so too should all legal wives 'who are maintained by their husbands'; if the guilty party was the client 'who buys a woman's favours . . . the husbands of many legal wives will be guilty'.[298]

But the Bolsheviks' increasing emphasis on discipline and top-down methods militated against Kollontai's approach. Like almost all sex reformers of the time, they initially saw libertarian and medical approaches as in harmony.[299] Yet from the start the two approaches were potentially in conflict. Communists sought both to give Soviet citizens freer and happier lives, and to turn Soviet Russia into a modern power – an urgent necessity, given the hostility of the surrounding capitalist world. As long as both these goals were blocked by

295   Healey 2001, pp. 68, 130, 168–9, 54, 36.
296   Healey 2001, p. 131.
297   Kollontai 1978, pp. 211, 255–6, 142.
298   Kollontai 1978, pp. 237, 271–2.
299   Lauritsen and Thorstad 1995, pp. 71–2 (citing Grigorii Batkis).

religious, feudal and bourgeois sexual prejudices, there was no tension between them. But in the hybrid Soviet society of the New Economic Policy (NEP) in the 1920s, where state ownership co-existed with private firms, the push for economic development entailed adopting a gamut of contemporary capitalist practices. These ranged from top-down, Taylorist management, which Lenin enthusiastically embraced, to the 'scientific' management of sexual life. As more and more emphasis was placed on reshaping society and families to meet the needs of breakneck industrialisation under bureaucratic discipline, especially from 1928 as the NEP gave way to the 'crude instrument' of the five-year plans,[300] the less room people were given to seek happiness in the ways they chose.

By the mid-1920s, modernising forces were winning out over libertarian ones. The strong influence of Hirschfeld's third sex theories combined with advances in endocrinology to push the Soviet health authorities towards medicalising sexual object choice and gender identity, rather than encouraging universally looser norms.[301] More broadly, by the mid-1920s Kollontai – due to her association in 1920–1 with an anti-bureaucratic opposition current and the lack of resources for the high-quality social services she insisted were indispensable (by 1925 only 3 percent of children received care outside the home) – was isolated. She warned that 'we cling to bourgeois lifestyles' – 'don't touch the family, don't try to change the family!' – and that 'the petty-bourgeois way of life and its ideology is swamping us'.[302] The fifth congress of the World League for Sexual Reform, originally planned for Moscow, had to be postponed and moved to Vienna.[303]

The acme of the Bolsheviks' modernising authoritarianism in the 1920s was their attitude towards sexual practices in the Soviet Caucasus and Central Asia. Lenin and other central Bolshevik leaders had fought hard during the civil war against the tendency of the Tashkent Soviet, a joint Bolshevik-Menshevik institution cut off for months from Soviet European Russia, to reproduce the anti-Muslim discrimination practised by tsarism.[304] But on sexual matters the new Soviet authorities perpetuated the old habit of treating Muslims' ways as 'backward' and 'primitive' – admittedly, an approach they applied even-handedly to the same-sex practices of the Russian Orthodox clergy. As a result, the decriminalisation of same-sex relations in Soviet Russia and the other European soviet

---

300   Hobsbawm 1994, p. 381.
301   Healey 2001, pp. 134–8.
302   Kollontai 1978, pp. 204, 206, 274, 301.
303   Lauritsen and Thorstad 1995, p. 74.
304   Carr 1985, pp. 331–9.

republics was not duplicated in the Caucasian and Central Asian republics, whose penal codes specifically targeted 'crimes constituting survivals of primitive custom'. In this way, the Bolsheviks replicated the Islamophobia of tsarist law enforcement, whose prosecutions for sodomy had disproportionately focused on Muslims, and the more general European colonial habit of setting out to stamp out 'sodomy' among subject peoples. The editors of the *Great Soviet Encyclopedia* also exempted the indigenous peoples of Siberia from their plea in 1930 for tolerance for same-sex practices.[305]

Communists in the 1920s

Outside Russia, Kollontai's radicalism often set the tone for Communists who focused on sexual issues, starting from the best of Kautsky's statements about the need to be the foremost defenders of women and other oppressed people. Specifically, German Communists were the homosexual movement's best allies in the 1920s. In a period when the emerging conceptions of homosexuality and inversion reflected a growing reification of gender and sex, Communists' defence of the rights of inverts and homosexuals suggested the possibility of a sexually free society beyond reification.[306] Unfortunately, the Communists' sexually libertarian period was all too brief, and many opportunities that could have been the source of creative sexual radicalism were doubtless missed.

The heteronormative worldview of the European labour movement was a constant brake on such possibilities. Social Democrats and Communists both succumbed again to the temptation of homophobia when Nazi SA head Ernst Röhm was available as a target. This was in part a response to the policies of middle-class homosexual leaders, who treated Nazis like Röhm with kid gloves. German homosexual activist Kurt Hiller, never a Communist himself, felt obliged to remind his supporters in 1930 that the Communist Party was by far the homosexual movement's most reliable ally in the Reichstag. Yet the homosexual movement in Weimar Germany failed to join in mobilising against fascism, partly in deference to self-identified homosexuals from middle-class

---

305 Healey 2001, pp. 153–4, 158–62, 254, 171.

306 Although the Second and Third Internationals did conceive of the working class in male and heteronormative ways, the history of the pre-Stalinist Marxist left belies Kevin Floyd's blanket assertion that there was a 'fundamental incommensurability' between traditional working-class and anti-heterosexist politics (1998, pp. 189–90).

backgrounds who often shared the conservative or right-wing nationalist politics of their class.[307]

The Communist milieu, in the period before the Stalinisation of Western European Communism, was in fact at least as open to sexual radicalism as other currents in the labour movement at the time. Early Communism, at least for a time, was appealing for many sexual radicals. There are examples from a number of countries, ranging from Stella Browne in England, to Crystal and Max Eastman and Floyd Dell in the US, to Wilhelm Reich in Germany. Browne, for example, a member of the British Communist Party in the early 1920s, repudiated in 1915 any 'wish to slight or depreciate the love-life of the real homosexual', though she did not want to 'force the growth of that habit in heterosexual people'. She also advocated separating female sexuality from motherhood, and questioned whether 'great love is the sole justification of sexual experience'.[308]

Communists' opposition to racism particularly attracted black sexual radicals. In the early 1920s, African-American writer Claude McKay, a leading figure of the Harlem Renaissance who included same-sex themes in his fiction and was active in Parisian homosexual circles,[309] was close to the radical African Blood Brotherhood and frequented the International Socialist Club while in London. He attended both the founding congress of the British Communist Party and the fourth congress of the Communist International.

Communists benefited from the fact that Soviet sexual legislation was widely viewed as enlightened in sex reform circles in the 1920s and that the Soviets played a prominent role in the World League for Sexual Reform. While there were doubtless pressures on sex radicals in the CP to tone down their sexual politics, those pressures were not necessarily greater in the mid-1920s than in other currents that were trying to reach a working-class audience. The German CP was exceptional in the support it gave in 1930–2 to Wilhelm Reich's German Association for Proletarian Sexual Politics (SexPol) – though the CP withdrew its support even before Hitler came to power,[310] and Reich was in any event no advocate of homosexuality.[311]

---

307 Herzer 1995, pp. 206–17.
308 Weeks 1981, pp. 175, 166.
309 Garber 1989, pp. 327, 330.
310 Lauritsen and Thorstad 1995, pp. 76–7.
311 In 'What Is Class Consciousness' (1934), Reich wrote that 'the stronger the homosexual tendency within [a juvenile] and also the more repressed his awareness of sexuality in general, the more easily he will be drawn toward the right' (1972, p. 297).

On the other hand, well into the 1930s at least one Spanish anarchist current held to a sexual puritanism out of keeping with anarchists' later image.[312] Even Goldman, rightly renowned for her defence of homosexuality, was not only discrete about her own passionate liaison in 1912 with Almeda Sperry, but complained in 1928 of lesbians' 'narrowness', calling them 'a crazy lot' whose 'antagonism to the male is almost a disease'.[313] Communist parties of the early and mid-1920s were no more sexually conservative than their social democratic and anarchist rivals.[314] All currents of the workers movement upheld the same basic heterosexual norm.

The variety of views on homosexuality among early Communists is strikingly illustrated in the writings of two heterodox Dutch Communists of the early 1920s: Henriette Roland Holst, a prominent poet and Marxist historian of bourgeois origin, and her close associate Jacques Engels, an activist of working-class origin.[315] Engels's view of homosexuality in his book *The Communist and Sexual Morality* (*De communist en zijn sexueele moraal*) (1926) was very much in keeping with contemporary 'scientific' opinion. Homosexuality was not 'a moral deviation', but an 'illness, which about 2 percent of the population suffers from', he wrote. 'Male homosexuals have feminine habits and inclinations, including in non-sexual questions ... Their sexual desires are oriented towards normal men, whose "wives" they want to be'. Engels called 'the elimination of the need to hide sexual relations of an unusual character ... one of the first preconditions for a healthy sex life and a healthy sexual morality'. He ended up making a backhanded case for a sort of same-sex marriage. 'Society can consider itself lucky when homosexuals have sexual relationships with each other, *thus preventing their having children with the same illness*', he reasoned, with typically eugenic logic.[316]

Roland Holst by contrast, though a close ally of Engels on many issues, had a number of supportive personal friendships with same-sex couples who did not necessarily fit the mould that Engels would have put them in. She wrote, for example, of the openly lesbian sculptor Saar de Sweet and her partner Emilie van Kerkhof, 'One cannot imagine any better neighbours than these two women'.[317] Roland Holst's and Engels's apparently divergent notions on homosexuality illustrate how gender and sexual roles were more polarised for longer

---

312   Cleminson 1995.

313   Faderman 1991, pp. 33–4.

314   On Dutch social democracy, for example, see Hekma 1995; on the US Socialist Party, see Battan 2004; on the British Labour Party, see Hall 2004.

315   Drucker 2004, p. 82.

316   Engels 1926, pp. 96–8, 168.

317   Etty 1996, pp. 158–9.

historical periods in working-class milieus, making a working-class Communist like Engels more likely to subscribe to a third sex-type theory of homosexuality than an elite Communist like Roland Holst. Nothing in either Holst's or Engels's work suggested that same-sex desires or relationships were of equal value to cross-sex ones. But then such a position was virtually unknown in their time, even in the work of an openly homosexual radical like Carpenter.

Libertarian Marxist influence extended in the 1920s as far as Japan, where the poet Yosano Akiko and the writer Miyamoto Yuriko celebrated 'woman's love for woman [as] part of a political and personal stance regarding women's equality and worth'.[318] However, almost all other voices combining Communism and sexual radicalism in the 1920s seem to have been European. Perhaps future researchers will find evidence of some isolated South African Communist's joining in miners' defence of their mine marriages, or of an Algerian Communist's grappling with same-sex intergenerational love. But Communism was only beginning to establish beachheads in the colonial world in the 1920s. In South Africa in the 1920s, for example, the early Communist movement was largely white, its Africanisation only beginning. In Latin America, José Carlos Mariateguí was exceptional in advocating a Communist orientation towards indigenous people.

Most of Communism's major breakthroughs in the dependent world would occur only in later decades, when the movement, thoroughly Stalinised, had adopted a lockstep model of stage-by-stage 'progress', in which non-reified same-sex patterns were denounced as 'backward' or 'degenerate'. Even in the 1920s, despite Lenin's battle against other Communists' colonial attitudes and Kollontai's against their sexual conservatism, the movement's abiding Eurocentrism and heteronormativity militated against a genuinely radical Communist sexual politics.

Reaction

The distinctive, hybrid same-sex subculture characteristic of the classical imperialist period in Europe was decimated by a new wave of repression following the outbreak of the economic crisis of the 1930s. In response to the deepening capitalist crisis of the 1930s, reactionary movements aimed to re-launch capitalism on a new basis by suppressing or regimenting labour, carrying out a systematic racist and nationalist programme and reinforcing the power of the state. They also had gender and sexual dimensions. Feminism

318 Schalow 1996, pp. 16–17.

and homosexuality were consistently viewed as enemies of these movements, and of their regimes once they took power. The proclaimed goal of one Italian fascist to restore to Italian men 'the warrior tradition of our race' was common to all these movements and regimes. 'The idea was to remake (male) human nature, to create a new type of man'.[319]

This was true of fascist and semi-fascist regimes in Europe – hostility to contraception, abortion and homosexuality were '*the* distinctive markers of fascist sexual politics'[320] – but also of nationalist dictatorships in dominated countries. It was true of not only those that allied with European fascism, but also those that allied with its supposedly democratic adversaries, and true of both those backed by the US during the Cold War and those that defined themselves as anti-imperialist. Even in bourgeois democracies in imperialist countries from the 1930s to the 1950s, the trend – especially but not only under conservative governments – was towards defence of a modernised version of unequal gender roles and of the newly established heterosexual norm.

The repression carried out by the Nazi regime is by now well known. Its spokespeople openly declared, 'The German uprising is a male phenomenon', drawing the corollary in 1928 that 'love between men or between women', like 'anything that emasculates our people ... we reject'.[321] Hirschfeld's Institute for Sexual Science was raided and its library burned in May 1933. At first a distinction seemed to be made between the left-leaning, gender-dissident community around Hirschfeld and the right-leaning, aggressively masculine gay circles around the Community of the Special, prominently represented in the new regime by Nazi SA head Röhm. However, Röhm was linked to the wing of Nazism that adopted an ostensibly anti-capitalist stance; Hitler's break with him in June-July 1934 began a general reign of terror against all same-sex practices. In 1935, Paragraph 175 was supplemented by a new provision criminalising even non-physical expressions of same-sex eroticism. Ultimately, about 100,000 men were prosecuted under these laws, close to half convicted, and thousands sent to concentration camps, where an estimated 5,000–10,000 died.[322]

Nazi sexual politics was not only viciously anti-homosexual, but also emphatically pro-heterosexual, as Dagmar Herzog has explained. 'For avowedly heterosexual, non-disabled non-Jews ... Nazi policy and practice turned out to be anything but sexually repressive'. Their overall goal was to reinvent sex as

---

319   Herzog 2011, pp. 61–2.

320   Herzog 2011, p. 60.

321   Haeberle 1989, p. 374.

322   Lauritsen and Thorstad 1995, pp. 44–9; Herzog 2011, pp. 72–4.

'an "Aryan" privilege'. By the early 1940s, the regime was openly encouraging premarital and extramarital sex, not only for the purposes of Aryan reproduction but also for pleasure.[323] In this sense, fascists were very unlike traditional conservatives; they were 'the revolutionaries of counter-revolution'.[324]

Campaigns against homosexuality similar to the Nazis' were carried out, though with less ferocity, under other fascist and semi-fascist regimes. In Italy, several thousand men were incarcerated for homosexuality, despite the lack of any specific law against it, in penal colonies, political concentration camps and local jails. In France, Pétain's Vichy regime in 1942 criminalised sexual acts between adults and people of the same sex under the age of 21. New repressive laws were also adopted in German-occupied regions defined as 'Aryan'; consensual adult homosexuality was banned in the Netherlands, for instance.[325]

In a cruel irony, the Stalinist regime in the Soviet Union repressed homosexuality as well, in the interests of bureaucratic rule but partly in the name of anti-fascism. Bolshevik policies of inconsistent toleration came to an end in the early 1930s with the consolidation of Stalinism. The Stalinist regime preserved the basic framework of inversion through which the Bolsheviks had seen sex and gender nonconformity in the 1920s. But whereas the attitude in the 1920s had been generally tolerant, the top-down, authoritarian industrialisation of the 1930s was seen as requiring of men a hyper-masculinity from which no deviation was accepted. Effeminate men – and men attracted to other men were generally associated with effeminacy – were viewed as shirking the heavy labour demanded by the five-year plans. Women's sexuality too was now 'subject to demands determined wholly by masculinist and natalist regime goals' (i.e. motherhood combined with waged labour). From 1929 on, an increasing number of campaigns were launched against the 'socially anomalous', which included prostitutes and gender dissenters. The People's Commissariat of Health was reorganised to put priority on fitting workers for labour, its leadership was replaced, and all the competing medical theories that had served to explain and legitimise same-sex sexualities – whether biological or psychological – fell into complete official disfavour. In 1933–4, male same-sex practices were re-criminalised throughout the USSR; in January 1934, there were mass arrests of men accused of them.[326]

---

323 Herzog 2011, pp. 67–70, 72–4.
324 Hobsbawm 1994, p. 117.
325 Herzog 2011, pp. 65–6, 63, 74.
326 Healey 2001, pp. 172–8, 255, 183–8; Lauritsen and Thorstad 1995, pp. 77–8.

This was the culminating act of 'a virtual moral counter-revolution'.[327] Court records provide evidence of the drive for labour discipline and thus productive manhood (reminiscent of mid-nineteenth-century Western European and North American gender roles) that underlay the Stalinist suppression of same-sex practices. One 1935 court ruling stated that the law was directed 'against sodomy not in the narrow meaning of the term, but against sodomy as an anti-social system'. After the initial wave of repression, courts often acquitted defendants who were not part of a 'closely tied group', or simply because they were married. Although the documentary record does not show this clearly, this pattern of persecution probably had a harsher impact on gender-dissident men and less on men perceived as more masculine. These more masculine men, often occupying useful positions in the workforce, were often given opportunities 'to rework ourselves, to foster in ourselves the new man... and new attitudes toward... daily life'.[328]

The link between the Stalinist crackdown on same-sex practices and the drive for disciplined and productive manhood is also suggested by the fact that it targeted lesbians far less. Same-sex acts between women were in fact not criminalised. Early Bolshevik tolerance towards productive, disciplined, masculinised women was sustained to a certain extent under Stalinism, as women's employment increased massively. Little attention was paid to stamping out lesbianism as such, although there was an occasional trial for lesbian seduction of a minor. At the same time, however, large families were encouraged, 'mistresses of the great Soviet home' praised, and women who shirked motherhood subjected to intense scrutiny and condemnation.[329]

In the Stalinist USSR, as in other parts of the world, sexual repression was linked to racism and nationalism. The drive to assimilate the Muslim regions to the predominant Russian culture built on but went beyond the Islamophobia present in earlier Bolshevik policies. At the same time, Stalinist anti-same-sex ideology associated gender and sexual nonconformity with the decadent West, fostering folkloric national identities that broke with the earlier Bolshevik emphasis on working-class internationalism.

The about-face on sexual issues in the USSR in the early 1930s was reflected within a few years in the international Communist movement, which was reduced almost everywhere to an instrument of Soviet foreign policy. The turn-about was glaring in Germany, where the Communist Party had in the 1920s been the staunchest champion of decriminalisation. After first denouncing in

---

327   Hobsbawm 1994, p. 316.
328   Healey 2001, pp. 192, 221–3, 227.
329   Healey 2001, pp. 196–202, 223–8.

1931 the Social Democratic press's attacks on Röhm's Nazi same-sex coterie, the Communist press joined in with a vengeance in 1932. After the Reichstag fire in February 1933, the Communists used left-wing arsonist Marinus van der Lubbe's homosexuality as a reason to take its distance from him and link him to the Nazis. From that point, Communists worldwide declared, 'Destroy the homosexuals – fascism will disappear'.[330]

The Communists' turn to homophobic politics contributed to a massive setback to sexual radicalism on the left. The World League for Sexual Reform dissolved in 1935 when its two remaining presidents adopted opposite attitudes on its future course, one favouring an apolitical stance, the other favouring an alliance with international socialism.[331]

Meanwhile, as the crisis of capitalism intensified and even capitalist democracies resorted to top-down economic interventionism and nationalism, repression of homosexuality was not limited to fascist or even dictatorial regimes. Prosecutions increased in Britain in the 1930s, for example.[332] While Germans fled to Switzerland to escape the Nazi persecution of homosexuality, the Swiss authorities harassed the publishers of the magazine *Freundschafts-Banner*.[333] In the US, the abolition of Prohibition in 1933 and the establishment of a new system of bar regulation provided the impetus for systematic crackdowns on homosexual gathering places.[334] In 1941, the US army and navy for the first time made it their policy 'to keep all homosexuals out of the service', and thousands of men received 'blue discharges' for homosexuality during the war.[335]

Open homosexuals played a role in anti-fascist resistance during the war, like the Dutch socialist Jef Last and the French surrealists Claude Cahun and Marcel Moore.[336] Yet the defeat of the fascist powers in the Second World War did not result in any sharp, lasting decrease in repression. The relative stability of the post-war period rested in part on the wartime discipline that had been instilled in the working class and general population, which tended to foster persistent sexual conservatism. In Europe, many interwar sex rights activists

---

330   Healey 2001, pp. 182–4.
331   Lauritsen and Thorstad 1995, p. 50.
332   Weeks 1981, p. 220.
333   Herzog 2011, pp. 75, 81.
334   Chauncey 1994, pp. 173, 334–49.
335   Bérubé 1989, pp. 387–9. This suggests that US gay historians' emphasis on the Second World War as 'a nationwide coming-out experience [that] properly marks the beginning of the nation's ... modern gay history' (D'Emilio 1989, p. 458) is somewhat overstated.
336   Latimer 2005, pp. 139–40, 144.

had been forced into exile or killed. This made it easier for Christian Democrats and other conservatives to 'present the re-establishment of traditional mores as a postfascist imperative.... Associating Nazism with sexual libertinism, promiscuity, and excess, the churches presented the restoration of sexual conservatism as an anti-Nazi program'. In West Germany and Austria, men who had been sent to Nazi camps for same-sex activity were denied reparations, pensions or reinstatement in their former jobs, and sometimes re-imprisoned. Post-war French governments retained the Vichy law criminalising male-male sex with anyone under 21 years of age; as late as 1960, the French National Assembly almost unanimously declared homosexuality a 'social scourge'.[337] And in England and Wales, the number of indictable male same-sex offences increased five-fold from the early 1940s to 1955.[338]

Anti-homosexual repression intensified in the US military with the end of the war, with about 500 women purged for lesbianism from the US forces occupying Japan, with similar purges taking place at US bases in Europe and elsewhere in Asia.[339] Soon civilians too were subjected to screening, with 1,700 people being denied federal employment in 1947–50 on grounds of homosexuality. In the 1950s, the Cold War climate produced a new wave of repression and witch-hunting, especially in the US. By the early 1950s, an average of 2,000 people a year were being purged from the armed forces for homosexuality.[340] Dismissals from federal civilian posts for homosexuality increased twelve-fold from the pre-1950 rate. Raids on gays bars led to thousands of arrests across the country each year;[341] a survey by the Institute of Sex Research showed that 20 percent of male homosexual respondents had had trouble with the police.[342] Symptomatically, the 1952 US McCarren Immigration and Naturalization Act, which in racial terms began a hesitant transition to greater ostensible liberalism, in sexual terms added new restrictions on homosexuals.[343] In Canada too, homosexuals were purged as a matter of policy from the federal civil service and Royal Canadian Mounted Police from the late 1940s to the early 1960s.[344]

---

337 Herzog 2011, pp. 153, 99, 119, 117, 120.
338 Weeks 1981, p. 239.
339 Bérubé 1989, p. 392.
340 D'Emilio 1983b, p. 44.
341 D'Emilio and Freedman 1997, pp. 293–4.
342 D'Emilio 1983b, p. 50.
343 Puar 2007, p. 119. Siobhan Somerville has commented that at this point sexuality replaced race in articulating 'the underlying fantasy of national purification – an unadulterated Americanness' (Meyerowitz 2002, p. 1280, n. 15).
344 Kinsman 1987, p. 121.

In Brazil, the authoritarian 'New State' headed by Gétulio Vargas from 1937 to 1945 promoted a ' "new" masculinity, which idealized strength, youth, and power'. Brazilian writings of this period linked homosexuality to sadism and both to African ancestry, and 'evoked racial anxiety, namely, the ominous image of dark, sinister forces preying on the purity of innocent, white Brazilian youth'. Although Brazilians avoided drawing the sharp racial divides characteristic of the US, Brazilians of partly African ancestry often tried to 'whiten' themselves, and sexologists particularly in the 1930s tended to 'de-whiten' the homosexuals they studied, 'implying that dark-skinned people were more likely to be homosexuals'.[345]

In hindsight, the US in particular was being transformed by a new long expansive wave that began at the beginning of the 1940s, several years earlier than in Western Europe and Japan.[346] Yet sexual change, out of synch, lagged behind, as the dominant forces in society worked 'manfully' to preserve or at least mimic the sexual regime of classical imperialism. 'One component of Cold War politics was the drive to reconstruct traditional gender roles and patterns of sexual behavior'.[347] This meant that 'fear of homosexuality kept heterosexual men in line as husbands and breadwinners'.[348] It was now 'almost a patriotic duty, Americans were told, to become "blissfully domestic" and to engage in a historically unprecedented, society-wide celebration of heterosexual romance'. A distorted version of Freudianism became 'the ideological bulwark of the sexual counter-revolution', with every attempt by a woman to escape economic dependence or sexual passivity being diagnosed as 'penis envy'.[349] Neo-Freudians fixated on 'the ability to have a durable intimate relationship with a person of the opposite sex' as *the* sign of psychic health, and agreed that homosexuals – 'the separate category of person that Sigmund Freud had insisted they were not' – were disturbed and needed to be cured.[350]

The gender conservatism of the 1950s had a major impact on attempts to organise homosexuals. In the US Mattachine Society in 1953 the same people who succeeded in driving its original ex-Communist founders from its leadership, demanding guarantees that they would not be 'infiltrated by Communists', also strongly rejected the founders' conception of homosexuals as culturally distinctive. They insisted on social integration 'as men and women whose

---

345   Green 1999a, pp. 142, 122, 73–4.
346   Mandel 1978, p. 145.
347   D'Emilio 1989, p. 459.
348   D'Emilio and Freedman 1997, p. 295 (citing Barbara Ehrenreich).
349   Coontz 2011, p. 68 (citing Betty Friedan).
350   Herzog 2014 (citing Edward S. Tauber).

homosexuality is irrelevant' and whose behaviour was in harmony with the existing 'home, church and state'.[351]

As capitalism emerged after the war from the long series of crises that had battered it from the 1870s to the 1930s, the restructuring that would give it a new relative stability had a lasting impact in several ways on same-sex desire and behaviour. Homosexuality would now develop in close relation to a reconfigured masculinity and femininity, and a newly consolidated culture of heterosexual romance and domesticity. It would rest on a deep divide between white people and the non-whites who formed a growing share of the world working classes, include same-sex patterns that colonialism and semi-colonialism had spread to Latin America, Asia and Africa, and contend with the persecution of same-sex patterns that colonial administrations had instigated. It would be forced to rely on, accept or rebel against the authority of 'scientific' sexology and psychology. And homosexuals would have to resist state repression that was virtually ubiquitous, on both sides of the Cold War, and in dictatorships and democracies alike.

Yet how homosexuality would develop in the post-war world was difficult to foresee. Even in hindsight, it is far from self-evident that gay identity was the wave of the future, and that other same-sex sexual formations were doomed to eventual extinction. To explore this question, however, we need to look at how lesbian/gay identity did take shape, above all in the second half of the twentieth century.

---

351   D'Emilio 1983b, pp. 79, 81.

CHAPTER 2

Fordism and Gay Identity

It was only after the Second World War that the gay/straight binary began to take the form it assumed in North America and Western Europe by the 1970s. The lesbian/gay identity that became dominant in imperialist countries in the 1970s, and in subsequent decades in much of the rest of the world, differed from the many other forms of same-sex identity that had existed in human history or even under capitalism.

Although in its earliest and most working-class forms, lesbian/gay identity overlapped with sexual inversion, its full-fledged form was reserved for people who had both sexual and emotional ties with their own sex; who generally did not conclude cross-sex marriages or form heterosexual families (unlike, say, latter-day gay icon Oscar Wilde); and who did not radically change their gender identity or sex role in adopting a lesbian/gay sexuality (unlike trans-gendered people in a great variety of cultures). In the same-sex relation-ships formed according to this pattern, extending over time from the middle class to a far broader range of the population, both partners considered them-selves part of the same lesbian/gay community, networks and even movement. This would have been a bizarre notion to millions of men around the world who penetrate transwomen or youths without considering themselves gay. It was unsettling to millions of women at the less explicit end of Adrienne Rich's 'lesbian continuum'.[1]

The new same-sex formation depended on the maturation of a new, Fordist regime of accumulation, notably involving rising wages and a welfare state. Fordism also provided a basis for racial liberalism and decolonisation, and a new black militancy, as well as a broader, society-wide transition from old conceptions of manhood and womanhood to a more 'performative' definition of gender, the second wave of feminism, and pervasive sexualisation linked to a commercial scene. These were the conditions for the establishment of a new, 'gay-dominant' same-sex regime, in which transgender and other patterns were marginalised.

In many neo-colonial countries and in the Soviet bloc, China and Cuba, however, the basic conditions for lesbian/gay communities were absent. There

---

1 Adam 1985, p. 658; Rich 1983; Wekker 1999. Fernbach gave an early and clear account of the uniqueness of lesbian/gay identity among historically existing forms of same-sex sexuality (1981, pp. 71–5).

the binary was imposed instead through the promotion of heterosexuality and repression of homosexuality. By the 1960s in Western Europe and the Americas, repression evoked a new wave of resistance – lesbian/gay liberation – linked to socialist, feminist, anti-imperialist and anti-racist movements and to the Nicaraguan, Mexican, Brazilian and South African left. A new gay left briefly challenged the gay/straight divide at the end of the 1960s and in the early 1970s, before the new sexual regime was consolidated in the later 1970s and 1980s.

Lesbian/gay identity thus originally had a dual and contradictory political character. Its foundations were laid almost invisibly and on a modest scale in Western Europe, North America and parts of Latin America in the two decades after the Second World War, through the expansion of a lesbian/homosexual commercial scene and the efforts of small 'homophile' groups. Homophile activists' approach was in continuity with the perspective of pre-war middle-class homosexuals, expressed in patient work in the 1950s to urge 'inverts' to conform to a more respectable model. In this respect, lesbian/gay identity was a precursor of today's gay normality.

But the big breakthrough for lesbian/gay identity in the years after 1968 was partly a break with middle-class homosexuality, inspired by a vision of libera-tion that at least for a few years was inclusive of trans people, hustlers and sexual outlaws generally. Lesbian/gay liberation was also initially consciously inspired by and connected to radical feminism and black and anti-imperialist struggles. By the late 1970s and 1980s (as discussed later in this chapter), radi-cal lesbian/gay politics was having at least a modest impact on the interna-tional radical left, including the Nicaraguan Sandinistas, the Brazilian Workers Party and South African anti-apartheid movements. Though this liberationist impulse was submerged in the 1980s by resurgent gay reformism, it can – and whenever it is uncovered anew, does – still serve as an inspiration for queer radicalism today.

Expansion and Sexualisation

The social backdrop of the post-war decades helps explain the dynamics of emergent lesbian/gay communities. Among the preconditions for their break-through on a mass scale were a general increase in people's living standards and economic security, made possible in part by the expanding welfare state, which made autonomous sexual lives possible for more people than ever before. The breakthrough also reflected a certain relative social homogene-ity in any one country of millions of people who came out around the 1970s, thanks in part to generational bonds and in part to the narrowing of economic divides in the 1950s and 1960s, so that there were fewer barriers to a common sense of identity. And it was made easier by a uniquely favourable political and cultural climate.

The gay/straight binary, absent from the vast array of pre-nineteenth century same-sex sexualities, came to typify the performative organisation of gender under late capitalism, consolidated on a mass scale only after 1945 under Fordism. All this occurred in a brief historical period, more a question of a few decades than of centuries. The 'straight-acting and -appearing gay male' was 'the distinctive creation of the period after the Second World War'.[2] This gay personage was the visible manifestation of the rise of a new same-sex formation.

The consolidation and spread of gay identity, especially among the mass of working-class people, took place to a large extent during what some Marxist economists refer to as the expansive long wave of 1945–73. This was a period in which world output of manufactured goods more than quadrupled and world trade in them grew more than tenfold.[3] It was also a period in which the global imperialist system, despite a largely static dividing line between dominant and dominated countries, changed its form in significant ways. Dozens of Asian and African countries achieved formal political independence, shifting from colonies or semi-colonies to neo-colonial nations that were nonetheless still economically dependent on the imperialist countries as a whole, sometimes closely bound to the former colonial power, and sometimes (as in much of former French Africa) politically and militarily under the old colonial power's thumb. But as part of this process, many Latin American and Asian countries began a massive process of industrialisation and urbanisation. This had major gender and sexual consequences.

As the imperialist powers vied during the Cold War to keep newly independent countries in their economic and geopolitical orbit, they recognised that the earlier blatant racism of their global order had become a liability. Open racism in the imperialist countries thus gradually and officially gave way to racial liberalism, which in Jodi Melamed's description viewed racial inequality as a problem, with solutions focused on 'abstract equality, market individualism, and inclusive civic nationalism'. Racial liberalism became an 'essential organizing discourse' of a system under US global hegemony.[4] With a substantial time lag and obvious major differences, this new ideology facilitated the development of a similar paradigm for lesbian/gay people. Yet like official

2   Halperin 1990, p. 9.
3   Hobsbawm 1994, p. 261.
4   Melamed 2006, pp. 2, 4.

anti-racism, the new rhetoric of sexual equality left many of the structural causes of oppression unaffected, and failed to dismantle the mechanisms by which prejudice was constantly reproduced among millions of the 'less enlightened' and more covertly put into practice by the ostensibly less racist ruling and middle classes.

Emerging gradually after a period of repression from the 1930s to the 1950s,[5] gay identity on a mass scale depended on the growing prosperity of the working and middle classes. It was catalysed by profound cultural changes from the 1940s to the 1970s that prosperity helped make possible. This meant that gay identity was shaped in many ways by the mode of capitalist accumulation that some economists call 'Fordism': specifically by mass consumer societies and welfare states.

After 1945, living standards in capitalist countries went up rapidly under the Fordist order, under which Henry Ford's model of assembly-line car production was extended to many other industries and many other parts of the world.[6] The consequent increases in labour productivity were matched to a large extent with increasing real wages that sustained rising effective demand. Various forms of social insurance cushioned the blows that hit working people during dips in the business cycle. As a result, for the first time masses of working-class people as well as students and others were able to live independently of their families, and give sexual object choice a greater role in their lives and identities.

On a lesser scale, these changes also occurred in many of the Latin American and Asian regions of dependent industrialisation. Following closely on the expansion of homosexual communities in Western Europe and North America in the 1950s and 1960s, and their displacement of pre-existing communities of 'inverts', such communities expanded as well in Argentina, Brazil and Mexico, despite interruptions due to social and sexual repression by dictatorships in the 1960s and 1970s. Though inflected by economic and cultural differences and less politicised, similar processes took place in Asian countries, both imperialist countries like Japan and dependent ones like Thailand.

These changes affected women as well as men, reflecting major changes under Fordism in the gender order. Despite the conservative ideology of the post-Second World War years and persistent legal obstacles – in France, for example, wives needed their husbands' permission to work until 1965[7] – women's labour force participation expanded in many countries beginning in

---

5 See, for example, Chauncey 1994, pp. 334–46.
6 Hobsbawm 1994, pp. 263–4.
7 Latimer 2005, p. 147, n. 20.

the 1950s. By the 1960s, middle-class women were also increasingly likely to work for wages. Women's levels of education rose too; by 1980, in many countries women were as likely as men to attend institutions of higher education,[8] and to enjoy the independence that this often conferred. These changes increased people's ability to imagine that women who were economically and even sexually independent might still be 'feminine', and that men who could no longer fulfil the role of *pater familias* and sole breadwinner might still be 'masculine'. In the 1950s, the largely middle-class lesbians and male homosexuals who led fledgling 'homophile' groups in Western Europe and North America set out to remould their constituencies in this framework as proper feminine women and masculine men. The breakthroughs of second-wave feminism in the 1960s (discussed later in this chapter) helped to vastly expand the scope for lesbian/gay community formation.

Although gays have often been perceived as more preoccupied by sex than others, the sexual self-definition at the heart of the new lesbian/gay identity did not make lesbian/gay people fundamentally different from many of the straight people around them. Following the rise of heterosexual romance beginning in the late nineteenth century, marriage and society in general were more explicitly and pervasively sexualised in the second half of the twentieth. Foreshadowed in the advertising boom of the 1920s, this trend burst out full-fledged in the post-Second World War expansive long wave. It began in the US, where a motivational psychologist explained that the challenge facing business was 'permitting the average American to feel moral ... even when he is spending' and adopting a 'hedonistic approach to his life'. The result was a 'large-scale invasion by entrepreneurs into the field of sex'. The 'capitalist impulse seized upon sexual desire as an unmet need that the marketplace could fill'. By the 1980s, the sex industry – narrowly defined as prostitution and pornography – was a multi-billion-dollar sector, while openly erotic images, male and female, were used to sell everything from jeans to phones.[9]

And going beyond the sex industry narrowly defined, repressively sublimated desire became the focus of much of cultural production: most books read for pleasure came to consist of 'mainly love-stories for women, thrillers of various kinds for men and perhaps, in the era of liberalization, some erotica or pornography'.[10] Beginning from the 1950s and burgeoning from the 1970s, a sex industry niche market of physique magazines, bars, bathhouses and

8   Hobsbawm 1994, pp. 310–11.
9   D'Emilio and Freedman 1997, pp. 305, 327–9.
10   Hobsbawm 1994, p. 513.

hustlers – and later videos, clothing, paraphernalia and a variety of novels – extended this process on a modest scale to homosexuals.

The dynamic of capitalist societies, as Jamie Gough and Mike McNair have pointed out, was increasingly for people to 'enter into sexual relations with each other as "free" individuals'. Yet there were continuous tensions between this growing sexualisation and atomisation of society, on the one hand, and the family institution that remained indispensable for reproduction (childcare, housework and inheritance), on the other.[11] This made sexualisation a problem in the eyes of millions of people.

If the sexualisation of human relations and society had meant a genuine eroticisation of everyday life, it would have been welcome. In reality, however, the sexualisation of life under Fordism entailed what Herbert Marcuse analysed as 'repressive desublimation', integrating sex into 'work and public relations' and thereby making it 'more susceptible to (controlled) satisfaction'.[12] It saw the embedding of sexual life in the consumer market and a set of unequal social relations, including class inequality, gender inequality, the heterosexual norm, and the family as a reproductive and consuming unit within a capitalist national space. In an economically dominated country like Indonesia, sexualisation meant the 'heterosexualisation' of the labour force, and it reinforced the 'family principle' as a core element of state ideology, with 'the family' consisting of 'husband, wife, and two children, with a car, a home with smooth white tile floors, a television set, and other paraphernalia of the new middle class'.[13] In an imperialist country like Canada, the growth of the welfare state anchored defence of the 'traditional' family even more in state policy, helping to buttress institutionalised heterosexuality.[14]

The objectification entailed in sexuality is itself neutral or even positive. Objectification – the alternate adoption of subject and object positions in an interplay between different human individuals – is inherent to sexuality. It was a sign of progress that in the late twentieth century billions of human beings decreasingly saw themselves as slaves to tradition and the imperatives of survival, and increasingly as 'beings defined by their pursuit of individual desire, including desires hitherto prohibited or frowned on'. Classical Marxism too 'envisaged the complete liberation and self-fulfilment of the individual'.[15] Criticising György Lukács's moralising tone in History and Class Consciousness,

---

11   Gough and MacNair 1985, pp. 48–9.
12   Marcuse 1964, p. 75.
13   Boellstorff 1999, p. 492.
14   Kinsman 1987, pp. 54–5.
15   Hobsbawm 1994, pp. 334, 467.

with his 'insistence that the objectification of persons is, by definition, dehumanizing', Kevin Floyd has pointed out the political importance of sexual practices that 'legitimate the use of the body as a pleasurable means'.[16] As Marx and Engels once remarked, those who entirely reject the treatment of human beings as objects combat 'not merely love but everything living, everything which is immediate, every sensuous experience, any and every *real* experience'.[17] Moreover, collective agency, far from being in conflict with objectification, in fact entails it.

Under capitalism, however, sexualisation has entailed not only objectification, but also reification, the treatment of humans as mere things and the petrifaction of specific roles and sexual identities, which is *not* inherent to sexuality.[18] And the connection between humans as things and other things for sale is never far away. Sex 'comes to define that which the consumer lacks'.[19]

Roots of Gay Identity

Under Fordism, the market was thus stimulating desire and romance in unprecedented ways. Yet at the same time, limits had to be placed on the expression of desire so that production and reproduction could carry on smoothly. Particularly given the uncertainties of life in the constant flux of capitalist society, people needed the security of stable relationships and families so that they could go to work in the morning with reasonable confidence that they would be cared for. The result was Marcuse's 'repressive desublimation': an uneasy combination of sexual freedom with a channelling of sexuality into forms

---

16 Floyd 2006, pp. 399–400. Floyd later (2009, p. 23) mentioned Lukács's 1967 self-criticism, in which Lukács acknowledged that objectification 'cannot be eliminated from human life in society' and is present in 'liberation as much as enslavement' (Lukács 1972, p. xxiv).

17 Marx and Engels 1975, p. 27.

18 Floyd has argued that sexual reification is a 'condition of possibility for... sexually non-normative discourses, practices, sites, subjectivities, imaginaries, collective formations, and collective aspirations' (2009, pp. 74–5). Having earlier recalled Lukács's later criticism of the conflation of objectification and reification in his *History and Class Consciousness*, Floyd here reproduced the conflation upside down: whereas Lukács rejected both objectification and reification, Floyd celebrated them both. It is true, as Floyd has argued, that the gay/straight binary was crucial to the development of twentieth-century gay politics (1998, p. 172). But the capital-labour relation was similarly crucial to the development of working-class politics. This does not mean that the gay/straight binary is anything to cheer about, any more so than capital's exploitation of labour.

19 Klotz 2006, p. 410.

compatible with the productive and reproductive order.[20] One form that this channelling took was fixed sexual identities: something narrower than free-floating erotic energy, but broader than desire for a specific person.

Building on the hetero/homo binary that had been taking shape for a century, the lesbian/gay identity that took shape in imperialist countries by the 1970s was a very specific form of sexual identity. Reciprocal sexual relationships between self-identified lesbian women or between self-identified gay men, in which 'masculine' and 'feminine' roles did not necessarily determine sexual identity, gradually became dominant in LGBT communities internationally. Although many lesbians and gay men continued to choose partners who differed from them 'in age or race or nationality or body type or preferred sexual role, reciprocal relations between adults and even persons of similar ages' became the norm for lesbian/gay male relationships 'in most bourgeois societies'.[21] With a range of differences across different societies that this chapter will explore, a 'new type of homosexuality' evolved, in which '*difference* (of age, class or gender behavior)' was no longer the 'erotic draw'. Gay men in particular developed 'a more masculine personal style' while seeking sex and relationships with other gay-identified men.[22]

Vital to sustaining a same-sex community organised along these lines was unprecedented prosperity – a prosperity that in part reflected a specific relationship of class forces. The role of popular resistance in defeating fascism had strengthened labour movements and democracies in post-war imperialist countries, while the role of mobilisation in winning political independence and sometimes a degree of economic independence in former colonies had produced populist regimes committed to fulfilling mass aspirations for better lives. As a result, post-war working-class living standards kept pace with rapidly rising productivity, and labour movements had more room for organising. This helped create a virtuous circle of rising wages and profits.

By the 1960s, the average level of unemployment in Western Europe was 1.5 percent.[23] Full employment meant more job opportunities for some people, including some homosexuals, who had previously been marginalised. And wages and living standards rose accordingly, with a host of social and sexual changes as a result. 'In these days of frozen foods ... compact apartments, modern innovations, and female independence, there is no reason why a woman should have to look to a man for food and shelter', one US lesbian wrote as early

---

20   Gough and MacNair 1985, p. 51.
21   Halperin 2002, pp. 139–40.
22   Herzog 2011, p. 123.
23   Hobsbawm 1994, p. 259.

as 1947. 'Never before have circumstances and conditions been so suitable for those of lesbian tendencies'.[24]

Propitious conditions did not consist of higher incomes alone. They also included unprecedented urbanisation: 42 percent of the world's population was urban by the mid-1980s, and in both imperialist and dependent countries public transport networks made urban residents more mobile than ever before. They included a massive extension of education: students in higher education expanded as a share of the total population from a tenth of a percent even in Germany, France and Britain before 1939, to 2 or 3 percent or more by the 1980s even in Peru, the Philippines and Ecuador. Whatever the educators' intentions, this helped people question received ideas and norms. It also spread the influence of middle-class homosexuality among people of working-class origin. They could learn at university 'how to talk politically and intellectually' about their homosexuality – giving their parents and peers a sense that they 'had entered elite worlds that were changing [them] beyond recognition'.[25]

Mainly but not exclusively in imperialist countries, the new conditions also included state welfare programmes – which by the late 1970s in some imperialist countries cost more than 60 percent of total state budgets – that dramatically decreased people's reliance on their traditional families.[26] The expansion of a social safety net made people less dependent on parents to support them when they were young, sick, disabled or unemployed, on spouses to help pay the rent, and on children to save them from poverty in old age.

The homogeneity of 1970s lesbian/gay communities was, of course, relative. Although they emerged early on in some Latin American countries, as well as in North America and Europe, they were more restricted and differentiated in the dependent world than in imperialist countries. Class, racial, gender and sexual differences always existed, and greater openness highlighted conflicts between gay employers and employees, gay landlords and tenants, gay men and lesbians, whites and blacks.[27] In retrospect, the model of reciprocal lesbian/gay sexuality was 'never perfectly embodied by anyone' and did not succeed for long in establishing a pattern 'wholly defined by sexual object-choice'.[28]

Same-sex relationships in which gender roles were less polarised nonetheless gradually became the norm internationally in the late twentieth century. Changes in working-class family structures and gender roles were key to

---

24   Faderman 1991, p. 129.
25   Bérubé 1997, pp. 58–9.
26   Hobsbawm 1994, pp. 293–5, 284.
27   D'Emilio 1989, p. 468.
28   Halperin 2002, p. 22.

allowing this to happen. For the first time since the mid-to-late nineteenth century – when the family wage had become a cherished ideal, and sometimes a reality, for broad working-class layers – the Second World War made waged work at least temporarily normal in many countries for even respectable working-class and middle-class women. Interrupted in the late 1940s, the increase in women's paid employment resumed and accelerated in the 1950s, so that in the US by 1955 a higher percentage of women worked for wages than ever had during the war. A combination of black poverty and long-standing African-American tradition made waged labour even more common among black women.[29] By 1981, women in the US were 35 percent of college and university teachers, almost 40 percent of bank officers, and almost 50 percent of real-estate brokers. Similar trends were at work not only in Western Europe, but even in many dependent countries: in Mauritius, for example, women's share in the waged workforce rose from very low levels to over 60 percent by the mid-1980s.[30]

Such changes came a bit later to European countries that experienced the war mainly as passive victims of German occupation. In the Netherlands, for example, married women's labour-force participation rates were still exceptionally low in the 1950s, while families were very tight-knit. Perhaps the lack of McCarthyist-style repression in such countries reflected the felt security of heterosexual family life, on which isolated homophile groups made little impression. The Netherlands, in any event, made up for lost time in the 1960s and 1970s.

Although as late as the 1960s, social programmes in imperialist countries tended to assume a male-breadwinner family – as in Daniel Patrick Moynihan's notorious 1965 report arguing that the way out of poverty for African-Americans led through escaping the 'tangle of pathology' towards 'the establishment of a stable Negro family structure' – from the 1970s both social policy and the capitalist economy increasingly took account of and even promoted lasting female participation in waged work.[31] By 'cheapening commodities... and lowering fertility', capitalist development 'reduced the domestic labor time necessary for reproduction', allowing women to work both inside and outside the home.[32] At the same time, by organising household consumption, women became 'key to the penetration of the family by the "new capitalism"'.[33]

---

29   Coontz 2011, pp. 59, 121–3.
30   Hobsbawm 1994, pp. 317, 311.
31   Moynihan 1965; Self 2012.
32   Brenner 2000, pp. 37, 223.
33   Weeks 1981, p. 257.

The increasing gender and racial diversity of the working class was most marked in the economic sectors that were growing most rapidly in imperialist countries by the 1960s, namely, the public and service sectors. In the US, 4 million workers were unionised between 1959 and 1980 in the public sector alone.[34] Although sectors like healthcare relied on and exploited women's traditional roles, in other ways gender and sexual norms were sometimes less solidly entrenched in the public and service sectors than in blue-collar industries. Organising in these sectors increasingly involved focusing on issues with links to racial and gender identity: pay equity for women, comparable worth, childcare, non-discrimination, affirmative action.[35] At the same time, the growing numbers of women working in blue-collar jobs, often segregated in women-only units with lower pay, increasingly took militant action in the 1960s as well, as in the Ford women machinists' equal pay strike of 1968.[36]

In the interwar years in some imperialist countries, a shift to more corporate and bureaucratic forms of capitalism had begun a shift among some middle-class people from conceptions of 'manhood' and 'womanliness' to forms of masculinity and femininity more focused on behaviour, dress and consumption. But despite the questioning of gender roles by the most radical strand of the women's movement (including someone like Alexandra Kollontai), and Freud's daring assertion that gender was not pre-given, this 'performative' form of gender remained a minority phenomenon before the Second World War. Under Fordism, it spread rapidly. Post-war capitalism needed many more managers and professionals, which the mushrooming of higher education produced. The swelling public and service sectors were more conducive to performative gender. And even the industrial working class was more thoroughly incorporated into corporate and bureaucratic structures, and more permeated by a consumer culture that moulded feminine and masculine styles in ways that responded to advertising and increased economic demand.

This helped make a dent in the pronounced gender polarisation that had been characteristic of both working-class heterosexuality and homosexuality in the first decades of the twentieth century. Differences between men and women became less significant as women increasingly not only worked for wages but wore trousers and, by the early 1960s, could have premarital sex or divorce with less social stigma. An anthropologist like Margaret Mead reflected these changes by pointing out that 'sex roles' varied from one society to the next. Following sexologist John Money's coinage in 1955, scholars increasingly

---

34   Krupat 1999, p. 15.
35   Krupat 1999, p. 16.
36   Duggan 2013, p. 11.

adopted the word 'gender' to distinguish social masculinity and femininity from biological sex. Feminists followed suit in the 1970s,[37] even more so following an influential article by Joan Scott in 1986.[38]

Traditional boundaries between male and female were stubbornly defended, entailing as they did all sorts of male social and legal benefits – as a committee of the New York Academy of Medicine explicitly noted in a 1966 opinion opposing any change in the birth certificate of a post-operative transsexual.[39] But alongside lingering traditionalism came the rapid spread of performative expressions of gender, together with 'greater opportunities for consumerism, increased aspirations for fun, and the rise of a romantic model of marriage, accompanied by the growing acceptability of premarital sex'.[40] In a country like Britain, young people's real wages rose at twice the rate of average real wages, and greater prosperity contributed to falling ages of sexual maturity.[41] More generally, mass education created a social layer of youth larger than ever before in human history, which besides being seen as a key market share also constituted a technological, cultural – and sexual – cutting edge.[42]

The combination of increased economic possibilities and a reconfiguration of gender roles helped many more people in imperialist countries in the 1950s and 1960s shape a sexually hedonistic culture extending beyond the largely middle-class limits of the earlier nonconformist milieu of the 1910s and 1920s. The changes freed growing numbers of women to assert their perceived sexual needs, though 'largely within a heterosexual framework and in the terms allowed by commercialism'.[43] By the early 1960s in the US, *Cosmopolitan* editor Helen Gurley Brown was relegating marriage to the role of 'insurance for the *worst* years of your life', while in the best years men were 'cheaper emotionally and a lot more fun by the dozen'.[44] Heterosexuality was clearly no longer mainly procreative; the search for sexual pleasure was increasingly central.[45]

Changing attitudes towards sex and relationships were dramatically reflected in divorce rates, which rose in England and Wales from one divorce for every 58 weddings in 1938, to one for every 2.2 weddings in the mid-1980s.

---

37   Meyerowitz 2002, pp. 3, 114–18, 128, 262–3.
38   Scott 1986.
39   Meyerowitz 2002, pp. 242–5.
40   Herzog 2011, p. 106.
41   Weeks 1981, p. 252.
42   Hobsbawm 1994, pp. 326–8.
43   Weeks 1981, p. 258.
44   D'Emilio and Freedman 1997, pp. 303–4.
45   D'Emilio 1983b, p. 248.

In Italy, divorce became legal in 1970, as did the sale of contraceptives in 1971, and abortion in 1978.[46] For a time in the 1960s and 1970s in many imperialist countries, 'mini skirts, the pill, group sex [and] mate swapping' made it almost seem as if straights were rivalling gays in sexual trailblazing. For a time in the 1960s, in fact, US lesbians seemed 'more conservative than heterosexual society had become'[47] – though lesbians were in a sense freer, as the sexual revolution initially put pressure on straight women to give up their 'right to say no' to men. Women did at least gain the right to say yes: from fewer than a quarter in the 1950s, the proportion of people in the US accepting cross-sex premarital sex rose to three-quarters by the 1970s. Unmarried heterosexual cohabitation became three times more common in the US in the 1970s than it had been in 1960, and doubled again from 1980 to the mid-1990s.[48]

The counterculture reflected the same trends in intensified form, with one US newsweekly reporting, 'There are no hippies who believe in chastity, or look askance at marital infidelity, or see even marriage itself as a virtue'.[49] Yet the counterculture too could be blatantly sexist, as when male hippies in Berkeley's People's Park demanded 'Free Land, Free Dope, Free Women'.[50] In Britain as well, personal liberation and general eroticisation had its limits, with sex roles rarely challenged and sexual liberation 'confined to the heterosexual libido'.[51]

Yet same-sex sexual relations burgeoned in these years. Within the broader hedonistic culture it became possible for a growing minority to form same-sex relationships and networks. Since no extensive surveys were published before the Second World War, it is hard to draw comparisons about the number of same-sex relationships in one period as compared to another. But the surveys that began to appear after the war, whether or not they registered any substantive change, at least brought a reality to light that surprised most contemporaries. In 1948, Alfred Kinsey's study of US male sexuality found that 50 percent of his subjects acknowledged experiencing same-sex attraction, over a third had had an adult same-sex encounter resulting in orgasm, and one in eight had had predominantly same-sex experience for at least a three-year period;[52] for women the figures were 28 percent, 13 percent and somewhat under half

---

46   Hobsbawm 1994, pp. 321, 323.
47   Faderman 1991, pp. 201, 186.
48   D'Emilio and Freedman 1997, pp. 309, 333, 331, 370.
49   D'Emilio and Freedman 1997, p. 307.
50   Faderman 1991, p. 203.
51   Weeks 1981, pp. 282–3.
52   D'Emilio and Freedman 1997, pp. 291–2.

the male figure.[53] From the late 1940s, sexual surveys in Britain, France and Italy were also tracking and to some extent legitimising a broadening range of sexual behaviour.[54]

An Expanding Subculture

Whatever the trends in same-sex behaviour, the homosexual subculture expanded. In medium-sized US cities from Massachusetts to Kansas and Colorado, the first known homosexual bars opened in the 1940s.[55] Even in the repressive climate of the 1950s, homosexuality continued to become more visible and lesbian and gay bars more numerous and more crowded. Butch lesbians in particular responded to attacks with increased determination to stand their ground.[56]

By the 1960s, traditional arguments against homosexuality, undermined by broad shifts in class and gender relations, were further weakened by several social and cultural factors. The increasing availability of contraceptives meant that 'the possibility of reproduction no longer defined most heterosexual encounters'. Practices like oral and anal sex were increasingly taken up by straight people, while growing numbers of straights accepted sexual desire and experience outside marriage.[57] Nor was the 1960s counterculture as uniformly heteronormative as the slogans of Berkeley People's Park suggest; part of it was influenced by the example of San Francisco's 1950s beats, including a consciously Whitmanesque, openly gay figure like Allen Ginsburg.[58] By the 1970s, a sexual morality centred on straight marriage seemed seriously shaken. It had taken 150 years to establish romantic, male-breadwinner marriage as the dominant model, as Stephanie Coontz has observed; it 'took less than 25 years to dismantle it'.[59]

The diversification of consumer marketing that Fordism entailed created space for the 'underground circulation of homoerotic images' in 'an increasingly less underground gay male [and lesbian] network'.[60] In the 1950s, the

---

53   D'Emilio 1983b, p. 35.
54   Herzog 2011, pp. 107, 109–10.
55   D'Emilio and Freedman 1997, pp. 290–1.
56   Davis and Kennedy 1989, pp. 439, 428.
57   Herzog 2011, pp. 169–70.
58   D'Emilio 1983b, pp. 177–81.
59   Coontz 2005, p. 247.
60   Floyd 2009, p. 174.

market niche of physique magazines, lesbian romances and lesbian and homosexual bars was still modest – though the superficial appearance of small-scale
enterprise was belied in some cities by the role of organised crime, in some
ways a sinister simulacrum of corporate capitalism. In any event, by the 1970s,
there was what seemed at the time a 'spectacular expansion of the commercial
subculture', particularly in major metropolitan centres and affluent milieus[61] –
though in turn it would be dwarfed by what followed in later decades. Over
time, Fordist mass markets came to coexist comfortably with a growing range
of niche markets, including the gay niche market. By the 1970s and 1980s, the
gay niche market in imperialist countries included newspapers, publishing
houses, professional services, travel agencies, resorts, sports leagues, theatre
companies, clinics and even, in a sense, churches.[62]

Women's growing role in the economy undermined the gendered dynamic of
capitalism, in which men's involvement in production and many women's confinement to domesticity historically made 'the public space of cities ... male
space'.[63] But given women's still lower participation in this period in the waged
workforce, their lower wages, the fact that many women attracted to women
had children, and the threat that known lesbianism would pose to mothers,
lesbian communities were smaller than gay male ones.[64] They emerged largely
in regions where women were entering the waged workforce and thus achieving a measure of economic independence, including East and Southeast Asia
by the 1980s.

Under Fordism, homosexual possibilities expanded in regions beyond
Western Europe and North America. Asia's first commercial homoerotic magazines appeared in Japan in the 1950s as the Fordist regime began emerging
there.[65] Japan constituted an intriguing special case: despite rapid capitalist
development after the Second World War, with living standards comparable
to those of Western Europe and North America, the first gay pride march was
held in Tokyo only in 1994, at about the same time that a spate of novels and a
TV drama on gay themes suddenly reached broad audiences. The unique forms
that Fordism took in Japan, involving lifetime employment for a substantial
proportion of the workforce and a tight network of corporate and family ties
that even in big cities left less space for purely independent social ties, may
have accounted for the delay. Despite the 'efficient commodification of an

---

61   Weeks 1981, p. 286.
62   D'Emilio 1983b, pp. 238–9.
63   D'Emilio 1989, p. 458.
64   D'Emilio 1983b, pp. 105–6.
65   Jackson 1989, p. 392, n. 60.

amazing range of sexual practices and erotic fetishisms from the 1920s' to the 1990s, and a widespread network of heterosexual prostitution, none of this significantly shook the apparently smooth surface of heterosexual family and public life.[66]

Even before the Second World War there were areas of industrialisation in some economically dominated countries as well. The long post-war expansion led to urbanisation and industrialisation in many upper-tier dependent countries, often fostered by development programmes that were, though capitalist, almost always state-planned or state-sponsored.[67] These countries included Mexico, Puerto Rico, Argentina, Uruguay, Brazil, South Africa, South Korea, Taiwan, Thailand and Malaysia. These countries' and regions' economic transformation created conditions similar to those that allowed the emergence of Fordist lesbian/gay communities and identities in imperialist countries. And in fact these communities' emergence began in the 1960s and 1970s. In Turkey, for example, with a level of economic development higher than the average in the Middle East, gay subcultures emerged in the big cities: Ankara, Istanbul and Izmir.[68]

A gay identity took shape among middle-class men in big Brazilian cities in the 1960s as the country rapidly industrialised and urbanised (with 56 percent of the population in urban areas in 1970 as compared with 36 percent in 1950). A gay scene emerged in Rio's Copacabana neighbourhood in the early 1960s, with a newspaper, O Snob, publishing from 1963 to 1969 that identified itself as aimed at entendidos (discreet homosexuals). A 1958 study of mostly discreet middle-class self-identified homosexuals in São Paulo found that 27 percent said they were sexually flexible (both insertive and receptive), and another 10 percent exclusively insertive – men who in earlier periods would probably not have self-identified as homosexual at all. By the 1970s, there was a range of publications promoting the new identity, as bars, discos and saunas proliferated, generally escaping repression by the military dictatorship that ruled Brazil throughout the decade.[69] Middle-class Brazilian gay men tended to argue that michês (macho men rejecting gay identity and insisting on their insertive role in male sex) were just closeted gay men. Yet the tradition of 'taking turns', in which slightly younger boys were supposed to be penetrated by older ones, persisted in many urban areas.[70]

---

66   Miller 1996, pp. 7, 136.
67   Hobsbawm 1994, p. 351.
68   Drucker 1996, p. 90.
69   Green 1999a, pp. 7 (citing Peter Fry), 147, 155–6, 183–6, 165–6, 268–9, 245, 248–51.
70   Mitchell 2011, p. 675 (citing Donna M. Goldstein, Richard Parker and João S. Trevisan).

A similar process began in Cuba before the victory of the revolution in 1959. There too, discreet, more masculine-appearing *entendidos*, particularly in Havana's large middle class, rejected what they saw as trans people's 'self-oppressive' behaviour – though paradoxically they also 'envied the freedom of the *locas* to be themselves' and sought out and often paid for sex with supposedly macho straight men. Despite anti-LGBT repression under the new regime after 1959, which continued to disproportionately target gender dissenters, closeted *entendidos* survived among professionals and even officials. The younger and more educated they were, the more likely they were to identify as *completo* (reciprocal in sex) and reject sexual role-playing.[71]

Lesbian/gay communities in Southeast Asia grew rapidly during the period of prosperity there from the 1970s to the early 1990s. Thailand, and especially Bangkok with its urban population of almost 10 million, became the 'undisputed gay capital of Southeast Asia' and a centre for LGBT migration and tourism. Bangkok and New York were in some ways comparable 'ports and nodes of regional and international transport and communications'. In a time of rapid dependent capitalist development, a gay identity linked to reciprocal sexuality gradually took hold in Thailand alongside the enduring strength of transgendered *kathoey* patterns. In the mid-1970s, a Bangkok newspaper column initially focusing on *kathoeys* expanded to a broad audience including self-identified gay men and lesbians, and by the early 1980s the production of major gay commercial media began in Bangkok.[72]

All these changes contributed to the decline of the same-sex formation of homosexuality/inversion characteristic of the era of classical imperialism, and the rise of a Fordist same-sex formation with lesbian/gay identity at its centre. In the earlier regime, homosexuality/inversion had been seen mainly as a failure to play a proper gender role, in sex and in other ways. In the new regime, homosexuality/gay sexuality was seen mainly as an expression of desire paralleling heterosexuality. Among psychologists, the rise of lesbian/gay communities and movements helped discredit neo-Freudians' homophobic departures from Freud's original, normalising but not pathologising positions; by 1963, Theodor Adorno, a prominent representative of the Frankfurt School noted for its synthesis of Marx and Freud, was declaring, 'Precisely when it is not warped or repressed, sex harms no one' – adding that prejudice against sexual minorities had helped create the mass base for Nazism.[73]

---

71   Lumsden 1996, pp. 30–1, 35–6, 152, 149–50.

72   Jackson 1989, pp. 241, 370, 373–7.

73   Herzog 2011, p. 129.

The paradigm shift under Fordism to a gay-dominant regime encouraged a trend towards decriminalisation in some of the countries where the French Revolution and Napoleonic expansion had not already led to the elimination of sodomy laws – though at first, as in the Napoleonic Code countries, decriminalisation took forms that reaffirmed the primacy of the heterosexual norm and guarded against homosexual seduction. This was the case with decriminalisation in Denmark in 1933, in Switzerland in 1942, and in Sweden in 1944. The 1963 West German anthology *Sexuality and Crime (Sexualität und Verbrechen)* used these Western European examples of reform to argue for founding sexual legislation on concepts of consent and privacy.[74] In 1964, the International Congress on Penal Law joined in calling for decriminalisation.[75]

The British Wolfenden Commission, convened in 1954, recommended decriminalisation in its report in 1957, though this only finally occurred in 1967 – with an age of consent of 21, an exception for the military, and a focus on dangers to youth that brought about a quintupling of prosecutions among men under 21 in the years after law reform.[76] Decriminalisation in Illinois, the first US state to adopt it, in 1961, had little impact on arrest figures, since arrests for vagrancy, disorderly conduct, public lewdness and solicitation increased.[77] Decriminalisation in Canada, proposed by the Trudeau government in 1967 and passed in 1969, fit a similar pattern: it helped 'demarcate a distinct sphere of private, adult homosexuality', regulated by psychiatrists instead of police.[78] Even France, a century and a half after decriminalisation, had an age of consent of 21 and regulations that until 1975 banned public display of the relatively tame homophile magazine *Arcadie*. In 1960, a motion describing homosexuality as a 'social scourge' passed the French National Assembly unanimously.[79] In Latin America, where formal decriminalisation had largely been achieved in the nineteenth century,[80] police raids and roundups were common until late

---

74   Herzog 2011, pp. 77, 81, 78, 128.

75   D'Emilio 1983b, p. 144.

76   Weeks 1981, pp. 242–4, 267, 274–5; Herzog 2011, pp. 124–5.

77   D'Emilio 1983b, p. 146.

78   Kinsman 1987, pp. 166, 168, 171.

79   Herzog 2011, pp. 119–20.

80   Once Ecuador's Constitutional Tribunal overturned the country's sodomy law in 1997, and Chile repealed its law in 1998, Nicaragua and Puerto Rico were the only Latin American countries left with such laws, both of them due in some sense to US intervention. Puerto Rico only repealed its law in 2005, after the US Supreme Court had declared it unconstitutional in 2003. Nicaragua repealed its law in 2008 after the Sandinistas returned to office.

in the twentieth century through much of the region, usually on the basis of vague laws about 'immoral and indecent behaviour'.[81]

Decriminalisation, however hedged about with restrictions, helped establish homosexuality as a form of sexuality parallel to, if not on a par with, heterosexuality. At the same time, the growing sexualisation of society and awareness of homosexuality virtually eliminated what space remained for purportedly non-sexual same-sex life partnerships, particularly among women. This development was often viewed with dismay and alarm by older, non-lesbian-identified female couples in the US who had lived together respectably into the 1970s, largely in women's professional milieus, with 'enough status to be beyond reproach in the world in which they moved'.[82] At the same time, gender-dissident and other patterns were being established as somehow inferior to proper lesbian/gay sexuality.

Lesbian/Gay and Gender

As homosexuality was originally defined in the age of classical imperialism, real men were not supposed to desire other men.[83] But this gradually gave way in the twentieth century to a different gay/straight binary, in which either straight women or gay men can desire masculine men.

This new lesbian/gay pattern usually took hold first among middle-class men and women who identified as homosexual. This reflected middle-class homosexuals' wish and need for discretion. In Montreal in the early 1950s, professionals and managers were mainly 'secret' homosexuals, keeping their distance from homosexual networks, while more open same-sex behaviour and identification were mainly characteristic of clerks and salesmen, artists, waiters and hairdressers.[84] Much the same pattern prevailed in the US even in the late 1960s.[85] The economic pressures on middle-class homosexuals influenced their cultural style. In the US by the 1940s and 1950s, many upper-class and professional lesbians found butch/femme 'aesthetically repulsive' and 'tacky' – attitudes that contributed to class segregation among lesbians. Fear of visibility

---

81   Mogrovejo 2000, pp. 84–5.
82   Rupp 1989, pp. 406–8.
83   Floyd 2009, p. 164.
84   Kinsman 1987, pp. 116–19 and Rubin 2011, pp. 322–3 (citing Maurice Leznoff and William Westley).
85   Rubin 2011, p. 341 (citing Esther Newton).

and exposure sometimes contributed to an aversion to butch/femme among lesbian professionals like teachers and social workers.[86]

Early on in imperialist countries, 'homophile' organisations, largely middle class in composition or at least leadership, began to play a disciplinary role in facilitating homosexuals' transition to more standard gender norms. As early as the 1930s, the Swiss *Freundschafts-Banner* began warning its male readers against 'effeminate' behaviour.[87] In the late 1940s and 1950s, the Dutch gay organisation COC and US homophile groups played similar disciplinary roles.[88] The US homophile Mattachine Society and lesbian Daughters of Bilitis (DOB) reflected the worldviews of their largely college-educated, professional leaders[89] and the 'accomodationist, conformist spirit of the Eisenhower era'. 'DOB regularly counselled lesbians to grow their hair long and wear dresses'.[90] One DOB leader recalled that getting one member to wear feminine clothes for a convention was celebrated as 'some great victory'. Its publication, railing against trousers and short hair, suggested that lesbians should do 'a little "policing" on their own'.[91] In Brazil in the 1960s the columnist Hélio waged an ongoing battle in *O Snob* against *bicha* effeminacy.[92]

The homophile groups of the 1950s set in motion a process of 'unhinging' working-class homosexuals from their own communities.[93] The US lesbian journal *The Ladder* evoked resentful complaints in the 1950s from working-class lesbians with its attacks on butch/femme as 'the worst publicity we can get'. In 'something of a class war', butches and femmes complained that 'these "kiki" women were ... buckling under by dressing like conventional women'.[94] African-American writer Lorraine Hansberry called for an end to the lecturing. Men also protested; a man from Nevada decried the attempt to get 'all homosexuals to act like bourgeois gentlemen'.[95] The class war even existed in an oddly distorted form among US transvestites in the late 1960s, between professional female impersonators who limited their gender transgression strictly to the stage and looked down on 'street fairies' as 'tacky', meaning 'cheap,

---

86   Faderman, pp. 175, 178.
87   Herzog 2011, p. 81.
88   Warmerdam and Koenders 1987, pp. 125, 153, 169; Floyd 2009, pp. 167–8.
89   Valocchi 1999, p. 217.
90   D'Emilio 1989, p. 460.
91   D'Emilio 1983b, pp. 106, 113.
92   Green 1999a, pp. 190–2.
93   Valocchi 1999, p. 216.
94   Faderman 1991, pp. 179–81.
95   D'Emilio 1983b, p. 114.

shoddy, or of poor quality ... indirectly a class descriptive term'.[96] Transgender relationships also sometimes faced disapproval in immigrant communities in imperialist countries, not only from straights but also from some people in same-sex relationships who resisted 'extreme role conceptions'.[97]

Supplementing the attempts of early lesbian/gay groups to discipline their members' gender norms, the second wave of feminism was key in reining in the butch/femme patterns that were still largely hegemonic in 1950s lesbian subcultures (or at least in turning them into 'a subterranean game').[98] Some early second-wave feminists were paranoid about lesbian-baiting to the point of trying to exclude lesbians from the women's movement or render them invisible – like Betty Friedan, first president of the US National Organisation for Women, who tried to keep lesbians out of public roles and vehemently opposed taking up lesbian issues.[99] Lesbians soon won more acceptance and leeway in feminist circles, but at the price of accepting some parameters. 1970s feminists often rejected butch identities as 'male identification', and cross-dressing, taking hormones and sex-reassignment surgery as 'personal solutions' to social problems.[100] The San Francisco Daughters of Bilitis and West Coast Lesbian Conference were both deeply divided in 1973 by the presence of a male-to-female transsexual; the Daughters of Bilitis, whose vice-president she had been, even expelled her.[101] In 1978, feminist theologian Mary Daly called transsexuality a 'necrophilic invasion' of women's space, and in 1979 Janice Raymond compared transsexuality with rape and Nazism.[102]

A temporary relaxation of gender norms in the 1960s created some space for playful gender-bending. The violence that erupted against drag queens in Brazil during Carnival in 1957 gave way to growing tolerance in the early 1960s, and by 1968 and later to a particularly striking and enduring gay and trans appropriation of Carnival. Even as the word 'gay' gained currency in the 1960s, its meaning often overlapped considerably in Brazil with *bicha*. In the US, the Kinks' 1970 hit 'Lola' proclaimed that 'girls will be boys and boys will be girls'.[103] There was a countercultural style even among men of 'bright, flowing fabrics, long hair, and love beads', and even a brief vogue of avant-garde

---

96   Rubin 2011, p. 242 (citing Esther Newton).
97   Wekker 2006, p. 196.
98   Califia 2003, p. 3.
99   Coontz 2011, p. 157.
100 Stryker 2008, pp. 100, 2.
101 Meyerowitz 2002, pp. 259–60.
102 Stryker 2008, pp. 105–8.
103 Meyerowitz 2002, p. 233.

182

drag, exemplified by rock star David Bowie and Warhol stars Candy Darling and Holly Woodlawn.[104] As gender in general became more performative, drag and gender-bending became its most conscious and explicit expression.

But despite the proliferation of ways in which women and men were expected to exert themselves to perfect and display their femininity and masculinity, most people continued to accept and insist that it all 'came naturally' to them. Full-fledged drag, already frowned upon by the most would-be respectable homosexuals in the 1950s, once more began to seem anomalous and even embarrassing in the context of the androgynous imagery that was in vogue through much of the 1970s. Many gay liberationists saw trans people as 'not liberated'. By 1973, the San Francisco Pride celebration split, with the larger event banning drag, and a trans leader was forcibly prevented from addressing the celebration in New York.[105] In some of the most industrialised areas of the dependent world, such as South Africa and the Southern Cone, where lesbian/gay cultures resembling those of imperialist countries became somewhat more prominent, forms of same-sex sexuality identified as 'lesbian' or 'gay' were still more limited to middle-class layers of the population, while transgender patterns often tended to be more prevalent among poor and working-class people.[106]

The invention of the transsexual was a first step towards separating out transgendered people from gays and lesbians. Despite the first partial sex-change operations and hormone treatments in the 1910s and 1920s (described in chapter 1), and a few more in the US in the early 1940s, the word 'transsexual' was only coined in 1949 and widely popularised with Christine Jorgensen's pioneering gender-reassignment surgery in 1952. Jorgensen's operation (performed in Denmark thanks to a 1935 statute permitting castration) was a media sensation in the US. Jorgensen capitalised on the gender shifts of the war years (she was called an 'ex-GI'), growing faith in science in the atomic age, and a typically American story of individual triumph over adversity. In a significant shift from earlier European discourses on inversion, US sexologists now characterised transsexuals as people whose 'psychological sex' differed from their physical sex, and increasingly concluded that their psychological sex was decisive.[107] The public's willingness to accept this showed that sexual behaviour and feelings now trumped potential parenthood in popular

104   Stryker 2008, pp. 95, 91.
105   Stryker 2008, pp. 98, 102.
106   Carrier 1975, pp. 120–1; Mejía 2000, p. 49; Oetomo 1996, pp. 265, 268; Boellenstorf 2005.
107   Meyerowitz 2002, pp. 48, 5, 42–4, 1, 60, 51–3, 62–9, 41, 131, 99, 112–14.

conceptions of sexual identity; otherwise Jorgensen could never have been so widely accepted as a woman.

Jorgensen's surgery was followed by others in the 1950s, and the number of operations multiplied in the late 1960s. Sex-reassignment surgery's big step forward in the US was due largely to the publication in 1966 of the book *The Transsexual Phenomenon* by Harry Benjamin – a German-born associate of Magnus Hirschfeld – followed within a few months by the establishment of the country's first sex-reassignment programme at the Johns Hopkins University Medical School. Growing informal networks that served as 'training grounds of sorts' for cross-dressing, hormone use and surgery[108] culminated in the formation in San Francisco in 1967 of the first US transsexual peer support group, Conversion Our Goal.[109] Although the Johns Hopkins clinic had an extremely restrictive approach – in its first two and a half years, of the 'almost 2000 desperate requests' for surgery it received, it acceded to only 24[110] – by the 1970s and early 1980s more than forty North American gender clinics, often university-affiliated, offered programmes leading to surgical reassignments[111] and over 1000 transsexuals had had operations.[112]

By a certain point, a female who felt she was 'a man trapped in a woman's body' might more likely consider herself a victim of 'gender dysphoria', a transsexual rather than a lesbian,[113] though no one counted as transsexual without seeking full surgical reassignment. Transsexuals in this period were supposed to conform to traditional gender stereotypes[114] and define themselves as straight, in keeping with a medical establishment that often included heterosexuality as an 'intrinsic attribute and defining feature' of transsexuality.[115] Jorgensen was typical of many transsexuals in expressing moralistic and religious objections to homosexuality, though she did characterise herself as homosexual at one point before her surgery and defended gay rights afterwards. Although Kinsey initially studied transsexuals together with transvestites and homosexuals, he eventually came to consider them a separate category.[116] Transsexuals were in fact, with the alteration of their genitals, supposed to feel themselves reborn

---

108   Meyerowitz 2002, pp. 82–8, 97, 215, 45–6, 7, 218–21, 169, 186–96.

109   Stryker 2008, pp. 73–5.

110   Meyerowitz 2002, pp. 142, 221–2.

111   Bolin 1994, p. 453.

112   Meyerowitz 2002, p. 222.

113   Faderman 1991, p. 304.

114   Meyerowitz 2002, pp. 225–6.

115   Bolin 1994, p. 460.

116   Meyerowitz 2002, pp. 7, 57, 59, 183, 170–2.

as new people, in a vision that 'made anatomy destiny, with genitality at the centre of the individual's identity'.[117]

Under the Fordist same-sex formation, transvestites were still often included (sometimes against their will)[118] under a gay umbrella, though increasingly viewed as atypical or even freakish, since gender nonconformity was increasingly seen as something with no intrinsic connection to a lesbian/gay sexual orientation. The very word 'transvestite' suggested a narrowly defined clothing fetish not necessarily linked to sexuality (many transvestites are of course straight) or to broader issues of gender identity – which was a more dubious implication. Doctors often lumped transvestites and transsexuals together, though again to some transvestites' displeasure. On the other hand, transsexuality could have 'overtones of upward mobility', expressing a desire for a 'normal' life and career rather than life as a 'freak'.[119] To the extent that transvestites were perceived as genuine gender and/or sexual dissidents, they were seen by transsexuals as people who lacked the ability or determination to 'go all the way' to surgery.[120] As for effeminate homosexuals, they did not disappear but became a sometimes-stigmatised minority on the gay scene.[121] While the word 'transgender' was attested as early as 1971, the concept did not catch on widely until the 1990s.

As transsexuality was separated out, and transvestism and other forms of gender dissent marginalised, there was a shift across societies from patterns of inversion to more characteristic lesbian/gay ones. Among young US lesbians by a certain point, their 'upbringing in the unisex 1960s made the polarities of masculine and feminine particularly alien to them'.[122] One Mexican study found students engaged in same-sex relations in the early 1970s – presumably middle class in aspiration if not in origin – particularly likely to abandon gender polarisation, with three-fourths rejecting exclusively active or passive roles.[123] Many LGBT people in the dependent world seemed to be increasingly giving up traditional sexual distinctions in the later twentieth century, as has been observed, for example, in Lebanon.[124]

The crucial question was not whether people had been straying covertly from the old sexual roles; that had always been the case. Among US butches

---

117 Bergero, Asiain and Cano-Caballero 2010, p. 59.
118 Meyerowitz 2002, 179–81.
119 Meyerowitz 2002, pp. 175, 181–2, 184.
120 Bolin 1994, pp. 458–9.
121 Hekma 1994, p. 238.
122 Faderman 1991, p. 187.
123 Carrier 1975, pp. 120–1.
124 Makarem 2007, p. 100.

and femmes in the 1950s, for example, dress and public behaviour were reputedly unreliable as a guide to who was a butch or femme sexually.[125] In Mexico, there was a word, *hechizos*, for 'real men' who had become open to reciprocal sex.[126] Brazilians spoke of '*bofe panquecas* – roughly, "studs who flip", the seemingly masculine, straight men who once in bed turn over and want to be penetrated anally'.[127] As long as this was a matter of private practice and gossip, its impact on the social understanding of gender and sexual roles was limited.

Of far greater social importance was the moment when the issue of who played what role moved from something to be insisted on to something of little significance, while the gender both partners had in common became the defining element of both of their sexual identities. Once that happened, it hardly mattered whether role-playing that had become unfashionable persisted more or less discreetly or whether people just operated with 'fuzzily bounded categories'.[128]

Migration from dependent to imperialist countries sometimes hastened the transition to lesbian/gay patterns. Many Afro-Surinamese women who had played the male role in *mati* relationships in Suriname adapted after several years in the Netherlands to the white Dutch rejection of roles. The shift could also be to a situation where women did not need to depend economically on men and *mati* pairs could have exclusive relationships. This could lead younger women to reject *mati* bisexuality as 'untrustworthy, self-serving, and too pragmatic, too interested in money'.[129]

Even if the extent of the shift from gender-dissident to reciprocal sexuality varied, the rise of more visible LGBT communities became possible wherever businesses catering to same-sex networks were established. Once such networks grew, it became more likely for a broad group, including gender dissenters, to spend more time in an LGBT community and identify with it.

Racial Liberalism and Neo-Colonialism

The development of Fordism in the US was rife with paradox. As the very name indicates, the US economically pioneered the new regime of accumulation. Antonio Gramsci, in prison in Italy in the 1930s, wrote at length about Fordism in the US. New Fordist sexual regimes also began emerging relatively

125   Davis and Kennedy 1989, p. 432.
126   Lumsden 1991, pp. 45–6.
127   Klein 1998, p. 29.
128   Makarem 2007, p. 101.
129   Wekker 2006, pp. 235, 234.

early there following the changes in production. But despite massive African-American migration beginning in the 1910s from the US South to the mass production plants in the industrial North, the transition from open racism to racial liberalism did not proceed any more rapidly in the US than elsewhere, even in the North; far from it. This shows the extent to which racial developments, like sexual ones, are autonomous from changes in regimes of accumulation that make them possible, and how variable the lag can be.

The fact that white homosexuals in the mid-twentieth century sought out same-sex scenes among African-Americans in Harlem could sometimes be motivated in part by an anti-racist impulse among people who were themselves outcasts and rebels, prefiguring the racial liberalism that Fordism eventually fostered. But it was also tainted by the exoticism that has often attributed a more 'natural' or 'primitive' sexuality to oppressed people. Harlem needed white tourism for economic reasons, and many venues that whites flocked to refused to serve blacks.[130]

Gradually and unevenly after the Second World War, however, the Fordist order increasingly fostered pressures to do away with formal racial and colonial distinctions. Particularly over the course of the 1960s, it became clear that under Fordism the white ruling classes of imperialist countries did not need colonial empires to maintain their position at the top of the global hierarchy or to ensure that blacks and immigrants would continue to disproportionately populate reserve armies of labour. This made it easier, once courageous activism and determined mobilisation applied sufficient pressure, for open colonialism to give way to neo-colonialism and forms of *de jure* racism like Jim Crow in the US to be dismantled.

Clearly this did not eliminate racial prejudice from the world. On the contrary, the reality of greater poverty and structural inequality among non-white and formerly colonised peoples continually reproduced and incited racist ideology about them in multiple ways, which remained an acute and understandable grievance among the rulers of decolonised states and the minority of blacks and immigrants who began to achieve middle-class status in imperialist countries. But racist ideology was decreasingly central to the operation of a racially liberal system. Although racial discrimination remained pervasive, the mechanisms that continually reproduced disproportionate black and immigrant poverty and unemployment were more camouflaged.

The ideology of formal racial equality provided a matrix that was also applied to formal gender equality and even, beginning in the 1970s, to equality across different 'sexual orientations'. Here too a wave of organising and years

---

130   Faderman 1991, pp. 68–72.

of mobilisation were needed to sweep aside discriminatory laws and institutions. But LGBT people insisted – together with women, blacks and others – on
their recognition and inclusion in the post-war frameworks for democracy and
civil rights that had initially excluded them. Lesbian/gay movements seized
an opportunity that had ripened. In this way, the new gay-dominant same-sex
regime was reinforced by the growing acceptance of formal gay equality.

In this domain too, however, the ideology of equality did not slow the continual reproduction of prejudice through all sorts of mechanisms, ultimately
deriving from a situation of structural gender inequality and heteronormativity.
The facts that lesbians and gays were less likely to have children, for example,
or more likely than straights to have certain jobs, or forced to go to clubs and
other places explicitly in search of sexual partners – all clearly consequences
of the realities of exclusion from a straight-dominated world – furnished arguments to stigmatise them. Within the emerging gay world, the new egalitarian
model also masked 'vectors of power' like racism, which nonetheless continued to shape erotic fantasies and sexual relationships, notably between black
and white men.[131]

The Fordist same-sex regime never took the same form across the entire
planet that it did in the imperialist countries. By the 1920s, imperialism had
established its way over virtually every part of the world except the embattled and isolated Soviet Union. By contrast, there were parts of the world that
the massive industrialisation, urbanisation and rising wages characteristic
of Fordism never reached. Most of Sub-Saharan Africa, in many cases only
formally decolonised in the 1960s, remained largely a source of agricultural
products and raw materials for the world market (where it was not completely
isolated from the world market and dependent on subsistence agriculture
and livestock herding). The same was true of parts of capitalist Latin America
(Andean, Amazonian and Central American areas), much of the Caribbean,
and big swathes of capitalist Asia. By the 1960s, capitalism had been overthrown in about a third of the world, notably the Soviet Union, Eastern Europe,
China and Cuba, which followed different paths. Almost all of these regions
would experience neoliberal sexual regimes from the 1990s without having
gone through Fordism. And more generally in the dependent world, combined
and uneven social construction ensured that the homogeneity of LGBT communities was always less than in imperialist countries.

The rapid growth of lesbian/gay communities in imperialist countries in
the Fordist period thus proceeded more slowly, sometimes far more slowly,
in dependent countries. This was true even in more prosperous dominated

---

131   Cervulle and Rees-Roberts 2010, pp. 125–6 (citing Alan Sinfield).

countries where urbanisation and dependent industrialisation did lead to the emergence of such communities. Even where reciprocal lesbian/gay sexuality did emerge, it often came later and took different forms, for several reasons: later and more limited industrialisation; later entry of women into the paid labour force; the greater strength of family structures due in part to less developed welfare states; and poverty, which limited people's participation in a gay ghetto founded on consumption. In Thailand, for example, the rapid rise of a gay community did not completely marginalise trans people, despite the introduction of gay publications, terms and trends into the *kathoey* world.[132] Lesbian/gay communities could be slow to spread to provincial cities, let alone the countryside.

While European or North American influence may at times have facilitated the emergence of lesbian/gay communities, the process of dependent capitalist development was at least as significant. If anything, dependence on imperialist economies helped delay development of the material basis for lesbian/gay communities, by delaying the achievement of higher wages and expanded welfare states that crucially facilitated life outside existing families.[133]

Economic ups and downs often slowed lesbian/gay community formation even in regions of the dependent world that had embarked upon widespread industrialisation. LGBT communities in the dependent world are particularly vulnerable to economic crises, which hit harder and deeper there, with all the social and political tensions they create. Communities' fragility helps explain why the first wave of Latin American LGBT movements – beginning in Argentina in 1969, Mexico in 1971, and Puerto Rico in 1974 – proved so vulnerable. Some movements were destroyed by dictatorships, as in Brazil from 1969[134] and Argentina after 1976. The rest retreated in almost every country in the aftermath of the 1982 debt crisis and the 'lost decade' that followed. Same-sex communities and identities were generally able to flourish only later in the 1980s, and by the 1990s were being reshaped by the different economic and social climate of neoliberalism.

Different paces of secularisation were another factor in more rapid or slower emergence of LGBT communities. The power of Protestant fundamentalists in the US and the Catholic Church in Latin Europe contributed to a process that lagged behind the most secularised societies of Northern Europe, though nominally Catholic countries like Belgium and Spain quickly caught up with nominally Lutheran Scandinavia. The example of Turkish cities like Istanbul,

---

132 Jackson 1989, pp. 6–7, 12.

133 Drucker 1996, p. 77.

134 Green 1999a, pp. 196–8.

Ankara and Izmir showed the importance of secularisation (in the Turkish case the outcome of an anti-colonial revolution) to the rise of LGBT identities in the Islamic world; the commercial scenes and organising efforts there had no parallel as late as the 1990s even in major metropolises like Cairo and Karachi.[135]

In India, despite formal secularisation with independence, the enduring social hegemony of Hinduism and to a lesser degree Islam (abetted by British policies of divide and rule) impeded the public affirmation of LGBT identities, especially with the rise of communalism from the 1990s.[136] Lebanon was an interesting intermediate case: despite the institutionalisation of religious communalism under French rule, the 'multi-religious, multi-confessional' nature of the society sometimes allowed more scope for LGBT scenes and communities.[137]

It is not clear how much continuity there was in general between traditional Arab sexual culture and that of the later-twentieth-century Arab region. Although self-identified lesbians and gay men were beginning to emerge there, distinctive lesbian/gay identities did seem less visible in Arab countries, as a high proportion of Arab men reportedly continued to have sex with other men without identifying at all as gay, transgendered or even bisexual. With sex tourism in the Maghreb, the usual assumption seemed to be that foreign men's Arab sex partners were playing the active role, going through a youthful phase, or both. Some men penetrated transgendered or other males.[138]

Still, the space for less reified same-sex formations, which had been fairly broad under classical imperialism in regions from Suriname to South African mining communities to the Islamic world, narrowed internationally under Fordism. Even in the Arab region, the forms taken by discreet sex between men sometimes suggested a slippage towards reciprocal lesbian/gay roles. For example, some Egyptian men spoke of 'face-to-face' sex, meaning that anal intercourse was avoided so as to evade issues of masculine or feminine roles.[139]

But the slowness with which the lesbian/gay patterns that became hegemonic under Fordism took root in parts of the world where industrialisation was later and dependent did not mean that an invert-dominant regime simply persisted there. Gender roles and sexual patterns were going through profound changes in the dependent world as well. But by contrast with the Russian Bolsheviks, who had connected their country's own same-sex patterns with

135   Van Grinsven 1997, p. 15; Khan 1997, p. 275.
136   Joseph and Dhall 2000, pp. 170–1.
137   Makarem 2011, p. 100.
138   Massad 2007, p. 364.
139   Van Grinsven 1997, p. 37.

some of the most advanced sexology and sexual emancipation movements in Germany, Fordist-era populist and bureaucratic regimes sought to 'modernise' their countries' family and sexual lives by repressing whatever failed to fit their top-down models.

Decolonisation and national liberation struggles led to shifts in sexual ideology in the dependent world. In economically dominated countries after decolonisation, the rise of a stronger state apparatus made possible more thorough sexual repression. The attempt to create nuclear family structures, seen as a crucial dimension of modernisation, was often a motive. Ironically, many governments playing on anti-imperialist sentiment associated same-sex eroticism with the resented West. Some colonised people associated same-sex relations with sex-segregated institutions such as prisons and migrant-labour compounds, which had spread with colonisation.

An ongoing tug-of-war began to define what in all this was global, national and local. In these debates, the idea of religious and/or ethnic 'tradition' or 'culture' was far from neutral; it reflected struggles for power, both between colonised and coloniser and among the colonised themselves.[140] A newly independent nation in particular had to act simultaneously as a modernising force and as the 'custodian of a fixed (in all senses of the word) identity-conferring precolonial past, in short, as the repository of tradition'.[141] Often in fact the traditions in question were inventions of the nineteenth or twentieth centuries, as many African 'tribal' traditions are as well.[142] African presidents like Zimbabwe's Robert Mugabe, for example, learned that homosexuality is 'un-African' as part of their Christian mission educations. Both the task of modernising and the task of affirming national identity could entail suppressing sexual realities at least as much as revealing, exploring or freeing them.

Before the Second World War, colonial ideology had pathologised the sexualities of non-European peoples, portraying non-European men in particular (like African-American men in the US) as sexually unbridled and threatening. Anti-colonial movements tended to turn the imagery upside down, exposing the falsehood of the sexual charges that justified repression of non-European men and the reality of sexual violence against and exploitation of colonised women. Unfortunately, this shift rarely brought any solace to those involved in same-sex relationships.

Anti-colonial struggles produced 'a narrative of "traditional sexuality" in which a hearty yet wholesome heterosexual appetite stood in proud opposition

---

140   Rofel 1999, p. 456.
141   Hoad 1999, p. 565.
142   Ranger 1992, pp. 211–62.

to the dominant, emasculating colonial discourse'.[143] This was already visible early in the twentieth century in Iran's Constitutionalist movement, when men who were seen as failing to adequately defend their country's freedom were threatened with being covered in women's headscarves. Oppression was 'linked to transgressions against women's sexual integrity, defined as men's honor'. A Constitutionalist leaflet in 1909 charged that Iranian soldiers 'look like men but are not men'; they were transgendered, womanly *mukhannas*.[144] A similar rhetoric characterised later authoritarian populist regimes, like the PRI regime in Mexico and Peronism in Argentina, that masked their subservience in practice to US imperialism with fervent protestations of their cultural authenticity and moral purity.

This kind of rhetoric also marked national liberation movements. Sexual 'blinders' led a revolutionary like Frantz Fanon to claim that 'there is no homosexuality in Martinique'.[145] As late as the mid-1980s in South Africa, a United Democratic Front spokesman said publicly that homosexuality was a product of apartheid's deformation of the African family that would disappear in post-apartheid society. Gays and Lesbians of Zimbabwe have denounced such attitudes as 'Victorian dogma', which African political leaders 'have the audacity to claim is the backbone of our African cultural heritage'.[146]

The falsehood of this sort of upside-down Eurocentrism was manifest in the Islamic world. The fact that Egypt and Pakistan both experienced colonial rule (by Britain), which Turkey escaped, helped account for the earlier growth of lesbian/gay formations in Turkey, even though European settlement in an Egyptian city like Alexandria was as great or greater than in any Turkish city, and the Christian minority in Egypt was proportionally far larger than in Turkey. British rule in Egypt and Pakistan left Islamic social hegemony unaffected or even strengthened, while Turkey went through a profound process of secularisation in the process of defending itself from European colonisation after the First World War. It was thus no accident that Turkey became, along with Indonesia, the Muslim-majority country where lesbian/gay communities were the strongest.[147]

In Egypt, there was a heteronormative paradigm shift in the work of Nobel Prize-winning author Naguib Mahfouz. While Mahfouz's 1947 novel *Midaq Alley* portrayed same-sex sexuality as commonplace but public awareness of

---

143   Epprecht 2009, p. 1262; see also Puar 2007, p. 49.
144   Najmabadi 2005, pp. 212–13, 216, 218–19.
145   Shohat 2006, p. 272.
146   Hoad, pp. 568, 566.
147   Drucker 2000a, p. 29.

it as shameful, his 1957 novel *Sugar Street* portrayed male same-sex desire as an 'illness'. And Arab literature after the defeat in the 1967 war with Israel was pervaded by images of humiliating, emasculating penetration of Arab men.[148] Iranian society too, where same-sex intimacy was pervasive for centuries, gradually came under European influence to see it as abnormal, at the same time as women's portrayal as companionate wives and modern mothers undermined 'homosocial Iranian motherhood'.[149] This was not a 'straightforward imposition of European sexual mores on non-European societies', but rather a case of mimicry in the service of rebellion: 'becoming like them to overthrow them'.[150]

Nevertheless, these repressive strategies were bound to fail in eliminating desire or purging culture. Often the forbidden same-sex patterns were hidden in plain sight. Popular Egyptian and other Arab male singers of the 1950s and 1960s still used the word 'beloved' in the masculine form, for example, even when the songs ostensibly referred to females.[151]

LGBT people in the most urbanised regions of Latin America by the 1970s were the most successful of any communities in neo-colonial countries in throwing off the association between homosexuality and imperialist influence. This probably had something to do with their ties with US lesbian/gay liberation, whose identification with anti-imperialism and solidarity was at its height in those years. The Brazilian movement, for example, though rejecting indiscriminate borrowing of North American terminology, welcomed the contributions of British/US activist Winston Leyland when he came in an explicit spirit of solidarity in the late 1970s.[152] Emerging LGBT communities in Asia, both at a greater cultural distance from Europe and North America and less politicised, were less likely to try to combine open LGBT identities with resistance to cultural neo-colonialism – perhaps because anti-imperialist tendencies were influenced in this period by Maoism, with its strong record of homophobia.

China and Cuba

If populist regimes in dependent capitalist countries were persistent in their efforts to stamp out homosexuality, bureaucratic regimes in countries where

---

148   Massad 2007, pp. 272–90; and see Drucker 2000a, pp. 31–2, 34.
149   Peirce 2009, pp. 1335–6.
150   Rao 2012.
151   Drucker 1996, p. 86.
152   Green 1999a, pp. 272–3.

capitalism was overthrown were ruthless. Despite the general relaxation of repression following Stalin's death in 1953, this pattern did not change fundamentally in the USSR before its collapse. Although there was perhaps a bit more room, for example, for a butch/femme subculture attested in a study in the late 1950s and early 1960s, men who had been convicted for sodomy were not included in the massive amnesties and waves of prisoner release in the mid-to-late 1950s. There was no question, then or later, of a return to the gender neutrality and lack of stigmatisation that had characterised the 1920s.[153] Although a controlled decriminalisation took place in Czechoslovakia and Hungary in 1961, and in East Germany in 1968, there was no move in this direction in the USSR. Only Gorbachev's *glasnost* policies in the late 1980s would make a public debate on decriminalisation possible once more.[154]

The Chinese Revolution of 1945–9 brought an unremittingly anti-lesbian and anti-gay regime to power. The Chinese bureaucratic state prosecuted homosexuality as 'hooliganism' or as 'activities that involved "roaming" beyond appropriate social borders'. While the Maoist regime split Chinese society along class lines that overrode kinship, the family remained crucial to individuals' social status through the inheritance of a 'class label'.[155] While after 1949 in the People's Republic ideas about homosexual abnormality were couched in Marxist terms, similar attitudes existed in Taiwan and Hong Kong.[156]

The Cuban Revolution, given its importance for revolutionaries all over Latin America, played a particularly negative role in associating the left with persecution of LGBTs. US imperialism helped foster this association in several ways. Given the fierce repression in the US in the 1950s, same-sex life was often 'channelled into illegal and lucrative offshore markets like the Havana underworld'. This pre-revolutionary sex tourism reinforced prejudice among Cuban revolutionaries, who had little familiarity with the kind of intellectual and artistic homosexual milieu that existed at the time in Mexico, Argentina or Brazil. US backing for a counter-revolutionary fifth column in Cuba in the early 1960s helped ensure that 'private space was invaded as never before'. The Soviet Union and Cuba's own Stalinist Popular Socialist Party also helped to fuel repressive attitudes,[157] as did a growing tendency to apply the Soviet model.[158]

---

153 Healey 2001, pp. 256–7, 241–3, 229–30, 249–50.
154 Healey 2001, pp. 245–9.
155 Rofel 1999, pp. 459, 464.
156 Hinsch 1990, p. 167.
157 Arguelles and Rich 1989, pp. 444–5, 447–8.
158 Lumsden 1996, pp. 180, 182–3.

Repression in revolutionary Cuba not only perpetuated and acted out existing prejudices against gender-dissident *maricones*, but also to a certain extent
froze an invert-dominant model in Cuba at a time when urbanised regions
in Mexico, Argentina and Brazil were beginning to shift towards a different
one. After a certain point, in any event, the Castro regime's macho attacks on
effeminate males as counter-revolutionary became a self-fulfilling prophecy.
One revolutionary intellectual declared that 'no homosexual [can represent]
the revolution, which is a matter for men, of fists and not of feathers'. In 1961,
the government began rounding up 'pederasts, prostitutes, and pimps'.[159] In
these conditions, even sexual and gender dissenters who had backed the revolution found themselves pushed toward ties with the anti-Castro underground,
one of the few places where they could escape their isolation.

The height of the regime's persecution came when gay men and trans
people were among those rounded up into the Military Units to Aid Production
(UMAP) in 1965. Although these camps were closed in 1968, other repressive
measures followed in the late 1960s and early 1970s: LGBT people were purged
from teaching, the arts, delegations abroad, medicine, the foreign ministry and
the Communist Party. Although the Supreme Court in 1975 overturned the
decree justifying the mass firings and some financial compensation was given,
habitual or public homosexuality was only decriminalised to some extent
in 1979 (softening a law passed in 1938). Teaching remained closed to people
convicted of any kind of sexual offence, and the ban on party membership
remained.[160]

Official policies on women's equality only partially mitigated anti-LGBT
attitudes. While women made advances in technical and other professions –
compared to only 13.7 percent of adult women in waged work on the eve of the
revolution – relatively few women had high positions in the regime. Welfare
programmes only supported sick, old or unemployed people if they had no
family to support them, severely limiting women's and LGBT people's independence.[161] While the regime encouraged women to work for wages and men
to share domestic work, anti-LGBT persecution 'reinforced the very *machismo*
that the family law was supposed to combat'.[162] In any event, the Family Code
was premised on the heteronormative nuclear family.[163]

159   Lumsden 1996, pp. 53–4, 58.
160   Lumsden 1996, pp. 65–71, 74–5, 77, 81–4, 93–4; Farber 2011, p. 214. Fidel Castro confessed
        in an interview in 2010 that he had been negligent in not stopping these anti-LGBT cam-
        paigns (Farber 2011, p. 221).
161   Lumsden 1996, pp. 24, 37, 60, 56.
162   Franco 1998, p. 11.
163   Arguelles and Rich, p. 449.

Moreover, self-organisation by blacks, women or LGBT people remained a taboo, so that the regime always set the limits, which were narrow. The leader of its women's organisation famously commented in 1974 that it was 'feminine, not feminist'.[164]

Yet development, secularisation and education have had effects on LGBT identity in China and Cuba that were neither foreseen nor welcomed by the Chinese and Cuban regimes, especially as cautious liberalisation (both economic and cultural) began. As one Nicaraguan lesbian recalled, 'It's contradictory, because ... in Cuba I found a *massive* community. ... I'd never seen so many lesbians and gay men in my life'.[165]

Castroist anti-LGBT prejudices were nevertheless reflected in Latin American liberation movements under Cuban influence, such as the Nicaraguan Sandinista National Liberation Front (FSLN). Pre-revolutionary Nicaragua had a transgender tradition of *locas* who did 'women's work', expressed, for example, in a traditional annual parade of men in drag in the city of Masaya. On the other hand, US sex tourism – on a very small scale – and male prostitution existed in a few bars in Managua.[166] Distaste for trans people in the countryside and for the sometimes-exploitative sexuality in Managua bars compounded the FSLN leaders' homophobic attitudes, which were particularly in evidence during the Sandinista government's first years.[167]

Repression and Resistance

In the early 1960s, in imperialist countries as in dependent ones, the constraints of the law, police, employers, landlords and social pressures of many sorts prevented most people from living openly lesbian/gay lives. Some of the remaining legal constraints were removed by reforms in the course of the decade. The lesbian/gay movements of the 1960s and 1970s in the imperialist countries and much of Latin America, and somewhat later elsewhere, inspired by a wave of other social rebellions, revolted against those bans that survived and against the legal restrictions that had accompanied decriminalisation.

Ironically, post-Second World War anti-homosexual witch-hunts in the US contributed to the establishment of a larger subculture when thousands of people with 'undesirable' discharges, facing ostracism and joblessness if they returned home, settled in port cities like San Francisco, Los Angeles, New York

---

164   Lumsden 1996, pp. 185–6; Farber 2011, p. 193.
165   Randall 2000, p. 99.
166   Drucker 1996, p. 99; Adam 1993, pp. 172–3.
167   Randall 2000, pp. 95–6.

and Boston.[168] The 1953 US federal executive order banning employment of homosexuals applied to around 20 percent of the total US work force.[169] 'The tightening web of oppression in McCarthy's America helped to create the minority it was meant to isolate'.[170]

In the US, persecution and resistance in the 1950s spurred lesbians to bond with one another, while tests meant to detect female homosexuality branded women as lesbians who had never imagined they were. Suddenly many women could become part of a lesbian subculture, Lillian Faderman has written, yet also 'suddenly there were more reasons than ever for the subculture to stay underground'.[171]

Sexual repression was even more vicious in countries where all popular movements were being repressed, as in the anti-gay campaigns of the Chilean junta between 1973 and 1989,[172] and the intimidation and closure of gay businesses under the Argentinean military dictatorship from 1976 to 1983. A wave of censorship and arrests and torture of oppositionists by the Brazilian military junta led to the closure of the fledgling Brazilian gay press in 1969.[173] In Brazil, Colombia, Ecuador, Peru and El Salvador, right-wing death squads carried out 'social clean-up' murders, particularly of male prostitutes and transvestites.[174]

Repression prompted two decades of struggle, at first by 'all too often utterly isolated individuals', later by lesbian/gay movements that refused to continue accepting their exclusion from social citizenship. These movements' victories in the 1970s made mass, open lesbian/gay communities possible in imperialist countries for the first time in history.[175] In the US, by the late 1970s the victories included the repeal of sodomy laws in about half the states, dozens of local anti-discrimination ordinances, the elimination of the ban on federal civil service employment of LGB people, and the removal of homosexuality from the American Psychiatric Association's list of disorders.[176] Trans legal victories included a 1968 New York court decision allowing a post-operative transsexual to legally change her name, a 1977 California court law with the same effect, and the striking down of various US laws against cross-dressing.[177]

---

168   Faderman 1991, p. 126.
169   Valocchi 1999, p. 214, n. 3.
170   D'Emilio 1989, p. 459.
171   Faderman 1991, p. 157.
172   Gough and McNair 1985, p. 88.
173   Green 1999a, pp. 248, 231, 197–8.
174   Drucker 1996, pp. 91–2.
175   Herzog 2011, p. 219.
176   D'Emilio and Freedman 1997, p. 324.
177   Meyerowitz 2002, pp. 208, 274, 245–7.

Anti-discrimination laws – beginning in Canada in Quebec in 1977,[178] in the US in the District of Columbia in 1973, and in Europe with the French law adopted in 1985 – and the equalisation of age of consent had a far greater social impact than the long process of decriminalisation that had begun in France in 1791. As late as the 1970s and 1980s, two-thirds of US lesbians believed that they would lose their jobs if their sexual orientation was known;[179] only with full legal and social equality did the mere absence of repression gradually give way to an effective right to sexual identification and expression. This shifted the boundary between private and public realms that had been so carefully drawn with decriminalisation.

Even if laws did not fully stamp out discrimination, they gave same-sex erotic expression rights in the public sphere. Paradoxically, this right meant the most where working-class job security was weakest, like most of the US, where it is still 'perfectly legal to refuse to hire or to fire someone for any reason or no reason at all, as long as the refusal or the firing does not violate any of a list of specifically-enumerated prohibitions' against discrimination (or the provisions of a union contract).[180]

The rise of political militancy across the capitalist world in the 1960s found expression among lesbians and gays as well, with groups like the Homophile League of New York abandoning the discretion of 1950s homophile groups and picketing publicly.[181] In San Francisco, bar owners united in 1962 to form the Tavern Guild. The nonconformist North Beach bar The Black Cat and its drag star José Sarria provided the base for Sarria's 1961 campaign for city supervisor and the founding in 1964 of the Society for Individual Rights, though the bar owners' backing faded once police harassment of bars largely ended in the mid-1960s. In 1965, the Washington DC chapter of the Mattachine Society broke with the group's tradition of discretion and moderation and began organising picket lines, press conferences and court challenges.[182]

In 1968, a US national conference of gay groups signalled the new militant mood by adopting the slogan 'Gay Is Good'. The meaning of 'coming out' was extended from joining a self-contained homosexual world to the 'open avowal of one's sexual identity, whether at work, at school, at home, or before television cameras', as 'a profoundly political act'. Within a few years the movement,

---

178   Kinsman 1987, p. 213.
179   Faderman 1991, p. 156.
180   Blum 2011/2012.
181   Faderman 1991, p. 191.
182   D'Emilio 1983b, pp. 187–92, 205, 164–5.

rooted in a rapidly expanding gay scene, 'not only provided a model to imitate but offered at last the safety of numbers'.[183]

At least as important in preparing the ground for the explosion of lesbian/ gay liberation in 1968–9 was the growing rebelliousness of groups like drag queens and male hustlers, who were beyond the pale for even the most militant homophile groups, focused as they were on forging a gender-normative homosexual identity. Militancy was growing up among trans people in the 1960s in different parts of the world. Pakistani transgendered *hijras* organised successfully in the early 1960s against a ban on their activities by the Pakistani government.[184] Indonesian *waria* were also organised in the 1960s, before there was any attempt to organise a gay movement as such.[185] Similar trans organising was going on in the same years in the US, with the magazine *Transvestia* launched in 1960, providing a basis for the Los Angeles Hose and Heels Club in 1961 and the national Foundation for Personality Expression in 1962. Resistance mounted on the streets as well, with drag queens and male hustlers fighting the police at Cooper's Donuts in Los Angeles in 1959, cross-dressing teenagers committing civil disobedience at Dewey's lunch counter in Philadelphia in 1965, and drag queens, hustlers and runaway teens fighting the police and rioting in and around Compton's Cafeteria in San Francisco in 1966.[186]

Susan Stryker has shown how the Compton's rebellion in particular was rooted in the broader radicalisation of the 1960s: growing resistance to police repression, which had intensified with military crackdowns on Vietnam-era soldiers' patronage of trans prostitutes; non-white people's resistance to racist 'urban renewal' schemes, notably in San Francisco's Tenderloin; grassroots campaigns for economic justice; and the formation in 1966 of the trans/hustler 'street power' youth group Vanguard, which met at Compton's.[187] Trans people who had in the 1950s often downplayed sex completely were also more often highlighting their sexuality by the late 1960s, bolstered by a growing eroticisation of transwomen in books, tabloids and photography.[188] This background makes clear that the 1969 Stonewall rebellion in New York, considered a founding moment of lesbian/gay liberation, continued a series of trans revolts linked to broader social radicalisation. Although Greenwich Village was not as economically depressed as San Francisco's Tenderloin, it too attracted 'drag

---

183   D'Emilio 1983b, pp. 199, 235, 246–7.
184   Naqvi and Mujtaba 1997, p. 265.
185   Oetomo and Emond 1992, p. 23.
186   Stryker 2008, pp. 53–5, 59–65.
187   Stryker 2008, pp. 65–73.
188   Meyerowitz 2002, pp. 61, 168–9, 196–204.

queens, hustlers, gender nonconformists of many varieties, gay men, a smattering of lesbians, and countercultural types who simply "dug the scene" ' – many of them non-white.[189]

These people's role in the rebellion is by now well known. It was both a gay and a trans insurrection – a rising of both newly confident homosexuals and of the 'outlaws of an already outlawed world'.[190] As trans participant Sylvia Rivera later recalled, activists could unexpectedly say, 'The revolution is finally here!'[191] Or in a more precise if somewhat more prosaic summary: 'A mass movement was born almost overnight'.[192]

The New Gay Left

The lesbian/gay liberation movement linked a rebellion against the growing commercialisation and gender-normativity of the emerging homosexual milieu with broader anti-capitalist movements. The link was made in large part by young gay students and hippies who were 'virtually immune to the penalties that kept homosexuals in line' – rejection by the military, dismissal from the civil service, an arrest record – because they had 'broken with the values of American society and scorned the rewards that success in America offered'.[193]

With May 1968 in France and the Stonewall rebellion in 1969, leftists began once more to play a prominent role in the lesbian/gay movement, through local collectives in cities including London, Los Angeles and New York and publications like *Gay Left* (London), *Gay Community News* (Boston) and *Body Politic* (Toronto). The US Homophile Action League declared, 'We are living in an age of revolution'.[194] Within weeks of Stonewall, the Gay Liberation Front was formed in New York as a self-proclaimed revolutionary group; in 1970, gay liberationists invaded the annual meeting of the American Psychiatric Association and interrupted a paper on aversion therapy with shouts of 'Genocide!' and 'Torture!'[195] Similar groups formed in 1970–1 in Anglophone Canada, Quebec,[196]

---

189   Stryker 2008, p. 83.
190   Shah 2011/2012.
191   Feinberg 2006, pp. 96–7, 109.
192   D'Emilio 1989, p. 466.
193   D'Emilio 2002, p. 55.
194   Faderman 1991, p. 193.
195   D'Emilio 1983b, pp. 232–5.
196   Kinsman 1987, p. 181.

Belgium and Italy; in 1972, sixteen groups from ten countries created an international gay revolutionary network.[197] In France, the Homosexual Front for
Revolutionary Action (FHAR) was vocally active from 1971, the same year that
the newly founded British GLF disrupted the Christian fundamentalist 'Festival
of Light' with a kiss-in in drag.[198]

The impact of the New Left and youth revolts in 1968 and after was as crucial
in parts of Latin America as in Europe and North America, in Argentina beginning in 1969, followed by Mexico in 1971 and Puerto Rico in 1974. In Argentina, a
Homosexual Liberation Front was founded in 1971. In the year before it ceased
publication in 1969, the Brazilian gay *O Snob* became increasingly politicised,
with one report on a march against the military government in 1968 describing the 'emotional sensation … when we feel the brotherhood of an ideal in a
totality never imagined, the shivers throughout our body, the tears that come
to our eyes, and that strange feeling that we are not alone'.[199] In Mexico, the
first gay activism and consciousness-raising in 1971 followed soon after the
student demonstrations of 1968 and strong protests against the regime. By
the late 1970s, there was a vibrant lesbian/gay left, with thousands taking part
in pride marches. Lesbian and gay organisations such as Lambda, Oikabeth
and the Homosexual Revolutionary Action Front (FHAR) grew rapidly.[200]

The actions of the new lesbian/gay left marked an at least temporary revolt
against the emerging gender-normative, predominantly middle-class homosexual identity that 1950s homophile groups had been helping to consolidate.
They expressed a camp sensibility that ' "denaturalizes normality" and makes
fun of heterosexuality'.[201] Martha Shelley of New York GLF wrote, 'We are
women and men … in revolt against the sex-role structure and nuclear family
structure', a striking contrast with homophile groups that had worked in the
1950s to make homosexuals adapt to the sex-role structure. Allen Young of GLF
demanded 'an end to the gender programming which starts when we are born',
and declared that 'in a free society everyone will be gay'[202] – that is, would tran-
scend the categories of heterosexual and homosexual. The Mattachine Society
by contrast, even in its initial, most radical months and even its most radical
chapters in the mid-1960s, had not gone further than defending the rights of a

197   Bréville 2011.
198   Herzog 2011, pp. 168–9; see also Weeks 1981, pp. 285–6.
199   Green 1999a, pp. 182, 195.
200   Lumsden 1991, pp. 60, 63–5.
201   Kinsman 1987, pp. 146–7.
202   D'Emilio and Freedman 1997, pp. 321–2.

homosexual minority. Now lesbian/gay liberation was rejecting the minority-group model, in favour of a vision of universal sexual liberation.

The new gay radical left was international, as part of a broader, global new left operating in a 'genuinely global' world. Activists in this world read many of the same books and saw GLF actions in New York and FHAR actions in Paris or Mexico City, like revolts at the Sorbonne, in Berkeley and in Prague, as 'part of the same event in the same global village'.[203] Radical lesbian/gay groups took their place from the beginning in anti-war and radical student actions;[204] shortly after its founding, New York GLF formed lesbian/gay contingents at anti-war marches in New York and Washington in 1969.[205]

The FHAR in France was particularly notable for its anti-imperialism, reacting against the ways the French racist far right linked the twin dangers of Arab immigration and homosexuality (especially among student activists who were supposedly 'inviting little brown-skinned lads into their bedrooms'). Gay leftist Jean Genet turned the prejudice upside down in an interview, speculating that perhaps going 'to bed with Algerians' had helped him realise that 'Algerians are no different from other men' and reinforced his sympathy for the Algerian struggle. The FHAR among other things made a graphic connection with the recent Algerian war of liberation with a manifesto of '343 sluts' who declared, 'We've been buggered by Arabs. We're proud of it and we'll do it again'. Far left intellectual Daniel Guérin among others embraced the impulse of solidarity that inspired the statement, and announced in signing it, 'All my life I have practiced a solidarity with Arabs based on shared oppression'[206] – though many radical intellectuals and even FHAR members criticised the essentialist and even racist way it reduced Arab men to a means of expression for white French gay men. A similar one-sided erotic charge permeated Genet's solidarity with the Palestinian fedayeen and Black Panthers.[207]

Lesbian leftists played an integral and visible role in a rising socialist feminist current, as exemplified by Charlotte Bunch's linkage of lesbianism to a 'real commitment to class struggle' in a speech to a socialist feminist conference in Antioch, Ohio, in 1975.[208] Lesbian feminists easily understood that freedom and equality for lesbians required women's emancipation, so that women would have other options than marriage and economic dependence

203   Hobsbawm 1994, pp. 446–7.
204   D'Emilio and Freedman 1997, p. 321.
205   D'Emilio 1983b, p. 233.
206   Shephard 2012, pp. 95–7, 103, 106, 114, 107.
207   Cervulle and Rees-Roberts 2010, pp. 61, 126 (citing Alan Sinfield).
208   Hennessy 2000, pp. 177–8.

on men. These concerns helped explain the links that Latin American lesbian activists made in the 1970s between lesbian/gay liberation, socialism and feminism, demanding 'a socialism without sexism'.[209] US lesbian feminists developed such a strong class-consciousness that they even became defensive if they had middle-class backgrounds, feeling obliged to become *'nouveau pauvre* or at least downwardly mobile'.[210] This class-consciousness had its limits, however. In hindsight, as Amber Hollibaugh has observed, the kinds of lesbians she worked with in the 1980s who were most at risk for AIDS – many of them sex workers, many 'endlessly incarcerated' – had never been visible in the lesbian feminist milieu.[211]

Hollibaugh was also a participant in northern California's Bay Area Gay Liberation (BAGL), founded in 1975,[212] which she has recalled as 'a socialist, primarily faggot organisation [that] set the tone of struggle, maintaining links between the gay male community and third-world communities', with 'a model for coming together, and taking up sexism and racism'.[213] The first three US national marches for lesbian/gay rights, in 1979, 1987 and 1993, were led by the left, with exemplary democratic decision-making processes and a wide range of progressive demands. These platforms spoke for tens of thousands of activists, if not for the mass of apolitical LGBT people.

Feminism and Black Militancy

Among the factors that were crucial in the emergence of the new lesbian/ gay left, links to feminism and black movements were particularly important. Moving beyond the narrow conception of activism that prevailed in unions and parties, feminism was key in replacing a narrow, 'economistic view of justice with a broader three-dimensional understanding, encompassing economy, culture and politics'.[214] By insisting on the political nature of personal life, 'even the way we make love and with whom', feminists began to 'break down the barriers which kept so many people, especially women [and LGBT people], out of politics'.[215] The women's movement also influenced gay activists in the

---

209   Mogrovejo 2000, p. 72.

210   Hennessy 2000, pp. 46–7, 177–8; Faderman 1991, pp. 236–7.

211   Shah 2011/2012.

212   Laird 2012.

213   Hollibaugh 1980, p. 212.

214   Fraser 2009, p. 103.

215   Rowbotham, Segal and Wainwright 1979, p. 13.

way it pioneered a freewheeling 'countercultural democratizing movement – anti-hierarchical, participatory and demotic'.[216] Both movements viewed democracy not simply as a procedural issue, but as a question of equal power within movements as well as society at large.[217]

The links between lesbianism and radical feminism were strong and clear from the first days of lesbian/gay liberation. As the women's movement radicalised, feminists too saw the link. In an implicit response to Friedan's homophobia, US leader Gloria Steinem warned, 'As long as we fear the word "lesbian" we are curtailing our own strength and abandoning our sisters'.[218] In 1974, a conference of the British Women's Liberation Movement added the right to a 'self-defined sexuality' and an end to anti-lesbian discrimination to its core demands.[219]

By questioning gender categories, radical feminists 'paved a smoother road' for lesbians and gays who were also challenging them. Lesbian feminists could sometimes be a bridge between feminist and lesbian/gay movements[220] – although the relative ease with which women and men coexisted in the early years of gay liberation lasted only until women became too fed up with gay men's treating them as the 'ladies auxiliary of the gay movement',[221] as did the women in the London Gay Liberation Front in 1972.[222] Lesbian feminism became the source of a 'broader and more diffuse social radicalization' with a 'broader social vision'.[223] It so cogently related gender and sexual oppression that both the women's and the gay movement drew on lesbian feminist analysis, along the way making the women's movement 'a "breeding ground" for lesbians'.[224]

Feminists with same-sex desires had a special stake in combating 'the patriarchal insistence that women be the sexualized object of exchange between men', expressed notably in the sexual harassment and rape of women who refused to be exchanged.[225] Some feminists saw erotic and emotional ties between women as, in Adrienne Rich's term, a 'lesbian continuum' of resistance to male domination. While rejecting the way Rich's conception of 'compulsory

216   Fraser 2009, p. 105.
217   Rowbotham, Segal and Wainwright 1979, p. 77.
218   Faderman 1991, p. 213.
219   Duggan 2013, p. 14.
220   D'Emilio 1983b, pp. 226, 237.
221   Faderman 1991, p. 189.
222   Arruzza 2013, p. 78.
223   Kinsman 1987, p. 17.
224   D'Emilio 1989, p. 467.
225   Hennessy 2000, p. 198.

heterosexuality'[226] oversimplified relations between black men and women, many black women celebrated women's 'alternative and parallel sexual culture' and their spirit of economic and social independence.[227] Lesbian socialist feminists at the same time insisted on the specific situation of women-loving women that could not be subsumed by the categories 'queer' and 'gay': their subjection to the gendered division of labour and to many forms of women's oppression.[228]

One source of affinity between feminist and lesbian/gay movements was the hostility they initially faced from the left, not only the traditional Stalinist left, but also much of the New Left. In an early feminist essay, Marge Piercy described the way female staff were routinely recruited for New Left groups as '[f]ucking a staff into existence'. In 1969, at a US radical rally, feminist theorist Shulamith Firestone's attempt to speak evoked cries to 'take her off the stage and fuck her'. This widespread machismo on the left created a propitious atmosphere for questioning the existing left's conception of politics.[229]

All socialist feminists agreed on the need for an independent women's movement that would choose its own leadership and chart its own course alongside an independent labour movement – in both of which socialist feminists needed to fight for their politics. LGBT socialists came to understand that an independent LGBT movement, similarly, was a key safeguard against the manipulative practices of some groups that had helped discredit Marxism in LGBT and other movements – not to mention the neglect of LGBT issues that had led many LGBT activists to question the left's relevance altogether.[230] Within the socialist movement, challenging male bias also meant criticising 'the artificial separation between work and everyday life', in which only events at the workplace or in formal politics were deemed worthy of political attention[231] – another vital point for LGBT struggles.

Feminists went on to challenge the full range of male domination, not only in politics and workplaces, but also in families and sexual relationships. The starting point was that 'the personal is political'.[232] One of the central props of the heterosexual norm for women was undermined from the moment Mary

226   Rich 1983.
227   Wekker 2006, pp. 68, 2–3.
228   Hennessy 2000, pp. 175–6.
229   D'Emilio and Freedman 1997, pp. 310–11.
230   See Cohen 2005, p. 28.
231   Rowbotham, Segal and Wainwright 1979, p. 60.
232   D'Emilio and Freedman 1997, pp. 310–1.

Jane Sherfey,[233] Anne Koedt and others, taking off from the work of William Masters and Virginia Johnson, began exposing the 'myth of the vaginal orgasm', the notion that penetration by a male was either necessary or sufficient for female sexual pleasure. Koedt wrote that the recognition of the clitoral orgasm would 'threaten the heterosexual *institution*' by making clear that 'sexual pleasure was obtainable from either men *or* women'.[234] In France, in 1974–5 a celebrated trial of three French men for raping two young Belgian lesbians made it possible to make political links between a feminist analysis of rape as male violence against women and a lesbian/gay liberationist analysis of 'corrective' rape as a tool for imposing compulsory heterosexuality.[235]

Gradually feminists came to see lesbianism as 'a test of female autonomy'.[236] In the US by the late 1970s, notably in northern California, western Massachusetts and Iowa City, there were largely lesbian women's communities with bars and coffeehouses, dozens of newspapers and journals, thriving presses, bookshops, collectives and for-profit businesses.[237]

Bunch declared that lesbianism was 'a political matter of oppression, domination, and power'.[238] New York Radicalesbians described lesbians in 1970 as rebels against the female role and as 'the rage of all women condensed to the point of explosion'. A strong current among lesbian feminists, represented, for example, by the Italian group Female Revolt, even began arguing that lesbianism was the 'necessary first step' for feminists searching for a free sexuality. They increasingly saw lesbianism as the only 'noble choice' a feminist could make, and heterosexuality as a sign of female masochism.[239] In Italy in 1977, a series of lesbian separatist groups sprang up in different cities, denouncing women who continued to have sexual relationships with men.[240]

Radical feminists moved on to wrestle with the reality that there is no 'homogeneous imaginary lesbian', since the position of women under gendered capitalism was very different among 'the haves' and 'the have-nots'.[241] Lesbians in or from the dependent world emphasised how gender inequality and dependent

233 Weeks 1981, p. 284.
234 D'Emilio and Freedman 1997, pp. 312–3.
235 Herzog 2011, pp. 163–4, 166–7.
236 Weeks 1981, p. 285.
237 Rubin 2011, p. 356.
238 D'Emilio and Freedman 1997, p. 317.
239 Faderman 1991, p. 206; Herzog 2011, pp. 170–1; Faderman 1991, pp. 207, 205.
240 Arruzza 2013, p. 76.
241 Hennessy 2000, pp. 201–2.

development reinforced each other, resulting in a female labour force in dominated countries that was 'cheaper than cheap'.[242]

Latin American lesbian feminism developed in conjunction with Latin
American women's movements generally.[243] The growth of feminism in the
1970s was crucial for the foundation of the first Mexican lesbian group in 1977,
for example.[244] In Chile, under the Pinochet dictatorship, the Ayuquelen
Lesbian Feminist Collective for several years after 1984 was the sole voice of
Chilean lesbians and gays, beginning from a feminist analysis.[245] In Brazil, the
rise by 1978 of feminist groups linking class and gender issues served as a stimulus to a similar approach in the lesbian/gay movement.[246] In Asia too, lesbian
movements often spun off from feminism, as in Thailand and the Philippines,
and were not necessarily linked to gay male activism.[247] Lesbian networking
at the 1983 Latin American Feminist Gathering and the 1985 UN women's
conference in Nairobi contributed to making possible the first Latin American
and Caribbean Lesbian Gathering in 1987, and the first Asian Lesbian Network
conference in 1990. These international gatherings sometimes inspired women
to found the first lesbian groups in their own countries after they returned
home, for example in El Salvador.

Lesbian feminists tried in their heyday to forge a liberated, feminist sexuality, an attempt that proved frustrating in the absence of the full material
conditions for women's liberation – and in the presence of some strikingly traditional conceptions of women's sexuality. Calls to get rid of the 'male-model
of penetration and orgasm' ran up against many lesbians' unwillingness to be
satisfied with hugging, holding hands, kissing and '[l]ocking souls with women
by looking deep in their eyes'. Calls to reject monogamy as 'men's way of keeping women enslaved' ran up against most women's socialisation and died down
for a time in many lesbian feminist communities by the 1980s, only to resurface
in different settings in later decades. Special nights for lesbians organised at
gay bathhouses by pro-sex feminists failed to catch on either.[248]

Politically too, lesbian feminists' attempts to carve out a separate realm
became bogged down in disagreements. The concept of 'male-identified
women' was uncontroversial when applied to right-wing women devoted

242   Wekker 2006, p. 57.

243   Mogrovejo 2000.

244   Lumsden 1991, pp. 63–5.

245   Robles 1998, p. 37.

246   Green 1999a, pp. 244–5.

247   Altman 2000, p. 140.

248   Faderman 1991, pp. 231–4, 254, 256–7.

to defending male-dominated institutions, or to conventional married women defending male-dominated families. But it was contested when extended to women seen as too masculine. 'I, for one, did not join the women's movement to be told how to be a good girl', Gayle Rubin argued in opposition to what she baptised 'femininism'. 'A strongly masculine butch will not necessarily identify politically with men', she would later argue. 'In fact, it is sometimes the most masculine women who confront male privilege most directly and painfully and are most enraged by it'.[249]

Not only lesbians but even gay men after 1968 focused on sexism as the root cause of their oppression.[250] Lesbian/gay liberationists fought for a world in which women would have as much power as men, be as strong as men, and play as great a role in public life, while men would be as gentle and emotional as women, play an equal role in the home and be as nurturing for children. They used drag and 'genderfuck' to cross and confuse gender boundaries. If masculinity and femininity could come to be seen as arbitrary distinctions, they reasoned, a fixed preference for a masculine or feminine partner (in sex, love or life) could be seen as neither more normal nor stranger than a fixed preference for blonds or brunettes. In a liberated culture everyone would in principle be open to erotic ties with men or women, and any preference that might exist would lose its social significance. In this sense, everyone and no one would be gay. As one classic early text of lesbian/gay liberation put it, 'the categories of homosexuality and heterosexuality would disappear'.[251]

For Marxists active in lesbian/gay liberation, integrating a purely social conception of gender required overcoming an aversion among earlier Marxists that had deep roots in the Marxist tradition. Almost all Marxists in the Second and Third Internationals, including pioneering thinkers on women's liberation like Clara Zetkin and Alexandra Kollontai, had dismissed feminism as a middle-class ideology. They rejected the idea of a broad, cross-class, independent women's movement 'indiscriminately embracing all women' – although Kollontai rebelled against the Marxist orthodoxy of her day by insisting that gender and sexual issues were political and indifference to them 'unforgivable', by challenging the sexual double standard and men's refusal to 'see a woman as an independent person', and by stressing the importance of a new morality for the working-class cause.[252] Kollontai's discussion of childrearing under socialism came very close to the later socialist feminist view of gender roles as

---

249   Rubin 2011, pp. 127, 244.
250   D'Emilio 2002, p. 56.
251   D'Emilio 2002, p. 155.
252   Kollontai 1978, pp. 51, 239, 243–4, 249.

purely social constructions. But only in the 1970s did socialist feminists begin to forge a new synthesis of Marxism and feminism, which gradually won over many Marxist currents and was useful for lesbian/gay liberation.

But although gender norms relaxed to a certain extent in the 1960s and 1970s, this led to a true devaluation of masculinity and femininity only in the context of a strong feminist critique, which was never entirely hegemonic in gay male circles.[253] The history of early lesbian/gay liberation suggests that among gay men, both gender-subversive and gender-conformist potentials were present from the start.

The two tendencies clashed, for example, in the 1969 split in New York between the substantively radical, multi-issue Gay Liberation Front and the tactically radical but single-issue Gay Activists Alliance. Alongside gay male New Leftists who admired macho straight revolutionaries, there were anti-macho groups like the Effeminists, Flaming Faggots, Street Transvestite Action Revolutionaries (STAR)[254] – founded in 1970 by trans activists Sylvia Rivera and Marsha Johnson, also active in GLF – and the Queens' Liberation Front.[255] Radical feminism pervaded other US 'second-wave' trans groups like the Transexual Counseling Service, the Transsexual Action Organization, and others.[256] France's FHAR showed strong 'effeminist' tendencies: its male members believed that particularly the receptive role they played in anal sex enabled them to understand 'the psychosexual position of women' and, much more broadly, the 'sexual misery from which we all suffer, homos, women, blacks, Indians, immigrants, proles, high schoolers, youth, the insane'.[257]

In the US by the mid-1970s, as the New Left shrank and its remnants turned to Maoist and other forms of 'party-building', the anti-machos had largely lost out among gay activists. The gay movement began to marginalise and exclude the trans people and gender dissenters who had played a key role from the 1966 Compton's rebellion through Stonewall.[258] In retrospect, the years of lesbian/gay liberation, with its rejection of the conception of a fixed gay minority, was only a brief interlude.[259] Increasingly, even as gender-bending continued to be a central defining element of many gay men's subculture and sense of style, the growing lesbian/gay movement seemed in continuity with the more militant

---

253   Cf. Floyd 2009, pp. 177–8.
254   Floyd 2009, pp. 168–70.
255   Stryker 2008, pp. 85–7.
256   Meyerowitz 2002, pp. 234–41.
257   Shepard 2012, pp. 110–11.
258   Stryker 2008, pp. 85–7.
259   Valocchi 1999, p. 217.

strand of homophile activism from the mid-1960s, not with the full diversity of the Stonewall rebellion.

Gender dissenters particularly suffered from the increasingly conservative climate in the course of the 1970s, as even legal victories 'both accommodated transsexuals and contained the threat', preserving legal and social gender distinctions. Agencies increasingly demanded medical and court documents before granting any recognition to trans people. In 1977, the fifth International Symposium on Gender Identity refused to seat a trans person on its Standards Committee of six doctors. Trans organisations fell apart one by one. In 1979, symbolically, the Johns Hopkins gender clinic stopped performing sex-reassignment surgery altogether, following charges that the operation gave 'no objective advantage in terms of social rehabilitation'.[260]

Not only feminism but also black consciousness was important for early LGBT organising, for example, in Brazil.[261] The links between LGBT organising and black struggles against apartheid in South Africa are striking. In the US, the civil rights struggle provided Frank Kameny and other mid-1960s gay militants with 'compelling evidence of the success of direct action',[262] manifest, for example, in the New York Mattachine Society's 'sip-in' at Julius' bar in 1966 (obviously modelled on the civil rights movement's sit-ins) against the liquor authority's policy of requiring that bars refuse service to open homosexuals.[263] In a more radical vein, Black Power marked the birth of identity politics.[264] It was the militancy of blacks (and students and the poor) in the 1960s that 'ignited' lesbian/gay liberation. Yet African-American and Latina lesbians often felt marginalised among lesbian feminists and impelled to give priority to their ethnic communities' struggles or to form their own lesbian groups.[265]

By contrast Rivera, herself Puerto Rican, has recalled a 1970 protest against police repression by the Puerto Rican Young Lords as 'one of the first times the STAR banner was shown in public': 'I ended up meeting some of the Young Lords that day. I became one of them'. That same year Black Panther leader Huey Newton issued a statement challenging anti-gay prejudice and calling for full participation of the gay and women's movements in revolutionary politics.[266] Radical lesbian/gay groups reciprocated by marching in solidarity

---

260 Meyerowitz 2002, pp. 253, 252, 248, 254–8, 267–70.
261 Green 2000, p. 59.
262 D'Emilio 1983b, p. 223. See also D'Emilio 2002, pp. 27–8.
263 Simon and Leitsch 2008.
264 D'Emilio 2002, p. 171.
265 Faderman 1991, pp. 195, 240–3.
266 Feinberg 1998, pp. 108, 123.

with the Black Panthers; a GLF member addressed a rally in 1970 in support
of imprisoned Panther leaders.[267] The Black Power slogan 'black is beautiful'
provided a model for gay pride.[268]

At universities, only the centrality of African-American and Latino revolts
to the rebellions of the 1960s in the US (given the comparative weakness of the
explicitly working-class left) explains the rapid proliferation of Black, Latino
and ethnic studies programmes since the 1970s. The rise of women's and
queer studies largely took advantage of an academic space that Black and
Latino studies had opened up. The striking hegemony of the US in academic
queer studies worldwide indirectly reflects in this sense the centrality of racism to the US political economy – despite the ongoing reality of racism inside
LGBT communities and movements.

In later years, as lesbian/gay movements grew more quickly in Europe and
North America, influences from diasporas there, for instance from US Latinos,
became a stimulus to community formation in some dependent countries, at
least in regions where LGBT communities had not yet emerged in the 1970s.
The emergence of South Asian LGBT groups in North America and Europe in
the mid-1980s paralleled organising in South Asia itself, for example.[269]

... and Changes on the Existing Radical Left

Initially in the 1960s and 1970s, the new gay left was an autonomous phenomenon, with only limited influence on existing radical and revolutionary
organisations. The old left's deep-rooted prejudices often restricted or wholly
blocked its convergence with lesbian/gay resistance. The same applied to feminism and even to a certain extent to black and immigrant struggles, but heterosexist prejudices were especially blatant.

From the 1930s on, the Stalinist, Maoist and later Castroist currents that
dominated the international anti-capitalist left had fostered anti-gay prejudice, inevitably undermining socialists' standing among LGBT people. Few
LGBT people remembered the days in the 1920s when not just Communists
but the bulk of activists in the world's 'sex reform' movements viewed Soviet
Russia as a beacon of enlightened sexual policies. However, LGBT people were
increasingly aware that the record of anti-capitalist movements and regimes in
the twentieth century on sexual issues was, for the most part, poor.

---

267   D'Emilio 1983b, p. 233.
268   D'Emilio and Freedman 1997, pp. 320–1.
269   Joseph and Dhall 2000, pp. 161–2.

After the Second World War, Communist and Maoist parties around the world continued to propagate anti-gay attitudes, and many leftist currents that were not pro-Soviet or Maoist unthinkingly took up the anti-gay tradition. Although the Communist tradition had a strong influence on Harry Hay and other ex-Communists who founded the US Mattachine Society in 1950–1 – from Mattachine's initially clandestine structure to the Popular Front tone of its broader campaigns and its conception of gays as an oppressed minority – Hay had to leave the CP before starting gay organising.[270] African-American poet Audre Lorde faced prejudice as a lesbian among US CP members in 1953 when she was working on a committee to free Julius and Ethel Rosenberg,[271] as did Bettina Aptheker. In the 1940s and 1950s, several lesbian and male homosexual CP members were asked to leave on the grounds that they could be blackmailed into informing for the FBI.[272] Anti-Stalinist Marxist currents that were less hostile to LGBT struggles (Niek Engelschman, founder of the Dutch gay organisation COC, for example, had been chair of the youth group of the pre-war Revolutionary Socialist Workers Party) were small and isolated.

Anti-LGBT attitudes were in evidence for many decades in many other parties under Soviet or Chinese influence. The Brazilian Communist Party and its large Maoist offshoot in the 1970s shared the attitude that homosexuality was a form of 'bourgeois decadence' and that fighting homophobia would divide the movement against the dictatorship.[273] In the US, in the early 1970s the Maoist Revolutionary Union (later the Revolutionary Communist Party) wrote in a special pamphlet on the issue that homosexuals were 'not prepared, in principle, for the arduous task of class transformation'.[274] As late as 1994, a women's organisation affiliated to the Communist Party of India condemned a conference for South Asian gay men as an 'invasion of India by decadent western cultures'.[275]

The major revolutionary organisations that grew up in Latin America in the 1970s under Cuban influence were hardly better. For example, in Argentina in 1973 when right-wing posters linked Marxist urban guerrillas to homosexuality and drug addiction, the left responded at a demonstration by chanting, 'We're not faggots, we're not junkies'.[276] In Chile too, the first public gay march in

---

270   D'Emilio 1983b, pp. 62–6, 69.
271   Faderman 1991, p. 144.
272   Aptheker 2008.
273   Green 1999a, pp. 271, 275; Green 2012, p. 450.
274   Rubin 2011, p. 122.
275   Joseph and Dhall 2000, pp. 163–4.
276   Drucker 1996, p. 94.

1972 in Santiago, under Salvador Allende's Popular Unity coalition of reformist socialists and pro-Soviet Communists, was broken up by the police and ridiculed in the left press.[277]

Machismo prevailed among Cuban-inspired revolutionary guerrillas in Brazilian jails in the 1970s, in a country where society and sexuality had begun changing rapidly by the 1960s and a new gay culture was developing. As the military dictatorship consolidated itself in the late 1960s and increasingly clamped down on the cultural, musical and sexual ferment of its society, dissenters 'trifurcated' between apolitical hippies, sell-outs and political diehards. Leftists who decided that only armed struggle could overthrow the regime dismissed cultural dissent as merely 'alienated', despite revolutionary leaders' own occasional weakness for the Beatles. They set out to create the socialist 'new man'. Their cult of Che Guevara allowed them to preserve aspects of their alternative lifestyles – long hair and free heterosexual love, for example – while putting their militant, working-class masculinity beyond question – and putting their few female comrades in all sorts of quandaries.[278]

The ethos of this self-enclosed revolutionary subculture, embracing a model of masculinity characteristic of the somewhat different Cuban sexual order in a slightly different period, imposed 'compulsory heterosexuality or at least an appearance of it'. Herbert Daniel, who would later come out as gay, recalled concluding in this period, 'I had to "forget" my sexuality'. Women had to prove themselves in this milieu by being as macho as the men, only to find that the men wondered if their 'overly masculine demeanor' might mean that they were closeted lesbians. Only in the late 1970s in Paris did Daniel and others launch a debate about same-sex love among the several hundred exiled Brazilian revolutionaries – a debate that deeply divided them for a time.[279]

The issues that divided the existing Communist and socialist organisations from LGBT, feminist and black movements went beyond machismo and other forms of prejudice. Linked to reformist, Stalinist and Maoist parties' orientation to winning and holding state power was an insistence that only 'the' party had a scientific, global vision of society, which automatically justified their playing a leadership role in all 'partial' movements. This led Communist and other parties to see politics as their private reserve and to try to limit social movements to their own 'specific problems'.[280] Socialist feminists among

---

277   Robles 1998, p. 36.
278   Green 2012, pp. 446–8, 463–4, 458–9, 454–5.
279   Green 2012, pp. 461, 452, 455, 465.
280   Rowbotham, Segal and Wainwright 1979, pp. 7–8 (citing Fernando Claudín).

others, however, refused to accept that their insights could only be validly applied to women's issues.

Beginning in the 1970s, however, accelerating in the 1980s and definitively with the collapse of the Soviet Union in 1991, Stalinist hegemony over the international left ended and space opened up for more democratic anti-capitalist currents. Although repression and orthodox Maoist hegemony on the far left was an effective obstacle to Marxist influence in Asian LGBT communities, there began to be openings in the Americas and Western Europe in the 1970s. The conviction began to spread on the left that Soviet, Chinese and Cuban vanguardist models, sexism and heterosexism reflected these regime's departures from Marxism's democratic essence, rather than Marxism's inherent nature.

Given the stress that Lenin and the Communist International had placed on black and other national liberation struggles, the rise in the 1960s of independent black movements was particularly hard for parties in the Leninist tradition to ignore or dismiss. It was the rise of black militancy and anti-imperialist struggles in the 1960s that first effectively challenged socialist organisations' subordination of autonomous movements.[281] By the mid-1970s, feminism too was provoking major debates on the left, notably in Western Europe, with Eurocommunist parties reconsidering their relationship to the women's movement. For the Italian far left organisation Lotta Continua, one of Europe's biggest Maoist groups, feminism even played a central role in its divisions and dissolution in 1976.[282] Among Trotskyist currents, the Fourth International was notable in adopting a long resolution on women's liberation in 1979 that recognised that women's liberation 'posed a profound challenge' to all working-class currents, declared it 'a life-and-death matter for the workers movement', supported women's autonomous self-organisation 'not subordinate to the decisions or policy needs of any political tendency', called for challenging sexist attitudes in its own national sections, and specifically included a positive account of lesbian feminism.[283]

Lesbian/gay liberation was particularly hard for the existing left organisations to address. But this too began to happen in the 1970s – although even in the best of cases the old left came to terms only with the more respectable aspects of emerging lesbian/gay identity, rarely with lesbian feminism's full challenge to male supremacy or with the most radical sexual impulses of trans and hustler revolts. Still, the left was sometimes profoundly reshaped by

281   Rowbotham, Segal and Wainwright 1979, p. 87.
282   Arruzza 2013, p. 75.
283   Fourth International 1979.

its encounter with lesbian/gay activism, in Latin America and South Africa as well as imperialist countries.

The confrontation of LGBT radicals with the existing left's prejudices was played out, for example, on the small stage of Nicaragua. As one Nicaraguan lesbian recounted, the Sandinista Revolution 'opened up a space'. International lesbian/gay solidarity, particularly from San Francisco's lesbian/gay Victoria Mercado Brigade, played a role in widening possibilities. The rise of a US movement against AIDS about the time that the disease appeared in Nicaragua created an opening for the fledgling LGBT movement. In 1988, lesbians and gay men organised an AIDS collective with support from the ministry of health.[284] In 1989, they marched openly as a contingent in the revolution's tenth anniversary celebration.[285] Even after the Sandinistas lost power and over the years moved to the right, they confirmed and sustained their support for LGBT rights.

In Mexico, by 1982 the LGBT movement linked up with the Revolutionary Workers Party (the section of the Fourth International), which ran several LGBT leaders as candidates in the elections that year.[286] On a bigger scale in Brazil, after a military dictatorship that broke the LGBT movement's continuity for almost a decade, the liberalisation of the regime and rise of the opposition converged with the rise of a new Brazilian gay left from 1976, culminating in 1980 with the first national gathering of gay groups and a few weeks later an LGBT contingent in a May Day rally in support of a São Paulo general strike.[287] The new Workers Party (PT) founded at the start of the 1980s worked well with the LGBT movement, with its candidates being elected with open LGBT backing and explicitly pro-gay programmes. The PT had the advantage of being a newly founded party that did not include the older, more anti-LGBT currents of the CP and Maoists.[288] Its leader Ignacio Lula da Silva declared at its first congress in 1981, 'We will not permit homosexuality to be treated as a sickness, much less as a case for the police'.[289]

Another breakthrough for radical lesbian/gay organising took place in black townships in South Africa, in the wake of the 1976 Soweto uprising. The issue of LGBT rights came to the fore in 1984 when one of several African National Congress members on trial for their lives, Simon Nkoli, was revealed to be gay. This provoked a split in the South African LGBT movement. Anti-apartheid

---

284   Randall 2000, pp. 101, 94, 96.

285   Drucker 1996, p. 99.

286   Lumsden 1991, pp. 60, 63–5; Drucker 1996, p. 94.

287   Green 1999a, pp. 271–6.

288   Green 2000, pp. 62–3.

289   Green 2012, p. 466.

lesbian/gay groups such as the Gay and Lesbian Organisation of the Witwatersrand and the Organisation for Lesbian and Gay Action (OLGA) were founded, and in 1990 the United Democratic Front admitted OLGA as an affiliate. The first Johannesburg Lesbian and Gay Pride celebration took place in 1990 – the same year that Nelson Mandela was released and the ANC legalised. A ban on discrimination on the basis of sexual orientation was included in the new South African constitution in 1996.[290] The ties forged in struggle between LGBT movements and the FSLN, PT and ANC would survive when these parties took power – though as in other countries, their increasingly moderate politics would raise issues on both sides.

The radical left would continue in later decades to come to terms with lesbian/gay communities, as the lesbian/gay identity that emerged under Fordism continued to take hold and spread. Other trends of the Fordist period would continue as well in the years that followed: the growing sexualisation of society and commercialisation of sexuality; decriminalisation and the adoption of anti-discrimination laws in more countries; and the increasing dissociation of lesbian/gay identity from gender nonconformity. The collapse of the Soviet bloc, major changes in China and Cuba, and the weakening of populist regimes in economically dominated countries would even remove barriers to the further spread of gay patterns. But from the 1980s on, neoliberalism would drastically undermine several of the foundations of the gay-dominant regime: rising real wages; expanding welfare states; and radicalised and growing anti-imperialist, black and feminist movements. The consequences of these changes for the same-sex formation would be profound.

---

290   Drucker 1996, pp. 95–6; Gevisser 2000, pp. 111, 119–20.

PART 2

Gay Normality Under Neoliberalism

∵

Homonormativity and Queer

Once the specificity of lesbian/gay identity has been explored and its emergence mapped, the question arises: is this the end of the story? Especially as gay normality has spread not only in imperialist countries, but also in other regions, some have wondered whether all other forms of same-sex sexuality are surrendering to what Dennis Altman has critiqued as the triumphant 'global gay', a monolithic figure riding the wave of capitalist globalisation.[1] In much the same way that *homo sapiens* was once viewed as the culmination of biological evolution, and liberal democracy (especially in the 1990s) as the culmination of human history, one might have sometimes imagined that all roads of LGBT history led to Castro Street in San Francisco. Queer theorists have tried to undermine any such monolithic vision of gay identity.[2] But their abstract championing of 'difference' has rarely engaged concretely with the historiography that sometimes seems to suggest that LGBT history is a one-way street. Queer theorists have too often focused on the production of discourse rather than the social relations underlying it.[3]

Part 2 of this book shows that lesbian/gay identities have in fact continued to spread and LGBT people have continued to carve out social space for themselves under neoliberalism since the 1970s. But spreading and consolidating gay identities have increasingly been 'warping', reflecting deepening class disparities and the even more intensive commercialisation and commodification of sexuality of the past several decades. A materialist approach can chart not only the emergence of lesbian/gay identities by the 1970s, but also shifts in LGBT identities in recent decades. It can explore connections between trends in the LGBT world and recent developments in gendered capitalism: specifically, in the mode of accumulation and kinds of societies that have taken shape since the recessions of 1974–5 and 1979–82.[4]

Chapter 3 maps the ways in which same-sex patterns have been adapting under neoliberalism to an increasingly fragmented working class, and to a gender order in which direct male domination of women is camouflaged in superficially gender-neutral institutions. In imperialist countries, the dominant

---

1 Altman 1996, pp. 77–8.
2 For example, Seidman 1997, p. 195.
3 Reynolds 2003.
4 Mandel 1978 and 1995.

lesbian/gay identities have become increasingly 'homonationalist', taking their place in an intensifying global hierarchy and an unequal world. Especially in some regions where LGBT rights have become most solidly established and particularly among the middle class, gay identity has morphed into a new gay normality, characterised by growing ghettoisation, gender conformity, the exclusion of trans people and sexually marginalised queers, a racist and Islamophobic integration into dominant nations and the formation of normative families founded on marriage. I call this current same-sex regime 'homonormative-dominant'.

The rise of homonormativity by no means implies that the larger societies are less heteronormative; on the contrary, homonormativity reflects and adapts to the heterosexual norm. The superficial multiculturalism characteristic of neoliberalism barely masks growing racial inequality, fuelling waves of homophobic reaction in the Islamic world and Africa and among racialised others. In imperialist countries too, backlashes against the advance of some lesbian/gay people's integration into society continue to occur, unpredictably and sometimes ferociously. Yet as chapter 4 shows, LGBT movements have been hindered in responding to homophobic backlashes by their own homonormative adaptation to the neoliberal order. This adaptation afflicts not only the newly emergent gay right and centre, but also the social-liberal centre-left and even to some extent the radical left.

Meanwhile low-income and rebellious LGBT people have formed an oppositional subculture of gender and other queers, which occupies a subordinate place in the homonormative-dominant regime. While neoliberalism has created the social conditions for the definition and consolidation of a new, specific constellation of gay normality, the antisocial impact of neoliberalism has given many LGBT people a wide range of reasons to question gay normality as it took shape from the 1990s. Analysing the material roots of queer dissent can provide a more solid basis for addressing a central political concern of recent queer theory – the defence of nonconformist or less privileged LGBT people against homonormativity – than queer theory itself offers. It can even help challenge the reification of desire manifest in the commercialisation of sexuality, repressive desublimation and the gay/straight binary, and help lay the foundation for a queer anti-capitalism.

Foundations of Neoliberalism

The depressive long wave that began by 1974–5 was met in the late 1970s with a neoliberal offensive, which is still continuing today. This offensive included (to be very schematic): a shift to 'Toyotist', 'just-in-time' production techniques and to 'lean production' generally; economic globalisation, liberalisation and deregulation, taking advantage of new technologies that 'accelerated the speed and dispersed the space of production';[5] privatisation of many state-owned companies and social services; an increase in the wealth and power of capital at labour's expense; an increase in inequality among countries (through the debt crisis and structural adjustment policies) and within countries (through regressive tax and welfare 'reforms' and attacks on unions); and luxury consumption that increasingly replaced mass consumption as a motor of economic growth.

These changes involve more than just globalisation. Even more centrally they reflect 'capital's increasing flexibility, mobility, and concentrated power'.[6] In short, anyone living through the last several years or decades has witnessed 'the increased centralisation of capital in the hands of the rich' and brutal cuts to services.[7]

This offensive has among other things fragmented the world's working classes. Big differences have (re)surfaced between better- and worse-paid workers, permanent and temporary workers, white and black, native-born and immigrant, employed and unemployed.[8] Deindustrialisation was devastating to millions of blue-collar workers in some regions of imperialist countries, not only men but also (sometimes butch) women who had found economic niches

---

5 Hennessy 2000, p. 6.
6 Brenner 2000, p. 317.
7 Rosenberg and Villarejo 2012, p. 1.
8 In Britain under Thatcher in the 1980s, for example, the 10 percent best-paid workers gained, while the bottom 20 percent were relatively worse off than they had been a century earlier, as mass poverty and homelessness re-emerged. In the US, the hourly earnings of the lowest 10 percent of the population fell by 16 percent in the 1980s (Hobsbawm 1994, pp. 308, 406, 573). One study of wage trends showed that among US manufacturing workers inequality soared in the 1970s and 1980s, reaching far higher levels than the 1930s, while the post-1994 recovery brought inequality down to only slightly lower levels (Galbraith and Cantú 2001, p. 83). Mike Davis noted 'extreme income/skill polarization' in the growing US healthcare, business service, banking and real estate sectors, resulting in a 'split-level economy' and 'reshaping the traditional income pyramid into a new income hourglass' (1986, pp. 214–18). Figures from the US Federal Reserve show that income inequality increased further at the end of the 1990s (Andrews 2003). Inequality became even more extreme in countries like Malaysia, Mexico, Peru, the Philippines and Sri Lanka, where the top 10 percent of earners accounted for a third or more of total income – not to mention Brazil, where the top 10 percent accounted for almost half of total income, the top 20 percent for almost two-thirds, and the bottom 20 percent for 2.5 percent (Hobsbawm 1994, p. 407).

in blue-collar jobs.[9] The less pronounced differences in income and job security in national working classes in the 1960s, which were the backdrop to the rise of lesbian/gay identity, became things of the past.

New technologies – especially cheaper means of transport and new communications media – have been crucial for neoliberal strategies to restore profits by fragmenting and dispersing production and distribution, as capital seeks out locations offering the cheapest labour and the most accommodating policies. Capital accumulation has been 'pumped up with new cyber subjects as its prime promoters'. Virtually everyone is aware of how these technologies have transformed cultures worldwide, especially for those with the incomes needed to acquire new gadgets. The growth of health, food, fashion and athletic markets has entailed the deeper 'penetration and commodification of the body and identity'. Sales have increased above all of goods that reshape the space and time of everyday life, like microwave ovens, mobile phones and MP3 players.[10]

Neoliberalism has also transformed the global division of labour and hierarchy of regions. Beginning in the 1970s, the open colonial empires of classical imperialism and the neo-colonialism of Fordism gave way to a new international division of labour, with a new wave of industrialisation in a number of dependent countries.[11] This ultimately took the form of neoliberal globalisation, under which no single country serves any more as capital's centre. Neoliberal globalisation is unprecedented, Robert Went has concluded, inasmuch as it has internationalised not only the circuits of commodity capital (trade) and money capital (finance), as in earlier cycles of capitalist internationalisation, but also the circuit of productive capital itself.[12] The result was 'for the first time in history...a single, increasingly integrated and universal world economy largely operating across state frontiers'.[13]

This new global economic order has steadily exacerbated inequalities of income and wealth both in and between states. From 1960 to 1987, the dependent countries' real per capita GDP fell from 9 percent to 5 percent of the imperialist countries' GDP. Real per capita GDP actually fell in the 1980s in Africa and Western Asia.[14] Globalisation has also widened the gap between rich and poor worldwide.

9   Feinberg 1998, p. 60.
10   Hennessy 2000, pp. 6, 3, 106–7 (citing Martyn Lee).
11   Hobsbawm 1994, pp. 205, 362.
12   Went 2001, esp. pp. 83–7, 149–50.
13   Hobsbawm 1994, pp. 277–81, 9–10.
14   Hobsbawm 1994, pp. 424, 405.

The flip side of globalisation is localisation, the subjection of particular localities to the demands of global capital. This often involves celebrating local communities and cultures. Insofar as the celebration of the local inhibits regional and global alliances against the sway of capital, however, it tends to promote political projects that 'keep the structures of capitalism invisible'.[15]

The dominant states under neoliberal globalisation are not in every case the colonial or neo-colonial powers of the past. This can sometimes obscure the continuing unequal and imperial nature of the world order. The occasional humiliating setback for imperialist countries has been experienced even by their less powerful and prosperous subjects – especially men – as 'psychic wounds'. This sense of humiliation can be played out in gendered and sexual ways.[16] Yet in reality most imperialist countries – if not their inhabitants – have benefited in relative terms from the rapid increase in the extent of global inequality, which has reversed and rolled back the modest decrease in inequality that took place in the neo-colonial period.

Similarly, while racial liberalism has morphed under the new regime of accumulation into neoliberal multiculturalism as a dominant ideology, this has by no means fostered an increase in material equality between people of different 'races' or 'cultures'. On the contrary, given the weakening of labour movements and their general lack of conscious anti-racist solidarity, mass migration has contributed to greater inequality and tensions within working classes.[17] Nor have the causes of structural inequality for and prejudice against LGBT people disappeared. On the contrary, the emergence since the 1990s of homonormative images of lesbians and gays in more and more parts of the world – increasingly portrayed as not only 'normal' but even privileged and/ or affluent – has continually fuelled prejudice, discrimination and violence against LGBT people, compounding the prejudice that structural differences between gay and straight were already fostering under Fordism.

One added twist of the neoliberal offensive has been the way in which the marketplace undermines conservative moralising, even if the space that neo-liberalism offers to sexual dissidents largely depends on their ability to fit 'the specifications of the consumer niche assigned to [them] by mercantile interests in the pursuit of profit'.[18] Sometimes traditional authority and morality seem to constitute an obstacle to capitalist expansion. In these circumstances, main-stream or liberal women's and gay challenges to traditional authority could,

15   Hennessy 2000, pp. 7–8.
16   Hennessy 2000, pp. 158–9 (citing Laura Kipnis).
17   Hobsbawm 1994, pp. 309–10.
18   Burt 1998, p. 16.

partially and often unwittingly, serve the interests of neoliberalism.[19] This was apparent in the way that the Pinochet dictatorship in Chile – a pioneer of neoliberal economics, as well as a notorious bastion of repression – coincided with the emergence of Chile's first gay dance clubs, as regular police raids failed to suppress Santiago's same-sex nightlife.[20] By the 1980s and 1990s, as South American dictatorships fell, an open LGBT scene and movement could spring up quickly. In Argentina too, where the LGBT movement took off in the early 1990s and had links to the radical left,[21] Buenos Aires banned discrimination based on sexual orientation after winning municipal home rule in 1996.

The contradictions of advancing women's and LGBT movements in a time of working-class weakness and growing inequality were played out in many of the ideological debates of the 1980s and 1990s. Women's equality and racial equality became steadily more established as political commonplaces (in rhetoric if not in reality) at the same time that redistributive and counter-cyclical economic policies, far less controversial forty years ago, were dismissed as outmoded and counterproductive – at least until the 2008 crisis prompted massive redistribution of wealth to the world's biggest banks and various forms of government stimulus. This has made it difficult for the right to roll back some of the gains of black, women's and LGBT movements. Yet profits continued to flow from 'a very traditional source – the gendered and racialised division of labor'. Racially oppressed people in particular continue to bear a 'great share of the burden for the production of surplus value'.[22] In the US, 'the pathologisation of women of color – the Black welfare mother in particular – was intrinsic to the shift from Keynesianism to neoliberalism'. In Europe today, 'hierarchized labor structures ... do not merely use, but produce ethnic difference'.[23]

The meaning of gender under neoliberalism is extraordinarily contradictory. Under capitalism, the family has traditionally served as a mechanism both for inculcating hierarchical and authoritarian social relations and for reproducing the workforce through women's unpaid labour.[24] Heteronormativity has facilitated both of these basic functions of the capitalist family. However, neoliberalism in many ways undermines the direct and obvious domination of wives and daughters by husbands and fathers and the Fordist gender regime, under which men in the 1950s and 1960s had a privileged position in the wage labour

---

19   Fraser 2009, p. 115.
20   Robles 1998, p. 37.
21   Brown 1999, p. 112.
22   Hennessy 2000, pp. 3–4, 105.
23   Ferguson and Hong 2012, pp. 1061, 1060 (citing Fatima El-Tayeb).
24   Seccombe 1993, pp. 5–20; Coontz 1988, esp. pp. 287–365.

market and women in many families a correspondingly constricted sphere in the home.[25]

Under neoliberalism, the 'traditional mandate that women serve others' is contradicted by the imperative that they 'compete with others as fully autonomous individuals'. Women can increasingly be found exercising authority as corporate managers, lawyers and top officials. Unemployed or underemployed fathers can increasingly be found doing childcare or unpaid domestic labour.[26] Neoliberalism thus to some extent undercuts the family's effectiveness as a site for inculcating traditional hierarchies. Feminists have described this tendency as a shift from 'private patriarchy' to 'post-modern' or 'public patriarchy', in which male power is exercised less within families and more collectively through the male-dominated state, market and professions.[27] 'Where once men who were wounded in their work-based masculinity might have found some compensation in their dominance at home', Ellen Willis has observed, 'now they are likely to feel unmanned in both public and private spheres'. In the absence of either class privilege or a working-class collective fight-back, the outcome for straight men can be 'unmitigated grief'.[28]

This is reflected in the contradictory impact of neoliberal policies on women. The increased prosperity and economic independence of a layer of bourgeois and middle-class women is bolstered by the cheap labour of other women, above all black and immigrant, who continue to labour in 'pink-collar ghettoes' at substantially lower average wages than men.[29] The growth of female labour, where (as is often the case) women are more vulnerable and exploitable, has been used by capital in its drive 'to deskill productive sectors and lower labour costs, to worsen working conditions and implement casualization of work'[30] – notably in Latin America, where women have formed the bulk of the work force in Mexican maquiladora assembly plants and played a key role in the growth of Brazilian industry. A swollen informal sector has maintained downward pressure on industrial wages and conditions.[31]

Even for women in the most prosperous working-class layers, as real hourly wages stagnated female waged work 'became what it had long been for the

---

25   Brenner 2003, pp. 78–9.
26   Hennessy 2000, pp. 5, 23–4.
27   Brown 1981.
28   Willis 1999.
29   Dequeecker 1994.
30   Arruzza 2013, p. 126.
31   Dashner 1987, pp. 63, 62.

poor, a way of making ends meet'.[32] As women have 'poured into labour markets around the globe', the ideal of the family wage has been replaced[33] by the 'low-wage, multi-earner family of Walmart times'. Rightward shifts in some feminists' agendas have sometimes facilitated the process, for example, as the call for high-quality, not-for-profit, twenty-four-hour childcare has given way to arguments for childcare as a service for employees and employers.[34] Yet studies have consistently shown that even women working outside the home do a disproportionate share of housework – one UK study showed that in 2006, while men did four times as much housework as in 1942, women still did about twice as much – and of 'emotional labour'. As a result, many working-class women have had to make a shift from housewife to superwoman. Housewifery, once experienced by many women as a prison, has for some become a romanticised dream.[35]

The institution of marriage has also been reshaped. On the one hand, the state continues to use marital status to channel many financial benefits to couples, especially prosperous ones: life insurance benefits and exemptions from capital gains and inheritance taxes.[36] On the other hand, when it comes to welfare and unemployment benefits, the neoliberal state increasingly evades its responsibilities by penalising couples – sometimes married couples, sometimes all couples, but always disproportionately working-class, low-income and poor people.[37] As marriage has increasingly given way in many countries to cohabitation, it has come to make less practical difference; whether cohabitation is viewed as in principle more egalitarian, a trial marriage, or simply a way of avoiding wedding costs, it tends for most practical purposes to be modelled on marriage and involve comparable burdens for women.[38] Given their lower wages and still disproportionate responsibility for children, working-class women are often 'a man away from poverty'.

At the same time, neoliberal gender arrangements are the basis for forms of sweatshop labour and tourist-trade sex work.[39] Neoliberalism also reinforces the family's role as a site where basic needs, such as care for old people, are met

---

32   Hobsbawm 1994, p. 319.
33   Fraser 2009, p. 110.
34   Sangster and Luxton 2012, pp. 290–1.
35   Barker 2012, pp. 147, 130, 149.
36   Barker 2012, p. 29.
37   Hennessy 2000, pp. 63–4.
38   Barker 2012, pp. 153–4.
39   Hennessy 2000, p. 91.

in privatised ways.[40] By imposing cuts in social spending – education, health-care, childcare – Structural Adjustment Programmes in economically domi-nated countries in the 1980s, austerity imposed later through the Maastricht criteria in the European Union, and austerity policies demanded by capital everywhere all displaced the costs of social reproduction even more onto women in the family.[41] Worldwide neoliberal policies have thus made the fam-ily more crucial than ever to the reproduction of capital,[42] re-establishing it as 'a cushion to absorb the social effects of hard times, and repersonalizing economic dependency, incentive, savings and work'.[43] All this has a negative impact on women, especially working-class and poor women.

In all these ways, gender functions as a continuing and even deepening divi-sion within neoliberal capitalism. Twenty-first-century studies show that peo-ple are just as often labelled by gender as they were over thirty years ago, and that parents persistently (and often unconsciously) encourage and discourage different behaviour in boys and girls.[44] This contributes to the persistence of a sexual gender gap, a difference in how men and women live and experience their sexual lives. Studies consistently show that men claim to have more sex-ual partners than women, and to have more frequent orgasms,[45] though pure physiology would lead one to expect the opposite. The explanation has to be social. Women's greater burden of domestic labour, combined with increasing waged labour and higher poverty rates, simply give them less time and fewer resources for sexual exploration. Moreover, even the heralded sexual eman-cipation of women has not fully eliminated the low sexual expectations that were inculcated in women for centuries, and that still limit most women's pur-suit of self-expression and pleasure.

In middle-class strata in imperialist countries, overconsumption accentu-ates the performative character of gender. In other ways, a more performative kind of gender has spread among the working class; for example, it fits 'the mobility, adaptability, and ambivalence required of service workers today'.[46] However, more 'performative' does not always mean more fluid; sometimes it means more rigid. A host of pop-culture manifestations kick in from the moment of birth to drive home to the new human being all the ways in which

---

40   Barker 2012, p. 159.
41   Barbosa, Dashner, Duggan, McAllister and Nikell 1994, pp. 8–9.
42   Burt 1998, p. 16.
43   Hennessy 2000, p. 75.
44   Jordan-Young 2010, pp. 251–2.
45   D'Emilio and Freedman 1997, p. 372.
46   Hennessy 2000, p. 109.

she can and must 'enjoy being a girl'. Judith Butler has discussed this intensive 'girling', begun by doctors at or before the moment of birth and 'reiterated by various authorities and throughout various intervals of time', as 'at once the setting of a boundary' and 'the repeated inculcation of a norm'.[47] In a dependent society like India, 'girling' takes forms that are brutally, existentially coercive, as about 60 percent of ' "girled" fetuses [identified through sonograms] are being immediately aborted or murdered upon birth'.[48]

LGBT People and Class

As the forms of gender oppression have changed under neoliberalism, so have the forms of heteronormativity. The decline of Fordism has also had implications for LGBT identities, communities and politics. Given the privatisation under neoliberalism of the satisfaction of social needs, wherever LGBT people are excluded from or marginalised in families, they must struggle harder to have their basic needs met. However, neoliberalism has had a differentiated impact on LGBT people and their communities.

Many of the institutions that define LGBT communities and produce their self-images tend to reproduce and defend a unifying lesbian/gay identity in apparent continuity with the identity that took shape in the 1970s. But even a schematic analysis can show that lesbian/gay subcultures and identities were put under pressure or into question in various ways by the decline of Fordism. Ultimately, as the class and social reality of LGBT communities became more fragmented and conflict-ridden, so did their ideological and even sexual expressions. In the end, the 'mode of production of material life condition[ed] [their] social, political and intellectual life process in general'; their 'social being... determine[d] their consciousness'.[49]

On the one hand, commercial gay scenes and sexual identities compatible with these scenes have advanced and been consolidated in many parts of the world, particularly among middle-class layers, as part of the ongoing commercialisation and commodification of sexuality under neoliberalism. The commercialisation of gay life is propelled by the expansion of the gay market. While far removed from the scale of major multinationals, the gay market under neoliberalism has dwarfed the market niches of the 1970s, not to mention the 1950s. Corporate advertising in US LGBT publications rose by 319 percent in

---

47   Butler 1993a, pp. 7–8.
48   Ebert 1996, p. 360.
49   Marx 1968, p. 182.

the 15 years from 1996 to 2011, for example, with LGBT press revenues reaching $307 million.[50] The commercial scene crosses class boundaries, but within it middle-class gay men and lesbians have the bulk of the buying power and thus set the tone.

On the other hand, commercial scenes have not been equally determinant for the lifestyles or identities of all LGBT people. In the dependent world, many poor people simply have a hard time taking part in commercial gay scenes. In imperialist countries, while commercial scenes are more accessible to even lower-income LGBT people, growing economic inequality has meant divergent realities in LGBT people's lives. Alienation has mounted among some LGBT people from the overconsumption increasingly characteristic of many aspects of the commercial gay scene, which inevitably marginalises many LGBT people. Alternative scenes of various sorts (not always necessarily less commercial) have proliferated.

Within some of these alternative scenes, a queer identity has coalesced that is seen at least in part as in opposition to existing lesbian/gay identities. It embraces some increasingly visible transgender identities and a variety of other identities linked to specific sexual practices or roles. These identities are extraordinarily diverse. But some of them are in tension with neoliberalism's dominant sexual regime. Their rootedness in characteristics of contemporary capitalism can be detected in a number of more or less common features. Whether or not they are explicitly defined as queer, they respond to the increasingly repressive character of the neoliberal order through their stubborn affirmation of sexual practices that are still – or increasingly – stigmatised. They also reflect the growing inequality and polarisation of neoliberal capitalism by making sexual power differentials explicit, and above all through gender nonconformity.

Like the commercial gay scene, with which its boundaries are fuzzy, the queer scene crosses class divides. There are certainly middle-class self-identified queers, including a disproportionate number of students and academics. Many middle-class or working-class queers can and do 'pass' as normal gays and lesbians at work and in other social settings. But the class atmosphere of the queer scene, while not exactly working class, is different from that of the commercial scene. The prevalent queer rejection of overconsumption, respectability and conformity puts queers in opposition to neoliberal gay normality. And queer spaces offer more room to, or at least solidarity with, LGBT people who have lost out under neoliberalism.

---

50   Prime Access 2012, p. 9.

By contrast, the end of the Fordist expansive long wave was not bad news for everyone by any means, and not for all LGBT people specifically. Not that life can ever be entirely privileged or wholly pain-free for LGBT people in a society where desire is a basis of classification, and where exclusively heterosexual desire is supposedly the norm; in a heteronormative society every LGBT person must confront a moment of acknowledging difference, which can often be traumatic. Even in 2013, a survey by the Pew Research Center has revealed, 39 percent of LGBT people in the US reported rejection by a family member or close friend because of their sexual orientation or gender identity.[51] But the discomfort of difference was softened among some middle-class and upper-working-class social layers that prospered in the 1980s and 1990s, especially but not only in imperialist countries, where commercial gay scenes continued to grow and to foster lesbian/gay identity.[52]

Market-friendly lesbian/gay identities prospered in commercialised spaces, in the construction of two-income households among better-off gays and (to a lesser extent) lesbians, and in the more tolerant public space fostered by gay rights victories. The combination of commercialisation with growing social tolerance for some normalised gay and lesbian identities is the driving force of homonormativity – the imposition of a set of norms that defines some LGBT people as at home in neoliberal society and excludes or marginalises others. The rise of homonormativity by no means weakens the heterosexual norm. The explosion in 2013 of opposition to same-sex marriage in France showed how much anti-gay prejudice still lurks beneath the surface, more or less visibly in different regions at different times, even in countries where gay normality seems solidly established. But homonormativity has been and is transforming LGBT life in a big swathe of the world.

Among those whom homonormativity defines as insiders in neoliberal society are many relatively better paid lesbian/gay people who benefited from both economic success and gay rights reforms. They have some cause to be contented with the progress they have made: 'inside a cozy brownstone, curled up next to a health-insured domestic partner in front of a Melissa Etheridge video on MTV, flipping through *Out* magazine and sipping an Absolut and tonic, capitalism can feel pretty good'.[53] By the 1980s, such people in the US were forming networks of lesbian/gay professionals, with forums on such topics as travel, estate planning and buying real estate; many lesbian/gay community

51 Pew Research Center 2013.
52 Altman 1982, pp. 79–97.
53 Gluckman and Reed 1997, p. xv.

institutions became dependent on their philanthropy.[54] In Canada, the rise of networks of openly gay doctors, lawyers and academics was accompanied by the founding in 1978 of Toronto's Lambda Business Council.[55]

For decades, capital in the US has been discovering the profits to be made from the lesbian/gay market, as reflected in *New York* magazine's 1993 'Lesbian Chic' cover, the frequent attention in the *New York Times*' 'Style' section, and *Fortune*'s praise of this 'wonderful market niche'.[56] Advertising promises gays and lesbians 'full inclusion . . . through personal consumption'.[57] But as Rosemary Hennessy has pointed out, 'as in most marketing strategies, money, not liberation, is the bottom line'. The predominant gay images in consumer culture have increasingly produced a 'class-specific gay subjectivity for both straight and gay audiences'.[58]

Neoliberal globalisation has compounded the divergences and inequalities that uneven capitalist development has helped produce. It reinforces and reproduces inequalities.[59] In the dependent world specifically, the rise in economic inequality has been accompanied by increased cultural tensions and class differences within both established and emerging LGBT communities.[60] These have included sexual divergences, as commercial gay scenes and the disproportionately middle-class lesbian/gay communities oriented towards them have consolidated and expanded. Often in these conditions a supposedly 'premodern, prepolitical, non-Euro-American queerness must consciously assume the burdens of representing itself to itself and others as "gay" in order to attain political consciousness, subjectivity and global modernity'.[61]

Many dependent countries, even some very poor ones, have developed sizeable middle classes in recent years. Countries like South Africa and Brazil have had prosperous middle classes, with incomes many times their countries' average, for decades; in both countries, class is linked to 'race', though in different ways. Other poor countries whose income distribution used to be less inequitable have converged in recent years with a global pattern of growing inequality. Millions of middle-class people in poor countries are now able to buy consumer goods and services, though usually at levels below those of rich

54   Faderman 1991, pp. 277–8.
55   Kinsman 1987, pp. 186, 182.
56   Hennessy 2000, pp. 134–5, 137.
57   Puar 2007, p. 63 (citing Alexandra Chassin).
58   Hennessy 2000, p. 112.
59   Mtewa 2003, p. 39.
60   Lind and Share 2003, p. 60.
61   Wekker 2006, p. 245 (citing Arnaldo Cruz-Malavé and Martin Manalansan IV).

countries. This has made it possible for gay ghettos of a sort to emerge in the dependent world. The existence of these ghettos can have an impact on LGBT culture in general; tastes and trends can trickle down from them to people who often cannot afford to set foot in such areas.

Middle-class gay discos and clubs in dependent countries often do their best to imitate Paris or San Francisco. This raises issues about the cultural dimension of neoliberal globalisation. Countries like Brazil and India have very large culture industries, including export industries, so there is no economic reason why they should not be able to meet the demand for LGBT images. But where domestically produced images are not plentiful or positive enough, people go looking for foreign ones, and sometimes they find foreign images more appealing even when local ones do exist. Reading a European book, watching a US video or wearing a leather jacket you could see in a Sydney bar does not make people's identities and lives the same as Europeans' or Australians'. Local and global imagery and identities are in constant, sometimes contradictory, interaction. But for LGBT people in the dependent world, artefacts from imperialist countries can be markers of cosmopolitanism, sexual identity and class status. Foreign TV channels, DVDs and internet sites have become accessible even in small towns in India, and have been 'instrumental in creating significant lifestyle changes', especially among young people.[62] Rock videos and the internet, US and French posters, magazines and films play a significant role in the Southeast Asian LGBT scene as well.[63]

The new class-specific gay subjectivity, as Jasbir Puar has argued, constructs the gay 'subject as a queer liberal one, invested in consumption, property ownership, and intimate, stable sexual relationships, relying on an archaic formulation of public/private divides'. The private-public divide is a cornerstone of bourgeois ideology, and the fact that sexuality under capitalism is generally consigned to the private sphere is not ideologically innocent. In the US, for example, the logic of the Supreme Court ruling striking down laws against the sexual conduct of stable partners in private, served to reaffirm the possible criminality of public sex, casual sex, sex parties and clubs, and other 'queer acts'.[64] Even in contexts where homonormativity barely exists – like India, where the Delhi High Court ruling in 2009 striking down the country's sodomy law provoked nationwide and justified LGBT celebration – this public-private divide is embedded within the framework of decriminalisation under bourgeois law. It has the potential to later help shape a new, constricting gay

62   Joseph and Dhall 2000, p. 158.
63   Altman 2000, p. 139.
64   Puar 2007, pp. xxvi, 123 (citing Katharine Franke).

normality, if and when conditions are ripe – if, among other things, the Indian Supreme Court ruling in 2013 recriminalising homosexuality is eventually overturned.

Even as gay men and lesbians have benefited from growing tolerance of their private sexual behaviour, they have increasingly been divided along class and racial lines between those who are entitled to privacy and those who are not. LGBT people receiving welfare benefits, for example, like straight recipients, are more and more racialised in Western Europe, as they almost always were in the US. Consequently, increasing recognition of same-sex partnerships also means increased policing of LGBT benefit recipients to check if their same-sex partners' income might justify cutting their benefits. Privacy is certainly not a right respected, whatever people's sexuality, for prisoners (who are, in the US, rightly characterised as inhabitants of the 'prison-industrial complex').[65] Nor is privacy guaranteed to those in North America and Europe whose Muslim background leads to increased surveillance for potential complicity with terrorism.[66]

The growing class divides in LGBT communities go beyond issues of consumption, culture and privacy. The class-specific character of supposedly gay-friendly capitalism is visible at a company like Levi's. Its marketing and policies are gay-friendly; it provides health benefits to its employees' same-sex partners and has a lesbian/gay employees association. But its LGBT and straight workers face equally gruelling conditions in the sweatshops of Saipan, and its LGBT ex-workers in Texas are in equally big trouble now that their jobs have been moved to the Caribbean.[67] IKEA too markets to same-sex couples while cutting the wages and benefits of both LGBT and straight workers by employing the undocumented and moving production to low-wage regions.[68]

The growth of a privileged lesbian/gay middle class also has an impact on urban geography, in the US in any event, through the spread of middle-class lesbian/gay neighbourhoods. The middle-class re-conquest of city centres, and the consequent displacement of less affluent populations, has been a much-noted aspect of neoliberal political economy since the 1980s, as has the lesbian/gay role in the process. One study of a gentrifying neighbourhood in Madrid has suggested that the gay community 'neutralizes homophobia by playing the role of urban rescuer: gentrification is the due gays pay to society'.[69]

65   Davis 1998; Alexander 2010.
66   Puar 2007, pp. 124, 126.
67   Hennessy 2000, p. 139.
68   Cervulle and Rees-Roberts 2010, p. 115 (citing Miranda Joseph).
69   Mitchell 2011, p. 670 (citing Gabriel Giorgi).

Since 9/11, state repression directed at immigrant communities targeted as sources of support for terrorism has become an added factor in this displacement, as large-scale arrests of immigrants in a neighbourhood like Jackson Heights in New York helped accelerate its transformation into a 'gay mecca'.[70]

Less affluent queers can just as well be among the displaced, 'competing with other low-income groups for the limited supply of cheap and moderate housing' – a source of racism, homophobia and violence. Rapidly rising rents and the spread of internet-based contacts may also be 'undermining the viability and centrality of bars as gay social institutions',[71] in any event for those less able to afford upscale clubs. Ultimately, this can lead to shrinking LGBT public space, undermining the basis for queer community, and strengthening pressures towards assimilation into straight society. These dynamics were ironically manifested in New York's Greenwich Village, not far from the site of the Stonewall rebellion, when the city planned a park along the Hudson River that would mainly serve luxury condominiums and displace LGBT people of colour, homeless youth and men in search of sex who had for decades congregated around waterfront piers.[72]

As the relatively inclusive if unequal lesbian/gay culture of the 1970s spread worldwide and consolidated, it was almost imperceptibly transformed into something else. A gay upper crust fitting into the neoliberal order has asserted its hegemony, which LGBT people at large have sometimes resisted but often accepted. Gradually the gay-dominant same-sex regime has given way to a different one, which we can call 'homonormative-dominant'.

While all social relations under capitalism are reified – distorted so that relations between people are perceived as relations with or even between things – the shift under neoliberalism to economic growth founded increasingly on middle-class overconsumption has raised the reification of human relations among neoliberalism's beneficiaries to new heights. This applies notably to sexual and emotional relations among some middle-class gay men and lesbians.

Without in any way minimising the ongoing importance for capitalism of household consumption, now including gay/lesbian household consumption, we can see that capitalism today also profits greatly from products for the 'consumer without kin', who today is sometimes a gay man or lesbian.[73] Consumerism under neoliberalism feeds on and fuels 'narcissistic fantasies of

---

70   Puar 2007, p. 150.
71   Rubin 2011, pp. 167, 345–6.
72   Mananzala 2011/2012.
73   Puar 2007, p. 28.

availability and control'.[74] In the former East Germany, sexologists have complained of a 'fast food fast sex' culture arriving from the West.[75]

At the same time, Volker Woltersdorff has described a 'flexibilization of sexual and gender norms' that allows fantasies a freer range than ever before over aspects of gender and sexuality, which are treated more than ever before as an economically 'productive and exploitable resource'.[76] Global neoliberalism demands (at least in some locations and social strata) more 'porous, gender-flexible, and playful subjects'. The art collective GANG summed up the spirit of the time when it proclaimed, 'Our bodies should be playgrounds, not just battlegrounds'.[77] The slogan is ambiguous: looking to the future, it summons up a vision of polymorphous liberation; in the context of the present, it risks reducing bodies to marketable playthings.

The abiding gender gap between men and women, and the difference in their relative economic status, are reflected in differences between gay male and lesbian (and trans) sexuality. Studies consistently show that gay men have more sexual partners than any other category of people, whether or not they are in long-term or primary relationships. Occasional rapid jumps in celibacy and monogamy in response to AIDS (in the US from 1984 to 1987, for example) have not changed this overall pattern. The freedom to have multiple partners without fear of legal consequences is a victory for gay liberation; ongoing gay male rejection of monogamy shows that the new gay right has not managed to impose its moralism (often even on its own adherents). At the same time, the pursuit of sex in isolation from social and emotional contact can sometimes fit the mould of Marcuse's repressive desublimation, with the growing commercialism of the gay male subculture in synch with the 'consumerist values that had already made sex a marketable commodity'.[78]

Global Gay Normality

Gay/lesbian middle-class overconsumption has acquired an imperial dimension through the tourist market. Tourism is 'a leisure activity that presupposes its opposite, namely regulated and organized work'.[79] It embodies the

---

74   Woltersdorff 2011, p. 170.
75   Herzog 2011, p. 206.
76   Woltersdorff 2011, pp. 164, 168.
77   Hennessy 1994, pp. 104–5.
78   D'Emilio and Freedman 1997, pp. 339–40, 356, 323.
79   Cervulle and Rees-Roberts 2010, pp. 62–4 (citing John Urry).

contradictions in the lives of people who spend much of their waking lives working for wages, which they value largely for the ability they earn to escape. But leisure (like work) has class and racial dimensions, for LGBT people – self-interestedly portrayed by the gay tourist industry as 'TurboConsumers™'[80] – as for others. Casualisation of wage labour and the growth of the informal sector in dependent countries under neoliberal globalisation have included the growth of the sex trade. Economic internationalisation has included the rise of international sex tourism, in two directions: the arrival of tourists from imperialist countries taking advantage of cheap sex for sale, and the arrival in imperialist countries of sex workers. Undocumented immigrants form a high proportion of sex workers in much of Europe; trans people form a high proportion of same-sex sex workers almost everywhere. Wholesale exclusion of trans people from most sectors of formal employment is one reason for this. And the tourist industry, which disproportionately targets high-income travellers, is increasingly central to many economies, reinforcing the centrality of luxury consumption in general under neoliberalism.

Of course, straight people account for the great majority of tourism from imperialist to dependent countries, and straight men for most sex tourism. In any event, there is no reason to gloss over the exploitative aspects of this tourism, which implicates both straights and gays, or to buy into the ideology that travel equals freedom.[81] Tourism is particularly marketed to gay men with images of 'newly hypersexualised natives', thus contributing to a certain 'aestheticisation of social precariousness'.[82] Sexual exploitation has been particularly visible in both newly capitalist Eastern Europe, where Prague has become a 'boyopolis' for Western European gay sex tourists, and Western Europe, where a high proportion of male prostitutes are now Eastern Europeans. Meanwhile some of the middle-class minority of Eastern Europeans who are beneficiaries of the new order have joined the flow of sex tourists to East Asia and Latin America,[83] further sexualising their societies and commercialising sexuality. Sex tourism from the US, Japan and Europe has grown to be a major industry in the Caribbean, Brazil, North Africa and Southeast Asia, while the domestic sex trade is important in countries in South Asia where sex tourism is proportionally less important. The spread of market relations has also fostered the

---

80   Mitchell 2011, p. 672.
81   Puar 2007, pp. 66, 65.
82   Cervulle and Rees-Roberts 2010, pp. 16–17.
83   Herzog 2011, p. 187 (citing Stan Persky).

sex trade in China,[84] creating distaste among middle-class Chinese gays for 'money boys' from the countryside.[85]

Issues involved in gay tourism exploded in scandal in France in 2009 when the media jumped on revelations in a previously published book by culture minister Frédéric Mitterand (nephew of the former president) about 'boys' he had encountered during trips to Thailand. While rightly censuring the homophobia that was focused on him, Mitterand hardly looked critically at the economic inequality, exploitation and exoticism involved in sex tourism. In fact, he mentioned a Moroccan immigrant worker who had taken 'revenge' on him in a bathhouse thirty years earlier as one of his persecutors.[86]

Ironically, as in Lebanon, a regime can simultaneously legalise or tolerate businesses that attract foreign gay tourists and repress its own people's same-sex communities.[87] This sex tourism perpetuates the centuries-long imposition of sex on dominated peoples. People who 'freely' chose to cater to it are often submitting to the veiled coercion of poverty. Admittedly, the sex trade may give those who work in it greater resources, greater freedom or both; in Brazil, male prostitution is 'increasingly a viable and known path out of poverty', offering chances for conspicuous consumption that functions as a 'mode of inclusion'.[88] But recognising the agency of sex workers and refusing to reduce them to mere victims[89] should not get in the way of acknowledging that they are, nonetheless, subject to economic constraints, and that their sex with tourists is 'infused with economic difference'.[90]

The story grows still more complicated when sex tourism is viewed as a form of activism or an affirmation of a stigmatised identity, or even shades into love tourism. Some of the African-American gay tourists to Brazil with whom Gregory Mitchell talked in his fascinating research defended their tourism as a civil right, a boon to the local economy and a way of promoting pro-gay feelings – usually failing to acknowledge the distorted picture of gays that such skewed encounters can also foster. As Mitchell has pointed out, one can and should endorse boycotts of anti-gay companies without arguing

---

84   Chou 2000, pp. 199–201.

85   Rofel 1999, p. 466.

86   Cervulle and Rees-Roberts 2010, pp. 11–15.

87   Makarem 2011, p. 100.

88   Mitchell 2011, p. 668.

89   As Khun Chutchai of the Asia-Pacific Sex Workers Network legitimately demanded during the Mitterand scandal (Cervulle and Rees-Roberts 2010, pp. 15–16).

90   Mitchell 2011, p. 670.

that gays 'deserve rights because they are valuable consumers'.[91] One can also support African-American working-class men's right to earn enough to visit Brazil or Africa, and to have sex and seek love when they get there, and at the same time encourage critical reflection on how exactly they spend their hard-earned money.

As black men looking for the blackest, most masculine Brazilian men they could find, the African-American gay tourists were sometimes on a sort of 'pilgrimage' in search of authentic African identity. They usually failed to acknowledge the self-disparaging attitudes implicit in their beguilement with 'images of exotic and overendowed dark-skinned natives', and in their lack of erotic interest in self-identified Brazilian gay men whose skin colour was often closer to their own. Gay tourist promoters play on such attitudes with slogans like 'you go East [to Asia] for boys, and South [to Latin America] for men'. Some of the African-Americans fell in love with their Brazilian boyfriends – feelings that could be reciprocated with at least a certain fondness – to the point that one of them, a middle-aged, skilled factory worker, worked overtime and gave up one of his visits to Brazil to pay for his Brazilian boyfriend's mother's surgery. Yet, ironically, the gay African-Americans often settled for 'shifting, conflicting, unstable relationships with "straight" men' who gradually morphed 'into precisely the middle-class, consumer-oriented, gay or bisexual' men they previously rejected.[92]

The visibility of (relatively) high-income lesbians and particularly gay men raises delicate issues that require careful analysis. Commodity fetishism in capitalist culture, and especially in the neoliberal culture of overconsumption, tends to privilege money and the products it can buy as *the* measures of social status – and for those lacking them, as occasions for stigmatisation, envy and resentment of those who have them. However, these markers of status should not be confused with the real measures of wealth and power under capitalism, which are the possession of accumulated capital and the occupation of key positions of power in corporate and state apparatuses. By these measures, while gay people are clearly present and even increasingly accepted in the global ruling class, those identified as straight still have a number of significant advantages, notably those derived from dynastic and other kinship networks.

The spread of corporate 'pride networks', paralleling corporate women's networks, shows alertness to the advantages of less prejudiced managerial recruitment, but is also testimony to enduring disadvantages that need to be compensated. Claims that anti-LGBT discrimination is likely to undermine

---

91   Mitchell 2011, pp. 667, 678.
92   Mitchell 2011, pp. 671, 678, 676, 670, 674, 678.

performance and is therefore 'bad for business',[93] whatever the kernel of truth they may contain, serve ideologically to mask the mechanisms of exclusion that were and are part and parcel of capitalism's day-to-day functioning. Even if gay and lesbian children are less routinely being deprived of their inheritances, heterosexual marriage to an heir or heiress still works better as an accumulation strategy than same-sex partnership, and being born into a ruling-class family is still a safer and far more common road to wealth than adoption by one of its gay scions.

The new gay normality has not been absent from Latin America, South Africa and East and South Asia, but it has been especially bounded there by class and geography. Given that dependent countries on the whole suffered greatly with the decline of the old forms of capital accumulation since the 1970s, LGBT communities and identities there have taken on very contrasting forms.[94] The period of slower growth internationally was a time of recurrent and devastating crisis in many dependent countries even before the generalised crisis of 2008 – notably in Latin America after 1982, in Mexico again after 1994, in much of Southeast Asia after 1997, in Brazil for several years after 1998, and in much of Africa with scarcely a breathing space. But this did not prevent the growth of middle classes in some regions with incomes far above their countries' averages and linked to global consumer capitalism – including gay consumer capitalism.

Commercialised, Western-oriented lesbian/gay identities in this context seem to have a complex and contradictory relationship with other same-sex sexualities that co-exist with them in the dependent world. In many ways, 'gay' and 'lesbian' are still largely middle- or upper-class concepts, even if they have sometimes provided a reference point in struggles for sexual emancipation.[95]

These contradictions have also been visible in China, as capitalism was largely restored in that country after the 1989 Tiananmen Square massacre, and China has grown to play a key role in the global neoliberal economy. Open LGBT organising has continued to be repressed, as is all organising outside party-state control. Just knowing that feminists and lesbians would attend the 1995 Beijing women's conference led the government to isolate it far away from the urban centre, forbid Chinese women university students from attending, and arrest gay activists who tried to make contact with delegates. But the growth of civil society, due to economic development, neoliberal globalisation

---

93   Moriarty 2007, p. 2007.
94   Drucker 2009, pp. 826–8.
95   Altman 2000; Oetomo 1996, pp. 265–8.

and market reforms, has created more room for a gay scene, despite police harassment, corruption and social disapproval.[96]

Despite all the diversity of China's self-identified lesbians and gays, almost all of them are relatively young, only coming of age once the transition to capitalism was well underway. They also share a rejection of rural queers, perceived as people of 'low quality' out for money, in a society where vast income differences between the coastal cities and the interior are reinforced by a system of virtual legal apartheid directed against rural migrants.[97] Reflecting the intra-Chinese dimension of globalisation – the synergy between the bourgeoisifying layers of the bureaucracy, and the overseas Chinese bourgeoisie of Hong Kong, Taiwan, Singapore and beyond – Hong Kong plays an outsized role in Chinese LGBT culture.

An equally contradictory dynamic has been at work in newly capitalist Eastern Europe. Sexual repression was far from uniform under the former Stalinist regimes: Poland had never criminalised homosexuality; Hungary and Czechoslovakia had decriminalised it in 1961, East Germany in 1968 (a year before West Germany). But none of these countries had ever known anything like the extensive Western European gay commercial scene or community organisations. The restoration of capitalism in the 1990s made their development possible, in neoliberal conditions of rapidly increasing inequality. The European Union and its member states also funded a new gay civil society in its own homonormative image and increasingly put direct political pressure on Eastern European governments to model their legislation on a Western European homonormative pattern. In the cynical words of LGBT rights activist Scott Long, Eastern European governments see the EU as 'a rich eccentric uncle' whose 'every crotchet must be humored', even if this means improving the treatment of 'homosexuals or other nonexistent creatures'.[98]

This has brought many benefits to Eastern European LGBT people. At the same time, it has helped reactionary nationalists like the Polish Catholic right, who are homophobic for many reasons, to manipulate popular resentment of the arrogant West to promote anti-LGBT campaigns. LGBT marches have been banned in countries including Latvia, Moldova, Poland, Russia and Serbia, or violently attacked by the far right, often with police connivance, where they have been officially permitted.[99] Well-intentioned Western European solidarity can sometimes backfire and reinforce the alien image of Eastern

---

96   Rofel 1999, p. 459.
97   Rofel 1999, pp. 451, 466–7, 473–4, n. 18.
98   Herzog 2011, pp. 184–5.
99   Moriarty 2007, p. 7.

European LGBT people. The first Moscow Pride in 2006, for example, consisted of 'a handful of Russians supported by foreign elected officials and gay activists'.[100] At least one Russian LGBT leader has warned that calls to boycott Russia to protest the 2013 law against 'gay propaganda' risk having the same effect of fuelling repression.[101]

In both imperialist and dependent capitalist countries, the ideological and cultural sway of homonormativity in LGBT communities has spread beyond the more privileged social layers in which people's lives fit it most comfortably. LGBT media in dependent countries rely to some extent on lesbian/gay media in the capitalist heartlands for their material and imagery.[102] In the imperialist countries, despite the proliferation of websites and zines defining identities and subcultures for minorities within the LGBT minority, the most widely circulated books, periodicals and videos tend to be those most closely linked to the new, predominantly middle-class gay mainstream. Even those who are economically least well equipped for the commercial gay scene are often dependent on it as a market for potential (short- or long-term) partners. More fundamentally, even celibate or monogamous people, who are at least temporarily not in the market for a partner, still tend to define themselves in the culturally hegemonic categories of lesbian, gay, bisexual or straight. Even poor trans and queer people whose lives are most remote from the images of the gay mainstream sometimes incorporate aspects of gay mainstream culture into their aspirations and fantasies, constructing their identities in part from images that may be borrowed and adapted from very different social realities.

This hegemony of gay normality over much of the LGBT world, and the physical coexistence of LGBT people of different classes in lesbian/gay spaces, provides arguments to those who downplay the importance of class in LGBT communities.[103] It is true that the class segregation that characterised early twentieth-century LGBT scenes eased in the Fordist period. Thanks to past struggles, working-class LGBT people now sometimes earn enough to buy things that once only middle-class people could afford (in itself something to celebrate). But cultural commonalities and cross-class relationships do not make LGBT identity and spaces class-neutral, any more than the existence of sexual relationships between masters and slaves meant that slavery was not a significant factor in them. In Brazil, for example, cross-class same-sex relationships, which are often interracial as well, tend to be organised around

---

100   Cervulle and Rees-Roberts 2010, pp. 36–7.
101   Alekseyev 2013.
102   Drucker 2000a, pp. 26–7.
103   For example, Seidman 2011.

status and power. A well-off São Paulo resident 'might hire a male hustler from a working-class family for a night of sex, but the social gulf between them would likely preclude a lasting relationship'.[104]

Most portrayals of gay life assume middle-class experience as the norm, and promote it as 'a script for how gay life should be conceived and lived'.[105] Lesbian/gay spaces are not islands, but heavily influenced by the structures of the surrounding societies. Research on young LGBT people's schooling in Britain, for example, has identified class as 'a major axis of power which positions LGBT people unequally and unjustly'.[106] Moreover, the sexual fracturing of LGBT scenes in recent decades also has a class dimension.

The Neoliberal Ghetto

Throughout the world capitalist system, lesbian/gay identity took new forms from the 1980s, acquiring a hegemonic position in a new same-sex formation that fit increasingly well into the emerging neoliberal order. Five homonormative features defined the newly hegemonic pattern: the lesbian/gay community's self-definition as a stable minority; an increasing tendency towards gender conformity; demarcation from and marginalisation of trans people and other minorities within the minority; increasing integration into the nation; and the formation of newly normal lesbian/gay families.

Lesbians' and gay men's self-definition as a minority group has built on the steady consolidation of the distinct categories of gay and straight over the course of the twentieth century, particularly under Fordism. At the same time, it expressed a profound social fact that became an even more pronounced feature of lesbian/gay life under neoliberalism. To the extent that lesbians and gays were increasingly defined as people who inhabited a certain economic space (went to certain bars, bathhouses and discos, patronised certain businesses, and, in the US at least, even lived to some extent in certain neighbourhoods), they were more ghettoised than before, more clearly demarcated from a majority defined as straight.

The fact that a fair proportion of those in the bars and bathhouses were always people with at least one foot in the straight world, sometimes even in cross-sex marriages with children, was always an open secret, but one that few people announced with fanfare. These boundary-crossers were generally seen

---

104   Green 1999a, pp. 283–4.
105   Heaphy 2011.
106   McDermott 2011, p. 64.

as people who were still more or less 'in the closet'. They tended to be discreet in order to avoid unpleasantness, and were in any event generally marginal to the developing lesbian/gay culture. The fact that people continued to come out and join the community at all ages – or for that matter sometimes formed cross-sex relationships before, after or at the same time as same-sex relationships – was also none too visible.

The tendency of many early theorists of lesbian/gay liberation to question the categories of heterosexuality and homosexuality, emphasise the fluidity of sexual identity, and speculate about universal bisexuality tended to fade away with time as the community's material reality became more pronounced. The more same-sex desire was seen as the virtual monopoly of a lesbian/gay minority, the less its manifestations – however open and unashamed – had to be seen as posing any questions about the feelings, relationships or way of life of the straight majority. Paradoxically, as apparent acceptance of a lesbian/gay minority grew, willingness to act on same-sex desire could even decline among the majority: German surveys in 1970 and 1990 reported that in 1970 18 percent of 16- and 17-year-old males admitted to at least one same-sex sexual experience, but that in 1990 the number had dropped to 2 percent.[107] The lesbian/gay rights movement accordingly ran less risk of seeming sexually subversive of the broader sexual order of gendered capitalism. The minority model was also well suited to 'an American style of interest-group politics'.[108]

The decline of butch/femme role-playing among lesbians, and of camp culture among gay men, also contributed to hardening the gender boundaries that remain central to capitalist societies. Drag queens rebelling against the post-war tightening of gender discipline had played a leading role in the 1960s uprisings, culminating in the 1969 Stonewall rebellion. But in the 1970s and later, they found that as social tolerance of lesbians and gays in general began to increase, social tolerance for gender nonconformity in many lesbian/gay spaces decreased. As the decline of Fordism put welfare state programmes under pressure, a renewed emphasis on the centrality of the family to social reproduction helped put a brake on the relaxation of gender norms that had characterised the 1960s. This conservative turn in the broader society was accompanied by a shift among gay men away from the largely androgynous imagery and occasional gender-bending of the early 1970s.

---

107   Schmidt 2001. Gert Hekma has linked Schmidt's work to his own research showing a decline since the 1960s in the number of Dutch males engaging in sex with other males (posting by Hekma to H-Histsex, 4 November 2013).

108   Valocchi 1999, p. 219.

In what Gert Hekma has called 'a revolution in models of gay desire', gay men began to adopt a 'macho' style, as ' "macho" men and "clones" had sex with each other', abandoning the 'older model of queen and trade'.[109] Susan Stryker has identified 1973 in the US as the year that the masculine ' "clone look" of denim, plaid, and short haircuts replaced radical hippie/fairy chic', signalling the return of a more gender-normative gay male style.[110] Feminine forms of self-presentation that lesbian feminists had once frowned upon also became more common and acceptable among 'lipstick lesbians' by the 1990s. This 'celebration of femininity' made them less easily distinguishable from straight women; Gayle Rubin, for one, thought it could reinforce traditional gender roles.[111]

In itself the macho look was 'merely a new form of "drag" ', and the same applied to lipstick lesbianism.[112] But the new norms were increasingly and pervasively enforced. In the earlier, smaller community of the immediate post-Stonewall years, non-gender-conforming LGBT people, less able or inclined to hide, had made up a higher proportion of the visible LGBT milieu. As lesbian/gay communities expanded, the influx of more 'normal-seeming' lesbians and gay men diluted the presence of those who only a few decades earlier had been called 'inverts' – and in fact had been seen as the predominant type of homosexual, and not yet separated out as transgendered. While some gay men remained accepting, many others viewed effeminate homosexuals as 'dinosaurs, the last remnants of a soon-to-be extinct species'.[113] A recent study showed that most gay and lesbian activists actively distinguish themselves from trans people and other gender dissidents to prove their own respectability and mental health.[114] Trans people have been increasingly barred from gay clubs (an issue for organising in Argentina, for example).[115] Given the greater prevalence and persistence of trans identities among working-class and poor people, this kind of exclusion was also a form of class discrimination.

---

109   Hekma 1994, p. 238.
110   Stryker 2008, p. 95. The clone look did not triumph all at once, however. As late as 1980, artist Keith Haring was stencilling 'Clones Go Home' on the pavements at transitions between New York's Greenwich Village gay ghetto and the more down-and-out East Village (Carr 2012, p. 166). The East Village scene of the 1980s foreshadowed in some ways the queer milieu of the 1990s.
111   Faderman 1991, p. 273; Rubin 1992, p. 214.
112   Kinsman 1987, p. 188.
113   Halperin 2002, p. 18.
114   Jordan-Young 2010, p. 265 (citing David Valentine).
115   Sarda 1998, p. 41.

Within the medical establishment, ironically, increased willingness to accept homosexuality as not intrinsically pathological went together with a sharper focus on gender nonconformity, further distinguishing and isolating trans people from gays. The flourishing, university-based gender clinics of the 1970s were far more concerned with 'restabilizing the gender system, which seemed to be mutating all around them in bizarre and threatening directions, than they were in helping that cultural revolution along'. Beginning in California in 1977, sex-reassignment surgery increasingly became legal grounds for changing birth certificates. But it was only 'grudgingly permitted for the few' to shore up 'the gender binary for the many'.[116]

Neoliberalism created both new possibilities and new dangers for transsexuals. The availability and use of hormones spread (through official or unofficial channels); by 1993, in the Netherlands one in 11,900 people born male and one in 30,400 born female had taken hormones to alter their sexual characteristics. As many university-based clinics in the US succumbed to gender conservatism to the point of stopping sex-reassignment surgery in the late 1970s, private clinics rushed to fill the gap. Often less concerned with screening candidates for surgery or imposing their own norms for surgery, the new private clinics could be more receptive to transsexuals' own wishes. But they were less tightly regulated, and sometimes gave free rein to incompetent, assembly-line or careless butchers. And many were cut-rate operations geared to maximising profits.[117]

Soon the pathologisation of trans people expanded, when the 1980 edition of the American Psychiatric Association's *Diagnostic and Statistic Manual of Mental Disorders* – the first one to appear since the 1973 edition that had removed homosexuality from the list – added the new category of Gender Identity Disorder (GID). The medical profession's growing interest in 'trying to understand, engineer, and "fix" gender' was in part 'an attempt to stuff the feminist genie back into its bottle'. The ideology of GID as a pathology presented trans people with a lose-lose situation: while many resisted medicalisation, many also sought forms of care for which a diagnosis of GID was a prerequisite.[118] The ideology also gave a scientific stamp of approval to 'the idea that there are two natural genders', with a 'right' sexuality corresponding to them.[119]

Paradoxically, part of what made it possible to reassert sharp distinctions between men and women, masculine and feminine, was the fact that under neoliberalism the range of permissible masculinities and femininities

116   Stryker 2008, pp. 93–4.
117   Meyerowitz 2002, pp. 9, 256, 271–4.
118   Stryker 2008, pp. 111, 113, 13–16.
119   Beccalossi 2012, p. 227.

has expanded somewhat. Shifting gender roles made it a bit easier and more comfortable for lesbians and gay men to live within the somewhat more flexible bounds of 'normal' masculinity and femininity. Not only has it become acceptable for women to wear trousers, they can more easily demonstrate 'strength and even muscle', and if they are unhappy with remaining sex role restrictions then they can identify as feminist rather than butch.[120] A growing market for health and fitness has resulted in a revised 'body ideal' featuring 'toned muscles and taut physiques': 'new embodiments of womanhood'[121] for straight women and cisgendered (non-trans) lesbians. The spread of forms of body modification – like preventive mastectomies and the use of performance-enhancing drugs – also broadened the range of masculine and feminine body imagery.[122]

This offered more choices to more women and men, but it also brought into sharper relief the choices of those who went the extra distance to put their masculinity or femininity in question. If they identified as gay or lesbian, they were seen as 'a vestige from the pre-modern past'[123] – or they could identify as something else.

Lesbian/gay communities thus increasingly defined themselves in ways that placed trans people – whose communities predated the new lesbian/gay identity by centuries – and other visible nonconformists on the margins, if not completely out of bounds. Despite the simultaneity of different constructions of gender and sexuality in any given society at a given time, a specific configuration of the relationship between gender and sexuality can be forcefully imposed at particular times and locations and in particular social strata. The cusp of the transition from Fordism to neoliberalism (roughly the late 1970s and early 1980s) was the time in imperialist countries when space for trans identities was at a historical nadir.[124]

---

120 Faderman 1991, p. 304.

121 Bolin 1994 p. 478.

122 Stryker 2008, p. 19.

123 Halperin 2002, p. 18.

124 It was also a low point for the 'ongoing, radical uncertainty' that Kevin Floyd has noted about whether 'gay male sexual practice feminizes any of the men involved' (2006, p. 64). This uncertainty has been most pronounced at transitional moments or locations, between a transgender model that insists that same-sex practice *does* feminise one partner, and a gay model that can insist just as emphatically that it does no such thing. Floyd himself gave an example (91) of a moment in this transition, when one male character in Hemingway's *The Sun Also Rises* remarks to another in Spain, 'I'm fonder of you than anybody on earth', adding, 'I couldn't tell you that in New York. It'd mean I was a faggot' (Floyd 2006, p. 91).

By the 1990s, the consolidation of the new lesbian/gay identity, combined with the stubborn persistence of gender nonconformity in same-sex communities, spurred on the definition of distinct trans identities, as the word 'transgender' came into widespread use. In the mid-1990s, 'LGBT' began to become a new portmanteau identity, one that 'reifies identities without interrogating them'.[125] The acronym thus incorporates trans people as a subordinate minority within an umbrella minority. Prejudice helped ensure that trans people were disproportionately illiterate, under-educated, poor and involved in crime. In a vicious circle, this justified further prejudice, which took especially deadly forms in the dependent world. In the lives of Brazilian trans people, for example, the result is 'recurring cycles of violence' and the 'centrality of violence'.[126] In Argentina, police killed over a hundred trans people between 1983 and 2000.[127] Accounts of so-called 'corrective rapes' of lesbians usually fail to note their transphobic dimension, with both butches in South African townships and tomboys in the Philippines being victimised to 'show' that they are 'still women'.[128] In the US too, trans people as a group have continued to experience one of the highest rates of violence and murder, with an average of one trans person dead from a hate crime every month.[129]

State enforcement of the gender binary has resulted in trans people's inability 'to marry, for example, or to cross national borders, or qualify for jobs, or gain access to needed social services, or secure legal custody' of their children.[130] Requirements for legal recognition of a gender change – in some countries this is legally impossible under any circumstances – have varied enormously, and included long lists of all sorts of arbitrary criteria: in Western European countries, for example, a psychological assessment and diagnosis, 'expert' statements, hormone therapy, surgery or plans for surgery, official panel or court approval, divorce and/or sterilisation.[131] Failure to jump through all these hoops can result in, among other things, denial of vitally needed healthcare, or violence: a 2008 US survey revealed that 40 percent of trans people had been harassed on presenting identification at variance with their perceived gender,

125   Dyer 2010, pp. 6–7.
126   Klein 1998, p. 30.
127   Moraiarty 2007, p. 8.
128   Pokade 2012, p. 472; De Vela, Ofreneo and Cabrero 2012, p. 357.
129   Stryker 2008, p. 142.
130   Stryker 2008, p. 6.
131   Verkerke 2012, pp. 15–17.

and 3 percent had been physically attacked.[132] In Leslie Feinberg's words, 'Bigotry exacts its toll in flesh and blood'.[133]

More broadly, what trans people experience as society's stigmatisation and marginalisation of those who fail to fit the gender binary takes a heavy psychological toll. While heteronormativity is reflected in much higher suicide rates among young LGBT people in general, suicide rates among trans people specifically are higher still. For example, in Ireland, 78 percent of the trans people surveyed have considered suicide, and 41 percent actually attempted it; the percentage of suicide attempts is also 41 percent in the US, and 34 percent in France.[134]

Lesbians and gay men who continued to flirt with gender dissent increasingly faced a stark choice, analogous in some ways to that faced a century earlier by women and men involved in same-sex romantic friendships as the concept of homosexuality increasingly impinged on people's consciousness. Should somewhat butch lesbians or somewhat effeminate gay men identify as trans themselves, or were they 'cisgendered' (as trans people began to call the rest of the world)? Should they at least express solidarity with trans people, or were the economic, social and even physical risks of being lumped in with them too great? The distinction of trans from LGB people reinforced the idea that 'homosexuality and bisexuality were by definition "gender normative", and that anyone who deviated from the conventional identities of "man" and "woman" automatically belonged in the transgender category'. As lesbian/gay people who conformed to gender norms seemed 'poised for mainstream acceptance', the price to be paid for gender nonconformity rose higher.[135] Transphobia provided powerful disincentives to lesbians and gay men's identifying as transgendered, or challenging or even questioning gender boundaries.

David Halperin has pointed out that the much-vaunted 'gay style' has persistently expressed a 'refusal of canonical masculinity' and a 'sly and profound critique of what passes for normal'.[136] But in many countries, straight men have also become freer in the twenty-first century to conduct themselves in ways that not long ago would have been seen as unmanly. If straight men can use cosmetics and spend more money on clothes, this gives gay men more leeway to behave in similar ways without risking being perceived as transgendered or even effeminate. They can simply take their place alongside, or even set the

---

132   Grant, Mottet and Tanis 2011, p. 5.
133   Feinberg 1998, p. 3.
134   Verkerke 2012, p. 14.
135   Stryker 2008, pp. 138, 152.
136   Halperin 2012.

tone for, the straight 'metrosexual', the term coined in 1994 by Mark Simpson and defined by him in 2002 as a 'young man with money to spend, living in or within easy reach of a metropolis – because that's where all the best shops, clubs, gyms and hairdressers are'.[137]

Shifts in gender under neoliberalism not only marginalised trans people within LGBT communities, but also increasingly gave class inflections to gay men's masculinity and lesbians' femininity. As the Indian gender queer group LABIA has pointed out, class – and in India particularly, caste and religion as well – determine 'the spaces that you can access and the ways in which you are allowed to behave in them', 'the amount of transgression that is allowed, and to whom and in what situations'.[138] 'The styles of masculinity executive and professional men favor differ sharply from those of truckers and carpenters'.[139] More prosperous gay men may find a professional brand of masculinity to be a more comfortable fit than a blue-collar masculinity that they could never manage.

Lesbians too have increasingly faced stylistic choices as the ostensibly class-less lesbian feminist communities of the 1970s and 1980s gradually came apart in classed ways. Many collectives made the transition to for-profit businesses; some lesbian-owned businesses experienced bitter labour-management conflicts; lesbian shops were driven out of neighbourhoods where commercial rents began to 'skyrocket'. Those lesbians who survived and profited in the new economic climate, like their middle-class lesbian forerunners of the 1950s, could disdain their less stylish lesbian sisters as 'tacky'.[140] The 1970s lesbian world declined along with the left and movements from which it had sharply separated itself, with fragments of it finding their place in the milieu of neoliberal women's or gay business.

Besides gender differences, a range of sexual preferences increasingly became the basis under neoliberalism of niche markets, subcultures and sub-identities, from SM to 'bears' to 'chubbies' and their 'chasers' and more. Besides the internet's significance for LGBT teenagers exploring their identities,[141] for the expansion of the transgender movement in the mid-1990s, for intersex people,[142] and in forging links in dependent countries between activists and

---

137 Simpson 2002.
138 Shah, Raj, Mahajan and Nevatia 2012, p. 225.
139 Rubin 2011, p. 246.
140 Rubin 2011, p. 356.
141 D'Emilio and Freedman 1997, p. 373.
142 Stryker 2008, p. 146; Feinberg 1998, pp. 90–1.

'regular gay men and women looking for a safe space',[143] it has facilitated the organisation of 'highly specialized communities of sexual interest'.[144] There was room for some of these sub-identities under the umbrella of 'normal' lesbian/gay identity. For others, insufficiently compatible with a stable position in the job market and neoliberal public space, marginalisation loomed – and queerness beckoned.

Homonationalism

Alongside demarcation as a stable minority, growing gender conformity and the separation of gay from trans, a fourth feature of the new gay normality has been the increasing incorporation of some lesbians and gay men into the imperialist nation. Here gender identity and sexuality were still closely linked, especially for men. For centuries, masculinity has been defined in feudal and capitalist societies by a positively valued propensity for violence, whether in the military, in everyday interactions with other men, or in sublimated form in sport. Incompetence at fighting and sport, and exclusion from the military, were therefore markers of insufficiently masculine men – while atypical competence, athleticism and military careers were markers of insufficiently feminine women.

Exclusion from the military, and therefore from the ranks of full male citizens, has often been one of the last forms of discrimination to fall. It was explicitly reaffirmed, for example, when homosexuality was decriminalised in Britain in 1967 (and only lifted in 2000), and perpetuated in US President Bill Clinton's curiously contradictory 'don't ask, don't tell' policy, adopted in 1993 and only lifted in 2011. The demand to eliminate discrimination based on sexual orientation in the military has been a constituent element of a new, nationalist homonormativity. This has been particularly evident in Israel, where Jewish open gay men's inclusion in the army was a marker of their incorporation into the Zionist project – understandably viewed without enthusiasm by Palestinian queers, who like other Palestinians in Israel face pervasive discrimination on the grounds of their exclusion from military service.

Jason Ritchie has recounted his discovery that each gay bar in Tel Aviv has a 'sort of checkpoint ... manned by a queer agent of Israeli nationalism, whose job it was to determine who belongs in this gay/Israeli space and who does not'. More broadly, gay Israelis 'consolidate their membership in the nation' by

143   Makarem 2011, p. 102.
144   Woltersdorff 2011, p. 169.

acting as 'gatekeepers at a metaphorical checkpoint, where queer Palestinians are inspected, policed, and occasionally admitted into the fold of Israeli gayness as "victims" of Palestinian culture' – or more often 'denied entry as excessively Arab or insufficiently "gay" '.[145]

More generally in the twenty-first century, the instrumentalisation of lesbian/gay rights in the service of imperialist and Islamophobic ideologies, which Puar has defined as 'homonationalism', has played a crucial role in integrating lesbian/gay people into the neoliberal order.[146] Its upshot, or at least its intended upshot, is a 'seemingly seamless articulation of queerness with an imperial nation state'.[147] Particularly, but not only, in countries like the Netherlands[148] and Denmark, where both same-sex partnership rights and anti-immigrant racism are strongly developed, this homonationalism has been key to consolidating and taming lesbian/gay identity. More broadly, it is an integral part of the neoliberal multiculturalism that masks capitalism's reliance on regional and racial hierarchies.[149] More generally in Europe, sexuality has become 'the sign of the European Union's benevolence' and a justification for prejudice against non-Europeans.[150]

Blatant racism has hardly disappeared; it continues notably in the form of stereotypes of black sexuality.[151] Increasingly in the last two decades, however, popular and right-wing racism based on skin colour has made way for a racism that is more often pseudo-cultural than pseudo-biological, and particularly for Islamophobia. It coexists in Northern Europe and North America with an ersatz form of multiculturalism that blurs the persistent, deniable, shifting but still crucial global divide between dominant and dominated groups and nations.

The French variant is an intensified emphasis on 'republican universalism', which relegates expressions of difference to the private sphere. The French LGBT mainstream has embraced this republican ideology in a way that obscures social and economic inequality and racism among LGBT people, which are making sexual relationships and ties of solidarity across class and race lines more difficult. A recent survey in the French gay magazine *Têtu* showed that LGBT people of immigrant origin had trouble finding white sex

145   Ritchie 2010, pp. 557, 560–1.
146   Puar 2007, pp. xxiv, 38–9.
147   Rosenberg and Villarejo, p. 10.
148   Mepschen, Duyvendak and Tonkens 2010; Jivraj and De Jong 2011.
149   Rosenberg and Villarejo, p. 2.
150   Ferguson and Hong 2012, p. 1060.
151   Wekker 2006, p. 249.

partners for more than one-off encounters or brief affairs. Across the imperialist countries, ethnic minorities and working-class people are eroticised, notably in pornography, while the dominant gay image becomes increasingly white and middle class in increasingly racialised societies.[152]

A growing number of gay men and lesbians have been prepared to accept such exclusions, or at least look the other way, as they pursued professional, business or political careers in a number of capitalist societies. Without necessarily renouncing or hiding their difference from the social norm, many of these people have preferred not to 'flaunt' it. Even the lesbian/gay middle-class layers that lived off gay businesses and non-profits – far from all of whom were among the real economic winners of recent decades, but who tended to be spoken for by those among them who were – preferred in general to keep lesbian/gay community expressions culturally inoffensive. Another layer of middle-class or middle-class-identified lesbian/gay people, who were making *their* careers inside mainstream businesses and institutions, sometimes cringed at manifestations of an LGBT community that marked them off too much from other people of their class. Many of these people wanted to pursue their careers in straight companies and institutions while being open about their same-sex relationships – fewer of them were willing than in the past to contract cross-sex marriages and to keep their same-sex lives hidden – but otherwise deny or minimise differences between them and the white, middle-class norm.

The rise of lesbian/gay professionalism has taken different, subtler forms in the mutation of academic lesbian/gay studies. While the initial radicalism of Black and Latino studies in the US in the 1960s and 1970s gradually and partially morphed into the ethnic pluralism of neoliberal multiculturalism, some lesbian/gay academics whose fields had been modelled on Black and Latino studies followed a comparable trajectory. The fact that the space for queer approaches has expanded more quickly in literature departments than in the social sciences has sometimes helped accentuate a turn towards cultural celebration and away from challenges to the powers that be. And the fact that queer studies is far bigger, relatively and absolutely, in the US than anywhere else has helped spread the post-modern inclinations of US queer studies internationally.

Despite an often enduringly confrontational rhetoric, a professional layer has provided the solid social base for the most moderate currents of LGB movements. Joining the movement from the 1980s when it became safer, moderates

---

152 Cervulle and Rees-Roberts 2010, pp. 17–18, 80, 23, 134, 69, 71, 146.

further reinforced its moderation and made professionalism a 'sign of accomplishment' rather than, as it often was in the 1960s and 1970s, suspect.[153]

Normal Gay Families

Such moderates have often seen same-sex marriage as the culminating moment in the process of gay emancipation. While the rights to marry and to adopt children do bring immediate, practical, crucial benefits to same-sex couples from many different class backgrounds, they can be the culmination of *some* gay people's integration into the productive and reproductive order of gendered capitalism. The call for these rights is a demand for equality, but also in some cases for equal class and racial privilege – and 'rights of property and inheritance in particular'.[154]

Paradoxically, neoliberalism has in many ways been loosening family ties. Just as ties to a single company and a single occupation have been eroding, neoliberalism fosters a kind of 'modular... *lean relationship*' parallel to lean production networks.[155] Ironically, therefore, same-sex marriage has become possible in more capitalist societies at a time when the significance of marriage has in some ways substantially declined. In Sweden and other Northern European countries, 'cohabitation and marriage became virtually indistinguishable legally and socially'.[156] At the same time, neoliberal cutbacks in social services, by privatising the provision of basic needs, have been restoring the centrality of the family unit to the social reproduction of labour – in classed ways.

Legal same-sex marriage or partnership can in this context secure not only much needed benefits for same-sex couples generally, but also specific advantages for middle-class and more secure working-class lesbians and gays. In this situation, limiting the 'horizon of queer politics to the right to marry', despite the intrinsic justice of the demand, props up not only a heteronormative model of monogamy but also the 'bourgeois articulation of privacy with property'.[157] One Canadian study showed, for example, that legal recognition of same-sex partnerships resulted on average in higher incomes for high-income LGBT people and lower incomes for low-income ones. This pattern also correlates

---

153   Faderman 1991, pp. 274–5.
154   Puar 2007, p. 29.
155   Woltersdorff 2011, pp. 175–6.
156   Coontz 2005, pp. 271–2.
157   Floyd 2006, p. 398.

with race.[158] The restriction of state recognition of same-sex relationships to couples thus produces new forms of exclusion.[159] For those most dependent on the welfare state in countries like Britain and the Netherlands, legal recognition of their partnerships can lead to cuts in benefits. The German government classifies all forms of cohabitation as 'communities of need' entailing an obligation to provide support, fusing the neoliberal 'offer of individualization . . . with the privatization of caretaking'.[160] Financial obligations often continue after a relationship ends; the first major legal case granting same-sex couple recognition in Canada involved alimony.[161]

As same-sex marriage spreads, other forms of partnership recognition that imitate the marriage model less slavishly are often eliminated, thus shanghaiing couples who seek any benefits or recognition into the existing marriage model. In any event, as with cross-sex couples, the practical differences between marriage and other forms of cohabitation have been shrinking. Nicola Barker has identified the French PACS ('civil solidarity pact') as one of the most flexible forms of legal recognition, since it allows couples some leeway to structure their relationship by agreement. Yet it too requires mutual assistance between partners, joint liability for debts and spousal support even after the couple breaks up.[162]

Consolidating partnerships can reinforce inequality within couples as well as between them. A study in San Francisco in the 1990s showed that the idea that same-sex couples are inherently egalitarian, often expressed by the couples themselves, was belied by the reality of an unequal division of labour in the home. When one partner worked for wages in a female-gendered occupation and the other in a male-gendered occupation, the partner (of whatever gender) in a female-gendered occupation tended to do more housework. Where the division of labour was more equal, this was often because someone else was paid for housework.[163] Even middle-class same-sex couples can find homonormative patterns unexpectedly constricting. Stephanie Coontz has told the story of a prominent gay historian whose stay-at-home boyfriend found himself 'trapped in personal dependence', lacking 'independent meaning in

---

158   Barker 2012, p. 100.
159   Woltersdorff 2011, p. 178.
160   Browne 2011; Woltersdorff 2011, p. 177.
161   Barker 2012, pp. 79, 162.
162   Barker 2012, pp. 55–8.
163   Barker 2012, pp. 155–6, 199 (citing Christopher Carrington).

his life', and suffering from the same anxieties as the housewives Betty Friedan had profiled in *The Feminine Mystique* in 1963.[164]

Even in the early, pioneering days of lesbian parenthood (through custody battles, adoption or resorts to donor insemination), the spread of parenting in lesbian/gay communities could sometimes have a conservatising impact. Part of a lesbian generation concluded – rightly or wrongly – that motherhood demanded 'a more moderate approach to life'.[165] More recently, among more prosperous lesbians and gays, those who are willing to forego the economic benefits and freedom of remaining childless can, like increasing numbers of the most prosperous parents generally, 'outsource support and caretaking'.[166] They are thus giving a new lease of life to the situation described by Alexandra Kollontai in which bourgeois parents placed their children 'in the care of hired labourers: nannies and governesses'.[167]

Not that middle-class parents are fated by their class position to hire cleaners and nannies; personal values and political choices are major factors in such decisions. But in the neoliberal economy, outsourcing care is easy and tempting for people with high enough incomes. Those lesbians and gays who make this choice are buying into the 'return of the servant classes'.[168] Those doing the caretaking today are naturally likely to be immigrants and/or non-white, in a home that presupposes 'the racial formation of domestic labor, the gendered division of labor, and the colonial differentiation of the wage scale'.[169] And even middle-class lesbian and gay parents without nannies can buy into the obsessive, expensive pursuit of 'the best for their children' – a pursuit that often expresses middle-class parents' anxiety at the prospect that their children might fail to inherit their class privileges.[170] The benefits of hired help and/or exclusive kindergartens are rarely available to working-class same-sex parents who cannot afford childcare, and thus must juggle wage work with parenting when they cannot or do not want to find others to share parenting.

In general, as the number of children being raised in households headed by same-sex couples rises, same-sex marriage and adoption can serve to legitimise and regulate the growing role that lesbian and gay couples are playing in social production, consumption and reproduction. They can 'simulate

---

164   Coontz 2011, p. 162.
165   Faderman 1991, p. 291.
166   Woltersdorff 2011, p. 176.
167   Kollontai 1978, p. 145.
168   Angell 2014, p. 20.
169   Reddy 1998, p. 356.
170   Angell 2014, p. 21.

heteronormative paternity through the purchase of reproductive technology' – 'in vitro, sperm banks, cloning, sex selection, genetic testing' – or take advantage of the global hierarchy by resorting to transnational adoption. This suggests that 'the capitalist reproductive economy...no longer exclusively demands heteronormativity as an absolute; its simulation may do'.[171] Yet the rise of same-sex-couple-headed nuclear families redefines and even reinforces rather than overcomes the gay/straight divide, since the ways in which lesbians and gay men form families (through sperm donorship, adoption, the break-up of straight families or other trajectories) necessarily remain distinctive.

Marriage has changed over time; it has no 'fixed, universal essence'. But marriage, as it has taken shape under gendered capitalism, and especially in recent decades under neoliberalism, can only be stretched a limited distance towards including less normative forms. There are always limits to the partners' legal scope to negotiate or alter the terms of their relationship, for example. Marriage is an extensive package that the spouses have to accept as a whole. In the US, the General Accounting Office has counted 1,138 consequences of marriage under federal law alone. The consequences of marriage everywhere include the transmission of wealth among the haves and a privatised obligation of support that is a particular burden for the have-nots. Although the ease of divorce varies, marriage is always intended to be stable and relatively hard to dissolve. In England, for example, boredom, incompatibility, inability to communicate or no longer having anything in common are explicitly *not* sufficient grounds for divorce.[172]

Conservative advocates of same-sex marriage celebrate its role in encouraging 'responsible' sexuality and specifically in 'civilising' gay men: an example of regulation through normalising and 'responsibilising'. As same-sex marriage gains acceptance and an LGBT person is no longer automatically categorised as a ' "bad" or dangerous sexual citizen', other sexual outsiders are assigned that role. However, the process is still underway of redefining what sexual behaviour is compatible with a stable, privatised partnership unit and what behaviour is threatening to it. Clearly still a legal marriage needs to entail a primary commitment that is in some sense, as the Massachusetts Supreme Court has stressed, '*exclusive*'. As one British judge observed, 'transient, irresponsible and insecure relationships' do not qualify. But sex outside marriage is decreasingly defined as automatic grounds for divorce; in current English

---

171   Puar 2007, pp. xiv, 30–1 (citing David Eng).
172   Barker 2012, pp. 5, 181–2, 22, 28, 26.

law, adultery can end a marriage only if one partner 'finds it intolerable to live with the respondent'.[173]

This suggests that marital law may be relaxing enough to embrace many gay male couples' longstanding emphasis on emotional rather than sexual fidelity:[174] an agreement that casual, one-off sex with others may be acceptable, but close ties outside the relationship that are both sexual and emotional are too threatening. In this framework, even sexual three-ways can serve to reaffirm the emotional and domestic primacy of the romantic couple. While less rigid than pure monogamy, this model does not necessarily constitute a more decisive break with heterosexual marriage than did the widespread Victorian tolerance of husbands' resort to prostitutes. Sexual exclusiveness is less a core characteristic of bourgeois marriage than is the privatised provision of basic human needs for practical or emotional nurturance.

In sum, a number of developments – the stabilisation of the gay/straight binary, the masculinisation of gay men and feminisation of lesbians, the marginalisation of trans people and others, the rise of homonationalism and the formation of lesbian/gay families fulfilling the function of privatised social reproduction – have been laying the basis of a new kind of gay normality. The same-sex formation founded on this normality fits into a neoliberal accumulation regime, as an earlier variant of lesbian/gay identity fit with Fordism. It is particularly congenial to middle-class and more secure working-class LGB people in parts of the world where lesbian/gay rights have been best secured – since in regions of greater persecution, the way of life that gay normality presupposes is only available to the most closeted and/or sheltered, generally upper-class, gays.

While LGBT people who have adapted to the new normality may be politically moderate or conservative and/or personally religious, they by no means have to uphold reactionary norms of masculinity and femininity or be sexually puritanical (or even strictly monogamous). On the contrary, a hallmark of homonormativity is identification with emancipation, modernity and 'liberal' attitudes (in the broad cultural sense). A normal gay lifestyle is generally far removed from the gay-negativity that characterised Reaganism or Thatcherism thirty years ago. Its affinity for neoliberalism is a subtle adaptation, visible almost exclusively when its boundaries need defending against forms of gender and sexual dissent that are incompatible with holding down a job or being

---

173 Barker 2012, pp. 94–5 (citing David Halperin), 169–70 (citing Steven Seidman), 175, 35, 173, 25–6.

174 Barker 2012, pp. 178–9 (citing Jeffrey Weeks, Brian Heaphy, and Catherine Donovan).

visible and comfortable in heteronormative public space (which includes the vast majority of public spaces in the world today).

'Homonormative' is, of course, not a label that people choose for themselves. Since people are not (and cannot be) always consistent in their attitudes, there is no simple litmus test to distinguish upholders of gay normality from LGBT people at large. No one has the option of living entirely free of norms. Nor does it make sense to label every LGBT person who is not visibly, confrontationally queer at any given moment as homonormative, or to condemn every working-class gay person with a reasonable income for overconsumption.

In any event, the fact that neoliberalism is overwhelmingly hegemonic in the world does not mean that the hetero- and homonormative forms that fit best with it are everywhere, fully, solidly established. Gay normality, queer and many intermediate gradations are still taking form as people shape their sexual identities day by day in response to a constantly shifting series of pressures and counter-pressures. It makes no sense to try to separate the sheep from the goats on the basis of sexual practices, gender identity, skin colour or income; comforting as this may be to those who like belonging to an in-group, it is neither analytically possible nor politically desirable. Rather, the point is to identify the pressures that are at work in all our lives, and in which directions, with what consequences, so as to facilitate critical reflection in one's own life and practical solidarity with others.

Fractures

The apparent uniformity of lesbian/gay culture as Fordism reached its end in fact helped disguise social and economic fractures opening up among LGBT people as neoliberalism emerged. As a result, the relatively homogeneous lesbian/gay identities that had taken shape in North America and Western Europe by the 1970s were challenged and fragmented over the following decades, though to different degrees in different countries. In particular, there has been a proliferation of alternative sexual or gender identities, more or less outside the mainstream commercial scene and the parameters of normalising lesbian/gay identity. Some, though far from all, of these alternative identities represent challenges to the gay/straight divide that emerged and was consolidated through much of the twentieth century.

Contrary to much anti-gay rhetoric, the prosperous couples focused on by glossy lesbian/gay magazines were never typical of most LGBT people. Data gathered by the US National Opinion Research Centre in the 1990s suggested that lesbian and bisexual women were still far less likely than other women to have professional or technical jobs and more likely to have service-sector or blue-collar jobs. Gay and bisexual men were more likely than other men to have professional/technical, clerical/sales or service jobs, but less likely to have managerial jobs.[175] The heteronormative constraints of many economic sectors – the pressures to abide by a heterosexual norm of behaviour – seemed to drive many LGBT workers to accept a lower wage in return for the 'relative comfort of working in a queer environment'.[176]

Whatever the causes (less ability or willingness to meet gendered job expectations, migration to more competitive job markets, discrimination), the net result refuted the unfounded claims made not only by anti-gay ideologues, but also by some gay publications. At least in the US, both gay men and lesbians were under-represented in the higher income brackets, while gay men in particular were over-represented in the lower income brackets.[177] A more recent study showed that 39 percent of LGBT adults in the US in 2013 had incomes under $30,000, compared with 28 percent of adults in general.[178] While women in same-sex couples earn more on average than straight married women, their income is, of course, less than men's.[179]

Trans people are even worse off. A 2006 study found that in San Francisco 60 percent of trans people earned less than $15,300 a year, only 25 percent had fulltime jobs, and nearly 9 percent had no source of income.[180] There are doubtless many millions of LGBT poor people in the world, disproportionately transgendered, disproportionately non-white and disproportionately female. Hard data are scarce, however. LGBT poverty is a topic that the queer academy has neglected,[181] although the Williams Institute at the University of California Los Angeles School of Law published a report on the subject in 2009. In any event, studies have shown that poverty rates are particularly high among LGBT people who are non-white, old or living in rural areas. In New York City, an estimated 20 to 40 percent of homeless youth are LGBT.[182]

The expansion of LGBT communities centred on gay commercial scenes has not improved the situation of lower-income LGBT people. On the contrary, as Jeffrey Escoffier has noted, the gay market, like all markets, tends to 'segment

---

175   Badgett 1997, p. 81.
176   Sears 2005, p. 106.
177   Badgett and King 1997, pp. 68–9.
178   Pew Research Center 2013.
179   Wolf 2009, p. 241.
180   Wolf 2009, p. 147.
181   Hennessy 2000, pp. 140–1.
182   DeFilippis 2011/2012a.

the...community by income, by class, by race and by gender'.[183] This is particularly true of same-sex couples, particularly same-sex couples raising children together, since two women living together are in a sense doubling the
economic disadvantages they both experience as women. Moreover, LGBT
people are more likely to be cut off from family support networks. As the
social safety net has frayed, inequalities resulting from wage differentials have
affected them with particular intensity.[184]

Across the capitalist world, the welfare state has been shredded, unions
have been weakened, and inequality has grown. Neoliberalism has meant all
this and more. It has been a 'wide-ranging political and cultural project – the
reconstruction of the everyday life of capitalism, in ways supportive of upward
redistribution of a range of resources'. The neoliberal project has racial, gender and sexual consequences. While its ideology separates supposedly value-
neutral economic precepts from politics and culture, in practice the economy
cannot be abstracted from the state or the family. Unfortunately, much of the
left has been inattentive to the connections among economics, politics, culture
and sexuality.[185]

In dependent countries, consumer society under neoliberalism is restricted
to narrower social layers than in imperialist countries. Trans people and
lesbians in particular, but also many gay and bisexual men, usually have
incomes too low to spend much on housing or going out. Even the most prosperous 'emerging economies', like South Korea, have less developed welfare
states than Western Europe, Canada or Australia.

In this context, polarisation within LGBT communities has been particularly great, even at the point of production. Same-sex identities intersect in
differentiated ways with class relations on the shop floor of Mexican maquila-
doras, for example. Gay male workers, initially if informally excluded from the
maquiladora workforce, began to be hired in the expansion of the 1990s, but at
the bottom rung of the workforce hierarchy, as the 'new women'. Yet there are
now gay men in management who play different roles and have a very different
status. Meanwhile the spectre of lesbianism is used to keep women workers in
line: 'Many women who become organizers so disrupt normative heterosexual
machista culture that they are threatened by their husbands and accused of
being lesbians'.[186]

---

183   Escoffier 1997, p. 131.
184   Jacobs 1997.
185   Duggan 2003, pp. xi, xiv, xvi.
186   Hennessy 2006, pp. 393–4.

What holds true in the workplace is equally visible in society at large. Lower-income LGB people, trans people, street youth and LGBT people of colour have been under assault in various ways in recent decades, as attacks on poor people and minorities have multiplied, racism has intensified even more in the US, and new forms of antagonism to black and immigrant communities (especially of Muslim origin) have grown up in European countries. Young LGBT people and sex workers in particular have been victims of intensified forms of coercive policing.[187]

Economic and social polarisation has appeared among LGBT people even in Cuba, as the economic crisis after the disappearance of the Soviet Union led people increasingly to resort to the underground economy as a survival strategy and, more recently, the regime began opening to the market. In the 1990s, semi-public gay 'ten-peso parties' with paid admission became common, as did *jinterismo*, the use of gifts as a means of seduction – particularly by foreigners with far greater resources – traditionally seen as stopping short of professional prostitution. Less innocently, the gulf has grown between middle-class gays – not so much professionals, whose salaries have little value, as those with hard currency and/or government connections – and poor black and working-class LGBT people in Old Havana. Dark skin is identified with sexual potency, but also with lack of education, culture and money.[188]

Sex Wars

Social polarisation within LGBT communities has coincided with greater prominence for forms of sexual identity and practice that focus explicitly on gender and power differences. Obviously these shifts did not reflect an instantaneous, spontaneous sea change in all LGBT people's felt desires or sexual practices. But when sexual identities and imagery took on more unequal and gender-polarised forms at just the time when the surrounding societies were undergoing a sharp, long-term rise in inequality, it would be implausible to dismiss the correlation as pure coincidence.

One of the first notable mutations in LGBT identity with the rise of neoliberalism was the role that SM and leather played in the more masculine culture that took hold among gay men in imperialist countries by the early 1980s, alongside the more mainstream 'clone' scene. While one gay male leather bar opened in New York as early as 1955 and more followed by the early 1970s, only

---

187   Sears 2005, p. 103.
188   Lumsden 1996, pp. 140–2, 138, 146–8.

from 1976 on did leather culture become a subject of attention and debate in the broader lesbian/gay community,[189] as gay male SM and leather parties 'reached new pinnacles of organization, sophistication, and capital investment'. Leather became a broad category including gay men who did SM or fist-fucked or were fetishists or simply preferred a butch image for themselves or sought it in their sexual partners.[190] By the 1980s there was an association in many people's minds between SM and male homosexuality, partially displacing the earlier association with effeminacy.[191] SM clubs like New York's Mineshaft became 'an arena for the masculinization of the gay male'.[192] They could also reinforce the growing emphasis among gays on consumption, since the cost of the wide panoply of gear involved in SM could mount up for practitioners who were not especially technically gifted.

The growing popularity of SM among gay men provoked widespread dismay in feminist communities and movements. In 1980, the US National Organisation for Women condemned SM along with intergenerational sex, pornography and public sex. In response, Rubin denounced a feminist current that 'condemned virtually every variant of sexual expression as antifeminist'.[193] US women's music festivals were disrupted in the 1980s by disputes over lesbian SM, as its practitioners sought allies among gay male sex radicals in general and gay men into SM in particular.[194]

Paradoxically at this stage, while divisions between 'tops' and 'bottoms' that would earlier have been widely rejected on liberationist grounds became acceptable and sometimes blatant, virtually all the men in the scene were masculinised in the process. It was as if SM served as a ritual of catharsis, of both acting out and exorcising the growing violence and inequality of the broader society.[195] Lesbians into SM, for their part, insisted on their feminist politics and their opposition to all gender hierarchies; as one said, roles as tops and bottoms were 'not social roles. They're just sexual'.[196] As Rubin put it, 'class, race, and gender neither determine nor correspond to the roles adopted for S/M play'.[197] A 'sexual ethics of negotiation' fosters SM participants' being

---

189   Rubin 2011, p. 132; Califia 1982, pp. 280, 244–8.
190   Rubin 2011, pp. 225, 308.
191   Altman 1982, p. 191.
192   Moore 2004, p. 20.
193   Rubin 2011, pp. 124, 172.
194   Faderman 1991, pp. 251–2, 254–6.
195   Altman 1982, p. 195.
196   Faderman 1991, pp. 260–3.
197   Rubin 2011, p. 134.

treated equally even across sharp disparities in social power, as SM at times 'makes visible previously invisible institutionalized power inequalities'.[198]

By the early 1980s, forms of sexuality that diverged from the perceived feminist norm also affected the kind of feminist culture previously hegemonic among lesbians. Lesbian feminist culture in a sense already struck a divergent note in the 1970s, as the sense persisted that lesbians in general were less involved in commercial scenes than gay men and persevered more in trying to sustain alternative ones. But while lesbian feminists had put women under great pressure in the 1970s to abandon butch/femme relationships that had been common among them for decades, some lesbians began in the 1980s to defend butch/femme vigorously,[199] at about the same time that some lesbians took a visible part in SM culture. However, the butch/femme subculture that arose in the 1980s was more diverse and flexible than the 1950s scene had been. While older and working-class lesbians seemed more likely still to insist that they were butch or femme by nature, younger and middle-class lesbians were more likely to play with roles as 'taboo-smashers and iconoclasts', out of 'a sense of adventure, a longing to push at the limits'. As with lesbian SM, butch and femme roles often did not correspond to domestic or economic ones[200] – even if the resurgence of role-playing was related in more subtle ways to growing social inequality.

The resurgence of butch/femme and the rise of SM dovetailed with a general upheaval in the lesbian world through conflict between currents that defined themselves as 'anti-pornography' and others that defined themselves as 'pro-sex', seeing sex as a terrain of both 'pleasure and danger'.[201] A pioneering article like Rubin's 'Thinking Sex'[202] moved beyond a narrow focus on gender and lesbian/gay identity to look politically at public sex, intergenerational sex, prostitution, fetishism and SM. A range of publications and film production companies put theory into practice by producing lesbian pornography. Cultural feminists responded that these trends 'validated the system of patriarchy, in which one person has power over another or objectifies her', and constituted a backlash against feminism. Yet the once self-contained and hard-edged lesbian feminist culture weakened over the decades.[203]

---

198 Woltersdorff 2011, pp. 174–5 (citing Darren Langdridge and Trevor Butt).
199 Nestle 1989; Hollibaugh and Moraga 1983, pp. 397–404.
200 Faderman 1991, pp. 263–5.
201 Vance 1984; Linden et al. 1982; Califia 1982, pp. 250–9.
202 Rubin 2011, pp. 137–81.
203 Faderman 1991, pp. 258–9, 250–1.

There has unquestionably been an explosive rise under neoliberalism of the production of commercial pornography, including violent pornography and clearly sexist pornography. 'Most pornography *is* sexist', Rubin wrote. But a group like Women Against Violence in Pornography and Media condemned not only violence and sexism, but also consensual SM and 'even the most banal pornography [which] objectifies women's bodies'. Andrea Dworkin defined pornography as 'the ideology that is the source of all the rest'.[204] Curiously, anti-pornography feminists like Dworkin succumbed to the same fallacy as a Marxist like György Lukács, identifying the objectification inherent in all human relations (sexual or otherwise) with the particularly intense and dehumanising reification characteristic of capitalism. To see the steadily advancing commercialisation of sex and sexual images (however deserving of criticism) as the 'source of all the rest', moreover, was to confuse cause and effect.

The proliferation of minority sexual identities within the LGB minority was no more universally welcomed in LGB communities than among feminists. Amber Hollibaugh has recalled that the 'drag queens, stone butches, S/M lesbians and leather men, high-femme dykes and queer sex workers, radical fairy boys and bisexual activists, and others too strange to name or categorize... were too far outside the norms established even by "gay" standards'. They represented the outlawry that many lesbian/gay people feared, and were only 'passively tolerated'.[205] The most explosive issue in the 'sex wars' was, briefly, the issue of intergenerational sex, which was the subject of a major confrontation during the organisation of the first US national lesbian/gay rights march in 1979. Going beyond legitimate concerns about coercion and abuse of authority, some currents perceived power differences between adults and youths as precluding the possibility of consent to sex.

In hindsight, the clone culture, lipstick lesbianism and sex wars of the 1980s were only an initial phase in a longer-term fracturing of LGBT identity. The consolidation of Reaganism and Thatcherism by the mid-1980s coincided for LGBT people with the onslaught of the AIDS epidemic, a trauma experienced as a sharp generational break. The epidemic gave an early, brutal example of the implications, for healthcare and for social protections in general, of neoliberal governance and the accompanying victim-blaming climate. As Simon Watney later recalled, 'We saw the sick pilloried, and the worst abuse reserved for the most severely devastated communities'.[206] These included sex workers,

---

204   Rubin 2011, pp. 271, 210, 269.
205   Hollibaugh 2011/2012a.
206   Herzog 2011, p. 177.

who faced calls for mandatory HIV testing,[207] reminiscent of the nineteenth-century regulation of prostitutes in the interests of clients. Gay bathhouses, even those that actively distributed condoms and safe-sex information, were closed in many cities. This supposed public-health measure 'drove men to the streets and alleys and parks, which were arguably less safe' than the clubs had been.[208]

Since global crises like AIDS hit the dependent world hardest, popular impulses to find scapegoats there were especially strong. The syndrome's global advance continually replicated the divides of class, race and planetary inequality, with Africa being the most devastated continent. It also reinforced the tendency, which already existed in dominated countries, to associate same-sex sexuality with disease, corruption and imperialism. AIDS not only killed a number of gay male leaders of the 1970s; in a time when an incurable disease linked death to sexuality, 'all forms of transgressive sexuality' were represented as 'both horrific and deadly'.[209]

After the devastation of the first years, however, the epidemic contributed to trends in some parts of the world towards broader acceptance of some LGB people. Some Western European governments designed or at least funded safer-sex education campaigns that eroticised condom use. This helped show that the 'lines between daring and dull, kinky and vanilla, promiscuous and monogamous, quite apparently ran *through*, not between, each group'.[210] In the US, even the trans community benefited from funding for 'culturally competent' prevention and harm-reduction strategies.[211] And as chapter 6 will discuss, AIDS sparked some of the most radical and even anti-capitalist queer organising that has ever been done.

Yet much LGBT work around AIDS focused on service provision and avoided politics, as communities were overwhelmed with the tasks of caring for sick and dying people on whom the neoliberal lean state was turning its back. The epidemic provided many lesbian/gay health professionals, as well as largely self-educated experts who emerged from activism, not only with years of long, hard, devoted labour, but also with openings for career advancement. And in gay male communities at large, many men who escaped or survived infection decided as they grew older that the time had come to 'get serious', live healthier and less adventuresome lives, and focus on settling down and making a living.

---

207   Shah 2011/2012.
208   Rubin 2011, p. 238; see also Drucker 1984.
209   hooks 1990, p. 196.
210   Herzog 2011, pp. 179–80, 182–3.
211   Stryker 2008, pp. 132–3.

For those with the right education, class background and resources, this could mean an intensified focus on middle-class careers.

The Emergence of Queer

Many young people who came of age in the era of AIDS and neoliberalism found the road to a secure middle-class existence strewn with obstacles. Beginning in the mid-1980s, a queer social milieu emerged, made up to a large extent of young people at the bottom of the unequal social hourglass that was resulting from economic restructuring.[212] One aspect of the underlying social reality was that the lower young queers' incomes were, and the more meagre their job prospects, the less on average they identified with or wanted to join the lesbian/gay community that had grown up since the 1960s and 1970s. For many young queers, as Torvald Patterson noted, economic restructuring meant more part-time and contract work, which left many 'unable to see a place for themselves in the by then established gay middle class'.[213]

Above all initially in English-speaking developed capitalist countries – the imperialist countries where social polarisation was greatest – young queers resisted disco culture, a bar-centred ghetto, and the kind of segregation that fit with ethnic-style minority group politics. Self-identified queers refused to be comfortable in the ghettos.[214] English-speaking queer scenes have been echoed in some ways by queers in squatters' milieus in continental Western Europe. This generation had also grown up in more diverse and changeable family structures, which made the notion of modelling same-sex households on traditional straight ones all the more implausible for them. In some milieus of young rebels, gender and sexual categories became more fluid than would be usual in mainstream straight, gay male or lesbian scenes.

Economic marginalisation and cultural alienation were closely interlinked in the emergence of a queer milieu, making it hard in many cases to say to what extent poverty was a cause of alienation, to what extent the choice of a queer lifestyle contributed to more or less voluntary poverty, and to what extent some queers were middle-class gays – particularly students and academics – dressing and talking like down-and-outs, in some cases perhaps only for a period of a few years of 'float[ing] in and out of deviance or propriety'.[215] In other cases,

---

212   Drucker 1993, p. 29.
213   Patterson 2000.
214   Seidman 1997, p. 193; Drucker 1993, p. 29.
215   Califia 2003, p. xiv.

queerness may be defined so much by dress, style or performance that it becomes as much a matter of consumer choice and an expression of reification as the middle-class gay identities it rejects.[216] Nevertheless, there has been an overall correlation between lower incomes (if not working-class identity) and queer self-identification.

If economic pressures made integration into the dominant lesbian/gay culture a dubious proposition for many young and disadvantaged queers in developed countries, the barriers have been all the greater for poor and working-class LGBT people in Asia, Africa and Latin America. They were less likely than middle-class LGB people to have identities (let alone incomes) that facilitated their integration into a Westernised, commercialised gay scene.[217] They were also more likely to be transgendered, to be subject to violence, and to be dependent on family and/or community structures for survival.

The economic marginalisation that they experienced tended to make post-Fordist, normal lesbian/gay identity at least as problematic and alien for them as for young self-identified queers in North America or Britain. For example, lower-class Brazilians, 'many of whom are of African descent, still find themselves with far fewer opportunities to circulate in the gay world'. One sign of this beginning in the early 1970s was the rapid spread of sex work. Prosperity gave more middle-class men the wherewithal to buy sex, on the one hand, while others, excluded from the Brazilian 'economic miracle', were forced by poverty into prostitution as cross-dressing or masculine hustlers.[218]

Various sexually dissident communities, such as increasingly militant trans people in much of Latin America and South and Southeast Asia, have become more visible and vocal. While they were slow at first to adopt the label 'queer', in the twenty-first century it has become increasingly common at least in LGBT academic milieus in Asia. It also became popular in Taiwan in the 1990s before being picked up in the People's Republic in the twenty-first century.[219] In India, in 2002 the lesbian group Stree Sangam changed its name to LABIA and its self-definition to a 'queer and feminist collective of lesbian, transgender and bisexual women'.[220]

These LGBT people in the dependent world have been forced to fight, socially and sometimes even politically, on one or two different fronts. Many of them have been fighting against prejudice and repression, which have been fuelled

216   Hennessy 2000, pp. 140–1.
217   Oetomo 1996, pp. 265–8.
218   Green 1999a, pp. 284, 251–2, 254–5.
219   Jackson 1989, p. 388 n. 3; Rofel 1999, p. 465.
220   Shah, Raj, Mahajan and Nevatia 2012, pp. 189–90.

by the dislocation of societies all over the world with the collapse of Fordist-based social and political orders. In this fight, neoliberalism in its most pro-gay forms may sometimes appear as a force working in their favour, inasmuch as it undermines local structures that oppress them. Images of the apparently prosperous and free lesbian/gay communities of Western Europe and North America can exercise a powerful attraction.

Yet at the same time, many LGBT people in dependent countries have been resisting attempts to claim them for the homogeneous, middle class-dominated lesbian/gay community that neoliberalism has been shaping, to purge them of 'old-fashioned' aspects of their identities, or to make them come out in ways that would tear them away from their families and communities without providing them with equivalent support systems. Chilean writer Pedro Lemebel, for example, has expressed his identification with Santiago's down-trodden *locas* and his rejection of the gay male model he encountered in New York.[221] One upwardly mobile man in Beijing burst out at one point, stating that 'all of us low-quality (*suzhi*) [queers] should form a group and talk about our problems being low-quality'.[222]

Class differences among LGBT people also overlap with differences along lines of race, immigrant origin, disability and age. The more visible lesbians there were, the more the realisation spread that 'a shared sexual orientation alone does not guarantee that its members will have much in common'. Anger and organising against racism and other forms of discrimination have spread since the 1980s.[223] Immigrant women sometimes rebel against the 'economic, emotional, and psychological dependency' in which they are trapped.[224] Others rebel against the narrow model of youthful, able-bodied attractiveness that prevails in neoliberal markets for sex and relationships.

Marginalisation of millions of LGBT people worldwide because they are poor, young or black has impelled many of them towards developing or adopting identities that have, to some extent, broken with homonormative patterns of gay identity. As we have seen, the dominant trend since the 1970s, based particularly on the reality of more prosperous LGB people's lives, was for the lesbian/gay community to define itself as a stable and distinct minority, to tend increasingly towards gender conformity, to marginalise its own sexual minorities, to integrate into the nation and to form homonormative families. By contrast, the nonconformist sexual and gender identities that have grown

---

221   Mansilla 1996, p. 23 (cited in Palaversich 2002, p. 104).
222   Rofel 1999, p. 467.
223   Faderman 1991, pp. 286, 288–90.
224   Wekker 2006, p. 242.

up among more marginalised layers have tended to be non-homonormative: to identify (culturally and sometimes politically) with broader communities of oppressed or rebellious people, to resist dominant gender norms (without being able to escape them entirely, given the realities of gendered capitalism), to highlight power differentials that dominant lesbian/gay imagery tends to elide, and to form alternative families and communities. While different counter-identities can and do sometimes clash with one another,[225] they share features that correspond to structural similarities in their bearers' positions under neoliberalism.

Marginalised, anti-homonormative identities defined by age, class, region and/or ethnicity overlap with sexual subcultures that are marginal in the commercial scene because they constitute (sometimes extensive) niche markets at best and illicit markets at worse. The relationship between alternative identities and marginalised sexual practices is elusive, but there does seem to be a correlation. Of course, many LGBT people limit their sexual rebellion to the safety of a particular type of bar. But the more attached people are to their sexual identities, the more reluctant many of them become to give them up at work or in public.

The more visible gender and sexual dissenters are, the less likely they are in most societies to get one of the well-paid, permanent, full-time jobs that have become scarcer and more coveted commodities in post-Fordist economies. Moreover, some people are virtually or entirely incapable of hiding aspects of their identities – particularly effeminacy in men or butchness in women – that are often rightly or wrongly associated with sexualities that are neither straight nor 'normally' gay. Voluntary or involuntary, tell-tale signs of gender or sexual deviance often lead to management's excluding people from professional or service jobs, or to fellow workers' hostility that impels people to avoid or flee certain workplaces.

Paradoxically, in the absence of general guarantees for workers' job security or free expression at work, anti-discrimination laws that protect LGB people in general may be of less than no use to sexually marginalised queers.[226] As Ruthann Robson has noted, 'If a company employs four lesbians, a new manager can fearlessly fire the one who has her nose pierced or who is most outspoken or who walks the dykiest'.[227] People who are 'erotically unconventional'

---

225 See, for example, Drucker 1993, p. 29.

226 McCreery and Krupat 1999, p. 6.

227 Robson 1997, p. 175, n. 13.

risk losing or not getting jobs. The more important and higher paid the job, the less will employers tolerate 'overt erotic deviance'.[228]

These factors help explain the correlation that exists between positions at the bottom of the social ladder and various alternative sexual scenes and identities that do not fit the standard moulds of gay normality. This is not a straightforward correlation between non-homonormative identities and working-class locations. On the contrary, working-class LGBT people and LGBT people of colour (who can, of course, be the same people) have sometimes reacted against self-defined queer or other sexually dissident groups. Sometimes queers have insisted on visibility in ways that make the lives of working-class LGBT people and LGBT people of colour more difficult in particular workplaces or communities.[229] But there is a correlation between queer identities and particular sectors of the working class – on average younger, less unionised and lower-paid – that have expanded since the 1970s.

Part of the younger queer generation has championed, to varying extents and in new ways, some of the sexual practices that were under attack during the sex wars of the early 1980s. SM has been less at the forefront of this new sexual rebellion than it once was. It seems less politically laden now than it was in the sex wars of the early 1980s. Perhaps it has become less central to LGBT scenes as it has increasingly in diluted form come to permeate the broader culture, as seen in the spread of piercing, tattooing, and leather fashion and accessories. By contrast, the queer generation has tended more to play with issues of gender, inequality and power difference in other ways that expose their artificiality and facilitate their subversion. Gender-bending and trans identities are particularly prominent.

Queers have thus rebelled against 'confining straightjackets' that accept some LGBT people as 'tolerated "others"' while marginalising those who fail to fit the criteria.[230] Queer can include a new category of 'perverts' who 'traverse or confuse hetero-homo divisions'.[231] In short, in a variety of ways queer can both express a revolt against the commercialisation and commodification of sexual life, and subvert the gay/straight binary that takes especially acute forms under neoliberalism. In particular, the new concept of queer helped to revitalise transgender politics in the 1990s.[232]

---

228   Rubin 2011, p. 163.
229   Drucker 1993, p. 29.
230   Sears 2005, p. 100.
231   Hennessy 2000, p. 113.
232   Stryker 2008, pp. 122–3.

Gender Queers, Other Queers

The contradictions of gender and power have been particularly visible in transgender and gender-bending subcultures since the 1990s. Drag has always to a certain extent subverted mainstream gender roles through 'veneration of the strong woman who defies social expectations to assert herself'.[233] Butler has argued, by contrast, that drag is not *necessarily* subversive: it can serve to denaturalise gender norms or to idealise them, in the sense that 'all gender is like drag'.[234] But drag does expose gender as something artificial: 'In imitating gender, drag implicitly reveals the imitative structure of gender itself – as well as its contingency'.[235]

Forms of gender-bending have shifted over the decades. In the 1980s, Hollibaugh declared that her vision of butch/femme was not a reaffirmation of existing gender categories, but rather a new system of 'gay gender'. More recently, younger trans people seem more likely to take on gender identities that are difficult to subsume at all under existing feminine or masculine roles. 'Today lesbian butch/femme is acquiring more flexibility than it had in the '70s when I came out', Patrick Califia has said, thanks in part to a cross-pollination of butch/femme with SM, which creates space for 'butch bottoms' and 'femme tops'.[236] This flexibility was built into the very definition of the term 'transgender'; at least as defined in the early 1990s, the term is not just a different way of saying 'transsexual', but encompasses a whole spectrum of gender diversity. Gloria Anzaldúa has added an intersectional dimension to this flexibility with her focus on 'hybridity' and a brand of feminism that values the power of being mixed or impure, of crossing borders, of subverting established categories.[237]

These more flexible and ambiguous transgender patterns can be associated both with the myriad forms of transgender that have existed for millennia around the planet and with queer milieus that have only emerged since the late 1980s in rebellion against the lesbian/gay mainstream. Globalisation has heightened awareness of worldwide gender diversity and fostered a transnational trans outlook.[238] Today's trans identities are thus in a sense very old and very new. Indian *hijras*, for example, today sometimes take hormones to

---

233   Altman 1982, p. 154.
234   Butler 1993a, p. 125.
235   Butler 1999, p. 175.
236   Califia 2000, pp. 186–9.
237   Stryker 2008, pp. 123–5 (citing Holly Boswell).
238   Stryker 2008, pp. 25–6.

accentuate their femininity, dress like modest housewives, and are faithful to their cisgendered male 'husbands' – or more often do not, so as to emphasise their ambiguous gender identity.[239] Younger black queers also often 'use the global as their field of operation much more intensely'.[240]

New transgender patterns – whose adepts increasingly call themselves 'gender queers' – contrast with the old forms of transvestism and the forms of transsexuality that arose in the 1950s and 1960s, which were defined by a medical establishment that urged transsexuals to adapt to the norms of their new gender.[241] Today, in the spectrum of performative gender that permeates the neoliberal sexual order, gender queers occupy the most conscious and explicitly performative end of the spectrum.

Queer-identified trans people do not necessarily reject hormone treatments or surgery, for example, but they can be selective in what they do or do not choose for themselves. In fact, only a minority of trans people (12.5 percent in the Netherlands, for example) opt for sex reassignment – not necessarily because the possibility is denied them or they lack the courage, but sometimes because they are comfortable as they are.[242] This new trend among transpeople owes something to SM people's attitude towards 'body modification': 'A new sort of transgendered person has emerged, one who approaches sex reassignment with the same mindset that they would obtaining a piercing or a tattoo'.[243]

The result can be ' "intermediate" bodies, somewhere between female and male'[244] on a 'continuum ranging from extremely masculine to extremely feminine, with a wide, more or less undefined zone between the two extremes'.[245] Some gender queers cannot be placed at any specific spot on a continuum, because of their choice to mix and match different gender characteristics in unique ways. Michael Hernandez, whose 'body remains a mixture of secondary female and male characteristics', has said: 'I just am. The name and the fit aren't that important anymore'. Others say, with Feinberg, 'I don't believe I should have to change my body to "match" my gender expression so that the authorities can feel comfortable'.[246]

239   Nanda 1994, pp. 404, 397–8.
240   Wekker 2006, p. 50.
241   Califia 2003, pp. 52–85.
242   Verkerke 2012, p. 28.
243   Califia 2003, p. 224.
244   Rubin 2011, p. 251.
245   Bergero, Asiain and Cano-Caballero 2010, p. 61 (citing Kim Pérez).
246   Feinberg 1998, pp. 75–6, 19.

For some of these people, as Holly Boswell put it in a seminal article of 1991, trans identity can be 'a viable option between cross-dresser and transsexual person, which also happens to have a firm foundation in the ancient tradition of androgyny'. This shift was hastened in the US by the closing in the 1980s of the old university-affiliated gender clinics and their replacement by independent, more client-centred clinics, where a wider range of treatment options facilitates an ongoing 'decoupling of gender and sex'.[247] More broadly, it is part of the proliferation of new possibilities created by biomedical technology,[248] spurring debates about its potential for expanding sexual and reproductive freedom and/or intensifying capitalist commodification.[249] The intensifying commodification is particularly evident for cross-dressing sex workers, for example, in Brazil, whose clients want someone who 'looks like a woman, but acts like a man in bed'.[250] This can make the combination of female breasts with a male erection a significant business asset.

This all reflects a profound change that Woltersdorff has formulated as follows: While gender is 'detached from the body' and its 'presumed naturalness ... cast into doubt', new medical technologies 'allow bodies to be created that call into question the traditionally arranged dimorphism of *sex*'.[251] Often today's trans people do not see themselves as transitioning from male to female or vice versa, but rather as trans as opposed to male or female. People of 'various gender-transposed identities', with similar concerns around stigmatisation and treatment, have converged around a more or less shared 'trigender paradigm'.[252] This is beginning to be reflected in official documents, as in Germany where 'other' is now an option alongside male and female – a limited and contradictory step that helps some people subvert gender while reaffirming it for others.

As transgender identity has gradually gained acceptance in many societies, it has tended to be defined in ways that eliminate or minimise the gender ambiguity and gender subversion practised by gender queers. Just as, for most people, by the 1980s 'gay' had been stripped of its liberationist content and virtually reduced to just another word for 'homosexual', 'transgender' is today being reduced to just another word for 'transsexuals' 'trapped in the wrong body' – with even the 'tolerant' reacting with bewilderment at or repugnance

247   Bolin 1994, pp. 467, 593, n. 46, 463, 465.
248   Stryker 2008, p. 28.
249   Arditti, Klein and Minden 1984.
250   Green 1999a, p. 254.
251   Woltersdorff 2001, p. 171.
252   Bolin 1994, pp. 461, 485.

for gender queers who fail to see sex reassignment as the solution to their 'problem'. This limited tolerance in reality can be a mechanism of exclusion and can serve to mystify relations of power.[253] Attitudes of tolerance and sympathy for trans people specifically can mask their exclusion from lesbian/gay communities, and their marginalisation and lack of power in relation to other LGBT people. These attitudes help maintain a wall of separation between trans people and lesbian/gay people whose touches of gender ambiguity are limited to a bit of 'gay style'.

For their part, many traditional poor and working-class trans people have often struggled for years to save money for operations, including in dependent countries, or have simply changed each others' genitals without resorting to official medicine. The thousands of *hijras* in South Asia, increasingly visible and militant among the poorest people of their region and notably at the 2004 World Social Forum in Mumbai, do not always share gender queers' interest in transcending or blurring gender categories – though some do. For that matter, even many intersex people (whose bodies complicate their identication as unambiguously male or female) 'are perfectly comfortable adopting either a male or female gender identity'[254] – though again, not all. And for intersex people who do rebel against male or female identity, some social space is opening up in some countries for a distinct intersex identity – though thus far, not much.

As in late nineteenth-century Germany, the dependent world's first open same-sex communities often largely consisted of gender-dissident people – with the difference that they are now living in a neoliberal global order. Trans people around the world know all too well from their own experience that the advent of globalisation does not necessarily put an end to their marginality or their high risk of poverty. A century and a half ago, Karl Marx noted the structural dependence of capitalism on a 'reserve army' of human beings it can shuck off in times of decreased profitability. This reserve army tends to be larger in those countries that are marginal to the global economy or that occupy a subordinate place in it. To be surplus, to be a disposable human being under capitalism, is to be 'raced, gendered, and sexualized . . . "in ways both old and new"'.[255]

The constraints on life for gender queers in conditions of pervasive inequality are visible in trans cultures across the dependent world. Class shapes gender queer identities in differentiated ways. In Thailand's *tom-dee* (butch/femme)

253   Mepschen 2009 (citing Wendy Brown and Slavoj Žižek).
254   Wolf 2009, p. 230.
255   Rosenberg and Villarejo 2012, p. 13 (citing Grace Kyungwon Hong).

subculture, consumption is important for the butch *tom* role: shopping malls are key sites for *tom-dee* socialising, and small businesses provide some *toms* with the economic basis vital for their sexual autonomy. Nevertheless, 'Most tom – like most unmarried women from Bangkok – do not earn enough to rent their own apartments and so continue to live at home'.[256] Generational differences are also important: in the burgeoning lesbian community of Jakarta, young people are increasingly likely to call themselves trans while older women use terms like 'butchie' or 'tomboy'.[257] In neoliberal India, where growing inequality has partly crosscut and partly reinforced the economic function of caste, the *hijra* world as a quasi-caste has provided an alternative model, with *hijras* living in 'houses' that substitute families and communities, led by *naiks* (chiefs) who supervise the joint activities of performance, begging and prostitution[258] – and of visible dissent and transgression.

Butch/femme is also pervasive among lesbians struggling for survival and dignity in South Africa's black townships.[259] In Cuba, trans people bore the brunt of the regime's oppression in the 1960s and 1970s. But since the mid-1990s, in the midst of economic hardship and openings to the market that have heightened inequalities, there has been a significant opening for forms of trans self-expression, on stage if not on the streets.[260] In 2013, an open trans person was even elected to a municipal council.

In Suriname, a particularly severe crisis – falling bauxite prices, incomes that fell by almost two-thirds from 1984 to 1997, slashed social services, dependence on remittances from the Netherlands or on sex work – has preserved same-sex *mati* relations among Afro-Surinamese women while accentuating class differences. The crisis if anything reinforced the unlikelihood of Afro-Surinamese women's marrying men, with only 9 percent of Creole women with steady male partners married to them in 1992. Women remained likely to be single, poor heads of household, even if they had jobs. This has meant the decline of traditional *mati* institutions like birthday parties and outings, decreased sexual opportunities for Surinamese 'male' *mati*, and starkly unequal relationships between *mati* with and without Dutch sources of income.[261]

The disproportionate dependence of trans people on the sex trade, especially in the dependent countries, is a complicating factor. Where healthcare

---

256   Jackson 1989, pp, 364–5, 369 (citing Ara Wilson).

257   Agustine, Sutrisno, Sugianto, Maria, Augustine, Sigit and Mariani 2012, pp. 311, 324.

258   Nanda 1994, pp. 409–10, 415–16.

259   Pokade 2012, pp. 474–6.

260   Lumsden 1996, pp. 195–7.

261   Wekker 2006, pp. 221, 62–4, 136, 60, 118, 66, 207–9.

systems do not fund transitions (which is the case in most places), the sex trade is a frequent way for transsexuals to fund their treatment.[262] The stigma associated with the sex trade probably varies in intensity depending on the indigenous sexualities that preceded it. In Thailand, for example, the sex trade has apparently led Thais to more readily associate transgendered *kathoeys* with prostitution, thus lowering their status.[263] In Latin America, where *locas* were always stigmatised and their sexuality commodified, it has probably not made as much difference. However, there are constants in the hypocrisy surrounding the hierarchy of sex work, in which repression is directed most intensely at those (like streetwalkers) whose earnings are most meagre and precarious, and the threat of violence, which shows how much sex workers are seen 'as nothing, as dispensable'.[264]

With trans people as with others, class can inflect the meaning of gender identity. A female-to-male transsexual executive or lawyer in New York is in a very different position from a *hijra* sex worker in Mumbai. More or less marginal, more or less prosperous gender queer writers and artists can occupy a range of social positions. But to a greater or lesser extent, different transgender patterns are radically subversive of the lesbian/gay identity that emerged under Fordism, in a way that the would-be all-encompassing acronym LGBT fails to successfully subsume in a single social subject. Transsexuals who identify as straight (albeit 'born in the wrong body') often question what they have in common with lesbians, gays or bisexuals. South Asian *hijras*, identifying with neither gender, cannot be legitimately classified as either gay or straight. Nor can gender queers who insist that they have moved beyond male and female.

Although on average trans people tend to have lower class positions than those who identify as lesbian or gay, this does not mean that self-identified lesbian/gay people's identities fit seamlessly into global, middle-class gay normality, especially in poorer countries. A shift to lesbian identity does not necessarily imply an embrace of European-style lesbian normality. Instead, lesbianism can be 'infused with other meanings when new groups claim the term'.[265] The adoption of the word 'gay' often disguises identities that are less global and homonormative than the label. The words 'gay' and 'lesbian', and various indigenous words in different languages, are often not mutually exclusive. The same Chinese who call themselves '*tongzhi*' ('comrades', with same-sex connotations) in some contexts can use the word 'gay' in others,

262   Shah 2011/2012.
263   Jackson 1989, p. 227.
264   Shah 2011/2012 (citing Ignacio Rivera).
265   Wekker 2006, p. 240.

particularly when they are identifying with international lesbian/gay culture.[266] The Hindi word *sakhi* has a comparable ambivalent and complementary relationship to 'lesbian'.[267] Some Filipinos in gay groups see themselves in other contexts as transgendered *bakla*.[268] In Brazil, some people have simply used 'gay' as a new way of saying *bicha*.[269]

Tom Boellstorff has explained that in Indonesia, while transgendered *waria* have identities that they see as indigenous to Indonesian culture, self-identified lesbian/gay people feel part of a national and international community, even if they are working class and have never travelled. Often US films and television programmes (thousands of which are broadcast on Indonesian TV) provide defining moments for lesbians' and gays' self-identification. Yet basic economic and social constraints prevent Indonesian *lesbis* and *gays* from fully matching their international counterparts. For example, self-identified Indonesian gay men usually marry women and have children with them. 'Most *gay* men want to marry' women, in fact, 'but they also scheme how to delay or avoid it and how to maintain *gay* friendships and sex partners once married'.[270]

In Africa too, someone can be 'proudly out [and] yet at the same time desire to marry and have children'.[271] Among African-American women in relationships with women, it is middle-class women who tend to identify more as lesbian – though they sometimes tend to adopt the identity later in life and be discreet about it. Working-class African-American women in such relationships, by contrast, even when not self-defined as trans, tend to present themselves as more masculine and define themselves as 'straight-up gays'.[272]

Some queer communities embrace a wide range of identities. The young victims of homophobia, racism, and economic and sexual exploitation in New York portrayed in the documentary *Paris Is Burning* included gays, trans people, transsexuals and other queers of colour. But all the inhabitants of their 'houses' affirmed their rejection of their original families and their antagonism to the ideologies of the homes they were driven out of. These young queers' alternative homes, headed by 'mothers' looking after kids 'turning tricks on the corner', gave a 'new meaning of family' to 'kids ... without parents', 'embracing

---

266   Chou 2000, p. 194.
267   Thadani 1999, p. 86.
268   Altman 2000, p. 141.
269   Green 1999a, p. 269.
270   Boellstorff 1999, pp. 480–3, 485, 488–91.
271   Epprecht 2009, p. 1271.
272   Moore 2011.

collectivities founded precisely on heterogeneity and nonidentity'.[273] They showed some striking parallels with the houses of *hijras* a world away in India – in other interstices of the same global, neoliberal economy.

The lives of both *hijras* in India and homeless queer youth in New York reveal the hollowness of neoliberal promises. The seductive images of sexualised commerce mostly promote overconsumption only by a minority, and even for them only in intervals stolen from the race to accumulate. Neoliberal globalisation and neoliberal multiculturalism in practice marginalise the great majority of the world's black and immigrant LGBT people and of the poorer four-fifths of LGBT people worldwide. Homonationalism suggests that true lesbian/gay identity is a privilege reserved for citizens of imperial powers. Gender-normative lesbian/gay identity not only excludes trans people and gender queers, but confines LGBT people in general in a masculine or feminine straitjacket. And the promise of same-sex marriage and normal lesbian/ gay family life offers a stacked deck to working-class LGBT people, who find their incomes stagnant, their social benefits cut, their services privatised and childcare making great demands on their overstretched time and incomes.

The social realities of neoliberal societies have provided the basis for a neoliberal sexual politics, which translates the imperatives of homonormativity into the politics of the pro-neoliberal gay right and centre, and the social-liberal policies of the gay centre-left. In chapter 4, we examine this neoliberal and social-liberal sexual politics in greater depth.

---

273   Reddy 1998, pp. 373, 370.

The Sexual Politics of Neoliberalism

The rise of gay normality has had a political impact when it has been used to define a sexual politics that adapts to the sexual parameters of neoliberalism rather than challenging them. All the social and sexual components of homo-normativity described in chapter 3 have political correlates, which this chapter will delineate. Homonationalism, for example, is a core element not only of lesbian/gay identity in imperialist countries, but also of the politics of the modernising right, including the gay right. Not only is normal same-sex partnership a foundation of today's middle-class lesbian/gay lifestyle, a moderate approach to same-sex marriage is a cornerstone of the social-liberal politics of the lesbian/gay mainstream. Queer rebellion, too, is not only a subculture, but also a politics. The marginal place of queer sexualities in the homonorma-tive-dominant regime makes queers a potential component of a broad anti-neoliberal alliance.

But so far, unfortunately, queer radicalism is marginal in the LGBT political landscape. No real break with the existing order is in prospect in the short term, and adjustments to it are ever more widely accepted. This makes the right and centre more serious contenders for LGBT people's allegiance than they used to be. It means that the left faces major challenges in becoming a vehicle for queer radicalism. This chapter surveys the landscape of neoliberal same-sex politics.

The rightward trends that gathered momentum around the world from the 1970s increasingly prevailed in LGBT movements in many countries by the dawn of the twenty-first century, and even more so during the post-2001 'war on terror'. Alongside the anti-gay, often fundamentalist right, a new gay right has emerged, enthusiastically embracing neoliberalism. The gay, social-liberal centre and centre-left, for their part, have largely made their peace with neo-liberalism. The radical left, weakened since the 1980s, has so far failed to present a compelling alternative to gay normality or link up with queer resistance. A queer radicalism has grown up since the 1990s that *is* challenging gay normality, but various features of it have helped perpetuate its marginality and inhibited the development of an effective queer anti-capitalism.

The overview presented in this chapter may not give reasons for short-term optimism. But it suggests how the dynamics of heteronormativity and homo-normativity are played out at different points of the political spectrum. It also gives us a clear sense of the tasks and the stakes as we try to craft a queer anti-capitalism that can overcome the limits of existing LGBT political currents.

The Anti-Gay Right

LGBT politics today, like LGBT life in general, has been twisted out of shape by neoliberalism. Politically and ideologically, the neoliberal offensive began with Thatcherism, Reaganism, and the retreat of reformist social democracy and left-liberalism to a pale social-liberalism (heralded by the about-face of the social-democratic Mitterand government in France in 1983). The fall of the Berlin Wall in 1989 and the collapse of the USSR in 1991 were not the causes of this process; in hindsight, the right's victory had been won on a global scale by the mid-1980s. But they did put the ideological icing on the cake, making it somewhat more credible to declare the 'end of history'.

Neoliberal policies, as Lisa Duggan has pointed out, promote the privatisation of the costs of social reproduction through 'personal responsibility exercised in the family and in civil society – thus shifting costs from state agencies to individuals and households'. To create a base of political support for such unpopular policies, neoliberal politicians have linked ' "culture wars" tactics with strategies to shrink public institutions and align their practices with business priorities'.[1] People with AIDS were 'accused of irresponsible sexual behavior and left to die without support'.[2]

Yet the politics of neoliberal austerity comes in different cultural flavours. It has proved compatible with both a cultural conservatism, which defends the family forms it defines as 'traditional', and a more broad-minded view that allows some room for same-sex variants. Sexual conservatism was the initial stance of the resurgent right, particularly in the US where mobilisations against abortion and gay rights in the late 1970s provided much of the mass base for reaction under Ronald Reagan in the 1980s. Neoconservative intellectual Norman Podhoretz made the link intellectually in 1977 in an essay blaming homosexuality for alleged US appeasement of the Soviet Union.[3] It was made on a mass scale beginning in 1977 in Dade County, Florida, where a reactionary campaign succeeded in overturning a lesbian/gay anti-discrimination ordinance, which led to a string of similar defeats in a series of US cities. In response to AIDS, the US right proposed to quarantine HIV-positive people and

1   Duggan 2003, pp. 14, 34.
2   DeFilippis 2011/2012b.
3   Rubin 2011, pp. 290, 144.

imposed mandatory testing of immigrants and military personnel. Reacting in 1996 against the first possible victory for same-sex marriage, a right-wing Congress passed (and Democratic President Clinton signed) the Defence of Marriage Act, denying federal benefits to same-sex married couples.[4]

Right-wing anti-gay campaigns at times have singled out especially stigmatised sexual practices as a way of condemning LGBT people in general. For a time in the late 1970s and 1980s, SM was a particular target. In 1978, Canadian police raided the Barracks, a leather-oriented bathhouse in Toronto, charging the men there under 'bawdy-house' laws on the grounds that the sex acts taking place there were inherently 'indecent'. A range of similar raids followed elsewhere in Canada in the next few years. In the US, the CBS documentary *Gay Power, Gay Politics* portrayed SM as a 'dangerous and often lethal activity', central to gay male sexual practices, and a beneficiary of gay political clout in San Francisco.[5] The right also focused on intergenerational sex, as shown in the repeated prosecutions of the Canadian gay paper *Body Politic* for simply discussing the issue in print, and US Senator Jesse Helms' successful move to block UN recognition of any LGBT group that condones 'paedophilia'.[6]

Sexual conservatism clearly has a bourgeois and middle-class base, just as sexual radicalism – a cross-class phenomenon – has some support among the working class and oppressed. But the reactionary right has used sexual conservatism to gain support among working-class and oppressed people to whom neoliberal economic policies have little or no appeal. Sometimes this sexual conservatism has blatantly appealed to white racism, as when French National Front leader Jean-Marie Le Pen claimed in 2011 that North African immigrants were out to 'sodomise the President'.[7] More indirectly, Gary Kinsman has suggested that the Canadian state used police raids on gay bathhouses in the 1970s and 1980s to hone the militarised force needed to contain racial and ethnic as well as sexual minorities and to safeguard plans for city centre redevelopment.[8]

At other times, the religious right's anti-gay campaigns among working-class, Latino, African-American and Asian populations in cities like New York have used LGBT people as a scapegoat for the frustrations caused by racism and poverty.[9] US reactionaries have spread their homophobic ideas not only domestically, but also globally, prolonging the centuries-old European and US tradition

---

4   D'Emilio and Freedman 1997, pp. 346–7, 354–5, 364.
5   Rubin 2011, pp. 114–16.
6   Rubin 2011, p. 218.
7   Shepard 2012, p. 80.
8   Kinsman 1987, p. 208.
9   Hennessy 2000, p. 165.

of exporting persecution. The victory of the US-backed right in Nicaragua in 1990 was followed by the rollback of the tentative gains for LGBT rights under the Sandinistas and the criminalisation of same-sex relations,[10] which was only repealed in 2008 after the FSLN returned to office. Similar right-wing Christian fundamentalism has spread – in Brazil, for example – where evangelicals have united since the 1980s with the Catholic hierarchy to block gay rights laws.[11]

Often fundamentalist groups based in imperialist countries have joined with politicians or the media to instigate or manipulate moral panics, which, as Scott Long has pointed out, are 'not "cultural" eruptions from primeval magma', but rather political responses to social and political anxieties.[12] A 2012 report on US right-wing campaigns in Africa revealed how US Christian right-wing groups – Catholics, Mormons and evangelicals – were 'expanding the U.S. Christian Right infrastructure on the African continent', hiding 'an American-based agenda behind African faces'. The result has been a rise in anti-gay violence in much of sub-Saharan Africa, notably the 2011 murder of David Kato of Sexual Minorities Uganda,[13] and the 2013 murder of Eric Lemembe of the Cameroonian Foundation for AIDS.

Gender and sexuality also serve as markers between Western and Eastern Europe. Catholic and Orthodox churches and political currents linked to them have capitalised on resentments among Eastern Europeans of the consequences of capitalist restoration and neoliberal inequality, with LGBT people as favoured targets. In this climate, violence against Eastern European lesbian/gay pride events has been partly the work of neo-fascist groups who believe that the EU is 'run by "fags" '.[14]

Homophobia also characterises Islamic fundamentalist forces that claim to combat Zionism and 'Crusaders', even as they adopt their own versions of neoliberal economics. Afsaneh Najmabadi has observed that the Islamic Republic of Iran is 'haunted by the spectre of homosexuality', tracking down and repressing erotic ties between women as well as cross-dressing by rebellious female teenagers.[15] The rise of Islamic fundamentalist homophobia has also encouraged anti-LGBT persecution by ostensibly secular regimes in the Islamic world. The May 2001 Queen Boat raid in Egypt, for example, only a few months before 9/11, was in part an attempt by the increasingly unpopular and

---

10   Lumsden 1996, p. 202.
11   Green 1999a, p. 283.
12   Long 2013.
13   Kaoma 2012, pp. 1, 3.
14   Herzog 2011, pp. 190–1.
15   Najmabadi 2005, pp. 244, 58.

embattled Mubarak regime to outflank the Muslim Brotherhood and other Islamic fundamentalists.

The Gay Right

In some imperialist countries, however, especially in Western Europe, sexual reaction has lost traction even as economic neoliberalism gained it. In this social climate, some same-sex relationships have been increasingly less problematic for one, modernising wing of the right. A gay-positive conservatism is still difficult to reconcile with the dominant worldview of the US Republican Party, which links attacks on the welfare state to reliance on a supposedly self-sustaining male-breadwinner family.[16] But it is more compatible with the kind of pro-neoliberal 'feminism' that celebrates the advances made by bourgeois and middle-class women, defends gender equality within the family, and nonetheless sees care within the family as a substitute for public social services, while ignoring or minimising the burden that this model places on poor and working-class women.

Nancy Fraser suggested in 2009 that in hindsight second-wave feminism had overdone its 'needed corrective to economism' just when 'redoubled attention' to economics was needed. As a result, it was 'conscripted' to legitimate the rise of 'a new form of capitalism: post-Fordist, transnational, neoliberal'.[17] Canadian feminists Joan Sangster and Meg Luxton have gone further, arguing that liberal feminism had been a powerful and consciously pro-capitalist force within the women's movement all along, 'long before neoliberalism'. They cited Johanna Brenner's warning in 1989 of a 'bourgeois feminist revolution' that was being reduced to 'the right to compete and contract'.[18] By 2010, Brenner was writing of mainstream feminism as an 'unwitting handmaiden to the capitalist class'.[19]

In retrospect, even Thatcherism did not respond to the rise of lesbian/ gay communities with unambiguously repressive policies. The Thatcher government's Section 28, which banned the promotion of homosexuality and 'pretended families' in schools and government-funded programmes, in fact distinguished ' "responsible" (private, closeted, discrete) gays from "dangerous" ones'. The transitional mind-set manifest in Section 28 was not fundamentally different from the one enshrined in US Democratic President Clinton's 'don't

16   Self 2012.
17   Fraser 2009, pp. 108–9, 99.
18   Sangster and Luxton 2012, pp. 289, 293, 297, 293.
19   Brenner 2010, p. 57.

ask, don't tell' policy for the US military (or, for that matter, the Russian law against 'gay propaganda' adopted in 2013).[20] Even the right-wing US Congress of the mid-1990s was, in hindsight, restrained in its pursuit of an anti-LGBT agenda; it 'preserved the status quo rather than turned back the clock of sexual change'.[21]

In the twenty-first century, in both Western Europe and the US, even the right has increasingly made some room for LGBT people. The dominant framework that has taken shape for same-sex politics in this period is a 'stripped-down, redistributive form of "equality" designed for global consumption', which 'supports "diversity" and "tolerance", but defines these in the narrowest' neoliberal terms.[22] Within this framework, the gay right argues that 'increasing lesbian and gay representation in dominant institutions lifts all queer people', in what Duggan and Richard Kim have called 'the trickle-down theory of gay rights'.[23]

Such theories have a social base. The lesbian/gay middle-class layers that live off gay businesses and non-profits prefer in general to keep queer community expressions politically moderate. Another layer of middle-class or middle-class-identified lesbian/gay people, who are making *their* careers inside mainstream businesses and institutions, can see even reformist gay rights movements as at best an unfortunate necessity. This is at least one basis for an agenda limited purely to pursuing anti-discrimination measures, with same-sex marriage as its upper limit, while avoiding any connection with other movements of the oppressed. Middle- and upper-class gays can be even more cautious and conservative in countries where basic gay rights have still not been won, as the Lebanese LGBT group HELEM for one has discovered. Contrary to assumptions by outsiders who assume that gay identity in Lebanon is 'the creation of the Westernized middle class', upper-class men who have sex with men avoid any links with HELEM.[24]

New opportunities have emerged for gay conservatives in the US despite the entrenched homophobia of the Republican Party. This was manifest in a sea change that took place in national lesbian/gay politics late in the 1990s. The fourth national lesbian/gay march in 2000 marked a drastic change in leadership, style and programme from earlier left-led initiatives. The right-leaning Human Rights Campaign Fund (now the Human Rights Campaign, HRC) and the Fellowship of Metropolitan Community Churches seized the initiative

20   Hennessy 2000, p. 152 (citing Anne Marie Smith).
21   D'Emilio and Freedman 1997, p. 366.
22   Duggan 2003, pp. xii, 21.
23   Duggan and Kim 2011/2012.
24   Makarem 2007, p. 105.

with a mobilisation around the theme 'faith and family' that brought hundreds of thousands of lesbians and gays to Washington. The organising was top-down and not open to debate; the contrast with the carefully inclusive organising leading up to the 1979, 1987 and 1993 US national marches (and the 1994 march on the UN) was striking. The US LGBT left has yet to succeed in regaining the initiative. As a result, the push for same-sex marriage and military service has pushed aside the broader array of issues that the US movement once highlighted.[25]

Several well-known US gay writers – Andrew Sullivan, Camille Paglia, Norah Vincent – in various ways and on various issues have identified with the political right. Sullivan, in particular, has made attacks on 'New Left feminism', bemoaning in a 2001 lecture 'the emasculation of gay politics'.[26] The US gay right's ideology was formulated by the Independent Gay Forum (IGF) in a manifesto, 'Forging a Gay Mainstream', that declared its attachment to 'the fundamental virtues of the American system', notably the 'market economy'. The IGF denied that 'gays and lesbians pose any threat to social morality or the political order' or that they should support radical change. IGF member Bruce Bawer argued that 'much of gay America's hope resides not in working-class revolt but in its exact opposite – a trickling down of gay-positive sentiments from elite corporate boardrooms'.[27]

Internationally too, the last few years have witnessed increasingly open manifestations of a new gay right, with few links even to mainstream lesbian/gay organisations and often ambivalent attitudes toward existing manifestations of LGBT community and identity. The meteoric rise of the Dutch political party around openly gay right-wing populist Pim Fortuyn in 2002 was perhaps the most spectacular example. More broadly in Europe, an increasingly visible minority of politically active gays identifies with the secular right that is defined in continental Europe as 'liberal'; for example, a significant proportion of Dutch lesbian/gay leaders now identify with the right-liberal VVD party. There have been similar developments in Denmark.

Nor is the rise of the new gay right limited to countries like the Netherlands and Denmark, where at least superficial acceptance of gays is almost a universal article of political faith. In parties of the Western European right, like the British Conservatives and German Christian Democrats, pro-gay stances have in the last few years become commonplace,[28] as the push for same-sex

25 Duggan 2003, p. 45. See also Cohen 1999, p. 115.
26 Goldstein 2002, p. 11; Duggan 2003, p. 63.
27 Duggan 2003, pp. 48, 54.
28 Herzog 2011, p. 197.

marriage by British Conservative Prime Minister David Cameron has shown. There were, of course, lesbians and gays advocating same-sex marriage for years before Conservatives and Christian Democrats began even considering it. But today the actual achievement of same-sex marriage is increasingly a collaborative effort by a mainstream lesbian/gay advance guard in alliance with a centre-left or centre-right main force.

The gay right is not the purveyor of a specific same-sex identity. In fact, it has projected strikingly different sexual attitudes in different countries. Clearly the moralistic preaching of fidelity and conformity is not universal even in the US gay right; this is only one face of neoliberal gay normality, and not necessarily the dominant one. In the Netherlands, Fortuyn embodied a sexual libertarianism and was uncritically, openly celebratory of some queer sexual practices – one more sign that non-monogamy does not in itself necessarily challenge the instrumental attitude towards human relations typical of neoliberal society. But in most countries, the gay right tends to downplay queer identity and sexuality, and advocate 'normality': integration into existing families and churches. It was no accident that the lesbian/gay 2000 march in the US took place under the banner of 'faith and family'.

However much the gay right's sexual attitudes may vary, it seems to have no capacity to link up with any alternative queer community or to contribute to defining any alternative queer identity. It can only oscillate between celebrating gay capitalism and defining queer sexuality as a purely private matter, preferably to be confined to a same-sex marital bedroom. This has precluded, at least so far, the rise of anything like a true queer right. On the contrary, the rise of the gay right has helped close the interregnum of 1968–73 lesbian/gay liberation, when the consolidation of a gender-normative lesbian/gay identity was briefly interrupted by a prominent and sometimes key role for trans and other gender-dissident activists in radical lesbian/gay groups.

Spreading from the gay right to the LGB centre and centre-left, an interpretation of 'lesbian/gay' has taken hold that makes it virtually indistinguishable from the homophiles' old, gender-normative conception of the homosexual. Ironically, as John D'Emilio has pointed out, an initially anti-capitalist gay liberation movement 'opened the door to legitimate investment in gay sex' and created the conditions for a new gay capitalism. This accounts for some striking continuities between the homophile movements that grew up before the mid-1960s and the gay right of recent decades[29] – leapfrogging over the radical legacy of the liberationist interregnum between them.

---

29   D'Emilio 2002, pp. 69, 227.

The Right and Homonationalism

The gay right as a whole is homonationalist. In the Cold War years, the US military had become a mainstay of racial liberalism, symbolised by Colin Powell's rise to its command, and even a certain kind of feminism, incarnated in the George W. Bush administration by Condoleezza Rice. Imperialism acquired a gender dimension, portraying women in the US as 'saviors and rescuers' of oppressed women elsewhere. Imperialist ideology has also always had a sexual dimension. The novelty is that it now has a same-sex dimension. The general orgy of patriotism in the US after 9/11 was picked up in US LGBT communities as well: 'The American flag appeared everywhere in gay spaces, in gay bars and gay gyms, and gay pride parades [featured] the pledge of allegiance, the singing of the national anthem, and floats dedicated to national unity'. Many middle-class gays and lesbians also responded to appeals to save the US by continuing to buy, 'marking this homonational consumer as an American patriot par excellence'.[30]

Neoliberal multiculturalism also wards off, in Jodi Melamed's words, any mobilisation against the neoliberal order by 'the racialized poor ... by portraying this class as strangely susceptible to terrorist seduction'. In the words of the 2006 US National Security Strategy, 'In some democracies, some ethnic or religious groups are unable or unwilling to grasp the benefits of freedom otherwise available in society'.[31]

It is a commonplace to observe that with 9/11 the Arab and Islamic world supplied North American and Western European rulers with the enemy image they needed after the Cold War. This enemy image is often gendered. Examples of the sexual repression of women in different parts of the world or segments of the population are exploited ideologically as evidence of the supposedly more civilised character of imperialist countries. Campaigns to free Muslim women (with or without their participation or enthusiasm) are one obvious example. The US Feminist Majority Foundation tried to enlist Afghan women in the US war, leading the Revolutionary Association of the Women of Afghanistan to condemn it as a manifestation of 'hegemonic, u.s.-centric, ego driven, corporate feminism'. There was a flurry in 2006 of condemnations of anti-gay repression in Iran – the details of the specific incidents involved were disputed among international human rights observers, though the repressive

---

30   Puar 2007, pp. 40, 5 (citing Inderpal Grewal), 2, 43, 66–7.
31   Melamed 2006, pp. 16–17.

character of Iranian sexual legislation was not – just in time to provide ammunition for the US Bush administration's campaign for military intervention.[32]

Condemnations of homophobic measures fall on fertile ground among LGBT people. Resentment of religious bigotry runs deep in LGBT communities, particularly among people who themselves suffered from it during their own Catholic, Protestant or Jewish upbringings. Indignation at anti-LGBT persecution by Islamic fundamentalist regimes and movements is a logical consequence of opposition to Christian bigotry. The political problem arises when people's resentment is projected away from their own context and experience, and focused on the Islamic world – as if Islam were inherently more homophobic than Christianity, a notion flatly contradicted by the preponderance of the historical evidence – especially when that resentment is manipulated to fit an imperialist agenda. The resentment can become poisonous when it is generalised to extend to all people of Muslim origin and/or Arabs, independently of any positions individuals take on LGBT issues.

The litany, 'Homosexual acts are against Islamic law' – eliding the question of what individual Muslims or groups of Muslims think or do – has been used to create a monolithic image of Muslims and Arabs. This essentialism is sometimes used to violent and even deadly effect. Anthropologist Raphael Patai's *The Arab Mind*, and especially its chapter on sexual taboos in Arab culture, served not only as the neoconservative bible on Arab behaviour, but also as a justification for forcing Iraqi prisoners to engage in same-sex acts as a way to turn them into informants. Whereas a century ago, images of pervasive Arab homosexuality served as a pretext for European colonial repression (or homosexual sex tourism), in Abu Ghraib the '(perverse) repression of the Arab prisoners [was] highlighted in order to efface the rampant hypersexual excesses of the U.S. prison guards'.[33]

In the space of a decade or two, the place of sexuality in the hegemonic European and North American view of the Islamic world has been virtually flipped upside down. Today, Europe and North America are seen as bearers of sexual enlightenment – mainly women's emancipation, and to a lesser extent LGBT rights – to an Islamic world seen as benighted and backward. The issue of same-sex formations among people of Muslim origin and in the Islamic world became even more of a political and intellectual minefield after 9/11. In a bizarre twist, neoconservatives and other rightists who for decades were hostile to feminism and the lesbian/gay movement have repackaged themselves as defenders of oppressed Arab women and gays. This ideological prism seriously

32   Puar 2007, pp. 6, ix–xi.
33   Puar 2007, pp. 4, 138–9 (citing Seymour Hersh), 83–4, 94.

distorts the interpretation of Arab sexualities, as Will Roscoe and Stephen Murray have pointed out, and does no justice to the historical 'variety, distribution, and longevity of same-sex patterns in Islamic societies'.[34] Islamophobia masquerading as support for women's equality rears its head in the most surprising places, as in remarks by Fidel Castro – no fan of either neoliberalism or the 'war on terror' – blaming the persistence of machismo in Cuba on 'Moorish' influences via Spain.[35]

The irony is that while the 'heteronormalisation of society was seen to be a marker of modernity in the 19th century, the exact opposite has become the case' now. Yet there is a constant: 'the "West" continues to arrogate to itself the power to define the content of modernity, to shift the goalposts of modernity . . . as it sees fit'.[36]

9/11 gave the right in Europe and North America a unique opportunity to redefine itself as feminist and sexually tolerant. Military intervention in the Islamic world has been legitimated in part by portraying Muslims as 'sexually deviant – whether repressed and frustrated or polygamous and sexually excessive or both simultaneously'.[37] This has helped many rightists, after acting as a not especially effective brake on feminist and sexual change for half a century, to reinvent themselves in short order as defenders of Western enlightenment, women and even gays against 'Islamic fascism'. LGBT and feminist movements have been harnessed to a political project aimed at obscuring responsibility for colonialism and global inequality by focusing instead on the allegedly unique misogyny and homophobia of non-Western countries.[38]

Anti-LGBT attitudes on the part of some non-white and poor people allow middle-class white gays who are drifting rightwards to pose as champions of LGBT blacks and immigrants while stigmatising other blacks and immigrants as homophobic.[39] In countries like the Netherlands and Denmark, right-wing forces have shown since 2001 how Islamophobia can be used to win right-wing acceptance or even hegemony in mainstream lesbian/gay organisations – unwittingly abetted by Muslim fundamentalists like Rotterdam imam Khalid El-Moumni, who in 2001 declared that Europeans who condoned same-sex marriage were 'less than pigs and dogs'.[40]

---

34   Roscoe and Murray 1997, pp. 4–6.
35   Lumsden 1996, p. 46.
36   Rao 2012.
37   Jakobsen 2012, p. 25.
38   Cervulle and Rees-Roberts 2010, p. 144.
39   Puar 2007, pp. 28–9.
40   Herzog 2011, p. 201.

In France, the immigrant suburbs of Paris and other major cities are portrayed as breeding grounds of homophobia, 'a few zones where the light of republican liberty had not yet penetrated' – mysteriously, since the media tend to focus on religious prejudice and downplay discrimination and poverty.[41] The suburbs abruptly forfeited their supposed monopoly on prejudice in 2013, when mass mobilisations against same-sex marriage revealed the depth of homophobia among millions of white French people. The norm defined by gay ghettos like the Marais in Paris or the Castro in San Francisco, magnets for LGBT people in the far larger heteronormative communities around them, nonetheless works to reinforce a straight norm in the larger society, white or non-white.

Even in the US, neoconservatives – the Republican faction least ideologically committed to Christian fundamentalism – have shed their former secular brand of social conservatism and homophobia[42] and repackaged themselves as virtual feminists. The fact that the right was at least temporarily shaken and divided by its debacle in Iraq opened more space for gay voices in the centre and centre-right of US politics.

The new homonationalist right is also fervently Zionist. Unfortunately, broader international and regional lesbian/gay networks, especially those in or run from the imperialist countries, have tended to embrace Israeli homonationalism and ignore or sidestep Palestinian objections, as in InterPride's decision to hold World Pride in Jerusalem in 2006.[43] This tendency has been very strong in North America, as witnessed by Toronto Pride's decision in 2010 (later reversed) to ban Queers Against Israeli Apartheid from marching, and the New York LGBT Centre's decision in 2011 to ban a Palestine solidarity group from meeting there – enforced by a director from a corporate rather than a grassroots background – later transformed into a moratorium[44] that was only lifted in 2013. A similar mind-set was visible in the decision of the International Gay and Lesbian Travel Association to hold its 2009 conference in Tel Aviv, over the protests of groups like the Lebanese LGBT HELEM.[45] In general, mainstream Israeli, Western European and North American lesbian/gay groups have been complicit in 'pinkwashing': celebrating Israeli gay life and rights in a way that includes Israel in the charmed circle of the enlightened, while explicitly or implicitly excluding Palestinians, other Arabs and Muslims.

---

41   Cervulle and Rees-Roberts 2010, pp. 39, 141–3.
42   See, for example, Dicter 1980.
43   Puar 2007, p. 16.
44   Schulman 2012, pp. 117–18, 121, 157–8, 170.
45   Schulman 2012, p. 116.

The emerging homonationalism of sections of the Western European and North American hard right has led it to selectively ignore the neoliberal agenda of many of the world's most homophobic forces. The Mubarak regime responsible for the 2001 Queen Boat raid in Egypt, and the ensuing wave of anti-LGBT repression a few months before 9/11, was, of course, one of the key US allies in the Middle East and one of the main Arab proponents of neoliberal policies. The newly pro-gay right has also generally avoided noticing the ongoing homophobic repression by US allies like Morocco, the Gulf States and the Saudi kingdom (the world's single most theocratic state and the oldest US ally in the Middle East).[46] European and North American media have failed to report the blatant homophobia of the imperialist-linked, anti-Syrian bloc in Lebanon (which expelled gay activists from its 'Freedom Camp') since 2005, or the widespread prejudice or cowardice of Western-funded human rights organisations in failing to defend LGBT victims.[47]

US right-wing lip service to lesbian/gay rights is worse than useless to LGBT Arab people. The Shiite parties, militias and gangs that dominate Iraq today are guilty of vicious repression of people engaged in same-sex sexualities, which the US occupiers have hardly lifted a finger to stop. In one incident in 2007, an Iraqi LGBT activist heard Americans talking in the next room while Iraqi police were torturing him.[48]

Gay Social-Liberalism

The combination of growing homonationalism and gender conformity in LGBT communities with growing straight tolerance for gay normality has helped open up mainstream space for a lesbian/gay rights agenda. The weakening of the radical left has helped fray what ties it had with LGBT movements. Yet even as the modernising right has opened up to homonormative politics, many LGBT groups are held back from aligning with it by memories of the right's history of homophobia. As political partners for LGBT activism, this mostly leaves the broad array of forces that can be called 'social-liberal': forces accepting the basic parameters of neoliberalism but trying to put a more human, social face on policy. These include the Democratic Party in the US and social-democratic, green and left-liberal parties in Europe. They also include a once-radical force like the Brazilian Workers Party (PT), the latter-day populists of the Mexican

---

46   Achcar 2002, pp. 31–5.
47   Makarem 2011, pp. 102–7.
48   Ireland 2007.

Democratic Revolutionary Party (PRD), and a former national liberation movement like the South African ANC.

Many Western European social-liberal governments in the last few decades have cautiously promoted lesbian/gay rights legislation. Even Tony Blair's New Labour used pro-gay pronouncements as a cheap way to show its progressivism, despite its continuity with many of Thatcher's economic policies and its family values rhetoric on social issues generally. US President Barack Obama, despite his caution on LGBT issues through most of his first term, jumped on the bandwagon of same-sex marriage in time for his re-election campaign in 2012, thus helping polish his otherwise much-tarnished progressive image. Since 2006, the French Socialist Party has picked up the tactic of pushing same-sex marriage and adoption, albeit with nationalist, republican rhetoric.[49] They were eventually enacted in 2012 by president François Hollande, alongside a range of austerity measures. The combination of neoliberal economics and gay rights legislation has been duplicated here and there on other continents as well. South Africa under the ANC, for example, became the first country on earth to ban discrimination on the basis of sexual orientation in its constitution.

Following decriminalisation and anti-discrimination legislation as headline items on lesbian/gay reform programmes, same-sex domestic partnership and marriage have been particularly well suited in some ways to a social-liberal agenda. On the one hand, they seem to eliminate discrimination that is increasingly hard to justify. On the other hand, they go together with an ideological commitment to family structures that are supposed to take over welfare functions that the state is abandoning. Same-sex partnership and marriage enable European social-democratic and green parties to give themselves a progressive aura at a much lower cost than a more general extension of retirement benefits, immigration rights and so on would involve. This helps explain how it has been possible to win same-sex marriage in a series of countries and regions, starting with the Netherlands and Belgium in Europe, Canada in North America, South Africa in Africa, and Mexico City in Latin America.

The passage of laws for same-sex civil union in a series of countries since the 1990s, and more recently laws for same-sex marriage, has been presented as the culminating achievement of lesbian/gay emancipation. Civil union legislation in France and Germany followed mobilisations by LGBT movements that brought hundreds of thousands of people into the streets, in response to the injustice felt when survivors were thrown out of their homes after their same-sex partners' deaths from AIDS and other blatant examples of inequality. Yet curiously, the first two European countries to open marriage to same-sex

---

49   Cervulle and Rees-Roberts 2010, pp. 21, 31–4.

couples (the Netherlands and Belgium) did so without any substantial LGBT mobilisation. In fact, the Dutch LGBT movement had traditionally advocated 'pluriformity of relationships' rather than same-sex marriage, while the Flemish LGBT movement took a critical distance from Belgian same-sex marriage legislation. Clearly, something else is going on besides victory in an LGBT struggle.

Partnership laws are in fact double-edged. Only the rise and strength of LGBT movements have made them possible. Yet they were not necessarily LGBT movements' first priority or their initiative. In the forms that existing governments have accepted and pushed through, they are also measures that fit into a vision in which LGBT people become monogamous, moral and well regulated. They are supposed to be normalised, to fit into a broader 'pro-family' agenda, and to contribute, by supporting their partners, to the neoliberal privatisation of social responsibilities.

David Boaz of the US libertarian Cato Institute has argued for same-sex marriage on the explicit grounds that marriage in conjunction with an unfettered market imposes discipline and privatises dependency among the poor.[50] Even the mainstream UK LGBT lobby Stonewall has argued that same-sex couples, like cross-sex ones, should be 'liable to maintain each other'.[51] The sermon that marriage offers an escape route from poverty is preached to social benefit recipients in compulsory workshops in many US states.[52] This is falsified by the racialised and criminalised character of poverty in a city like Washington, DC, where the three out of four African-American men who have spent time in prison are legally denied jobs, housing or public benefits.[53] In the US as a whole, 'heterosexual marriage promotion has utterly failed to put a dent in poverty rates'.[54]

Combined with the fact that working-class, poor and black people, at least in the US, are in general less likely to marry or to stay married,[55] this makes it unsurprising that same-sex marriage advocacy is disproportionately middle-class and white, despite the undeniable benefits it offers to many working-class people as well. Nor is it surprising that same-sex marriage is not a popular cause among LGBT people who have pioneered 'constructed families' or 'families of choice': families based not on existing kinship structures, but on arrangements improvised in the interests of joint survival by people who feel

---

50   Duggan 2003, p. 64.
51   Barker 2012, p. 99.
52   Sidel 2012, pp. 14–15.
53   Alexander 2010, p. 4.
54   DeFilippis 2011/2012a.
55   D'Emilio and Freedman 1997, pp. 370–1.

an affinity.[56] Although the power of romantic ideology sometimes distorts most LGBT people's perception of their own interests, the reality of their lives makes clear that the right to marry is a 'narrow and utterly inadequate solution for the problems that most queer people face'.[57] It is a bit surprising that same-sex marriage advocates so rarely note the dangers of marriage promotion programmes, which could conceivably put pressure on lesbian mothers or domestic violence victims to marry former male partners whom they do not want in their lives or in their children's lives.[58]

Besides fitting into a neoliberal social agenda, same-sex marriage also helps define a new international hierarchy among states. It has become 'yet another marker in the distance between barbarism and civilization': between Eastern and Western Europe, and between the Islamic world and Europe.[59]

On issues other than partnership, the social-liberal left has often been just as conservative as the right. Despite growing attention in many imperialist countries to the isolation and harassment of LGBT teenagers, often leading to suicide, fears and taboos limit the discussion of youth sexuality across the political spectrum. Virtually no Dutch politician protested, for example, in 2012 when a Dutch court dissolved the foundation Martijn on the grounds that even advocating social acceptance of intergenerational sex and legislative change in this area posed a threat to public order. The chilling effect of this climate leads to LGBT groups fearing even allowing the presence of people over and under the age of 16 at the same gathering.

Yet none of social-liberal parties' shortcomings on LGBT issues have weakened LGBT movements' tilt in their direction. This reflects a change within the LGBT movement. The major lesbian/gay rights organisations that were built in the 1970s and 1980s in imperialist countries, and since the late 1980s in South Africa, much of Latin America, and South and Southeast Asia, initially saw their mission as challenging their societies' heterosexual norms, and tended to see other social change movements, particularly feminist movements, as allies. But women's and other movements failed to keep pace with lesbian/gay movements' gains, as in the 1980s and 1990s left-of-centre parties proved open to decriminalisation of homosexuality, anti-discrimination laws and even legal recognition of same-sex partnerships. This made a strategy of broad alliances increasingly seem more of a hindrance than a help to winning some gay rights.

---

56   Holllibaugh 2011/2012b.

57   Duggan 2011/2012b.

58   DeFilippis 2011/2012b.

59   Puar 2007, p. 20.

An agenda of far-reaching social change was not much use in winning political friends and influencing people at the end of twentieth or beginning of the twenty-first century. While often still proclaiming their commitment to a broader progressive agenda, the major LGBT organisations came to function more and more as a lobby linking middle-class LGBT layers to the strongest social-liberal political forces.

A political agenda has thus gained strength among lesbian/gay movements that focuses on legal reforms to the exclusion of deeper social change – the kind of social change that most LGBT people, who are not middle- or upper-class and who have suffered in economic hard times, need. The hegemonic, social-liberal wing of LGBT movements has treated legal reforms not just as a tool to challenge discrimination, prejudice and oppression, but also as a way to secure a certain kind of social status and social mobility for a minority. In that sense, the agenda of reforms has become an agenda of adaptation. The people who staff and lead major lesbian/gay organisations may not always subscribe to an agenda of adaptation; at least initially they often at least paid lip service to long-term, deeper change, and in some cases may still genuinely believe in it as individuals. But in practice they have largely succumbed to moderation because of the weight of money and social pressure behind it. The agenda of gay adaptation is hegemonic today on the Western European and Canadian centre-left, and has been making major inroads in Latin America, the US and a growing number of other regions.

Lesbian/gay rights have been picked up by the European Union, for example, particularly since sexual orientation rights were written into the Treaty of Amsterdam that took effect in 1999. While the initiative in this field within the EU first came mainly from social democrats, left-liberals and greens, it has since been taken up more broadly. The EU's leaders, many of whom see the EU as a major power (albeit one reliant mainly on non-military 'soft power'), need to foster some sort of European identity. But what can a European identity consist of? Not a strong labour movement and welfare state – even though these are European traditions; the EU's Lisbon Agenda aims at undermining them in the interest of greater competitiveness in the global economy. One possibility is a 'community of values' enshrined in human rights principles that do not actually cost money (such as secularism, opposition to the death penalty, and the formal elimination of anti-gay discrimination).

Intangible values were particularly useful in distinguishing Europe from the US under George W. Bush, as well as from the neighbouring Muslim world. They continue to be useful as an alternative, more appealing face for the EU during the crisis, when more and more Europeans associate European integration with harsh austerity. So in a sense, LGBT rights are part of the democratic decoration that is on offer to Europeans while their markets are forced open and many of their social protections stripped away.

This has yielded some positive results, such as the striking down of anti-gay laws in several EU countries (at first Ireland and Austria, lately mainly Eastern European states) and pressure to equalise same-sex and cross-sex ages of consent. Claiming a modern, secular European identity can help win LGBT victories over anti-gay forces like the Catholic Church, which fiercely opposed same-sex marriage in Portugal, mobilised massively against it in Spain, and has been resisting any prospect of it (so far successfully) in Italy. But meanwhile the same political forces that have backed these reforms have taken part – more or less hesitantly, more or less shamefacedly – in an assault on poor people and minorities, including lower-income LGB people, trans people, street youth and LGBT people of colour.

The US Democratic Party was slower to prove useful to a mainstream gay rights agenda, at least at the national level, from the days of the Clinton administration to most of the Obama administration's first term. It thus alienated a major organisation like the National Gay and Lesbian Task Force, which was to some extent an exception to an international trend towards greater gay integration into the political system. The 1993 national US lesbian/gay march in many ways targeted the Clinton administration as much as the Republican right. Only with the 2000 march did the US movement's centre of gravity swing from a position to the left of the Democratic Party to a point, if anything, to its right. Obama's backing for same-sex marriage has opened the way for a broad range of US LGBT forces to fall back in line behind the Democratic Party.

Some space for LGBT political activism in social-liberal frameworks is also available in several dependent countries. In Brazil, where the Workers Party (PT) pioneered pro-LGBT positions in the 1980s, it has remained a reference point for LGBT politics after becoming a social-liberal party since 2002 under Presidents Lula Ignacio da Silva and Dilma Rousseff. But the PT's policies in office have been as cautious on sexual issues as on economic ones. For example, anti-discrimination laws have been passed in some states and municipalities but not at federal level. While some PT politicians have pressed for same-sex marriage, the party leadership has preferred not to antagonise the Catholic or evangelical churches or the right, leaving it to the federal Supreme Court in 2011 to grant same-sex couples the same rights as different-sex married couples. The Mexican Democratic Revolutionary Party has gone further at least in Mexico City, where it passed same-sex marriage in 2009.

In most Asian and African countries, however, there are no major social-liberal parties available as political partners for LGBT activism. In many countries, links between LGBT NGOs and foreign social-liberal patrons (mostly in

Europe) are the closest available equivalent. These NGOs face the peculiar seductions involved in funding from imperialist countries, particularly from Dutch and Scandinavian governments (directly or indirectly) and lesbian/gay foundations. Trends in international feminism have contributed to these pressures through the NGO-isation of women's movements,[60] leading to wrenching debates over issues of legitimacy and representation among Latin American feminists in general and lesbians in particular.[61] When the World Bank, Dutch or Scandinavian governments or development agencies fund social movements, there is a danger that governmental or non-governmental donors will 'dictate terms and conditions'.[62] There is a real risk that movements will be funded from imperialist countries based on identities and models that homonormative groups in imperialist countries can see and recognise. Such identities are the most middle class, most in harmony with commercialised lifestyles, and least liable to challenge neoliberalism.

Since foreign funders can be crucial in enabling LGBT movements in dependent countries to do their work, it is inevitable that movements will respond to them and negotiate with them. The question is to what extent NGOs are using foreign funds to defend LGBT people, and to what extent they are promoting funders' agendas to LGBT people. The Lebanese LGBT group HELEM initially resisted these pressures by refusing any conditional funding and avoiding direct funding linked to specific policies or attempts at political influence. Yet embattled LGBT groups in the Arab region, as elsewhere, have not always been immune from the 'rampant commercialization and image creation, the shift to the right toward institutional identity politics, and disengagement from the real needs of the community' characteristic of many European and North American funders and advisers.[63]

The As-yet-unqueered Left

Beyond the social-liberal politics of the centre-left, LGBT radicals have the option of taking part in the anti-neoliberal or even anti-capitalist left. However, the scope for political action that this option has offered in recent years has been limited. Despite victories for lesbian/gay rights that have bucked the general rightward tide, the LGBT left of the 1970s and 1980s grew weaker as the left

---

60   Alvarez 2000.
61   Mogrovejo 2000, pp. 85–7.
62   Joseph and Dhall 2000, p. 174.
63   Makarem 2011, pp. 105–6, 110.

in general went into retreat. Nowhere in the past twenty years has the radical left played a role in LGBT struggles or debates comparable to the role of the Soviet and German Communist Parties in the sex reform movements of the 1920s, of (mostly independent) Marxists in lesbian/gay liberation in 1968–73, or even of the Revolutionary Workers Party (PRT) in the Mexican lesbian/gay movement in the early 1980s. In the US, for example, Urvashi Vaid's tenure as director of the National Gay and Lesbian Task Force was the apogee of progressive LGBT leadership – which shipwrecked in 1993 on Clinton's betrayal, during his first months in office, on the issue of gays in the military.[64]

In Western Europe, the major parties of the more militant reformist left have rarely distinguished themselves on LGBT issues from the social-liberal centre-left. Often they have at best tried to catch up on the issue of same-sex marriage by castigating the centre-left for its delays and hesitations; they have hardly ever managed to put forward, much less mobilise around, a radical critique. Marxist currents that have done significant theoretical work and adopted good positions[65] have seldom had the organisational weight to make a substantial political impact. With occasional exceptions, the radical queer groups that have sprung up here and there since the early 1990s have not been closely linked to the rest of the radical left. There have not even been strong links between radical queer groups and non-partisan formations contemporary with them like Occupy or the *indignad@s*, despite some active LGBT caucuses and initiatives in some Occupy groups.[66]

In Latin America, some of the founders in 1991 of Chile's Homosexual Liberation Movement (MOVILH) had been members of the Communist Party, and the country's first lesbian/gay radio programme was based for a time at a station linked to the CP.[67] Yet the party has done little more than pledge in 2011 to vote for same-sex marriage. The Bolivarian radicalisation in Venezuela, the strongest challenge to neoliberalism posed in Latin America or perhaps anywhere so far in the twenty-first century, has yielded more for LGBT people. But it has also revealed the limits of a process largely dependent on a single charismatic leader and an entrenched state apparatus, a process that has still not reached the point of a decisive break with the global order.

---

64   Vaid 1995, pp. 148–77.

65   Like the Fourth International, which has adopted a fairly comprehensive text on LGBT liberation (2003).

66   Occupy Boston, for example, had an LGBT working group that put on consciousness-raising events like a special General Assembly, and several very active trans activists (email from Carolyn Magid, 2 August 2013).

67   Robles 1998, pp. 38–9.

Venezuela has not seen anything like the heterosexism that characterised the early years of Sandinista rule in Nicaragua in the early 1980s. On the contrary, discrimination on the basis of sexual orientation was banned in one of the early measures of Hugo Chávez's presidency, the labour law adopted in 1999. Yet pressure from the Catholic Church and the right, and the lack of substantial LGBT mobilisation, defeated attempts to include pro-LGBT provisions in the constitution in 1999 and again in 2007. Maria Gabriela Blanco of the Revolutionary Alliance for Sex-Gender Diversity (founded in 2009) commented in 2012 that 'after 7–8 years of revolution no one was talking about sexual diversity; the revolution is still too conservative'. She cited the example of a public recreation centre that 'will not let same-sex couples hold hands because they say that it is a "place for families" and that "there are children present"'.[68]

Links between the Southeast Asian radical left and LGBT activism initially seemed promising after the outbreak of the 1997 economic crisis, notably in the Philippines and particularly Indonesia. Sex workers took part in demonstrations in 1998 that brought down the Indonesian dictator Suharto, and the leftist People's Democratic Party supported and worked for a time with the Indonesian LGBT movement.[69] Unfortunately, the Southeast Asian radical left failed to take off in later years.

The most striking recent example of links between Asian queer organising and the radical left comes from Nepal, where the abolition of the monarchy as part of a peace process with Maoist guerrillas ushered in changes leading to legal recognition and rights for trans people. As part of this process, a leader of the country's LGBT Blue Diamond Society was elected to the Constituent Assembly for the Communist Party of Nepal (United) (one of the country's many Communist parties). The assembly subsequently established a committee on sexual and gender minorities. When the major Communist Party (Maoist), in keeping with long-established Maoist doctrine, expelled two women from its camps for having a sexual relationship, the Blue Diamond Society was able to prevail on it to relent and allow the couple to return – a remarkable break with Maoist tradition.[70] A recent split in the Maoist movement, however, signals difficulties in moving forward with an anti-capitalist agenda. This can narrow the space for developing a Nepalese queer anti-capitalism.

---

68   Blanco, Spronk and Webber 2012.
69   Oetomo 1999.
70   Peterson and Pokharel 2009.

Queer Marginality

As long as alliances with broader forces of the anti-capitalist left remain few and limited, radical queer activists face the task themselves of working out positions for queer anti-capitalist politics and translating them into public organising and activism. Self-identified radical queer groups have existed, at least intermittently, for the past quarter-century, as a 'punky, anti-assimilationist, transgressive movement on the fringe of lesbian and gay culture',[71] and a milieu that is 'disgusted by marriage and military and that longs to return' to a radical vision.[72] Politically, a wave of Queer Nation groups, following on the 1987 March on Washington and the rise of ACT UP, originated in the US as part of the largest and most militant wave of LGBT activism since the 1970s. The different forms of AIDS activism and queer activism that emerged initially in the US and Britain in the late 1980s and early 1990s posed a radical challenge to established lesbian/gay rights organisations. Self-defined queer activist groups have also appeared more recently in a number of countries in continental Europe. The Pink Panthers in Paris and Lisbon[73] have forged a dynamic, Latin European variant of international queer radicalism. Queer-identified groups are also beginning to spring up here and there in dependent countries.

But queer radicals' ability to contend for influence in LGBT movements or to set the agenda of sexual politics more generally has been held in check by a number of factors. Queer radicalism emerged in an overall context of societal reaction, in which LGBT militancy was largely isolated from and unsupported by its logical allies. This led to some disturbing ambiguities. Queer ideology has been hard to pin down. In the imperialist countries that have so far been radical queers' main base, the predominant ideological current among them has been a fairly diffuse anarchism. Queer groups have yet to show much of an orientation towards large-scale mobilisation, to take root among the racially and nationally oppressed, or to prove their lasting adaptability to the dependent world.[74] While large anti-capitalist parties have rarely made links with queer radicalism, queer radicals have rarely found their way to a broad political audience. In this sense, the limits of anti-capitalist parties and of small radical queer groups mirror each other.

---

71   Morton 1996, p. 15 (citing Dennis Cooper).
72   Schulman 2012, pp. 143–4.
73   See http://www.pantheresroses.org/ and http://panterasrosa.blogspot.nl/.
74   For discussions from an anti-capitalist perspective of the potential and limits of early Queer Nation groups and of today's queer radical milieu, see Drucker 1993 and Drucker 2010.

The early Queer Nation groups reflected a certain break in the movement's memory. Although many of the practical stands and philosophical or theoretical points they made had originally been made by an earlier generation of the lesbian/gay liberation movement, young queers were often unaware of this. The emergence of Queer Nation as a distinctive, insurgent current thus showed the failure of lesbian/gay liberation to transmit its history, to make its values prevail in actually existing LGBT communities, or to sustain a vibrant left wing in the LGBT movement.

By comparison with early lesbian/gay liberationists, early Queer Nation groups had an even more voluntarist or even idealist mind-set. They tended to see queer identity as consciously chosen and crafted. Many LGBT identities have in fact had a voluntary dimension. In some cases, this has distinguished LGBT oppression from oppression based on race, gender or disability, which are generally not chosen but visible, material and unavoidable. But this is only one aspect of LGBT oppression. The fact that women living apart from men have lower living standards is not chosen; the fact that even the most closeted LGBT people could for generations lose their jobs or homes was not chosen; the fact that the great majority of LGBT people still grow up in straight families is not chosen.

Many trans people, however well they fit into a queer milieu as 'gender queers', also do not feel that they have chosen their identities. As early as 1992, failure to tackle trans issues effectively in Queer Nation San Francisco led to the formation of a separate Transgender Nation, though overall the queer milieu proved more supportive than lesbian/gay and feminist milieus had been in the 1970s. The intersex community, which began organising politically with the founding in 1993 of the Intersex Society of North America,[75] seems less easy to include under a queer umbrella, largely because intersex people usually have no choice at all about being intersex.

Despite its implicit and increasingly explicit opposition to neoliberalism, queer radicalism has also had an ambivalent relationship to the commercial gay scene. It has resisted the assimilationism that it sees the commercial scene as promoting. But a whole series of Queer Nation actions in the 1990s focused on invading shopping malls and modifying logos on t-shirts – a tactic that risked replacing critiques of consumerism with alternative forms of consumption.[76] This contrasted with more frontal rejections of consumerism that were also present in queer direct action groups, like the chant 'We're here,

75   Stryker 2008, pp. 135–6, 138–9.
76   Hennessy 2000, pp. 127–8.

we're queer, we're not going shopping!' used by ACT UP San Francisco a few years earlier.

The sexual radicalism of queer politics has had a complex and contradictory relationship to the realities of gender, race and class. Initially, ACT UP reflected the manifest need to respond to AIDS with 'a new kind of alliance politics...across the dividing lines of race and gender, class and nationality, citizenship and sexual orientation'.[77] Yet queer activism has sometimes obscured rather than highlighted these realities, with an exclusive focus on sex that can erase its intersections with gender, class and race. This erasure can be facilitated by queer politics' slippage from radical anti-separatism to one more form of identity politics, which can rest on 'an unspoken appeal' to a white middle-class model.[78]

For women in particular, the emphasis on sexual agency that has always been central to queer, while avoiding seeing women exclusively as victims, risks divorcing 'pleasure and sexuality...from the social structures that organize them'.[79] Although the name Queer Nation and its angry separatist spirit were reminiscent of Lesbian Nation, only 20 percent of the original group was lesbian. Its lesbian, working-class and black members began reproaching it early on for being oblivious to their concerns.[80] Barbara Smith complained that for Queer Nation 'racism, sexual oppression and economic exploitation [did] not qualify' as queer issues.[81] Queer politics in the late 1980s and early 1990s largely failed to appeal to alternative scenes and identities rooted among people of colour and women; a number of Queer Nation groups split amid charges of racism and sexism. Nor did the queer contingents and groups that emerged within or joined in the global justice movement, particularly after the 1999 Seattle protests – a promising component of the queer left – succeed to any great extent in linking up with or contributing to shaping alternative queer identities.

Clearly there is no straightforward correlation between queer radicalism and working-class politics as such. On the contrary, LGBT working people and particularly non-whites have sometimes reacted against queer radicalism when it demanded visibility of them that would make their lives more difficult in their communities, families or unions. The problem arises when the alternative to assimilation or homonormativity is defined not as organised resistance

---

77   Stryker 2008, p. 134.
78   Hennessy 2000, p. 227 (citing Wendy Brown).
79   Hennessy 2000, p. 178.
80   Faderman 1991, pp. 300–1.
81   Cohen 2005, p. 36.

in forms compatible with long-term survival, but as 'transgression' or 'freedom from norms'. This implies the exclusion of those who are 'positioned as *not free in the same way*'.[82]

Even when queer anti-capitalists work inside existing queer radical groups, they need to put forward a distinctive approach that challenges the limitations of these groups' politics. Resisting the retreat from class in LGBT activism, queer anti-capitalists should challenge not only heterosexism among straights and gay normality, but also blanket hostility to straights and non-queer-identified gays where it exists among some self-identified queers. When directed against gay men, this hostility risks selectively reproducing traditional homophobic stereotypes of gays as privileged and powerful: images that are seductive in a time of rising homonormativity, but problematic if they do not reflect the ongoing reality of gay oppression. Avoiding all these pitfalls will require seeking new tactics and forms of organising within queer groups.

This means refusing to replace a simple gay/straight dichotomy with an equally simple queer/straight dichotomy. As Cathy Cohen warned in the mid-1990s, queer activism had a tendency to 'reinforce simple dichotomies between the heterosexual and everything "queer"'.[83] Perhaps this reflects the constant process noted by David Halperin, in which new 'critical vocabularies are helplessly overwhelmed and reabsorbed ... by older and more familiar ones', and doctrinaire tendencies drown out 'anti-dogmatic, critical, and experimental impulses'.[84] Alongside its impulse to challenge the gay/straight binary, queer radicalism from the beginning has contained a strain of the most blatant essentialism. This strain was visible, for example, in 1990 in 'Queers Read This!', seen as one of Queer Nation's founding or at least prefigurative manifestos, which proclaimed, 'We've given so much to [the] world: democracy, all the arts, the concepts of love, philosophy and the soul'.[85] This kind of chauvinist, self-isolating ideology, unconsciously mimicking the lesbian separatism of the 1970s,[86] risks making it impossible for queer radicals to escape from their own subcultural ghetto.

A global, multidimensional perspective can hold queer radicalism to its promise of 'the destabilization and even deconstruction of sexual categories'. It can insist, in Cohen's words, on 'sustained and multi-sited resistance

---

82 Puar 2007, p. 22 (citing Sara Ahmed).
83 Cohen 2005, p. 22.
84 Halperin 2002, pp. 86, 46.
85 Halperin 2002, p. 16.
86 See, for example, Faderman 1991, pp. 237–9.

to systems' that 'normalize our sexuality, exploit our labor, and constrain our visibility'.[87]

So far, most existing queer radical groups lack the strength and clarity to do this. And the existing, as-yet-unqueered radical left lacks the strength and clarity needed to be a consistent and significant ally of queer anti-capitalism, or to challenge the now established hegemony of the gay right and centre. As in the early years of lesbian/gay liberation after 1968, queer leftists themselves will therefore have to draw on the Marxist and feminist traditions and other radical paradigms to lay a solid foundation for the necessary politics, working where possible with those on the existing radical left and in queer radical milieus who see the urgency of this task. Perhaps it is in part on this foundation that a new radical left – better equipped for the sexual and other challenges of the new century – can rise again.

---

87   Cohen 2005, p. 24.

PART 3

Challenges for a Queer Anti-Capitalism

:.

Towards a Queer Sexual Politics

So far, Parts 1 and 2 have only traced the origins of gay normality, diagnosed the ills with which it afflicts LGBT people today, and criticised the assimilationist politics that it underpins. Worldwide in this time of crisis, as we have seen, lesbian/gay identity has been both consolidating and fracturing. As it is seen in more regions and milieus as normal, it has increasingly been adapted to the neoliberal economic, gender and racial order.

At the same time, a diverse set of alternative sexual identities has been diverging more and more from this gender-conformist, consumerist gay normality. Some of these alternative identities – the ones we can group together as queer – implicitly challenge the very basis of the gay/straight binary. Queer identities can be the staring point for developing an effective queer anti-capitalism and a global rainbow politics. In Part 3, I turn to the task of describing the challenges that such a queer anti-capitalist politics will face, and present some ideas about how to meet and overcome these challenges. Chapter 5 explores directions for a specifically queer sexual politics and lays out a five-part agenda for issues ranging from transgender liberation to global queer solidarity to polyamory. Chapter 6 suggests how broader, class-based and other social movements – like healthcare struggles and labour – as well as the political arena can and should be 'queered' in order to shape a vital sexual dimension of societal transformation. Without this queering of broader movements and of democracy itself, radical sexual visions will remain purely utopian.

Queer has a radical potential that is historically unprecedented, due to its combination of gender-bending and sexual flexibility. The sex reformers of a century ago saw homosexuality as out of synch with the dominant gender roles, but as long as inverts' gender dissent was seen as innate and not 'infectious', its radical potential was limited. The lesbian/gay liberationists of a half-century ago emphatically saw their sexual transgressions as relevant to all of humanity, but the radical potential of *their* challenge was rapidly reined in as lesbian/gay identity was dissociated from gender-bending. Today's queers tend to see themselves as transgressive on the terrains of both gender and sex, and increasingly as anti-neoliberal and anti-homonationalist as well. This makes them a potential threat to gendered capitalism as it is structured today. This queer threat to the existing structures of oppression is the focus of chapter 5.

Queer radicalism also poses a challenge to most existing LGBT movements. The dominant strand of LGBT politics has ceased or failed to combat the ways neoliberalism constantly renews the wellsprings of prejudice, allows only a distorted and constrained kind of sexual freedom, and consigns LGBT people to the status of a perpetual minority. The hegemonic lesbian/gay currents limit themselves largely to combating the overt prejudice and discrimination that are merely symptoms of society's underlying heteronormativity. Sometimes they even respond to anti-gay attacks by supporting repressive measures that can play into a right-wing tough-on-crime agenda. These currents actually embrace the status of a tolerated minority and the limited liberal conception of freedom.

LGBT movements will therefore have to be rebuilt and restructured as, like labour and other social movements, they come to grips with a transformed global context. An effective queer left can only emerge as part of this process. It will involve a combination that cannot yet be foreseen of organising on the basis of diverse identities and of initiatives that mobilise a broader set of communities. If it meets this challenge successfully, it has the potential to fulfil the radical promise of early twentieth-century sexual emancipation movements, post-1968 lesbian/gay liberation, LGBT engagement with the South African ANC, Nicaraguan Sandinistas and early Brazilian PT, and the wave of organising in response to AIDS. But to achieve this, it has to come to grips with an increasingly fragmented and contested LGBT political landscape.

Despite its potential, its activist commitment and its intellectual vibrancy, the queer radical left today still only occupies a small corner of the global LGBT political scene. While lesbian/gay identity has lost the central place it occupied in the LGBT world of the 1970s and 1980s, it is still far from marginalised. On the contrary, the new gay normality shows no signs of succumbing to queer assaults in the foreseeable future. Far from returning to the subordinate place it had in the construction of homosexuality in the half-century before 1940 – when gender-dissident inversion (analogous to what we would today call transgender identity) was the predominant form – it seems to be retaining its hegemonic position in the same-sex constellation, as the same-sex pattern best suited to the dominant order. Yet it is less secure, and certainly more contested, than it was in the 1970s and 1980s. The same-sex politics of our time is largely a clash between the politics of neoliberal gay normality and the politics of queer.

Chapter 3 summed up the new gay normality in five features. As the introduction noted earlier, and as chapter 5 will explore in depth, the key imperatives of a radical queer sexual politics can be identified in opposition to those five features, point by point.

Neoliberal gay normality	Radical queer sexual politics
Stable or lesbian/gay minority / neoliberal ghetto	Blurring the boundaries / polymorphous perversity
Gender conformity	Subverting gender / third-wave socialist feminism
Exclusion of gender & other queers	Queer inclusion / trans and youth liberation
Homonationalism	Global and anti-racist solidarity
Homonormative families	Queering intimacy & domesticity / polyamory / love-comradeship

The five features of a radical queer sexual politics are not yet accomplished facts; they are still tasks to be tackled, dimensions to be fleshed out. While queer radicalism is inherently a politics of sexual liberation – which is the queerest thing about it – a queer *politics* has to involve more than being visibly, defiantly sexual in queer ways. Each of the five tasks for a queer politics has to take shape in organising tactics, as well as changes in personal and community life. To achieve full sexual liberation, a queer politics has to challenge and win power at the level of the economy, state and other sites where power is concentrated. Without a strategic project, queer radicalism dooms itself to perpetual marginality. Queer politics in this sense has barely begun to be invented.

Defining queer politics in this way contradicts common-sense thinking about sexuality, and what has largely become common sense even among radical queers. For capitalist cultures organised around the divide between public and private, the sexual is pre-eminently private. Radical queers disagree, of course; we understand that heterosexuality is publicly 'flaunted' every day, and that genuine queer equality demands bringing queer sex into the public sphere and insisting on its public recognition.[1] But most queers see the sexual as predominantly cultural. Disgusted with what passes for politics under neoliberal hegemony and leaning towards a wholesale anarchist rejection of the politics of large-scale organisations and state institutions, many queers see sexual politics as a domain of individual or small-group action and cultural production. Inventing a true queer politics must begin by challenging this dichotomy and refuting this fallacy.

---

1   Barker 2012, p. 187.

The cultural and the personal do not exist in a separate realm apart from the economic, the political and the social; they are constantly deployed and manipulated by the powers that be to produce economic, political and social outcomes that are in *their* interests. '*Neoliberalism was constructed in and through cultural and identity politics*', as Lisa Duggan has pointed out. Moreover, radical cultural and personal change is only possible by transforming the state, economy and other structures that form the foundation of cultural and personal life, at both the micro level of individuals and small groups and the macro level of the city, nation, region and planet. Transformation will not be possible as long as '*cultural and identity issues are separated, analytically and organizationally, from the political economy in which they are embedded*'.[2]

An agenda for a radical sexual politics therefore has to address multiple cultural, social, economic and political issues. In subverting gender, it has to be closely connected to a socialist feminist programme for reproductive freedom. In practising queer inclusion and global and anti-racist solidarity, it needs to focus on cutting-edge struggles like those of queer youth and trans people, and solidarity campaigns against Islamophobia, cuts in aid to poor countries and the 'pinkwashing' of Israel as a pro-gay state. At the same time, it should start from visions of queer intimacy and 'families of choice' to define a radical yet unifying approach to the issue of same-sex partnership. This means opposing the privatisation of care and the transmission of class privilege, while exploring new ways of supporting parents and creating flexible forms for intimate relationships.

Blurring the Boundaries

Today there is a push in many countries to incorporate lesbian, gay, bisexual and even trans people into the prevailing sexual and family order. That order is structured under gendered capitalism by having the vast majority of children raised and socialised by at least one biological parent in families formed by sexually and romantically linked heterosexual couples. Particularly in regions where the nuclear family has been consolidated as the predominant capitalist household form, these are the families in which the great majority of LGBT children grow up. This means that at best, even in the most supposedly enlightened enclaves, LGBT people are bound to face a period of differentiation and alienation in coming to terms with their distinct identity. Their own process

---

2   Duggan 2003, p. 3, original emphasis.

of family formation is bound to be exceptional and complex. In short, the best this order can offer LGBT people is a kind of second-class citizenship.

LGBT lives in this situation entail a constant choice between, or more accurately a varying combination of, adaptation and ghettoisation. Most LGBT people can only survive, let alone prosper, by doing waged work in heteronormative companies or institutions. Their survival is made easier if they find steady partners who also have steady jobs, and even easier if they both have reasonably supportive heterosexual family networks to fall back on. But work and family life of this kind involves a constant process of adaptation, of having or failing to correct spoken or unspoken assumptions and weighing one's own words and gestures. Even the places where most people spend their free time are heteronormative – witness the hostility evoked by queer kiss-ins in straight bars and sometimes by any public signs of same-sex affection. This is not necessarily a reflection of straight people's prejudice or unwillingness to understand; it is simply the result of the heteronormative ways in which life is structured. So most LGBT people escape from the dominant forms of work, family and leisure or complement them with life in a separate LGBT world, made up of more or less mainstream gay bars, clubs and associations, and more or less alternative queer and trans scenes. Even in the absence of prejudice or discrimination, this is what gay normality consists of: a combination of life in a heteronormative world and retreat into an LGBT ghetto.

In contrast to the homonormative model of lesbian/gay people as a minority caught between adaptation and ghettoisation, a queer radical politics can look to a future beyond the gay/straight binary. This is in keeping with the early objectives of lesbian/gay liberation, and with Herbert Marcuse's vision of a generalised freeing up of human eroticism. It is in LGBT people's interests to contest the heteronormative order and develop alternatives to it: not just a queerer ghetto, but communities beyond norms and ghettos. Radical queers challenge the social frontiers between gay and straight in different ways. One way is simply acting sexually in ways or settings that transgress society's heterosexual norm – same-sex tongue-kissing in straight singles bars, for example. They assert what Scott Tucker once called 'our right to the world'.[3] The full range of issues and adversaries that they take on comes across in the list of focus groups that Queer Nation San Francisco had at its height: the streets; the media; the military; government institutions; universities; suburban malls; communities of colour; other countries.

Some queers have questioned whether distinctive LGBT communities and subcultures are desirable even in existing heteronormative societies, arguing

---

3 Tucker 1997, pp. 25–39.

that the notion of a sexual identity necessarily 'carries deep strands of permanency, stability, fixity, and near-impermeability to change'.[4] The identification of sexuality with core selfhood has come to be deeply rooted in European cultures. But it is not unique to Europe. Transgendered *kathoeys* in traditional Thai culture were also perceived as having natural, unchanging identities, to the point that changing *kathoeys* to men or men to *kathoeys* was forbidden in Buddhist scriptures as a form of witchcraft.[5] There are thousands of trans people on every continent who have little choice about developing a separate identity, since a separate identity is thrust upon them from a very young age. However unfashionable the concept of a 'true self' is in queer studies, transsexuals' perseverance through the decades and across national boundaries in pursuing bodily change underlines their 'deeply rooted sense of who they were'.[6]

On the other hand, membership in an LGBT community does not necessarily imply a one-sided, unchanging sexual orientation. Many people who consider themselves bisexual live partly in and partly out of such communities. Others continue to have a same-sex identity and take part in LGBT communities even while having long-term – even primary – cross-sex relationships, a choice accepted by some and viewed suspiciously by others in their communities. All this is evidence of the fluidity of sexual desire and behaviour, which in many people's lives changes over time and in different circumstances.

Given this reality, it is not always clear to LGBT people in many parts of the world that 'coming out' is a key moment in winning their liberation. In some cases, they have never been 'in the closet'. Girls who become involved sexually with other girls need not always struggle with how to tell their mother: sometimes 'Mother . . . is not told; she has eyes to see'.[7] In a culture where people can engage in same-sex sexual behaviour without necessarily identifying as gay, for example, it is questionable what it means to call on them to come out. People whose lives include both same-sex and cross-sex relationships, straddling or confusing the gay/straight binary, have to be free to decide when, where and how they speak out. Tactical flexibility in proclaiming sexual identity can be a way of blurring the gay/straight binary.

In other cases, LGBT people feel that some discretion is a reasonable way of sustaining a way of life in which same-sex relationships are only one part. This too can be a way of blurring the boundaries between gay and straight. Many LGBT people feel free to express their same-sex desires in an LGBT

---

4 Wekker 1999, p. 132.
5 Jackson 1989, p. 26.
6 Meyerowitz 2002, pp. 138–9.
7 Wekker 2006, p. 187.

milieu without 'having a unified, unchanging identity in all situations'.[8] They can have a 'complex double life' that enables them to belong to a 'semi-clandestine sexual and social subculture', while maintaining close relationships to their families of origin.[9] In the Netherlands, LGBT immigrants from the Islamic world have spoken of a 'powerful double life' in which they can celebrate their sexualities at some times and places, while preserving important ties to their original families and ethnic communities.[10]

This is not to say that such double lives are easy. Ghadir, a leading member of the Palestinian lesbian group Aswat, lived a lesbian life in Israel for years exclusively with Israeli Jewish women, then returned to her Palestinian city where she married and had a child, then got divorced and joined Aswat – without discussing her sexuality with her family of origin or her closest Palestinian straight friends.[11] Reticence about coming out has special meaning among Palestinians living next door to Jewish Israelis who insist on it. 'Western strategies like visibility and "coming out" are irrelevant for us', Haneen Maikey has said. 'In different places, we can be different people. We can have this flexibility in our identity without having the "ceremony" of coming out. We are not a Christian culture, we don't have this tradition of confessing'.[12] She has described the 'coming-out narrative' as an oppressive standard by which to tag people: those who are out are labelled 'healthy, strong, mature', those who are not, 'weak, immature, backward'.[13]

A choice not to seek out personal confrontations with families of origin need not preclude public expressions of queer identity. But publicity does entail the risk of involuntary coming out if the news finds its way back home.[14] Even if it does, parents have their own choice to make, between confrontation, silence, subtle acknowledgement and more or less explicit support – each of which can start a process of queering the family. Sometimes queering can proceed by way of the economics of 'conditional acceptance', when parents reluctantly accept children's queerness simply because queer children prove to be 'more responsible and reliable than ... "normal" children'.[15]

---

8   Boellstorff 1999, p. 496.
9   Green 1999, p. 281.
10   Drucker 2000b, p. 216.
11   Schulman 2012, p. 138.
12   Maikey and de Jong 2011.
13   Schulman 2012, p. 153.
14   Pokade 2012, p. 482.
15   De Vela, Ofreneo and Cabrero 2012, p. 360.

Calls for completely breaking with existing identities and communal forms sometimes ignore the class privilege required for such complete breaks.[16] Family ties, if preserved and adapted, can even be a source of strength and support to LGBT people. In pre-revolutionary Russia and the Soviet Union of the 1920s, for example, there were cases of fathers and siblings providing hospitable homes for their gender- and sexually-dissident daughters and sisters.[17]

In the US too, many LGBT people of colour resist a model of coming out that jeopardises family and community ties – especially in the face of the AIDS crisis, which often makes family and community key for survival.[18] US experience suggests that mainstream LGBT organisations sometimes 'encourage young people to come out' without any 'real comprehension of the hostile forces they are likely to confront' or 'commitments to addressing their needs'.[19] In any case, people can be understandably sceptical of the notion that coming out in itself decreases prejudice. After all, women, blacks and Jews have almost always been 'out', and it is questionable whether this has limited prejudice against them. Judith Butler has questioned the extent to which anyone can be completely 'out' anyway, given that there are always aspects of one's identity that cannot be fully disclosed: '*the closet* produces the promise of a disclosure that can, by definition, never come'.[20]

Houria Bouteldja of the French Party of the Natives of the Republic argued in 2012 and 2013, for example, that while there are same-sex practices in French immigrant neighbourhoods, they do not imply the existence of a universal gay identity. She rejected the charge that a refusal to come out is evidence of homophobia. Instead she portrayed many LGBT immigrants' choice for a cross-sex marriage, with either a straight or LGBT partner, as a legitimate act in defence of a family and community order threatened by racism in many forms. Bouteldja even refused to take a position on the 'white agenda' of same-sex marriage, declaring that unlike issues of unemployment, police harassment, discrimination and housing, 'this question does not concern me' as an immigrant. Few immigrants showed up for the big demonstrations for or against same-sex marriage, she said, because they knew that even if it passed, its impact in immigrant neighbourhoods would be minimal.[21]

Yet black and immigrant communities are not isolated islands; they are caught up (more or less for different individuals) in broader trends in the sur-

---

16   Cohen 2006, p. 34.
17   Healey 2001, pp. 57–8.
18   D'Emilio 2002, pp. 186–7.
19   Christian and Mukarji-Connolly 2011/2012.
20   Butler 1993, p. 309.
21   Bouteldja 2012.

rounding societies, including sexual trends. There is therefore no single tactic
for queering families that can or should be expected among all people of black
or immigrant origin. In response to Bouteldja, another French person of immigrant origin, Madjid Ben Chikh, while endorsing her rejection of the 'white
agenda', insisted that those like him, a 'Kinsey 6' (exclusively gay person), 'are
everywhere'. He rejected the invisibility that Bouteldja would impose on him.
He insisted on the necessity of gay political identity as a means of survival
in a – Western – homophobic society: an identity linking him with a black gay
man like James Baldwin and with LGBT Palestinians. And he called for a dialogue on a basis of mutual respect.[22]

The tactics advocated by Bouteldja and Ben Chikh, respectively, each have
their risks and advantages. The tactic of working within existing families and
communities risks demanding too much sexual self-sacrifice. It is possible to
respect the tactical decisions people make without glossing over the oppression that often contributes to their choices. The choice of women who love
women to continue to have sex with men, who are sometimes abusive, may in
some cases be largely determined by their poverty and economic dependency
as women. A Chinese woman's statement that being open about her sexuality
would make her 'a devil in people's minds' and be seen as 'failing in my obligation and responsibility as a wife, daughter and mother' may suggest that the
'harmonious family order' she sought to preserve was based in part on her own
sacrifices.[23] Yet people's links to their families and communities of origin can
be a source of strength, for them as individuals and in struggles for liberation.
On the other hand, the tactic of claiming a public LGBT identity, though it risks
cutting off blacks and immigrants from their families and ethnic communities,
can be a source of strength in leading queer lives and building queer alternatives. Each person has to make this choice for him- or herself, and their different choices can ultimately lay the foundation for a powerful strategy based on
a multiplicity of tactics.

From a radical queer perspective, both the tactic of queering existing communities from within and the tactic of claiming public queer space can assume
that the straight world is 'never immune to the seduction of homoerotic desire'.[24]
This gives queers the potential to sustain a vision of universal sexual liberation, across a diversity of tactics, if they can keep an ultimate goal in mind.
As Marcuse described it, this ultimate goal is overthrowing the supremacy of
genitally-focused heterosexuality so as to make possible a return to 'polymorphous perversity': the undifferentiated receptivity to erotic pleasure that Freud

---

22   Ben Chikh 2013.
23   Chou 2000, p. 201.
24   Chou 2000, p. 206.

had seen as the preserve of infants. 'No longer used as a full-time instrument of labor, the body would be resexualized ... in a reactivation of all erotogenic zones', Marcuse wrote. 'The body in its entirety would become ... a thing to be enjoyed – an instrument of pleasure'. He explicitly included same-sex eroticism among the forms he envisaged in a post-capitalist 'high civilization'.[25] This is very different from either the normality of today's gay ghettos or the heterosexual norm assumed in almost all the rest of the world. Blurring the boundaries between gay and straight, difficult as that may seem today, can begin to undermine that binary.

One could imagine queer communities emerging both within communities of oppressed people and from rebellions against gay ghettos, sharing in their diversity a conception of selfhood as 'multiple, malleable, dynamic, and possessing male and female elements'.[26] Queer communities could be defined by identities that are allowed to be fluid, rather than being obligatorily fixed. Queer movements could be defined as embracing everyone who wants to fight for greater sexual freedom, rather than as proclaiming and defending ghettos. Existing same-sex identities could be neither repudiated nor fetishised, but respected and built upon as stepping-stones towards liberation – stepping-stones that could lead in a range of different directions.

This dialectical approach to identity would involve different tactics in different situations. But the key to the dialectics of identity everywhere would be accepting that change and variability are inevitable, legitimate sources of enjoyment and occasions for celebration. The scope for queer identities could be particularly great in locations where the reification of desire into heterosexuality and homosexuality is still incomplete or resisted, and where elements of more free-floating patterns have survived the twentieth century.

The possibility of communities that are not ghettos, and liberation that does not imply segregation, often goes together with the idea of an LGBT community that discards much of the economic and cultural baggage of consumer capitalism that predominates in today's same-sex formation. Mark Gevisser has written of 'the tantalizing possibility that South Africa, with its fusion of individualist Western rights-politics and African communal consciousness, might show the world a far smoother way of integrating gay people into society, even if this is at the cost of the kind of robust gay subculture that dominates cities like New York and San Francisco'.[27] A Costa Rican living in Nicaragua has contrasted the society that LGBT Nicaraguans wanted in the wake of the

25   Marcuse 1966, pp. 201, 203.
26   Wekker 1999, p. 132; Wekker 2006, p. 192.
27   Gevisser 2000, p. 136.

Sandinista Revolution with the kind of gay ghetto she saw emerging in Costa Rica: 'we've wanted to push society, so it will make a place for us, not carve a place out which is only for lesbians and gay men'.[28] In the right conditions, this could converge with the radical potential of queer politics as 'an "in your face" rejection of proper sexual identities that is both anti-assimilationist and anti-separatist'.[29]

Subverting Gender

A central axis of radical queer as well as feminist politics is subverting gender, which structures the reproduction of the heteronormative family, of human beings as producers and thus of capitalism as a whole. Even more clearly than sexuality, gender is not merely a cultural phenomenon or something that can be successfully challenged at a purely personal level. It structures not only the family, but also the workplace, state and every other social institution – including the institutions that define today's gender-normative gay normality. Subverting gender is therefore simultaneously a personal, cultural, collective and political project. A radical queer approach to partnership and marriage, for example, is impossible except as part of a radicalised feminist alliance.

Obviously women and women's movements are central agents in this project, with lesbians playing a key role. Lesbian self-organisation within queer milieus reflects their special insights on gender issues. Women are quick to feel the need to organise their own groups to avoid enduring men's (sometimes blatant, sometimes subtle) misogyny, or being relegated to subordinate positions. Lesbians also have little patience for 'internalised lesbophobia, as much from heterosexual feminists as from closet lesbians'.[30] In fact, autonomous lesbian organising need not stand in the way of alliances with GBTs. For example, the Palestinian LGBT organisation Al Qaws works together with Aswat, a group of Palestinian gay women that is in turn an independent part of a feminist organisation. This cooperation comes naturally: LGBT organising intrinsically involves challenging the patriarchal character of Palestinian society, sexual taboos and the pervasive racism of Israeli society.[31] In Latin America, while some lesbians have reacted to male misogyny by boycotting mixed groups

---

28   Randall 2000, p. 100.
29   Hennessy 2000, p. 52, echoing Hennessy 1994, p. 87.
30   Mogrovejo 2000, p. 75.
31   Maikey and De Jong 2011.

and events, others choose to remain in mixed groups to serve as their 'critical conscience'.[32]

Similarly, some Latin American lesbians have continued despite lesbophobia as 'loyal daughters to their mothers' to 'fight for space ... within the feminist movement'.[33] Solidarity through women's organising has been significant for the development of lesbian movements internationally. For example, at the UN Women's Decade Conference in Nairobi in 1985, at several times during the packed lesbian workshops, a Kenyan woman got up to say, 'In our country it does not exist' – and other Kenyan women would shout, 'Yes it does! Yes it does!'[34]

Even as socialist feminist and lesbian feminist currents as such grew weaker, LGBT movements have continued to learn from the deepening insights of left feminist theorists. Today, following a first wave of women's struggles and theorising about a century ago, which included Marxists like Zetkin and Kollontai, and a second wave in the 1960s and 1970s, which included the first socialist feminists, a third wave is challenging some of the wrong turns of neoliberal feminism, in ways that hold tremendous promise for LGBT politics.

Some third-wave feminists are calling into question 'the usefulness of "woman" as the foundation of all feminist politics'. Some theorists have suggested that gender is like language: 'while we have a biological capacity to identify with and to learn to "speak" from a particular location in a cultural gender system, we don't come into the world with a predetermined gender identity'. Despite ongoing tensions, more feminists are taking some distance from the anti-transgender dogmatism of some activists in the 1970s, and re-examining the sex wars debates in more nuanced ways. They are increasingly sensitive to how historical, variable and contingent gender can actually be, and how arbitrary it can be to 'reduce the wide range of livable body types into two and *only* two genders'.[35] They are recognising that gender identity can be 'fluid and open, resisting dichotomised labels of "masculine" and "feminine"'.[36] And in Vreer Verkerke's words, they are seeing that feminism can be an ally for transgender activism when it acknowledges that it 'is not just about women, but about gender'.[37]

32   Sarda 1998, p. 41.
33   Mogrovejo 2000, p. 87.
34   Drucker 1996, pp. 96–7.
35   Stryker 2008, pp. 3, 4, 11–12.
36   Bergero, Asiain and Cano-Caballero 2010, p. 63.
37   Verkerke 2012, p. 13.

'To me', Leslie Feinberg has written, 'gender is the poetry each of us makes out of the language we are taught',[38] with the caveat that many of us 'grow up thinking and "speaking" the "wrong" gender dialect'.[39] For decades, studies have suggested that if gendered behaviour can be 'achieved by the "wrong" sex, it logically follows that it is in reality also achieved, not inherited, by the "right" sex'.[40] The experience of trans people also demonstrates the relational character of gender: apart from any external cues of visible body types, clothing and behaviour, no gender identity has been satisfactorily achieved until and unless it is recognised by others and reflected in the way people are treated as they interact with others.[41]

Recent theory has undermined the once ostensibly clear distinction between a biological, permanent, hard-edged category of sex and a social, historically constructed, fuzzier category of gender – a dichotomy that is 'probably culturally bound and scientifically misleading'.[42] Queer theory, notably in the work of Butler, through its study of intersex people – estimated to include one in 2,000 human beings, who are increasingly struggling against automatic surgery meant to assign all infants a male or female identity[43] – and others, has shown how influential social, cultural and historical factors can be for the classification of people by biological sex. 'Human anatomy continues to burst the confines of the contemporary concept that nature delivers all babies on two unrelated conveyor belts'.[44]

A socialist feminist understanding of how class and gender are intertwined in women's struggles should inform a radical queer understanding of LGBT struggles. Movements for reproductive freedom were defined from the 1970s as embracing not only abortion rights and the fight against sterilisation abuse, but also sexual self-determination. By 2004, even the UN Special Rapporteur on health declared that violence and discrimination against sexual minorities was a barrier to sexual and reproductive health.[45] These battles entail confronting the neoliberal state in the midst of a crisis.[46] They therefore require new forms of feminist organising, mobilising more widely and resolutely, 'based on the

---

38   Feinberg 1998, p. 10.
39   Newton 1989, p. 292.
40   Rubin 2011, p. 340 (citing, for example, Esther Newton).
41   Bergero, Asiain and Cano-Caballero 2010, p. 60.
42   Herdt 1994, p. 21.
43   Stryker 2008, p. 9.
44   Feinberg 1998, p. 7.
45   Moriarty 2007, p. 25.
46   Young 1981, pp. 63–4.

self-activity of working-class women'.[47] This kind of feminist organising would be the natural ally of queer organising based on the self-activity of LGBT working people.

For years, left feminists have been proposing ways of challenging neoliberalism, both by improving conditions in wage work and placing a higher social and economic value on care work. Attacking the debilitating spiral that links women's traditional responsibility for childrearing, most women's second-class status in labour markets, and unequal power in the family would disrupt 'market-mediated processes of subordination [that] are the very lifeblood of neoliberal capitalism'.[48] This kind of left feminism has the potential to converge with LGBT efforts to challenge both ghettoisation and adaptation to the existing family order, by building alternative households and communities founded on more humane and expansive values than romantic bonding in the interests of successful market competition. Only such an alliance can make it possible to move beyond the mainstream lesbian/gay agenda, to a broader vision of a truly liberated sexuality, truly liberated homes and a truly liberated culture.

Queer Inclusion

Part 1 of this book, and chapter 3 in particular, analysed the origins of the gay normality that is hegemonic in the homonormative-dominant regime of neoliberalism, and exposed the deep roots of the fracturing of same-sex identities that has ensued. It showed that LGBT communities are being fractured as a result of fundamental changes in the productive and reproductive order of gendered capitalism. The process has put young, low-income and poor queers, trans people and other marginalised groups in different situations from those encountered by people in the consolidating gay mainstream. The political implication is that these groups have a special role to play in an anti-capitalist sexual politics. This raises questions for radical politics in general.

The forms taken by alternative, non-homonormative sexual identities do not necessarily win them easy acceptance among feminists or socialists. The lesbian/gay identity that emerged by the 1970s had much to commend it from the broad left's point of view (once the left had largely overcome its initial homophobia). By contrast, gender and other queers can raise the hackles

---

47   Brenner 2000, p. 205.
48   Fraser 2009, pp. 115–17.

of many on the left, since their sexuality strikes many as at variance with the mores to be expected and hoped for in an egalitarian, peaceful, rational future.

But no sexuality existing under capitalism can serve as a model for sexualities to be forecast or desired in a truly free society. Nor is it useful to privilege any particular existing form of sexuality in present-day struggles for sexual liberation. The aim of radicals should not be to replace the traditional 'hierarchical system of sexual value' identified by Gayle Rubin[49] with a new hierarchy of our own. 'In history as in love', David Halperin has written, 'the real harm in power imbalances comes not from the dissymmetry itself but from its sentimentalization or institutionalization, from the denial of the reality of unequal power through its normalizing as the truth of gender, class, race, status, beauty, wealth, romance, professional authority, national identity, historical difference'.[50] Pleasure that does not harm others is its own sufficient justification. Rubin's 'pluralistic sexual ethics', judging sexual acts by 'the way partners treat one another, the level of mutual consideration, the presence or absence of coercion, and the quantity and quality of pleasures they provide',[51] is fully in keeping with the ethos expounded by Alexandra Kollontai during the Bolshevik Revolution.

As Amber Hollibaugh pointed out many years ago, sexual history has first of all to be able to 'talk realistically about what people *are* sexually'.[52] Radicalism is 'not only about making a new future, it is also about making space for what is'.[53] There is no ' "pure" revolutionary subject lying somewhere outside [the] constraints' of existing sexual categories.[54] We need to see 'diversity as a gift [and] anomalies as precious'.[55] And in radical struggles over sexuality, as in radical struggles over production, the basic imperative is to welcome and stimulate self-organisation and resistance by people subjected to exploitation, exclusion, marginalisation or oppression, in the forms that their own experience proves to be most effective.

This is not to say that queer anti-capitalists should simply adopt a liberal attitude of unthinking approval of sexual diversity in general, in a spirit of 'anything goes'. Our central concern should be to advance the sexual liberation and empowerment of those situated to transform society, who today

---

49 Rubin 2011, pp. 149–50.
50 Halperin 2002, p. 21.
51 Rubin 2011, p. 154.
52 Hollibaugh and Moraga 1983, p. 396.
53 Crosby et al. 2012, p. 144 (Heather Love).
54 Kinsman 1987, p. 220.
55 Rubin 2011, pp. 175, 253.

include among them straights, LGBT people and – particularly among society's most oppressed – gender and other queers. The 1960s ideal of liberation needs to be reclaimed, cleansing it of the taint of neoliberal 'freedom'.[56] An ideal of queer freedom needs to be developed and deepened, which is available not only to those with purchasing power or those who imagine themselves to be already free of gender or sexual norms, but to people in general, who need a material foundation for their personal and sexual freedom.

The post-Stonewall LGBT movement waged an effective fight against discrimination and won many victories on the basis of a lesbian/gay identity widely shared by those engaged in same-sex erotic or emotional relationships. But this classic lesbian/gay identity has not been the only basis in history for movements for sexual emancipation. In the German homophile struggle from 1897 to 1933, for example, Magnus Hirschfeld's Scientific-Humanitarian Committee, the wing of the movement closest to the working-class left, tended to put forward polarised 'third sex' theories.[57] This is what one might predict on the basis of the evidence that reciprocal gay identities were at first primarily a middle-class phenomenon, while transgender and gender-polarised patterns persisted longer among the working class and poor.[58] Today in the dependent world as well, transgender identities seem to be more common among those of lower class status, who are less plugged in to globalised networks.[59] Rather than privileging same-sex sexualities more common among the less oppressed, however superficially egalitarian, the left should be particularly open and attentive to those same-sex sexualities more common among the most oppressed, however polarised.

The queer rejection of a homogenised, assimilationist homonormative sexuality need not be the preserve of a marginal subculture in imperialist countries; it could eventually be compelling for LGBT people worldwide. Especially in the economically dominated countries in which most human beings live, LGBT communities are unlikely ever to become homogenous, and there are too many diverse subcultures to marginalise them all – especially the trans people and sex workers who play a disproportionate role in the dependent world. The great diversity of identities gives substance to the idea of a radical *alliance* of all the sexually oppressed, rather than a movement around a single sexual identity. While the extent of diversity does not allow for a 'monolithic discourse',[60] a commonality of oppression could ultimately be the wellspring

56   Jakobsen 2012, pp. 20–1.
57   See Fernbach 1998, p. 51; Drucker 1997, p. 37.
58   Chauncey 1994.
59   Oetomo 1996, pp. 265–8.
60   Chou 2000, p. 203.

of a powerful oppositional force. Within a broad alliance of the sexually oppressed, each group has a distinctive contribution to make to an overall programme. Strengthening autonomous organising within LGBT groups of trans people, blacks and immigrants, the young and old, people with disabilities or marginalised sexual practices can foster a more democratic and pluralist community.[61]

The need for autonomous organisation by LGBT youth, for instance, is crucial. The fight against youth poverty and for economic independence for young people must take account of the specific importance of this demand for LGBT young people. Self-organisation by LGBT youth could also make possible discussions that are difficult or impossible in broader LGBT organisations. Young people can and must insist on the essential role they need to play in their own liberation, against older people's paternalistic inclination to protect them by imposing restrictions on them. They can, for example, constantly point out that the sexual liberation of youth requires more access to information and images, not less.[62]

This could enable a new approach to intergenerational relationships, beginning from the flexible conception of sexual maturity adopted in 1920s revolutionary Russia,[63] as supposed to an arbitrary age of consent. The reforms to age-of-consent laws that were briefly explored in the 1990s could also be re-examined. In the Netherlands between 1991 and 2002, for example, an older person having sex with someone aged 12 to 15 was legally exempt from prosecution unless a complaint was made by the younger partner, the younger partner's parent or guardian, or a child welfare agency. The Soviet Russian approach of the 1920s and the Dutch approach of the 1990s could be combined in a legal definition of sexual maturity that defines readiness for different sexual acts in a flexible and differentiated way, with the young person's own awareness and initiative given priority over 'expert' opinion.

In the dependent world particularly, the diversity of LGBT communities has resulted in an alliance model of organising as an alternative or a supplement to the model of a single, broad, unified organisation. Shifting alliances among autonomous groups can be the basis of a united front between those whose identities fit the basic parameters of the gay/straight divide and those whose identities do not. This can facilitate the development of a truly queer conception of a 'multiple, malleable, dynamic' sexuality.[64]

---

61   Kinsman 1987, pp. 223.
62   Fourth International 2003, point 13.
63   Healey 2001, p. 122.
64   Wekker 1999, p. 132.

Trans and Bi Inclusion

Among the different queer constituencies with a special role to play, trans people are increasingly central today to the radical queer project of subverting gender. Butler's insight that even sex, and not just gender, can be socially constructed is crucial for transgender and intersex activism.[65] These analyses have made clear that transgender is a '*movement across a socially imposed boundary away from an unchosen starting place* – rather than any particular destination or mode of transition'. It is not simply a form of same-sex sexuality, but instead cuts across sexual orientation: a transman could be gay or straight or bisexual. Failing to recognise this reinforces the idea that LGBT identities are necessarily gender-normative.[66] In reality, trans people reside on a 'span of identities' ranging from androgynous and feminine men to drag queens and straight male cross-dressers.[67]

The increasing integration of trans issues into feminist theory and activism is crucial given the disproportionate and growing importance of transgender patterns in dependent countries, especially among poorer people. In imperialist countries too, by the late 1990s trans issues were seen as cutting-edge.[68] This suggests that despite all the setbacks for lesbian/gay liberation since the 1970s, the categories of lesbian/gay, bisexual and straight, and even the categories of male and female, may already be losing some of their centrality for sexual politics. Now feminist analysis needs to make sexuality more central to its own project. As Afsaneh Najmabadi has written, early feminism in Iran, for example, was 'deeply enmeshed in disavowal, denial, and eradication of male homoeroticism'; now feminism needs to inquire more deeply into its affinities with 'sexual others'.[69]

Fights for trans rights, besides their importance for trans people themselves, should also be viewed as potentially significant ways of subverting the existing gender order. The example of the US Employment Non-Discrimination Act, introduced in Congress repeatedly since the 1970s as an attempt to ban discrimination on the grounds of sexual orientation, shows the crucial need

---

65   See Girard 2009.

66   Stryker 2008, pp. 1, 131, 137–8. Among other things, Stryker was criticising Gayle Rubin for treating transsexuals and transvestites in 1982 as a 'despised sexual caste' rather than a gender category (Stryker 2008, p. 149). Accepting the justice of this criticism, Rubin pointed out in mitigation in 2010 that transgender studies did not yet exist in 1982 (Rubin 2011, pp. 215–16).

67   Feinberg 1998, pp. 55, 47, 16.

68   Stryker 2008, p. ix.

69   Najmabadi 2005, pp. 235, 243.

for trans autonomous organisation: in 2007, its gay Democratic sponsor decided not to include gender identity in the act, after years of growing support for inclusion, and the mainstream Human Rights Campaign reversed its previous support for inclusion.[70] At the same time, the link between the fights against anti-trans and anti-gay discrimination poses an implicit challenge to the effort to separate sexual from gender identity, and thus to gay normality as such. Because every group trying to win anti-discrimination legislation has to decide whether to add 'gender identity' after 'sexual orientation', transgender inclusion has become an unavoidable issue for LGBT rights activists. The left should be clear that sacrificing trans people to homonormative expediency is unacceptable.

In the absence of trans self-organisation, defining movements as LGBT is no guarantee of full and genuine inclusion. It can even be a way of evading a badly needed critique of homonormativity. Autonomous trans organisation can facilitate the process of negotiating unity between trans people and cisgendered lesbian/gay people (or, for that matter, cisgendered self-defined queers, who also exist).[71] Self-organisation by trans people does not imply that cisgendered LGBT people are an adversary, but simply that trans people can more clearly and effectively address certain issues among themselves, often in preparation for raising these issues in broader LGBT forums.

Trans organising has a long history in the dominated countries, as well as a growing presence today. One of the earliest prominent leaders of the LGBT movement in Turkey, Demet Demir, was a transsexual who also played an important role in sex workers' organising, the feminist movement and HIV/AIDS advocacy. In 1991, Demir was the first person ever to be recognised as an Amnesty International prisoner of conscience due to persecution on account of sexual orientation.[72] Since 1993, Brazilian trans people have both organised themselves independently and forced the LGBT movement to open up to them.[73] The rise of queer radicalism in the US in the early 1990s gave a fresh impetus to trans activism as well, as groups were founded with names like Transgender Nation and Transexual Menace and more mainstream LGBT groups began picking up transgender demands.[74] Global organising began with the holding of the first international transgender congress in 1987.[75]

---

70   Stryker 2008, pp. 150–2.
71   Califia 2003, p. 256.
72   Drucker 2000ob, p. 218.
73   Green 1999b, p. 104.
74   Meyerowitz 2002, p. 283.
75   Bolin 1994, p. 472.

A ban on discrimination on grounds of gender identity is only one key trans demand. Other demands include full access to freely chosen medical care, education, and safe and accepting homes for trans young people, protection in prison from rape and other forms of violence, safe toilets and gender-neutral pronouns for those who do not identify as either male or female.[76] The media has to be called to account for sensationalist, transphobic coverage that fosters violence and suicide. Trans and intersex people have a long way to go before the medical industry meets their needs: one study revealed that children with intersex conditions found medical exams 'intrusive and dehumanizing', while adults in another study used words like 'rape', 'invasion' and 'violation' to describe clinic visits.[77] The lists of demands that have come out of trans organising in Argentina have been particularly comprehensive; some of the demands have been won. In 1998, for example, the city of Buenos Aires adopted a measure against police harassment of transvestites and sex workers. Other demands have included funding by public health services of sex change operations and a reduction the number of documents and occasions when people are classified as male or female, since such classifications often serve no legitimate purpose – a clear challenge to gender divides.[78]

This last demand raises especially complex issues around positive discrimination and women's-only space, which many women experience as a precious area of safety in sexist societies. As members of the Indian gender queer group LABIA have observed, in such spaces 'a body that is not keeping with the norm may seem threatening and out of the ordinary, even when the person's gender does not seem transgressive'. Such situations can even lead to violence.[79] It should be possible to address the issue in ways that recognise the importance of women's-only space without essentialising female identity – that is, while accepting self-identification as a woman as the decisive criterion.

There can be significant connections in same-sex organising between transgender people and other groups. In the right political circumstances, trans people can even become politically active along with their cisgendered partners. Non-gay-identified 'men who have sex with men' (MSMs) often recoil from the possibility of being publicly linked to those with whom they have sex and sometimes sexual relationships, in defence of their own masculine identities and for fear of losing their status within their heterosexual families. Signs of respect and recognition for their trans partners can be major steps

---

76   Feinberg 1998, pp. 133, 71.
77   Jordan-Young 2010, p. 242.
78   See Fourth International 2003, point 18.
79   Shah, Raj, Mahajan and Nevatia 2012, p. 227.

forward in queering their broader societies. Breakthroughs are most likely in times of major social transformation, as, for example, when the abolition of South African apartheid also helped break down barriers for social participation by LGBT people. As a result, some South African MSMs – such as the Zulu *injonga* partners of trans *skesanas* – became willing to be publicly identified with LGBT people, even leading the 1992 Johannesburg Pride parade.[80]

When trans people's sexual partners have cross-sex relationships at the same time, they can be seen as bisexuals, who have also been organising and demanding more recognition for many years now. But in contexts where trans people's partners do not identify as bisexual, their relationship to LGBT movements can be different from that of bisexuals; sometimes they are unique. *Injongas* are exceptional in having a distinctive identity and a traditional word they use to refer to themselves. But perhaps macho men or femme women who have sex with trans people in Latin America or Asia could also one day play a visible role in LGBT organising, if and when LGBT movements become strong and popular enough.

Perhaps macho Brazilian *michês*, who reject gay identity and insist on their insertive role, are taking a tentative step towards a distinctive LGBT identity when they describe themselves as 'bi', sometimes in deference to their African-American boyfriends. Scepticism about their machismo is fuelled by the common assumption that they will 'bottom' for the right price. But openness to a distinctive definition of *michê* identity has to be distinguished from a homonormative insistence that *michês* are really gay 'deep down' and should just come out. This insistence on a uniform gay identity can just increase stigma and hold back more openness – as witness the pervasive urban legends warning Costa Rican male sex workers not to enjoy the sex too much or associate with gays too much if they want to avoid becoming gay themselves.[81]

Still, it would be a major blow to heteronormativity – and to heteronormative conceptions of family – for men and women in cross-sex marriages to openly acknowledge their own same-sex relationships. Replacing the suspicions, tensions and sometimes even contempt between trans people and the cisgendered people who have sex with them – all the more when class differences are at work – with respect and solidarity would be an especially big step.[82]

The radicalism of trans organising is in no way diminished by focusing on legal reforms like anti-discrimination laws that can be vital to trans people's

---

80   McLean and Ngcobo 1994, pp. 164–5.
81   Mitchell 2011, pp. 668–70, 675, 677, 667–8, 675, 676 (citing Jacobo Schifter).
82   The workshop on Algeria and Morocco at the 1999 Euromediterranean Summer University on Homosexualities in Luminy, France, helped me get more of a sense of these dynamics.

lives. The limited victories that have been won so far – allowing changes in gender identification at least for post-operative transsexuals; the inclusion of trans people in at least a few US municipal anti-discrimination ordinances; the recognition in the 1994 *Diagnostic and Statistical Manual* (DSM) of the existence of gay trans people – are tributes to persistent organising by trans groups like the US GenderPAC.[83] They have paved the way for more radical campaigns. Beginning in 2008, for example, a global Stop Trans Pathologisation campaign worked (unfortunately with only limited success) to remove 'gender dysphoria' altogether from the fifth, 2012 edition of the DSM.[84]

At the same time, there needs to be an emphasis on base-building outside institutions instead of only lobbying within them. Above all, a constant effort is needed to push beyond reforms that can sow divisions among trans people (for example, between those who do and those who do not opt for surgery) and that can be incorporated into existing, if slightly reconfigured, gender norms.

Eliminating surgery or medical treatment as a requirement for legal gender change may seem like a limited demand, for example. The law Portugal adopted in 2011, requiring only a declaration of gender dysphoria, went a fair distance towards granting the demand for identification papers that reflect people's own gender identity. Recent regulations in the US have moved in the same direction, for passports in 2010, for new California birth certificates in 2011, for residence and work permits in 2012, and for the Social Security Administration in 2013. But as the Ecuadorian organisation Different Bodies, Equal Rights has argued, eliminating the requirement for 'expert' sanction can be a major victory over the imposition of Eurocentric forms of masculinity and femininity.[85] It also poses a challenge to the security state, which especially since 9/11 has faced trans people with impossible dilemmas. If the gender indicated on a driving licence or passport did not correspond to their biological sex, they were often committing an offence for which they could be fined or jailed; if it did not correspond to their perceived gender, they could be prevented from driving or travelling.[86]

More generally, winning the freedom for legal gender change on demand can open up a process of 'denaturalising "normal bodies"' and finding new words to make trans 'thinkable ... without resort to images of illness'.[87] And it can put an end to the appalling situation in which simply using a public

---

83   Stryker 2008, pp. 121, 142–3, 148–9, 120, 141.

84   Verkerke 2012, pp. 5–6.

85   Verkerke 2012, pp. 16, 29.

86   Feinberg 1998, p. 20.

87   Witty 2012, p. 11.

toilet – either a men's room or a women's room – can lead to confrontations and even violence.[88]

The liberating effects of overcoming gender restrictions apply to everyone, without distinctions among LGBT people or different subsets of trans people. With trans autonomy and genuine inclusion, the broader LGBT movement can tackle forms of oppression that also hurt cisgendered LGB people, and in fact everyone. As Feinberg has noted, preconceptions about 'what a "real" woman or man should be' impose 'a life sentence in a gender straightjacket' on everyone, so that everyone's 'individual journey … is shunted into one of two deeply carved ruts'. 'Trans liberation has meaning for you – no matter how you define or express your sex and your gender'. This militates against the practice of according special status to perfect 'gender queers' and lesser status to trans-sexuals. It is not possible to 'force all people to live outside of femininity and masculinity'. 'We all have the right to find our place on the circle of sex and gender, and still defend every other point on its circumference'.[89]

Undermining gender differences, one of the original goals of lesbian/gay liberation in the 1970s, has been increasingly neglected as a goal by lesbian/gay movements. But the trans community at least insists on viewing 'gender and sex systems as relativistic systems imposed by society'. Transgender has thus assumed the mantle of gender nonconformity that the lesbian/gay main-stream shucked off in the course of the past thirty years. Perhaps trans people are a 'harbinger of our future'.[90] Even in the short run, challenging gender roles should help dissident queers resist an assimilationist politics, which always seems to leave them behind.

Gender dissent both poses challenges and provides opportunities for femi-nism. 'Why should we as feminists deplore or deny the existence of masculine women or effeminate men?', asks Esther Newton. '[S]hould we not support those among us, butches and queens, who still bear the brunt of homophobia?'[91] Madeline Davis and Elizabeth Kennedy have gone further, stressing that 'butch-femme roles created an authentic lesbian sexuality appropriate to the flourishing of an independent lesbian culture', and arguing that these roles express women's 'concern with the ultimate satisfaction of other women' in a way that 'is part of a strong sense of female and potentially feminist agency'.[92]

---

88   Feinberg 1998, pp. 68–9.
89   Feinberg 1998, pp. 3–4, 99, 6, 5, 118.
90   Bolin 1994, pp. 447, 470 (citing Holly Boswell).
91   Newton 1989, p. 292.
92   Davis and Kennedy, pp. 431, 437.

Transgender also highlights basic feminist issues about the role of gender in structuring the labour market.

Gender queers may not be 'dismantling the categories of man and woman' entirely. But in 'opening up a world of possibilities in addition',[93] they can vastly enlarge the space for those who refuse to identify as entirely the one or the other. This can move us closer to a world in which the social significance of gender distinctions is markedly diminished, and power differentials based on gender vanish altogether.

Global and Anti-Racist Solidarity

Queer solidarity across racial and national boundaries is only possible through building anti-racist and global solidarity. For anti-capitalists, solidarity rests on the basic understanding that all oppressed people are contending with a global capitalist and neoliberal order, which can only be effectively resisted and defeated through a unified global fight-back. Because capitalism has now conquered the entire planet, opposition to it has to take account of the 'interpenetration of ... local arrangements with capital's global structures'.[94] In other words, human beings' sexual lives worldwide need to be understood as part of a global totality, and at the same time as overdetermined by a wide array of local factors. LGBT people in the world today have converged enough to have a certain real commonality. This is an objective basis for solidarity in oppression and struggles. Yet bitter experience has taught that global unity needs to be based on autonomy for and leadership by blacks, people of immigrant origin, and people in the economically dominated countries if it is not to be a cloak for control by white Europeans and North Americans.

Over the past century and more, racism and nationalism have repeatedly proved extremely potent as sources of division, within LGBT communities as well as among working people. In imperialist countries under neoliberalism, homonationalism has emerged as a key component of the new homonormativity. Traditional calls by labour and socialists to overcome these differences and unite in multiracial movements have often been ineffectual. Marxists' insistence on focusing on the big picture has at times been seen as Eurocentrist, eliciting fierce opposition from revolutionary nationalists. The question has even been asked whether speaking of totality – of the global system as a

---

93   Feinberg 1998, p. 58.
94   Hennessy 2000, p. 9.

whole – at all necessarily implies an 'imperial, American universalism'.[95] The question can and should be turned around, however: is it possible to effectively challenge an imperial, Eurocentric universalism without constructing a powerful, anti-imperialist, anti-Eurocentric alliance? Queer scholars of colour in the US and Britain particularly have done a good and vitally necessary job of exposing racist and Eurocentric assumptions and dynamics within queer studies and within LGBT communities. The task remains of demonstrating the full centrality of anti-racism to global anti-capitalist struggles today.

Especially since the 1960s, the balance of opinion on the left has shifted towards seeing self-organisation of the nationally and racially oppressed as an important, even indispensable condition for unity. From the intersectional perspective of rainbow politics, identity groups should be seen as potential coalitions in waiting. An African-American movement, for example, is in a sense a coalition of African-American men and women, LGBT and straight.[96] Similarly, every queer group should be seen as a coalition of white and non-white queers, male, female and trans. This has implications, for example, that critical self-reflection and community organising lay the groundwork for effective coalition.[97] Coalition-building, based on conscious grappling with diversity, can be the starting point for a new queer movement on a global scale. Building blocks for a global queer politics already exist in creative LGBT analysis and organising on every continent, notably by LGBT blacks and immigrants in imperialist countries, drawing on not only concepts arising out of lesbian/gay liberation and queer studies, but also their own unique experience.

One challenge in devising a truly global anti-racist strategy is grasping the full diversity of racism around the planet. While categories of class and gender are structurally embedded in the gendered capitalist mode of production and reproduction, categories of nation and race, however ideologically central, are constructed in a bewildering range of ways. For example, in politically aware British and South Africans circles, 'black' is used to cover roughly the same groups that are referred to in the US as 'people of colour', while 'Black' is largely reserved in the US for African-Americans. Stuart Hall was taken aback when he left his native Jamaica, where he was 'coloured' and thus a step above 'black', to arrive in England, where he was still 'coloured' and nonetheless as 'black' as anyone.[98] Other differences in racial construction go even deeper. In continental Europe in the twenty-first century, for example, where Islamophobia

---

95   Crosby et al. 2012, pp. 140 (Roderick Ferguson), 138 (Kevin Floyd).
96   Crenshaw 1993, p. 1299.
97   Collins 1998, p. 934.
98   Hall 1985, p. 108.

has become the single most powerful form of racism, the people of Muslim origin who are its victims by no means have a consensus on defining themselves as 'black', 'people of colour' or even 'non-white'. The categories of 'black', 'colour' and 'white' are equally problematic when trying to grasp, for example, the racialised antagonisms between mestizos and indigenous people in much of Latin America. Only a truly global solidarity founded on an understanding of imperialism as a system can make it possible to navigate these complexities successfully.

LGBT organising in dependent countries and among oppressed groups in imperialist countries needs to take account of the role of religion for their constituencies. The US radical queer group Southerners on New Ground, for example, noted in one of its campaigns in North Carolina that 35 percent of their 16,000 volunteers identified as religious, often continuing to take part in religious structures and even incorporating same-sex partners into them. The group had to be consciously inclusive of these people, 'while still holding firm to our politics and our fight against religious supremacy and fundamentalism'.[99]

LGBT people of black, immigrant and Muslim origin have been organising in a number of countries to assert their dignity and demand visibility and inclusion. The French multiracial LGBT organisation Kelma was founded in 1997 with the aim of creating 'a mixed space, beyond the dictatorship of looks, cash or skin colour'.[100] Stigmatisation has greatly complicated the struggles of European LGBT Muslims, who have been increasingly visible in the twenty-first century, for example, in the Dutch foundation Yoesuf, German immigrant dance parties and the British soap opera *EastEnders*. They face the joint insistence of Islamophobes and Muslim fundamentalists that their very existence is a contradiction in terms.[101]

Queers on the radical left have increasingly made solidarity with LGBT blacks and immigrants a priority. In Denmark in 2010, for example, the Queer Committee of the anti-capitalist Red-Green Alliance disassociated itself from that year's Pride march, which it said was being used to provide LGBT cover to Islamophobia. Much more visibly, Judith Butler generated international shock waves in 2010 by refusing the Civil Courage Prize offered to her by the Berlin Christopher Street Day Committee. 'The host organizations refuse to understand antiracist policies as an essential part of their work', Butler said; 'I must distance myself from this complicity with racism, including anti-Muslim

---

99   SONG 2011/2012.
100   Cervulle and Rees-Roberts 2010, pp. 130–2.
101   Herzog 2011, p. 203.

racism'. Rightfully, she said, the award should go to LGBT immigrant groups that were mobilising in Berlin's Transgeniale (Alternative Pride).[102]

Internationally too, the reality of imperialism requires a great deal of sensitivity to the many ways in which well-intentioned interventions from imperialist countries undermine rather than support the agency of LGBT people in dependent countries. The sequence of events around the founding of a Namibian LGBT NGO led some Namibians to see homosexuality as 'a Norwegian conspiracy', for example, suggesting a sort of 'unwitting conspiracy between homophobic regimes and local and international activists' in imposing a hetero/homo binary.[103] One egregious example was the protest at the Egyptian embassy organised by ACT UP Paris in response to the 2001 Egyptian Queen Boat raid. The protest's slogans included a demand to 'free our lovers': hardly helpful for the Egyptian defendants, who were not defending themselves as open queer men, let alone as men with European lovers. Such blunders can only be avoided through more communication and coordination between activists in imperialist and dominated countries, in a way that allows Africans and Asians – in all their political and cultural diversity – to teach Europeans and North Americans 'how to do rights work'.[104]

Related issues were highlighted in 2011 by the announcement by British Conservative Prime Minister David Cameron's government that it would cut aid to African governments that violated LGBT rights. A long list of African activists and organisations responded with a statement denouncing the threat. The decision to cut aid disregarded the agency of African LGBT movements and created the 'real risk of a serious backlash', the statement said. 'Donor sanctions are by their nature coercive and reinforce the disproportionate power dynamics between donor countries and recipients'. The British assumptions about African sexualities behind the policy also helped cut off LGBT people from broader civil society and lent credence to the notion that 'homosexuality is "unAfrican"'. The statement called instead for tactics that took account of the history of colonialism.[105] Yet threats of aid cuts multiplied after Ugandan president Yoweri Museveni signed an anti-gay law in 2014.

Opposing the imposition of 'strings-attached' development aid poses, in acute form, the question of who sets the priorities. 'As long as Western liberal democracies can name "gay rights" as the new litmus test for an appropriate twenty-first century democracy, we can obsess about "anti-gay" legislation in

---

102   Schulman 2012, pp. 115, 128–9.
103   Hoad 1999, p. 572.
104   Abolafia 2013.
105   Nana, Abbas, Muguongo, Mtetwa and Ndashe 2011.

Nigeria and say nothing about the violence and economic exploitation of the Shell Oil Company on the land and bodies of Nigerians'.[106] An agenda for LGBT equality is 'reductive and distorting', Scott Long has written, when it would only win LGBT people equal rights to the poverty and violence of a fundamentally unequal world. Cutting aid to Africa, specifically, is a gesture in favour of sexual equality that risks deepening economic inequality, thus making 'some people less equal in the name of making others more so'.[107] Not to mention the political inequality that is underscored when whole African nations are penalised for violations of LGBT rights, when no one suggests penalising the whole of the United States (for example) for the murder of a trans person each month.

More discussion is needed about what tactics actually work. At the least, LGBT rights should be situated in the broader framework of sexual and reproductive rights, so that civil rights issues are not severed from their social and economic context. More thought should also be devoted to the risk that condemnations and retaliations from Europe and North America might further isolate LGBT Africans in their own countries. A British and German refusal of aid to Malawi following arrests in 2009, for example, led to increased homophobia and threats to LGBT activists, who had to go into hiding.[108] The result can be, in Long's words, 'More blood. More pain'. LGBT Africans need to have more of a say over their degree of visibility, if international solidarity is not to be reduced to 'defending the defenders after they're dead'. Finally, while the right of asylum for persecuted LGBT people must absolutely be affirmed and honoured far more than it now is, exile can mean for activists the destruction of 'the way people live as connected and implicated beings in their cultures, contexts, communities' – 'social death'.[109]

Nevertheless, where LGBT communities are under siege, LGBT refugees and migrants to other countries can help defend and sustain queers in their countries of origin. Although the UN High Commissioner for Refugees has included sexual identity among the grounds for 'well-founded fear of persecution' entitling people to refugee status,[110] LGBT refugees' rights are routinely ignored and denied as anti-immigrant prejudice spreads in country after country. In addition, restrictions on movement, especially since 9/11, have highlighted commonalities between trans people and immigrants, refugees and the

---

106   Farrow 2011/2012.
107   Long 2013.
108   Abolafia 2013.
109   Long 2013.
110   Moriarty 2007, p. 25.

undocumented. Defending LGBT people thus involves joining campaigns that link fights against gender-normativity and homonationalism to resistance to state policing of gender and national boundaries.[111]

Solidarity between LGBT movements in imperialist and dependent countries has often piggybacked on the strong cultural influence traditionally exerted by imperialist cultures. The International Lesbian, Gay, Bisexual, Trans and Intersex Association (ILGA), initially founded and run largely by lesbians and gay men in imperialist countries, has contributed to the growth of movements in the dependent world by carrying out solidarity actions, sending materials and money, and 'twinning' richer and poorer groups. International solidarity has also been a source of support for LGBT activism in the Soviet Union and the Russian Federation, and Eastern Europe more broadly.[112] Yet sometimes the vision and solidarity of European and North American activists have had unfortunate limits, as when the 1985 ILGA conference in Toronto rejected a resolution supporting anti-imperialist movements. More recently, more leadership for ILGA at world level has come from Latin America, Asia and Africa – but resources have flowed disproportionately to ILGA's European region, which receives funding from the European Union.

In recent years, interaction among LGBT movements within specific regions has become at least as important as connections to imperialist countries. The Asian Lesbian Network's first conference in 1990 and Asian gay conferences beginning in 1986 helped consolidate Asian organising; Asian networking has continued in the face of obstacles, most dramatically the Islamic fundamentalist attack on the ILGA Asia conference in Surabaya, Indonesia in 2010.[113] Latin American and Caribbean Lesbian Gatherings beginning in 1987 played an even bigger role in their region. LGBT movements in the dependent world have sometimes been spurred on by compatriots returning from imperialist countries or helped by immigrants in North America or Europe who have organised in solidarity with them. For example, the first two LGBT South Asian organisations were founded in 1985–6 in the North American diaspora and then spread back to India.[114]

The solidarity shown by Lebanese and Palestinian LGBT groups towards the rest of the Arab region has also been significant. One tragic factor in this region has been the mass movement of refugees, including LGBT refugees, across the Middle East. The Lebanese group HELEM has provided support to Iraqi

---

111   Stryker 2008, p. 150.
112   Healey 2001, pp. 246–7.
113   Mazdafiah 2012, p. 246.
114   Drucker 1996, p. 97.

refugees fleeing persecution based on their sexual orientation, and campaigned for the rights of Palestinian refugees in Lebanon, who face major discrimination. HELEM has remained open to everyone living in Lebanon, even at the cost of losing some Lebanese members.[115]

Solidarity becomes more complicated in the Arab region when the issue arises of working with Israeli LGBT groups. Maikey of the Palestinian group Al Qaws has said that 'unfortunately, many of the Israeli LGBT groups have come to accept the nation and strive to become integrated in it'. Al Qaws has preferred working with Israeli anti-Zionist groups. For many queers worldwide, the Palestinian struggle is also a fight against Israeli self-legitimation through highlighting lesbian/gay rights in Israel ('pinkwashing'), a fight waged by the coalition Palestinian Queers for BDS (boycott, divestment and sanctions). 'Israel commits human rights violations and occupies another people and then abuses my difficulties and my name by saying my society is backward and homophobic', Maikey has said. 'My struggle is dismissed and my people are demonized'.[116]

All these struggles benefit from queering history in anti-Eurocentric ways, uncovering Asia, Africa and Latin America's same-sex past. In the last few decades, scholars have been busily uncovering what many nationalist forces had spent even longer burying. A wealth of material has been emerging about same-sex formations in, for example, Africa and Asia. They have also been busily linking together what Eurocentric and nationalist historians had worked to separate out, for example, showing the centuries-long sexual interactions among captives, converts, renegades, diplomats, expatriates, tourists and their captors or hosts in Europe and the Islamic world,[117] and the great influence of Europe and the US on both colonised and non-colonised Asia and of Chinese sexual culture on other East and Southeast Asian countries.[118] And they have been demonstrating the enormous range of sexual formations in, for example, Africa.[119]

Against Islamophobia

In responding to right-wingers repackaging themselves in recent years as defenders of oppressed Arab women and even gays, the left has sometimes

115   Makarem 2007, p. 105.
116   Maikey and De Jong 2011.
117   Peirce 2009, p. 1326.
118   Loos 2009, pp. 1312–13.
119   Epprecht 2009, p. 1259.

been divided. When international human rights or LGBT groups have issued alerts about persecution of Middle Eastern LGBT people (for example, in Iran), some LGBT anti-imperialists have denounced the critics for contributing to the US war drive.[120] Others have insisted on the importance of both opposition to US intervention and solidarity with LGBT people. Yet international LGBT movements have been hamstrung by their relative weakness in and ignorance of the Arab region. The ill-thought out tactics and sometimes 'outright colonialist mentality' of some LGBT groups in imperialist countries may sometimes even play into the hands of repressive forces.[121] There is an urgent need to link imperialism, gender and sexuality.

One key point is that there is neither a historical nor a logical connection between anti-imperialism and cultural nativism. The British Empire was careful not to interfere with Islamic domination of civil society in countries it ruled such as Egypt and Pakistan. By contrast, Muslim Turkey's fierce resistance to colonisation after the First World War and Muslim Indonesia's struggle for independence after the Second World War involved far-reaching secularisation, albeit from above by authoritarian regimes. It is no accident that Turkey and Indonesia have stronger LGBT communities and movements today than the Arab countries, almost all of which enjoyed the dubious benefits of European colonialism.[122]

The relative rarity of LGBT identities in Arab countries today is not due to lack of European and North American influence; European influence has been stronger in the Arab region than in a country like Thailand, with its burgeoning LGBT scenes. On the contrary, as Joseph Massad's wide-ranging analysis of nineteenth- and twentieth-century Arabic literature has shown, in the colonial period European influence was mobilised to promote heterosexuality and suppress the centuries-old wealth of Arab same-sex forms.[123] Factors like the

---

120   In a related argument, Joseph Massad has blamed repression in the Arab region largely on the lesbian/gay groups and human rights organisations that he calls the 'Gay International', asserting: 'By inciting discourse about homosexuals where none existed before, the Gay International is in fact *heterosexualizing* a world that is being forced to be fixed by a Western binary' (Massad 2007, p. 188). Protests by international groups have been more a reaction than a cause, however; their power is derisible compared to that of imperial powers or multinational capital. Moreover, in 'dismissing self-identified Arab queers as essentially inauthentic replicas of their Western counterparts, Massad overlooks their capacity to act as conscious agents' (Ritchie 2010, p. 567). In any event, the 'gay genie is out of the bottle ... regardless of whether it was human rights groups, global media, or grassroots activists who rubbed the lamp' (Mitchell 2011, p. 674).

121   Makarem 2007, p. 104.

122   See Drucker 2000a, p. 29.

123   Massad 2007, p. 416.

region's relatively low rate of female paid employment, which limit women's sexual independence and help narrow men's leeway for gender dissent, have probably been more important in holding back the rise of LGBT identities. Another obvious factor is what Gilbert Achcar has called 'the Arab despotic exception': the fact that the US continued for so many years before the 2011 Arab Spring to back dictatorships in the Middle East, due to its vital economic and geopolitical interests there, rather than risk the kind of transitions to nominal democracy that it allowed in much of Latin America, Sub-Saharan Africa and other parts of Asia.[124] The result has been less freedom for political and social organising, and specifically for LGBT organising, in the Arab region.

Linking queer and anti-imperialist organising is therefore crucial. The example of the Lebanese LGBT group HELEM shows how effective LGBT participation in broad anti-imperialist movements can be in integrating LGBT people and their issues into a society and discourse of resistance. Based on the conviction that 'sexual liberation cannot be achieved through imperialism [or] detached from the wider struggle for democracy', in 2003 HELEM joined Lebanese mobilisations against the Iraq war, flying a rainbow flag at one demonstration and receiving prominent media attention. In 2006, HELEM joined the grassroots solidarity movement against the Israeli invasion of Lebanon and became part of the largest independent resistance and refugee and war victim relief campaign. Beirut's LGBT community centre became part of Beirut's busiest relief headquarters during four weeks of bombing. One LGBT supporter of the campaign reported feeling 'happiness like never before' when an official of the Shiite fundamentalist Hizbollah thanked him for his work – a striking contrast with the homophobia expressed by the liberal forces behind the Cedar Revolution. Unfortunately, HELEM's appeal for solidarity to an international LGBT conference meeting at the time in Montreal elicited strong opposition, as well as support.[125]

Beyond these promising beginnings, no one can know how or in what forms Arab LGBT communities and movements will develop. In particular, no one knows what proportion of Arabs who have sex with people of the same sex identify or will come to identify as lesbian, gay, trans or bisexual. But this is no argument for privileging either those who have LGBT identities or those who pursue their same-sex desires without such identities. Nor is it an argument for withholding solidarity, on the pretext of a sort of 'reverse Orientalism' that would reserve LGBT identities to Europe and the Americas.[126]

---

124 Achcar 2004, pp. 69–74.
125 Makarem 2011, pp. 107–9.
126 Makarem 2007, p. 110.

There have in fact been examples of anti-imperial solidarity beyond the Islamic world, in defiance of the strong tendency towards homonational-ism among LGBT people in imperialist countries. Several international LGBT organisations, including the International Gay and Lesbian Human Rights Commission and the international Muslim group al-Fatiha, joined in 2003 in opposing the US war in Iraq. Yet, in general, radical queers have shown more of an urge to international solidarity than mainstream LGBT NGOs. In the US, it was Queers for Peace and Justice, and the Audre Lorde Project (a group of LGBT people of colour), which created nationwide LGBT anti-war coalitions.[127]

Radical queer solidarity was visible in Israel at the start of the second Palestinian intifada in 2001 when an Israeli queer group marched in Pride with a black banner declaring, 'There Is No Pride in the Occupation'.[128] Queer solidarity with Palestine took on an international dimension in 2006, when in response to InterPride's decision to hold World Pride in Jerusalem, a New York queer coalition declared, 'It's not "World" Pride without Palestinian and Arab queers, and we refuse to pit our queer celebrations against Palestinians' freedom'.[129] Ultimately, 22 LGBT organisations boycotted the Jerusalem event. In 2010, LGBT activism succeeded in minimising attendance at a special, Israeli consulate-funded San Francisco Jewish Film Festival series for Israel Pride Month, and in barring a Tel Aviv municipal float from Madrid Pride. The formation of Palestinian Queers for Boycott, Divestment and Sanctions in Ramallah in 2010 was a crucial spur towards both international LGBT solidarity and recognition of LGBT people in Palestinian society. Their first global campaign in 2011 led the International Gay and Lesbian Youth Organisation to cancel a gathering planned for Tel Aviv.[130]

A serious base of support for US queer solidarity with the Palestinian strug-gle was built by a US tour of Palestinian LGBT leaders in 2011, beginning at the National Gay and Lesbian Task Force Creating Change conference. The tour was a breakthrough, not only in making Palestinian LGBT people visible, but also in making them the central spokespeople about their own lives and for their own struggle. These events culminated in 2011 when Palestinian BDS leader Omar Barghouti declared in an interview in New York that BDS was 'about building a better society [which] by definition must be inclusive and must recognize people's rights... and... identity, be it gender, sexual identity [or] any other

127   Puar 2007, pp. 44, 246, n. 25.
128   Schulman 2012, p. 131.
129   Puar 2007, p. 16.
130   Schulman 2012, pp. 115–17, 120–1, 126–7, 176.

form of identity'.[131] However, identity is not the core issue. For example, the police rarely know whether the people they harass, arrest or torture identify as gay. The sequence of cause and effect is the reverse, as historians have shown: the common experience of repression can contribute to the development of transgender, gay, lesbian and queer identities.

In the age of neoliberal globalisation, power relations between colonisers (witting or unwitting) and colonised cut across LGBT movements, anti-imperialist movements, and the Marxist left. The fact remains that *all* the victims of oppression today badly need allies in the imperialist countries, who have access to far greater resources. Cultural sensitivity and respect for self-determination are essential. But neither should stand in the way of solidarity with the victims of repression by regimes whose vicious sexual puritanism often goes hand in hand with their subservience to an imperial agenda. Ultimately, queer anti-capitalists in both imperial and dominated countries should join forces to resist empires, and along with them the mirror-image plagues of homonormative arrogance and homophobic repression that the division of the world fosters.

Queering Intimacy and Domesticity

Confronted with the construction of 'normal', nuclear gay families, queer radicals face the challenge of making it possible to organise personal and domestic lives in ways that are freer, more flexible and more open to the wider community. Today, the prevailing family and community structures worldwide are organised in ways that maintain and perpetuate male domination of women, heteronormativity and other inequitable social relations, though sometimes in more subtle forms. As a result, families and communities often exert a conservatising influence in society, in rich countries as well as poor ones, even where poor and working people mobilise in large numbers against the dominant economic policies. Sustained and transformative mobilisation requires changes at the household and community level, so as to change conservatising influences into emancipatory ones. This means that family and community structures dictated by ideology and tradition need to be modified, starting from the dynamics of struggle and self-organisation. Struggle at the elemental household and community level is one of the core dynamics of a queer anti-capitalism.

The feminist dictum that the personal is political means that struggles over power are at work in the smallest social units and in every human relationship.

---

131   Schulman 2012, pp. 106, 109, 172.

One benefit of Michel Foucault's influence has been an increased focus on the analysis of power at the micro level. For LGBT people, this means, besides the individual couple, the household and community, where the transformational force of queer dissent is frequently felt. Queers are adopting a range of strategies for intimate relationships and domestic life that provide alternatives to creating homonormative families. There is, of course, no automatic connection between the dynamics at work in an erotic relationship, a friendship or a group of housemates and the broader realm of politics – no automatic translation to issues of reform or revolution. But a feminist and anti-capitalist politics ultimately can and must link these micro-level transformations to the macro level, where they should ultimately be reflected in every site of economic, social and political power.

Queering intimate relationships and domestic units is often the starting point, with changes that can be impelled by a variety of different queer tactics. One tactic – often the only one available to trans people in many countries – is to form or join alternative households and communities of sexual dissidents. In many cases, these sexually dissident communities are economically marginal, confined to the informal sector and sometimes the sex trade. Yet whether among South Asian *hijras* or runaway young people in New York, they are challenges to existing heteronormative families. They can empower people to create and defend homes and communities independent of normatively defined families and communities. As *hijras* join the *hijra* community, they 'simultaneously distance themselves from their former friends and relatives'.[132] Paradoxically, this can earn them respect from people still enmeshed in normative families, who see the narrowness and corruption that traditional family loyalty can entail. This perception of *hijras* as less corrupt has been one factor in their electoral appeal: one *hijra* ran for office in Pakistan in 1990, and another was elected to the city council in the northern Indian city of Hissar in 1995.

Alongside alternative queer relationships, friendships, and domestic and community structures, there is also a molecular process – a process that is at work neighbourhood by neighbourhood, family by family, or even individual by individual – of queering existing living units. Even within some traditional families, women who live more or less in a separate women's sphere of domestic labour and household production bond with each other in all sorts of emotional and erotic ways.[133] As long as women's intimate relationships with each other take place privately and beyond men's field of vision, they can be entirely

---

132   Nanda 1994, pp. 403–4.
133   Rich 1983, pp. 192–3.

compatible with conservative family ideology. But if and when women begin to speak publicly about their ties with each other inside existing families, a queering process gets underway, which need not have any explicit sexual component but *can* include a sexual or affective dimension.

Social and particularly political mobilisation by women can foster female solidarity and bonding, for example, when women cooperate in public to get fuel or water or milk for their children or health services (such as abortion or contraception), or to resist genital mutilation of their daughters. In Latin America in particular, feminism has widened its self-definition to embrace such forms of women's self-organisation, even if they are not initially defined as feminist.[134] The movements' sexist adversaries often recognise the queer potential of female bonding, and lesbian-bait the movements in order to thwart them. Activist women react all too often by stressing their own heterosexuality and femininity, marginalising, rendering invisible or excluding the lesbians, bisexuals and transmen among them. The same heterosexist dynamic can be at work in women's informal and communal production networks, which facilitate women's survival when they are excluded from or disadvantaged in formal economies.[135] But the potential to replicate heteronormativity exists alongside a potential for queering. Cultural factors, personal ties and conscious choices can all help determine which potential wins out.

The processes of queering existing families and communities, and of building and sustaining distinctive LGBT relationships and households, come together when LGBT and other households and communities intersect. This requires overcoming the stigmas and taboos that mark off separate LGBT networks.[136] Queering households, communities and larger societies lays bare the socially constructed, ideological character of gender, family and sexual structures. It can show how the traditional heterosexual family 'in privileging the intimacy of close kin...has made the outside world cold and friendless, and made it harder to sustain relations of security and trust except with kin'.[137] People can then begin to pose questions, not so much about what is 'natural' or 'part of our culture', as about what kinds of networks best meet their material, social, emotional and sexual needs. Networking and organising can begin to trump biology.[138]

134   Dashner 1987, pp. 67, 70, 72–3, 79–81.
135   Lind and Share 2003, pp. 61, 64.
136   McLean and Ngcobo 1994, pp. 164–5.
137   Barker 2012, p. 143 (citing Michèle Barrett and Mary McIntosh).
138   Jolly 2000.

Heteronormativity takes different forms in different contexts, even within the same social formations, depending on whether or not existing families and communities bend to accommodate different forms of LGBT sexuality and identity. In dependent countries, people tend to be more dependent on their families and communities, even in big cities, where networks based on kinship, ethnicity, and region of origin are often crucial for day-to-day survival. This makes breaking with families or communities harder, and means it can have more drastic consequences when it occurs. LGBT people are more often challenged to find ways to cope with existing family structures and change them without wholly surrendering their own needs and identities. In the absence of welfare states, family is more important in poorer countries for simple survival. Marriage and children are the only form of old-age or health insurance in many poor countries. This has meant that even when extramarital sexuality is tacitly tolerated, it is important that it not be mentioned, so as not to put parenthood and family order in question.[139] Similar constraints affect many African-American lesbians for whom membership in sometimes-homophobic African-American churches is vital to their sense of community.[140]

The growing affluence of some people in some dependent countries is creating more possibilities for some LGBT people to live independently of their families of origin.[141] But even with the rapid recovery in Asia after the economic crisis in 1997, and Asia's initial resilience in the face of the crisis since 2008, the living standards of the great majority remain far below those even of imperialist countries in crisis. This still makes it difficult for most LGBT people to separate from family and community. Molecular queering – the process of infiltrating queer intimacy into existing families while trying to avoid complete breaks – will thus remain a preferred tactic for many.

Persistently wrestling with existing families, without simply acquiescing and pretending, can have an impact over time, importing bits of queer intimacy into otherwise homonormative forms. Sometimes refraining from blurting out awkward facts can help to make surprisingly flexible solutions possible. One Chinese parent whose gay son had never mentioned his sexuality encouraged the son after a time to participate more in AIDS activism.[142] Another pair of Chinese parents invited their son's male lover to eat with the family and eventually even move in.[143] There are similar stories of lovers moving in with

---

139   Epprecht 1996, p. 15.
140   Moore 2011.
141   Altman 2000, p. 143.
142   Rofel 1999, p. 461.
143   Chou 2000, pp. 196–7.

the family in South African black townships and Brazilian *favelas*. One queer Palestinian in an eighteen-year-long relationship with an Israeli Jewish man would bring his partner to weddings and other family gatherings, without ever explicitly naming their relationship.[144] Arguably, arrangements like these can do more to change a society's sexual culture than would moving away to some other city with a lover, even if that were an option. In any event, these arrangements have the potential to do far more than a lesbian or gay couple would, especially when the latter forms a normal same-sex nuclear family, which can duplicate many of the dynamics of a heterosexual nuclear family.

Finally, queers who neither choose to continue living in their families of origin nor are forced into sexually outlawed communities engage in a day-to-day process of experimentation with other ways of shaping their 'families we choose'.[145] Fighting for the freedom to experiment can involve difficult tactical debates and decisions. This was clear in 2006 when the majority of drafters of a radical US statement on queers and immigration decided against privileging conjugal couples, same-sex or cross-sex, in their demands. Instead, they called for recognition of 'the flexible kinship and friendship networks within which LGBT immigrants live and work'. This led to several major organisations declining to endorse the statement, and may have limited mobilisation around it.[146] Yet the goal of moving beyond dominant family forms is one worth fighting for.

Discussions of sexual liberation in queer milieus increasingly focus on the idea of polyamory, of '(usually long-term) intimate and sexual relationships with multiple partners simultaneously'.[147] Its advocates take up the call of early lesbian/gay liberation for non-monogamy, while being less subject to co-optation by commercialised sex on demand because more insistent on ongoing emotional bonds. The ideal of polyamory strikingly resembles the vision Kollontai put forward a century ago. ' "Love" has many faces and aspects', many 'shades of feeling', she cautioned. Kollontai welcomed the unprecedented variety of sexual relationships she saw around her, opposing 'any formal limits on love', any distinction between long- and short-term relationships and any imposition of monogamy as a norm, since 'a frequent change of partners by no means signifies sexual intemperance'. She argued that the complexity of love was best recognised through an ideal of 'love-comradeship' that was non-exclusive and valued mutual respect, mutual sensitivity and the ability to

---

144   Ritchie 2010, p. 565.
145   Barker 2012, p. 179 (citing Kath Weston).
146   DasGupta 2011/2012.
147   Barker 2012, p. 176 (citing Jin Haritaworn, Chin-ju Lin and Christian Klesse).

listen, 'based on the unfamiliar ideas of complete freedom, equality and genuine friendship'.[148]

None of this amounts to a blueprint. Neither friendship nor desire can be dictated or rationally prescribed; no one can say with certainty when or why the two will or will not coincide. It is at least possible now to resist the dogmas that (as the ancient Athenians believed) friendship necessarily excludes sex, that (as in the Boston marriages in the past) intimate same-sex friendships must look sexless to the outside world, or that (for some gay men especially in the 1970s) only ex-lovers can be friends. Now friendship should be possible to combine with a spectrum of physical affection, in which questions of genitality and penetration need not be decisive – thus fostering polymorphous perversity and undermining the gay/straight binary. A wide range of configurations has to be allowed for, of different numbers of friends and/or lovers in various emotional and sexual combinations. Sometimes they can even blur the distinction between friends, lovers and 'families we choose'.

All these configurations constitute forms of resistance to the most intimate manifestations of the new gay normality: specifically, the new domestic paradigm and new 'love doctrine' now being propagated by supposedly gay-friendly psychoanalysts. In the face of this 1950s neo-Freudianism revived for the new millennium, there is a need to return to the defence of sexual outlaws and dissidents,[149] and a crying need for 'just trying to think outside the box'.[150] Queering domesticity means rejecting the impulse to form 'normal' gay/lesbian families founded on the romance of the couple and of overconsumption.

At the same time, queer radicals need to resist the tendency that still exists in the radical left to treat sexual relationships and close emotional ties as non-political and to relegate them to the private realm. Besides the real and sometimes vital material benefits that recognition of relationships can entail in capitalist states, the impulse to celebrate and share love – sexual or not – is a positive human impulse and helps strengthen broader communities. A queer politics of relationship should be linked to what the US statement 'Beyond Same-Sex Marriage' in 2006 called 'the widespread hunger for authentic and just community' and 'a sense of caring community and connectedness'.[151]

Besides an emotional relationship, queer kinship is also an intensely practical relationship. 'Economic justice and queerness, when truly brought together, say that we are connected across love and the deepest forms of self-expression

---

148   Kollontai 1978, pp. 241, 287, 289, 288, 291, 229.
149   Herzog 2014 (citing Kenneth Lewes).
150   Shah 2011/2012 (citing Ignacio Rivera).
151   Abramovitz et al. 2006.

and ... also ... in the ways we support each other'. This includes the networks that provide childcare and eldercare, and the people who choose to share living space and transport.[152] The catch is that while care is 'essential and mutually enriching', under capitalism it is also risky for the carer, who by 'using her fixed resources – time, money, paid or unpaid leave from work – ... reduces her ability to protect herself against the normal vagaries of life'. Legal marriage can give carers a form of insurance,[153] but one enmeshed in existing structures of inequality. The illusion should always be resisted that ideal personal solutions are possible in a neoliberal society that constantly eats away at the time, space, stability and emotional energy needed to sustain friendships and loving bonds.[154]

Partnership

A project of queering intimacy and domesticity should be the basic matrix for queer positions on same-sex civil unions and marriage, rejecting and moving beyond marriage as a middle-class strategy for advancement in neoliberal society. LGBT commitment ceremonies do often break with the conventionality of most weddings, and LGBT parenting often involves calling on adults who are not blood kin to share childcare.[155] Demanding that recognition of same-sex love be enshrined in the right to marry, however, often entails a celebration of romantic love, which is a very specific kind of kinship. The ideal of romantic love has a specific European history, from medieval chivalry to Protestant ideals of domesticity to nineteenth-century romantic novels. European and North American ideals of marriage are one product of that history. These ideals have been spread by global media, and they influence LGBT people as well. But many sexual relationships have as much to do with satisfying desire, holding together family and community, or surviving economically as they do with romance. As queers formulate their demands, they do not have to privilege relationships based on romantic love as the universal prism through which struggles around intimacy and domesticity must be refracted.

Instead a queer anti-capitalism can and should reaffirm the strand of utopian libertarianism on sexual matters that flourished in the early years of the Russian Revolution. It should uphold Kollontai's libertarian view of a future

---

152   Raffo 2011/2012.
153   Vaid, Duggan, Metz and Hollibaugh 2013.
154   Sears 2006/7.
155   D'Emilio 2002, p. 190.

eros 'freed from the constraints of private property, sex inequality, and hypo-critical moral convention', and her acknowledgement of 'the value of experi-mentation in ... love relationships'.[156]

This does not mean replacing the current model of normal gay families with a fully worked-out blueprint for a different setup. The model of a lesbian/gay community presented to us by moderates is antiseptic, commercial, and based on the 'pink market'. However, many LGBT people are not unequivocally loyal to either that model or a radical vision of queer freedom. Most people are not ideologues. They often hold contradictory ideas, some moderate, some radical, which they do not always even see as contradictory. Radical ideas can some-times be effectively promoted and moderate ones undermined by mobilising the LGBT community broadly.

For example, two men or two women who get married mimicking the forms of heterosexual marriage, with a 'bride' in white, are not necessarily a purely reactionary phenomenon. The ceremony can be, in Nicola Barker's words, 'framed as a demand for positive recognition of *difference* rather than same-ness', as a way of 'queering marriage' – all the more so when it includes explicit vows to fight homophobia, or men dancing down the aisle carrying flowers.[157] Didier Eribon made a comparable call in 2006 for a 'resignification' of marriage that would 'shake the existing order'.[158] But while a same-sex ceremony can and should deconstruct and undermine heterosexual marriage, it does not do so necessarily or exclusively. It does different things at once, some consciously, some unconsciously. For example, a man who wants to marry another man, or a woman who wants to marry another woman, is probably not looking for a legal license to rape, even though in some countries today there is still legally no such thing as rape in marriage. The partners presumably want to affirm their love, their relationship, and the legitimacy of same-sex desire – all of which are positive – and are not necessarily conscious of the negative sides of the institution they are reinforcing.

In this sense, Kevin Floyd is right: same-sex marriage is not 'inherently con-servative or assimilationist', and it 'deserves to be taken more seriously than it has within queer politics'. But it does not follow that the question is merely one of 'political vocabulary'.[159] So far, the issue of equal marriage rights has been predominantly framed in a way that legitimates marriage as an institution, pri-vatises social needs that could and should be addressed collectively, and thus

---

156   Healey 2001, pp. 110–11.
157   Barker 2012, pp. 93, 125–6.
158   Cervulle and Rees-Roberts 2010, pp. 28–9.
159   Floyd 1998, p. 197.

fits the issue into a neoliberal, individualist vision. The challenge for the left is to demand changes in partnership laws that go beyond reform, designing a challenge to inequality in rights to marriage that also challenges the broader inequalities of which marriage is part and parcel.

A vigorous defence of equal rights for same-sex marriage, founded on the urgency of same-sex partners' practical needs for health benefits, tax breaks, immigrant status and housing rights, should therefore be accompanied by a politics that at least implicitly critiques the institution of marriage and the way the capitalist nuclear family privatises the satisfaction of social needs. However much marriage has evolved over the past century, it is still part of the nuclear family. That suggests the need for a dual agenda: defending people's right to civil marriage, as a basic question of equality, and at the same time stressing that the human impulse to celebrate a loving relationship can be honoured in ways that dissociate it from state-sanctioned marriage. A fight for equal rights to marriage can at the same time highlight the limitations of the privatised provision of childcare and human needs, and the insistence on stability with scant regard for emotional or intellectual needs, that the institution embodies.

A radical queer approach to partnership also demands a sophisticated analysis of its sexual side, recognising the increasingly flexible attitudes towards sexual fidelity that many romantic and domestic couples have today. A radical queer alternative should affirm such attitudes while going beyond them, exploring ways of celebrating, supporting and defending friendship and community, open to varying degrees and in varying ways to erotic possibility and sexual transgression, against the exclusive demands of couplehood *and* the seductions of commodified sex.

It is never too soon to start formulating further demands, more radical demands that go beyond the limits of same-sex marriage laws that have been won so far. This could mean a continuing, widening, and more inclusive mobilisation, based on an understanding of the limitations of the rights that existing laws grant, and reaching out to those in LGBT communities whose needs are least addressed by them. It would be 'tragic to allow marriage equality to destroy or marginalize the pioneering work of queer families who have taught us that family is more complicated and more fulfilling than traditional models of marriage can ever capture'.[160]

In the longer run, a radical queer approach should lead to the demand formulated in the US 'Beyond Same-Sex Marriage' statement for '*access to a flexible set of economic benefits and options regardless of sexual orientation, race,*

---

160   Harris-Perry 2013, p. 10.

gender/gender identity, class, or citizenship status'.[161] This could take the form of a multi-tiered system with a range of possible 'designated family relationships',[162] reframing equality as 'the right to form a family and share household resources inside and outside marriage'.[163] This means demanding recognition and support for a much more varied range of sexual, emotional and living arrangements, de-linking issues of who people have sex with, who they cohabit with, who they share income and expenses with and who they raise children with. In the end, it dovetails with radical demands like: 'Disestablish marriage. Get the state out of the business. Abolish the legal category' – and instead 'create an intimate union status expressly tailored to protecting intimate care in various forms'.[164]

This can give the radical left an angle to tackle the issue of same-sex marriage differently from the right and centre-left. We should not turn our backs on all the same-sex couples who yearn for marriage equality; as long as there are practical or symbolic benefits to be gained by marrying, same-sex couples should have an equal right to them. But we can take a transitional approach to the issue, supporting the demand for equality in a way that points beyond marriage.

This should mean, for example, mobilising LGBT parents, who are often divorced from cross-sex spouses and not always in new couples with same-sex partners, and particularly lesbian mothers. The neoliberal state may be increasingly tolerant of alternative family forms as long as they, like heterosexual nuclear families, shoulder the economic cost of caring for their members' needs. But the fundamental interest of the state in a capitalist society – especially the neoliberal lean state – in ensuring the privatised reproduction of the labour force is likely to perpetuate the second-class status of same-sex and single parents. By far the most effective way of ensuring that parents will do the hard, unpaid work of raising children is to rely on the deep-rooted ideological sense of the natural – meaning biological – bond between parent and child. Even as more room opens up for lesbian and gay parenting and other alternative family forms, there are strong pressures to continue to define alternatives as exceptional and conditional.

These pressures are manifest in the many ways LGBT parents are treated as second-class and hemmed in by heteronormative rules. Even in countries where same-sex marriage has been won, for example, a fierce battle is almost

---

161   Abramovitz et al. 2006.
162   Barker 2012, pp. 201–2 (citing Nancy Polikoff).
163   DeFilippis 2011/2012a.
164   Vaid, Duggan, Metz and Hollibaugh 2013.

always required to win the right to medically assisted reproduction, which undermines the stubborn privileging of genetic parenthood.[165] So far, no partnership or marriage law has recognised birth mothers' female partners as fully equal. Often co-mothers are offered only access to expensive, time-consuming adoption procedures. At best (as in the Netherlands since 2013) the law allows automatic legal parenthood for co-mothers only in cases where there is an anonymous sperm donor (an option that is actually impeded by the current law).[166] A radical demand would be automatic parental rights for all female co-mothers from the moment of birth, while leaving rights and responsibilities open for the biological father and other co-parents in forms the mothers could choose from a range of legally defined options.

The left should at the same time demand that children receive support from the community as a whole; hundreds of millions of stressed parents should welcome this. We should demand that the rights and responsibilities of social parenthood be uncoupled from the often-questionable fact of biological fatherhood. This would make the left a natural voice not only for all the lesbian mothers who are today denied equal parenting rights, but also for millions of LGBT people who remember how alienating it was to grow up in families structurally defined as straight.

A radical queer approach would also entail demanding individualisation of rights for LGBT people who are not in couples and may not want to be part of couples, particularly for those who choose not to be financially dependent on someone else. Rights to healthcare, welfare benefits or legal residency, for example, should not depend on living with someone with a job. Nor should single people have to subsidise people in couples. These demands imply an attack on the neoliberal agenda, because social provisions require money and cut into profits. They are radical left demands that correspond to real needs of real LGBT people. They could also make the left the champion of still more millions of people who are single by circumstance or choice.[167]

In short, a radical queer approach should not be limited *either* to tinkering with or queering legal marriage or partnership, *or* to purely social and economic demands without regard to partnerships. Without adequate levels of social support, the most ideal partnership will still leave the people in it alienated and isolated; without sustaining emotional and sexual bonds, even people whose material needs are fully provided for will still be lonely. So we

---

165   Barker 2012, pp. 50–1.
166   Hofman 2013, p. 39.
167   This approach to the issue of same-sex marriage is outlined in Fourth International 2003, point 17.

need both to look at the wider society beyond marriage and to challenge core elements of marriage as an institution. For example, demands for marriage equality should be combined with demands to provide benefits to individuals without regard to marital status, thus eliminating humiliating forms of dependency that the law now creates and perpetuates, and to tax capital gains and inheritance much more progressively, thus avoiding turning marriage equality into a further boon for those who already have too much. This would make it possible to attack the heteronormative aspect of marriage without accepting it as an appropriate mechanism for distributing social resources.[168]

A two-pronged approach to partnership, both queering it and looking beyond it, would avoid the pitfall of seeing legal experts as the 'technocrats of an unfolding Utopia'. It would, for example, save us from getting too bogged down in the details of same-sex marriage versus other forms of legal partnership recognition. Unfortunately, the steady forward march of same-sex marriage is often eliminating the small degree of flexibility that other forms of recognition have sometimes offered. For example, same-sex civil marriage in South Africa has undermined any push for same-sex inclusion in customary or Muslim marriage, which can have great social importance.[169] Without exaggerating the importance of the differences among various forms, radical queers can use what existing flexibility there is now as evidence in advocating for a far greater range of possibilities in the future.

A simultaneous focus on queering partnership and moving beyond it can also avoid one of the least helpful of possible debates: over whether a same-sex couple who get married are doing 'the right thing'. As György Lukács argued almost a century ago, a true understanding of how the bourgeois state functions should allow us to 'slough off both the cretinism of legality and the romanticism of illegality', leaving questions of engaging or not engaging in legal forms 'to be resolved on the spur of the moment ... on the basis of *immediate expediencies*. In this wholly unprincipled solution lies the only possible practical and principled rejection of the bourgeois legal system'.[170]

Queer anti-capitalists clearly face a formidable array of tasks in developing a radical sexual politics. We need to blur the boundaries of the gay/straight binary by queering public space, and at the same time by more or less discretely queering the structures of personal life within communities of the oppressed. We need to subvert gender and defend a left feminist agenda by helping to build a working-class movement for reproductive and sexual freedom, and

168   Barker 2012, p. 197.
169   Barker 2012, pp. 169 (citing Carol Smart), 108–9.
170   Lukács 1972, pp. 270, 264.

through the struggles of lesbians, bisexuals, trans and intersex people, fighting for all the demands for reform and for more sweeping transformation that these struggles entail. We need to push to fully include a range of sexual and gender dissenters in queer communities, for example, by supporting the self-organisation and sexual autonomy of young queers. We need to champion global and anti-racist queer solidarity in fights in defence of queer refugees and migrants and against aid conditionality, Islamophobia and pinkwashing. And we need to queer intimate and domestic life through building queer alternative communities, queering existing families, shaping polyamory and working for queer alternative proposals on partnership and parenting.

Yet even this exhausting agenda is not exhaustive. Beyond the specifically sexual programme of a queer radical politics, queer anti-capitalists also need to push sexual and social transformation by queering a range of other, less directly sex-focused movements. This additional set of tasks is the subject of chapter 6.

Queering Broader Movements

Queers' intransigent affirmation of the claims of desire immediately ran up against a major contradiction of neoliberal consumerism. Neoliberal societies summon up a myriad of desires and suggest they should be easily fulfilled. But in real life, 'the satisfaction of these desires must be borne by the individuals themselves, as much as they can afford'. In insisting on the legitimacy of queer desire, queers implicitly demand that desire be capable of realisation, independently of the money and privilege needed to have wants fulfilled in a neoliberal order. Queer activism thus had a tendency from the start to contest neoliberalism.[1]

If it is to successfully help challenge and defeat neoliberalism, a queer politics cannot be a merely personal or cultural project. As chapter 5 showed, it requires an independent queer political movement that fights for radical sexual demands. At the same time, it requires a social transformation that LGBT people cannot bring about in isolation. Queers need allies. To be effective allies for a queer politics, broader, class-based and other social movements need to be queered: opened up to queer people, queer leadership, queer issues and queer approaches to organising. Chapter 6 focuses on the prospects for queering these broader movements.

Only queered movements can address basic LGBT needs like housing for queer relationships, and safety and independence for queer youth. Movements around healthcare from ACT UP to the South African Treatment Action Campaign have been exemplary cases of queered social movements. Going beyond these movements, since the working class in the broad sense is indispensable to social transformation, labour activism too has to be queered. This can involve work-related organising that existing unions are not yet tackling – in the sex trade, for example. At the same time, the queering of existing unions should be linked to challenges to bureaucracy and class collaboration.

Given how embattled individual social movements have been under neoliberalism, the twenty-first century has witnessed the rise of an attempt to join different anti-neoliberal movements into a unified force: the global justice movement. It too needs to be queered. So does the anti-capitalist left, which remains necessary to provide political direction in the battle against capital and the state, but needs to be rebuilt and imbued with a new dynamism if

---

1 Woltersdorff 2011, pp. 178–9, 165.

it is to be made fit-for-purpose and overcome its current weakness. Finally, this chapter argues, democracy itself needs to be queered, to make it inclusive of all those whom neoliberal democracy today excludes, and to make it embrace sexual and other realms of life that capitalism declares out of bounds to democracy.

Basics of Queer Anti-Capitalism

This overview makes clear that while personal politics is undoubtedly important, a radical queer politics also has to involve organising and activism in the public sphere. LGBT people have the potential to play a significant role in challenging the existing world order. Mobilisation and self-organisation of those who suffer most directly from neoliberalism, though offering no panaceas, are nevertheless indispensable. Self-organisation, including LGBT self-organisation, needs to take place in the most basic units of society – families (traditional kinship-based families or 'families of choice') and communities – so as to counter policies imposed from above by the state and capital.

Another core dynamic has to be solidarity. Far-reaching queer demands that do not fit into any existing government's or mainstream current's agenda can only be won by building a powerful oppositional force. A credible prospect of realising and sustaining alternatives to neoliberal sexual politics requires deploying a broad constellation of social forces. An intersectional or transversal politics, including alliances against sexism, racism and neoliberal globalisation, is not just a practical requirement for making headway in LGBT politics; it is constitutive of what an effectively radical queer force would be. Queer people cannot be themselves in most workplaces or lead healthy lives except as part of queered labour and healthcare movements. Genuine democratic participation by queers is only possible as part of a broader movement to transform formal, manipulative democracy into genuine, substantive democracy.

So what would a queer anti-capitalism look like? It would necessarily have some things in common with the existing anti-capitalist left. In any event, it would not turn its back on LGBT people who are older, or those in steady relationships, or those with decent-paying jobs. Queer anti-capitalists are a natural component of the '99 percent' that movements like Occupy and the *indignad@s* have worked to rally against the crisis. The potential of queer anti-capitalism was manifest in the visible LGBT presence in the massive protests in 2013 in Brazil and Turkey. Negatively, as Ghassan Makarem has noted, the Egyptian revolution has raised issues of gender and sexuality 'from day one', mainly because both the old regime and Islamic fundamentalists have used gender and sexual prejudice against the uprising. Over time, this can have a positive impact on young rebels' feminist and queer consciousness.[2]

A queer anti-capitalism cannot give up the battle for legal reforms. Not every sexual issue lends itself to legal reform, of course; sometimes, individual action or changing the social climate is what counts. But often stopping state repression and wresting resources from the state are crucial, in basic fights against violence, criminalisation and discrimination, as well as more ambitious struggles for equality, for example, in parenting. These fights demand the broadest possible unity across different LGBT identities. It is in the interests of all LGBT people to unite against the discrimination that still exists to some extent in all societies; victories over discrimination bring greater or lesser gains to all sexual and gender dissenters, at least potentially. On other issues, LGBT rights can be best defended by working and demanding space within still broader movements, such as trade unions, the women's movement and the global justice movement. So a concrete, radical approach to specific LGBT issues involves looking for strategies and tactics that are effective in mobilising people and promoting unity on specific issues.

At the same time, a queer anti-capitalist approach to reforms has to look beyond reforms. It requires a focus on the longer term, on the systemic change that is indispensable to defending and deepening reforms in the face of the system's dynamic of reining them in and hollowing them out. And genuine unity in the fight for reforms has to fully include people who are neither rich, nor professional, nor respectable, who are often marginalised by the fake unity of mainstream organisations. A queer anti-capitalist approach to winning reforms must be based on an understanding of the imperatives of gendered capitalism and the need to resist them. It means fighting for the broadest possible LGBT unity – in the sense of a mobilising and inclusive unity against neoliberal heteronormativity.

In general, an alternative to the reformist vision of lesbian/gay rights has to be an integral part of an alternative global vision: a vision of a more social, more democratic, more feminist world. The starting point in realising this vision is the self-organisation of oppressed people in social movements. LGBT people have created social movements of their own; at the same time, LGBT movements crosscut other social movements in ways that need to be made explicit. Queering the social movements is an enormous task that remains to be tackled worldwide, with a view to developing multi-issue coalitions.[3]

---

2   Email from Ghassan Makarem, 21 July 2013.
3   Feinberg 1998, p. 104.

The way neoliberal globalisation sets working people at opposite corners
of the earth in cutthroat competition with each other throws up barriers to
self-organisation. Nevertheless, discontent with their fate under neoliberalism, combined with the upheavals and questioning resulting from economic
restructuring, have spurred the subordinate actors within traditional families
and communities – women and LGBT people – to organise themselves. Self-
organisation of LGBT people, though encountering even greater resistance
and taking place on a more modest scale than women's self-organisation, has
a similar potential to help bring about needed changes at the grassroots level.
Women's and LGBT self-organisation, whether in separate women's or LGBT
spaces or in existing institutions, always risks replicating or mimicking existing relations of domination as long as such inequitable relations prevail in the
larger society. But as Penelope Duggan has pointed out, they can also pose a
challenge to the habits and organisational forms of traditionally straight-male-
dominated, gender-normative and heteronormative trade unions and movements for change.[4]

At the local level, the New York group Queers for Economic Justice, founded
in 2002, was for twelve years a unique example of a new, promising, alternative queer way of organising. Its goal, as defined in its mission statement, was
to 'challenge and change the systems that create poverty and economic injustice in our communities, and to promote an economic system that embraces
sexual and gender diversity'. Upholding the principle that access to social and
economic resources is a fundamental right, it took up a wide range of social
issues. Its grassroots organising, 'always informed by the lived experiences and
expressed needs of queer people in poverty', sought to overcome the invisibility of poor queers in both LGBT rights and economic justice movements.[5]
In the words of its executive director, Amber Hollibaugh, she wanted a movement that 'queers the reality of Walmart line jobs, sex work and homeless shel-
ters', that focuses on queer economic survival and on LGBT lives shaped by
capitalism.[6]

Social movements fighting for housing, education and welfare programmes
need to follow this example, recognising the LGBT people among those they
are fighting for and the specific importance of social movement demands
for sexual liberation. Specific demands must be formulated on a range of
economic issues so as to reflect LGBT experience, needs and creativity. This
chapter cannot undertake a comprehensive survey of queer social movement

---

4   Duggan 1997.
5   DeFilippis 2011/2012a.
6   Vaid, Duggan, Metz and Hollibaugh 2013.

organising, but it can attempt to set out a general approach: mobilising broadly for reforms in ways that point beyond mere reforms. It showcases a few specific movements, for different reasons in each case. It discusses housing organising because of the vital importance of living space to the possibility of living queer lives. It discusses healthcare organising because of the especially inspiring queer politics that have been developed in that movement. And it looks at workplace organising because of the strategic centrality of working people to transforming and queering society.

LGBT people have a specific stake in winning recognition in practice of the human right to housing, since physical space is a precondition for the flourishing of human sexuality and relationships. Decent and affordable housing for poor and low-income people, an important goal in itself, must take account of the diversity of households and communities. In South African black townships, for example, where families often sleep eight to a room, 'there is simply no space to be gay'.[7] LGBT people's need for physical space for same-sex relationships is also evident in Cuba, where same-sex couples cannot find space of their own in the overcrowded housing or even rent hotel rooms together except by grace of a well-disposed manager. They have had to resort to beaches, rooftops, empty lots or public toilets.[8] Even in Cuba, with its vaunted healthcare and education, hard times since the 1990s and linkages between welfare provision and heteronormative family structures have made LGBT people even more dependent on their families of origin for space to live in.[9]

This makes it crucial to assert the right of LGBT people and unmarried people generally to housing. In Venezuela, for example, linkages between the renters' movement and the Revolutionary Alliance for Sex-Gender Diversity won the adoption of two articles of the housing law banning discrimination on the basis of sexual orientation.[10] In New York's Greenwich Village, the grassroots youth group FIERCE, made up largely of young LGBT people of colour, has resisted the displacement by luxury development plans of LGBT people of colour, homeless youth and men in search of sex. FIERCE won a few tentative victories in 2007 and 2008 for the inclusion of its constituents' space in the development plans.[11] Queers for Economic Justice won other victories in New York on this front in the last several years. For example, they secured a policy that gives homeless trans people the right to choose for either the men's or

---

7   Gevisser 2000, pp. 126–7.

8   Lumsden 1996, pp. 155–6, 189; Arguelles and Rich 1989, pp. 452–3.

9   Lumsden 1996, p. 194.

10   Blanco, Spronk and Webber 2012.

11   Mananzala 2011/2012.

women's side of the emergency shelter system. Another policy gives registered domestic partners the same right as married couples to emergency family shelter.[12] At some point, queer housing organising needs to go further, to challenge a housing market structured around the pursuit of profit, which has never produced enough affordable housing for those whose need is greatest and whose incomes are lowest.

Efforts to fight poverty among older people must recognise LGBT seniors' specificity: the relatively greater weakness of their support from children and from family and kinship networks, their concentration in more expensive urban centres, and lack of pensions resulting from livelihoods gained in non-traditional or non-professional fields more open to LGBT people.[13] Queering social movements can even be a fruitful approach to issues that are usually not seen as social movement issues at all. The San Francisco LGBT group Community United Against Violence has pioneered alternatives to a repressive approach to violence, linking hate violence on the streets to domestic violence and state violence. In New York City, the Audre Lorde Project's Safe Neighbourhoods Campaign emphasises community accountability in combating both street and police violence.[14] Queer organising against violence directly confronts heteronormativity, since it is those who most openly deviate from the heterosexual norm who are most often targets of queer-bashing. It also indirectly undermines homonormativity, since lesbians and gays able to pass as 'normal' tend to suffer less from attacks on the street and by police.

The response of governments to such demands, when it is not simply denial and repression, is often that 'the money just isn't there' to implement them. This smokescreen needs to be blown away. LGBT people along with others need to highlight the frightful contrast between, for example, the relatively small sums needed to treat AIDS and other deadly diseases worldwide (according to a 1994 United Nations estimate, US $5–7 billion a year for ten years),[15] and the gargantuan amounts that every year go to debt service and to military spending ($1.56 trillion in 2013, with the US, as chief enforcer of the neoliberal world order, spending 39 percent of the global total).[16]

Queering from within social movements has its potential limitations. Grassroots social movements have the advantage that the people with the most urgent and direct stake in change have a close relationship to them, but

12   Duggan 2011/2012a.
13   Hollibaugh 2011/2012b.
14   Whitlock 2011/2012.
15   Toussaint 1999, pp. 238–9.
16   See http://en.wikipedia.org/wiki/List_of_countries_by_military_expenditures.

the disadvantage that their social base can put them under pressure to achieve quick results and keep to the narrowest possible focus. This can come at the expense of long-term, fundamental sexual and social change. As a result, in LGBT as in feminist movements, grassroots groups can become 'primarily *advocates for* rather than *mobilizers of* their constituency'.[17] There are risks of bureaucratisation, dependence on donors, and subordination of trans people and other sexual minorities. One key safeguard is to consistently orient organising to the long-term interests of the working class as a whole, since even the most privileged working people ultimately share interests antagonistic to capital and to the bureaucracies that shield capital. Another is to build strong links between solid LGBT activist bases in social movements, on the one hand, and radical political movements, on the other.

Queering Healthcare Organising

The politics of healthcare is probably the best example so far of the queering of a grassroots social movement. LGBT people, particularly those who are HIV-positive or at great risk of seroconversion, have a high stake in insisting that consumers of healthcare must have a decisive voice in its provision. They understand from their own experience how crucial it is that healthcare is considered a right, not a commodity. The fight against pharmaceutical multinationals and the rest of the global medical industry is based on the insistence that the human right to healthcare prevail over 'intellectual property rights' and profits. The logical extension of this insistence is the demand that access to every form of healthcare be universally guaranteed worldwide as a right, not a privilege, and provided as a basic public service rather than commercially. While queer healthcare organising is still far from winning these essentially socialist demands, it has put challenges to the prerogatives of private property on the political agenda on several continents. It has even succeeded in reining in the logic of for-profit pharmaceutical research and development and intellectual property rights.

LGBT people's pioneering of safer sex and changes in the marketing of anti-retroviral drugs have increasingly meant that sex between males need not mean infection, and infection need not mean death – but lifetime HIV treatment costs in the US were estimated not long ago to be around $600,000. A report of 2012 concluded, 'No population in the developed world has been as heavily affected by HIV as Black men in the U.S. who have sex with other men

---

17   Brenner 2003, p. 81.

(MSMs)', who constituted almost one in four of new HIV infections in the US, one in six of people living with HIV, and 22.4 percent of new US infections.[18] Instead of care, those most vulnerable to AIDS often face repression. 'Sex work and street-level drug dealing and drug use are the places that produce the most risk around HIV', with a disproportionate presence of black people and women, and 'places that have been targeted for the heaviest forms of policing'.[19]

Trans people too have suffered disproportionately from AIDS, particularly if they depend on sex work for survival or share needles for injecting hormones. As a result, they now have one of the world's highest HIV infection rates.[20] Care disparities have been worst in countries without virtually universal care, including many dependent countries, but also the US. Healthcare organised for profit cannot 'make even the remotest dent in racial and economic disparities' in a system based on capitalism: 'the business models just won't work'.[21]

Although for a few years AIDS diverted LGBT attention from conventional politics, AIDS and AIDS-inspired repression quickly became forceful stimuli to organising. The spread of AIDS has highlighted and increased the role of LGBT community networks in many countries in securing healthcare for their members. In most dependent regions, LGBT access to commercial or official healthcare has been anything but automatic. In country after country, existing LGBT networks have been crucial to securing care for seropositive people, not only through political battles, but also through ongoing, day-to-day service provision.

LGBT organising in a number of dependent countries laid the basis for grassroots queer healthcare movements, in some cases creating LGBT movements in countries where they had never existed before. Inadequate or repressive responses by health authorities to AIDS sometimes provided the spark. In Costa Rica, for example, the health ministry's raids on gay bars, mandatory testing, and several murders in 1987 gave rise to a wave of protest and the founding of the country's first LGBT groups.[22] AIDS also prompted the formation of groups in Guatemala, Kenya, Malaysia, Singapore, Thailand and Vietnam, which, while not strictly speaking gay, were in fact their countries' first tolerated, largely-LGBT public organisations. Safer-sex workshops enabled the originally predominantly white Gays and Lesbians of Zimbabwe (founded in 1990)

---

18   Black AIDS Institute 2012, pp. 37, 9, 15.
19   Hollibaugh and Singh 1999, p. 82.
20   Stryker 2008, pp. 113–14.
21   Black AIDS Institute 2012, p. 22 (citing David Malebranche).
22   Schifter Sikora 1989.

to make contact with an informal black gay network.[23] AIDS activism was also part of the emergence of gay organising in the Soviet Union in the 1980s.[24] A striking case was the cooperation that took place between LGBT activists and the ministry of health in Sandinista Nicaragua.[25] In China too, AIDS work with gay men has become possible, though the first person to attempt it (in 1994) was sacked by the Chinese government.[26]

AIDS activism in the dependent world has largely followed the trajectory of women's activism. In Latin America, for example, beginning in the 1980s women's movements were increasingly channelled into NGOs focused on apolitical service provision,[27] moving from solidarity to advocacy and from identity to policy, sometimes sacrificing democracy to expediency.[28] Sometimes they have been complicit in the ways international financial institutions have used ' "women's empowerment" to distract attention from [their programmes'] distinctly disempowering effects'.[29] AIDS activism has also been embraced by international development agencies and financial institutions, with contradictory results. Aid from international agencies, health ministries and private foundations has turned many struggling AIDS activist groups into well-established NGOs since the 1980s.[30] In general, the result has been an ongoing tension between their founders' impulses for sexual liberation and pressure from donors to tone down the message.

The transnational character of HIV/AIDS organising is manifest, and frustrated, by restrictions on entry and residence by HIV-positive people, imposed by 64 countries around the world. The battle against such restrictions continues – buoyed by the overturning of the US ban in 2010 after years of dogged organising.[31]

In the US, the 1987 LGB March on Washington by 600,000 people showed that the crisis was generating a new anger and militancy.[32] The AIDS Coalition to Unleash Power (ACT UP), founded in New York that same year, provided an international impetus to a militant, visibly queer movement around healthcare. Following the 1987 march, other ACT UP groups were founded, not only

23   Drucker 1996, p. 95; Mburu 2000, p. 187.
24   Healey 2001, pp. 245, 247.
25   Randall 2000, pp. 96–7.
26   Rofel 1999, p. 452.
27   Dashner 1987, p. 70.
28   Alvarez 2000, pp. 3–4, 23.
29   Brenner 2010, p. 60.
30   Lind and Share 2003, p. 56.
31   Ordover 2011/2012.
32   D'Emilio 1989, p. 472.

in major US cities like Los Angeles and San Francisco, but also smaller ones like Oklahoma City, Shreveport and Orlando. Together they transformed the way drugs were tested and approved in the US, and won protection for HIV-positive people under the Americans with Disabilities Act.[33] Cathy Cohen cited ACT UP New York's needle exchange and prison projects as prime examples of the potential of 'principled transformative coalition work'.[34] For a time in the early 1990s, ACT UP New York worked with trade unions and the National Organisation for Women on organising a national march for universal healthcare – a far more progressive programme than the one finally adopted almost two decades later under Barack Obama's presidency – only to see the effort stall due to lack of commitment from ACT UP's allies.[35]

Soon after the founding of ACT UP New York, and of similar ACT UP groups in other North American cities, the direct action movement against AIDS began to demonstrate its internationalist spirit and potential. Activist AIDS groups took the name ACT UP in Paris and Amsterdam, while groups elsewhere with other names picked up some aspects of the ACT UP model. The model has shown remarkable success in challenging both heteronormativity and the power of major multinational corporations. AIDS activists internationally joined in Durban, South Africa, in July 2000 to denounce the international financial institutions and their policies of trade liberalisation as responsible for the 'millions [who] have died of AIDS and tens of millions...infected with HIV'.[36]

The apogee so far of grassroots queer HIV/AIDS activism has probably been reached with South Africa's Treatment Action Campaign (TAC). TAC built on earlier links between LGBT and anti-apartheid activism to put the ANC government under pressure and eventually win an unprecedented (though still inadequate) degree of access to HIV drugs for poor and low-income people in a dependent country. Even more impressively, if that were possible, TAC became a central player in the fight against drug patents in the hands of pharmaceutical multinationals and against intellectual property rights, a key component of the free trade agenda of international neoliberalism. It has been an outstanding example of the queering of a social movement agenda. The fights for access to anti-HIV drugs in all countries, especially poor ones, and against US

33   D'Emilio and Freedman 1997, pp. 366–8.
34   Cohen 2005, p. 45.
35   Conversations at the time with ACT UP New York activist Steve Ault, confirmed by email 26 February 2013.
36   ACT UP 2000.

attempts to make countries give up their hard-won rights to produce or import generic drugs remain key, and implicitly anti-capitalist, demands.[37]

A revealing contrast can be drawn between AIDS care in South Africa since TAC's victories and in non-capitalist Cuba. The standard of healthcare for the poor majority in Cuba is far higher than in South Africa; the availability of anti-HIV drugs was virtually taken for granted rather than a hard-won victory. Despite the least justifiable, most restrictive aspects of the Cuban quarantine of HIV-positive people, public health measures (along with the embargo) have helped ensure a far lower rate of HIV infection than in other Latin American countries, let alone South Africa. Yet *machista* and heteronormative assumptions have made it hard to conduct safer-sex education in Cuba and have placed disproportionate reliance on professional, centralised medicine, and the percentage of male infections due to same-sex contact has risen[38] – though the situation has improved somewhat recently due to the work of the National Sex Education Centre led by Mariela Castro.

Including and moving beyond HIV and AIDS, there is still a major fight to be waged to win equality in healthcare for trans people, who face systematic discrimination – tragically illustrated by the case of US transman Robert Eads, who died of ovarian cancer after being unable to get healthcare because of his transgender history.[39] Intersex people are waging a comparable battle against routine surgery on intersex newborns (treated in nine cases out of ten 'as girls because "it's easier" '). The issue was highlighted in 1996 when a bill before the US Congress to prohibit clitoral surgery on daughters of African immigrants was worded to permit ongoing surgery on intersex newborns, despite protests by the Intersex Society of North America. The debate exposed the hypocrisy of a law that only targeted 'irrational and unscientific' Africans.[40]

The point is not to stigmatise people working in healthcare. On the contrary, changing healthcare requires a dialogue with healthcare workers.[41] More generally, labour-community alliances are vital to defending, improving and transforming social services.

---

37   See Fourth International 2003, point 16.
38   Lumsden 1996, pp. 160–77.
39   Stryker 2008, p. 140.
40   Feinberg 1998, pp. 89, 91 (citing Cheryl Chase).
41   Feinberg 1998, p. 82.

Queering Workplace Organising

The utopian potential of queer radicalism depends on social movements, including current queer focuses on 'coalition building between and among queer resistance, anticapitalist and antiracist work, immigrant rights, anticolonial struggle, and movements for national self-determination'.[42] But alliances broad enough to seriously challenge, let alone overthrow, the rule of capital will need to go even further, organising on a vaster scale than anyone has managed so far. In particular, they will have to tackle the dimensions of gender and sexuality while mobilising the full transformative potential of class-based organising. LGBT activism in workplaces, the main location where the working class organises to identify as a working class, is crucial to queering overall social transformation. Although LGBT labour organising has already been more successful than most existing queer radical groups in appealing to women, blacks and immigrants, so far a radical queer perspective has not been brought to bear much on workplaces.

The challenge remains to make explicit and foreground the implicit class and anti-racist content of sexual radicalism. Sex radicals like Hollibaugh, Cherrie Moraga and Joan Nestlé did this in the 1980s by explicitly linking their own working-class origins to their butch/femme sexualities. Gender queers today could do the same by highlighting the class oppression of trans people and allying much more with trans organising in the dependent world and racially oppressed communities. This would facilitate a redefinition of queer to make it more genuinely global, broader and thus more truly radical. It is no accident that a working-class sex radical like Hollibaugh later became a central figure in New York's Queers for Economic Justice.

Queer interest in class issues goes far beyond labour organising narrowly defined. Any issue that speaks to the interests of people who have to work for a living is a working-class issue. Though neglected by mainstream LGBT organisations, these issues are important to millions of LGBT people. The workshop on class at the annual conferences of the US National Gay and Lesbian Task Force is always packed.[43] There are many links that can be made, for example, between same-sex partner benefits and a living wage for all workers, even single workers, whatever their sexual orientation.[44]

A queer working-class perspective needs to challenge standard definitions of who constitutes the working class. For example, the definition needs to

---

42   Rosenberg and Villarejo 2012, pp. 4–5.

43   Shah 2011/2012.

44   Cohen 1999, p. 116.

be expanded to include people working in the sex trade. For them as for any other oppressed group, self-organisation is a key element of change. Efforts at self-organisation in the US, which began in the 1970s with the group COYOTE (Call Off Your Old Tired Ethics), have revived more recently with groups like SWANK (Sex Workers Action New York) and SWOP-NYC (Sex Workers Outreach Project – NYC). This is an issue that would probably be more of a focus for queer activism if the taboo around it could be overcome among activists themselves. As Hollibaugh has commented from her own experience, the sex trade was at times crucial for her survival as an activist – preferable in any event to the 'just miserable' alternatives available to her: 'in dry-cleaning plants, cleaning floors at night in big corporate buildings, picking fruit, or ... cleaning fish for tuna-canning plants'.[45]

Beyond the stigma, there are more than enough issues to organise around in the sex industry, including but going beyond prostitution. Besides the demand for decriminalisation (as distinct from state control or regulation) as a precondition to legal organising, workers in the industry need to organise to resist the harassment, violence and exploitation to which they are subjected. For the women who make up the great majority of these workers, this is basic to a feminist politics that can fight the forms of gender inequality specific to this industry. There is an obvious need for information and resources around safer sex and AIDS and STI prevention. An anti-capitalist feminist politics for the sex industry would need to go still further, in search of transitional demands leading ultimately to abolishing commercial sex along with commercial everything else.[46] Yet crackdowns on the sex trade implemented without sex workers' participation, as in post-revolutionary Havana or Ho Chi Minh City, can be experienced as being even more oppressive than the sex trade itself. Effective and lasting abolition of sexual commerce can only be the achievement of those working in it themselves. One day, like all working people, they should win freedom from the need to prostitute their bodies, brains or talents in order to survive and lead the lives they want.

LGBT organising in workplaces around workplace issues is done through existing trade-union structures, by multi-issue queer groups or a combination of both. There are advantages to LGBT labour organising by queer groups instead of or alongside trade unions. For one thing, it avoids the need to go through the process of queering a heteronormative structure. Autonomous queer campaigns can be especially effective for LGBT-specific workplaces like bars and bookshops, making it easier to organise community support and

---

45   Shah 2011/2012.
46   Rubin 2011, pp. 272–3; Rubin opposes eliminating commercial sex as a goal.

boycotts.[47] The US campaign starting in 1975 to get gay bars and their customers to boycott Coors beer, whose owners were both anti-union and anti-gay, was a well-known and successful example of labour-queer synergy.[48] In the early 1990s in San Francisco, Queer Nation organised in support of workers at the bar EndUp. Later in the 1990s, Queer Nation campaigned against the restaurant chain Cracker Barrel, which had openly anti-gay employment policies.[49]

There are also undeniable advantages to harnessing the resources of established trade unions to LGBT workplace organising. Since the 1980s, through the heyday of anti-AIDS organising, Queer Nation and beyond, LGBT caucuses have grown steadily inside trade unions in many countries, culminating in periodic international queer labour gatherings (Workers Out!) in 1998, 2002, 2006 and 2009. LGBT labour is potentially an important component of a new queer left. At the same time, for better and for worse, it currently embodies much of the diversity of the working class – and the political limitations of the broader labour movement. The benefits of LGBT union work would be far greater if unions could be queered as part of a broader upsurge that brings a broad, social-movement, class-struggle current to leadership in existing unions. In the end, the process of queering unions – of ensuring that LGBT people and issues are fully integrated into their struggles – can only succeed if it is linked to a radicalisation of the union movement that moves beyond workplace reforms to make labour a dynamic force for sweeping social change.

By now there are many examples of campaigns with a variety of approaches inside the unions. In 1981, the Canadian Union of Postal Workers became the first union in the country to win a contract ban on anti-gay discrimination (at a time when only Quebec had an anti-discrimination law); in 1985, two decades before legal same-sex marriage was won in Canada, a local of the Canadian Union of Public Employees won recognition of same-sex spouses in their contract.[50] A victory in 1982 in winning same-sex partner benefits for employees of the New York alternative weekly *Village Voice* was secured by openly gay staff writer Jeff Weinstein, backed by straight colleagues on the bargaining committee. The same union, the United Auto Workers, dropped the same demand in contract talks with Chrysler in 1996, due in part to the lower visibility of LGBT workers in the blue-collar car industry.[51] Yet there were gains for LGBT workers in contract talks with Chrysler three years later.[52]

47 Cohen 1999, p. 117.
48 Laird 2012.
49 McCreery and Krupat 1999, p. 1.
50 Moriarty 2007, pp. 19–20.
51 Krupat 1999, pp. 17–18.
52 McCreery and Krupat 1999, p. 4.

There is an emerging, broad international consensus on LGBT issues that unions can and should address. These issues include refusal of employment, dismissal and denial of promotion on grounds of gender or sexual identity or HIV status, and LGBT people's self-exclusion from certain workplaces or jobs (for example, involving work with young people or vulnerable groups). Partner benefits are another whole set of issues, including health, childcare, leave, pension, insurance and bereavement; they need to be equally available to all, whether their relationships are cross-sex or same-sex, legally recognised or not. Harassment is a constant issue – from homophobic or transphobic jokes to verbal abuse to false accusations to violence – that needs to be addressed with clear and forceful policies. Trans workers need to be supported through whatever transitions they choose and in their interactions with co-workers, managers and clients,[53] in particular respecting their confidentiality and their right to decide who they tell what and when. Once they are ready, the union and fellow workers need to respect and support trans workers' choice of name, dress and gendered facilities (like toilets).

To make open LGBT workplace organising possible through existing unions, those unions need first to be queered, overcoming their heteronormative culture and the assumption that their members are all straight. Most LGBT people are still not out at work or in their union. Many LGBT people quit or fail to join unions that do not welcome or defend them. There are union activists and even leaders who keep their same-sex lives private; that is their choice to make, depending on circumstances, and unions should protect their members' privacy. But LGBT union members are more likely to be active, and thereby make their union stronger, when they can freely choose to be open. Visibility in union policies, leaflets, posters, journals and offices is crucial. So is union education of members on LGBT issues.[54]

Only in this way can being open about one's sexuality in a union be not 'a trial by fire but an opportunity for new and creative forms of organizing'.[55] If workers 'are terrified of speaking out, of ever articulating the particularities of their own lives', their 'spirit is broken precisely in the place where they need to have a voice'.[56] This is a vital issue for unions themselves. After years of decline, the union movement has to address the concerns of a diverse workforce if it is to regain its strength and vitality. This will require deepening 'a dynamic conception of class...defined as much by social identity as by

---

53   Moriarty 2007, pp. 9, 19, 21–3.
54   Moriarty 2007, pp. 5, 10, 14, 16, 34.
55   McCreery and Krupat 1999, p. 7.
56   Hollibaugh and Singh 1999, p. 74.

economic position'[57] – starting from the understanding that racial, gender and sexual affinities have always been tools in building solidarity.[58] It will require rejecting the 'stifling economism' of most unions, and building a 'class culture with very different dynamics', 'an alternative social world' with a 'transformative political culture'.[59]

Union visibility at LGBT events is important in queering the unions and enabling a working-class presence in LGBT communities. There are many examples of this by now worldwide. To mention one example, the nurses' union in São Paulo, Brazil has worked with organisers of the city's annual Pride event to make it more political. Unions can and should do work with LGBT groups to respond to repression or demand change, for example, in commemorating International Day against Homophobia and Transphobia and Transgender Day of Remembrance.[60] They can also be a place where workers can go for information on HIV and safer sex; union training programmes could include issues around preventive sexual health maintenance.[61]

The understanding needs to be won that LGBT 'workers' rights are trade union rights and trade union rights are human rights'. In 2007, the International Labour Organisation implicitly recognised this when for the first time it included data and analysis on anti-LGBT discrimination in its report *Equality at Work*.[62] At the same time, more LGBT people need to understand that since queer workers need economic security to live open queer lives, the queer movement needs to 'join the battles over power in the workplace'.[63]

Given that unions almost always start as heteronormative organisations, self-organisation by LGBT members is a prerequisite for queering them. Self-organisation can take different forms: LGBT members' own networks and initiatives, email lists, working groups, workshops and conferences. Some of these may appropriately be limited to self-identified LGBT people, while others may be open to anyone interested in exploring or working on LGBT issues. Whatever their form, all these groups deserve union acceptance and recognition, and support through granting of union funds, space and facilities. They should not be used to ghettoise LGBT people or issues, however; instead they

57   McCreery and Krupat 1999, pp. 5, 2.

58   Krupat 1999, p. 15.

59   Hollibaugh and Singh 1999, pp. 75, 77, 80, 83.

60   Moriarty 2007, pp. 17, 16.

61   Hollibaugh and Singh 1999, pp. 78, 82.

62   Moriarty 2007, pp. 5, 6.

63   Blum 2011/2012.

should be a springboard to including LGBT members and issues in union bargaining and leadership bodies and discussions.[64]

When unions do stand up for their LGBT members, they can be part of
an effective response to prejudice in the surrounding society. In Warsaw, following a proposal in 2007 by a deputy minister to 'prohibit the promotion of
homosexuality and other deviance' in Polish schools, 12,000 education workers
joined with LGBT rights groups to protest government discrimination against
teachers on the grounds of sexual orientation and political beliefs.[65]

Often, however, union LGBT organising is hemmed in by the bureaucratic
approaches characteristic of so many union full-timers (who have a vested
interest in minimising the risks that sharp conflicts entail) and leaderships,
especially in the defensive climate fostered by the neoliberal offensive.
Education and public-sector unions are a special case. It has been easier for
them to take the lead on LGBT issues, as shown by their prominence in international LGBT labour networking and the extensive declaration on LGBT labour
work they adopted at a gathering in Porto Alegre, Brazil in 2004.[66] On the other
hand, their particularly close ties to the state give them strong inclinations
to choose behind-the-scenes lobbying and public information campaigns
over more confrontational tactics like strikes. Queer unionists should fight to
have public-sector unions ally with communities suffering from austerity and
anti-social policies, rather than reach accommodations with government that
neglect community interests. In education, for example, labour-community
alliances, like the one built in the 2013 Chicago teachers' strike, should also
include links with activism among LGBT pupils and the spread of 'gay-straight
alliances', which are challenging the still overwhelming heteronormativity of
schools and demanding safety and dignity for LGBT pupils.[67]

In general, the best safeguard against bureaucratic co-optation or restriction of LGBT labour organising is to 'press uncompromisingly for the union to
take an active campaigning role on lesbian/gay rights issues, which will keep it
engaged in mass activity, and to continue to encourage lesbian/gay workers to
mobilize to advance their own demands, not allowing "friendly" bureaucracies
to take over, and using success in one as a stepping stone to the next'.[68]

---

64   Moriarty 2007, pp. 13–16.
65   Moriarty 2007, p. 7.
66   Moriarty 2007, pp. 12–13, 32–4.
67   D'Emilio 2002, p. 177.
68   Fourth International 2003, point 12.

Queering Global Justice

In the wake of the 'battle of Seattle' in 1999, a range of radical social movements began gathering in global, regional, national and local Social Forums to coordinate resistance to neoliberalism. The Social Forums were the organisational expression of an international movement for 'global justice' or 'a different globalisation'. Although they have had their ups and downs over the years, the success of some World Social Forums have showed their continuing potential to connect with and bring together anti-neoliberal rebellions that are breaking out around the world during the current crisis, and at times to move towards more clearly anti-capitalist demands. At some of these Social Forums, LGBT activists have had a significant presence, with highlights including the massive participation of *hijras* in the World Social Forum in Mumbai in 2004, and queer participation in the World Social Forum Free Palestine in Porto Alegre in 2012. Refracting a global justice agenda through the prism of all the queer demands that have been proposed for it, and the queer demands that still remain to be formulated and accepted, has the potential to change it drastically.

For a time, the global justice movement raised significant strategic issues for both anti-capitalists and queers. For example, calls for 'deglobalisation', and particularly for subjecting capital and the state to 'constant monitoring by civil society',[69] raised the question of what movements and communities have not usually been included in civil society. Concepts like democracy, civil society and community have been central to the global justice movement; queering them would involve rethinking them in basic ways. LGBT movements have not so far given a strong impetus or sense of direction to a process of queering the Social Forums. This is a challenge that merits taking up. Queering the politics of global justice could be a way to tackle the queering of the whole concept of development, which would require re-imagining the economy and the planetary hierarchy inherent in the neoliberal – and ultimately capitalist – order.

LGBT activists found allies as well as adversaries even before Seattle in some of the NGO gatherings that debated the directions taken by international civil society. Explicit recognition for lesbians was initially included in the Action Platform of the Fourth World Conference on Women in Beijing in 1995, for example, only to be dropped from the final document. Yet the presence of hundreds of lesbians there 'galvanized semipublic explorations of gay identities', and was soon followed in 1997 by the opening of China's national gay hotline.[70] Despite controversy, the World March of Women included lesbian demands in

---

69   Bello 2000; cf. Bond 2003.
70   Rofel 1999, p. 452.

its platform.[71] In 2013, the international peasant movement Via Campensina also called for an end to homophobia.[72] Ecuadorian and Brazilian delegates at the UN World Conference Against Racism in Johannesburg in 2001 backed calls to fight discrimination based on sexual orientation, which the preparatory Dakar African NGO Forum also took up, while others resisted.[73] LGBT activists have seized the opportunities provided by these gatherings to network and highlight the links between sexual liberation and global justice, for example, in the fight against the Free Trade Area of the Americas.[74] Those from the dependent world have pushed these same links at international LGBT gatherings.[75]

The global justice movement is indebted to the LGBT movement for creative forms of direct action that ACT UP used from 1987 on to protest against policies around the AIDS epidemic, drawing in its turn on earlier experiences of civil rights, peace and anti-nuclear movements. Beginning in Seattle in 1999, many similar tactics spread around the world, though ironically LGBT people have not often been very visible in global justice actions.[76]

The World, regional, national and local Social Forums, despite their ups and downs, remain an interesting laboratory for observing developments in global social movements. Compared with traditional social organisations and political parties, the Social Forums offer a space where diverse movements can meet and exchange in a less hierarchical way.[77] They are seen explicitly as spaces for forms of solidarity that cut across the usual boundaries between issues and currents. This has made it somewhat easier for sexual issues to get a hearing.

There has been a significant though uneven level of LGBT participation in the Social Forum process. Much of the greatest progress has been made at Latin American Social Forums, notably at the second World Social Forum in Porto Alegre, Brazil in 2002, and again at the third Porto Alegre Forum in 2003, where thousands of people visited the LGBT space. An even bigger breakthrough took place at the World Social Forum in Mumbai in 2004, where thousands of transgendered *hijras* processed through the streets and made their presence felt in the tents where discussions took place. Unfortunately, their presence was not translated into LGBT representation at the level of the World Social Forum's International Council or other central bodies of the Social Forum process. The

---

71 World March of Women 2001.

72 Via Campesina 2013.

73 Mtewa 2003, pp. 37–8, 41–2.

74 GLBT South-South Dialogue 2003b.

75 GLBT South-South Dialogue 2003a.

76 Shepard and Hayduk 2002.

77 Rousset 2005.

problem may be in part that LGBT organisations in dependent countries lack the solid structures and finances of the biggest NGOs, trade unions and movements that play the main roles in, and especially between, Forums – and that the bigger forces have never taken action to improve representation of LGBT people and other oppressed groups.

The first European Social Forum in Florence in late 2002 brought together dozens of queer groups, particularly from Italy and Portugal, but also from other countries, including nearby Eastern European countries. The queer radicals assembled in Florence defined themselves primarily as economic and social outsiders. A call eventually endorsed by thirty-odd organisations declared, 'The accelerating neoliberal and right-wing offensive in Europe is a threat to our lives as LGBT people' – for example, 'cuts in social services and privatisations are a special threat to LGBT people, inasmuch as they shift basic social responsibilities onto families (while our families of origin often do not support us, and we do not have the right to form new ones)'. 'But resistance movements against neoliberal globalization hardly take us into account', the call added. 'This situation has to change, and fast!'[78] The Florence Call expressed a clear identification with queer labour organising and immigrant and transgender struggles. Lesbians played a prominent role, in particular through the central role of the Italian national organisation ArciLesbica, whose leader Titti di Simone also represented the Party of Communist Refoundation in the Italian Senate at the time. Unfortunately, LGBT assemblies at subsequent European Social Forums have lacked the infrastructure to ensure continuity and focus.

The US Social Forum in Detroit in 2010 also provided an opportunity for networking on the radical queer left. Among the People's Movement Assemblies that emerged from it was a Queer People's Movement Assembly that met at the Creating Change conference in Baltimore in 2012.[79]

Gradually, LGBT NGOs and movements have begun to have an impact. The Yogyakarta Principles drafted in 2007 by an international group of experts reflected the growing coordination and weight of international LGBT civil society.[80] Although the structures of the United Nations express the will and interests of states – today, virtually all of them capitalist – rather than peoples or civil societies, the accepted role of NGOs in their deliberations makes possible a certain, indirect influence by organising and mobilisation. This was visible in the breakthrough resolution on same-sex rights adopted by the UN Human Rights Council in 2011. Interestingly, the crucial role of countries like Brazil and

---

78   ArciLesbica et al. 2002.

79   SONG 2011/2012.

80   Alston et al. 2007.

South Africa in creating a majority for the resolution, otherwise backed mainly by the European and North American 'usual suspects', resulted in a text whose wording was more genuinely global in tone than many supposedly international LGBT declarations. It focused more on issues of violence and survival than on the purely legal issues (which imperialist governments often fetishise), and discussed sexual minorities rather than 'homosexuality' or 'gays'.[81] For all the limitations of UN institutions, the Human Rights Council vote could be an indirect, tentative beginning of a process of global political queering.

Similar dynamics are at work at regional levels. The Organisation of American States, for example, passed its first resolution supporting LGBT and intersex rights in 2013, following a campaign by Argentina, Brazil, Canada, Chile and Uruguay. The resolution was made possible by a series of national victories, from Ecuador's protection of sexual orientation in its constitution to Peru's enshrinement in law of LGBT people's right to form a family.[82]

Building a Queer Left

Since the 1970s, socialist feminists in particular who had organised independently of the existing left, taking refuge from its sexism and other shortcomings, have recognised that there is nonetheless no substitute for building broad, overarching, albeit transformed, radical left organisations. Their own movement experience convinced them of the 'vulnerability and limitations inherent in ... an isolated localism'. They saw the need for 'a common programme of political and social change, meeting the needs of all oppressed groups, ... gathering together the social power of the community with the industrial power of those in production, and pitching this popular power against the existing state'. At the beginning of a time of attacks and cutbacks that has now lasted over three decades, they saw the dangers of marginalisation in the absence of broad, militant alliances. Sheila Rowbotham concluded that the women's movement on its own (or for that matter labour or any other movement on its own) could not produce a 'finished alternative', however much feminist practice and process could contribute to developing one.[83] Just as building autonomous communities and groups should be combined with working in broader movements that have the social weight to bring about change, working in broader movements ultimately gives rise to the need for a political vehicle that

---

81   UN Human Rights Council 2011.

82   Strother 2013.

83   Rowbotham, Segal and Wainwright 1979, pp. 10–11, 5–6, 203, 45.

can unite their forces in order to fundamentally transform the power structures of society.

For queer radicals, this means building a queer left. This work is being done in part by queer anti-capitalists' autonomous efforts inside social movements, grassroots revolts like Occupy and the *indignad@s* and the global justice movement. But they can and should also intervene inside the existing organisations of the radical left and the LGBT movement. James Green has concluded from the Brazilian experience that safeguarding the LGBT movement's autonomy can be combined with collaborating politically with the left.[84] Although there are few recent examples of successful LGBT cooperation with the radical left, past advances made through working with the Mexican Revolutionary Workers Party, the Sandinistas and the ANC showed that making connections while being visible and vocal could pay off.

Today, the queering of radical left organisations remains a challenge to be addressed everywhere, with many dimensions. The association between LGBT activists and the left was a constant through much of the twentieth century, from Edward Carpenter in Britain and Magnus Hirschfeld in Germany, to the Soviet role in the World League for Sex Reform, to lesbian/gay liberationists' attraction to Marxism, to connections with the South African ANC and Brazilian PT. But it is an open question as to how much that connection will amount to in the twenty-first century. The anti-capitalist left has yet to establish connections with queer activism that are as solid as the links Communists made in the 1920s with sex reformers, or those that gay/lesbian liberationists made in 1968–73 with the New Left. So far, the radical left, in its weakened state, is not doing much to expose the limitations of today's gay normality, or to build an alliance that includes radical queers who reject it. And LGBT people, even the most politically conscious and organised among them, are no longer a constituency that the left can take for granted. Even radical queers who refuse to be satisfied with fiddling within heteronormative parameters do not automatically identity with the left as they encounter it.

With the number of open LGBT people in many countries now exceeding the number of radical leftists, this should matter to leftists. Unless the left does better in meeting the challenge of sexual politics and developing a well thought-out, inspiring programme for it, the rightward realignment of the lesbian/gay movement could continue and advance even further. Masses of LGBT people could be lastingly co-opted into mainstream social-liberal and neoliberal politics, while radical queers remain isolated and embittered on its

---

84   Green 2000, p. 68.

fringes. The alternative to rightward realignment is the mobilisation of LGBT people as part of the anti-neoliberal and anti-capitalist left.

To be credible forces in queer politics, organisations of the radical and revolutionary left need to make a deeper commitment to supporting the sexually oppressed, like the *hijras* who intervened in the World Social Forum in Mumbai, or the trans people and gender queers whose actions are spreading. They need a public profile that is visibly queer, colourful and anti-heteronormative, including the visibility of queer spokespeople and leaders. The Mexican Revolutionary Workers Party made a start on this in the 1980s, but only briefly, and its example has rarely been followed. There have been a few more recent cases. In Latin America, one of the parts of the world where resistance to global neoliberalism sprang up most quickly in the 1990s, the Zapatista rebellion in Mexico gave an early example of how a radical LGBT agenda can be integrated into a resurgent broad left, as LGBT people participated in the Zapatistas' Aguascalientes Convention[85] and Subcommandante Marcos publicly hailed the work of congresswoman Patria Jiménez for LGBT rights.[86] Yet these few examples still stop far short of a full-fledged queering of the radical left.

Today, the forms of self-organisation in different movements are very different, diverse and distinct. The question that people now ask in many movements is often how they can safeguard the forms, places and atmosphere in which they feel comfortable as a specific oppressed group. In other words, at this historical moment, democratic control is often seen less as a matter of power and effectiveness, and more as a matter of identity. Anti-capitalist parties cannot hope to attract LGBT activists in this situation unless they are the accountable instruments of radical social movements that are themselves well on their way to being queered. Radical left organisations need to give queer issues a prominent place in their programmes and activities. Internally they need to educate their membership, discuss queer activism and issues at base and leadership level, and challenge prejudices wherever they arise, as well as the pervasive assumption that any member not publicly proclaimed LGBT is therefore straight.[87]

Just as social movements need to remain accountable to the communities that constitute their base, political organisations need to be constantly called to account by the movements whose interests they are supposed to represent,

---

85   Mejía 2000, pp. 52–3.
86   Lamas 1998, p. 21.
87   The Fourth International (2003, Part IV) has at least offered a good summary of what
      needs to be done.

including queer movements. Otherwise, the state that is supposedly to be transformed can end up transforming, co-opting, corrupting and subordinating the political organisation instead. Once this happens, anti-capitalist parties risk following in the wake of more mainstream parties in Western Europe and North America, which have begun opening up to a crop of lesbian/gay politicians virtually indistinguishable from their straight counterparts. These gay politicians often leave sexual issues dangling somewhere at the bottom of their agendas, and adopt personal styles that make them walking, talking embodiments of homonormativity. This has nothing to do with transcending the gay/straight binary; it is simply surrendering to straight hegemony. For radical left parties to ward off this spectre it is crucial, for queer anti-capitalists as for anti-capitalists generally, that they have centres of gravity outside the state.

Laying out this whole agenda, and comparing it to the reality of the existing radical left, risks making it look utopian. But queer activists, for their part, are ill-advised to sit and wait for a broader radical left to come along that meets their needs and demands. There is no hope of winning the radical queer agenda without a broad, queered radical left, so queers need to take up the task of challenging, engaging with and building the broader anti-capitalist left. Admittedly, LGBT leftists run occupational risks: a double burden of activism and a tendency towards split personalities. Only as their numbers grow, and understanding grows in both LGBT and anti-capitalist organisations, will the burdens and pressures on them ease.

Besides in social movements, grassroots revolts, the global justice movement and the as-yet-unqueered radical left, queer anti-capitalists face complicated tactical choices in relating to other, existing LGBT forces. To the extent that there ever was one, broad LGBT movement, this is rarely the case today. Where the new gay right has organised autonomously or achieved hegemony over a supposedly broad LGBT organisation, like the Human Rights Campaign in the US, there is clearly no place for queer anti-capitalists in its ranks. In other broad LGBT organisations under centre-left leadership, there may be more space for anti-capitalists, as long as the organisations' agendas include independent LGBT mobilisation and not just lobbying the state for reforms within the limits of what mainstream political forces consider acceptable. In the US, the Creating Change conferences organised by the National LGBT Task Force have proved a useful venue for radical queers to exchange ideas. At the global level, the International Lesbian, Gay, Bisexual, Trans and Intersex Association (ILGA) has included left-leaning currents particularly from Latin America and South Africa. The relationship of forces is less favourable in ILGA's European region, which is the best funded, the most integrated into state and quasi-state institutions (notably the EU), and more social-liberal in outlook.

The dominance of Pride marches in many cities by right-leaning and commercial forces constantly poses dilemmas for queer radicals about the relative merits of critical participation and alternative organising. In hindsight, the US LGBT left's decision in 2000 to boycott an undemocratic, right-wing-dominated national march left the march's conservative leadership unchallenged and underscored the left's defeat. The focus of many recent Prides on same-sex marriage has rarely elicited a creative radical response; leftists have alternated between largely uncritical participation and complete absence. Yet the truth is that queer groups' support base is often uninterested in events it sees as off-putting, commercialised and homonormative, while the bulk of participants in Pride are often there to celebrate and have a good time, not to hear criticism. And the centrifugal tendencies in the community are mostly not of queer radicals' making. In New York, for example, there are now a Dyke March, a Trans March and a Drag March held on different days and in different neighbourhoods from the corporate-sponsored LGBT March. Some divisions are simply unbridgeable, as in Tel Aviv, where since 2001 radical queers in solidarity with Palestinians have continued to organise either events separate from the main Pride event or separate contingents within the main event itself.

At the other end of the political spectrum, queer anti-capitalists can work with more subculturally-oriented, anarchist or semi-anarchist queers. These currents have played a major role, for example, in fighting pinkwashing and organising solidarity in imperialist countries with Palestinian queers. Theoretical or strategic differences between anarchists and Marxists should not be allowed to get in the way of queers' working together. However, problems can arise when there is a need to reach out broadly to working-class, black and immigrant LGBTs, often people with jobs and/or family ties and responsibilities that can be hard to reconcile with the 'do-it-yourself' approach of many queer milieus. Yet queer groups that do not reach out will perpetuate the limitations of their initial class, gender and racial composition, even if they do not stagnate or fold.

Queer anti-capitalists can be most comfortable working in or through groups like Queers for Economic Justice in New York, which had a largely anti-capitalist perspective and leadership itself. Unfortunately, there are not many places in the world as yet in which a critical mass exists for groups like this. Perhaps in the coming years outward-looking anti-capitalist and anti-imperialist queer groups will be founded in more places, begin networking and form an international pole of attraction.

The necessary dialogue between the queer current and other forces is further complicated by the development of a political culture in which disagreements among allies are addressed with the same rhetorical passion as confrontations

with open racists, sexists, homophobes and right-wingers. In this political culture, people who do not feel represented can quickly lose patience and adopt
confrontational tactics. Confrontational forms of public action that can be
effective ways to gain media attention can be habit-forming, spilling over into
situations where differences of opinion arise within progressive movements.
This kind of tactic has become more common among queer radicals. For the
new generations that are now emerging, nothing can be assumed; everything
must be demonstrated in practice at each decisive moment. Their attitude to
the forces they encounter can depend less on political or sociological analysis
than on vocabulary, organisational forms, and the age, gender, skin colour and
style of spokespeople.

Pointless clashes in the movement can sometimes be avoided through a
model of conjunctural alliances rather than an insistence on unified organisations. An alliance model has the advantage of flexibility, as different alliances
can be forged among different queer constituencies and a variety of other
groups depending on the issue at stake. The fight for partnership legislation
in recent years in a series of countries united a broad spectrum of LGBT communities, but some lesbians and radical queers held back, feeling that the issue
was not a priority for them. In a single, unitary organisation this could have led
to battles over priorities and resources; in an ad hoc alliance it did not have to.
Now where partnership rights have been won, concerns are being voiced by
LGBT people who are disadvantaged by the new legislation: lesbian mothers,
for example, whose parenting rights are still not equal to those of cross-sex
couples, and single people whose social benefits are now inferior to those of
coupled people. There may be potential here for building new organising alliances, which would not have to be narrowly class-based, but whose leadership
would more likely have to come from the queer left and would not necessarily
have to embrace the full range of LGBT communities.

Finally, an alliance strategy can allow queer radicals to more effectively
negotiate the most central divide in LGBT movements today: the divide
between newly 'normal' lesbians and gays who are finding their place in the
neoliberal order and queers who neither can nor want to fit into it. Without
corresponding neatly to class boundaries, this is in the last analysis a difference in class outlook. It cuts across all the other distinctions of gender, race,
ethnicity and sexual diversity. The category 'trans', for example, includes both
'homeless teenage drag queens rag[ing] against the cops who beat them merci-
lessly and then demand sex' and 'cross-dressers who own banks and railroads,
hold high-level government offices, and run television studios'.[88] No unified

---

88   Feinberg 1998, p. 132.

political organisation with a single leadership can possibly do full justice to the people on both sides of this abyss. The victims and adversaries of neoliberalism need to organise independently if they are not to be sold short and sold out.

Queering Democracy

The neoliberal age has seen the expansion of formal democracy to more countries, notably countries formerly ruled by post-capitalist, pro-imperialist or populist dictatorships. Yet even in many countries with multiparty elections and some opposition media, LGBT people have time and again experienced their exclusion from democracy on virtually every level: from supposed democratic institutions, from minimal democratic rights, even from movements fighting for democracy. Even when constitutions guarantee everyone's right to demonstrate and organise, police often attack LGBT demonstrations with impunity, while officials refuse to register LGBT organisations.

Moreover, making headway towards sexual freedom usually requires a deeper kind of democracy than minimal democratic freedoms. The formal democracies that have become more common in recent decades in much of the world still have little or no meaning for millions of the excluded, including homeless people, street children and trans people. Talk of democratic governance or participatory development rings hollow as long as these people's lives are ruled and sometimes destroyed by the whims of police, paramilitaries or thugs. Challenges to homophobia and particularly lesbophobia and transphobia are crucial to overcoming endemic repression of and violence against women, LGBT people and many other oppressed groups.[89]

Democracy means not just free media (the centrality of the internet has often been noted) and elections, but also a political culture in which there is room for activism outside institutions. This space must be won by mobilisation. The mobilisation of vast sectors of society in South Africa against apartheid, including LGBT blacks, created a dynamic political culture, despite the disappointments of the ensuing decades. The resulting gains for LGBT people are unique in Africa, including the first constitution in the world to explicitly ban discrimination based on sexual orientation. These gains have helped sustain LGBT organising, in a society where enclaves of gay normality exist alongside areas of violent homophobia. As one transwoman summed up the constitution's importance: 'You can rape me, rob me, what am I going to do...? Wave

---

89   Kleitz 2000.

the constitution in your face? I'm just a nobody black queen ... But ... since I heard about that constitution, I feel free inside'.[90] The resulting feeling of empowerment has made it possible not only to strike down discriminatory laws and win other reforms, but also to sustain grassroots organising against neoliberal policies and secure victories like those of the Treatment Action Campaign.

Mobilisations in other countries since the outbreak of the economic crisis in 2008, like the *indignad@s*, Occupy, the Arab Spring and revolts in Brazil and Turkey have all at times included a visible LGBT presence. 'In Gezi Park [in 2013] I saw LGBT organisations working together with groups that used to have contempt for them', a gay Turk observed, and others who 'didn't use to have much interest in the [LGBT] movement showed their support in the last Pride'.[91] This is a source of hope for comparable empowerment elsewhere. In the Arab region, for example, this means linking up with the Arab Spring and with anti-Zionism, which has been central to what exists so far by way of a genuinely international queer activism. This is most obviously the case among LGBT Palestinians, who see their struggle as 'challenging and breaking the current sexual and gender hierarchies in Palestinian society' as well as the Israeli occupation.[92]

Radical organising is very much called for, given the limits to sexual freedom in countries marked by deep social and economic inequality – which means an increasing proportion of the world. Full LGBT equality requires liberation from poverty and dependency. LGBT people also need jobs that can save trans and young people from dependence on the sex trade. AIDS cannot be overcome, in those countries where male-male sex is a major factor in the epidemic, without challenging the structural adjustment programmes that decimate healthcare. LGBT people cannot escape from or remould their families without the protection of a strong social safety net. Tackling any of these issues requires sustained mobilisation to deepen the social and economic content of democracy. LGBT liberation thus means not only legal rights achieved through the mechanisms of formal democracy, but also broader transformations achieved together with other social forces fighting against repression, racism, fundamentalism, neoliberalism and capitalism.

Even when queer activists see the need to join in these battles, however, it does not follow that other democratic and radical forces will welcome queer

90   Gevisser 2000, p. 136.
91   Delleman 2013, p. 51.
92   Maikey and de Jong 2011.

allies. Queers therefore need to organise autonomously from other movements. Independent queer organisations, initiatives and thinking are indispensable.

Queers also have a specific contribution to make in conceiving participatory democracy and its importance for anti-capitalism. Full and equal LGBT participation in democracy requires overturning at least two major barriers: gender-biased and heteronormative definitions of who gets to participate, and definitions of citizenship that do not take enough account of social and cultural difference. LGBT people have had an explicit place in 'thematic assemblies' on issues of 'social inclusion' in the participatory budget process in Porto Alegre and several other Brazilian cities.[93] But this remains an isolated example. Participatory development programmes engaging with the informal sector need to include trans people and LGBT participants in the sex trade.

LGBT movements also have lessons about democracy to share with social movements and the left more generally. For example, the three national lesbian/gay marches in the US in 1979, 1987 and 1993 were in many ways models of how full representation can be ensured. All the key organising decisions were taken by broad national conferences. These conferences were made up of carefully chosen delegations, with 50 percent representation for women, 25 percent for people of colour, regional quotas and so on. These structures were effective in facilitating broad mobilisation for the marches. Grassroots democracy should also be understood as a tool in impeding bureaucratisation of LGBT organisations themselves. It should help 'prevent the emergence of a professional/managerial elite', challenging 'the role of gay business control in the community and establish[ing] services under democratic community control'.[94]

At the same time, LGBT people feel the need to organise themselves to secure their inclusion in democracy, autonomously from the existing institutions that are supposed to embody it. The ultimate goal should be to transform institutions rather than be co-opted by them, to create institutions that are not just formally democratic but substantively and genuinely democratic.

Especially in Latin America, discussions of LGBT self-organisation, autonomy and democracy are bound sooner or later to raise the issue of Cuba. For all the progress made in recent years, the Cuban state is not prepared to countenance discussions in situations it does not control. The state's 'bureaucratic character [still] inhibits the autonomous, self-directed struggles that are needed';[95] LGBT people 'still cannot independently organize in defense of

---

93   Bruce 2003, pp. 98–9.

94   Kinsman 1987, p. 223.

95   Lumsden 1996, pp. 112, 117.

their interests to oppose government policy and actions'.[96] This is the chief obstacle that has stood in the way of attempts to form an LGBT organisation in Cuba since 1994, when the founders of the Gay and Lesbian Association of Cuba declared their determination to 'struggle against discrimination, abuses, and blackmail' and for 'cultural and personal liberation'.[97]

Only in 2012 did a Cuban CP conference embrace the aim to 'confront prejudices and discriminatory conduct on the basis of sexual orientation'. Starting in 1996, a national sex education centre was developed for Cuban schools, although director Mariela Castro of the National Sex Education Centre commented in 2012, 'It started out very tentatively; "sex education light" ... omitting themes of diversity for example. Today, their inclusion is still timid, and some resistance persists'.[98] The 1993 gay-themed film *Fresa y chocolate* was enormously popular in Cuba partly because its 'implied criticism of the regime's treatment of gay males [was] conjoined with a wider critique of other repressive, intrusive interventions of the Cuban state into everyday life'.[99] Anti-bureaucratic organising will be crucial to carving out a genuinely free space for LGBT people, as well as saving the gains of the Cuban Revolution from the regime's recent turn towards the 'Chinese model'.

In countries where formal democracy is largely a fig-leaf and LGBT people are under siege, as well as in countries where both bourgeois democracy and gay normality are well established, radical queer organising is needed to achieve the vast expansion of democracy required to defeat both hetero- and homo-normativity. Polymorphous perversity, the subversion of gender, queer inclusion, a world of solidarity, and queered families and communities cannot be simply the work of individuals, or even of an expanded queer subculture. They are only possible as the outcome of a collective project, involving intensive and prolonged processes of grassroots democracy, which includes a direct assault on the structures of gendered capitalism. This is what is ultimately at stake in the queering of democracy.

---

96   Farber 2011, p. 221.
97   Lumsden 1996, pp. 197–8, 211–14.
98   Reed 2012.
99   Lumsden 1996, pp. 181, 195.

Conclusion: The Principle of Hope

'Thinking', wrote Ernst Bloch in *The Principle of Hope*, 'means venturing beyond'.[1] One could hardly imagine a statement that is more urgent in our time – or more difficult. The neoliberal order is crumbling around us, yet virtually every government and the overwhelming majority of political and social forces continue in practice to uphold Margaret Thatcher's conclusion: 'There is no alternative'. At the same time, most of the alternative prospects that the radical left identified in the last century are gone or no longer attractive. Even twentieth-century sexual radicalism needs rethinking.

True, the global landscape seems to offer LGBT people today more than the average, meagre portion of hope. Even Barack Obama has eventually swung with the prevailing wind as far as allowing same-sex couples the 'audacity of hope' for equal rights to marriage. Yet such a pleasant surprise at the realisation of a hope that only a few years ago seemed implausible should not obscure the reality that the fulfilment of LGBT hopes remains, in many other ways, cruelly partial. Like so many other hopes under neoliberalism, most LGBT aspirations can only be achieved in practice by those who have the money to pay for them. The normality for which some yearn is only available to those who meet a number of criteria: upper or middle class or at least in the precarious ranks of the secure working class, employed and productive, lastingly coupled or at least aspiring to be, and preferably forming nuclear units mimicking heterosexual families. Even those who manage to jump through all of these burning hoops are bound to be scarred, to some extent, by the experience of childhood, youthful difference and alienation. And even after triumphantly being branded normal, they still face hostility and prejudice from those who see even or especially 'normal' gays as different, alien, privileged, rich, sinful, white(ned) and/or Western(ised).

Symptomatically, the seemingly breakneck progress towards LGBT rights in recent years has done nothing to reverse the virtual erasure of the word 'liberation' from the movement's vocabulary. Lesbians and gays' use of this word in the 1960s and 1970s in Paris, New York, Mexico City and Buenos Aires expressed a sense that life could be qualitatively freer and happier, for not only sexual dissidents but everyone. It expressed their desire to identify with women's liberation, black liberation and liberation struggles in places like Vietnam, Palestine and South Africa. Today, while open racism and sexism are generally taboo,

---

1 Bloch 1986, pp. 4–5.

there is hardly any sense that LGBT organisations or even radical queer groups are part of any broader fight for freedom.

Yet, in fact, true LGBT freedom would necessarily involve sweeping transformations affecting far more than just LGBT people. Specifically, it would require a reconfiguration of sexual life that abandons sex's supposed foundation in each individual's sexual orientation or 'sexuality'; a transformation of basic household units based on the abolition of gender as we know it; a transcendence of the global hierarchy of nations and 'races'; and a re-opening of the left's horizons to make it possible once more to challenge the parameters of capitalism.

Beyond Sexuality

A radical queer politics cannot simply propose a new same-sex formation to replace the homonormative-dominant one we are currently living under. Still less can it propose a return to any of the other sexual regimes that preceded it in human history. Historically, same-sex relationships have been neither less moral nor less healthy than cross-sex ones. But contrary to a certain gay mythology, they have been neither exempt from the oppressive structures of the surrounding social orders nor inherently more egalitarian than cross-sex ties. Transgender and intergenerational patterns, for example, by far the most common same-sex patterns in human history, have always been enmeshed in hierarchies of gender, age and social status. As class societies developed, their different same-sex formations have all had a negative feature in common: their focus on the gender of a sexual partner as at least one crucially significant criterion, within broader social orders that were always characterised by gender essentialism and gender inequality. The same-sex regimes of slave and feudal societies, for example, often linked love of youths to contempt for women, while even the beloved youths were not seen as possessing a right to pleasure on a par with their adult male lovers.

The distinctively capitalist same-sex regimes of the last century and a half have retained a focus on a partner's gender in intensified form, by defining a reified, gendered desire as integral to each individual's sexuality. Sexuality has been understood, to a historically unprecedented extent, under imperialism as a domain distinct from the rest of life and as permeating the whole of each human personality. In the invert-dominant regime of classical imperialism, the consignment of 'homosexuals' to the status of congenital freaks of nature served to uphold the proper, productive and reproductive manliness and womanliness of the newly 'heterosexual' men and women charged with maintaining the imperial race. In the gay-dominant regime of Fordism, lesbians and gays were gradually able to shed their status of freaks only by becoming proper men, women, producers and citizens themselves, accepting the status of a perpetual minority in their own commercialised ghetto, and casting off those who failed or refused to navigate this transition as new categories of freaks. The outcome of this process is the homonormative-dominant same-sex regime of today's neoliberalism.

In each period of this history, there were gender and sexual dissidents who rebelled against the frameworks being imposed on them. In the period of classical imperialism, *matis* in Suriname, mine husbands and wives in South Africa, and participants in intergenerational relationships in the Arab region, for example, failed to conform to the new gendered reification of desire and the homo/hetero binary it imposed. The early Bolshevik Revolution and its sex reformer allies, while accepting the binary, at least took major steps towards eliminating the moralism and discrimination that afflicted homosexuals. In the years from 1968 to 1973, lesbian/gay liberationists rebelled against the conformist respectability of the homophile groups, championed gender-bending and socialist feminism, and identified with the revolutionary left, briefly giving to the terms 'lesbian' and 'gay' connotations that differed from 'homosexual'. Today, queers continue these traditions with many different transgressions against homonormativity. Yet all these more or less inchoate rebellions have been under pressure and on the defensive.

A radical queer perspective should aim at fomenting more sustained and successful rebellions, which can win acceptance for the wide range of same-sex patterns today, including those of gender and other queers, which cannot be subsumed into gay normality. Today's alternative, non-homonormative sexualities often pose a challenge, at least implicitly, to the reification of sexual desire that the categories of lesbian, gay, bisexual and straight embody. They define a multitude of living human beings whose actual lives do not fit neatly into these categories. Queer radicalism needs to hone this challenge and make it explicit, in ways that question the consumerism entailed by gay normality. Just as the fantasies of consumers under neoliberalism should be challenged – for example, the belief that obtaining the 'right' commodities will define them as unique individuals and secure their happiness – so the romantic illusion that defines individuals and their happiness on the basis of a quest for the 'right' partner, and in particular a partner of the 'right' gender, must also be criticised. We need to remember that while 'the ideologies of romantic love and companionate marriage' make capitalism '(sometimes) survivable',[2] these ideologies are ultimately a form of adaptation to an unliveable order.

---

2   Crosby et al. 2012, p. 132 (Tavia Nyong'o).

Our attitude to all sexual identities should include a recognition of the need for what Rosemary Hennessy calls 'unlearning': uprooting 'the identities we take for granted... from ways of thinking that invite us to construe them as natural'. This does not mean 'a simple renunciation of identities – gay, straight, man, woman'. Rather, it means critically examining them, understanding their historical and material roots and limitations, and moving beyond them towards more expansive ways of living and loving.[3]

Only in this way can we begin to create the conditions of possibility for the erotic life that people have long dreamed of: polymorphously sensual rather than genitally obsessed; egalitarian rather than possessive.[4] This means re-situating sexual life in the wide panoply of human affection and connection. It means infusing human productive and reproductive activities in general with beauty and erotic energy. And it means breaking the gay/straight binary, so that same-sex desire is merged into a broader universe of desire that is welcomed and understood in all its diversity and commonality.

Herbert Marcuse was exceptional as a Marxist in recognising the potential role of 'perversions' in making true sexual freedom possible. Influenced by Marcuse, many of the most radical pioneers of lesbian/gay liberation in the 1970s saw their ultimate goal as the abolition of both heterosexuality and homosexuality as social categories.[5] Contemporary queer theorists have also been exploring the limits and taboos of contemporary same-sex sexuality, inspiring more boundary-defying queer activists. Like 1960s gay liberationists, today's queers critique the gay commercial scene, which is an integral part of what Marcuse saw as capitalist repressive desublimation.

The queer critique of the gay ghetto is not only a critique of its norms, but also implicitly a critique of its need to exist – ultimately, a questioning of the legitimacy of the straight world outside it, and of the straight identity and norm that prevail there. This does not imply any questioning of the legitimacy of cross-sex desire or behaviour, and still less any superiority of same-sex to cross-sex sexual desires or practices. It does not imply that there is anything illegitimate about someone's saying, 'I'm usually not attracted to people of my own gender', or 'I've never had sex with someone of my own gender', or 'I'm not looking for a same-sex relationship'.

---

3   Hennessy 2000, pp. 229–30.
4   D'Emilio 2002, p. 58.
5   See Altman 1971, pp. 227–38; Mieli 1980, pp. 23–31; Fernbach 1981, pp. 105–12. Unlike Kevin Floyd, many of these pioneers agreed with Marcuse in celebrating same-sex eros and other 'subversive utopian fantasies', but not separate gay identities (Floyd 2009, p. 150).

But in a heteronormative society, the statement 'I am straight' means both less and more than these other, specific statements. It means less because many people who call themselves 'straight' *have* experienced same-sex attraction or sex. And it means more because it conveys to fellow straights that 'I'm not one of them', and conveys to people open to same-sex possibility that 'I am off limits'. In short, *'straightness' is a denial of queer possibility*. The question thus arises: in a sexually free society, why would even someone who happened to be engaging exclusively in cross-sex sexual relationships have any need or desire to say, 'I am straight'? Why would the category even exist?

Contesting the categories of gay and straight, and developing an inclusive, queer conception of sexual freedom, can be a way of moving towards that truly free civilisation that Marcuse described a half-century ago in *Eros and Civilization*. In a sexually free society, he declared, 'all laws are self-given by the individuals', the values of 'play and display' triumph over those of 'productiveness and performance', and the 'perversions' can find expression in the eroticisation of the entire human personality.[6] While the new gay normality will not succumb quickly to queer assaults, a queer anti-capitalism can help us set a course towards a profound eroticisation of everyday life that can only be truly achieved beyond the constraints of capitalism – in that free society where 'everyone will be gay'.[7]

Finding new ways to challenge the reification of desire that the categories of lesbian, gay, bisexual and straight embody is ultimately in the interests of what Alexandra Kollontai called the 'many and varied bonds of love and friendship', based on 'love or fleeting passion' rather than on 'calculation, habit or even intellectual affinity'. Kollontai argued that 'the joys of a love unknown in the commercial society of capitalism' would be conducive not only to the happiness of those who experienced it, but also to a 'new attitude to life, society, work, art and to the rules of living'. She started from the understanding that 'love is a profoundly social emotion'. Comradeship and solidarity, she wrote, demand ' "warm emotions" – sensitivity, compassion, sympathy and responsiveness'. These impulses have to be drawn on to give people the strength and courage to face the difficulties of inventing polygamous and bisexual lives. The 'winged Eros' that Kollontai defended would embrace this full complexity of love.[8]

It would also put an end to the emotional impoverishment that characterises contemporary capitalism. Today, vital human needs for affection and

---

6 Marcuse 1966, pp. 191, 195, 203.
7 D'Emilio 2002, p. 57 (citing Allen Young).
8 Kollontai, pp. 231, 230, 259, 276, 278, 285, 288.

commitment are forms of 'outlawed need': the 'monstrous necessity' that 'haunts' capitalism.[9] The unprecedented atomisation of human beings in our societies results in an unprecedented dependence on romantic love for emotional survival. One terrible result 'when the loved ceases to love and leaves', in Kollontai's words, is a 'bitter and desperate feeling of desertion, of limitless loneliness'.[10] No love is eternal and unchanging, nor should it be expected to be so, and change can always entail pain. But a utopian vision of sexual freedom can offer a way out from the desperately cherished illusion of eternal and unchanging love.

Realising this utopian vision will require travelling a long and winding road. Along this road lie both the personal struggles of individuals, friends and lovers to live life differently, and broad social mobilisations for reforms that also look beyond reforms. Queer anti-capitalists will have to find ways to combine individual gender-bending with legislative change that frees trans people and others from rigid gender binaries. We will have to combine experiments in polyamory with measures to expand legal options for households and reverse the privatisation of care. We will have to resist homonationalism and racism in everyday life, while working to overthrow the global institutions of capital. And we will have to lead lives beyond overconsumption, while creating a society in which everyone has enough and resources are democratically controlled and justly allocated.

The challenges that lie along the road towards a queer anti-capitalism are daunting. But only by facing them can we hope to create a fundamentally different and better world. We need to tackle them with all the optimism of the will of which we are capable.

Beyond Gender and Nation

Challenging the gendered desire of the gay/straight binary entails a critical attitude towards the overarching structures of gender in today's world. It demands a 'queer union' of Marxism and feminism,[11] based on a commitment to the 'porosity of gender boundaries'.[12]

Looking to a world of porous gender boundaries does not imply expecting women and men, or even masculine and feminine attributes, to disappear off

---

9   Hennessy 2000, pp. 216 (citing Deborah Kelsh), 228.
10   Kollontai 1978, p. 69.
11   Arruzza 2013, p. 124.
12   Shah, Raj, Mahajan and Nevatia 2012, p. 234.

the face of the planet. It means challenging the still overwhelming expectation that every human being encountered should be instantly identifiable as either male or female, and that identifiable males and females will live within the outer limits of acceptable masculine and feminine behaviour, respectively. Instead, as gender queers are increasingly asserting, each person can embody a distinctive and fluctuating combination of masculine and feminine attributes; and as intersex and trans people are increasingly making visible, many people can have 'intermediate bodies', with distinctive and variable combinations of male and female physical characteristics. Once the expectation of universally single-gendered human beings (including lesbian and gay human beings) is shattered, a vast area of freedom could open up for a diversity of clothing, adornment, body types and behaviour. And in terms of desire, people could increasingly be open to being attracted or aroused by different aspects or junctions of masculinity, femininity or androgyny in different relationships or different phases or moments of their lives.

None of this can come about painlessly or at a purely individual or small-group level. Gender is not an accident of culture or history; it is an integral part of a gendered system of production and reproduction. Neoliberalism has in some ways made the gender dimension of capitalism more flexible and optional, but in other ways, by undermining more collective support mechanisms, it has made the elementary gendered units of society more inescapable. Even LGBT politics has been warped by three decades of neoliberalism. A radical same-sex politics will require moulding it into a new and different shape, making firm commitments to less popular struggles like those against anti-trans discrimination and for public funding of body modification surgery. It will also require re-engaging with the central issues of socialist feminism – gender, the family and the social reproduction of labour – and showing what is at stake in these issues for LGBT people's everyday lives and survival. LGBT liberation should be integrated into a comprehensive programme for reproductive freedom and socialisation of childcare and domestic labour – a programme that would clash with the prerequisites for maintaining profit rates and accumulating capital.

Socialised childcare and domestic labour, like all public services, require public resources. From capital's point of view, this is a drain on its revenue – certainly compared with unpaid labour in the family (still disproportionately done by women, albeit, when paid for, increasingly by black, immigrant and lower-income women), which is cheap – and especially in times of crisis. As the drumbeat of accusations against black, immigrant and poor families constantly reminds us, moreover, families still have the crucial function of shepherding children and young people into productive (profitable) employment and preventing any disruptive behaviour on their part. Any attempt on the part of LGBT people to meet their needs through claims on public resources or to assert the rights of non-homonormative households and communities, especially for LGBT young people escaping from heteronormative families and seeking independence, therefore involves a challenge to the reigning neo-liberal consensus. This does not just apply to demands for social support for alternative households, whether of South Asian *hijras* or New York runaways. It also applies to endeavours to foster the queering of existing families and communities from within. These efforts too depend on LGBT people having the economic resources and allies they need to strengthen their position within their families and communities of origin. In other words, they depend on jobs, incomes, networks and political organising.

Along with opposition to privatised domestic labour, resistance to exist-ing norms of masculinity and femininity poses just as much of a challenge to the heteronormative family. After all, the heteronormative family is one of the first places where male and female identities are assigned (where children are 'boyed' and 'girled'), and the rudiments of expected masculine and femi-nine behaviour are taught. Heteronormative families are also (increasingly these days) the place where children who deviate from gender roles begin to learn how they can achieve their own kind of lesbian, gay or transsexual nor-mality. Great as the role of media and schools is later, the experts agree, the family is key – as it is from the standpoint of queer counter-experts as well.

Many LGBT efforts to establish new family forms attempt a reconnection, against the atomising capitalist current, with broader communities. But suc-cess in this endeavour requires posing the revolutionary question: 'Are the present ways that capitalism orders life – the privatization of reproduction and childrearing; the demand that more and more adults be drawn into the labor market; the shrinking resources available to the nuclear family – the best way to do things?'[13]

Kollontai was convinced a century ago that the 'compulsive isolated family' was 'doomed to disappear' as 'not only useless but harmful'.[14] A radical queer politics today should converge with Kollontai's radical Bolshevism of a century ago in looking towards more conscious, more open, more collective ways of organising domestic life. This utopian vision should include ways for queers to join in creating economic alternatives,[15] in a world in which both com-munity *and* individual autonomy flourish. Creating LGBT-friendly domestic

---

13   D'Emilio 2002, pp. 190, 43.
14   Kollontai 1978, pp. 71, 226.
15   Jakobsen 2012, p. 32.

alternatives can contribute to meeting children's need for 'security and continuity...without replicating the intense, exclusive relationships of the nuclear family' – which can be just as intense and exclusive in a unit made up of a newly normalised same-sex couple plus kids. So genuine alternatives need to move beyond gay as well as straight normality. They need to affirm the value of freely chosen sexual and parental relationships – recognising that co-parents need not be sexual partners – while recognising that sexual autonomy and access to time and money are vital to achieving them.[16]

For all parents and would-be parents, whatever their sexualities and how-ever they become parents, there are great advantages to domestic forms in which people other than biological parents share both the tasks of caring for and raising children, and the pleasures of living with children. Kollontai believed that fatherhood 'should not be established through marriage' but voluntarily chosen, and that mothers could 'learn to be the mothers...of all' children. 'Communist society will take upon itself all the duties involved in the education of the child', she foresaw, 'but the joys of parenthood will not be taken away from those who are capable of appreciating them'.[17] A society where domestic life is organised more or less along these lines is the only one in which same-sex desire can be fully accepted and integrated in the house-hold units and communities people are raised in.

Achieving a truly queer world will also require creating a new kind of inter-nationalism, one that not only confronts imperial military and economic power, but also resists the ways imperialism distorts our conceptions of gender and sexuality. Queers today live in a global world, bound to each other by the transnational flow of images and artefacts, transnational tourism and the sex trade, and the migration of queer bodies across continents. Yet homonational-ism restricts 'true' lesbian/gay identity to a privilege of a minority of 'normal', largely white and middle-class men and women in the imperialist countries. Global and anti-racist solidarity is needed to shatter the barriers that homona-tionalism has erected. Then a global challenge to heteronormativity and homonormativity can be integrated into a global movement against capital-ism, creating the potential for a world where neither state boundaries nor skin colour nor religious background get in the way of an erotic culture binding together the planet.

---

16   Brenner 2000, pp. 215, 259.
17   Kollontai 1978, pp. 227–8, 230, 258.

Queering the Future

Sexual liberation has to include winning substantive, economic and social equality, in a world where really existing capitalism makes legal equal rights to employment, housing and accommodations empty for LGBT people who cannot afford them. Claiming a possible queer future, beyond gay and straight, and beyond heteronormative or homonormative families, therefore means claiming a possible future beyond capitalism. It means insisting on a utopian dimension of politics, in the positive sense pinpointed by Perry Anderson when he wrote that 'all creative socialist thought is likely to possess a utopian dimension'.[18] 'As we jut up against the impossibility of capitalist futures, we enact the negation of these futures in the name of another'.[19]

The demand for a queer future beyond capitalism is a demand for a society 'where autonomy and security do not preclude each other but coexist'. The material basis for such a society could be provided by 'community- or worker-controlled day-care, housing where privacy and community coexist, neighborhood institutions – from medical clinics to performance centers – that enlarge the social unit where each of us has a secure place'.[20] Deeply participatory democracy is the best basis for sustaining and governing such forms of social support, and for allowing individual autonomy to co-exist as harmoniously as possible with community. This vision should provide a horizon for the social movements that are being and need to be queered: the movements for healthcare that groups like ACT UP and the Treatment Action Campaign have globally reshaped, and movements for housing, education, and old and young people's rights whose queering is less advanced.

Meeting 'human needs is the baseline of history', Hennessy has reminded us: needs that develop historically, that can only be met through social relationships, and that include 'satisfaction of the human capacity for sensation and affect'. Alongside purely material needs and needs that can be satisfied collectively, there are needs for different kinds of love: 'the long-term commitment or the deep and lasting ties of affection between friends, the bond between a child and her caretaker, or any number of other loves'.[21] Satisfying all these needs should be part of a queer utopia: not a blueprint to be realised, but a set of goalposts to guide action. Yet it is no accident that 'utopia' in the

---

18   Anderson 1980, p. 175, n. 34.
19   Rosenberg and Villarejo 2012, p. 7.
20   D'Emilio 1983a, pp. 110–11.
21   Hennessy 2000, pp. 210, 205.

socialist tradition has a pejorative meaning as well as a positive one. Unless it plausibly points to an agency capable of creating such a future, the appeal to a post-capitalist future runs the risk of confirming the supposed inescapability of the capitalist present.

The Marxist tradition rightly insists that no such agency of transition is possible without the social power of the working class – the broad, expanding, diverse and fragmented category of those who need jobs to survive – at its core. This strategic understanding has often animated LGBT workplace activists as they have worked to queer the labour movement from without and within. Yet LGBT movements more broadly today almost never share it. In this respect, queers remain deeply marked by the retreat from class that began in the 1980s. Poststructuralists and postmodernists often referred to 'new' social movements like queers as they challenged, first and legitimately, the old left's economistic idea of the leading role of the working class and its vanguardist conception of 'the' working-class party. Then, more dangerously, they moved on to contest the claim of social movements in general to represent the oppressed.

Both mainstream LGBT organisations and more radical queer groups have been twisted out of shape by the retreat from class and postmodernist theorising, though in different ways. Mainstream organisations, especially in imperialist countries, often see themselves as lobbies rather than as true movements; queer groups often see themselves as subcultural and activist collectives that do not aspire to represent anyone but themselves. Both self-conceptions are denials of transformational hope. Queer anti-capitalists need to look towards re-founding LGBT movements on a different basis.

A working-class queer perspective, updated to reflect the realities of today's broad and diverse working class, could offer a persuasive alternative to both mainstream lobbies and marginal queer collectives. This would not mean a movement restricted to working-class people, even broadly defined, or one in which non-working-class queers have lesser status. Nor would it be a movement narrowly focused on workplace or economic issues. But given both the strategic role of the working class in transforming society and working people's claim to a powerful voice on straightforward democratic grounds, a genuine queer radicalism needs to inhabit spaces where working-class people feel at home. And it needs to infuse all its concerns and campaigns with a class orientation, closely interwoven with the gender, sexual, racial, cultural and community dimensions that are inextricable from class today.

By queering democracy, radical queers can show in practice that masses of people, including those most often excluded from the rituals of formal democracy, can participate in ways that genuinely express and advance their own ideas and interests. At various times since the 1960s, queer activists among others have in fact begun to demonstrate this. Such a queer contribution to grassroots democracy is particularly appropriate and needed in the global justice movement, which the Tunis World Social Forum in 2013 suggested could be reinvigorated by the upheavals of the Arab Spring and Southern European rebellions. It is equally needed in labour and other social movements stifled by bureaucracy and adaptation to the imperatives of life under neoliberalism. In all these frameworks, queer radicalism could and should be part of a militant left wing that reasserts the movements' common vocation as agencies of transformation.

Defining the potential of queer anti-capitalism in an expansive way puts in question the idea that there can ever again be 'a' gay movement, a sort of 'big tent' including the whole LGBT spectrum from left to right. When all sexual dissidents were outlaws, they all had a certain common interest in storming the walls of prejudice. Today, some gays seem to be scaling the walls if not safely inside them, and to feel that disreputable allies can only hold them back from gaining more wealth and power. Shifting alliances of different currents, and of people with varying sexual identities, issue by issue, may make more sense as an image of the LGBT future. Within this landscape, the broad radical left should become a reliable ally for a new queer left as it challenges the newly respectable lesbian/gay right.

A left that breaks with heteronormativity and fully supports queer self-organisation is key – together with LGBT rejection of the illusion that 'recently acquired gay rights can be secured, let alone expanded, when so many other rights are being trampled upon'.[22] Or as Cathy Cohen has put it, 'Don't believe their lie; our inclusion in and of itself will not make things different'. It will only mean that those 'deemed most deviant and aberrant [will] face yet another system of exclusion', while the privileged group permitted entry will have at best won inclusion in an oppressive society.[23]

This means that the left itself needs to be transformed. It needs to reclaim the almost forgotten liberationist impulses of the 1960s and 1970s, when radical politics embraced the whole of human experience, including its most intimate aspects, and the most despised of society's outcasts. And the left needs to purge its own culture of heteronormative attitudes and habits so that queers, for the first time, will feel equally and fully at home in its ranks. It needs to heed Amber Hollibaugh's call: 'Finally, let sex and desire be truly significant and alive in our politics, without compromise or condescension'.[24]

---

22   Lumsden 1996, p. xxi.
23   Cohen 1999, pp. 113–15.
24   Hollibaugh 2011/2012a.

A new radical queer politics will require moving same-sex structures and self-conceptions in a fundamentally different direction from the warped ones they have been taking in recent decades, both radicalising a broad segment of LGBT people and winning much of the radical queer milieu to a broader conception of social and political struggle. The most fruitful approaches to LGBT liberation will probably be those that combine sexual radicalism with coalition-building, link LGBT demands with strategies for broader social transformation, and build unitary left organisations alongside independent queer groups. LGBT working people, blacks, immigrants and people in the dependent world can all make their own, distinctive contributions to the re-foundation of a queer left, enriching the idea of sexual freedom with the 'imperatives of struggle, resistance, and social transformation'.[25]

If the queer left can address and meet these challenges, it can make a vital contribution to a rebirth of hope in a world that so badly needs it – hope for an escape at last from the confines of neoliberal crisis and violence, to a world of pervasive pleasure and genuine freedom. In the struggle for this new and better world, the queer left can see to it that the process of transformation is enduringly inspired by the dear love of comrades.

---

25   Gevisser and Cameron 1994, p. 5.

References

Abolafia Aguita, Luis 2013, 'We Recommend: Aid Conditionality and Respect for LGBT People['s] Rights', available at: <http://www.sxpolitics.org/?p=7369>.

Abramovitz, Mimi et al. 2006, 'Beyond Same-Sex Marriage: A New Strategic Vision for all our Families & Relationships', available at: <http://www.beyondmarriage.org/full_statement.html>.

Achcar, Gilbert 2002, *The Clash of Barbarisms: September 11 and the Making of the New World Disorder*, translated by Peter Drucker, New York: Monthly Review Press.

———— 2004, *Eastern Cauldron: Islam, Afghanistan, Palestine and Iraq in a Marxist Mirror*, translated by Peter Drucker, New York: Monthly Review Press.

ACT UP 2000, 'Treatment for all ... Now!' (20 July), available at: <http://www.actupny.org/reports/durban-access.html>.

Adam, Barry D. 1985, 'Structural Foundations of the Gay World', *Comparative Studies in Society and History*, 27(4): 658–71.

———— 1993, 'In Nicaragua: Homosexuality Without a Gay World', *Journal of Homosexuality*, 24(3–4): 171–81.

Adam, Barry D., Jan Willem Duyvendak and André Krouwel 1999, 'Gay and Lesbian Movements beyond Borders? National Imprints of a Worldwide Movement', in *The Global Emergence of Gay and Lesbian Politics: National Imprints of a Worldwide Movement*, edited by B.D. Adam, J.W. Duyvendak and A. Krouwel, Philadelphia: Temple University Press.

———— (eds.) 1999, *The Global Emergence of Gay and Lesbian Politics: National Imprints of a Worldwide Movement*, Philadelphia: Temple University Press.

Agustine, Sri, Evilina Sutrisno, Lily Sugianto, Ignatia Maria, Irene Augustine, Sigit and Afank Mariani 2012, 'Female Transgender: Gender & Sexual Identities among Transgender Female to Male Persons in Jakarta', in *Women-Loving-Women in Africa and Asia: Trans/Sign, Report of Research Findings*, edited by S.E. Wieringa, Amsterdam: Riek Stienstra Fonds.

Aldrich, Robert 2003, *Colonialism and Homosexuality*, London: Routledge.

Alekseyev, Nikolay 2013, 'Fighting the Gay Fight in Russia: How Gay Propaganda Laws Actually Only Help', *RT News*, available at: <http://rt.com/op-edge/russia-gay-rights-sochi-945/>.

Alexander, Michelle 2010, *The New Jim Crow: Mass Incarceration in the Age of Colorblindness*, New York: New Press.

Alston, Philip et al. 2007, *The Yogyakarta Principles: Principles on the Application of International Human Rights Law in Relation to Sexual Orientation and Gender Identity*, Geneva: International Commission of Jurists, available at: <http://www.unhcr.org/refworld/docid/48244e602.html>.

Altman, Dennis 1971, *Homosexual: Oppression and Liberation*, New York: Avon Books.

———— 1982, *The Homosexualization of America, The Americanization of the Homo-sexual*, New York: St. Martin's Press.

———— 1996, 'Rupture or Continuity? The Internationalization of Gay Identities', *Social Text*, 14(3): 77–94.

———— 2000, 'The Emergence of Gay Identities in Southeast Asia', in *Different Rainbows*, edited by Peter Drucker, London: Millivres/Gay Men's Press.

Althusser, Louis 1971, *Lenin and Philosophy and Other Essays*, translated by Ben Brewster, New York: Monthly Review Press.

———— 1979, *For Marx*, translated by Ben Brewster, London: Verso.

Alvarez, Sobia E. 2000, 'Translating the Global: Effects of Transnational Organizing on Local Feminist Discourses and Practices in Latin America', *Cadernos de Pesquisa*, 22: 1–27.

Amer, Sahar 2009, 'Medieval Arab Lesbians and Lesbian-like Women', *Journal of the History of Sexuality*, 18(2): 215–36.

Anderson, Perry 1979a, *Considerations on Western Marxism*, London: Verso.

———— 1979b, *Lineages of the Absolutist State*, London: Verso.

———— 1980, *Arguments within English Marxism*, London: Verso.

Andrews, Edmund L. 2003, 'Economic Inequality Grew in '90s Boom, Fed Reports', *New York Times* (23 January).

Angell, Marcia 2014, 'The Women at the Top', *New York Review of Books*, 61(5): 18–21.

Aptheker, Bettina 2008, 'Keeping the Communist Party Straight, 1940s–1980s', *New Politics*, 45: 22–7, available at: <http://newpol.org/content/keeping-communist-party-straight-1940s-1980s>.

Arditti, Rita, Renate Duelli Klein and Shelley Minden (eds.) 1984, *Test-Tube Women: What Future for Motherhood?* London: Pandora Press.

Arguelles, Lourdes and B. Ruby Rich 1989, 'Homosexuality, Homophobia, and Revolution: Notes Toward an Understanding of the Cuban Lesbian and Gay Male Experience', in *Hidden from History: Reclaiming the Gay and Lesbian Past*, edited by Martin B. Duberman, Martha Vicinus and George Chauncey, Jr., New York: Penguin.

Arruzza, Cinzia 2013, *Dangerous Liaisons: The Marriages and Divorces of Marxism and Feminism*, London/Amsterdam/Pontypool: Resistance Books/IIRE/Merlin Press.

Badgett, M.V. Lee 1997, 'Beyond Biased Samples: Challenging the Myths on the Economic Status of Lesbians and Gay Men', in *Homo Economics: Capitalism, Community and Lesbian and Gay Life*, edited by Amy Gluckman and Betsy Reed, London: Routledge.

Badgett, M.V. Lee and Mary C. King 1997, 'Lesbian and Gay Occupational Strategies', in *Homo Economics: Capitalism, Community and Lesbian and Gay Life*, edited by Amy Gluckman and Betsy Reed, London: Routledge.

Bannerji, Himani 2011, 'Building from Class: Reflections on "Race", Gender, and Class', in *Educating from Marx: Race, Gender, and Learning*, edited by Sara Carpenter and Shahrzad Mojab, New York: Palgrave Macmillan.

Bao, Daniel 1993, 'Invertidos Sexuales, Tortilleras, and Maricas Machos: The Construction of Homosexuality in Buenos Aires, Argentina, 1900–1950', *Journal of Homosexuality*, 24(3/4): 183–219.

Barbosa, Mariela, Heather Dashner, Penny Duggan, Carol McAllister and Eva Nikell 1994, 'Introduction: Women and Economic Integration', in *Women's Lives in the New Globalized Economy*, edited by Lisa Duggan and Heather Dashner, Amsterdam: IIRE.

Barker, Nicola 2012, *Not the Marrying Kind: A Feminist Critique of Same-Sex Marriage*, Basingstoke: Palgrave Macmillan.

Battan, Jesse F. 2004, ' "Socialism Will Cure all but a Bad Marriage": Free Love and the American Labor Movement, 1850–1910', in *Meetings & Alcôves: Gauches et sexualités en Europe et aux Etats-Unis depuis 1850*, edited by Jesse F. Battan, Thomas Bouchet and Tania Régin, Dijon: Editions Universitaires de Dijon.

Battan, Jesse F., Thomas Bouchet and Tania Régin (eds.) 2004, *Meetings & Alcôves: Gauches et sexualités en Europe et aux Etats-Unis depuis 1850*, Dijon: Editions Universitaires de Dijon.

Beachy, Robert 2010, 'The German Invention of Homosexuality', *Journal of Modern History*, 82(4): 801–38.

Beccalossi, Chiara 2012, *Female Sexual Inversion: Same-Sex Desires in Italian and British Sexology, c. 1870–1920*, Basingstoke: Palgrave Macmillan.

Bello, Walden 2000, 'From Melbourne to Prague: The Struggle for a Deglobalized World', available at: <http://www.corpwatch.org/article.php?id=367>.

Ben Chikh, Madjid 2013, 'Chère Houria Bouteldja', *Minorités*, 159, available at: <http://www.minorites.org/index.php/2-la-revue/1458-chere-houria-bouteldja.html>.

Bensaïd, Daniel 2001, *Les Irréductibles: Théorèmes de la résistance à l'air du temps*, Paris: Textuel.

———— 2013, *An Impatient Life: A Memoir*, London: Verso.

Benstock, Shari 1989, 'Paris Lesbianism and the Politics of Reaction, 1900–1940', in *Hidden from History: Reclaiming the Gay and Lesbian Past*, edited by Martin B. Duberman, Martha Vicinus and George Chauncey, Jr., New York: Penguin.

Bergero Miguel, Trinidad, Susana Asiain Vierge and Maria Dolores Cano-Caballero Gálvez 2010, '¿Hacia la despatologización de la transexualidad? Apuntes desde una lógica difusa', *Revista Norte de Salud Mental*, 8(38): 56–64, available at: <http://www.psiquiatria.com/articulos/psiq_general_y_otras_areas/50521/>.

Bérubé, Alan 1983, 'Marching to a Different Drummer: Lesbian and Gay GIs in World War II', in *Powers of Desire: The Politics of Sexuality*, edited by Ann Barr Snitow, Christine Stansell and Sharon Thompson, New York: Monthly Review Press.

———— 1997, 'Intellectual Desire', in *Queerly Classed*, edited by Susan Raffo, Boston: South End Press.

Besnier, Niko 1994, 'Polynesian Gender Liminality through Time and Space', in *Third Sex, Third Gender: Beyond Sexual Dimorphism in Culture and History*, edited by Gilbert Herdt, New York: Zone Books.

Black AIDS Institute 2012, 'Back of the Line: The State of AIDS Among Black Gay Men in America, 2012', available at: <http://www.blackaids.org/reports/back-of-the-line>.

Blackwood, Evelyn 1986, 'Breaking the Mirror: The Construction of Lesbianism and the Anthropological Discourse on Homosexuality', in *The Many Faces of Homosexuality: Anthropological Approaches to Homosexual Behavior*, edited by Evelyn Blackwood, New York: Harrington Park Press.

Blackwood, Evelyn and Saskia Wieringa (eds.) 1999, *Female Desires: Same-Sex Relations and Transgender Practices across Cultures*, New York: Columbia University Press.

Blanco, Maria Gabriela, Susan Spronk and Jeffrey R. Webber 2012, ' "Now Is the Time!": Struggle for Sexual Diversity in Venezuela', *The Bullet*, 683, available at: <http://www.socialistproject.ca/bullet/683.php>.

Bleys, Rudi C. 1995, *The Geography of Perversion: Male-To-Male Sexual Behavior Outside the West and the Ethnographic Imagination, 1750–1918*, New York: New York University Press.

Bloch, Ernst 1986 [1954], *The Principle of Hope*, Volume 1, translated by Neville Plaice, Stephen Plaice, and Paul Knight, Cambridge, MA: MIT Press, available at: <http://www.marxists.org/archive/bloch/hope/introduction.htm>.

Blum, Richard 2011/2012, 'Equality with Power: Fighting for Economic Justice at Work', *Scholar & Feminist Online*, 10(1/2), available at: <http://sfonline.barnard.edu/a-new-queer-agenda/equality-with-power-fighting-for-economic-justice-at-work/>.

Boellstorff, Tom 1999, 'The Perfect Path: Gay Men, Marriage, Indonesia', *GLQ*, 5(4): 475–510.

———— 2005, *The Gay Archipelago: Sexuality and Nation in Indonesia*, Princeton: Princeton University Press.

Bolin, Anne 1994, 'Transcending and Transgendering: Male-to-Female Transsexuals, Dichotomy and Diversity', in *Third Sex, Third Gender: Beyond Sexual Dimorphism in Culture and History*, edited by Gilbert Herdt, New York: Zone Books.

Bond, Patrick 2003, ' "Deglobalisation"? Sure, but What's Next?' *Green Left Weekly* (26 February).

Boswell, John 1980, *Christianity, Social Tolerance and Homosexuality: Gay People in Western Europe from the Beginning of the Christian Era to the Fourteenth Century*, Chicago: University of Chicago Press.

Bouteldja, Houria 2013, 'Universalisme gay, homoracialisme et "mariage pour tous" ', availableat:<http://www.indigenes-republique.fr/universalisme-gay-homoracialisme-et-mariage-pour-tous-2/>.

Breitman, George 1967, *The Last Year of Malcolm X: The Evolution of a Revolutionary*, New York: Merit Publishers.

Brenner, Johanna 2000, *Women and the Politics of Class*, New York: Monthly Review Press.

———— 2003, 'Transnational Feminism and the Struggle for Global Justice', *New Politics*, 9(2): 78–87.

———— 2010, 'Free-market Feminism', *Monthly Review*, 2010, 62(7): 57–63, available at: <http://monthlyreview.org/2010/12/01/free-market-feminism>.

Bréville, Benoît 2011, 'Homosexuels et subversifs', *Le Monde Diplomatique*, available at: <http://www.monde-diplomatique.fr/mav/118/BREVILLE/47101>.

Brown, Carol 1981, 'Mothers, Fathers and Children: From Private to Public Patriarchy', in *Women and Revolution: A Discussion of the Unhappy Marriage of Marxism and Feminism*, edited by Lydia Sargent, Boston: South End Press.

Brown, Judith C. 1989, 'Lesbian Sexuality in Medieval and Early Modern Europe', in *Hidden from History: Reclaiming the Gay and Lesbian Past*, edited by Martin B. Duberman, Martha Vicinus and George Chauncey, Jr., New York: Penguin.

Brown, Stephen 1999, 'Democracy and Sexual Difference: The Lesbian and Gay Movement in Argentina', in *The Global Emergence of Gay and Lesbian Politics: National Imprints of a Worldwide Movement*, edited by B.D. Adam, J.W. Duyvendak and A. Krouwel, Philadelphia: Temple University Press.

Browne, Kath 2011, '"By Partner We Mean...": Alternative Geographies of "Gay Marriage"', *Sexualities*, 14(1): 100–22.

Bruce, Iain 2003, *The Porto Alegre Alternative: Direct Democracy in Action*, London/Amsterdam: Pluto Press/IIRE.

Burt, Jo-Marie 1998, 'Sexual Politics in Latin America' [Introduction], *NACLA Report on the Americas*, 31(4): 16.

Butler, Judith 1993a, *Bodies that Matter: On the Discursive Limits of 'Sex'*, New York: Routledge.

———— 1993b, 'Imitation and Gender Insubordination', in *The Lesbian and Gay Studies Reader*, edited by Henry Abelove, Michèle Aina Barale and David M. Halperin, New York: Routledge.

———— 1999, *Gender Trouble: Feminism and the Subversion of Identity*, New York: Routledge.

Califia, Pat 1982, 'A Personal View of the History of the Lesbian S/M Community and Movement in San Francisco' in *Coming to Power: Writings and Graphics on Lesbian S/M*, edited by Samois, Boston: Alyson.

———— 2000, *Public Sex: The Culture of Radical Sex*, San Francisco: Cleis Press.

Califia, Patrick 2003, *Sex Changes: Transgender Politics*, San Francisco: Cleis Press.

Camfield, David 2014, 'Theoretical Foundations of an Anti-Racist Queer Feminist Historical Materialism', *Critical Sociology*, available at: <http://crs.sagepub.com/

content/early/2014/02/17/0896920513507790.abstract?rss=1&patientinform-links=y
es&legid=spcrs;0896920513507790v1>.

Carr, Cynthia 2012, *Fire in the Belly: The Life and Times of David Wojnarowicz*, New York:
Bloomsbury.

Carr, Edward Hallett 1985, *The Bolshevik Revolution, 1917–1923*, Volume 1, New York: W.W.
Norton & Company.

Carrier, Joseph 1975, *Urban Mexican Male Homosexual Encounters*, Irvine: University of
California, unpublished doctoral thesis.

Castronovo, Russ and Dana D. Nelson (eds.) 2002, *Materializing Democracy: Toward a
Revitalized Cultural Politics*, Durham, NC: Duke University Press.

Cervulle, Maxime and Nick Rees-Roberts 2010, *Homo exoticus: Race, classe et critique
queer*, Paris: Armand Colin.

Chauncey, George 1989, 'Christian Brotherhood or Sexual Perversion? Homosexual
Identities and the Construction of Sexual Boundaries in the World War I Era', in
Hidden from History: Reclaiming the Gay and Lesbian Past, edited by Martin B.
Duberman, Martha Vicinus and George Chauncey, Jr., New York: Penguin.

———— 1994, *Gay New York: Gender, Urban Culture, and the Making of the Gay Male
World, 1890–1940*, New York: Basic Books.

Chou Wah-shan 2000, 'Individual Strategies for *Tongzhi* Empowerment in China', in
Different Rainbows, edited by Peter Drucker, London: Millivres/Gay Men's Press.

Christian, Reed and Anya Mukarji-Connolly 2011/2012, 'What's Home Got to Do with
It? Unsheltered Queer Youth', *Scholar & Feminist Online*, 10(1/2), available at: <http://
sfonline.barnard.edu/a-new-queer-agenda/whats-home-got-to-do-with-it-unsheltered-
queer-youth/>.

Clark, Anna 1995, *The Struggle for the Breeches: Gender and the Making of the British
Working Class*, Berkeley: University of California Press.

Cleminson, Richard 1995, 'Male Inverts and Homosexuals: Sex Discourse in the
Anarchist *Revista Blanca*', in *Gay Men and the Sexual History of the Political Left*,
edited by Gert Hekma, Harry Oosterhuis and James Steakley, Binghamton: Harrington Park Press.

Cohen, Cathy J. 1999, 'What Is this Movement Doing to My Politics?', *Social Text*, 17(4):
111–18.

———— 2005, 'Punks, Bulldaggers, and Welfare Queens: The Radical Potential of Queer
Politics?', in *Black Queer Studies*, edited by E. Patrick Johnson and Mae G. Henderson,
Durham, NC: Duke University Press.

Collins, Patricia Hill 1998, 'The Tie that Binds: Race, Gender and US Violence', *Ethnic
and Racial Studies*, 21(5): 917–38.

Coontz, Stephanie 1988, *The Social Origins of Private Life: A History of American Families
1600–1900*, London: Verso.

———— 2005, *Marriage, a History: How Love Conquered Marriage*, New York: Penguin.

———— 2011, *A Strange Stirring:* The Feminine Mystique *and American Women at the Dawn of the 1960s*, New York: Basic Books.

Crenshaw, Kimberlé 1993, 'Mapping the Margins: Intersectionality, Identity Politics, and Violence against Women of Color', *Stanford Law Review*, 43(6): 1241–99.

Crompton, Louis 1985, *Byron and Greek Love: Homophobia in 19th-Century England*, Berkeley: University of California Press.

Crosby, Christina, Lisa Duggan, Roderick Ferguson, Kevin Floyd, Miranda Joseph, Heather Love, Robert McRuer, Fred Moten, Tavia Nyong'o, Jordana Rosenberg, Gayle Salamon, Dean Spade and Amy Villarejo 2012, 'Queer Studies, Materialism, and Crisis', *GLQ*, 18(1): 127–47.

DasGupta, Debanuj 2011/2012, 'Queering Immigration: Perspectives on Cross-Movement Organizing', *Scholar & Feminist Online*, 10(1/2), available at: <http://sfonline.barnard.edu/a-new-queer-agenda/queering-immigration-perspectives-on-cross-movement-organizing/>.

Dashner, Heather 1987, 'Feminism to the Tune of the Cumbia, Corrida, Tango, Cueca, Samba...', *International Marxist Review*, 2(4): 61–96.

Davis, Angela 1998, 'Masked Racism: Reflections on the Prison Industrial Complex', *ColorLines: News for Action*, available at: <http://colorlines.com/archives/1998/09/masked_racism_reflections_on_the_prison_industrial_complex.html>.

Davis, Madeline and Elizabeth Lapovsky Kennedy 1989, 'Oral History and the Study of Sexuality in the Lesbian Community: Buffalo, New York, 1940–1960', in *Hidden from History: Reclaiming the Gay and Lesbian Past*, edited by Martin B. Duberman, Martha Vicinus and George Chauncey, Jr., New York: Penguin.

Davis, Mike 1986, *Prisoners of the American Dream: Politics and Economy in the History of the US Working Class*, London: Verso.

D'Emilio, John 1983a, 'Capitalism and Gay Identity', in *Powers of Desire: The Politics of Sexuality*, edited by Ann Barr Snitow, Christine Stansell and Sharon Thompson, New York: Monthly Review Press.

———— 1983b, *Sexual Politics, Sexual Communities: The Making of a Homosexual Minority in the United States, 1940–1970*, Chicago: University of Chicago Press.

———— 1989, 'Gay Politics and Community in San Francisco since World War II', in *Hidden from History: Reclaiming the Gay and Lesbian Past*, edited by Martin B. Duberman, Martha Vicinus and George Chauncey, Jr., New York: Penguin.

———— 2002, *The World Turned: Essays on Gay History, Politics, and Culture*, Durham, NC: Duke University Press.

D'Emilio, John and Estelle B. Freedman 1997, *Intimate Matters: A History of Sexuality in America*, Chicago: University of Chicago Press.

De Vela, Tesa Casal, Mira Ofreneo and Marion Cabrera 2012, 'Surfacing Lesbians, Bisexual Women and Transgendered People's Issues in the Philippines: Towards Affinity Politics in Feminist Movements', in *Women-Loving-Women in Africa and*

Asia: Trans/Sign, Report of Research Findings, edited by S.E. Wieringa, Amsterdam: Riek Stienstra Fonds.

Decter, Midge 1980, 'The Boys on the Beach', *Commentary*, 70(3): 34–48.

DeFilippis, Joseph N. 2011/2012a, 'A New Queer Agenda: Introduction', *Scholar & Feminist Online*, 10(1/2), available at: <http://sfonline.barnard.edu/a-new-queer-agenda/introduction/>.

———— 2011/2012b, 'Common Ground: The Queerness of Welfare Policy', *Scholar & Feminist Online*, 10(1/2), available at: <http://sfonline.barnard.edu/a-new-queer-agenda/common-ground-the-queerness-of-welfare-policy/>.

Delleman, Lars 2013, 'Turks én homo: dat is een paradox', *GayKrant*, 667: 45–52.

Dequeecker, Ida 1994, 'Belgium: As Some Women Climb the Career Ladder, Others Are Sent Back to the Kitchen', in *Women's Lives in the New Globalized Economy*, edited by Penelope Duggan and Heather Dashner, Amsterdam: IIRE.

Downing, Christine 1989, *Myths and Mysteries of Same-Sex Love*, New York: Continuum.

Draper, Hal 1978, *Karl Marx's Theory of Revolution, Volume II: The Politics of Social Classes*, New York: Monthly Review Press.

Draper, Theodore 1986, *American Communism and Soviet Russia: The Formative Period*, New York: Vintage Books.

Drucker, Peter 1984, 'Warning Signs from San Francisco', *Gay Community News* (9 June): 5.

———— 1993, 'Gay Liberation's Second Wave: What is Queer Nationalism?', *Against the Current*, 43: 28–30.

———— 1996, ' "In the Tropics There is No Sin" ', *New Left Review*, 218: 75–101.

———— 1997, 'Gays and the Left: Scratching the Surface', *Against the Current*, 68: 35–37.

———— 2000a, 'Introduction: Remapping Sexualities', in *Different Rainbows*, edited by Peter Drucker, London: Millivres/Gay Men's Press.

———— 2000b, 'Reinventing Liberation: Strategic Challenges for Lesbian/Gay Movements', in *Different Rainbows*, edited by Peter Drucker, London: Millivres/Gay Men's Press.

———— 2004, ' "More Freedom" or "More Harmony"? Henriette Roland Holst, Jacques Engels and the Influence of Class and Gender on Socialists' Sexual Attitudes', in *Meetings & Alcôves: Gauches et sexualités en Europe et aux Etats-Unis depuis 1850*, edited by Jesse F. Battan, Thomas Bouchet and Tania Régin, Dijon: Editions Universitaires de Dijon.

———— 2009, 'Changing Families and Communities: An LGBT Contribution to an Alternative Development Path', *Development in Practice*, 19(7): 825–36.

———— 2010, 'The New Sexual Radicalism: Socialist Feminist Reflections on Queer Activism', *Against the Current*, 146: 23–8.

——— 2012, 'Byron and Ottoman Love: Orientalism, Europeanization and Same-Sex Sexualities in the Early Nineteenth-Century Levant', *Journal of European Studies*, 42(2): 140–57.

——— (ed.) 2000, *Different Rainbows*, London: Millivres/Gay Men's Press.

Duberman, Martin B., Martha Vicinus and George Chauncey, Jr. (eds.) 1989, *Hidden from History: Reclaiming the Gay and Lesbian Past*, New York: Penguin.

Duggan, Áine 2011/2012a, ' "Nobody Should Ever Feel the Way that I Felt": A Portrait of Jay Toole and Queer Homelessness', *Scholar & Feminist Online*, 10(1/2), available at: <http://sfonline.barnard.edu/a-new-queer-agenda/nobody-should-ever-feel-the-way-that-i-felt-a-portrait-of-jay-toole-and-queer-homelessness/#identifier_2_103>.

Duggan, Lisa 2002, 'The New Homonormativity: The Sexual Politics of Neoliberalism', in *Materializing Democracy: Toward a Revitalized Cultural Politics*, edited by Russ Castronovo and Dana D. Nelson, Durham, NC: Duke University Press.

——— 2003, *The Twilight of Equality? Neoliberalism, Cultural Politics, and the Attack on Democracy*, Boston: Beacon Press.

——— 2011/2012b, 'Beyond Marriage: Democracy, Equality, and Kinship for a New Century', *Scholar & Feminist Online*, 10(1/2), available at: <http://sfonline.barnard.edu/a-new-queer-agenda/beyond-marriage-democracy-equality-and-kinship-for-a-new-century/>.

Duggan, Lisa and Richard Kim 2011/2012, 'A New Queer Agenda: Preface', *Scholar & Feminist Online*, 10(1/2), available at: <http://sfonline.barnard.edu/a-new-queer-agenda/preface/>.

Duggan, Penelope 1997, *The Feminist Challenge to Traditional Political Organizing*, Amsterdam: IIRE (Working Paper no. 33).

——— 2013, 'Prologue', in *Dangerous Liaisons: The Marriages and Divorces of Marxism and Feminism*, by Cinzia Arruzza, translated by Marie Lagatta and Dave Kelly, London: The Merlin Press.

Duggan, Penelope and Heather Dashner (eds.) 1994, *Women's Lives in the New Globalized Economy*, Amsterdam: IIRE.

Dyer, Richard 2010, 'Préface', in Maxime Cervulle and Nick Rees-Roberts, *Homo exoticus: Race, classe et critique queer*, Paris: Armand Colin.

Ebert, Teresa 1996, 'The Matter of Materialism', in *The Material Queer: A LesBiGay Cultural Studies Reader*, edited by Donald Morton, Boulder: Westview Press.

Edge, Simon 1995, *With Friends Like These: Marxism and Gay Politics*, London: Cassell.

Ellmann, Richard 1988, *Oscar Wilde*, New York: Vintage Books.

Engels, Friedrich 1988, 'To Karl Marx (22 June 1869)', in *Marx-Engels Collected Works*, Volume 43, London: Lawrence and Wishart.

———— 2000 [1884], 'Origins of the Family, Private Property and the State', *Marxists Internet Archive*, available at: <http://www.marxists.org/archive/marx/works/1884/origin-family/cho2d.htm>.

Engels, Jacques [Jelle Boersma] 1926, *De communist en zijn sexueele moraal*, Overschie: Uitgeverij 'Iskra'.

Epprecht, Marc 1996, 'Outing the Gay Debate', *Southern Africa Report*, 11(4): 14–16.

———— 2009, 'Sexuality, Africa, History', *American Historical Review*, 114(5): 1258–72.

Escoffier, Jeffrey 1997, 'The Political Economy of the Closet: Notes Towards an Economic History of Gay and Lesbian Life before Stonewall', in *Homo Economics: Capitalism, Community and Lesbian and Gay Life*, edited by Amy Gluckman and Betsy Reed, London: Routledge.

Etty, Elsbeth 1996, *Liefde is heel het leven niet: Henriette Roland Holst, 1869–1952*, Amsterdam: Uitgeverij Balans.

Faderman, Lillian 1991, *Odd Girls and Twilight Lovers: A History of Lesbian Life in Twentieth-Century America*, New York: Penguin.

Farber, Samuel 1990, *Before Stalinism: The Rise and Fall of Soviet Democracy*, New York: Polity Press.

———— 2011, *Cuba since the Revolution of 1959: A Critical Assessment*, Chicago: Haymarket Books.

Farrow, Kenyon 2011/2012, 'A New Queer Agenda: Afterword: A Future beyond Equality', *Scholar & Feminist Online*, 10(1/2), available at: <http://sfonline.barnard.edu/a-new-queer-agenda/afterword-a-future-beyond-equality/>.

Feinberg, Leslie 1998, *Trans Liberation: Beyond Pink or Blue*, Boston: Beacon Press.

Ferguson, Roderick A. and Grace Kyungwon Hong 2012, 'The Sexual and Racial Contradictions of Neoliberalism', *Journal of Homosexuality*, 59(7): 1057–64.

Fernbach, David 1981, *The Spiral Path: A Gay Contribution to Human Survival*, Boston/London: Alyson/Gay Men's Press.

———— 1998, 'Biology and Gay Identity', *New Left Review*, 228: 47–66.

Floyd, Kevin 1998, 'Making History: Marxism, Queer Theory, and Contradiction in the Future of American Studies', *Cultural Critique*, 40: 167–201.

———— 2006, 'Lukács and Sexual Humanism', *Rethinking Marxism*, 18(3): 397–403.

———— 2009, *The Reification of Desire: Toward a Queer Marxism*, Minneapolis: University of Minnesota Press.

Ford, Clellan S. and Frank A. Beach 1951, *Patterns of Sexual Behaviour*, New York: Harper & Brothers.

Foucault, Michel 1973, *The Order of Things: An Archaeology of the Human Sciences*, New York: Vintage Books.

———— 1980, *The History of Sexuality, Volume 1: An Introduction*, translated by Robert Hurley, New York: Pantheon.

———— 1990, *The History of Sexuality, Volume 2: The Use of Pleasure*, translated by Robert Hurley, New York: Vintage Books.

Fourth International 1979, 'The Fourth International and the Struggle for Women's Liberation', available at: <http://www.internationalviewpoint.org/spip.php?article 1586>.

———— 2003, 'Resolution on Lesbian/Gay Liberation', available at: <http://www.internationalviewpoint.org/spip.php?article177>.

Franco, Jean 1998, 'The Long March of Feminism', *NACLA Report on the Americas*, 31(4): 10–15.

Fraser, Nancy 2009, 'Feminism, Capitalism and the Cunning of History', *New Left Review*, 56: 97–117.

Freud, Sigmund 1938, *The Basic Writings of Sigmund Freud*, translated and edited by A.A. Brill, New York: Modern Library.

Galbraith, James K. and V. Garza Cantú 2001, 'Inequality in American Manufacturing Wages, 1920–1998: A Revised Estimate', in *Inequality and Industrial Change: A Global View*, edited by James K. Galbraith and Maureen Berner, Cambridge: Cambridge University Press.

Garber, Eric 1989, 'A Spectacle in Color: The Lesbian and Gay Subculture of Jazz Age Harlem', in *Hidden from History: Reclaiming the Gay and Lesbian Past*, edited by Martin B. Duberman, Martha Vicinus and George Chauncey, Jr., New York: Penguin.

Garcia, J. Neil C. 1996, *Philippine Gay Culture: The Last Thirty Years*, Diliman: University of the Philippines Press.

Gay, Peter 1999, *The Bourgeois Experience: From Victoria to Freud, Volume 1: The Education of the Senses*, New York: W.W. Norton.

George, Rosemary Marangoly (ed.) 1998, *Burning Down the House: Recycling Domesticity*, Boulder: Westview Press.

Gevisser, Mark 1994, 'A Different Fight for Freedom', in *Defiant Desire: Gay and Lesbian Lives in South Africa*, edited by Mark Gevisser and Edwin Cameron, Johannesburg: Ravan Press.

———— 2000, 'Mandela's Stepchildren: Homosexual Identity in Post-Apartheid South Africa', in *Different Rainbows*, edited by Peter Drucker, London: Millivres/Gay Men's Press.

Gevisser, Mark and Edwin Cameron 1994, 'Introduction', in *Defiant Desire: Gay and Lesbian Lives in South Africa*, edited by Mark Gevisser and Edwin Cameron, Johannesburg: Ravan Press.

———— (eds.) 1994, *Defiant Desire: Gay and Lesbian Lives in South Africa*, Johannesburg: Ravan Press.

Girard, Gabriel 2009, 'Théories et militantismes queer: réflexion à partir de l'exemple français', available at: <http://www.europe-solidaire.org/spip.php?article14760>.

GLBT South-South Dialogue 2003a, 'South-South Recommendations, ILGA 20th World Conference' (Rome, July 2000), in *Globalization: GLBT Alternatives*, edited by Irene León and Phumi Mtewa, Quito: GLBT South-South Dialogue.

———— 2003b, 'Declaration on the Free Trade Area of the Americas (FTAA)' (Quito, October 2002), in *Globalization: GLBT Alternatives*, edited by Irene León and Phumi Mtewa, Quito: GLBT South-South Dialogue.

Gluckman, Amy and Betsy Reed 1997, 'Introduction', in *Homo Economics: Capitalism, Community and Lesbian and Gay Life*, edited by Amy Gluckman and Betsy Reed, London: Routledge.

———— (eds.) 1997, *Homo Economics: Capitalism, Community and Lesbian and Gay Life*, London: Routledge.

Gopinath, Gayatri 1998, 'Homo-Economics: Queer Sexualities in a Transnational Frame', in *Burning Down the House: Recycling Domesticity*, edited by Rosemary Marangoly George, Boulder: Westview Press.

Gough, Jamie and Mike MacNair 1985, *Gay Liberation in the Eighties*, London: Pluto Press.

Grant, Jaime M., Lisa A. Mottet and Justin Tanis 2011, *Injustice at Every Turn: A Report of the National Transgender Discrimination Survey*, Washington: National Center for Transgender Equality and National Gay and Lesbian Task Force, available at: <transequality.org/Resources/ntds_full.pdf>.

Green, James N. 1999a, *Beyond Carnival: Male Homosexuality in Twentieth-Century Brazil*, Chicago: University of Chicago Press.

———— 1999b, ' "More Love and More Desire": the Building of a Brazilian Movement', in *The Global Emergence of Gay and Lesbian Politics: National Imprints of a Worldwide Movement*, edited by B.D. Adam, J.W. Duyvendak and A. Krouwel, Philadelphia: Temple University Press.

———— 2000, 'Desire and Militancy: Lesbians, Gays, and the Brazilian Workers Party', in *Different Rainbows*, edited by Peter Drucker, London: Millivres/Gay Men's Press.

———— 2012, ' "Who Is the Macho who Wants to Kill Me?" Male Homosexuality, Revolutionary Masculinity, and the Brazilian Armed Struggle of the 1960s and 1970s', *Hispanic American Historical Review*, 92(3), 437–69.

Greenberg, David 1988, *The Construction of Homosexuality*, Chicago: University of Chicago Press.

Grémaux, René 1994, 'Woman Becomes Man in the Balkans', in *Third Sex, Third Gender: Beyond Sexual Dimorphism in Culture and History*, edited by Gilbert Herdt, New York: Zone Books.

Griffin, Peggy 2007, 'Sexing the Economy in a Neo-liberal World Order: Neo-Liberal Discourse and the (Re)Production of Heteronormative Heterosexuality', *British Journal of Politics and International Relations*, 9(2): 220–38.

Haeberle, Erwin J. 1989, 'Swastika, Pink Triangle, and Yellow Star: The Destruction of Sexology and the Persecution of Homosexuals in Nazi Germany', in *Hidden from History: Reclaiming the Gay and Lesbian Past*, edited by Martin B. Duberman, Martha Vicinus and George Chauncey, Jr., New York: Penguin.

Hall, Lesley 2004, ' "No Sex Please, We Are Socialists": The British Labour Party Closes its Eyes and Thinks of England', in *Meetings & Alcôves: Gauches et sexualités en Europe et aux Etats-Unis depuis 1850*, edited by Jesse F. Battan, Thomas Bouchet and Tania Régin, Dijon: Editions Universitaires de Dijon.

Hall, Stuart 1985, 'Signification, Representation, Ideology: Althusser and the Post-Structuralist Debates', *Critical Studies in Mass Communication*, 2(2): 91–114.

Halperin, David M. 1989, 'Sex before Sexuality: Pederasty, Politics, and Power in Classical Athens', in *Hidden from History: Reclaiming the Gay and Lesbian Past*, edited by Martin B. Duberman, Martha Vicinus and George Chauncey, Jr., New York: Penguin.

——— 1990, *One Hundred Years of Homosexuality and Other Essays on Greek Love*, New York: Routledge.

——— 2002, *How to Do the History of Homosexuality*, Chicago: University of Chicago Press.

——— 2012, 'Normal as Folk', *New York Times* (21 June), available at: <http://www.ny times.com/2012/06/22/opinion/style-and-the-meaning-of-gay-culture.html?_r=0>.

Harris-Perry, Melissa 2013, 'What Difference Will Marriage Equality Make?', *The Nation*, 296(15):10, available at:<http://www.thenation.com/article/173550/what-difference-will-same-sex-marriage-make>.

Hayes, Jarrod 2000, *Queer Nations: Marginal Sexualities in the Maghreb*, Chicago: University of Chicago Press.

Healey, Dan 2001, *Homosexual Desire in Revolutionary Russia: The Regulation of Sexual and Gender Dissent*, Chicago: University of Chicago Press.

Heaphy, Brian 2011, 'Gay Identities and the Culture of Class', *Sexualities*, 14(1): 42–62.

Hekma, Gert 1994, ' "A Female Soul in a Male Body": Sexual Inversion as Gender Inversion in Nineteenth-Century Sexology', in *Third Sex, Third Gender: Beyond Sexual Dimorphism in Culture and History*, edited by Gilbert Herdt, New York: Zone Books.

——— 1995, 'Homosexuality and the Left in the Netherlands, 1890–1911', in *Gay Men and the Sexual History of the Political Left,* edited by Gert Hekma, Harry Oosterhuis and James Steakley, Binghamton: Harrington Park Press.

Hekma, Gert, Harry Oosterhuis and James Steakley (eds.) 1995, *Gay Men and the Sexual History of the Political Left,* Binghamton: Harrington Park Press.

Hennessy, Rosemary 1994, 'Queer Theory, Left Politics', *Rethinking Marxism*, 7(3): 85–111.

———— 2000, *Profit and Pleasure: Sexual Identities in Late Capitalism*, New York: Routledge.

———— 2006, 'Returning to Reproduction Queerly: Sex, Labor, Need', *Rethinking Marxism*, 18(3): 387–95.

Herdt, Gilbert 1994, 'Preface' and 'Introduction: Third Sexes and Third Genders', in *Third Sex, Third Gender: Beyond Sexual Dimorphism in Culture and History*, New York: Zone Books.

———— (ed.) 1994, *Third Sex, Third Gender: Beyond Sexual Dimorphism in Culture and History*, New York: Zone Books.

Herzer, Manfred 1995, 'Communists, Social Democrats, and the Homosexual Movement in the Weimar Republic', in *Gay Men and the Sexual History of the Political Left*, edited by Gert Hekma, Harry Oosterhuis and James Steakley, Binghamton: Harrington Park Press.

Herzog, Dagmar 2011, *Sexuality in Europe: A Twentieth-Century History*, Cambridge: Cambridge University Press.

———— 2014, 'What Happened to Psychoanalysis in the Wake of the Sexual Revolution? A Story about the Durability of Homophobia and the Dream of Love, 1950s–2010s', in *Sexualities: Contemporary Psychoanalytic Perspectives*, edited by Allessandra Lemma and Paul Lynch, New York: Routledge.

Hinsch, Bret 1990, *Passions of the Cut Sleeve: The Male Homosexual Tradition in China*, Berkeley: University of California Press.

Hoad, Neville 1999, 'Between the White Man's Burden and the White Man's Disease: Tracking Lesbian and Gay Human Rights in Southern Africa', *GLQ*, 5(4): 559–84.

Hobsbawm, Eric 1987, *The Age of Empire, 1875–1914*, New York: Pantheon Books.

———— 1994, *Age of Extremes: The Short Twentieth Century, 1914–1991*, London: Michael Joseph.

Hobsbawm, Eric and Terence Ranger (eds.) 1992, *The Invention of Tradition,* Cambridge: Cambridge University Press.

Hofman, Paul 2013, 'Wet lesbisch ouderschap: uitstel of afstel?', *GayKrant*, 677: 38–9.

Hollibaugh, Amber 1980, 'Right to Rebel', in *Homosexuality: Power and Politics*, edited by Gay Left Collective, London: Allison and Busby.

———— 2011/2012a, 'Defining Desires and Dangerous Decisions', *Scholar & Feminist Online*, 10(1/2), available at: <http://sfonline.barnard.edu/a-new-queer-agenda/defining-desires-and-dangerous-decisions/>.

———— 2011/2012b, '2, 4, 6, 8: Who Says that Your Grandmother's Straight', *Scholar & Feminist Online*, 10(1/2), available at: <http://sfonline.barnard.edu/a-new-queer-agenda/2-4-6-8-who-says-that-your-grandmothers-straight/>.

Hollibaugh, Amber and Cherríe Moraga 1983, 'What We're Rollin around in Bed with: Sexual Silences in Feminism', in *Powers of Desire: The Politics of Sexuality*, edited by

Ann Barr Snitow, Christine Stansell and Sharon Thompson, New York: Monthly Review Press.

Hollibaugh, Amber and Nikhil Pal Singh 1999, 'Sexuality, Labor, and the New Trade Unionism', *Social Text*, 17(4): 73–88.

hooks, bell 1990, *Yearning: Race, Gender, and Cultural Politics*, Boston: South End Press.

Huusen, Arend H., Jr. 1989, 'Sodomy in the Dutch Republic during the Eighteenth Century', in *Hidden from History: Reclaiming the Gay and Lesbian Past*, edited by Martin B. Duberman, Martha Vicinus and George Chauncey, Jr., New York: Penguin.

Ireland, Doug 2007, 'Iraqi Gay Activist Arrested, Tortured', *Gay City News* (3 May), available at: <http://direland.typepad.com/direland/2007/05/iraqi_gay_activ.html>.

Jackson, Peter A. 1989, *Male Homosexuality in Thailand: An Interpretation of Contemporary Thai Sources*, Elmhurst: Global Academic Publishers.

——— 2009, 'Capitalism and Global Queering: National Markets, Parallels among Sexual Cultures, and Multiple Queer Modernities', *GLQ*, 15(3): 357–95.

Jacobs, Michael P. 1997, 'Do Gay Men Have a Stake in Male Privilege? The Political Economy of Gay Men's Contradictory Relationship to Feminism', in *Homo Economics: Capitalism, Community and Lesbian and Gay Life*, edited by Amy Gluckman and Betsy Reed, London: Routledge.

Jakobsen, Janet R. 2012, 'Perverse Justice', *GLQ*, 18(1): 19–45.

Jivraj, Suhraiya and Anisa de Jong 2011, 'The Dutch Homo-Emancipation Policy and its Silencing Effects on Queer Muslims', *Feminist Legal Studies*, 19(2): 143–58.

Jolly, Susan 2000, 'What Use is Queer Theory to Development?' Institute for Development Studies, University of Sussex, discussion paper, available at: <http://www.ids.ac.uk/files/dmfile/jollytalk.pdf>.

Jordan-Young, Rebecca M. 2010, *Brain Storm: The Flaws in the Science of Sex Differences*, Cambridge, MA: Harvard University Press.

Joseph, Sherry and Pawan Dhall 2000, ' "No Silence Please, We're Indians!" – Les-bi-gay Voices from India', in *Different Rainbows*, edited by Peter Drucker, London: Millivres/Gay Men's Press.

Kaoma, Kapya John 2012, 'Colonizing African Values: How the U.S. Christian Right is Transforming Sexual Politics in Africa', *Political Research Associates,* available at: <http://www.publiceye.org/publications/globalizing-the-culture-wars/pdf/africa-full-report.pdf>.

Karlinsky, Simon 1989, 'Russia's Gay Literature and Culture: The Impact of the October Revolution', in *Hidden from History: Reclaiming the Gay and Lesbian Past*, edited by Martin B. Duberman, Martha Vicinus and George Chauncey, Jr., New York: Penguin.

Katz, Jonathan Ned 1976, *Gay American History: Lesbians and Gay Men in the U.S.A.*, New York: Thomas Y. Crowell Company.

——— 1995, *The Invention of Heterosexuality*, New York: Penguin.

Kautsky, Karl 1900, 'Class War and Ethics', translated by J.B. Askew, available at: <http://www.marxists.org/archive/kautsky/1900/11/ethics.htm>.

———— 1918, 'Chapter VIII: The Object Lesson', in *The Dictatorship of the Proletariat*, translated by Henry James Stenning, available at: <http://www.marxists.org/archive/kautsky/1918/dictprole/ch08.htm>.

Kergoat, Danièle 2009, 'Dynamique et consubstantialité des rapports sociaux', in *Sexe, race, classe: pour une épistémologie de la domination*, edited by Elsa Dorlin and Annie Bidet-Mordrel, Paris: PUF, 2009.

Khan, Badruddin 1997, 'Not-so-gay Life in Pakistan in the 1980s and 1990s', in *Islamic Homosexualities: Culture, History and Literature*, edited by Will Roscoe and Stephen O. Murray, New York: New York University Press.

Kimball, Geoffrey 1993, 'Aztec Homosexuality: The Textual Evidence', *Journal of Homosexuality*, 26(1): 7–24.

Kinsman, Gary 1987, *The Regulation of Desire: Sexuality in Canada*, Montreal: Black Rose Books.

Klein, Charles 1998, 'Gender, Sexuality and AIDS Prevention in Brazil', *NACLA Report on the Americas*, 31(4): 27–32.

Kleitz, Gilles 2000, 'Why is Development Work so Straight?', Institute for Development Studies, University of Sussex, discussion paper, available at: <http://www.ids.ac.uk/files/dmfile/whystraight.pdf>.

Klotz, Marcia 2006, 'Alienation, Labor and Sexuality in Marx's 1844 Manuscripts', *Rethinking Marxism*, 18(3): 405–13.

Kollontai, Alexandra 1978, *Selected Writings*, translated by Alix Holt, Westport, CT: Lawrence Hill and Company.

Krupat, Kitty, 'Out of Labor's Dark Age: Sexual Politics Comes to the Workplace', *Social Text*, 17(4): 9–29.

Kumar, Arvind 1993, 'Hijras: Challenging Gender Dichotomies', in *A Lotus of Another Color: An Unfolding of the South Asian Gay and Lesbian Experience*, edited by Rakesh Ratti, Boston: Alyson Publications.

Laird, Cynthia 2012, 'Labor Leader Howard Wallace Dies', *Bay Area Reporter*, (22 November), available at: <http://ebar.com/news/article.php?sec=news&article=68274>.

Lamas, Marta 1998, 'Scenes from a Mexican Battlefield', *NACLA Report on the Americas*, 31(4): 17–21.

Latimer, Tirza True 2005, *Women Together/Women Apart: Portraits of Lesbian Paris*, New Brunswick: Rutgers University Press.

Lauritsen, John and David Thorstad 1995, *The Early Homosexual Rights Movement (1864–1934)*, New York: Times Change.

Lecklider, Aaron 2012, 'Coming to Terms: Homosexuality and the Left in American Culture', *GLQ*, 18(1): 179–95.

Lenin, Vladimir I. 1961 [1902], *What Is to Be Done? Burning Questions of Our Movement*, translated by Joe Fineberg and George Hanna, in *Collected Works*, Volume 5, Moscow: Foreign Languages Publishing House, available at: <http://www.marxists .org/archive/lenin/works/1901/witbd/iii.htm>.

———— 1964 [1915], *The Revolutionary Proletariat and the Right of Self-Determination*, translated by N.K. Krupskaya, in *Collected Works*, Volume 21, Moscow: Progress Publishers, available at: <http://www.marxists.org/archive/lenin/works/1915/oct/16 .htm>.

———— 1970 [1916], *The Discussion on Self-Determination Summed Up*, in *Collected Works*, Volume 22, London: Lawrence & Wishart, available at: <http://www.marx-ists.org/archive/lenin/works/1916/jul/x01.htm>.

León, Irene and Phumi Mtewa (eds.) 2003, *Globalization: GLBT Alternatives*, Quito: GLBT South-South Dialogue.

Lih, Lars T. 2006, *Lenin Rediscovered:* What Is to Be Done? *in Context*, Leiden: Brill.

Lind, Amy and Jessica Share 2003, 'Queering Development: Institutionalized Heterosexuality in Development Theory, Practice and Politics in Latin America', in *Feminist Futures: Re-Imagining Women, Culture, and Development*, edited by Kum-Kum Bhavnani, John Foran and Priya Kurian, New York: Zed Books.

Long, Scott 2013, 'Eric Ohena Lembembe: Not Again, or Never Again?', *A Paper Bird: Sex, Rights, and the World*, available at: <http://paper-bird.net/2013/07/19/eric-ohena-lembembe-not-again-or-never-again/>.

Loos, Tamara 2009, 'Transnational Histories of Sexualities in Asia', *American Historical Review*, 114(5): 1309–24.

Löwy, Michael 1998, *Fatherland or Mother Earth: Essays on the National Question*, Amsterdam/London: IIRE/Pluto Press.

Lukács, Georg 1972 [1922], *History and Class Consciousness: Studies in Marxist Dialectics*, translated by Rodney Livingstone, Cambridge, MA: MIT Press.

Lumsden, Ian 1991, *Homosexuality, Society and the State in Mexico*, Toronto: Canadian Gay Archives.

———— 1996, *Machos, Maricones and Gays: Cuba and Homosexuality*, Philadelphia: Temple University Press.

Lybeck, Mati M. 2009, 'Gender, Sexuality, and Belonging: Female Homosexuality in Germany, 1890–1933', *Bulletin of the GHI*, 44: 29–41.

Magdoff, Fred and Harry 2004, 'Disposable Workers: Today's Reserve Army of Labor', *Monthly Review*, 55(11), available at: <http://monthlyreview.org/2004/04/01/ disposable-workers-todays-reserve-army-of-labor#top>.

Maikey, Haneen 2012, 'Signposts from Al Qaws: A Decade of Building a Queer Palestinian Discourse', available at <http://alqaws.org/articles/Signposts-from-alQaws-A-Decade-of-Building-a-Queer-Palestinian-Discourse/>.

Maikey, Haneen and Alex de Jong 2011, 'Palestine: Resisting Homophobia and Occupation', available at <http://www.europe-solidaire.org/spip.php?article22232>.

Makarem, Ghassan 2011, 'The Story of HELEM', *Journal of Middle East Women's Studies,* 7(3): 98–112.

Mananzala, Rickke 2011/2012, 'The FIERCE Fight for Power and the Preservation of Public Space in the West Village', *Scholar & Feminist Online,* 10(1/2), available at: <http://sfonline.barnard.edu/a-new-queer-agenda/the-fierce-fight-for-power-and-the-preservation-of-public-space-in-the-west-village/>.

Mandel, Ernest 1978, *Late Capitalism,* translated by Joris de Bres, London: Verso.

——— 1995, *Long Waves of Capitalist Development: A Marxist Interpretation,* London: Verso.

Mansilla, Luis A. 1996, 'El ángel caído' (Interview with Pedro Lemebel), *Punto Final,* 23.

Marcuse, Herbert 1964, *One-Dimensional Man: Studies in the Ideology of Advanced Industrial Society,* Boston: Beacon Press.

——— 1966, *Eros and Civilization: A Philosophical Inquiry into Freud,* Boston: Beacon Press.

Martin, Robert K. 1989, 'Knights-Errant and Gothic Seducers: The Representation of Male Friendship in Mid-Nineteenth Century America', in *Hidden from History: Reclaiming the Gay and Lesbian Past,* edited by Martin B. Duberman, Martha Vicinus and George Chauncey, Jr., New York: Penguin.

Marx, Karl 1968 [1859], 'Preface to A Contribution to the Critique of Political Economy', in *Selected Works in One Volume,* by Karl Marx and Friedrich Engels, New York: International Publishers.

——— 1976 [1867], *Capital: A Critique of Political Economy,* Volume 1, translated by Ben Fowkes, Harmondsworth: Penguin Books.

Marx, Karl and Friedrich Engels 1968, *Selected Works in One Volume,* New York: International Publishers.

——— 1975 [1845], 'The Holy Family, or Critique of Critical Criticism: Against Bruno Bauer and Company', translated by Richard Dixon and Clement Dutts, in *Collected Works,* Volume 4, Moscow: Progress Publishers, available at: <http://www.marxists.org/archive/marx/works/1845/holy-family/ch04.htm #4.4.a>.

Massad, Joseph A. 2007, *Desiring Arabs,* Chicago: University of Chicago Press.

Mazdafiah, Siti 2012, 'To Support Activism: Building Communication among Lesbian Community in Surabaya', in *Women-Loving-Women in Africa and Asia: Trans/Sign, Report of Research Findings,* edited by S.E. Wieringa, Amsterdam: Riek Stienstra Fonds.

Mburu, John 2000, 'Awakenings: Dreams and Delusions of an Incipient Lesbian and Gay Movement in Kenya', in *Different Rainbows,* edited by Peter Drucker, London: Millivres/Gay Men's Press.

McCreery, Patrick and Kitty Krupat 1999, 'Out Front: Lesbians, Gays, and the Struggle for Workplace Rights (Introduction)', *Social Text*, 17(4): 1–7.

McDermott, Elizabeth 2011, 'The World Some Have Won: Sexuality, Class and Inequality', *Sexualities*, 14(1): 63–78.

McLean, Hugh and Linda Ngcobo 1994, 'Abangibhamayo bathi ngimnandi (Those who Fuck me Say I'm Tasty): Gay Sexuality in Reef Townships', in *Defiant Desire: Gay and Lesbian Lives in South Africa*, edited by Mark Gevisser and Edwin Cameron, Johannesburg: Ravan Press.

Mejía, Max 2000, 'Mexican Pink', in *Different Rainbows*, edited by Peter Drucker, London: Millivres/Gay Men's Press.

Melamed, Jodi 2006, 'The Spirit of Neoliberalism: From Racial Liberalism to Neoliberal Multiculturalism', *Social Text*, 24(4): 1–24.

Mepschen, Paul 2009, 'Against Tolerance: Islam, Sexuality and the Politics of Belonging in the Netherlands', *International Viewpoint*, available at: <http://www.europe-solidaire.org/spip.php?article14519>.

Mepschen, Paul, Jan Willem Duyvendak and Evelien Tonkens 2010, 'Sexual Politics, Orientalism, and Multicultural Citizenship in the Netherlands', *Sociology*, 44(5): 962–79.

Merrick, Jeffrey and Bryant T. Ragan, Jr. (eds.) 2001, *Homosexuality in Early Modern France: A Documentary Collection*, New York: Oxford University Press.

Meyerowitz, Joanne 2002, *How Sex Changed: A History of Transsexuality in the United States*, Cambridge, MA: Harvard University Press.

——— 2009, 'Transnational Sex and U.S. History', *American Historical Review*, 114(5): 1273–86.

——— 2010, ' "How Common Culture Shapes the Separate Lives": Sexuality, Race, and Mid-Twentieth-Century Social Constructionist Thought', *Journal of American History*, 96(4): 1057–84.

Mieli, Mario 1980, *Homosexuality and Liberation: Elements of a Gay Critique*, London: Gay Men's Press.

Miller, Stephen D. (ed.) 1996, *Partings at Dawn: An Anthology of Japanese Gay Literature*, San Francisco: Gay Sunshine Press.

Mitchell, Gregory 2011, 'TurboConsumers™ in Paradise: Tourism, Civil Rights, and Brazil's Gay Sex Industry', *American Ethnologist*, 38(4): 666–82.

Mogrovejo, Norma 2000, 'Lesbian Visibility in Latin America: Reclaiming Our History', in *Different Rainbows*, edited by Peter Drucker, London: Millivres/Gay Men's Press.

Moodie, T. Dunbar (with Vivienne Ndatshe and British Sibuyi) 1989, 'Migrancy and Male Sexuality on the South African Gold Mines', in *Hidden from History: Reclaiming the Gay and Lesbian Past*, edited by Martin B. Duberman, Martha Vicinus and George Chauncey, Jr., New York: Penguin.

Moore, Mignon R. 2011, *Invisible Families: Gay Identities, Relationships, and Motherhood among Black Women*, Berkeley: University of California Press.

Moore, Patrick 2004, *Beyond Shame: Reclaiming the Abandoned History of Radical Gay Sexuality*, Boston: Beacon Press.

Moriarty, Martin 2007, *Trade Unionists Together for LGBT Rights*, Ferney-Voltaire/ Brussels: Public Services International/Education International.

Morton, Donald 1996, 'Changing the Terms: (Virtual) Desire and (Actual) Reality', in *The Material Queer: A LesBiGay Cultural Studies Reader*, edited by Donald Morton, Boulder, CO: Westview Press.

———— (ed.) 1996, *The Material Queer: A LesBiGay Cultural Studies Reader*, Boulder, CO: Westview Press.

Moynihan, Daniel Patrick 1965, *The Negro Family: The Case for National Action*, Washington: US Department of Labor, available at <http://www.blackpast.org/?q=primary/moynihan-report-1965#chapter 4>.

Mtewa, Phumi 2003, 'GLBT Visions for an Alternative Globalization', in *Globalization: GLBT Alternatives*, edited by Irene León and Phumi Mtewa, Quito: GLBT South-South Dialogue.

Murray, Stephen O. 1990, 'Andean Cultures' and 'Haiti', in *Encyclopedia of Homosexuality*, edited by Wayne R. Dynes, Warren Johansson, William A. Percy and Stephen Donaldson, New York: Garland Publishing.

———— 1997, 'Gender-defined Homosexual Roles in Sub-Saharan African Islamic Cultures', in *Islamic Homosexualities: Culture, History and Literature*, edited by Will Roscoe and Stephen O. Murray, New York: New York University Press.

Najmabadi, Afsaneh 2005, *Women with Mustaches and Men without Beards: Gender and Sexual Anxieties of Iranian Modernity*, Berkeley: University of California Press.

Naqvi, Nauman and Hasan Mujtaba 1997, 'Two Baluchi *Buggas*, a Sindhi *Zenana*, and the Status of *Hijras* in Contemporary Pakistan', in *Islamic Homosexualities: Culture, History and Literature*, edited by Will Roscoe and Stephen O. Murray, New York: New York University Press.

Nana, Joel Gustave, Hakima Abbas, Wanja Muguongo, Phumi Mtetwa and Sibongile Ndashe 2011, 'Statement of African Social Justice Activists on the Threats of the British Government to "Cut Aid" to African Countries that Violate the Rights of LGBTI People in Africa', available at <http://www.blacklooks.org/2011/10/statement-of-african-social-justice-activists-on-the-decision-of-the-british-government-to-"cut-aid"-to-african-countries-that-violate-the-rights-of-lgbti-people-in-africa/>.

Nanda, Serena, 'Hijras: Al Alternative Sex and Gender Role in India', in *Third Sex, Third Gender: Beyond Sexual Dimorphism in Culture and History*, edited by Gilbert Herdt, New York: Zone Books.

Nestle, Joan 1989, 'The Fem Question', in *Pleasure and Danger: Exploring Female Sexuality*, edited by Carole S. Vance, London: Pandora.

Newton, Esther 1989, 'The Mythic Mannish Lesbian: Radclyffe Hall and the New Woman', in *Hidden from History: Reclaiming the Gay and Lesbian Past*, edited by Martin B. Duberman, Martha Vicinus and George Chauncey, Jr., New York: Penguin.

Ng, Vivien W. 1989, 'Homosexuality and the State in Late Imperial China', in *Hidden from History: Reclaiming the Gay and Lesbian Past*, edited by Martin B. Duberman, Martha Vicinus and George Chauncey, Jr., New York: Penguin.

Norton, Rictor 1992, *Mother Clap's Molly House: The Gay Subculture in England, 1700– 1830*, London: Gay Men's Press.

Oetomo, Dédé 1996, 'Gender and Sexual Orientation', in *Fantasizing the Feminine in Indonesia*, edited by Laurie J. Sears, Durham, NC: Duke University Press.

———— 1999, 'The Struggle for Lesbian and Gay Rights', in *Green Left Weekly*, 351, available at: <http://www.greenleft.org.au/node/20305>.

Oetomo, Dédé and Bruce Emond 1992, *Homosexuality in Indonesia*, translated by Sindhu Suyana, [n.p.].

Ordover, N. 2011/2012, 'Defying *Realpolitik*: Human Rights and the HIV Entry Bar', *Scholar & Feminist Online*, 10(1/2), available at: <http://sfonline.barnard.edu/a-new-queer-agenda/defying-realpolitik-human-rights-and-the-hiv-entry-bar/>.

Padgug, Robert 1989, 'Sexual Matters: Rethinking Sexuality in History', in *Hidden from History: Reclaiming the Gay and Lesbian Past*, edited by Martin B. Duberman, Martha Vicinus and George Chauncey, Jr., New York: Penguin.

Palaversich, Diana 2002, 'The Wounded Body of Proletarian Homosexuality in Pedro Lemebel's *Loco afán*', *Latin American Perspectives*, 29(2): 263–82.

Patterson, Torvald 2000, 'Queer without Fear', Amsterdam: [n.p.].

Peirce, Leslie, 'Writing Histories of Sexuality in the Middle East', *American Historical Review*, 114(5): 1325–39.

Peterson, Ben and Subash Pokharel 2009, 'Nepal's Blue Diamond Society: Hopes High for LGBTI Rights', *Links*, available at: <http://links.org.au/node/980>.

Pew Research Center 2013, 'A Survey of LGBT Americans: Attitudes, Experiences and Values in Changing Times', available at: <http://www.pewsocialtrends.org/2013/06/13/a-survey-of-lgbt-americans/>.

Pokade, Noman 2012, 'From the Horse's Mouth: Township Perceptions on the Black Butch Lesbian Identity', in *Women-Loving-Women in Africa and Asia: Trans/Sign, Report of Research Findings*, edited by S.E. Wieringa, Amsterdam: Riek Stienstra Fonds.

Post, Charles 2007a, 'The Labor Aristocracy: A Reply', *Against the Current*, 127, available at: <http://www.solidarity-us.org/site/node/490#N5>.

———— 2007b, 'U.S. Labor's Subterranean Fire', *Against the Current*, 131, available at: <http://www.solidarity-us.org/site/node/1186#R8>.

———— 2012, *The American Road to Capitalism: Studies in Class Structure, Economic Development and Political Conflict, 1620–1877*, Chicago: Haymarket Books.

Poulantzas, Nicos 1980, *State, Power, Socialism*, translated by Patrick Camiller, London: Verso.

Prime Access 2012, *2011 Gay Press Report*, Mountainside, NJ: Rivendell, available at: <http://rivendellmedia.com/documents/2011-Gay-Press-Report.pdf>.

Puar, Jasbir 2007, *Terrorist Assemblages: Homonationalism in Queer Times*, Durham, NC: Duke University Press.

Raffo, Susan 2011/2012, 'The Practical Day-to-Day Details of Being Queer', *Scholar & Feminist Online*, 10(1/2), available at: <http://sfonline.barnard.edu/a-new-queer-agenda/the-practical-day-to-day-details-of-being-queer/>.

——— (ed.) 1997, *Queerly Classed*, Boston: South End Press.

Randall, Margaret 2000, 'To Change Our Own Reality and the World: A Conversation with Lesbians in Nicaragua', in *Different Rainbows*, edited by Peter Drucker, London: Millivres/Gay Men's Press.

Ranger, Terence 1992, 'The Invention of Tradition in Colonial Africa', in *The Invention of Tradition,* edited by Eric Hobsbawm and Terence Ranger, Cambridge: Cambridge University Press.

Rao, Rahul 2012, 'On "Gay Conditionality", Imperial Power and Queer Liberation': available at <http://kafila.org/2012/01/01/on-gay-conditionality-imperial-power-and-queer-liberation-rahul-rao/#more-11088>.

Reddy, Chandan C. 1998, 'Home, Houses, Nonidentity: *Paris Is Burning*', in *Burning Down the House: Recycling Domesticity*, edited by Rosemary Marangoly George, Boulder, CO: Westview Press..

Reed, Gail 2012, 'Revolutionizing Gender', *MEDICC Review*, 14(2), available at: <http://www.medicc.org/mediccreview/index.php?issue=20&id=246&a=vahtml>.

Reich, Wilhelm 1972, *Sex-Pol: Essays, 1929–1934*, edited by Lee Baxandall, translated by Anna Bostock, Tom DuBose and Lee Baxandall, New York: Vintage Books.

Reynolds, Paul 2003, 'Some Thoughts on Marxism and the Social Construction of Sexuality', paper for the 'Socialism and Sexuality' Conference, University of Amsterdam, [n.p.].

Rich, Adrienne 1983, 'Compulsory Heterosexuality and Lesbian Existence', in *Powers of Desire: The Politics of Sexuality*, edited by Ann Barr Snitow, Christine Stansell and Sharon Thompson, New York: Monthly Review Press.

Ringrose, Kathryn M. 1994, 'Living in the Shadows: Eunuchs and Gender in Byzantium', in *Third Sex, Third Gender: Beyond Sexual Dimorphism in Culture and History*, edited by Gilbert Herdt, New York: Zone Books.

Ritchie, Jason 2010, 'How Do You Say "Come Out of the Closet" in Arabic? Queer Activism and the Politics of Visibility in Israel-Palestine', *GLQ*, 16(4): 557–75.

Robinson, Paul 2001, 'Freud and Homosexuality', in *Homosexuality and Psychoanalysis*, edited by Tim Dean and Christopher Lane, Chicago: University of Chicago Press.

Robles, Víctor Hugo 1998, 'History in the Making: The Homosexual Liberation Movement in Chile', NACLA Report on the Americas, 31(4): 36–40.

Robson, Ruthann 1992, Lesbian (Out)Law: Survival under the Rule of Law, Ithaca: Firebrand.

———— 1997, 'To Market, to Market: Considering Class in the Context of Lesbian Legal Theories and Reforms', in Queerly Classed, edited by Susan Raffo, Boston: South End Press.

Rodney, Walter 1972, How Europe Underdeveloped Africa, London: Bogle-L'Ouverture Publications.

Rofel, Lisa 1999, 'Qualities of Desire: Imagining Gay Identities in China', GLQ, 5(4): 451–74.

Romero, Adam et al. 2007, 'U.S. Census Snapshot', available at: <http://escholarship .org/uc/item/6nx232r4>.

Roscoe, Will 1994, 'How to Become a Berdache: Toward a Unified Analysis of Gender Diversity', in Third Sex, Third Gender: Beyond Sexual Dimorphism in Culture and History, edited by Gilbert Herdt, New York: Zone Books.

Roscoe, Will and Stephen O. Murray 1997, 'Introduction', in Islamic Homosexualities: Culture, History and Literature, edited by Will Roscoe and Stephen O. Murray, New York: New York University Press.

Rosenberg, Jordana and Amy Villarejo 2012, 'Introduction: Queerness, Norms, Utopia', GLQ, 18(1): 1–18.

Ross, Ellen and Rayna Rapp 1983, 'Sex and Society: A Research Note from Social History and Anthropology', in Powers of Desire: The Politics of Sexuality, edited by Ann Barr Snitow, Christine Stansell and Sharon Thompson, New York: Monthly Review Press.

Rousset, Pierre 2005, 'The World Social Forum: A New Framework for Solidarities', in Bandung 2005: Rethinking Solidarity in Global Society, Yogyakarta: Ghadjah Mada University/Yayasan Pondok Rakyat.

Rowbotham, Sheila 1977a, 'Edward Carpenter: Prophet of the New Life', in Socialism and the New Life: The Personal and Sexual Politics of Edward Carpenter and Havelock Ellis, by Sheila Rowbotham and Jeffrey Weeks, London: Pluto Press.

———— 1977b, A New World for Women: Stella Browne, Socialist Feminist, London: Pluto Press.

Rowbotham, Sheila, Lynne Segal and Hilary Wainwright 1979, Beyond the Fragments: Feminism and the Making of Socialism, London: The Merlin Press.

Rubin, Gayle 2011, Deviations: A Gayle Rubin Reader, Durham, NC: Duke University Press.

Rupp, Leila 1989, ' "Imagine My Surprise": Women's Relationships in Mid-Twentieth Century America', in Hidden from History: Reclaiming the Gay and Lesbian Past, edited by Martin B. Duberman, Martha Vicinus and George Chauncey, Jr., New York: Penguin.

Sangster, Joan and Meg Luxton 2012, 'Feminism, Co-optation and the Problem of Amnesia: A Response to Nancy Fraser', in *Socialist Register 2013: The Question of Strategy*, edited by Leo Panitch, Greg Albo and Vivek Chibber, London: The Merlin Press.

Sarda, Alejandra, 'Lesbians and the Gay Movement in Argentina', NACLA *Report on the Americas*, 31(4): 40–1.

Sargent, Lydia (ed.) 1981, *Women and Revolution: A Discussion of the Unhappy Marriage of Marxism and Feminism*, Boston: South End Press.

Saslow, James M. 1989, 'Homosexuality in the Renaissance: Behavior, Identity, and Artistic Expression', in *Hidden from History: Reclaiming the Gay and Lesbian Past*, edited by Martin B. Duberman, Martha Vicinus and George Chauncey, Jr., New York: Penguin.

Schalow, Paul Gordon 1989, 'Male Love in Early Modern Japan: A Literary Depiction of the "Youth" ', in *Hidden from History: Reclaiming the Gay and Lesbian Past*, edited by Martin B. Duberman, Martha Vicinus and George Chauncey, Jr., New York: Penguin.

———— 1996, 'Introduction', in *Partings at Dawn: An Anthology of Japanese Gay Literature*, edited by Stephen D. Miller, San Francisco: Gay Sunshine Press.

Schifter Sikora, Jacob 1989, *La Formación de una Contracultura: Homosexualismo y Sida en Costa Rica,* San José.

Schmidt, Gunter 2001, 'Gibt es Heterosexualität?', available at: <http://www.taz.de/1/archiv/archiv/?dig=2001/03/17/a0215>.

Schulman, Sarah 2012, *Israel/Palestine and the Queer International*, Durham, NC: Duke University Press.

Scott, Joan W. 1986, 'Gender: A Useful Category of Historical Analysis', *American Historical Review*, 91(5): 1053–75.

Sears, Alan 2000, 'Queer in a Lean World', *Against the Current*, 89, available at: <http://www.solidarity-us.org/site/node/965>.

———— 2005, 'Queer Anti-Capitalism: What's Left of Lesbian and Gay Liberation?', *Science and Society*, 69(1): 92–112.

———— 2006/7, 'Lean on Me? The Falling Rate of Friendship', *New Socialist*, 59: 36–7.

Sears, Laurie J. (ed.) 1996, *Fantasizing the Feminine in Indonesia,* Durham, NC: Duke University Press.

Seccombe, Wally 1992, *A Millennium of Family Change: Feudalism to Capitalism in Northwestern Europe*, London: Verso.

———— 1993, *Weathering the Storm: Working-Class Families from the Industrial Revolution to the Fertility Decline*, London: Verso.

Seidman, Steven 1997, *Difference Troubles: Queering Social Theory and Sexual Politics*, Cambridge: Cambridge University Press.

———— 2011, 'Class Matters ... but How Much? Class, Nation, and Queer Life', *Sexualities*, 14(1): 36–41.

Self, Robert O. 2012, *All in the Family: The Realignment of American Democracy since the 1960s*, New York: Hill & Wang.

Shah Chayanika, Raj, Shalini Mahajan and Smriti Nevatia 2012, 'Breaking the Binary: Understanding Concerns and Realities of Female Assigned/Born Persons across a Spectrum of Lived Gender Identities', in *Women-Loving-Women in Africa and Asia: Trans/Sign, Report of Research Findings*, edited by S.E. Wieringa, Amsterdam: Riek Stienstra Fonds.

Shah, Nayan 2005, 'Between "Oriental Depravity" and "Natural Degenerates": Spatial Borderlands and the Making of Ordinary Americans', *American Quarterly*, 57(3): 703–25.

Shah, Svati P. 2011/2012, 'Sex Work and Queer Politics in Three Acts', *Scholar & Feminist Online*, 10(1/2), available at: <sfonline.barnard.edu/a-new-queer-agenda/sex-work-and-queer-politics-in-three-acts/>.

Shepard, Benjamin and Ronald Hayduk (eds.) 2002, *From ACT UP to the WTO: Urban Protest and Community Building in the Era of Globalization*, London: Verso.

Shepard, Todd 2012, ' "Something Notably Erotic": Politics, "Arab Men", and Sexual Revolution in Post-decolonization France', *Journal of Modern History*, 84(1): 80–115.

Sheridan, Alan 1998, *André Gide: A Life in the Present*, London: Hamish Hamilton.

Shohat, Ella 2006, *Taboo Memories, Diasporic Voices*, Durham, NC: Duke University Press.

Sidel, Ruth 2012, 'We Don't Need a Piece of Paper from City Hall – or Do We?', *Women's Review of Books*, 29(6): 14–15.

Simon, Scott and Dick Leitsch 2008, 'Remembering a 1966 "Sip-In" for Gay Rights', National Public Radio interview, available at: <http://www.npr.org/templates/story/story.php?storyId=91993823>.

Simpson, Mark 2002, 'Meet the Metrosexual', *Salon.com*, available at: <www.salon.com/2002/07/22/metrosexual/>.

Smith-Rosenberg, Carroll 1989, 'Discourses of Sexuality and Subjectivity: The New Women, 1870–1936', in *Hidden from History: Reclaiming the Gay and Lesbian Past*, edited by Martin B. Duberman, Martha Vicinus and George Chauncey, Jr., New York: Penguin.

Snitow, Ann Barr, Christine Stansell and Sharon Thompson (eds.) 1983, *Powers of Desire: The Politics of Sexuality*, New York: Monthly Review Press.

SONG (Southerners on New Ground) 2011/2012, 'Our People Are Worth the Risks: A Southern Queer Agenda from the Margins and the Red States', *Scholar & Feminist Online*, 10(1/2), available at: <http://sfonline.barnard.edu/a-new-queer-agenda/our-people-are-worth-the-risks-a-southern-queer-agenda-from-the-margins-and-the-red-states/>.

Spector, Scott 2007, 'Where Personal Fate Turns to Public Affair: Homosexual Scandal and Social Order in Vienna, 1900–1910', *Austrian History Yearbook*, 38: 15–24.

Steakley, James D. 1989, 'Iconography of a Scandal: Political Cartoons and the Eulenberg Affair in Wilhelmin Germany', in *Hidden from History: Reclaiming the Gay and Lesbian Past*, edited by Martin B. Duberman, Martha Vicinus and George Chauncey, Jr., New York: Penguin.

Stern, Jessica 2011/2012, 'This Is What Pride Looks Like: Miss Major and the Violence, Poverty, and Incarceration of Low-Income Transgender Women', *Scholar & Feminist Online*, 10(1/2), available at: <http://sfonline.barnard.edu/a-new-queer-agenda/this-is-what-pride-looks-like-miss-major-and-the-violence-poverty-and-incarceration-of-low-income-transgender-women/>.

Strother, Emma 2013, 'Progress and Challenges to LGBT Rights in Latin America', available at: <http://www.coha.org/progress-and-challenges-to-lgbt-rights-in-latin-america-in-light-of-the-recent-sixth-resolution-on-human-rights-sexual-orientation-and-gender-identity/>.

Stryker, Susan 2008, *Transgender History*, Berkeley: Seal Press.

Thadani, Giti 1999, 'The Politics of Identities and Languages: Lesbian Desire in Ancient and Modern India', in *Female Desires: Same-Sex Relations and Transgender Practices across Cultures*, edited by Evelyn Blackwood and Saskia Wieringa, New York: Columbia University Press.

Thoresen, Beste (ed.) 2012, 'Inequality Watch', Oslo: Norwegian People's Aid, available at: <http://www.npaid.org/News/2012/Inequality-Watch-launched>.

Toussaint, Eric 1999, *Your Money or Your Life! The Tyranny of Global Finance*, London/Dar es Salaam: Pluto/Mkuki na Nyota.

Transgender Law Center and San Francisco Bay Guardian 2006, 'Good Jobs Now!', available at: <www.transgenderlawcenter.org/issues/employment/good-jobs-now>.

Trevisan, João S. 1986, *Perverts in Paradise*, translated by Martin Foreman, London: Gay Men's Press.

Trumbach, Randolph 1989, 'The Birth of the Queen: Sodomy and the Emergence of Gender Equality in Modern Culture, 1600–1750', in *Hidden from History: Reclaiming the Gay and Lesbian Past*, edited by Martin B. Duberman, Martha Vicinus and George Chauncey, Jr., New York: Penguin.

———— 1994, 'London's Sapphists: From Three Sexes to Four Genders in the Making of Modern Culture', in *Third Sex, Third Gender: Beyond Sexual Dimorphism in Culture and History*, edited by Gilbert Herdt, New York: Zone Books.

Tucker, Scott 1997, *The Queer Question: Essays on Desire and Democracy*, Boston: South End Press.

UN Human Rights Council 2011, 'Resolution on Human Rights, Sexual Orientation and Gender Identity' (A/HRC/17/L.9/Rev.1), available at: <http://www.ohchr.org/EN/NewsEvents/Pages/DisplayNews.aspx?NewsID=11167&LangID=E>.

Vaid, Urvashi 1995, *Virtual Equality: The Mainstreaming of Gay and Lesbian Liberation*, New York: Anchor Books.

Vaid, Urvashi, Lisa Duggan, Tamara Metz and Amber Hollibaugh 2013, 'What's Next for the LGBT Movement?', *The Nation*, available at: <http://www.thenation.com/blog/175015/whats-next-lgbt-movement#axzz2azsUV7NX>.

Valocchi, Steve 1999, 'The Class-Inflected Nature of Gay Identity', *Social Problems*, 46(2): 207–24.

Vance, Carole S. (ed.) 1989, *Pleasure and Danger: Exploring Female Sexuality*, London: Pandora.

Van der Meer, Theo 1994, 'Sodomy and the Pursuit of a Third Sex in the Early Modern Period', in *Third Sex, Third Gender: Beyond Sexual Dimorphism in Culture and History*, edited by Gilbert Herdt, New York: Zone Books.

——— 2007, *Jonkheer mr. Jacob Anton Schorer (1866–1957): Een biografie van homoseksualiteit*, Amsterdam: Schorer Boeken.

Van Grinsven, Iwan 1997, *Limits to Desire: Obstacles to Gay Male Identity and Subculture Formation in Cairo, Egypt*, Nijmegen: [n.p.].

Verkerke, J. Vreer (ed.) 2012, *Transgender: Wat is daar nou ziek aan?* Amsterdam: Vreerwerk.

Via Campesina 2013, 'The Jakarta Call', available at: <http://viacampesina.org/en/index.php/our-conferences-mainmenu-28/6-jakarta-2013/resolutions-and-declarations/1428-the-jakarta-call>.

Vicinus, Martha 1989, 'Distance and Desire: English Board School Friendships, 1870–1920', in *Hidden from History: Reclaiming the Gay and Lesbian Past*, edited by Martin B. Duberman, Martha Vicinus and George Chauncey, Jr., New York: Penguin.

Warmerdam, Hans and Pieter Koenders 1987, *Cultuur en Ontspanning: Het COC 1946–1966*, Utrecht: Interfacultaire Werkgroep Homostudies.

Weeks, Jeffrey 1981, *Sex, Politics and Society: The Regulation of Sexuality since 1800*, London: Longman.

——— 1989, 'Inverts, Perverts, and Mary-Annes: Male Prostitution and the Regulation of Homosexuality in England in the Nineteenth and Early Twentieth Centuries', in *Hidden from History: Reclaiming the Gay and Lesbian Past*, edited by Martin B. Duberman, Martha Vicinus and George Chauncey, Jr., New York: Penguin.

Wekker, Gloria 1999, ' "What's Identity Got to Do with It?" ', in *Female Desires: Same-Sex Relations and Transgender Practices across Cultures*, edited by Evelyn Blackwood and Saskia Wieringa, New York: Columbia University Press.

——— 2006, *The Politics of Passion: Women's Sexual Culture in the Afro-Surinamese Diaspora*, New York: Columbia University Press.

Went, Robert 2000, *Globalization: Neoliberal Challenge, Radical Responses*, Amsterdam/London: IIRE/Pluto Press.

——— 2001, *Essays on Globalization: A Journey to a Possibly New Stage of Capitalism*, Amsterdam: University of Amsterdam, unpublished doctoral thesis.

Whitlock, Kay 2011/2012, 'We Need to Dream a Bolder Dream: The Politics of Fear and Queer Struggles for Safe Communities', *Scholar & Feminist Online*, 10(1/2), available at: <http://sfonline.barnard.edu/a-new-queer-agenda/we-need-to-dream-a-bolder-dream-the-politics-of-fear-and-queer-struggles-for-safe-communities/>.

Wieringa, Saskia E. (ed.) 2012, *Women-Loving-Women in Africa and Asia: Trans/Sign, Report of Research Findings*, Amsterdam: Riek Stienstra Fonds.

Wilde, Oscar 1990 [1891], 'The Soul of Man under Socialism', in *The Works of Oscar Wilde*, Leicester: Blitz Editions, 1990, available at <http://www.marxists.org/reference/archive/wilde-oscar/soul-man/index.htm>.

Willis, Ellen 1999, 'How Now, Iron Johns?' *The Nation* (25 November), available at: <http://www.thenation.com/article/how-now-iron-johns#axzz2XgvPBXsP>.

Witty, Thijs 2012, 'Wat is normaal?' in *Transgender: Wat is daar nou ziek aan?*, edited by J. Vreer Verkerke, Amsterdam: Vreerwerk.

Wolf, Sherry 2009, *Sexuality and Socialism: History, Politics and Theory of* LGBT *Liberation*, Chicago: Haymarket Books.

Woltersdorff, Volker 2011, 'Paradoxes of Precarious Sexualities: Sexual Subcultures under Neo-liberalism', *Cultural Studies*, 25(2): 164–82.

World Bank 1994, *Enhancing Women's Participation in Economic Development*, Washington: World Bank.

World March of Women 2001, 'Demands of the World March of Women', available at: <http:/www.worldmarchofwomen.org/revendications/index_html/en/base_view>.

Young, Iris 1981, 'Beyond the Unhappy Marriage: A Critique of the Dual Systems Theory', in *Women and Revolution: A Discussion of the Unhappy Marriage of Marxism and Feminism*, edited by Lydia Sargent, Boston: South End Press.

Index

Except for some basic definitions, the index does not contain entries for the terms capitalism, class, gay, gender, heteronormativity, heterosexuality, homonormativity, homosexuality, lesbian, neoliberalism, normality, queer, sexuality or transgender, because these concepts are central concerns of the book as a whole.